وما أرسلناك إلا رحمة للعالمين

THE HIDDEN PEARLS

SEERAH

ENCYCLOPEDIA

VOL- 01

DARUSSALAM

YOUR AUTHENTIC SOURCE OF KNOWLEDGE

HEAD OFFICE

P.O.Box: 22743,
Riyadh 11416
K.S.A.
Tel: 00966 -11- 4033962
00966 -11- 4043432
Fax: 00966 -11- 4021659
E-mail:
info@darussalamksa.com
info@darussalampublishers.com
Website:
www.darussalampublishers.com
facebook.com/darussalam.sns

K.S.A. Darussalam Showrooms:

- **Riyadh**
  Olaya branch:
  Tel 00966-11-4614483
  Fax: 4644945
  Malaz branch:
  Tel 00966-11-4735220
  Fax: 4735221
  Suwaydi branch:
  Tel 00966-11-4286641
  Suwailam branch:
  Tel & Fax: 00966-11-2860422
  Riyadh Avenu Mall
  Lulu Market branch:
  Tel & Fax: 00966-11-4032296
- **Jeddah**
  Tel: 00966-12-6879254
  Fax: 012-6336270
- **Makkah**
  Tel: 00966-12-5376862
- **Madinah**
  Tel: 00966-14-8459266,
  Fax: 014-8550119
  Mobile: 0503417155
- **Al-Khobar**
  00966-13-8692900
- **Khamis Mushayt**
  Tel & Fax: 00966-17-2207055
- **Yanbu Al-Bahr**
  Tel: 0500887341 Fax: 014-3229188
- **Al-Buraida**
  Tel: 0503417156 Fax: 16-3268965

وما أرسلناك إلا رحمة للعالمين

THE HIDDEN PEARLS

SEERAH ENCYCLOPEDIA

VOL- 01

PATRON IN CHIEF

Abdul Malik Mujahid

AUTHORSHIP AND COMPILATION

Mohsin Farani
(M.A Urdu, Historian, Geographer & Linguist)

Hafiz Muhammad Ibrahim Tahir Kailani
(M.A Islamic Studies, Graduate Madinah University)

Maulana Tanveer Ahmad
(Graduate in Islamic Studies)

Hafiz Abdullah Nasir Madni
(Graduate in Islamic Studies)

Hafiz Iqbal Siddiq
(Graduate Madinah University)

Hafiz Abu Bakr Ahmad Khawaja
(Graduate Madinah University)

ENGLISH TRANSLATION

Muhammad Kamal Myshkat

CORRECTION, COLLATION & REVIEW

Maulana Irshad ul-Haq Athri
(Graduate & Researcher in Islamic Studies)

Prof. Muhammad Yahya
(B.A Honours, M.A Arabic, Senior Research Scholar Darussalam)

Maulana Muhammad Khalid Saif
Ret. Research Scholar Islamic Ideology Council, Islamabad

ASSISTANCE

Muhammad Anwar Awan
(M.A English, Islamic Studies, Political Science)

Maulana Abdul Wahhab Shihab
(Graduate Madinah University)

Mr. Ahmad Kamran
(Senior Journalist & Expert in Urdu Language)

Maulana Abdul Baseer Khalid
(Graduate in Islamic Studies)

بسم الله الرحمن الرحيم

In the Name of Allah,
the Most Gracious, the Most Merciful

King Fahd National Library Cataloging-in-Publication Data
Maktaba Dar-us-Salam
The Hidden Pearls Encyclopedia Vol 1. /
Maktaba Dar-us-Salam. - Riyadh , 2017
Pages: 640 Size: 17x24 cm
ISBN: 978-603-500-406-0
1-Prophets Stories 2- Muhammad, Prophet Life
I-Title
239 dc 1438/6300

L.D. no. 1438/6300
ISBN: 978-603-500-406-0

وأحسن منك لم تر قط عيني

وأجمل منك لم تلد النساء

خلقت مبرأ من كل عيب

كأنك قد خلقت كما تشاء

And my eyes have never seen
more beautiful than you.

And no mother ever gave birth
to a child more beautiful than you.

You have been born
free from all types of defects.

As if you have been created
just according to your own will

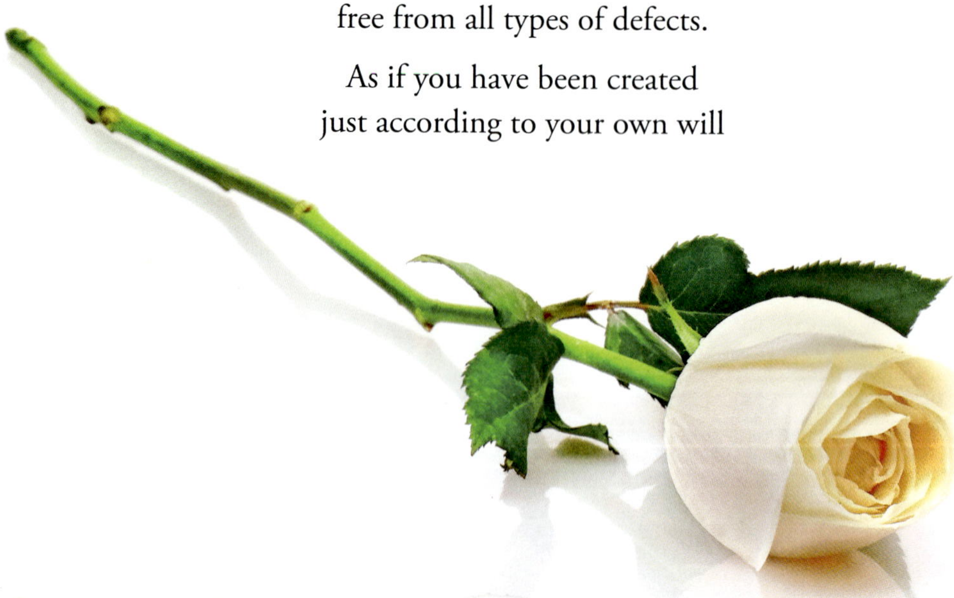

اللهم صل على

محمد

وعلى آل محمد كما صليت على إبراهيم

وعلى آل إبراهيم إنك حميد مجيد

اللهم بارك على محمد وعلى آل محمد

كما باركت على إبراهيم وعلى آل إبراهيم

إنك حميد مجيد

Table of Contents
VOLUME-01

Chapter 2

Chapter 3

The Hidden Pearls

Seerah Encyclopedia

Muhammad ibn Abdullah ﷺ began his prophetic mission in the seventh century of the Christian Era. This period was one of the darkest in human history – a time when humanity seemed to have lost sight of its purpose and sunk into a spiritual abyss, void of morality. Ignorance abounded, and the masses sought only the fulfillment of their desires. People had forgotten their true Lord and Creator. The message with which the prophets Abraham (ابراهيم), Moses (موسىٰ), and Christ (عيسىٰ) had come, had long blurred and faded into obscurity, preserved in the hearts of only a few rare individuals scattered throughout the world.

In the cities and in the deserts, mankind had forgotten of the life after death. Immersed in their worldly pursuits and selfish desires, they never paused to reflect or consider the purpose of their lives, the reason for which their Lord had placed them on earth, what they owed to Him, or what duties they were obliged to carry out.

For all the trappings of wealth and glory that empires around the world sported, there was an air of hopelessness and desperation felt keenly by rulers and commoners alike. At times, it was difficult to find even a single soul who cared about his faith, who worshipped the One True God, or felt deeply for his fellow people.

The reason for this terrible plight of mankind is best described by a Verse of the Qur'ān:

﴿ ظَهَرَ ٱلْفَسَادُ فِى ٱلْبَرِّ وَٱلْبَحْرِ بِمَا كَسَبَتْ أَيْدِى ٱلنَّاسِ لِيُذِيقَهُم بَعْضَ ٱلَّذِى عَمِلُوا۟ لَعَلَّهُمْ يَرْجِعُونَ ﴾

"Evil (sins and disobedience to Allāh) has appeared on land and sea because of what the hands of men have earned (by oppression and evil deeds), that He (Allāh) may make them taste a part of that which they have done, in order that they may return (by repenting to Allāh, and begging His Pardon)." Ar-Rūm 30: 41.

In the tenth year of the seventh century of the Christian Era, Allah sent His final Messenger, Muhammad ibn Abdullah ﷺ, to provide a guiding light through the murk of corruption, to enlighten mankind and lead them to a spiritual and behavioural reformation.

﴿ لَقَدْ مَنَّ ٱللَّهُ عَلَى ٱلْمُؤْمِنِينَ إِذْ بَعَثَ فِيهِمْ رَسُولًا مِّنْ أَنفُسِهِمْ يَتْلُوا۟ عَلَيْهِمْ ءَايَٰتِهِۦ وَيُزَكِّيهِمْ وَيُعَلِّمُهُمُ ٱلْكِتَٰبَ وَٱلْحِكْمَةَ وَإِن كَانُوا۟ مِن قَبْلُ لَفِى ضَلَٰلٍ مُّبِينٍ ﴾

"Indeed, Allāh conferred a great favour on the believers when He sent among them a Messenger (Muhammad ﷺ) from among themselves, reciting to them His Verses (the Qur'ān), and purifying them (from sins by their following him), and instructing them (in) the Book (the Qur'ān) and Al-Hikmah [the wisdom and the Sunnah of the Prophet (i.e. his legal ways, statements and acts of worship)], while before that they had been in manifest error." Āl-'Imrān 3: 164.

To this end did Allah send His last Messenger, the Seal of the Prophets, Muhammad ﷺ. He was born in Makkah in one of the noble tribes of Quraish, in the eighth decade of the sixth century CE. This book records the life, achievements and works of the leader of Allah's Creation, this brilliant star and guide to all mankind for the rest of time.

May Allah bless him and grant him salvation.

PUBLISHER'S Note

اَلْحَمْدُلِلّٰهِ نَحْمَدُهُ وَ نَسْتَعِينُهُ وَ نَسْتَغْفِرُهُ وَ نَعُوذُ بِاللّٰهِ مِنْ شُرُورِ أَنْفُسِنَا وَمِنْ سَيِّئَاتِ
أَعْمَالِنَا، مَنْ يَهْدِهِ اللّٰهُ فَلَا مُضِلَّ لَهُ، وَمَنْ يُضْلِلْ فَلَا هَادِيَ لَهُ، وَأَشْهَدُ أَنْ لَّا إِلٰهَ إِلَّا اللّٰهُ
وَحْدَهُ لَا شَرِيكَ لَهُ، وَأَشْهَدُ أَنَّ مُحَمَّدًا عَبْدُهُ وَرَسُولُهُ.

Praise be to Allah. Him we extol and His forgiveness we seek. His refuge we seek from the evils of our baser self (*Nafs*) and from evil deeds. He whom Allah guides, none can misguide him and him whom Allah misguides none can guide. I bear witness that there is no god except Allah, the One, without partner; and I bear witness that Muhammad is His slave and His messenger.

﴿ يَٰٓأَيُّهَا ٱلَّذِينَ ءَامَنُوا۟ ٱتَّقُوا۟ ٱللَّهَ حَقَّ تُقَاتِهِۦ وَلَا تَمُوتُنَّ إِلَّا وَأَنتُم مُّسْلِمُونَ ﴾

"O you who believe! Fear Allāh (by doing all that He has ordered and by abstaining from all that He has forbidden) as He should be feared. (Obey Him, be thankful to Him, and remember Him always,) and die not except in a state of Islam [as Muslims (with complete submission to Allāh)]." [1]

﴿ يَٰٓأَيُّهَا ٱلنَّاسُ ٱتَّقُوا۟ رَبَّكُمُ ٱلَّذِى خَلَقَكُم مِّن نَّفْسٍ وَٰحِدَةٍ وَخَلَقَ مِنْهَا زَوْجَهَا وَبَثَّ مِنْهُمَا رِجَالًا
كَثِيرًا وَنِسَآءً ۚ وَٱتَّقُوا۟ ٱللَّهَ ٱلَّذِى تَسَآءَلُونَ بِهِۦ وَٱلْأَرْحَامَ ۚ إِنَّ ٱللَّهَ كَانَ عَلَيْكُمْ رَقِيبًا ﴾

"O mankind! Be dutiful to your Lord, Who created you from a single person (Adam), and from him (Adam) He created his wife [Hawwa

1. Āl 'Imrān 3:102.

(Eve)], and from them both He created many men and women; and fear Allāh through Whom you demand (your mutual rights), and (do not cut the relations of) the wombs (kinship). Surely, Allāh is Ever an All-Watcher over you."[1]

﴿يَٰٓأَيُّهَا ٱلَّذِينَ ءَامَنُواْ ٱتَّقُواْ ٱللَّهَ وَقُولُواْ قَوۡلٗا سَدِيدٗا ٧٠ يُصۡلِحۡ
لَكُمۡ أَعۡمَٰلَكُمۡ وَيَغۡفِرۡ لَكُمۡ ذُنُوبَكُمۡۗ وَمَن يُطِعِ ٱللَّهَ وَرَسُولَهُۥ فَقَدۡ
فَازَ فَوۡزًا عَظِيمًا ٧١﴾

"O you who believe! Keep your duty to Allāh and fear Him, and speak (always) the truth. He will direct you to do righteous good deeds and will forgive you your sins. And whosoever obeys Allāh and His Messenger (ﷺ), he has indeed achieved a great achievement (i.e. he will be saved from the Hell-fire and will be admitted to Paradise)."[2]

Allah's blessings towards mankind are many and varied, but none is greater than that of Faith – making us believers and faithful followers of His last and final Messenger, Muhammad (ﷺ).

As humans, we are weak and fall into error, committing sins and transgressing against the rules that Allah has set for us. Yet despite these occasional aberrations, we continue to love our Messenger ﷺ. To a true believer, Allah's Messenger is dearer to our hearts than anyone else – more beloved to a believer than his parents, his wife, his children, himself, and indeed, the entire universe itself. This deep and abiding love is the mark of a true believer.

No matter how intense and profound this love

1. An-Nisā' 4:1.
2. Al-Ahzāb 71-33:70.

is, none have yet been able to truly describe and encompass in writing the sheer magnitude of the effect that this great man had on the world. The qualities of his life, his character, and his works can never be given the justice they deserve.

The same can be said of those who read his biography or hear it from others. No matter how often one reads or listens to stories from the life of the Prophet (ﷺ), there are always new insights and greater joys to be learned. One can never be satiated – every moment in the life of the Messenger (ﷺ) contains a lesson that refreshes and sustains the heart, mind, body and soul. The bliss that one attains merely by learning about the Messenger of Allah (ﷺ) is more quenching than the fabled elixir of life.

In these dark and disturbing times, the Muslim Ummah is confronted with innumerable challenges. The entire disbelieving world is arrayed against the believers, attempting to challenge and destroy Islam from the inside out. Through political and academic means, there are people working day and night in an effort to achieve this end. A global culture of instant gratification, fulfilling sexual desires and acquiring the latest entertainment technology has alienated Muslim youth from Allah's Messenger, pushing them to cut off their relationship to him entirely. The only solution to this terrible situation is to rekindle the love of Allah's Messenger in the hearts of every Muslim, illuminating their souls with an accurate account of his life and works.

The writer is very much aware of his defects and drawbacks and yet he is proud of the deep love Allah has created in his heart for His Messenger.

Since my childhood, I have been an avid reader of the many biographies of Prophet Muhammad (ﷺ). During my school days, Qazi Suleman Mansurpuri's book "Rahmatun-Lil-'Alameen" was my favourite book. Time passed, and my love for Allah's Messenger increased day by day until I arrived in Saudi Arabia. It was there that I had the chance to read many books and ultimately became a publisher myself. I am grateful to Almighty Allah that, by His grace, Darussalam has published many valuable books on the life and mission of Allah's Messenger (ﷺ).

Apart from publishing my own books on the life of the final Prophet of Allah ﷺ, I read with great interest any biography of the Messenger published by anyone and anywhere in the world, especially those written in Urdu and Arabic. In the course of my reading I came across the famous biography, "Ar-Rahīq Al-Makhtūm."

I was deeply impressed by it, and it was an unpredicted blessing from Allah that one day I came across the author of that biography, Safi-ur-Rahmān Mubarakpuri. He was a well-known figure and I knew him well, but I was delighted when he told me that he had already heard about me. We met occasionally and gradually became closer day by day.

In those days, he was working at the Seerah and Sunnah Center of the Islamic University of Madinah. However, some time later, he joined Darussalam and began working as the chairman of the Academic Committee of Darussalam. Though I could not spend as much time with him as I desired due to my heavy engagements, I would sometimes steal a few hours just to sit with him. I would spend those precious hours engaging in long conversations and seeking inspiration from him.

One day, in the course of my study of the Seerah, a brilliant idea struck me. I had discovered during my studies that although Hadith scholars and historians had described almost every event of the Messenger's life, their styles differed greatly. One historian dealt with an event briefly but another historian dealt with the same event in great detail while a third one, referring to the same event, added a several previously unmentioned details and a few more Ahādith. Considering this, I thought that it would be wonderful to write and publish a comprehensive book, based on authentic traditions covering every incident of the Prophet's life, and arranging it in a clear and orderly manner.

During a sitting with Shaikh Safi-ur-Rahmān, I took the opportunity to discuss the idea of publishing a comprehensive book on the life and mission of Allah's Messenger ﷺ. The Shaikh was an intelligent man and immediately understood the need for such a project. He swiftly approved the idea, despite the seemingly grandiose scope of the plan. He also mentioned that during his time at the Sunnah and Seerah Centre of the Islamic University in Madinah, he had done work for a similar project but had been unable to complete it for a variety of reasons.

Though he gave me a great deal of hope, I realized just what a tremendous job it would be, and stopped short of suggesting, "If Darussalam does it..." Collecting details of the events of the Messenger's life and mission, putting them together in one place in an easy-to-read way for the youth of modern times was no easy task. I knew of my own failings and incapacity to do such momentous work.

Despite all this, I remained excited by the idea. Even after I left the Shaikh, I thought to myself about the great potential of the project. Furthermore, I mused, I had the endorsement and even a figurative seal of approval from the great Shaikh himself!

Unfortunately, I could not immediately embark on this project. I had many other engagements and innumerable other publication projects to look after. So the grandiose Seerah project was deferred, although only temporarily, of course.

In the meantime, the Shaikh fell ill and had to shuttle frequently between India and Saudi Arabia. This was followed by yet another more heart-rending event. A Danish newspaper (or rather, a rag of a paper), published insulting caricatures of Allah's Messenger ﷺ, a sad event which immediately set in motion a flurry of outcry, protests, and marches worldwide. Seminars and conferences were held, condemning the perpetrators of this heinous crime, while many intellectuals stressed the need to present before the world a correct and true account of the life and mission of Prophet Muhammad (ﷺ).

There was a great commotion and a hectic flurry of activities during those days. The publication of the caricatures in the Danish rag had deeply upset the hearts and minds of the Muslims around the world. Everybody wanted to do something and contribute somehow to proactively combating the pernicious deeds of the hateful individuals behind the caricatures.

I too played a small role. I wrote to the editor of the daily Urdu News of Jeddah requesting him to publish an article on the Seerah (the Prophet's biography) everyday. A few days later I received a phone call from Mr Rauf Tahir, the editor of the paper's weekly magazine. He told me that it was difficult to write on Seerah everyday, but he offered to publish one article on Seerah in the weekly magazine of the paper regularly, providing I write it myself. I accepted the offer gladly and gratefully, and wrote 174 articles, in all. To write these articles, I had to study a great deal, which enriched my own knowledge.

In the course of my study of Seerah, I came across a book titled 'Maqalat Professor Abdul-Qayyum' (Essays of Prof. Abdul-Qayyum) wherein I found, to my surprise, the sketch or outlines of a plan to be followed in writing the Seerah. It was exhilarating indeed, for it fitted in exactly with the idea that I had continued to nurture in my mind. I became more determined than ever to pursue this challenging goal.

Once again, however, hurdles arose. The first snag was financing - I wanted to publish the encyclopedia in ten volumes and, later, its translation in several languages, including English. Nonetheless, in 2007, I made up my mind to implement this project.

To that end, I travelled to Syria and conferred with the religious scholars there. We exchanged ideas and I then assigned this task to a great religious scholar who, according to my plan, would consult other learned scholars and start this project.

They laid down the outlines of the project and proceeded with their work. I remained in constant touch with them, but when I reviewed their work after some time, I was deeply disappointed. Their output was not up to the mark.

In a second attempt, I turned to Egypt and conferred with the scholars there. Just as in Syria, a committee of scholars was formed, the outlines were made clear, and I requested that they continue work on the project. Once again, however, a review of their work did not elicit the satisfaction I had hoped for. Put plainly, the standard of work was unacceptable.

Failure paves the path to success. Keeping this in mind, I sought out the Lahore branch of Darussalam and set up a special committee for the Seerah encyclopedia. Later, when I reviewed the preliminary work of the scholars of Lahore, I felt that it was very much in line with what I desired. To begin this project formally, I went to Lahore myself.

Initially, Shaikh Muhammad Zulfiqar was recruited to undertake this important work. Later, for greater scope and ease, I gathered together a group of scholars drawn from Darussalam Research Centre of Lahore. Over a period of time, some changes were made in the committee several times for administrative and academic reasons.

The members of the committee, as it stands today, are: Muhammad Ibrahim Tahir Abdus-Salam Kaylani (graduate of Madinah University), Hafiz Abu Bakr Ahmed Khwaja (graduate of Madinah University), Iqbal Siddiq (graduate of Madinah University), Muhammad Abdullah Nasir (graduate, Islamic Sciences), Tanveer Ahmad (graduate, Islamic Sciences), Abdul-Wah'hab Shihab (graduate, Madinah University), Abdul-Baseer Khalid (graduate, Arabic and Persian) and Muhammad Anwar Awan (M.A English, Islamic Studies and Pol. Sciences).

How to proceed with this work, along what lines, how to collect authentic Hadiths and in what order should it be written - these were vital matters. To address these issues, Hafiz Abdul-Azeem (General Manager, Darussalam, Lahore) appointed Prof. M.Yahya, Senior Research Scholar of Darussalam, and Mr. Mohsin Farani, an eminent journalist, research scholar, historian and geographer, to guide and supervise this academic project.

I requested Prof. Irshad-ul Haq Asari, a prolific writer and research scholar, as well as Shaikh Muhammad Khalid Saif, senior research scholar of Islamic Ideological Council, to join the team. They were required to check, revise and correct the contents of the articles of this encyclopedia, which were to be written according to the methodology of Hadith scholars. I am grateful to Allah that both acceded to my request and did their job exceedingly well. May Allah reward them with the best of rewards.

These eminent scholars gave us valuable guidance, telling us the authentic from the weak narrations and highlighting the historical antecedents and many other imperative pieces of information.

Apart from these prominent figures, the other staff members of Darussalam, especially the reverend scholar and commentator of Qur'an, Hafiz Salahuddin Yusuf, made significant contributions to this historical work.

The encyclopedia begins with an article captioned 'Style of Writing and Methodology of Research,' which is intended to aid readers in their study of this encyclopedia.

This is followed by a very comprehensive and scholarly preface written by Professor Muhammad Yahya. In his preface, the learned professor has traced the development of Seerah writing over different periods of Muslim history, beginning from the era of pious Caliphs, how it was preserved, documented, referenced and arranged by the Muslim scholars and the principles and methodologies followed by Seerah writers and their style of writing. He also reviews in detail contemporary themes of modern times, stressing the need to take the methodology and style of Hadith scholars as a model which should be followed by the modern biographer, as an infallible criterion to establish the truth of whatever he writes.

Obviously, an objective and balanced study of the Prophet's biography is impossible without full knowledge and understanding of those ancient times, the Arab tribes of those days, their social and political conditions, and their cultural and intellectual contexts. In this connection, Mr. Mohsin Farani, assisted by Mr. Muhammad Anwar Awan did an excellent job. He has managed to highlight important locations by means of truly rare maps and given unique genealogical tables of important personalities and tribes.

This is all a brief history of the different stages through which this encyclopedia passed before it saw the light of the day. I am grateful to Allah for that.

Not a single event of the Messenger's life has been left or overlooked in this encyclopedia. Each and every event has been thoroughly researched, examined and vetted by the thirteen-member Committee and then written in an easy, flowing style.

Let me mention here, before I close this article, that I decided to open every chapter with a relevant Verse of Qur'an or part of it suited to the contents of that chapter. This was done by the famous calligrapher, Muhammad Abdur-Rahman (nicknamed Abdah).

I am deeply grateful to the many people who have worked together to make this project possible. I would like to especially mention Hafiz Abdul Azeem Asad for managing, organizing, and supervising the work on this noble project; as well as the the scholars and other helpers who worked tirelessly and carefully on their respective chapters.

Last of all, I pray to Allah to grace everyone who helped and co-operated in this great work with the Prophet's intercession on the Day of Judgment, raise us all from the dead on the Day of Resurrection as the devoted servants of Qur'an and Hadith and make this 'Encyclopedia of Seerah' a light for mankind. O, Allah, the Lord of the creations, grace this work with Your acceptance. You are the All-Hearing, the All-Knowing. Āmeen.

Abdul-Malik Mujahid
Servant of Qur'an and Sunnah
(Managing Director, Darussalam,
Riyadh - Lahore).
July, 2013

Methodology and Style of Writing

The Hidden Pearls, (اللؤلؤ المكنون) is a comprehensive, all-inclusive encyclopedia on the life and works of Muhammad (ﷺ). We have tried, to the best of our ability, to include in this momentous work all things relating to the final Messenger of Allah. We have neither overlooked nor trivialized a single minor event or secondary fact, chronicling every incident from his birth to his death.

In this book we have described in detail the social conditions of his times, the modes of life and the habits and the temperament of the inhabitants of Arabian Peninsula as well as the general conditions of the people living near or around them. All of this is essential to a proper understanding of the age in which he lived, the most brilliant epoch of human history, and to discover the reason for which Allah chose the Arabian Peninsula as his birthplace and the starting point of his sacred, universal mission.

In pursuing our goal, we have been impersonal and objective in all technical matters through this project, including in the methodology of this academic research work. By the grace of Allah, we hope that readers of

'The Hidden Pearl' will be transported mentally and spiritually to the era of the Prophet Muhammad (ﷺ). To feel as though one was experiencing that blessed age, being instructed, chastened, and refined morally and spiritually, to feel oneself being moulded into a dutiful slave of Allah by the supreme guide of mankind – that is what we hope each and every reader will experience as they read the biography of the greatest man who ever lived.

To this end, we have made the contents of the encyclopedia follow a chronological order. We have sought a style of writing that will effectively highlight the various events of the Messenger's life, giving them special significance by ensuring that the entire book has been written in a simple, appealing, and logical manner.

While writing, preparing and arranging the contents of the book, the following methods have been used:

Style of Writing

1. The book begins with a preface in which we have discussed in detail the subject of Seerah (biography of the Prophet), its value and importance, and the reason why it should be studied. Here we also touched upon the works produced by various biographers and Seerah writers in different periods of Muslim history. In the course of our discussion we have evaluated and assessed the writings of orientalists and their partisans on this subject.
2. Three sources are of vital importance to writing any book on Seerah: (A) Qur'an (B) Ahādith (C) Books of Seerah and Maghāzi (biographies and accounts of military expeditions).

In order to present deeper explanations and more accurate descriptions, comparisons, and analyses, we have also made use of the following sources:

- Commentaries on the Qur'an and Ahādith.
- Sacred books of other faiths (the Bible, including the Old and New Testaments).
- Books of history and geography.

- Books on the physical qualities and character (Shamā'il) of Muhammad (ﷺ).
- Books describing the miracles of Prophet Muhammad (ﷺ).

3. In cases wherein several different versions relating to a single event were found in the books of Hadith and Seerah, we chose from among them the most authentic and comprehensive narrations. If the most authentic narration was brief, we then referenced the different versions while mentioning their respective grades of authenticity. When different accounts of a single event were present, each with a different conclusion, we listed them all and made mention of the narration which had the greatest weight.

4. While quoting Ahādith, we have taken the utmost care to ensure the authenticity of the texts, the chains of narration, and the reliability of narrations. As much as possible, we have used only those narrations which Hadith scholars have considered worthy of attention. On occasions when there was a need to quote a weak narration to fill in a gap or explain a point, we have referenced the weakness of the narration.

For clarity and comprehension, we have taken the following measures to ensure that every reader is able to familiarize themselves with the encyclopedia and navigate it with assured expediency.

5. The Seerah has been divided into chapters, with each chapter featuring a new theme. A few lines following each chapter title give a brief introduction to the contents of the chapter. Some chapters also contain subtitles.

6. Every chapter of every volume of the Seerah begins with a Qur'ānic Verse or Hadith, featured in beautiful calligraphy that represents the basic subject of the respective chapter.

7. Each chapter and its subtitles begin with a new page.

8. The title of every chapter is written in large, bold letters.

9. Quotations have been written within inverted commas while Qur'ānic

Verses, translations of Ahādith and quotations from the Bible have been highlighted with indent.

10. Quotations from the Bible referring to the qualities of Allah's Messenger ﷺ and prophesying his coming have been highlighted with a grey line. Comments on the prophecies follow in the same order.

11. Qur'ānic Verses and Arabic texts have been printed in red to make them conspicuous.

12. Difficult words, names of tribes, and other proper names have been explained briefly in the margins. Unknown places have also been located and explained in the margins. These marginal notes have been given alphabetically at the end of each volume. The words in the text which have been explained in the marginal notes have been underlined.

13. Columns have been used for comparisons.

14. Qur'ānic Verses and Ahādith have been written separately in brackets.

15. The tribes of Adnān and Qahtān have been listed in separate genealogical tables.

16. Locations are illustrated by means of maps and, in some cases, with sketches.

17. When available, various important places have been shown with photographs.

Methodology of Research and Documentation

1. Referencing and documenting the Qur'ānic Verses, Ahādith, the events of the Messenger's life and his travels and military campaigns (Maghāzi) have been done in the following way:

    - Qur'an: the name of the Sūrah, its number, and the number of the Verse.
    - *Tafaseer* (commentaries of Qur'an): the name of the commentary, the name of the Chapter (Sūrah), its number and the number of the verse.

- Hadith: When referencing Bukhāri, Muslim, and other books of Sahih Ahādith – name of the book and number of the respective Hadith. When referencing Ahādith taken from other books of Hadith – volume of part of the book, page number, and number of the respective Hadith.

In case of one-volume books of Hadith commentary, Prophet's biography, his military campaigns (مغازی) physical and spiritual characteristics (شمائل) and miracles (معجزات): Name and page number. For multi-volume books: Name of the book, number of the volume, and page number.

- References to the Bible mention the name of the Gospel, the number of the chapter, and the number of the verse.

2. Apart from printed books, information has been gathered from electronic libraries, with the names of their respective websites mentioned accordingly. Since all the electronic information cannot be deemed reliable, we have taken only that information which is indispensable and which is verified by other authentic sources.
3. While documenting, Arabic references have been written in Naskhi (ordinary, cursive calligraphic) style. English references begin with a new line.

Method of cataloging and indexing

1. Each volume begins with three kinds of lists:
   - Table of contents. It contains every topic of the book as well as the maps, sketches, and genealogical tables arranged in the same order as they occur in the book.
   - Appendixes. A separate list of maps, sketches and genealogical tables has also been given.
   - Marginal references have been arranged alphabetically. They are of four kinds: Lists with proper names, locations, tribes, and miscellaneous items.
2. The last volume of the Seerah encyclopedia will consist of indexes

which will include the complete references of Qur'ānic Verses, Ahādith, sayings of the Companions, poetic verses and the topics as well as those of proper names, places, tribes, religions and sects, all alphabetically arranged, Allah willing.

The index volume will also contain a detailed collection of the source-references of this biographical encyclopedia.

Praise be to Allah. We rely on Him alone for the success of this noble project. May Allah bless His Messenger Muhammad ﷺ, his family, his companions, and his followers until the end of time, Āmeen!

وَاللّٰهُ وَلِيُّ التَّوْفِيقِ وَعَلَيْهِ التُّكْلَانُ وَبِهِ نَسْتَعِينُ وَنَسْتَغْفِرُهُ وَالْحَمْدُلِلّٰهِ رَبِّ الْعَالَمِينَ
وَصَلَّى اللّٰهُ وَسَلَّمَ وَبَارَكَ عَلٰى مُحَمَّدٍ وَّ عَلٰى اٰلِهِ وَأَصْحَابِهِ وَأَتْبَاعِهِ أَجْمَعِينَ .

Preface

﴿لَقَدْ مَنَّ ٱللَّهُ عَلَى ٱلْمُؤْمِنِينَ إِذْ بَعَثَ فِيهِمْ رَسُولًا مِّنْ أَنفُسِهِمْ يَتْلُوا۟ عَلَيْهِمْ ءَايَٰتِهِۦ وَيُزَكِّيهِمْ
وَيُعَلِّمُهُمُ ٱلْكِتَٰبَ وَٱلْحِكْمَةَ وَإِن كَانُوا۟ مِن قَبْلُ لَفِى ضَلَٰلٍ مُّبِينٍ﴾

"Indeed, Allāh conferred a great favour on the believers when He sent among them a Messenger (Muhammad ﷺ) from among themselves, reciting to them His Verses (the Qur'ān), and purifying them (from sins by their following him), and instructing them (in) the Book (the Qur'ān) and Al-Hikmah [the wisdom and the Sunnah of the Prophet (i.e. his legal ways, statements and acts of worship)], while before that they had been in manifest error."[1]

﴿ٱلَّذِينَ يَتَّبِعُونَ ٱلرَّسُولَ ٱلنَّبِىَّ ٱلْأُمِّىَّ ٱلَّذِى يَجِدُونَهُۥ مَكْتُوبًا عِندَهُمْ فِى ٱلتَّوْرَىٰةِ
وَٱلْإِنجِيلِ يَأْمُرُهُم بِٱلْمَعْرُوفِ وَيَنْهَىٰهُمْ عَنِ ٱلْمُنكَرِ وَيُحِلُّ لَهُمُ ٱلطَّيِّبَٰتِ وَيُحَرِّمُ
عَلَيْهِمُ ٱلْخَبَٰٓئِثَ وَيَضَعُ عَنْهُمْ إِصْرَهُمْ وَٱلْأَغْلَٰلَ ٱلَّتِى كَانَتْ عَلَيْهِمْ ۚ فَٱلَّذِينَ ءَامَنُوا۟
بِهِۦ وَعَزَّرُوهُ وَنَصَرُوهُ وَٱتَّبَعُوا۟ ٱلنُّورَ ٱلَّذِىٓ أُنزِلَ مَعَهُۥٓ ۙ أُو۟لَٰٓئِكَ هُمُ ٱلْمُفْلِحُونَ (١٥٧) قُلْ
يَٰٓأَيُّهَا ٱلنَّاسُ إِنِّى رَسُولُ ٱللَّهِ إِلَيْكُمْ جَمِيعًا ٱلَّذِى لَهُۥ مُلْكُ ٱلسَّمَٰوَٰتِ وَٱلْأَرْضِ ۖ
لَآ إِلَٰهَ إِلَّا هُوَ يُحْىِۦ وَيُمِيتُ ۖ فَـَٔامِنُوا۟ بِٱللَّهِ وَرَسُولِهِ ٱلنَّبِىِّ ٱلْأُمِّىِّ ٱلَّذِى يُؤْمِنُ بِٱللَّهِ
وَكَلِمَٰتِهِۦ وَٱتَّبِعُوهُ لَعَلَّكُمْ تَهْتَدُونَ﴾

"Those who follow the Messenger, the Prophet who can neither read nor write (i.e. Muhammad ﷺ) whom they find written with them in the Taurāt (Torah) (Deut, xviii 15) and the Injīl (Gospel) (John, xiv 16) with them, – he commands them for Al-Ma'rūf (i.e. Islamic

1 Āl 'Imrān 3:164.

Monotheism and all that Islam has ordained); and forbids them from Al-Munkar (i.e. disbelief, polytheism of all kinds, and all that Islam has forbidden); he allows them as lawful At-Tayyibāt (i.e. all good and lawful as regards things, deeds, beliefs, persons and foods), and prohibits them as unlawful Al-Khabā'ith (i.e. all evil and unlawful as regards things, deeds, beliefs, persons and foods), he releases them from their heavy burdens (of Allāh's Covenant with the Children of Israel), and from the fetters (bindings) that were upon them. So those who believe in him (Muhammad ﷺ), honour him, help him, and follow the light (the Qur'ān) which has been sent down with him, it is they who will be the successful. Say (O Muhammad ﷺ): ``O mankind! Verily, I am sent to you all as the Messenger of Allāh – to Whom belongs the dominion of the heavens and the earth. Lā ilāha illa Huwa (none has the right to be worshipped but He). It is He Who gives life and causes death. So believe in Allāh and His Messenger (Muhammad ﷺ), the Prophet who can neither read nor write (i.e. Muhammad ﷺ), who believes in Allāh and His Words [(this Qur'ān), the Taurat (Torah) and the Injīl (Gospel) and also Allāh's Word: ``Be!" – and he was, i.e. 'Īsā (Jesus) son of Maryam (Mary), عليه السلام], and follow him so that you may be guided."[1]

A unique era of human history began with the prophetic mission of Muhammad (ﷺ). The starting point and epicenter of that revolutionary call was the small town of Makkah, a distant town, relatively unknown by the great empires of the time, surrounded by desert and barren mountains.

Thousands of years ago, a House of Allah built exclusively for the worship of the One True God had been built, but at the time of the birth of the Prophet ﷺ, its purpose had been corrupted and the people of the land had filled it with the statues and images of their idols.

The people of Makkah and the surrounding areas had almost completely forgotten Allah. Though their city had been founded by

1 Al-A'rāf (7): 157-158.

the Prophets Ibrāhīm and Ismā'īl, who had spread the true message of *Tawheed* (monotheism) throughout the world, their descendants had parted from the path of truth and without divine revelation, the people of Arabia and of the world slipped into religions of desires and lies. Idolatry became popular to the point that there were few left in the world who even recalled the ancient religion dedicated to monotheistic worship. Wealth and power were what every man sought; accumulating both and enjoying the advantages that they brought. Engaging in gambling, drinking alcohol, and the pleasures of the flesh were the center of most peoples. In an ever-increasing obsession to fulfill their every desire, people did not flinch from committing any act, no matter how horrible.

Exploitation of the poor and disadvantaged, cruelty and injustice, cheating and lying, persecuting the downtrodden became a societal norm. Culture was twisted to the point that out of pride and greed men would bury their own daughters alive. They did not want to spend on daughters who will neither earn nor will be able to fight for the honour of the family and the tribe.

The Arabian Peninsula was a wild place, populated by tribes who were ever-ready to attack each other for any perceived slight. Security of life, property and honour were privileges that only the wealthiest and most powerful could afford. There was no system of governance, no central authority, no institution to render help to any aggrieved person. Every tribe was independent of the other, with no avenue to turn to for one to redress their grievances. In short, life was in chaos.

Yet in the very midst of anarchy and uncivilized immorality, there were a few noble souls who strove to protect themselves from common vices and tried hard to emulate and encourage virtue. From amongst these men was one man who rose above all others in honour and virtue. He abhorred lying and cheating, gaining a reputation for being 'the Trustworthy One'. He was the very embodiment of all that was pure and good, a matchless paragon of self-control, unselfishness, justice and fairness, compassion, honesty, integrity and truth. He was revered, in the society of Makkah, for his moral conduct and noble character.

Despite the fame that surrounded him due to his excellence of character, he never aspired to or sought any position of power or material benefit. He benefited others but sought no benefit for himself. The name of this great and unique personality was Muhammad bin Abdullah bin Abdul-Muttalib (ﷺ).

Revolutionary Mission

After forty years of his well loved and respected life in Makkah, Muhammad (ﷺ) went through a unique experience about which he had never thought for. It was his contact with the special Messenger of Almighty Allah, the Archangel Jibreel (Gabriel). He conveyed to him that Allah has chosen him as His last messenger to all the human beings for all times to come.

Now he was charged with a divine mission. It was his duty to act and call his countrymen, and all of humanity, to accept and believe in the truth. He had to call upon them to discard their wrong old beliefs and remodel their entire lives according to a new, perfect system, given by the Creator of the universe Himself. It was a revolutionary call for each and every human being to follow.

In working for the success of this great and universal mission, he had no means to support himself except the Message of Allah and the example of his own conduct, which has all the charm to attract all the mankind. To root out the entire centuries-old system of pagan beliefs and customs was no easy task. Though any other man would have needed strength of arms, wealth, or power to complete the job, he had nothing and no one except a few faithful followers who were themselves weak and oppressed.

The system prevalent in Makkah in those times was cruel, arbitrary, tyrannical, and discriminatory. Power belonged to the wealthy and the tribal chiefs. The new call, the call of Islam, posed a dangerous challenge to the established practices. The protagonists and the supporters of the old practices would brook no opposition to their hegemony.

Vicious and without mercy, they fell on the new converts with full force and flinched from no means, however cruel, to eradicate them root and branch. In a desperate effort to discourage anyone who considered the new religion, the pagans of Makkah tortured the Muslims cruelly.

The Messenger of Allah ﷺ spent the first thirteen years of his missionary life instructing and training the first converts amid agonizing and unbearable circumstances. During this time, knowing that they would not last long if the heightened persecution continued, he and his faithful followers sought a safe refuge from the tyranny of the arrogant disbelievers.

Their relief at finding a safe haven in the city of Madinah was short-lived, for the turmoil continued for another ten years. The Prophet Muhammad (ﷺ) spent those ten years in continuous defense of the faith, beating back the unrelenting onslaught of the Makkan pagans and other hostile Arab tribes.

In addition to militarily defending Islam, the Messenger of Allah's most difficult task was to set up and implement an ideal social system. This consisted of training the new converts and inculcating in their hearts and minds the right faith, transmuting the fighting tribes into a single, homogeneous, cohesive *Ummah* (community), strengthening their bond with Allah, and instilling in their hearts the love of fellow people. Moreover, he had to see to it that his mission continued across the succeeding generations, to ensure that if at any time it became weak through negligence or error, the Muslims had the capacity to recuperate and rejuvenate their faith.

The World's Most Successful Person

Three things were needed to defend and promote this new faith: what did have at his hand, in addition to the Book revealing the eternal truths, and his own personality who acted by each and every word of the Book, to accomplish the greatest mission in the history of mankind? Only a small band of disciples, trained and chastened by him, most of whom were shepherds, itinerant vendors, small traders, woodcutters, gardeners, farmers, daily workers, slaves and freed slaves.

These seemingly insignificant people, after they had been trained and disciplined, became exemplary rulers, warriors and generals, judges, diplomats, efficient administrators, big traders, scholars and teachers.

After reaching Madinah he had only ten years time in which he managed to transform entire societies, not only in Makkah and Madinah, but throughout the Arabian Peninsula and the rest of the world. Tribes known to be hot-tempered, bellicose, and aggressive began joining the fold of Islam. The Prophet's success, both militarily and diplomatically, had left them no choice except to accept the new faith and become a part of the greater *Ummah* (international Muslim community).

This new community that he had forged was faced with numerous hardships both during and after his lifetime. However, due to the purity of their faith and the strength of their characters, they were able to withstand the test of time – rebellion and apostasy were dealt with firmly, and in less than twenty years, they overthrew the most powerful civilizations and empires of the world. For centuries after, this *Ummah* remained the world's most distinguished power, encouraging virtue and discouraging vice, administering the world with justice and working for public welfare and common weal.

Focus of the World's Attention

How could a few weak and poor Muslims, persecuted for thirteen long years in Makkah, suddenly overwhelm the whole of Arabia in the next ten years? How could they possibly manage to convert previously hostile and uncooperative natives to the new faith, uniting them under one banner and one cause? How were they able to overthrow the two mighty empires, that of the Romans and the Persians, within the next fifteen to twenty years? And finally, how was it that the subjects of these fallen empires embraced the new faith so zealously?

The sheer force and continuous successes of the Muslim *Ummah* inspired amazement and awe. Both from within and without the

Muslim community, there were people curious enough about this unique phenomenon to investigate the history behind these events and the events behind the history. Historians scrutinized every aspect of the Muslim society, studying it in detail and reflecting on it. Obviously, their inquiries led them to the one man at the heart of this transformation. Whether one was angry or enlightened by this change of world events, none could deny that they were drawn to this great man and his charismatic personality.

There is no disputing the fact that Muhammad (ﷺ) was at the center of this societal metamorphosis. As a result, his life was recorded in every minute detail; his actions and his sayings were shared, written down, checked, investigated, and studied by different groups of men, with diverse motives, from various angles. Everything that he said about others, and what others said of him, were all noted, preserved in writing, and studied. In fact, it was the Prophet himself who allowed that every aspect of his life be observed and shared publicly, in order that others may take him as an example and follow him as much as possible.

Naturally, no one else could have allowed such a keen and critical observation of his personality; this would never have been possible with anyone except a Messenger of Allah.

In Makkah, where the Messenger of Allah began his mission, there were only a few men and women who viewed his mission with respect and sympathy. Amongst these people were those closest to him - his wife, his daughters, his cousin, his servants, and his most beloved friends.

Those who believed in the Prophet Muhammad (ﷺ) came from different levels of Makkan society. Some were slaves; others, the masters of slaves. Rich or poor, these selected individuals recognized the truth of Muhammad's message, accepted the call and spoke well of him. However, the rest of the Makkans, who formed the majority, were formidably hostile to the Prophet (ﷺ). The pagans of Makkah spoke of him with loathing and rancour. In spite of this hostility and bias they could find anything but virtues and characteristics which cultivate respect and admiration in human hearts.

Those Closest to Him, Loved Him Most

When you meet with someone frequently on a regular basis, interacting with him constantly and in various situations, you get to know his personality and his character thoroughly. You become deeply familiarized with him, aware of both his faults and his better qualities. The more time you spend with him, the less you are impressed by his behaviour. Such is the case with the majority of people all over the world and throughout time.

On the other hand, however, there are a few very special people in the world – those whose character is stunning, eliciting within others a desire to become close to and remain attached to these individuals. The more one spends time with such a personality, the more one is impressed and increases in love for him, respecting him for his excellent qualities. Those closest to him remember him often, love him deeply, and value him highly. Such a reaction leaves no doubt as to the caliber and greatness of the individual's character and personality.

In the same vein, no man can escape the piercing observation of his wife. Her scrutiny is ceaseless; she is aware of his defects of character as well as the motives behind his good works. No one can know a man's true disposition better than his wife. The Messenger of Allah (ﷺ) spent the first twenty-five years of his married life with Khadeejah bint Khuwaylid. She loved him deeply, adored him, and revered him till the end of her life. Even during the most difficult days of his life, when he was confronted by furious enemies hostile to his mission, her love of him never flagged or diminished. She comforted him, supported him, and constantly reassured him that his mission would succeed and that Allah would not fail him.

After Khadeejah's death, the Prophet Muhammad (ﷺ) was then observed by his other wives, of whom there were nine or ten. Many of them came from different tribes and even different countries. Some of these women were the daughters of his greatest enemies and most diehard pagans; Safiyyah bint Huyayy's father was the leader of a Jewish tribe while Māriyah Qibtiyyah was a Coptic slave girl from Egypt. All of these women who came from varying cultural and religious backgrounds were impressed, without exception, by the Prophet Muhammad's words and actions to the extent that they willingly transformed their lives and moulded themselves in accordance to his teachings. Furthermore, they themselves became teachers of the Prophet's way, advising and guiding others on how best to follow his great example.

In all of history, there was never an entire family who unanimously loved and followed the head of their household as it was done by the family of the Prophet (ﷺ), including his servants. They not only loved and followed him wholeheartedly; they encouraged everyone else to do so as well.

And so did his companions who came from different cultural backgrounds and distant places: Salmān from Zoroastrian Persia, Christian Suhaib from Byzantine Empire, 'Abdullah bin Salām, a Jew from Madinah, Bilal from Ethiopia, and Tufail bin 'Amr Dausi, a tribal chief of Tihāmah. As soon as they entered into his presence, they were enthralled by both his magnetic personality and the ringing truth of his message. They and others like them, immediately pledged themselves to him and his cause, keeping him constant company, modeling their lifestyles according to his, and became his helpers, lieutenants, and preachers.

Winning of Enemies' Hearts

Though the Prophet's implacable foes gathered all the pagan tribes of Arabia against him and tried to root out the new faith and destroy his companions, they were forced to acknowledge the nobility of his character and his deep, enduring love for his people and humanity at large. Many of them, such as Khālid ibn Waleed, turned to the Prophet (ﷺ) at some point in their lives, in search of a meaningful and blessed life.

Abu Jahl, the arch enemy of Muhammad (ﷺ), was killed in a battle. His son, 'Ikrimah, full of rancor and hatred, fled on the day of the Conquest of Makkah to Yemen. No military contingent was sent to arrest him. He came back of his own volition, at the motivation of his wife, hoping to be pardoned by the forgiving, merciful Messenger of Allah, and embraced the Islamic faith and sacrificed his life in its cause.[1]

'Ikrimah was no exception. Anyone who initially opposed the Prophet (ﷺ) became his follower eventually; the fiercest opponent becoming his most ardent follower and helper.

Beyond the Shores of Arabia

The same was true of the conquered nations beyond the borders of Arabia. The powerful empires of the time considered their civilizations to be superior to all others. They had their own values, their own criterions of vice and virtue, good and evil. Their conquests brought them joy and their setbacks spurred them on to act yet more resolutely to turn the tables on their victorious foes.

Thus, when news began to come of successful military campaigns from the Arabs, they paid little head. For centuries, they had considered the Arabs weak, backwards and uncivilized, and dismissed these new tidings as being merely insignificant forays and audacious incursions. In the manner of empires, they resolved to punish this seeming impudence, but as time passed and the Arab conquests continued, they realized that they had grossly underestimated this new force. Eventually overwhelmed and crushed, their hearts were filled with fear in addition to bitter hatred and vengeful loathing.

Human history consists of a long narrative of conquerors humiliating and crushing the conquered, looting, impoverishing and dishonouring them. Islamic history, however, presented quite a different scenario. The Muslim conquerors distributed the royal treasuries accumulated over centuries among the subjects of the conquered territories. They struck off the oppressive taxes and instead imposed the *Jizyah*, a light tax on

1 Sunan An-Nasā'i: 4072; and Al-Bidāyah Wan Nihāyah: 4/297.

non-Muslims in exchange for their exemption from military service. The conquered enjoyed the same rights as the conquerors. Both were at par at the bar of justice. It was a new system of government which evoked deep consideration and many questions in the minds of the conquered people. Amazed, bewildered, and intrigued, they wanted to know one thing – what was the cause of this new method of rule?

To every question they posed, only one answer was given: These were the teachings of the prophet who felt for all mankind; whose aim was to benefit humanity without distinction of colour or race; who desired nothing of this world for himself and who sought to give everyone an opportunity for temporal and spiritual bliss; who ensured to it that everyone, the conquerors and the conquered, shared equal opportunities and were entitled to basic human rights.

Witnessing this philosophy being turned into reality before their eyes, entire populations couldn't help but fall in love with the Prophet (ﷺ) and his message. Their initial spite turned into curiosity, then wonder, and finally, reverence and respect.

Centuries upon centuries have passed, but there has never been a decrease in people's love for Muhammad (ﷺ). There have always been, and always will be, multitudes of people who adore the ultimate paragon of virtue and want others to love him as they do.

People have vied with each other in extolling the virtues of this blessed man. His companions described every aspect of his life, whether personal or military, public or private. Those who heard about him thirsted for more details about him, seeking out the Prophet's close companions to learn more. Many devoted their entire lives to collecting and preserving any knowledge available about his life, in order to pass it down for future generations to benefit from. Is this aspect, there is no parallel to the Messenger of Allah (ﷺ) anywhere in human history. There has never been a man like him whose words and acts, character and conduct, habits and merits were written, taught and preached by so many men.

His life was not like that of any other person's. One of the most important things to know about him was that the divine revelation used to come according to his and his companions' circumstances; and that as soon as the divine inspiration was revealed, he would immediately put it into practice. His actions guaranteed his success.

No one, not even the most critical of observers, could find any discrepancy between the divine revelation and his own demeanor. The Qur'an and the Prophet's way of life were twin aspects of a single truth. Both were interrelated in theory and practice. The beauty of his conduct has never been matched by any other individual in existence. It is no wonder, then, that the Companions were so overwhelmingly impressed and captivated by him and why they, in turn, narrated the events of his life so clearly, perfectly and beautifully.

Poetic Tributes from Umm Ma'bad and Hassān

The Companions did not exaggerate in their descriptions of Prophet Muhammad (ﷺ). They described and narrated what they saw with their own eyes. Their accounts were not marred by verbosity. The beauty of the one whom they spoke of was so perfect and sublime that any attempt to exaggerate would be tantamount to defect. Affectation was out of the question, for the feelings inspired by the grace of the Prophet (ﷺ) were too sincere for pretence.

The spontaneity of Umm Ma'bad's praise, who was not yet a muslim, owed itself to the beauty and perfection of the Messenger's character and personality, her simple words glimmering with truth. Centuries have passed, but her words ring as sweet and true today as they did on the day she spoke them. Her words captivated the urbane and the rustic alike. How could it be? The mystery was solved by the poet Hassān bin Thābit, who had devoted his entire life to eulogizing the Messenger of Allah (ﷺ):

مَا إِنْ مَّدَحْتُ مُحَمَّدًا بِمَقَالَتِي　　　لٰكِنْ مَّدَحْتُ مَقَالَتِي بِمُحَمَّدِ

'I did not praise Muhammad with my words. Rather I made my words worthy of praise by (beauty of) Muhammad (whom I used my words to describe)'.

The flawlessness and perfection of his morals was impressive. Yet even more impressive was the beauty of his bondage to Allah. Whereas his morals concerned his relationship with fellow men, his spiritual conduct concerned his relationship with Allah Almighty.

When asked about the way he prayed during Ramadan, especially the eleven Rak'āt (units) of Tarāweeh, his eloquent wife Ayeshah replied:

فَلَا تَسْأَلْ عَنْ حُسْنِهِنَّ وَ طُولِهِنَّ

'Oh, don't ask me about their beauty and their length!'[1] In essence, the perfection and purity of his worship – just like everything else he did in his life – were simply indescribable.

It was this type of worship, sincere and beautiful, which the Prophet (ﷺ) advised his Companions to observe and replicate:

«صَلُّوا كَمَا رَأَيْتُمُونِي أُصَلِّي»

"Pray as you see me praying."[2]

and

«خُذُوا عَنِّي مَنَاسِكَكُمْ»

"Learn from me how to perform the ceremonies and rites of Hajj."[3]

It was the beauty of this worship which attracted the observers so strongly:

﴿وَأَنَّهُۥ لَمَّا قَامَ عَبْدُ ٱللَّهِ يَدْعُوهُ كَادُوا۟ يَكُونُونَ عَلَيْهِ لِبَدًا﴾

"And when the slave of Allah (Muhammad ﷺ) stood up invoking Him (his Lord - Allah) in prayer, they (the jinn) just made round him a dense crowd as if sticking one over the other (in order to listen to the Prophet's ﷺ recitation)."[4]

1 Sahīh-ul-Bukhāri: 1147; Sahih Muslim: 738.

2 Sahīh-ul-Bukhāri: 631.

3 Sahīh Muslim: 1297; As-Sunan Al-Kubra lil Baihaqī: 125/5. The wording of the Hadith is by the latter.

4 Al-Jinn 72:19.

Military Expeditions

The Prophet's life was multi-faceted and addressed each and every aspect of life and society. One of the greatest issues that the Prophet (ﷺ) faced was that of his armed struggle to defend the faith and the believers who were persecuted by their enemies.

The Companions of the Prophet (ﷺ) observed and recorded the Messengers behaviour in every sphere of life beginning with his formal worship, and then everything else from his social interactions and conduct with others, to his morals, manners, and the merits and rewards of good deeds. These subjects are all interlinked and imperative parts of a fully comprehensive and correct Islamic upbringing, education, and training; Muslim jurists and scholars of Hadith throughout history have followed this order when compiling their books and teaching their students.

The subject of military expeditions and wars carried out for the sake of Allah, however, differs somewhat from other central topics.

In military campaigns, as with everything else, the Prophet's conduct was the center of attention. He was not only a military commander, but a model of courage and bravery for others. In the heart of battle, the bravest of warriors took refuge behind him, as Barā' ibn 'Āzib related:

كُنَّا وَاللَّهِ! إِذَا احْمَرَّ الْبَأْسُ نَتَّقِي بِهِ، وَإِنَّ الشُّجَاعَ مِنَّا لَلَّذِي يُحَاذِي بِهِ، يَعْنِي النَّبِيَّ ﷺ .

> "By Allah, we shielded ourselves behind him. The brave amongst us was the one, who could stand alongside him (the Prophet ﷺ)."[1]

The Messenger of Allah (ﷺ) was a model in *Jihād* – the greatest warrior, the wisest commander, the most merciful conqueror. He made important decisions and took counsel with others when it was needed.

His followers fought alongside him with extraordinary zeal and courage. Their exploits of valour have left indelible marks on history, marks which are the proud heritage of the entire Muslim *Ummah*. The

1 Sahih Muslim: (79)- 1776.

way they fought was without parallel and the way they expressed their emotions in poetry was no less unique.

National epics are usually full of hyperbole, exaggerating and even lying; the poetry of *Jihād*, however, was eloquent narrations of the events that took place, expressed with truth and sincerity. The Companions spoke of what they did and felt without ever stretching the facts. At the same time, their epics were the true mirrors of their inner feelings.

The exploits and the sagas of the Companions of the Prophet (ﷺ), like their *Jihād* narrations, became the heritage of later-day Hadith scholars, jurists, and Qur'anic commentators who derived points of law from those very traditions. Historians and biographers also collected these narrations in detail for their own scholarly purposes.

The numerous Ahādith recording and reporting the events and details of battles and skirmishes were collected, categorized, and classified in accordance to the specific needs of the scholars. As the science of Ahādith evolved and grew in stages, the narrations of military expeditions were collected alongside accounts of events that took place immediately before, after, or interlinked with them. For example, due to the fact that most of the battles were fought outside Madinah, it necessitated that the Muslim warriors had to travel great distances across vast stretches of land. Thus, the reports of those journeys became an inseparable part of the many stories of *Jihād*, and also there were journeys for *Jihād* but no fighting took place. All these details were written down in accordance to their respective time frames.

Seerah A Closer Look

Meaning of Seerah

The Arabic word "Seerah" is derived from a root-word, "*Sair* (سَير)," which means "to start, to set out, to travel." The plural of *"Seerah"* is *"Siyar"*(سِيَر) ." Initially, the word *"Siyar"* was used for those travels which the Prophet (ﷺ) undertook for the purpose of *Jihād*. Subsequently, as the events of journeys and battles were recorded together, the categories which consisted of these narrations were then called *Maghāzī* and *Siyar*" (military expeditions and journeys).

"Seerah" is the noun derived from the verb "*Sāra Yaseero* (سَارَ يُسِيْرُ)." It means "bearing, attitude, and position." The word conjures up the idea of 'shape, form, condition' and so on. In the Qur'an it is used in that sense when the staff of Moses changed into a serpent and Allah told him to pick it up again:

﴿خُذْهَا وَلَا تَخَفْ سَنُعِيدُهَا سِيرَتَهَا الْأُولَىٰ﴾

"Grasp it and fear not. We shall return it to its former state." [1]

Since Siyar is the plural of Seerah, its general meaning include that of 'conditions, occurrences and the way of life.'

It should be noted that the narrations relating to *Maghāzi* and *Siyar* were of themselves a source of proof for *Ijtihād* and *Istinbat* in Islamic matters. In Islamic law, *Ijtihād* is a term which refers to making independent judgments in legal situations or to answer theological questions. This is based upon the acceptable interpretation and application of the principles of *Fiqh* (jurisprudence); and is the opposite of *Taqleed* (following previous statements or rulings). *Istinbat* means to infer or derive further points of law from existing laws. Both are vital and imperative factors in the consideration and implementation of Islamic law.

Apart from historians, many jurists wrote books on the military campaigns of the Prophet (ﷺ). Though they were categorized as books of *Siyar*, they contained rulings on important issues connected with *Jihad* and military expeditions. Examples include *"As-Siyar"* by al-Aazā'i (d. 157 AH) and *"Kitab as-Siyar as-Sagheer"* and *"Kitab as-Siyar Al-Kabeer"* by Muhammad bin Hasan Ash-Sheybani (d. 189 AH).

These books have been referred to as books of international law, by some such as Dr. Muhammad Hameedullah.[2]

1 Tāhā 20:21.

2 Khutbat-i-Bahawalpur, Khutba 5, P. 164-166. See also Sahih-ul-Bukhāri, *Kitab-ul-Jihad was-Siyar;* and Sahih Muslim, *Kitab-ul-Jihad was-Siyar*. Bukhāri described the battles and the events which occurred in the course of those battles in Kitab-ul-Maghāzi.

The art of writing books on the Seerah and military expeditions evolved over time. Historians expanded the categories and contents contained within these books, gradually moving on from certain standards of narrations until they included poetic Verses written about the Prophet (ﷺ), his personal and family history, accounts of his kinsmen, the events preceding and following his Prophetic mission, his merits, qualities, habits and character.

An interesting thing to note is that the word *Seerah* is expansive enough in its meaning that not only can it easily contain all the aforementioned information, but it also allows for one to deduce points of law from them and to derive conclusions based upon analytical study of those texts.

Evolution of Biographical Literature

Studying accounts of the Prophet's travels closely is not only fascinating, especially when noting their gradual evolution into full biographies, but is academically rewarding as well. Before beginning a formal study of the Messenger's Seerah, it is worth pausing to review the accounts of biographers during different periods of history in order to recognize the great importance that members of the *Ummah* gave to his life story, and to note how much care Muslim scholars took in documenting the events of his life.

Eyewitness Accounts of Prophet's Life and Military Campaigns

Reading of the Qur'an gives a reader, a general idea of the Prophet's personality, but the main and most detailed sources of information about his life and military campaigns are the eyewitness accounts of those people who were in his company during these events.

The records of the Prophet's expeditions as recorded in the authentic books of Ahādith and Sunan have been given mostly by Ali ibn Abi Tālib, 'Abbās ibn 'Abdul-Muttalib, 'Abdur-Rahmān ibn 'Auf, Abdullah bin Mas'ūd, Jābir bin 'Abdullah, Zaid bin Thābit, Abu Mūsā

Al-Ash'arī, Abu Qatādah, Salamah bin Akwa'ؓ and others.

Many of the events of the Battle of Hunain were narrated by Abu Qatadah ؓ. Details of the journey to Hudaibiyyah, found in Sahih Muslim and Sunan Abu Dawood were narrated by Salamah bin Akwa'ؓ. He also described the events of the campaigns of Dhi Qarad and Kheybar.

Talhah bin 'Ubaidullahؓ narrated occurrences of the Battle of Uhud, and Sahl bin Sa'dؓ related those of the Battle of the Trench. The Mother of the Believers 'Ā'ishah(ؓ) also spoke of those battles which she witnessed, such as when she provided water and first aid to the wounded soldiers of the Battle of Uhud.[1]Her narrations can be found in Sahih Al-Bukhāri.[2]

Many younger Companions such as 'Abdullah ibn 'Abbās, 'Abdullah ibn 'Umar, 'Abdullah ibn 'Amr ibn 'Ās, Anas ibn Mālik, Barā' ibn 'Āzib, and 'Abdullah ibn az-Zubairؓ also participated in these excursions and shared their observations.

Some detailed narrations come from Abu Hurairahؓ, who became a Muslim on the eve of the Battle of Kheybar and took part in every battle thereafter. He recounted not only those incidents which he experienced himself, but also those which he learnt from other Companions.

This sharing and passing down of narrations occurred frequently amongst the Companions, and was in fact a vital factor in the accurate recording of events. Some of the youngest Companions, most notably Anas ibn Mālik, 'Abdullah ibn 'Umar, and 'Abdullah ibn Abbāsؓ, related stories from their elders and others who had taken part in battles which they themselves were unable to participate in due to their young age.

Anas ibn Mālikؓ was present at Badr, but only as a servant to the Messenger of Allah, and was forbidden from actively fighting at the time. His son, Mūsā ibn Anas, later said that his father took part in

1 Sahih-ul-Bukhāri: 4064.
2 Sahih-ul-Bukhāri: 4065 and 4077.

eight battles[1] later on and narrated them in great detail, although he included stories that were told to him by other Companions as well.

The first battle which 'Abdullah bin 'Umar ﷺ witnessed was the Battle of the Trench, followed by *Bai'at* (the Pledge of) *Ar-Ridwān* and other skirmishes. During the era of the caliphs he travelled as far as Syria, Iraq, Persia, Egypt and Tunisia to fight for the cause of Allah. As for the battles preceding the Battle of Trench, he obtained information about them from his father and others and narrated them later.

'Abdullah bin 'Abbās ﷺ, the *Hibr* (learned scholar) of the Muslim *Ummah* narrated an extensive number of Ahādith from the Prophet(ﷺ), as well as stories about the events of his life and the battles that took place. He was, however, extremely young at the time and is considered to have been only fifteen years old at the time of the Prophet's death.

It is important to note here that he had been living in Makkah alone with his family until the Conquest of Makkah and migrated to Madinah only after the Conquest. Interpreting the Qur'anic Verse:

﴿ إِلَّا ٱلْمُسْتَضْعَفِينَ مِنَ ٱلرِّجَالِ وَٱلنِّسَآءِ وَٱلْوِلْدَٰنِ ﴾

"Except the weak ones among the men, women, and the children"[2],

He remarked:

كُنْتُ أَنَا وَأُمِّي مِنَ الْمُسْتَضْعَفِينَ : أَنَا مِنَ الْوِلْدَانِ وَأُمِّي مِنَ النِّسَاءِ .

'Me and my mother were considered helpless (i.e. we were forced to live among the infidels in Makkah because we were feeble). I was just a child and my mother a fragile woman.'[3]

Most of Ibn 'Abbās' narrations concerning the battles and the Prophet's life were based, aside from his own experiences, on what he avidly learnt from elder Companions. He shared his enthusiasm in learning the details of the Prophet's life with the following story:

"When the Messenger of Allah died, I said to an Ansarī (an Ausi or

1 Al-Isabah: 1/276.
2 An-Nisa' 4:98.
3 Sahih-ul-Bukhāri: 1375 and 4597; Tafsir At-Tabari, An-Nisa' 4:98.

Khazraji Muslim of Madinah): 'Let us go to the Companions of Allah's Messenger and inquire of them about him. There are many of them now.' He replied: 'O son of 'Abbās, do you think that people need you? There are many Companions of the Messenger of Allah ﷺ among them and you see them.'

So I went on without him and began gathering information. If I came to know of a Hadith and I knew the narrator, I would go to him. If I found him taking a noonday nap, I would tie up a sheet of cloth around my waist and knees and sit down, the wind blowing sands over me. As he came out of the house and saw me, he would exclaim: 'O cousin of the Prophet, what brought you here? If you had sent me a message, I would have come to you.' I would say: 'No. I have a better right to come to you myself.' Then I would ask him about the Hadith.

That Ansārī (whom I had asked to accompany me in the pursuit of knowledge) lived long enough to see me surrounded by people asking me questions about the Prophet's life and works. Thereupon, that Ansari commented: 'This young man proved to be wiser than me.'"[1]

It is quite clear from the above that the young Companions and their pupils were always eager to discover more about the life and works of Allah's Messenger(ﷺ). They collected every bit of information from eyewitnesses and transmitted them on words. The science of Seerah was an important branch of religious knowledge and that it kept evolving over time.

'Ikrimah, a famous Tābi'ee (of the generation after the Companions), said in praise of Ibn 'Abbās: 'He was a sea of knowledge. No academic issue was too difficult for him."[2]

This was only natural considering that the Prophet(ﷺ) had famously supplicated for him:

«اَللّٰهُمَّ! عَلِّمْهُ الْكِتَابَ»

1 At-Tabaqat li Ibn Sa'd: 367,368/2; Al-Mustadrak Lil-Hākim: 106,107/1. According to Dhahabī, the Hadith is authentic and fulfills the conditions laid down by Bukhāri.

2 Siyar 'Alām-un-Nubala': 3/354.

O Allah, teach him the Book (i.e Qur'an),"[1]and

«اَللّٰهُمَّ! عَلِّمْهُ الْحِكْمَةَ»

"O Allah, teach him the wisdom (i.e Hadith)."[2]

'Abdullah bin 'Abbās acquired knowledge from eminent Companions like 'Umar, 'Ali, Mu'ādh, 'Abbās bin 'Abdul-Muttalib, 'Abdur-Rahmān bin 'Auf, Abu Sufyān Sakhr bin Harb, Abu Dharr, 'Ubayy bin Ka'b and Zaid bin Thābit ﷺ. Later on, a large number of Tābi'een (the generation after the Companions) became his pupils and studied under him.

During the lifetime of Ibn 'Abbās, people used to put down in writing his narrations. Sometimes, some of the sub-narrators, who had written down his words, would have him check what they had written to ascertain the accuracy of their writings.

After Ibn 'Abbās ﷺ had lost his eyesight, the scholars of Tā'if came to him with the written texts of his narrations and told him they wanted to hear those narrations directly from him.

He acquiesced, but as he started reciting his Ahādith, he found that his sequence was different from that of the written copies. It was uncomfortable for him because he had to change the sequence of his narrations to comply with that of the written texts. In order to overcome this difficulty, he told them to recite the written Ahādith and said:

"If I affirm a Hadith, it will amount to my having narrated the Hadith to him.' They did as he told them and read out their texts to him.[3]

Barā' bin 'Āzib al-Ansāri ﷺ was also a young Companion and a friend of 'Abdullah bin 'Umar. Neither of them was allowed to take part in the Battle of Badr because of their young age. Though Barā' could not take part in the Battle of Badr, he did gather information about many events of the battle from those who took part in it, a fact that speaks for his enthusiasm for learning. Bukhāri included his

1 Sahih-ul-Bukhārī: 75.

2 Sahih-ul-Bukhārī: 3756.

3 Siyar 'Al ām-un-Nubalā': 3/354, 355.

narrations concerning Badr in his Sahih.

Barā' took part in the Battle of Uhud and spoke about many incidents that had taken place during it. These narrations are also recorded in Bukhārī. As well, Bukhārī and Muslim have both included Barā' bin 'Āzib's narrations about the journey of *'Umrat-ul-Qadā'* and the ceremonial rites of Hajj. Incidentally, these narrations also include many details about the Treaty of Hudaibiyyah. In the same way, Bukhārī, Muslim, Tirmidhī, and Abu Dawood collected the details of the Battle of Hunain as given by Abu Ishāq as-Sabee'ī on the authority of Barā' bin 'Āzib.

Moreover, Tirmidhī also quoted narrations regarding the events of the military campaigns of 'Alī bin Abi Tālib and Khālid bin Waleed in parts of Yemen, as given by Barā' bin 'Āzib.[1]

On the whole, Barā' bin 'Āzib took part in fifteen military expeditions[2] with the Messenger of Allah and narrated details from them all. His narrations come to a total of five hundred and three.

Abu Hurairah embraced Islam on the eve of the Battle of Kheybar[3]. Like other Companions, he also related the events of the Battle of Kheybar as well as the campaigns following it. He also recorded in great detail the events of the previous battles. For example, he described the Battle of Rajee', including the martyrdom of 'Āsim bin Thābit Ansārī, the maternal grandfather of 'Āsim bin 'Umar bin al-Khattāb ﷺ and the imprisonment of Khubaib and Zaid bin Dathnah ﷺ, followed by detailed description of how Khubaib was martyred.[4]

The massive amount of knowledge that he collected and shared with others displayed his devotion to the pursuit of knowledge. He took the greatest care in gathering information about every event that took place related to the Prophet (ﷺ) and his followers and passing this

1 Jāmi' at-Tirmidhī: 1704.

2 Musnad Abi Dawood at-Tayālasī: 92/2; At-Tabaqat Li-Ibn Sa'd: 368/4. The chain of narration is authentic.

3 Al-'Istī'āb li-Ibn Abdul-Barr: P. 852.

4 Sahih-ul-Bukhārī: 4086; Sunan Abi Dawood: 2660.

knowledge down to the newer generations of the Muslims.

It is clear from these facts that there was always a desire amongst the Companions, both during and after the lifetime of the Prophet (ﷺ), to inform themselves of the details of his life, including the battles waged for the sake of Islam, and to memorize them and transmit them to others.

Early Compositions of Seerah

Amongst the youngest Companions, there were several who were outstanding in their keen interest in the *Maghāzī* and *Siyar*. Among them Sahl ibn Abi Hathmah (b. 2AH) and Sa'eed ibn Sa'd ibn 'Ubādah Al-Khazraji left behind written tracts on the *Maghāzī* and *Siyar*. At the later stage, great scholars, such as Imam Ahmad, At-Tabarī, and Balādhuri would refer to these tracts.

Role of the Tābi'een

The Tābi'een consisted of the generation born after the death of the Prophet, and who learned their religion and their history from the Companions. They, in turn, developed the science of Seerah. Whatever they heard from the Companions, both in Ahādith and regarding the *Maghāzī*, they put into writing as well as committing to memory. This ensured the strong authenticity and high reliability of their narrations.

As a result, later authorities, such as Imam Al-Bukhāri would refer to these Tābi'een. He took details of the Prophet's journey on the eve of the Conquest of Makkah from 'Urwah ibn az-Zubair[1], who was born in the year 23 AH[2].

Similarly, Imam Muslim recorded the details of the Conquest of Makkah based upon the account of 'Abdullah ibn Rabāh who had, in turn, learned them from Abu Hurairah.[3]

Listed below are the names of other prominent Tabi'een and

1 Sahih-ul-Bukhārī: 4280.
2 Siyar 'Alām-un-Nubala': 4/422.
3 Sahih Muslim: 1780.

scholars who contributed to the recording and preservation of the Seerah.

- Sa'eed bin Musayyib al-Makhzūmi (d. 94 AH): He was a famous Tābi'ee, Muhaddith and jurist. He left behind several written works on the Prophet's life and conquests. Most of his writings were included by At-Tabari in his history.
- 'Abān bin 'Uthmān bin 'Affān (d. 101 AH): Imam Mālik took from him his accounts of the military campaigns. His narrations are to be found in Tabaqat Ibn Sa'd, Tabari's history, and Tāreekh Ya'qūbī, as well as in books of Hadith.
- Abu Fadalah Abdullah bin Ka'b bin Mālik (d. 97AH): Of those who wrote on the military campaigns, Ibn Ishāq and Tabari were the two most famous men who made use of his writings.
- 'Āmir bin Sharaheel Sha'bī (d.103 AH): Many writers including Abu Ishaq Sabee'i, Sa'eed bin Masrooq Thauri, 'A'mash, Qatadah and Mujālid bin Sa'eed etc. quoted his narrations.
- Qāsim bin Muhammad bin Abi Bakr as-Siddiq: His narrations have been preserved in the books of Hadith scholars as well as in the compilations of historians like Tabari, Balādhuri, and Wāqidī.
- Wahb bin Munabbih (d. 144 AH): His compilation of Hadith was discovered by Dr Hameedullah in Istanbul. He also composed a book on the military campaigns, a part of which is still extant in Heidelberg. His narrations are extant in the compilations of Ibn Ishāq, Ibn Qutaibah, Mas'ūdi, Maqdasi and Tabari.

By the beginning of the second century of the Hijra calendar, the art of writing the Prophet's biography and his military campaigns became quite refined and organized at the hands of the literate Tābi'een and became a part of the curriculum of the next generation. During this period there were also some other Tābi'een, younger than Wahb bin Munabbih, who specialized in Hadith, Sunan, biography and accounts of military campaigns. Some of them wrote books on these subjects. Their information was based on the narrations they had laboriously collected from the Companions and senior Tābi'een.

During the era of the successors of the Companions (Tābi'een), 'Āsim bin 'Umar bin Qatadah stood out as a very important figure. He was the grandson of Qatadah bin Nu'mān ﷺ, a famous Companion. He collected narrations from his grandmother, Rumaithah ﷺ, who was herself a Companion. In addition to her, he also collected narrations from Jabir bin Abdullah and Anas bin Mālik ﷺ, who had special interest in the military campaigns.

Men like Bakr bin Ashaj, Ibn 'Ajlān and Ibn Ishāq were his pupils. Ibn Ishāq narrated from him the story of the Jews' conversion to Islam in his book. For his deep knowledge of the military campaigns, 'Umar bin Abdul-Azeez appointed him an instructor in *Maghāzi* and *Manāqib* (military campaigns and glorious deeds) at the Jāmi' Umawi (Ummayad Mosque) Damascus.

Another luminary of this age was Imam Muhammad bin Muslim bin 'Ubaidullah bin 'Abdullah bin Shihāb Zuhri Qurashi. He was born in 50 AH and died in 124 AH. He acquired knowledge from Ibn 'Umar, Sahl bin Sa'd, Anas bin Mālik, Sā'ib bin Yazeed, 'Abdullah bin Tha'labah bin Su'air and Mahmūd bin Rabee'. He also spent eight years with Sa'eed bin Musayyib, a senior Tabi'ee. He took Ahādeeth from other Tābi'een, most of whom were the sons of the Prophet's companions such as Ali bin Husain, 'Urwah bin Zubair, Sālim bin Abdullah bin 'Umar, Muhammad bin Jubair bin Mut'im, Muhammad bin Nu'mān bin Basheer, Abu Salamah bin 'Abdur-Rahmān bin 'Auf, 'Ubaidullah bin 'Abdullah bin Utbah, Qāsim bin Muhammad, 'Āmir bin Sa'd, Kharijah bin Zaid bin Thābit, 'Udaidullah bin Ka'b bin Mālik and 'Abān bin 'Uthmān ﷺ.

Imam Zuhrī labored hard to collect narrations relating to Sunan, Maghāzī and Siyar from his eminent teachers. Historians tell us that he used to go to the house of each Ansāri, ask every companion of the prophet, man and woman, old or young, about the words and acts of Allah's Messenger.[1] Thus, the majority of his teachers were from the

1 Tahdheeb-ul-Tahdheeb: 9/397.

Companions of the Prophet (ﷺ).

Those who narrated from him were eminent Tabi'een such as 'Atā' bin Abi Rabah (who was older than him), 'Umar bin 'Abdul-Azeez (who died long before Zuhri), 'Amr bin Deenār, 'Amr bin Shu'aib, Zaid bin Aslam, and Mansūr bin Mu'tamar. Among his students were great Hadith scholars including Ma'mar bin Rāshid, Auzā'i, Shu'aib bin Abi Hamzah, Sufyān bin 'Uyainah, Mālik bin Anas, and Laith bin Sa'd ﷺ.

The leading authorities on the art of Maghāzī and Siyar, Musa bin 'Uqbah and Muhammad bin Ishāq, were the disciples of Imam Zuhri, And so were other experts in the field of Maghāzī: Yaqūb bin Ibrahīm, Muhammad bin Salih Tammār and 'Abdur-Rahmān bin 'Abdul-'Azeez. All of them left valuable tracts and books on *Maghāzī*.

Among Imam Zuhri's contemporaries were Abu Ishāq Sabee'ī, (d. 127 AH), Yaqūb bin 'Utbah bin Mugheerah Madani (d. 128 AH), Abu Rūh Yazeed bin Rumān Asadi Madani (d. 130 AH) and Abul-Aswad Muhammad bin 'Abdur-Rahman Madani (d. 131 AH or 137 AH). The writings of the latter scholars provided a rich harvest for the writers of the six canonical books of Hadith (Kutub Sittah) besides Ibn Sa'd, Tabari, Balādhuri, Ibn Hajar, Ibn Kathir, Ibn Qayyim and Ibn Sayyed-un-Nās. Hafiz Ibn Hajar quoted forty-eight narrations relating to Maghāzi and Siyar in his book, *Al-'Isabah*, from his book.

- Another great scholar of Hadith, *Maghāzi* and Siyar of this age was Musa bin 'Uqbah (d. 140 AH or 141 AH). He was initially, a slave of Zubair's family. He met Abdullah bin Umar and was the teacher of Imam Mālik. The latter acknowledged his skill in the field of Maghāzi and Siyar and encouraged people to learn this art from him.

- His narrations have been preserved in the six canonical books of Hadith and in the compilations of Ibn Kathir and Ibn Hajar. Eduard Sachau published a part of his *Maghāzī*, *Al-Muntaqa min Maghāzī Musa bin 'Uqbah,* in 1904. He had found the manuscript in Berlin.

- This age also saw the rise of many other stars like 'Abdullah bin Abu Bakr bin Hazm (d. 130 or 135 AH) an Imam of Maghāzī and teacher of many Hadith scholars and historians, Dawood bin Husain 'Umawi (d. 135 AH) and Sulemān bin Tarkhān Taimī (d.143 AH). The narrations of these scholars are to be found in the six canonical books of Hadith as well as in the compilations of Ibn Mu'tamir 'Ishbīlī and Ibn Hajar and Suhailī's *Ar-Raud ul-Unuf.*

He also wrote a book entitled *As-Seerat-as-Sahihah*. Seventy-seven pages of this book were published as an annex to Wāqidī's *Kitāb-ul-Maghāzī* in 1856, thanks to the efforts of the orientalist Von Krammer.

Evolution of the Art of Seerah Writing

Those mentioned above were the early writers of *Maghāzī* and *Siyar*. A review of the books of the next generation of writers who took narrations from them reveals an important stage in the evolutionary process of the art of Seerah writing.

By the end of the first century, and until the first quarter of the second Hijra century, the meaning of the word Seerah had become wider in scope. Seerah was no longer only an account of the Prophet's travels and military campaigns, but also contained a description of his genealogy, the prevailing socio-economic conditions at the time of his birth and those before it, the important events during his childhood, youth, and years before he began his prophetic mission.

A look at the first part of the Maghāzī of Ibn Ishāq (d. 151 AH) reveals that his Seerah begins with the Prophet's lineage going back to the Prophet Abraham, followed by accounts of the kings and tribes of Yemen, the propagation of idol-worship by 'Amr bin Luhayy, accounts of Bani Jurhum and their closure of Zamzam well, the latter's recovery by Abdul-Muttalib, accounts of the Prophet's relatives on his mother's side, the Prophet's birth, the event of Tubba' Himyarī, the assault of the People of the Elephant and the poetry concerning it, the Prophet's marriage to Khadeejah, the anxious waiting by the Jews of a coming prophet, and the incidental mention of Salmān Farsi's conversion to

Islam.

Next he describes the reconstruction of the Ka'bah, Warqah bin Naufal professing the Christian faith before the Prophet began his mission, how the Prophet passed his days in seclusion in the Cave of Hira, the beginning of the Revelation of the Qur'ān, finding out the exact date of the Night of Power *(Lailat-ul-Qadr)* when the Revelation began, the temporary cessation of the Revelation, names of the earliest converts to Islam, the persecution of the Muslims by the pagans, the economic boycott of the Prophet and his family, the migration to Abyssinia (modern Ethiopia), the mission of the Prophet, the death of Abu Tālib and Khadeejah, the marriage of his daughters, and the Prophet's wives, all in one place.

This is followed by a description of his enemies who ridiculed him and the signs proving that he was a Messenger of Allah. Together with all these things, he also describes such events as the conversion of Umm Shareek Dausiyah, Abu Hurairah ad-Dausī, 'Adi bin Hātim, and Jareer bin 'Abdullah. These events belong to a much later date but he has juxtaposed them with a description of the events relating to the people of Yemen as all these people belong to Yemen. These are followed by a description of the Isrā' (the Prophet's night journey from Makkah to Jerusalem). Immediately after that, he begins writing about the Prophet's military campaigns. The part of Ibn Ishaq's biographical work which has been retrieved now closes with an account of the Battle of Uhud.

- One of the notable teachers of Ibn Ishaq was Abdul-Malik bin Muhammad bin Amr bin Hazm Madani, an authority on the *Maghāzī*. He died in 176 or 177 AH, after the death of Ibn Ishāq.
- Another renowned contemporary of Ibn Ishāq was Ma'mar bin Rashid (d. 150 or 153 AH). Historians such as Baladhurī, Ibn Sa'd and Tabari, and famous Hadith scholars, benefited by his books. A complete copy of his *Maghāzī*, which is still extant in Chicago, was published by Nabeeh Abood with some additions. Copies of a part

of his book are extant in Istanbul, Rabat, and Damascus.

- Other contemporaries of Ibn Ishāq include Abu Muhammad Abdur-Rahmān bin 'Abul-'Azeez Hanafī (d. 162 AH), Muhammad bin Sālih bin Dinār (d. 168 AH), 'Abdullah bin Ja'far Makhramī (d. 170 AH), and Abu Ma'shar Sindi (d. 170 AH). Each one of them is considered authority on Seerah in his own right.
- Among Ibn Ishāq's famous pupils were Ziyād bin 'Abdullah Bakkā'ī (d. 183 AH), Salamah bin Fadl Abrash Ansāri (d. 191 AH), Yunus bin Bukair Shaibani (d. 199 AH) and Abul-'Abbās Wahb bin Jareer bin Hazim Azdi (d. 206 AH). They are the transmitters of Ibn Ishāq's Seerah. Amongst those who benefited by Bakkā'ī are great Hadith scholars such as Imam Ahmad, Ahmad bin Abdah Dabbī, Abu Ghassān Nahdī, Ismā'īl bin Taubah and 'Umar bin Zurārah and the writers of Maghāzī and Siyar such as Ibn Hisham. In the second century of the Hijra calendar, Seerah writing reached its peak.
- Other notable biographers of this era are Abu Ishāq Ibrāhīm bin Muhammad Fazāri (d. 186 AH) Yahya bin Sa'eed 'Umawi (d. 194 AH), and Waleed bin Muslim Dimashqi (d. 195 or 196 AH). All of these three men wrote biographies which were preserved in the compilations of the later historians and Seerah writers.

Untrustworthy (*Majrooh*) Biographers

During this time there were many writers of the Prophet's biography who, according to the scholars expert in the Science of Validation *(Al-Jarh wa-Ta'deel),* are extremely weak. For example:

- 'Ali bin Mujāhid bin Muslim Qadi Kabuli (d. 162 Ah): He is *Matrūk* (abandoned, whose narrations are not to be accepted). Tirmidhi, however, took from him only those Ahādith which he had narrated on the authority of Tha'labah.
- Muhammad bin Omar Waqidī (d. 207 AH): He is a famous historian and biographer, although many Hadith scholars were of the opinion that he is *Matrūk* (abandoned). Some Imams of the

Science of Validation dismissed him as a fabricator *(Waddā')* and liar *(Kadhdhāb)*.

- Haitham bin 'Adī bin 'Abdur-Rahman Tha'labī (d.207 AH), a contemporary of Waqidī, is also one of them. His narrations are found in the compilations of Tabari, Balādhari, Ibn Qutaibah, and Mas'ūdī but he, too, has been dismissed as a liar by the Imams of the Science of Validation.

Siyar and *Maghāzī*: Refining and Re-arranging

- An important stage in the evolution of Seerah writing began during the closing years of the second Hijra century and the beginning of the third. It can accurately be referred to as the stage of pruning, refining and arranging. This stage began with the work of the famous biographer Abdul-Malik bin Hisham bin Ayyūb Himyari (d. 213 or 218 AH). He revised, refined and re-arranged the contents of Ibn Ishāq and made some valuable additions to it, borrowing valuable details from the trustworthy authorities. The revised version came to be known later on by his name: *As-Seerat-un-Nabawiyyah li Ibn-i-Hishām*.

- Second important name in this connection is that of Muhammad bin Sa'd Katib Wāqidī (d. 230 AH) wrote his *At-Tabaqat* in eight volumes, of which the first two volumes are on Seerah. Ibn Sa'd was a Hadith scholar; although his mentor and teacher, Waqidi, is unreliable, Ibn Sa'd was considered to be trustworthy. He quoted narrations from Wāqidī; however, he included the chain of narrators for each Hadith and later scholars were easily able to single out those narrations and deduce which of them were authentic (Sahih). Moreover, Ibn Sa'd was very careful in his selection of narrations.

  During this period, some other scholars such as Ibn Habeeb Baghdadi (d. 245 AH) wrote books on history and biography with no chains of narration. His book Al-Muhabbar contains information not found in other books; but verifying the accuracy of that information was and is a difficult task.

- *Tareekh-ul-Yaqūbī* by Ahmad bin Ja'far bin Wahb (d. 292 AH) and another book, *Murooj-udh-Dhahb wa Ma'ādin-ul-Jauhar* by Abul-Hasan Ali bin Husain Mas'ūdi (who died in the middle of the following century) both fall under the same category. Neither quotes the chains of narration for any Hadith quoted within those books.

Biographies Written by Hadith Scholars

In addition to historians, several Hadith scholars also wrote books on Seerah. Most of these books are now nowhere to be found; however, some of their contents were preserved in the books of other authors. The most famous among them are:

- Sa'eed bin Mugheerah Massīsī (d. 220 AH): His narrations are found in Sunan an-Nasā'ī.
- Ahmad bin Muhammad Warrāq (d. 228 AH): His narrations have been quoted in Sunan Abu Dawood, Musnad Abi Ya'la and Musannaf Ibn Abi Shaibah.
- Muhammad bin 'Ā'idh Qurashi (d. 234 AH): Abu Dawood and Nasā'ī quoted his narrations.
- Abdullah bin Muhammad bin Ali bin Nufail Harrāni (d. 234 AH). He wrote a book on military campaigns (maghāzi). Abu Dawood quoted narrations from his book and so did Muslim and other Hadith scholars in their books, on the authority of Dhuhalī.
- Abu Bakr Ibn Abi Shaibah (d. 235 AH): His narrations occur in Bukhāri, Muslim, Sunan Abu Dawood and Sunan An-Nasā'ī. In addition to Al-Musannaf, a collection of Ahādith, he also wrote a book entitled *Awā'il-ul-Islam*, a copy of which is still extant in Berlin. His other book, *Al-Maghāzī*, has already been published.
- An important book from this era is *At-Tareekh* by Khalīfah bin Khayyāt 'Asfarī (d. 240 AH). The first volume of this book is on Seerah and has already been published. The contents of the book have been arranged in a chronological order, beginning from the

first year of the Hijra calendar and followed by a brief chapter on Seerah. He relied on the Seerah of Ibn Ishāq as transmitted by Bakr bin Salmān and Wahab bin Jareer. His biography of the Prophet (ﷺ) is brief, but he is very careful about the chains of narration, quoting only authentic and reliable Ahādith. Khalīfah bin Khayyāt was one of the teachers of Imām Bukhārī.

- Hishām bin Ammār (d. 245 AH): Bukhārī and Nasā'ī quoted his narrations.
- Sa'eed bin Yahya bin Sa'eed 'Umawi (d. 249 AH). A *Thiqah* (trustworthy) person and a Hadith scholar *(Muhaddith)*, he was also the author of a valuable book on *Maghāzī*.[1]
- Zubair bin Bakkār (d. 256 AH) wrote a book on *Seerah* as well as a book on the Prophet's wives, a subject considered to be an important part of *Seerah*.
- Ahmad bin Hārith Kharraz (d. 258 AH) was a highly reliable Hadith scholar *(Muhaddith)*. He left behind a valuable book entitled *'Maghāzī an-Nabi wa Sarāyāhu wa Azwājuhu* (the holy battles of the Prophet, his military expeditions, and his wives).
- Abdul-Mailk bin Muhammad Raqqāshī Basrī (d. 276 AH) wrote a separate book on *Maghāzī*. Ibn Mājah and Ibn Khuzaimah took some narrations from his book.
- Abu Bakr bin Abi Khaithamah Zuhair bin Harb (d. 279 AH) wrote a valuable book, *At-Tareekh-ul-Kabeer* [2], which also contains a brief biography of the Prophet arranged in chronological order. It served as a reference book for Tabari, Dhahabi, and Khateeb Baghdādi.
- Ibrahīm bin Ismā'īl Anbārī Tūsī (d. 290 AH) also wrote a book entitled *Al-Maghāzī*.
- Imam Abu Zur'ah Abdur-Rahman bin 'Amr bin 'Abdullah bin Safwān Nasrī Dimashqī (d. 281 AH). Besides a book on Hadith,

1 Siyar A'lām-un-Nubalā': 139/9; and Tahdheeb-ut-Tahdheeb: 86/4.

2 Tareekh Baghdād: 4/162-164; and Ghayat-un-Nihāyah fi Tabaqat-ul-Qurra', P. 23; and Lisan-ul-Meezan 1/277.

Al-Musannaf, he compiled an important book on history which contained a biography of the Prophet as well as the biographies of his successors (caliphs). This book, entitled *Tareekh Abi Zur'ah Ad-Dimashqī* has already been published and is currently in circulation.

- Imam Abu Ishaq Ibrāhīm bin Ishāq Harbi (d. 285 AH) wrote an important book on the life of the Prophet (ﷺ) during this same time period. In knowledge, piety, and asceticism, he is considered an equal of Imām Ahmad bin Hanbal.
- Abu Muhammad 'Abdullah bin Muslim bin Qutaibah Dīnavari (d. 276 AH) was another well-known author of this age. He wrote several books in the style of Hadith scholars; two of his books, *Al-Ma'ārif* and *'Uyoon-ul-Akhbār*, are considered source-books of Seerah. Another book alleged to be written by him, *Al-Imamah was-Siyāsah*, is disputed as to its authorship, with controversy as to whether it can be truly attributed to him or not. Khateeb Baghdādī said of him: 'He was trustworthy, religious, and learned[1]. On the contrary, Baihaqī and Hākim found fault with him, although Dhahabī defended him from some of his critics.

Imam Yaqūb bin Sufyān Fārsi Fasawī (d. 277 AH), the author of *Al-Ma'rafah wat-Tareekh*, devoted a part of his book to the biography of the Prophet. This part is no longer extant although the third volume of the book contains some excerpts of the missing parts collected from different books.

Seerah Books Written by Historians

- A notable figure of this age is the well-known historian, Ahmad bin Yahya Balādhuri (d. 279 AH) whose compilations are considered to be the source-books of Seerah. His book, Ansāb-ul-Ashrāf, is a history of genealogy and ancestry of the prophet and the different tribes of Arabia. His other book, *Futuh-ul-Buldān,* records the treaties and peace agreements made by the Prophet (ﷺ). Following the methodology of Hadith scholars, he was very careful about the

1 Tareekh Baghdād: 10/170.

chains of narration. Most of his narrations were considered to be authentic (Sahih) but he himself is considered to be weak by the experts in the Science of Validation *(Al-Jarh wat-Ta'deel)*.

- Close to the end of the third century, another important and detailed book on Seerah was compiled by the renowned Hadith scholar, commentator of Qur'an and historian, Muhammad bin Jareer Tabari (d. 310 AH). It was entitled *Tareekh-ul-Umam Wal-Mulook* (A History of Nations and Kings), a part of which was devoted to the Seerah of the Prophet. Although he usually followed the methodology of Hadith scholars and was extremely cautious about chains of narration, his main purpose for this book was simply to collect all the narrations on the subject, regardless of whether they were authentic or weak. It was left to later scholars, who wanted to benefit from his book, to undertake the hard job of assessing, evaluating, scrutinizing and grading the narrations.

When we review the works of Hadith scholars in the field of Seerah writing, we find that their works are better than others in that they gave due care to the authenticity of the chains of narration. They followed the principles of the Science of Validation and took only those Ahādith which met the standards of acceptability, and avoided doubtful or fabricated Ahādith.

Seerah Writers of Spain and Morocco

The fourth century of the Hijra calendar saw the emergence of eminent biographers from Spain and Morocco undertaking the Seerah, in the tradition of the Hadith scholars. During this particular period of time, they led the Muslim world in the science and art of writing the Seerah. They followed both trends previously set by biographers of the Prophet's life – that of comprehensive records of the Prophet's entire life, and that of analysing the incidents of his life.

- Abu Muhammad 'Abdullah bin Abi Zaid Qairawani (d. 386 AH) of Morocco wrote a comprehensive book entitled *Kitab-ul-Jāmi' fi-Sunan wal-Ādāb wal-Maghāzī wat-Taareekh*.

- Imam Ibn Hazm Andalusi (d. 456 AH), in Spain, following the method of *Talkhees* and *Tajreed,* compiled a book entitled *Jawāmi' as-Seerat-un-Nabawiyyah,* using his own authentic sources.

Ibn 'Abdul-Barr Namri Qurtubi (463 AH) wrote *Ad-Durar fi Ikhtisār-il-Maghāzī wa-Siyar,* around the same time as the above mentioned authors. It was followed by another book, *Al-Iktifā' bimā Tadammanahu min Maghāzī Rasoolillah wath-Thalāthatil-Khulafā'* written by Abu Rabee' Suleman bin Musa Kalā'ī Andalusī (d. 634 AH)

Biographical Works of the 6th & 7th Centuries

- *Al-Muntazam fi Tareekh-ul-Mulook Wal-Umam* by Abdur-Rahmān bin Ali bin Muhammad bin Ja'far Jauzi (d. 597 AH) was one of the most prominent books written in the eastern part of the Muslim empire during this period.
- The author began his work with a description of the creation of the earth, the mountains, oceans and rivers, the wonders of the earth, Jinn and other inhabitants of the earth during different epoches of history. It is interesting to note that in this part he also portrayed the horrors of the Hell. Describing the human settlement of the terrestrial globe, he started from Adam; the first man placed on earth by Allah Almighty, and comes finally to a detailed biographical history of the Prophet (ﷺ) arranged in chronological order.
- Later on, Ibn Atheer Jazari (d. 632 AH), a famous Hadith scholar, wrote *Al-Kamil fit-Tarīkh,* a part of which was devoted to the Prophet's biography.
- Yahya bin Humaidah (d. 630 AH) wrote a three-volumes biography of the Prophet known as *Seerah Ibn Abi Tayy.*
- Abu Zakaria Yahya bin Sharaf Nawawi, more famously known as Imam An-Nawawi, was the author of *Tahdheeb-ul-Asmā' wal-Lughat*. The book begins with the biography of the Prophet (ﷺ) and his physical traits *(Shamā'il)*. The author was extremely cautious in his selection of Ahādith; as a result, though this section was brief, it was extremely valuable. It has now been published separately under

a new title: *Tahdheeb As-Seerah an-Nabawiyyah*.

- Ali bin Muhammad bin Mahmūd Kāzroonī (Gazrooni in Persian) (d. 697 AH), a famous Shafi'i historian of the seventh century, wrote a history in seventeen volumes. Titled *'Raudat al-Arīb,'* it contained a detailed biography of the Prophet (ﷺ). Apart from this, he wrote a separate biography of the Prophet (ﷺ), *As-Seerat An-Nabawiyyah,* generally known as *Seerat-i-Kazrooni.*[1]

Biographical works of the 8th Century

- Hafiz Abul-Mu'min Dīmyātī (d. 705 AH) wrote *Al-Mukhtasar fi Seerat-i-Sayyed-il-Bashar,* currently known as *Seerat-i-Dimyātī*. Many an author of the later years benefited by it.
- Another book of this age was *Seerat Khilātī,* written by Allāmah Alā'ud-din Ali bin Muhammad bin Hasan Khilātī Qadoos (d. 708 AH)[2].
- Hafiz Shams-ud-Din Muhammad bin Ahmad bin 'Uthman Dhahabi (d. 748 AH), the most famous Hadith scholar and historian of his age, wrote a voluminous book entitled *Tareekh-ul-Islam*, a part of which was devoted to a detailed biography of the Prophet (ﷺ).
- Hafiz Ibn Kathir (d. 774 AH) wrote a book of the same genre, known as *Al-Bidāya Wan-Nihāyah*. It is one of the most important and highly reliable books of history, the first six parts of which are devoted to the biography of the Prophet (ﷺ). These parts have also been published separately under the title of *As-Seerat an-Nabawiyyah.*

Different Approaches of Biographers

Muhadditheen (scholars of Hadith) studied the personality of the Prophet from every angle possible. They left no aspect of his life alone; they closely observed and recorded his every word and every action. His devotional prayers, the way he worshipped, his dealings with the

1 Ad-durar-ul-Kāminah fi 'A'yān-il-Mi'ati-th- Thāminah: 3/119; Mu'jam-ul-Mu'allifeen: 7/232.
2 Ad-Durar-ul-Kāminah fi A'yān-il-Mi'ati-th-Thāminah: 101/3.

people, his morals and manners, his military campaigns, his habits, his merits, his family life, the way he ate and dressed – each topic has been the subject of intense scrutiny and immense research.

Historians and biographers also focused on these topics, although their approach differed from that of the Hadith scholars. The *Sunan* compiled by the latter began with the Prophet's mission, his message to mankind, his worship, and social dealing, which they described in detail for a variety of reasons. His military campaigns and his personality were noted later on in the books of Ahādith after the above mentioned topics.

Historians and biographers, however, began their works with the Prophet's lineage, his birth, his upbringing, youth, marriage and other personal incidents, as well as the details of his military campaigns and expeditions.

In other words, Hadith scholars in their Sunan concentrate first on his prophetic mission; while biographers and historians focus on his background and personality. The former focused on the Messenger as a prophet of Allah, while the latter looked at him basically as a human being, and at the same time as a prophet. These different approaches explain the variation in the sequence of subjects in their compilations. Though the facts remain the same, the order in which they are described varies.

The Prophet's Life as Described by Bukhārī

- When we look at the collection of authentic (Sahih) Ahādeeth collected by Bukhārī (d. 256 AH), we see that it opens with *Bad' al-Wahyi* (the beginning of the Revelation), followed by *Kitāb al-Imān* (Book of Faith) and *Kitāb al-'Ilm* (Book of Knowledge), followed by *'Ibadāt* (Religious Observances).

These subjects relate to the Prophet's personality as a Messenger of Allah. *Kitāb al-Jihād was-Siyar* (Book of *Jihād* and Travels) is separate from *Kitāb al-Maghāzī* (Book of Military Campaigns). *Kitāb al-Manāqib* describes his personal qualities, habits, personal matters, his illness and death.

Bukhārī lists authentic narrations, verifying the statements of genealogists tracing the Prophet's ancestry to Adam and the merits of Banu Kinanah, Quraish and Banu Hāshim. All the names from 'Abdullah up to 'Adnān are found in the books of genealogists and biographers. Bukhāri also wrote a separate chapter on *'Alāmāt an-Nabuwwah* (Signs of Prophethood) in his book of *Al-Manāqib*, while other writers compiled separate books on *'Alāmāt an-Nabuwwah*. In his books of Fadā'il ashāb an-Nabi and *Manāqib al-Ansār* he describes the Prophet's friends, companions and his kinsmen.

The contents of his other books, *Kitāb al-At'imah*, *Kitāb adh-Dhabā'ih was-Said, Kitāb al-Adāhi* and *Kitāb al-Ashribah,* also revolve around his personality and habits of the prophet, while *Kitāb ad-Da'wat* and *Kitāb ar-Riqāq* describe the details of his devotional worship and his life of abstinence, self-abnegation and piety.

In short, Bukhari tried to cover every conceivable aspect of the Prophet's life and chose for his book a name quite unique in his times: *Al-Jami' as-Sahih al-Musnad Min Hadith-i-Rasūlillah Sunanihi wa Ayyamihi*. According to another narration, the name he gave to his book was *Al-Jami' al-Musnad as-Sahih al-Mukhtasar min Umūr Rasūlillah (ﷺ) wa Sunanihi wa Ayyāmihī*.

Through this name he wanted to convey to the public at large that his Sahih recorded each Hadith with its chain of narration and that it covered all matters relating to the Prophet's life, including his lifestyle and his military campaigns.

The Prophet's Life as Described by Muslim

- Imam Muslim bin Hajjāj Qushairī (d. 261 AH) collected in his book all the authentic Ahādith relating to the Prophet's personal life as well as his lineage, morals, habits, merits, miracles, his life in Makkah and Madinah, *Jihad*, journeys, and his death.

Under the different chapters of the authentic collections of Bukhārī and Muslim, only those narrations which conform to the standard set by Bukhāri and Muslim have been taken. Alhough those narrations do not provide all the details, they do give the outlines of each topic. Remaining details have to be taken from other books of Hadith, biographies and history.

The Prophet's Personal traits and Other Physical Qualities

Many Hadith scholars, besides compiling books of Ahādeeth, wrote separate books on the personality of the Prophet and his character.

- Tirmidhī (d. 275 AH), a distinguished pupil of Imam Bukhārī, besides writing his Sunan comprehending all the above-mentioned topics, wrote a separate book on the Prophet's physical qualities and merits. This book was entitled *Ash-Shamā'il an-Nabawiyyah wal Khasā'is al-Mustafawiyyah,* and has been very well-received by scholars and biographers, and has been popular ever since. Many detailed commentaries have been written on it, which in turn have also become extremely popular.
- Numerous other concise books on the personal traits and physical characteristics of the Prophet were written by Hadith scholars during or before the times of Tirmidhī. Amongst them were Sifat un-Nabi by Abul-Bakhtari Wahb bin Wahb Asadī (d. 200 AH), *Sifat un-Nabi* by Abul-Hasan Ali bin Muhammad Madā'nī (d. 234 AH) and *Sifat wa Akhlāq un-Nabi* by Dawood bin Ali Asfahānī, a Hadith scholar and contemporary of Tirmidhi[1]. These books are no longer extant, although their contents became a part of other comprehensive books later on.
- In addition to Tirmidhī, several other Muhadditheen wrote books on the Shamā'il (personal traits and personal qualities of the Prophet). The following are some of the most notable ones:
- *Akhlāq un-Nabī wa Ādābihi* by Hafiz Abu Muhammad 'Abdullah

1 Al-Fihrist Li-Ibn-un-Nadeem P. 271, 272.

bin Muhammad bin Ja'far bin Hayyān Asfahāni (d. 369 AH), nicknamed Abush-Shaikh.

- *Sharaf al-Mustafa* by Abu Sa'eed 'Abdul-Malik bin Muhammad Nīshapuri (d. 406 AH), *Shamā'il un-Nabi* by Abul-'Abbās Ja'far bin Muhammad Mustaghfirī (d. 433 AH) and *Al-Anwār fi Shamā'il in-Nabiyy al-Mukhtār* by Hussain bin Mas'ūd Baghawī (d. 510 AH), who was a great scholar of Hadith.
- A very popular and important book on the topic was written by the famous Hadith scholar and commentator of Sahih Muslim, Qadi 'Ayād Yahsabī (d. 544 AH). The title of his book was *Ash-Shifā' bi-Ta'reefi Huqooq il-Mustafa*. It was well-received by the scholars of the *Ummah*. Commentaries of this book were written by knowledgeable people of every generation afterwards. The book describes the personal traits, physical characteristics, and various aspects of the Prophet's life. Among the commentators of this book are well-known figures like Taqiyyuddin Ahmed bin Muhammad Sam'ānī Hanafi (d. 832 AH), Mulla Ali Qāri (d. 1014 AH) and Shihāb Khifāji (d. 1096 AH).[1]
- In the sixth century, Ibn Muqrī Gharnātī (d. 522 AH) of Andalusia wrote *As-Shamā'il bin-Noor as-Sāti' al-Kāmil.*
- Another famous scholar of Andalusia, Al-Hafiz al-Imam Abul-Fat'h Muhammad bin Sayyid-in-Nās al-Ya'murī (d. 734 AH) wrote the biography *'Uyoon al-Athar fi Funoon al-Maghāzī wash-Shamā'il was-Siyar*. It is a comprehensive and popular book from which many scholars, biographers and historians benefited greatly.
- Muhammad bin Sayyid-in-Nās was a great Hadith scholar; hence, following the methodology of the Muhadditheen, he scrutinized the narrations and identified in the light of evidence those which had more weight.
- Since the book was not easily available for a long period of time, the scholars of later generations often quoted some of those narrations which had lesser weight. Unfortunately, this led to some confusion

1 Sharhu Ash-Shifa' li-Mulla Ali Al-Qari: 1/3.

regarding the book and its author. Some assumed that the book considered both the strong and weak narrations as being equal, although the truth is that the writer included the weak narrations only to analyze and compare to the authentic traditions.

- One of the most outstanding works on the Prophet's physical qualities and behaviour (Shama'il) is *Shama'il-ur-Rasool* by Ibn-Kathir (d. 774 AH).
- *Safar-us-Sa'ādah* by Majd-ud-Deen Ferozābādī (d. 817 AH) is also a popular book of Shamā'il, although regretfully, the author did not care over much to ascertain the degree of accuracy of the narrations he quotes.
- *Al-Khasā'is wal-Mu'jizāt un-Nabawiyyah* by Jalal-ud-Deen 'Abdur-Rahmān Suyūtī (d. 911 AH) is a medley of narrations of all kinds.

Miracles of the Prophet (ﷺ)

In addition to recording the Shamā'il of the Prophet Muhammad, the great Muhadditheen also penned various works regarding the miracles of the Prophet ﷺ, highlighting those marvels which made it undisputable that he was a genuine and true Messenger of Allah.

- According to the scholars, the first man to write a book devoted exclusively to the Prophet's miracles was a great Hadith scholar named Muhammad bin Yusuf Firyābī (d. 212 AH). He gave his book the title of *Dala'il un-Nabuwwah* (arguments of the Prophethood).
- He was followed by Ali bin Muhammad Madā'inī (d. 234 AH), the author of *Ayāt un-Nabi*, and by Dawood bin Ali al-Asfahānī (d. 280 AH), the author of *A'lām un-Nabuwwah*. Both of them also wrote books on the Prophet's personal traits and physical characteristics, *Sifat un-Nabi* and *Sifat wa Akhlāq-un-Nabi* respectively.
- Other writers on the same subject included Ibn Qutaibah (d. 276 AH), the author of *A'lām-u-Rasoolillah;* Abu Bakr Ibn Abi Dunya (d. 281 AH) and Abu Bakr Jafar bin Muhammad Mustafad Firyābī (d. 301 AH); the latter two authors each wrote a book of the same name, *Dala'il un-Nabuwwah*.

- They were followed by a famous Hadith scholar, Ibn Abi Hātim (d.327 AH), author of A'lām un-Nabuwwah; Abu 'Abdullah Muhammad bin Ishāq bin Yahya bin Mandah (d. 395 AH), author of Dalā'il un-Nabuwwah; and Abdul-Jabbār Mu'tazali (d. 415 AH), author of *Tathbeet Dalā'il in-Nabuwwah*.
- In the fifth century of the Hijra calendar, Abu Nu'aim Ahmad bin Abdullah Asbahāni (d. 430 AH) wrote his *Dalā'il un-Nabuwwah* while Abdul-Hasan Ali bin Fahd Māwardī (d. 450 AH) wrote an excellent book bearing the title *A'lām un-Nabuwwah*.
- In the same century, Abu Bakr Ahmad bin Husain bin Ali Baihaqi (d. 458 AH) wrote his famous and impressive book, *Dalā'il un-Nabuwwah*.
- Abu Umar Yusuf bin Abdul-Barr Al-Qurtubi (d. 535 AH) of Andalusia wrote a biography of the Prophet highlighting his miracles. In the ninth century AH, 'Umar bin Ali bin Mulaqqin (d. 804 AH) wrote two books of the same genre, *Khasa'is-u-Afdal il-Makhlooqeen* and *Ghāyat us-Sool fi Khasā'is ir-Rasool*.
- Shihab-ud-Deen Abul-'Abbās Ahmad bin Muhammad bin Abi Bakr bin Abdul-Malik Qastalāni (d. 923 AH), a commentator of Bukhari, wrote *Al-Mawāhib ul-Ladunniyyah bil Minah il-Muhammadiyyah*. It became very popular and remained a great reference work for the later generations. Although Qastalāni was a Hadith scholar, he compiled in his book all narrations on the topic regardless of authenticity.
- Jalāl-ud-Deen Suyūtī (d. 911 AH) wrote a detailed book on the same subject, entitled *Al-Khasā'is ul-Kubra*.
- These were some of the most important books written regarding the miracles and proofs of the Prophethood of Muhammad (ﷺ).

Commentaries on Prophetic Biographies

Following the books written specifically on the biography of the Prophet Muhammad (ﷺ), a new genre emerged. Islamic scholars began to produce series of explanatory commentaries written on important and popular biographies of the Prophet. The commentaries featured additional information provided under the headings of original books, as well as explanatory notes on the texts of the narrations, verses, and so on.

- Of all these commentaries, the most important one is *Ar-Raud ul-Unuf*, a comprehensive commentary on Ibn Hishām's biography of the Prophet (Seerat Ibn Hishām) by Abdur-Rahmān Suhaili.
- Later, another commentary on Seerat Ibn Hisham was written by Yahya bin Hamzah bin Ali Tālibi (d. 745 AH), a famous Imam of Zaidi Shiites of Yemen. It was entitled *Al-Anwār ul-Mudī'ah fi Sharh il-Akhbar in-Nabawiyyah*. He also wrote *Khulāsat us-Seerah*, an abridgment of Seerat Ibn Hisham.
- *Noor-un-Nibrās fi Seerat-i-Ibn-i-Sayyed in-Nās* is a well-known commentary on *'Uyoon ul-Athar* by Ibn Sayyed in-Nās. It was written by Abul-Wafā Ibrahīm bin Muhammad bin Khaleel Tarābulusi Halabī (d. 841 AH).
- An explanatory commentary on Qastalāni's *Al-Mawāhib al-Ladunniyyah* was written by Muhammad bin Abdul-Bāqī Zarqānī (d. 1122 AH) in eight volumes. It is a detailed commentary popularly known as *Sharh uz-Zarqāni 'alal-Mawāhib*. It is a collection of various narrations of differing authenticity.

Comprehensiveness:
A New Stage in the Development of Seerah Writing

It is a fact that Imam Bukhari and Imam Muslim were the first to write comprehensive biographies of the Prophet Muhammad (ﷺ). They in their Sahihain, dealt with every aspect of his life and missionary work, including every major and minor detail. They are to be the pioneers of this particularly detailed style of biographical writings.

- Biographical writing of the Prophet's life continued developing over the years, passing through different stages until it reached its fullest form in the eighth century AH. The best example is that of *Zad ul-Ma'ād* written by Ibn Qayyim (d. 751 AH), a disciple of Ibn Taimiyah, who himself benefited greatly from the works of Bukhari and Muslim. Like his mentor and teacher, Ibn Qayyim's mission was to educate all of mankind as to the life and station of the Prophet Muhammad ﷺ; and to encourage them to follow the Prophet's example for a blissful life in this world and the Hereafter without straying from the pathway charted by the prophet ﷺ.

In his book *Zād ul-Ma'ād,* Ibn Qayyim says about the Prophet Muhammad (ﷺ):

فَهَدَى (اللّٰهُ) بِهِ إِلٰى أَقْوَمِ الطُّرُقِ وَ أَوْضَحِ السُّبُلِ، وَافْتَرَضَ عَلَى الْعِبَادِ طَاعَتَهٗ وَ تَعْزِيرَهٗ وَتَوْقِيرَهٗ وَمَحَبَّتَهٗ، وَالْقِيَامَ بِحُقُوقِهِ، وَسَدَّ دُونَ جَنَّتِهِ الطُّرُقَ، فَلَنْ تُفْتَحَ لِأَحَدٍ إِلَّا مِنْ طَرِيقِهِ .

'Through him, Allah guided (mankind) to the most straight and the most clear path, made His slaves duty-bound to obey him, help him, honour and love him, discharge his rights; He closed all the ways to the paradise except the way of His prophet. None can enter the paradise except through his way'[1].

For Ibn Qayyim, a biography of the Prophet ﷺ is not just a book containing information about his person, his military campaigns and the momentous events of his life, but a clear map of guidance leading to salvation and temporal and spiritual bliss. He goes on to say:

وَإِذَا كَانَتْ سَعَادَةُ الْعَبْدِ فِي الدَّارَيْنِ مُعَلَّقَةً بِهَدْيِ النَّبِيِّ ﷺ، فَيَجِبُ عَلٰى كُلِّ مَنْ نَّصَحَ نَفْسَهٗ، وَأَحَبَّ نَجَاتَهَا وَسَعَادَتَهَا أَنْ يَّعْرِفَ مِنْ هَدْيِهِ وَ سِيرَتِهِ وَ شَأْنِهِ مَا يَخْرُجُ بِهِ عَنِ الْجَاهِلِينَ بِهِ، وَ يَدْخُلُ بِهِ فِي عِدَادِ أَتْبَاعِهِ وَ شِيعَتِهِ وَ حِزْبِهِ .

'Now if a man's bliss in this life and the next is inextricably linked to the Prophet's guidance, then it is incumbent on the one desiring his weal, salvation and bliss to acquire knowledge of his life and his guidance at least enough to separate himself from the ignorant and be counted among his followers and his partymen'.[2]

1 Zād-ul-Ma'ād: Preface: 1/34, 35.
2 Op.cit.: 1/69,70.

Any biography of the Prophet, according to Ibn Qayyim, should cover these three things; he himself named his book *Zād ul-Ma'ād fi Hadyi Khair il-'Ibād*. In his book, Ibn Qayyim wrote of the Prophet's lineage, his childhood and his youth, the events during his lifetime, his wives, offspring and servants, his dress, shoes, *Miswāk* (a small stick of wood, the tip of which is crushed and made soft to brush and cleanse teeth), his arms, personal belongings and means of carriage.

Alongside these, he described the Prophet's daily routine, how he spoke and when he kept quiet, how he performed ritual ablution and prayer, all in detail. From these details he also derived various points of juridical law.

Zād Ul-Ma'ād, like *Sahih Al-Bukhari,* encompasses every dimension of the Prophet's life. Thus, it too is considered to be a comprehensive biography of Prophet Muhammad (ﷺ).

The difference, however, lies in that unlike the authors of Sunan Ahādith who collected, classified, and arranged narrations, Ibn Qayyim wrote of the Prophet's life in a descriptive manner.

To understand the canonical works of Bukhāri and Muslim, commentaries are needed to explain the time period, circumstances, and other necessary details. The author of *Zād ul-Ma'ād,* however, provided his own commentary on the narrative, explaining and expounding matters by a process of deduction in great detail.

It should be noted that with regards to authenticity, *Zād ul-Ma'ād* does not come close to the works of Bukhāri and Muslim. The degree of authenticity of the latter two is very much higher than Ibn Qayyim's standards. Bukhari's deductions *(Istinbāt)* and conclusions and inferences *(Istintāj)* are points of reference and sources for Islamic scholars of every generation. However, Ibn Qayyim did make excellent use of the canonical works of Bukhari and Muslim.

- Although none matched Ibn Qayyim's work, it is evident that biographers during the ninth and tenth centuries of the Hijra calendar were extremely eager to collect as much information as possible regarding the Seerah.

- One of the most notable author of this age was Muhammad bin Yusuf Dimashqi Shāmi (d. 942 AH). He assembled all the information he could gather from books available in his times (more than three hundred in number), and named his compilation *Subul ul-Huda war-Rashad fi Seerat-i-Khair-il-'Ibād*. This encyclopedia, which has already been published in fourteen volumes, is an all-encompassing, comprehensive book and generally avoids fabricated narrations; however, it must be noted that no attempt was made by the writer to verify the authenticity of each and every narration he quoted.

Next to Muhammad Dimashqi was Ali bin Burhan-ud-Deen (Ibrāhīm) Halabi, the author of *Insān ul-'Uyoon fi Seerat il-Ameen il-Ma'moon,* known popularly as *Seerat al-Halabiyyah*. Unfortunately, it is full of weak *(Da'eef)* narrations and Israeli tales.

While reviewing the historical evolution of biographical writings during the first thousand years of Muslim history, only a few of those well-known books which were used by scholars during different ages, and are still being used, as vital sources and reference-works, were quoted.

It is beyond the scope of this work to list all such books; nor would these few pages be able to accommodate such a lengthy review.

The next stage in the long history of Seerah writing is with regards to the opponents and adversaries of Islam and the Muslims, and how they influenced newer generations of biographers of more recent generations.

Orientalists

The thirteenth century AH (equivalent to the nineteenth century of the Christian Era) saw the emergence of a new series of biographies of Prophet Muhammad(ﷺ). These burgeoning historians were in fact European Orientalists who studied the languages of the Muslims with the set purpose to acquire detailed knowledge about Islam and the

Muslims and, through this knowledge, promote their own national interests.

The Industrial Revolution of Europe, with its concomitant rush for colonies, led to a surge of their interest in the Muslim world. Their motive was not an objective study of the Muslim faith, but rather, they had their own military, political, economic and social interests in mind. In order to gain a more comprehensive knowledge and understanding of the Muslims, their way of thinking, and their points of strength and weakness, it was essential for them to know the person of Muhammad (ﷺ) and his mission: the person who is at the center of all Muslim thought and action.

Western scholars have long made claims about being objective in their study and evaluation of religious systems, but when it comes to Islam, they fail to dissociate themselves from their own deeply ingrained prejudices. Their historical animosity towards Islam bars them from analyzing the faith and its followers with neutral eyes.

With their goal being to impress the Muslims with their own intellectual methodologies and civilization, the Orientalists' first mission was to weaken the link that binds the Muslims to their beloved Prophet. They were intent upon impairing the Muslims' love for the person whose teachings were a guidebook in life for them.

Thus, they sought out and promoted those individuals within the Muslim community who were already enamored of Western philosophies and preferred Western intellectual attitudes over that of Islam. These people, with European support, set about spreading their self-made ideas and twisted mentalities, all in the name of an objective study of the Prophet's biography.

Their crusade against the Messenger of Allah ﷺ went to great lengths, and made every attempt to discredit his character, his morals, and his behaviour. One of their many ridiculous claims was that there exists no reliable and documented information relating to his biography.

The Orientalists made many statements and allegations against the Prophet Muhammad (ﷺ), which were widespread through their teachings and continue to be popular today. Some of these claims include the following:

- Islamic beliefs have been derived from those of the Jews and the Christians, and Muhammad (ﷺ) would borrow ideas from Christian and Jewish priests such as Waraqah ibn Naufal and Abdullah ibn Salām.
- The Qur'an is the word of Muhammad (ﷺ), not Divine Revelation from God.
- The rites and ceremonies of Islamic worship have been copied from other religious systems.
- The Prophet's marriage to Khadeejah was based on his desire for her wealth.
- He opposed the believers of other revealed faiths because he wanted himself to be acknowledged as the Messenger of God.
- He acknowledged the Israeli prophets in the beginning of his mission to solicit people's attention and finally declared himself to be their chief.
- He arrogated to himself a lineage going back to Ishmael (Ismā'īl) and claimed to be his descendent as a way of raising his status and legitimizing his claim to prophethood.
- During his missionary activity in Makkah, he took Moses as his model. Later on, he turned to Abraham and took him as his model.
- During his stay in Madinah, his prophethood changed into kingship.
- Islam spread by sword.
- Islam's allowance of polygamy (up to four wives) is a sign of hyper sexuality and that the Muslim men are sexually insatiable.
- The legal punishments prescribed by Islam are barbaric.
- The Muslims are naturally rapacious, murderers and robbers.
- Biographies of Prophet Muhammad (ﷺ) were written centuries later and, therefore, are unreliable.
- The miracles attributed to the Prophet are tales of fiction and

exaggeration.

All of these allegations were desperate attempts to insult and belittle Islam and undermine the basic foundations of its belief. However, the baselessness of their slurs was and is clear to even those fair-minded non-Muslims who interacted positively with the Muslims. The bigoted and biased writers who were the originators of the initial movement against Islam were followed by a new wave of Orientalists who used yet more subtle ways to denigrate Islam.

- William Muir employed a method different from that of Margoliath. Instead of outright lies, he used a mixture of both falsehood and truth.
- Joseph Schacht, an expert in Arabic language and literature, avoided direct criticism of the Prophet (ﷺ). Instead, he tried to find fault with the Sunnah, Hadith, Islamic jurisprudence, the four foundations of Islamic jurisprudence *(Usool-ul-Fiqh),* and the individual and independent opinions of Muslim jurists on questions of law *(Ijtihad).*
- William Montgomery Watt, basing his arguments on the Marxist concept of dialectical materialism, tried to misrepresent the life and mission of the Prophet.

These people are representatives of the Orientalist coterie in general. Many of them have their own disciples and followers who are working along the same lines, each of them in his own special field.

A common theme amongst the Orientalists is their constant criticism, doubt, and overall hatred regarding the Hadith and its sciences, especially that of verifying and grading chains of narration *('Ilm-ul-Asnad).*

These sciences are unique to the Muslims, who were the pioneers of these sciences which excited the envy of the Orientalists the most and became the main butt of their criticism. To degrade these sciences, they argue that the Muslims busied themselves with these sciences so much as that they neglected textual criticism.

The Qur'an has been translated into several European languages, as have many biographies of the Prophet Muhammad (ﷺ) originally written by Muslim scholars.

Despite the mud-slinging of prejudiced European writers and the hostility of Orientalists, despite the bad example set by non-practicing Muslims, the effect of those translated works on Western readers is amazing indeed. Thousands of them have already turned to Islam and this process of conversion continues today at an ever-increasing rate.

Influence of the Orientalists A New Stage in Biographical Writings

Initially, many Muslim intellectuals became influenced by the works of Orientalists and subsequently, their philosophies and worldviews. This influence was felt first in the Asian subcontinent (India and Pakistan) and later, in the Arab world, due to spreading colonization by European powers.

In the Indian subcontinent, a prominent example of the colonialist, the Orientalist impact was Sir Sayyed Ahmad Khan. His works display two contrary trends, each struggling with the other. On one hand, he was extremely concerned by the objections of the Orientalists about the Prophet and wanted to write in defense of him while, on the other hand, he was oddly impressed by their 'rational' and materialistic arguments. In short, he felt mentally shaken.

The Muslims, especially the Hadith scholars, had set a very high standard of accuracy while writing the Prophet's biography and history. Unfortunately, instead of defending them and replying to the superficial criticism of the Orientalist, Sir Sayyed Ahmad Khan succumbed to their arguments and became strongly influenced by them. Although he had his own views and wrote books representing his own opinions, which later on affected other academics, most knowledgeable Muslims rejected them.

Collectively, the Muslim *Ummah* was shaken by this attack on the Prophet's integrity. As a result, the scholars agreed that there was urgent need to re-discover and explore the life and mission of the Messenger of Allah (ﷺ). A series of excellent books on the subject of Seerah began to be printed regularly; one such example of these books published in the Subcontinent was Qazi Muhammad Suleman Mansūrpuri's *Rahmatun lil-'Alameen*.

The author's purpose was to make an objective study of the Prophet's life, present the events of his life in their true perspectives, dispel the cobwebs of suspicions and doubts created by rationalists in the minds of the masses, and reconnect bonds of true love between the Prophet and his followers. To that end, he composed a comprehensive work covering all the different aspects of the Prophet's life: military campaigns, travels, miracles, personal traits and natural disposition, character, and so on. The book has been the object of much deserving praise.

The author did not only rely on Muslim reference works, but went further and made use of old & new Testaments and books of other faiths. It is widely held that Qazi Mansurpuri was the pioneer of this new stage in the development of Seerah writing, and popularized the use of modern sciences such as mathematics, physics and astronomy to fix the calendar years and the timings of ceremonies of worship.

While writing on the Prophet's merits, nature and character and the unexcelled beauty and perfection of the Book revealed to him, he made use of new sources in addition to the traditional reference works normally used by Muslim writers. Books on subjects as diverse as comparative religions, world civilizations, and archaeology did not escape his attention. Qazi's monumental work is based on authentic sources and is entirely free from excesses and exaggerations. Events described in his book have been analyzed scientifically. Indeed, *Rahmatun lil-'Alameen* spearheaded a new direction for biographers, especially those from the Asian Subcontinent.

On the heels of *Rahmatun lil-'Alameen* came Dr. Muhammad Hameedullah's Le Prophete de l'Islam, a biography written in both

French and English. Thousands of Christian and other non-Muslim youth read his book and converted to Islam. Thanks to such efforts, the spell cast by the Orientalists as well as misguided Muslim historians, biographers and writers who came under their influence has been largely dispelled and remains at bay.

Allama Shibli

The first volume of *Rahmatun lil-'Alameen* was published in 1912 (1330 AH). According to Sayyed Suleman Nadvi, Allama Shibli started working the same year on his biography, which he had already planned to write several years ago.[1] Shibli died in 1916 CE.

By then, the manuscript of the first volume together with its preface was already complete and was published posthumously by Sayyed Suleman Nadvi. He also completed the remaining parts of the book.

Shibli's goal was to clear away the dust kicked up by the Orientalists and to write a detailed biography of the Prophet Muhammad (ﷺ) based on authentic sources. In his book Shibli refuted the objections of the Orientalists, exposed their mistakes, and expounded what they had misinterpreted and relied largely on authentic sources to describe events.

However, biographers of Allama Shibli noted that he was responsive and impressionable by nature and easily influenced. In many ways, he was influenced by Sir Sayyed Ahmad Khan and was in fact one of his admirers. Although he rejected Sayyed's views on religious matters, he was nonetheless influenced by the Orientalists' rational criticism of Islamic sources.

While replying to the charges made by the Orientalists against the biographical and Hadith literature produced by the Muslims with respect to textual criticism, Shibli, like Sir Sayyed, adopted a novel method of his own. He identified *'Ilm-ud-Dirayah* which is actually the evaluation of the chain of narrations, with the Orientalists'

1 Seerat-un-Nabi: Preface, First Edition: 1/15.

methodology of textual criticism, and in his bid to affirm that those methodologies are useful for evaluation of Ahādith; he looked for proofs and arguments for this purpose.

Whatever proofs Shibli thought are available in support of his views, he dilated upon in the preface of his biographical work. Rationalists whose mission it was to take human reason as the sole criterion to evaluate narrations exploited Shibli's views. As a result, they whimsically applied, what they called *Dirayah* (textual criticism) on the most authentic narrations which they did not want to buy and rejected them to invent a new edition of Islam which was a far cry from the pristine faith taught by the Prophet (ﷺ), hoping that this new, self-styled faith could easily pass as Islam.

Before Shibli's idea of *Dirayah* is reviewed, it is better to look first at the standard set by Hadith scholars to authenticate Ahādeeth. Thereafter, an examination of the Orientalist methodology and the ideas of Allama Shibli will commence.

Biographical Literature and Hadith Scholars' Criterion of Accuracy

The Prophet's entire life, in every aspect, is a model and guide for the Muslims. It was therefore necessary to ensure that any statement or action attributed to him was totally correct and reliable. To that end did the narrators of *Ahādeeth* give utmost care to the system of the chain of narration *(Asāneed)* and contribute to its evolution.

The Muhadditheen (scholars of Hadith) who narrated and studied these texts thus developed the science of authenticating these sayings. They laid down strict rules to ascertain the reliability of the narrators and the text narrated by them. They created a list of conditions and grades to be assigned to the narrators, based upon the degree of their reliability. This system came to be known as *Asmā'-ur-Rijāl* and *Al-Jarh wat-Ta'deel.*

By means of these stringent rules, it became possible for the Muslim scholars to deduce rulings and points of law from authentic Ahādeeth and also use them as a base for *Ijtihad* to find solutions for problems that might come up in the future.

This was in fact the methodology of the Companions of the Prophet and their senior successors *(Tābi'een)* from the very first day with respect to the Seerah of the Messenger of Allah as well.

As Seerah writing became an independent genre of religious literature and grew in popularity, scrupulous and cautious Muhadditheen were not the only ones involved in this field; less careful writers also joined the trend. Those writers could not keep the same high standard which was the distinctive mark of the Companions and *Tabi'een* during the early days of Muslim history.

Laxity had already set in during the times of Imam Az-Zuhri's pupils. It can be easily gathered from the comments given by Hadith scholars who determined the status of Ibn Ishāq, a pupil of Imam Az-Zuhri and an expert in the military campaigns of the Prophet. For example, Yahya bin Sa'eed 'Umawī, an Imam of Hadith and Seerah, said of him: 'Ibn Ishāq misspells names because he copied them from the (official) register'.[1]

This suggests that he did not know the persons whose names he copied, but simply took their names from the register and quoted their narrations.

A further charge against Ibn Ishāq is that he did not hear directly from Hisham bin 'Urwah bin Zubair's wife, Fatimah, the narrations which he attributed to her and quoted them in his biography of the Prophet. In any case, further inquiries could not prove the allegation and *Imam* Ahmad and several other *Imams* came to his defense on this count.

Cautious Hadith scholars scrutinized and sifted the narrations of Ibn Ishaq thoroughly and chose only those which were acceptable. They rejected Ahādith of a lower grade.

Imam Adh-Dhahabi's opinion was the most positive out of them

1 Tasheefat-ul-Muhadditheen 1/26; and As-Seerat-un-Nabawiyyah lil-'Umri: preface 1/57.

all, although he still did not support him completely. He said:

فَلَهُ ارْتِفَاعٌ بِحَسَبِهِ، وَلَا سِيَّمَا فِي السِّيَرِ، وَ أَمَّا فِي أَحَادِيثِ الْأَحْكَامِ فَيَنْحَطُّ حَدِيثُهُ فِيهَا عَنْ رُتْبَةِ الصِّحَّةِ إِلٰى رُتْبَةِالْحَسَنِ إِلَّا فِيمَا شَذَّ فِيهِ، فَإِنَّهُ يُعَدُّ مُنْكَرًا .

'His standard is high as regards biographical facts...As for the Ahādith concerning rulings; they rank down from *Sahih* (authentic) to *Hasan* (good), and only rarely when he opposes the most dependable narrations his narration is considered to be *Munkar* (denounced).[1]

He further said:

فَكِتَابُهُ مُحْتَاجٌ إِلٰى تَنْقِيحٍ وَّ تَصْحِيحٍ وَّ رِوَايَةِ مَا فَاتَهُ .

'His writings need to be reviewed and corrected and what he missed needs to be related'.[2]

He added:

كَانَ أَحَدَ أَوْعِيَةِ الْعِلْمِ حِبْرًا فِي مَعْرِفَةِ الْمَغَازِي وَالسِّيَرِ وَلَيْسَ بِذَاكَ الْمُتْقِنِ فَانْحَطَّ حَدِيثُهُ عَنْ رُتْبَةِ الصِّحَّةِ، وَهُوَ صَدُوقٌ فِي نَفْسِهِ مَرْضِيٌّ.

'He was a learned scholar, had a good knowledge of military campaigns and the details of the Prophet's life but he is not perfect. His Ahādeeth, therefore, rank lower than 'authentic' but he is truthful *(Sadooq)* and acceptable'.[3]

In *Meezan al-I'tidāl,* he comments on Ibn Ishaq's biographical work with these words:

صَالِحُ الْحَدِيثِ مَالَهُ عِنْدِي ذَنْبٌ إِلَّا مَا قَدْ حَشَا فِي السِّيرَةِ مِنَ الْأَشْيَاءِ الْمُنْكَرَةِ الْمُنْقَطِعَةِ .

'His own narrations are right and proper. I have nothing against him except that he filled his biography with *Munkar* (denounced) and *Munqati'*(whose chain is broken) narrations.'[4]

1 Siyar A'lām-un-Nubalā': 7/41
2 Siyar A'lām-un-Nubalā': 116/6.
3 Tadhkirat-ul-Huffāz: 1/130.
4 Meezān-ul-I'tidāl: 3/469.

If a man of the rank of Ibn Ishāq who is *Sadooq* (truthful) and *Mardi* (acceptable) can fill his biography with *Munkar* and *Munqati'* narrations, it takes no stretch of the imagination to realize what others lower in rank than him have done.

The Prophet's biography is no ordinary history. It is the narrative of the life and missionary activities of a prophet of Allah. It is imperative that anyone who seeks to record the events of his life be extremely careful in their pursuit.

According to Islamic faith – to attribute anything doubtful or unauthentic to Prophet Muhammad (ﷺ) is a sin. Any would-be biographer of the Prophet must keep to the standard of Hadith scholars, as no historian of the world ever could match Hadith scholars in terms of caution, care, and circumspection while recording facts and events relating to the Prophet's life.

According to the standard set by Hadith scholars, no word or report attributed to the Prophet ﷺ can be accepted unless the initial narrator has himself heard it from the Prophet ﷺ or was an eye-witness to it.

The methodology of the Companions was that they used to repeat a Hadith frequently in different gatherings at different times. Their listeners (i.e their pupils or *Tābi'een*) would commit to memory as well as write down the Hadith in the very words used by the Companions. This was the first step in the preservation of Ahādeeth.

Moreover, the *Tabi'een* would inquire of other Companions present at that time about the same Hadith in order to bring forth all the details and conditions relevant to the Hadith. If they detected any difference in the wordings of the Companions, they would turn to the same Companion from whom they had heard the first time and have the matter clarified. In this way, the *Tābi'een* were able to gather all the details concerning the Hadith.

It was not uncommon for Companions to tell their pupils to refer the Hadith to other Companions who were present at the time of the event. In case the Companion himself was not present at the time of the event, he would ask him to refer the Hadith to the person from whom he had heard it or any other Companion who was present at that time and at that place. The purpose of all this was to ensure that a particular event or a Hadith reached a wider public in a state which was clear and reliable.

This was also the way of the followers of the Companions and their followers *(Atbā' at-Tābi'een)*. In case the Companion was alive, they would, after they had heard a Hadith indirectly, try to hear it directly from the Companion himself. They would also try to hear the same Hadith from as many followers of the Companions' followers of different times as possible in order to make sure that the teacher narrated that Hadith at different times in his life time exactly in the same way without mixing up or confusing facts and wordings.

It was noted that the companions were very careful and the most dependable, all other were thoroughly checked with respect to their integrity *('Adālat)*, strength of memory, accuracy *(Dabt)* personal character, thoughts and views, and even their political and religious inclinations.

Hadith scholars took note of all these details and preserved them in their books. They also took further steps of inquiring to make sure whether the sub-narrator had actually met in his lifetime the person from whom he was narrating. The more cautious amongst them did not consider the meeting to be enough, but also verified whether he had actually heard the Hadith from him. They kept records of which narrator met which teacher and at what time. They also made inquiries as to who met his teacher (Shaikh) in his old age and the level of his retentive memory at that time. In order to determine whether a Hadith was sound or weak, they kept a record of which sub-narrators were accepted by how many trustworthy *(Thiqah)* and critical Hadith scholars and which sub-narrators were ignored by them.

Proud Islamic Heritage

This meticulous and accurate record of the Prophet's sayings and doings was the product of the collective efforts of the early Hadith scholars. No other people ever kept a record of the sayings of their prophets in such a foolproof way, nor devised such a system. Some nations did keep a record of the teachings of their prophets, but this was done by isolated men who were in no way connected with the events. Their records were mere collections of the reports of anonymous men, hearsays, fables and tales. Those who analyze their writings can easily detect discrepancies and even inconsistencies in their texts.

Western historians make critical studies of these writings in the light of semantic and syntactical contexts, the details of which will be discussed later, and then accept what look reliable to them and reject the rest. However, in their studies and as evidenced by their statements, these historians are invariably and almost unconsciously influenced by their own views and other religious, national and social considerations. It is difficult, if not impossible, for them to remain impersonal and objective.

Western historians, while writing the history of the mediaeval or pre-mediaeval times, keep in mind the prevailing civilization and the social, political and economic conditions of those times. They also research the views of important individuals of those times, the main schools of philosophy, and the general intellectual conditions that prevailed. Studies are done on relics such as old coins, inscriptions, architecture, and more.

Historians also examine the legends of the particular time period, and contrast them with the statements of other historians, and other stories and fables which do not conflict with the basic views generated about the civilization. These narratives are all collected, compared and contrasted, and merged together to form a more easily understood timeline of events.

This is called the methodology of textual criticism in the West. However, this particular methodology invariably leads to different conclusions and conflicting opinions by different scholars. Each new writer opposes vehemently the one preceding him and offers a new theory regarding what they believe is the actual sequence of events. Such history cannot be accepted unequivocally due to the large margin for error.

The methodology of textual criticism has had numerous unfortunate results. It has come to the point that some Western historians argue over the personalities of Moses and Jesus (ﷺ), and in fact doubt their very existence. Those who do accept that these men existed depict them in such a way that they appear lower in standing and stature than actual prophets. As a result, modern followers of Judaism and Christianity do not accept them as individuals deserving absolute and unconditional obedience.

On the other hand, Muslim scholars invented the novel methodology of verifying all narrators of historical incidents. This system involved examining, assessing and grading the chain of narrators and sub-narrators according to their degree of reliability, a system which barred personal inclinations and views from influencing any decisions.

The final result was that historical personalities were represented accurately, emerging with their characters intact; naturally, the beauty of their qualities immediately evoked love, admiration, and reverence for them. Through truthful historical narrations, the personality of the Prophet ﷺ shone so brilliantly that no honest human being could help believing in him as the true Messenger of Allah.

Hadith Scholars and Textual Criticism

The scholars of Islam had a different approach to the methodology of textual criticism. One major advantage that they had over Western, non-Muslim scholars was the fact that Islamic texts were preserved and filtered through an intensive system before being put through further rigorous tests.

The preservation of Ahādith followed a certain formula which ensured the absolute authenticity of every narration. Students were required to memorize the text of a Hadith and its chain of narration, and would have them written down as well. Only after a Hadith had already been preserved in memory, as well as in writing, was the principle of textual criticism applied.

Each word of a Hadith was checked and verified by comparing it with the statements of different narrators. Any narration containing a *Shādh* word (a word not conforming to words found in Ahādith on the same subject from other narrators) was rejected. A text containing any *'Illah* (hidden defect) was also rejected. Any narration weak in wording or meaning or inferior in eloquence to that of the Prophet (ﷺ), was likewise rejected. Textual confusion *('Idtirāb-ul-Matn),* interpolation of extraneous words *(Mudraj),* and even errors of dots or vowel-marks *(Tasheef)* were noted down and scrutinized.

These were all points that came under the umbrella of textual criticism; the energy and detail devoted to the science of Hadith displays how the Muhadditheen were extremely cautious in all matters relating to the textual criticism. This attention to detail and scrupulousness is also exemplified by the particular wording of Hadith scholars in regards to their statements. For example, the statement 'This Hadith has a sound chain of narration,' does not mean that the Hadith and its *Sanad* are both authentic; rather, it implies that the scholar had verified the chain of narration alone and not the *Matn* (text) itself, which would require separate scrutiny.

Muhadditheen further developed textual criticism in the context of Hadith sciences. After the determination of authentic narrations, these Ahādith were collected, compared, and contrasted for further examination.

First, a scholar would collect all the reliable texts of a particular Hadith and arrange them according to his own particular system. In the case that an inconsistency is encountered due to lack of information, the scholar would then collect all the details relating to the event from narrations which are not weak *(Da'eef),* non-conforming *(Shadh),* denounced *(Munkar)* or fabricated *(Maudoo').*

If the scholar was able to find details in the statements of several narrators that would remove the inconsistency or discrepancy, he would note them down and resolve the issue. If, in another case, he was able to find some kind of basis upon which to reconcile the apparently conflicting statements, he would do so.

Hadith scholars have been following the principles of scrutinizing and verifying the chain of narrators as well as the texts of Ahādeeth for centuries. While following these principles, never had they had to reject entirely a Hadith with an authentic chain of narration.

Hadith scholars also used the principle of *Tarjeeh* (giving more weight to one of the several Ahādeeth available). This methodology was followed when they were confronted with several Ahādeeth of varying degrees of strength and as a result, there appeared discrepancies regarding dates of events or places of events.

For example, most of the writers of *Maghāzī* (military campaigns) say that the Battle of Bani Mustalaq took place in 6 AH; however, Mūsā bin 'Uqbah, a Hadith scholar and historian, and later on, Ibn Qayyim and Dhahabī, dated the event to the year 4 AH. Their argument was that, according to many authentic narrations, Sa'd bin Mu'ādh took part in this battle and he was martyred soon after the Battle of Banu Quraizah. That made a sound foundation to apply the principle of *Tarjeeh*.

Following the same principle, Imam Al-Bukhārī, in opposition to writers of Maghāzī such as Ibn Ishāq and Waqidī, asserts that the Battle of Dhat-ur-Riqā ' took place after the Battle of Kheybar. His argument was that, according to more authentic Ahādeeth, Abu Musa Al-Ash'arī and Abu Hurairah took part in this battle, and it is established beyond doubt that they had come to the Prophet ﷺ for the first time immediately after the conquest of Kheybar. *Tarjeeh* consists in giving precedence to the authentic Ahādeeth over the weak one, to the more authentic over the less authentic.

A Muslim historian or biographer or a Hadith scholar builds his conclusions upon material which is sound, its text authenticated, and its chain of narration verified. He has no need to select serviceable, convenient pieces from a mass of conflicting, contradicting, unverified and unreliable material.

Unlike the research scholars of the West, a Muslim scholar needs to rely upon no guesswork, conjecture, or preferences when scrutinizing his texts. He uses reliable material retained in memory and preserved in writing by trustworthy scholars of old. Thus, a Muslim scholar's methodology of textual criticism is vastly different, and certainly superior, to the methods employed by non-Muslim scholars.

The Inappropriateness of Western Methodology

An unconditional rational approach to life, its intricacies, complexities, and miraculous phenomena has its limits. If presented with too difficult a situation, the only result is an 'explanation' of utterly ridiculous proportions, made due to a desperate attempt to deny any and all acknowledgement of a Higher Power and the true nature of the miracles.

Examples of the rationalist approach to Islamic history are many. In every case, explanations are brought forth to wave away any acceptance of Divine intervention. One such case is that of the Battle of Badr. Why and how were a little more than three hundred, poorly armed men able to defeat well-equipped army of one thousand soldiers? How was it possible for the meager Muslim forces to kill seventy of their enemy and capture another seventy? Rationalist historians claim that this was only possible due to the pagans' lack of water, and being on the verge of death already due to thirst. However, it is known and recorded that the pagan soldiers themselves testified to the fact that it had rained before the night of the battle, and that they had no paucity of water, nor any other resources. Indeed, it was the Muslims themselves who had been suffering from lack of a water supply, and the Quraish had benefited most by the rainfall.

These Orientalist historians also doubted the number of those pagans killed and captured by the Muslims, though the elegies of the pagans themselves testified as to the tragedy that befell them. There was hardly a single household in Makkah that did not count one of their members among those killed. Unfortunately, some Muslim historians and biographers were deeply impressed by the rational methodology of textual criticism, which biased Western scholars adopted to suit their own purposes. Two main examples of such Muslim historians are Ahmad Ameen in the Arab world and Shibli Nuʿmānī in united India. Both they and their followers tried hard to prove that in textual criticism, the Muslims did not lag behind the West and that they too followed the rational approach!

Shibli's Error

To prove his point, 'Allama Shibli argued that in the terminology of Hadith the Science of Narration *('Ilm-ur-Riwāyah)* is the name of the science that scrutinizes the chain of transmission *(Asāneed)* according to the rules of the Science of Validation *(Al-jarh wat Ta'deel);* on the other hand, *'Ilm-ud-Dirāyah* is a branch of knowledge by means of which Ahādeeth are examined on rational grounds, and that any narration in conflict with reason, no matter how sound the Hadith is, can be rejected.

This is gravely incorrect, as all Islamic jurists and Hadith scholars are unanimous that *'Ilm-ud-Dirāyah* is the very name of the science that examines, checks and scrutinizes the chain of narration and the narrators according to the rules of *Al-Jarh wat-Ta'deel* (Science of Validation) and, in the light of the conditions laid down by them, decides as to whether a particular Hadith is authentic or weak. On the other hand, *'Ilm-ur-Riwāyah* is the name of the science by which we study, learn, remember and narrate the words and actions of the Prophet ﷺ.

In the course of his argumentation, Shibli quotes frequently from Imam As-Suyūtī's famous book *Tadreebr-ur-Rāwī*. In this book Suyūtī writes, quoting Ibn-ul-Akfānī (d.794):

عِلْمُ الْحَدِيثِ الْخَاصُّ بِالرِّوَايَةِ: عِلْمٌ يَّشْتَمِلُ عَلٰى أَقْوَالِ النَّبِيِّ ﷺ وَ أَفْعَالِهِ وَرِوَايَتِهَا وَضَبْطِهَا وَ تَحْرِيرِ أَلْفَاظِهَا .

'Ilm-ur-Riwāyah (Science of Narration) covers the words and acts of the Prophet ﷺ, narrating them, remembering them and writing them.'

Then he defines *'Ilm-ud-Dirāyah*:

وَ عِلْمُ الْحَدِيثِ الْخَاصُّ بِالدِّرَايَةِ : عِلْمٌ يُّعْرَفُ مِنْهُ حَقِيقَةُ الرِّوَايَةِ وَ شُرُوطُهَا وَ أَنْوَاعُهَا وَأَحْكَامُهَا وَ حَالُ الرُّوَاةِ وَ شُرُوطُهُمْ، وَ أَصْنَافُ الْمَرْوِيَّاتِ، وَمَا يَتَعَلَّقُ بِهَا .

'Ilm-ud-Dirāyah is the science by means of which we know the

true nature of a Hadith, its conditions, its kinds, the relevant rulings, state of its narrators, their conditions, kinds of narrations and other connected things.'

Expounding further, As-Suyūtī writes: The true nature *(Haqeeqah)* means the method of transmitting a tradition and using words like *Haddathana* (حدثنا) or *Akhbarana* (اخبرنا) to describe its way of narration. The conditions of *Dirāyah* refer to the way how a Hadith was obtained, for example, by *Simā'* (سماع) (reading by the teacher) or *'Ard* (عرض) (reading by the student before the teacher) or *Ijazah* (اجازه) (permission to transmit). By 'types' we know whether a Hadith is connected *(Muttasil)* or broken *(Munqati')* and so on. By 'rulings' we mean whether a Hadith may be accepted (sound) or rejected *(Da'eef)*. 'State of narrator' refers to whether he is a man of integrity *('Ādil)* or unreliable *(majrooh)*. By 'conditions', we mean how a narrator received the Hadith or how he transmitted it on to others. 'Kinds of narrations' refers to whether a Hadith occurs in *Musnad, Mu'jam* or *Juz'* etc. or whether they are the sayings of the Prophet ﷺ or the words of his companions (اثار). 'Connected things' refers to the terminology of Hadith science.[1]

In short, *'Ilm-ud-Dirāyah* is the branch of knowledge by which we know whether a narrator and his narration are acceptable (sound) or unacceptable (weak).[2]

Fallacy of Shibli's Arguments

Allama Shibli twisted the meaning of *Dirāyah* in order to argue in favour of rejecting a sound Hadith if it did not conform to anybody's reason. According to his definition, while writing on the origin of *Dirāyah,* he claimed that this rule of rejecting a Hadith on rationalist ground was initiated by Qur'an itself. He writes:

"When the Hypocrites slandered 'Ayeshah ﷺ, they circulated the news in a way that deluded some of the Companions themselves. According to Bukhāri and Muslim, even Hassān bin Thābit رضي الله عنه was

1 Tadreeb-ur-Rāwī: 1/21,22.
2 Taujeeh-un-Nazar ila Usool-il-Athar: 1/729.

among those who slandered 'Ayeshah ﷺ. That is why he was given the legal punishment prescribed by Islam for slandering. The Qur'ān says it explicitly:

﴿إِنَّ ٱلَّذِينَ جَآءُو بِٱلْإِفْكِ عُصْبَةٌ مِّنكُمْ﴾

"Surely, those who brought forth the slander are a group among you."[1]

According to *Tafseer ul-Jalālain, "Minkum"* (منكم) (among you) means: a group of believers. That is, the slanderers are a group of believers.[2] The Qur'ān revealed Verses exonerating her and declaring her purity. One of them says:

﴿وَلَوْلَآ إِذْ سَمِعْتُمُوهُ قُلْتُم مَّا يَكُونُ لَنَآ أَن نَّتَكَلَّمَ بِهَٰذَا سُبْحَٰنَكَ هَٰذَا بُهْتَٰنٌ عَظِيمٌ﴾

"And, why did you not, when you heard it, say: "it is not right for us to speak of this. Glorified are You (O Allah)! This is a great lie."[3]

"A normal way to ascertain the truth could have been to inquire about the names of narrators, make sure that they were trustworthy and then ask them to testify but, according to the verse, Allah asked the believers (as to) why they did not dismiss this news as mere calumny as soon as they had heard it the first time. This proves that a thing which does not conform to reason should be rejected outright as utterly wrong. This mode of inquiry, that is, *Dirāyah,* had already started in the era of the Companions."[4]

Shibli translated the Verse [Surely, those who spread the slander] as 'those who slandered.' And he translated the following Verses according to it. But Shah Abdul-Qādir translated it as 'Those who brought forth this storm.' These words, as well as the context of the Qur'ān, make it quite clear that the Qur'ān is not referring to the slanderers but those who spread the slander. The original slanderers were the evil hypocrites who wanted the slander to spread among the Muslims and, to that end, made use of simple-hearted Muslims.

1 An-Nūr 24: 11.
2 Tafseer-ul-Jalāl'ain: An-Nūr 24:16.
3 An-Nūr 24:16.
4 Seerat-un-Nabī, Preface 1/39

Here are the relevant Verses of Qur'an:

﴿إِنَّ ٱلَّذِينَ جَآءُو بِٱلۡإِفۡكِ عُصۡبَةٞ مِّنكُمۡۚ لَا تَحۡسَبُوهُ شَرّٗا لَّكُمۖ بَلۡ هُوَ خَيۡرٞ لَّكُمۡۚ لِكُلِّ ٱمۡرِيٕٖ مِّنۡهُم مَّا
ٱكۡتَسَبَ مِنَ ٱلۡإِثۡمِۚ وَٱلَّذِي تَوَلَّىٰ كِبۡرَهُۥ مِنۡهُمۡ لَهُۥ عَذَابٌ عَظِيمٞ ﴿١١﴾ لَّوۡلَآ إِذۡ سَمِعۡتُمُوهُ ظَنَّ ٱلۡمُؤۡمِنُونَ
وَٱلۡمُؤۡمِنَٰتُ بِأَنفُسِهِمۡ خَيۡرٗا وَقَالُواْ هَٰذَآ إِفۡكٞ مُّبِينٞ ﴿١٢﴾ لَّوۡلَا جَآءُو عَلَيۡهِ بِأَرۡبَعَةِ شُهَدَآءَۚ فَإِذۡ لَمۡ يَأۡتُواْ
بِٱلشُّهَدَآءِ فَأُوْلَٰٓئِكَ عِندَ ٱللَّهِ هُمُ ٱلۡكَٰذِبُونَ ﴿١٣﴾ وَلَوۡلَا فَضۡلُ ٱللَّهِ عَلَيۡكُمۡ وَرَحۡمَتُهُۥ فِي ٱلدُّنۡيَا وَٱلۡأٓخِرَةِ
لَمَسَّكُمۡ فِي مَآ أَفَضۡتُمۡ فِيهِ عَذَابٌ عَظِيمٌ ﴿١٤﴾ إِذۡ تَلَقَّوۡنَهُۥ بِأَلۡسِنَتِكُمۡ وَتَقُولُونَ بِأَفۡوَاهِكُم مَّا لَيۡسَ لَكُم بِهِۦ
عِلۡمٞ وَتَحۡسَبُونَهُۥ هَيِّنٗا وَهُوَ عِندَ ٱللَّهِ عَظِيمٞ ﴿١٥﴾ وَلَوۡلَآ إِذۡ سَمِعۡتُمُوهُ قُلۡتُم مَّا يَكُونُ لَنَآ أَن نَّتَكَلَّمَ بِهَٰذَا
سُبۡحَٰنَكَ هَٰذَا بُهۡتَٰنٌ عَظِيمٞ ﴿١٦﴾ يَعِظُكُمُ ٱللَّهُ أَن تَعُودُواْ لِمِثۡلِهِۦٓ أَبَدًا إِن كُنتُم مُّؤۡمِنِينَ ﴿١٧﴾ وَيُبَيِّنُ
ٱللَّهُ لَكُمُ ٱلۡأٓيَٰتِۚ وَٱللَّهُ عَلِيمٌ حَكِيمٌ ﴿١٨﴾ إِنَّ ٱلَّذِينَ يُحِبُّونَ أَن تَشِيعَ ٱلۡفَٰحِشَةُ فِي ٱلَّذِينَ ءَامَنُواْ
لَهُمۡ عَذَابٌ أَلِيمٞ فِي ٱلدُّنۡيَا وَٱلۡأٓخِرَةِۚ وَٱللَّهُ يَعۡلَمُ وَأَنتُمۡ لَا تَعۡلَمُونَ ﴿١٩﴾ وَلَوۡلَا فَضۡلُ ٱللَّهِ عَلَيۡكُمۡ
وَرَحۡمَتُهُۥ وَأَنَّ ٱللَّهَ رَءُوفٞ رَّحِيمٞ ﴿٢٠﴾﴾

"Verily, those who brought forth the slander (against 'Āishah رضي الله عنها the wife of the Prophet ﷺ) are a group among you. Consider it not a bad thing for you. Nay, it is good for you. To every man among them will be paid that which he had earned of the sin, and as for him among them who had the greater share therein, his will be a great torment. Why then did not the believers, men and women, when you heard it (the slander), think good of their own people and say: "This (charge) is an obvious lie?" Why did they not produce four witnesses against him? Since they (the slanderers) have not produced witnesses! Then with Allāh, they are the liars. Had it not been for the Grace of Allāh and His Mercy to you in this world and in the Hereafter, a great torment would have touched you for that whereof you had spoken. When you were propagating it with your tongues, and uttering with your mouths that whereof you had no knowledge, you counted it a little thing, while with Allāh it was very great. And why did you not, when you heard it, say: "It is not right for us to speak of this. Glorified are You (O Allāh)! This is a great lie.' Allāh forbids you from it and warns you not to repeat the like of it forever, if you are believers. And Allāh makes the Ayāt (proofs, evidences,

verses, lessons, signs, revelations, etc.) plain to you, and Allāh is All-Knowing, All-Wise. Verily, those who like that (the crime of) illegal sexual intercourse should be propagated among those who believe, they will have a painful torment in this world and in the Hereafter. And Allāh knows and you know not. And had it not been for the Grace of Allāh and His Mercy on you (Allāh would have hastened the punishment upon you). And that Allāh is Full of Kindness, Most Merciful."[1]

It is clear from the foregoing verses that 1.the evil baseless story being spread was not "news" (i.e. true), but rather an awful slander; 2.The slanderers had an evil purpose, but Allah knew their plans and instead changed it into something good for the believers; It was made clear that every believer is innocent unless otherwise proven through proper evidence. Slanders are not to be propagated. 3.Those who were behind this plan secretly are the greatest criminals; 4.If a believer, man or woman, is slandered, (and no witness is brought forward) one should not give ear to it but keep one's good opinion of him or her; 5.Those who slander but fail to produce four witnesses shall be considered liars; 6.Allah's doom could have befallen those who spread this slander because it was an evil thing; 7. when they had heard this baseless accusation, they should have immediately dismissed it as a mere slander and said 'we won't spread it any further'.

Allama Shibli's attempt at 'proving' rationalism as being a part of, or the basis of, *'Ilm ad-Dirāyah* is inherently flawed. He deliberately changed the word 'slander' *(buhtan)* to 'news,' and again mistranslated the word 'witnesses' into 'narrators' in order to make his point regarding the correct course of inquiry would be to inquire about the names of the tale-bearers and then to determine their degree of reliability.

The argument Shibli makes has various implications. To begin with, he has twisted the meanings of the words 'slander' and 'news' to suit his own purposes, when the Qur'ān itself clearly distinguishes between the two. Allah says,

﴿إِن جَآءَكُمۡ فَاسِقُۢ بِنَبَإٖ فَتَبَيَّنُوٓاْ﴾

1 An-Nūr, 24: 11-20.

"If an evil-person comes to you with any news, verify it." [1]

It is clear from this Verse that any news (referred to in *Sūrah Al-Hujurāt*) has to be verified while a slander (referred to in *Sūrah An-Noor*) calls for four witnesses. The two cases are different, and subsequently, are to be treated differently.

According to Shibli's interpretation, however, a slander should have been treated as mere news (information), verified first, then treated as slander, and the stage of producing four witnesses would come at the very end. Shibli was forced to resort to this method of argumentation because he sought to find some ground in the Qur'ān to justify his view of *Dirāyah*.

Shibli took further steps to justify his concept of *'Ilm ud-Dirāyah*. He referred to a conversation that took place between Abu Hurairah and Ibn 'Abbās ﷺ as to whether eating food cooked on fire invalidates ritual ablution.

Ibn 'Abbās ﷺ said: 'If eating food cooked on fire invalidates ablution, shall we have to perform ablution after eating ghee or drinking boiled water?' To this Abu Hurairah replied: 'Dear nephew, when you hear the Hadith of the Prophet ﷺ, act, and do not give examples'.[2]

Although this was a purely academic discussion between two Companions, Ibn 'Abbās was bringing forward a difficulty in understanding the real implication of the Hadith narrated by Abu Hurairah. Shibli interpreted it to mean that Ibn 'Abbās ﷺ rejected Abu Hurairah's Hadith on the basis of its contradiction to 'reason.'[3]

Tirmidhi, while narrating this conversation, also quoted other Ahādeeth, similar in meaning, narrated by six other Companions (Umm Habeebah, Umm Salamah, Zaid bin Thābit, Abu Ayyub and Abu Mūsā ﷺ). Hence, the conclusion is that Abu Hurairah was not the lone narrator, nor did Ibn 'Abbās reject the narrations of all the other six. Many other senior Companions like Ibn Umar, Abu Talha, Anas Ibn Malik, Abu Musa, Ayeshah and Zaid bin Thābit ﷺ held that eating food on fire makes

1 Al-Hujurāt, 49: 6.

2 Jami' At-Tirmidhī: 79; and Sunan Ibn Mājah: 485.

3 Seerat-un-Nabi: Preface: 1/39, 40, 54.

it obligatory to renew ablution.[1]

Similarly, there were many other Companions who disagreed on the matter and had differing arguments to support their view. Neither side rejected the Hadith quoted by the other party.

Thus, Shibli's attempt to use this point and the conversation between Ibn 'Abbās and Abu Hurairah ﷺ, as an example of simply the superiority of 'reason' as compared to narration of authentic narrators is moot.

Another implication of Shibli's arguments is that if his first example is accepted, then so too must it be accepted that the differences of opinion among the Prophet's Companions over different academic matters meant that each of them rejected the Hadith advanced by the other to support his own opinion. Of course, this argument itself is completely untrue.

Choosing Between Sound and Weak Ahādeeth

Shibli also quoted Ibn Jauzī and Mulla Ali Qāri (d. 1014 AH) as having said that any narration contrary to observation, feelings or axiomatic and self-evident truth should be considered a weak *(Da'eef)* Hadith.[2]

This is a grave error. None of the listed Hadith scholars ever said that any person by his own opinion, feelings, observations and his self-styled rules may decide about a Hadith and grade it sound or weak.

The fact of the matter is that Hadith scholars reviewed all the Ahādeeth with respect to their chains of transmission, and collected all the other signs of weakness, in addition to those in the chains of transmission. That is, apart from the weakness in the chains of transmission, they identified other types of weaknesses that impair a Hadith and make it weak.

Mulla Ali Qāri collected in his book some Ahādith, and after evaluating them according to the standard set by the Science of Transmission *('Ilm-ul-Asānīd),* made a general review of them. In his conclusions, he enumerated several other signs indicative of fabrication.

1 Tuhfat-ul-Ahwadhī: 1/229.
2 Seerat-un-Nabi: Preface 1/40, 41

One of those signs is that those Ahādith speak of things which are uncommon, unusual, against human observation and, as a whole, repugnant to the universally accepted truths and norms of human reason.[1]

In other words, he pointed out some drawbacks usually found in fabricated Ahādith, but he, in no way, described the rules of examining and evaluating Ahādeeth. It should be noted that those signs are never found in any Hadith reported by reliable narrators or any Hadith free from error or non-conformity *(Shudhūdh)* and hidden defects *('Illah)*. (A *Shādh* or errant Hādeeth is the one which does not conform to similar Ahādith, narrated on the same topic, whose chains are stronger).

Rationalism is Not the Norm

It is true that many authentic Ahādeeth describing the miracles of the Prophet ﷺ, such as his ascent to the seventh heaven *(Al-Mi'rāj)* do not look reasonable to Orientalists and other rationalists; however, they are completely credible to the believer who firmly accepts that Allah, who creates man in the womb of his mother, nourishes him, and brings him alive on the earth, can easily summon a human being to the heavens. Every Companion, Hadith scholar, jurist and learned scholar, including Ibn Jauzi and Mulla Ali Qāri, have all believed unconditionally in the Ahādeeth relating to the Prophet's ascension and other miracles and, in fact, the miracles of all other prophets, as true and authentic.

No one except the Orientalists and Modernists influenced by them, have ever rejected a Hadith or dubbed it as weak *(Da'eef)* simply because it is considered to be 'irrational' or does not conform to anybody's reason. Every passing day adds to the sum total of human knowledge. With the constant progress of scientific inquiry, new evidences are emerging, proving the validity of many a phenomenon which appeared to be irrational previously. Human reason is not infallible. If it were the standard of faith and belief, then the entire religion of Islam or even Christianity or Judaism–based upon belief in God, divine revelation, angels, the afterlife, resurrection, paradise and

1 Al-Maudooāt-al-Kabeer by Mulla Ali Qāri, P. 155.

hell – would be completely thrown out of the window. Those who take human reason as the yardstick to measure every truth, are the ones, who also deny the existence of God. Furthermore, human reason and level of intellect is not equal nor exact amongst all mankind. No two men have an equal degree of intellect; every person has different mental capabilities, and each person on earth thinks, rationalizes, and makes decisions differently and according to different patterns of rationale.

All jurists and Hadith scholars are unanimous that the Ahādith which are authentic as to their chain of transmission, are in accord with the sound reason of a believer. Faults are found only in weak and fabricated Ahādith. The goal of Hadith scholars was to see that the statements and actions of the Prophet ﷺ are reported exactly and accurately. They took utmost care to ensure that whatever they reported about the Prophet ﷺ, his words or actions, were unaltered, unmixed, and that no extraneous element crept into it. Their criteria were complete, absolute truthfulness. To achieve this goal, the Muhadditheen set before them a very strict standard and criterion to evaluate Ahādeeth.

Human reason is only a means to comprehend properly an authentic Hadith and seek a way to act by it. It is in no way a judge over it. It benefits by it, expands the frontiers of its comprehension, admires its beauty, seeks and describes the fine points of it. A man of sound intellect feels delighted to act by it while, on the other hand, whimsy rejection and doubt only confuse the mind. They give him no peace of mind.

Shibli says in his preface later on, elaborating his view of *Dirāyah*: "The truth is that it is difficult to categorically decide this matter. The common opinion is that a Hadith whose narrators are trustworthy and authentic, the chain of narration being in no way broken *(Munqati')*, cannot be rejected even though it is in conflict with reason." By way of example, he quotes the statements of Hafiz Ibn Hajar and Allama Qastalani, commentators of Bukhāri, to prove that an authentic Hadith can in no way be rejected just because it does not conform to human reason (at some stage of time).[1]

It is strange for Shibli to refer to the well-considered opinions of such great scholars supported with proofs as 'common opinion.' It is no common opinion, but rather the well-established and universally accepted rules of Hadith scholars. Those Muhadditheen, who did an excellent job of performing the difficult task of preserving Ahādith – they memorized them, wrote them down, documented them, wrote commentaries, and lay down the stringent rules of probing and evaluating them, a science unique in the history of mankind. Hence, reason demands of us to accept the authority of Hadith scholars as to whether a Hadith may be accepted or rejected. With regard to the issue under discussion, the verdict of Hadith scholars is what Shibli himself said before the quoted excerpt:

'Reason cannot be identified or specified. The defenders of Ahādith claim that if this word is expanded further, anyone may reject a Hadith on the ground that it is not in conformity with his reason.'

The Prophet's Companions and Rationalism

Shibli divided the Companions into two groups and stated that one of the two groups was wary and hesitated to accept some Ahādith on rational grounds. To support his view, he gave several examples, one of them being the foregoing dispute between Abu Hurairah and Ibn 'Abbās رضي الله عنهما. Below are a few others:

Ibn 'Abbās رضي الله عنهما saw a few rulings attributed to Ali ibn Abi Tālib رضي الله عنه. Ibn 'Abbās started copying them but skipped some of them, saying: 'By Allah, it cannot be Ali's ruling or, else he strayed from the (straight) path.' Moreover, a book containing Ali's rulings was brought to Ibn 'Abbās. Except for a space about three feet long, Ibn 'Abbās deleted the whole of it.[2] "Obviously," comments Shibli, "Ibn 'Abbās guessed from the contents that those rulings could not have been given by Ali رضي الله عنه. Therefore, he felt no need to make inquiries about the narrators or

1 Seerat-un-Nabi: Preface 1/53, 54.
2 Sahih Muslim, Preface 22,23.

trace the chain of narration."[1]

However, Ibn "Abbās ﵄ did not care to trace the chains of narration because the rulings had come from unspecified sources. The very words of the narration prove it. Moreover, those rulings had been penned down but they did not mention the names of narrators or witnesses. Ibn 'Abbās ﵄, who had spent a large part of his lifetime with Ali ﵁, knew of his rulings more than others. It is obvious that when he was shown those rulings, he kept intact those which he knew were right and struck off the rest. There was no mention of narrators, in which case, how could he make inquiries about them?

Mahmūd bin Rabee' ﵁ narrated a Hadith: 'Whoso says that there is no God except Allah (the missing part being: يَبْتَغِي بِذَالِكَ وَجْهَ الله 'seeking thereby the pleasure of Allah), Allah shall keep him safe from the Fire'. On hearing this Hadith, Abu Ayyūb al-Ansāri ﵁ replied: 'By Allah, I do not think what you say is the statement of the Prophet.'[2]

Commenting on this Hadith Shibli remarked: 'Though Mahmūd bin Rabee' ﵁ came to Madinah and verified the Hadith from the narrator ('Utbān), as mentioned in Bukhārī, it does not affect the essence of the matter. Abu Ayyūb ﵁ could well have doubted 'Utbān ﵁ for the same reasons for which he doubted Mahmūd bin Rabee' ﵁. Abu Ayyub did not think Mahmūd was wrong, but thought that the latter may have misunderstood the Hadith.'[3]

Mahmūd bin Rabee' ﵁ had met the Prophet ﷺ when he was only a child. He was five years old when the Prophet ﷺ passed away. He had heard this Hadith from 'Utbān, but Abu Ayyūb ﵁ had not. Thus, when the latter heard it from the child Mahmūd, he commented what he commented. It is a mere presumption of Shibli that Abu Ayyūb ﵁ would make the same comment even if he had heard it directly from 'Utbān or that his comment was based on the irrationality of the Hadith. This Hadith is not in conflict with reason in any way. Surely, Allah may forgive whom He will for any sin other than the sin of

1 Seerat-un-Nabi: Preface 1/54,55.
2 Sahih-ul-Bukhari :1186; Sahih Muslim: (264) - 657.
3 Seerat-un-Nabi: Preface 1/55.

ascribing partners to Allah.

In fact, What Mahmūd bin Rabee'ﷺ said was one of the established principles of Islam. The Qur'an states very clearly:

﴿ إِنَّ ٱللَّهَ لَا يَغۡفِرُ أَن يُشۡرَكَ بِهِۦ وَيَغۡفِرُ مَا دُونَ ذَٰلِكَ لِمَن يَشَآءُۚ ﴾

"Surely, Allah forgives not that partners should be set up with Him (in worship). But he forgives except that (anything else) to whom He wills." [1]

How could Abu Ayyūb think of a Verse of the Qur'ān as repugnant to reason? Many other Companions also reported Ahādeeth similar in meaning. The conclusion is that Abu Ayyūb's purpose was only to stress the need for utmost caution while attributing a statement to the Prophet ﷺ, which was why Mahmūd bin Rabee'ﷺ referred the Hadith once again to 'Utbān ﷺ for verification. Had the Companions set before them the criterion of rationalism and reason to decide the soundness of a Hadith rather than the accuracy of reporting, then Mahmūd bin Rabee' would obviously have had no need to turn to 'Utbān for verification; instead, he could have simply convinced Abu Ayyūb by means of rational arguments.

Hadith of Dry Ablution (*Tayammum*)

Umar's comment, اِتَقِ الله يا عمارُ "Fear Allah, O 'Ammār!" upon hearing 'Ammār's narration concerning dry ablution *(Tayammum)* was not a rejection of a sound Hadith on rational grounds. It is also wrong to say that 'Umar was not satisfied by 'Ammār's explanation.

The truth is that 'Umar did not remember all the details of dry ablution, which was why 'Ammār reminded him that once, during a journey, both of them had become ritually unclean and both needed to perform dry ablution for want of water. 'Umar did not do so, while 'Ammār rolled in dust and prayed. When the latter returned to Madinah, he told the Prophet what he had done. Thereupon, the Prophet told him that in such a situation dry ablution was enough for him. 'Ammār tried to remind Umar of that event, although the latter

1 An-Nisā' (4): 48.

could not recollect it.[1]

Thus, 'Umar's statement towards 'Ammār was not to deny the Hadith, but rather enjoining caution to the narrator as he reported the event. Thereupon, 'Ammār said to 'Umar: اِتَقِ الله ياعمارُ 'If you wish, I will not report the Hadith.' To this 'Umar replied: 'We entrust you with this responsibility which you have undertaken to bear'.[2] That is, he advised him to be cautious while reporting this Hadith. Obviously, there seems to be no ground for Shibli to infer from this event that companions rejected a Hadith because they thought it conflicted with their reason!

Mourning the Dead

'Ayeshah ﷺ objected to the Hadith which says that mourning torments the dead, on the ground that it conflicts with the verse of Qur'an:

﴿ وَلَا تَزِرُ وَازِرَةٌ وِزْرَ أُخْرَىٰ ﴾

"No bearer of burdens shall bear the burden of another." [3]

She did not reject the Hadith on rational grounds; in fact, many of the Companions differed over this matter.

Later, the Hadith scholars reconciled between the Verse of the Qur'ān and the Hadeeeth, saying that if a dead man instructs his relatives and friends to hold mourning sessions as it was the practice in *Jahiliyyah* (Period of Ignorance), he shall be tormented in his grave.

'Ayeshah ﷺ objected to 'Umar's Hadith: "They (the pagans killed at Badr) are hearing what I am saying to them now," saying that it was in conflict with the verse of Qur'an [You cannot make hear those who are in graves][4]but again, she did not reject it on rational grounds. She objected because she was not told the other part of the Hadith: "Allah has now returned their souls to their bodies and they are hearing my words better than you." This missing part of the Hadith removes her objection.

1 Sahih-ul-Bukhārī: 338 and 347.
2 Sahih Muslim: 368.
3 Al-An'Ām 6: 164; Sahih-ul-Bukhari: 1288.
4 Sahih-ul-Bukhari: 3979-3981.

Is a divorced woman entitled to support allowance during the *Iddah* period? 'Umar ﷺ did not act by what Fatimah bint Qais narrated, not because he rejected her narration on rational grounds, but because he doubted her memory. He is reported to have remarked:
" لاندرى لعلها حفظت اونسيت " 'We don't know if she remembered it or forgot it.' Then he quoted the Quranic Verse:

﴿ لَا تُخْرِجُوهُنَّ مِنۢ بُيُوتِهِنَّ وَلَا يَخْرُجْنَ إِلَّآ أَن يَأْتِينَ بِفَٰحِشَةٍ مُّبَيِّنَةٍ ﴾

> *"Expel them not from their houses nor let them go forth unless they commit open immorality."*[1]

and, arguing from the generality of the Verse, said that a divorced woman shall be given maintenance allowance.[2]

Hadith scholars explained that the Hadith of Fatimah bint Qais was authentic because it related to a woman irrevocably divorced (مطلقة ثلاثة بائنة) (who is not entitled to maintenance allowance), while the Quranic Verse (quoted above) relates to a woman given a revocable divorce (مطلقه رجعيه).

Imam Ahmad bin Hanbal's ruling matched what Fatimah bint Qais had said. He remarked that there is no Verse in Qur'an prescribing maintenance allowance for a woman irrevocably divorced. Jurists take this Hadith as a basis and have inferred from it many a point of law.

It is true that some Companions occasionally expressed surprise on hearing an authentic Hadith, or sought further verification, or doubted a narrator's memory; however, this should not be construed to mean a rejection of Hadith on rational grounds.

Similarly, in case of some difficult Ahādith, comments made by Companions such as, 'it is difficult to understand,' or 'it raises another problem,' should not be taken as a rejection of the respective Hadith. It is rather an acceptance of Hadeeth, along with an acknowledgement of their inability to understand it perfectly well.

1 At-Talāq 65:1
2 Sahih Muslim: 1480; Fath-ul-Bari: 9/594,595.

Narrations of Child Companions

Writing in his preface under the title 'Level of witness and the type of event,' Shibli says: "If a reliable narrator narrates an ordinary, commonplace event, his narration will easily be accepted, but if he narrates an extraordinary, out-of-the common event not consistent with the environment, then an 'ordinary level of reliability' is not enough. He goes on to say: "Scholars debate over whether there is an age-limit prescribed for a narrator. Most of the Hadith scholars maintain that a five-year old boy may narrate a Hadith or, for example, if a five-year-old Companion reports some word or act of the Prophet, his narration shall be accepted."[1]

Once again, Shibli mixes up different concepts. He confuses child-narrators with child-Companions, questioning the reliability of both despite the fact that age is only a barrier in acceptance of Ahādith for child-narrators, and not child-Companions. In point of fact, Hadith scholars who were in favor of accepting narrations from child-narrators advanced the case for child-Companions, and argued that if the latter were acceptable, the former would be even more so. Shibli quotes frequently from the book *Fat'h-ul-Mugheeth* to support his view, although ironically, even a brief look at the same book makes the opposite argument clear.

The book states:

وَرُدَّ عَلَى الْقَائِلِينَ بِعَدَمِ قَبُولِ الصَّبِيِّ بِإِجْمَاعِ الْأَئِمَّةِ عَلٰى قَبُولِ حَدِيثِ جَمَاعَةٍ مِّنْ صِغَارِ الصَّحَابَةِ مِمَّا تَحَمَّلُوهُ فِي حَالِ الصِّغَرِ كَالسِّبْطَيْنِ وَهُمَا الْحَسَنُ وَالْحُسَيْنُ ابْنَا ابْنَتِهٖ فَاطِمَةَ الزَّهْرَاءِ، وَالْعَبَادِلَةِ ابْنِ جَعْفَرِ بْنِ أَبِي طَالِبٍ، وَابْنِ الزُّبَيْرِ، وَابْنِ عَبَّاسٍ، وَالنُّعْمَانِ بْنِ بَشِيرٍ، وَالسَّائِبِ بْنِ يَزِيدَ، وَالْمِسْوَرِبْنِ مَخْرَمَةَ، وَأَنَسٍ، وَمَسْلَمَةَ بْنِ مُخَلَّدٍ، وَ عُمَرَ بْنِ أَبِي سَلَمَةَ، وَيُوسُفَ بْنِ عَبْدِاللّٰهِ بْنِ سَلَامٍ، وَأَبِي الطُّفَيْلِ وَعَائِشَةَ وَنَحْوِهِمْ رَضِيَ اللّٰهُ عَنْهُمْ مِّنْ غَيْرِ فَرْقٍ بَيْنَ مَا تَحَمَّلُوهُ قَبْلَ الْبُلُوغِ وَبَعْدَهٗ.

"The argument of those who oppose taking narrations from children is rejected by some scholars who maintain that all

1 Seerat-un-Nabi: Preface 1/48.

the Imams are unanimous that the Ahādeeth which the child-Companions acquired or narrated during their childhood days are acceptable, such as Hasan and Husain ﷺ, the Prophet's grandsons from his daughter Fatimah ﷺ; all the three Abdullahs ('Abdullah bin Ja'far bin Abi Tālib, 'Abdullah bin Zubair, and 'Abdullah bin Abbās), Nu'mān bin Basheer, Sā'ib bin Yazeed, Miswar bin Makhramah, Anas, Maslama bin Mukhallad, 'Umar bin Abi Salamah (son of Umm Salama, the Mother of the Believers), Yūsuf bin 'Abdullah bin Salām, Abu Tufail, 'Ayeshah ﷺ, and others. It does not matter whether they learned (and narrated) Ahādith before coming of age or after it."[1]

Contradicting His Principles

By confusing and mixing up minor Companions with other child narrators, Shibli raised a controversy over the narrations of child-Companions and ruled them as a low-level testimony for important events. Logic demands that he should have kept to his own self-styled rules and refused to rely on the narrations of child-Companions but, on the contrary, he often based his arguments on their narrations.

For example, while writing on the Migration *(Hijrah)*, he said: "The story of migration is very moving. It is for this reason that Bukhāri, who is generally very concise, dwells upon this event at great length, quoting 'Ayeshah ﷺ. Though Ayeshah was seven or eight years old at that time, her narrations are, in fact, those of the Prophet ﷺ and Abu Bakr ﷺ themselves because she must have heard the details from them. Moreover, she was herself a witness to those events in the beginning."[2]

'Ayeshah was only six years old then and had just begun her seventh year.[3] She was not seven or eight years old, as Shibli claimed. Moreover, the way she described the early part of the event indicates quite clearly that she was a witness to that event. Concerning the Migration, Shibli relied upon the entire narration of 'Ayeshah ﷺ, who was a minor at the time!

1 Fat'h-ul-Mugheeth: 2/150, 151.
2 Seerat-un-Nabi: 161/1.
3 Al-Isabah: 8/231,232.

All Narrations of child Companions are Authentic

It is the unanimous opinion of all Hadith scholars that a child-Companion who saw or heard from the Prophet ﷺ, according to the conditions of those times, were indeed completely focused on the words and actions of the Prophet (ﷺ). They also listened to Ahādeeth from their relatives and other Companions with rapt attention, and later, verified what they heard and expanded their knowledge. Whatever Ahādeeth they narrated later in their lives are all considered to be authentic.

Shibli's confusion and mixing-up of child-Companions with child-narrators, his discussions on personal opinions of narrators colouring their narrations, and his view on whether the Companions were divided over the acceptance of Ahādeeth on rational grounds, are clearly issues he kicked up only so that he could argue in defense of those legal rulings which are based on analogy *(Qiyās)* but which are contrary to clear and authentic Ahādeeth.

To begin with, Shibli began with narrators of 'ordinary level of reliability' and said that their narrations, in case they are not in harmony with the environments of the event, are objectionable.[1]

Later, he goes on to say: 'The European rules of re-examining and checking witnesses are very much different from ours. Europeans do not care a lot as to whether a narrator is truthful or a liar, about his character and his habits, and the strength of his retentive memory. To them this type of inquiry is neither possible nor necessary. They only note as to whether the statement of a narrator fits in with the event and the context. If a confirmed liar narrates an event and his narration appears to be right in the context of the environs, his statement running smooth, with no break or inconsistency, the event he describes should be accepted as true. That is the view and the practice of the Europeans.

On the contrary, a Muslim historian and, in particular, a Muslim scholar of Ahādith does not care for the quality of a narration. First and foremost, he inquires about the reliability of a narrator. He refers

1 Seerat-un-Nabi: Preface 1/48.

to books of biographical science to find out whether he is listed there as a trustworthy narrator or not.[1] If he is not trustworthy (ثقة), his narration deserves no attention.[2]On the contrary, the narration by a trustworthy narrator, though apparently in conflict with the context and reason[3], shall be accepted.[4]'

Hadith Scholars on the Rationality of Authentic Ahādith

Many of the comments Shibli makes about Hadith scholars are incorrect, and often in contradiction with his own statements. Giving his own interpretation of the term *Dirāyah,* he acknowledges that Hadith scholars believe that any Hadith which is against human 'reasons' *(Uqool)* or against the established principles is fabricated. In this connection he quotes the words of Imām Ibn Jauzī[5].

With reference to a Hadith being in conflict with reason, Ibn Jauzī was very cautious in his choice of words. He said: "A Hadith in conflict with human 'reasons', not reason." That is, he used the plural number because in this case a single man's reason cannot be the arbiter or the criterion. Unreliable narrators are they who narrated Ahādeeth against human 'reasons', Qur'an and *Sunnah,* and absolute consensus *(Ijmā' Qāt'i)*. Reliable narrators are those, who never narrate a *Munkar* (denounced) Hadith in which the foregoing defects are found.

For Hadith scholars, as already explained before, trustworthiness is one of the basic criteria. The most important condition of trustworthiness is that a narrator should never narrate a *Munkar* (denounced) Hadith.

---

1 Narrator's name is not easy to list except after thorough and intensive investigation and after it has been proved beyond doubt that he never narrated anything contrary to established truths.

2 Next to *Thiqah* (trustworthy) is *sadooq* (truthful) and *Maqbool* (acceptable). Their narrations are accepted if there is only a slight weakness and they are free from blame of lying or fabricating Ahādeeth and that there are other corroborating evidences to support them. Their narrations are accepted after scrutinizing the text of the Hadith.

3 If his narrations are in conflict with contexts *(Qarā'in)* and established truths, this will affect the degree of his trustworthiness.

4 Seerat-un-Nabi: Peface 1/69,70.

5 Seerat-un-Nabi: Preface 1/40.

Hadith scholars never consider a narrator trustworthy if he narrates Ahādeeth contrary to 'reason of the majority of the people' *('Uqool),* established rules, senses and common observation. There is no need to look for proof to invalidate such narrators because investigation has revealed that such narrations come only from blameworthy *(Majrooh)* persons.

It is clear from Shibli's writings that he did not give due thought to every aspect of what he wrote about *Dirāyah* and *Qiyās* (Analogy). Often, he would say something at one point and later on, would contradict his own statements.

He gives several examples of his self-styled notion of *Qiyās* and *Dirāyah,* some of which have already been mentioned and criticized. As for others, they relate to a difference of opinion among the Companions regarding some legal issues, or to the ignorance of the entire Hadith or some parts of it, none of the events mentioned therein had anything to do with the Companions rejecting a Hadith because they thought it to be repugnant to reason or deduction by analogy (*Qiyās*).

Unfair Criticism of Muhadditheen

Shibli has also been found to make claims regarding the *Muhadditheen* which are contrary to reality. For example, he writes: "We need to follow the rules of *Dirāyah* set by Hadith scholars very strictly, the rules which they themselves ignore sometimes."[1]

Such a claim is blatantly dishonest – there have been none in the entire history of mankind to be as strict, cautious and inflexible with respect to the scrutinizing of narrations. The Hadith scholars never ignored their principles, and indeed, Shibli did not give a single example of the alleged laxity of Hadith scholars.

The truth is that Shibli's concept of *Dirāyah* is his own, a self-styled concept, quite different from that of Hadith scholars. The latter never ignored it while scrutinizing Ahādeeth.

The issue is not that of Hadith scholars accepting a Hadith repugnant

1 Seerat-un-Nabi: Preface 1/70.

to the minds of wise good-natured believers in Allah or their rules, sense or observation; rather, the issue is that of some persons giving precedence to their own opinions over authentic Ahādith, opinions which Hadith scholars cannot accept and for which they cannot reject an authentic Hadith. The matter is not one of human reason but one of personal opinions. Obviously, Hadith scholars cannot reject an authentic Hadith for the sake of personal opinions or preferences.

Holy Battles and Principles of Hadith Scholars

After discussing the aforementioned topics, Shibli described the rules he followed in the Prophet's biography. He kept the Qur'an at the forefront of his sources, followed by authentic Ahādeeth. He informs us that he laboured hard to collect authentic Ahādeeth relating to the Prophet's biography, and that he felt no need to take narrations found in biographies if he could find authentic Ahādith. He also claimed that he made full inquiry into all those commonplace events which were significant one way or another.[1] No doubt, these are unanimously accepted principles.

However, later on under the heading of 'References,' he writes: 'Regarding events which are somewhat significant, I referenced them to authentic Ahādeeth or reliable historians but, while describing the details of ordinary events or military campaigns, I did not labour hard as Hadith scholars do."[2] His latter remarks display a callous and careless understanding of the Prophet's Seerah; not a single event in the Messenger's life can be called "ordinary," and his every word and action have special significance and must be followed. It is unseemly for one who claims to study the Prophet's biography to be lax or negligent with regards to any incident whatsoever of the Prophet's life.

Orientalists and Arab Authors

When the imperial powers of the West had fully colonized the Muslim world and imposed their own educational system on them, a spate of Arabic books emerged, bearing the imprint of the Orientalists' thought

1 Seerat-un-Nabi: preface 1/71.
2 Seerat-un-Nabi: preface 1/72.

and style.

Among such books, some were quite prominent, such as *Hayāt-o-Muhammad* (Life of Muhammad), written by a well-known Egyptian man of letters, Muhammad Husain Haikal. Writing about his own book, the author says:

إِنَّنِي لَمْ آخُذْ بِمَا سَجَّلَتْهُ كُتُبُ السِّيرَةِ وَالْحَدِيثِ، لِأَنَّنِي فَضَّلْتُ أَنْ أَجْرِي فِي هٰذَا الْبَحْثِ عَلَى الطَّرِيقَةِ الْعِلْمِيَّةِ .

> "I did not take (anything) from what has been recorded in biographies and books of Ahādeeth because I chose to follow the scientific method in my research work."

How could one ignore sources which contain hard facts, and instead turn to conjecture, probability, and guesswork? Is the Seerah of the Prophet Muhammad (ﷺ) a scientific enquiry? Surely, invertion of ones own history is no scientific research.

Another famous Arab author, Muhammad Fareed Wajdi, wrote a series of articles entitled *As-Seerat-ul-Muhammadiyyah Tahta Dau il-'Ilm-i-wal-Falsafah* (Biography of Muhammad in the light of science and philosophy). His words bespeak his views:

وَقَدْ لَاحَظَ قُرَّآؤُنَا أَنَّنَا نَحْرِصُ كُلَّ الْحِرْصِ فِيمَا نَكْتُبُهُ فِي هٰذِهِ السِّيرَةِ عَلَى أَلَّا نُسْرِفَ فِي كُلِّ نَاحِيَةٍ إِلَى نَاحِيَةِ الْإِعْجَازِ، مَا دَامَ يُمْكِنُ تَعْلِيلُهَا بِالْأَسْبَابِ الْعَادِيَةِ، حَتَّى وَلَوْبِشَيْءٍ مِّنَ التَّكَلُّفِ .

> "Our readers must have noted that while writing this biography we very much desire to explain events in a normal, ordinary way as much as possible and not exaggerate in describing any aspect of it as a miracle even if we have to constrain ourselves in this regard."

In other words, Mr. Wajdi thought it necessary to deny the miraculous content of the Prophet's mission and works even at the cost of inconvenience. Hence, he did his best to interpret the facts in a way that would deny the miraculous nature of the events.

How does mankind distinguish a prophet from an ordinary man? Surely, the best proof of a man claiming to be a prophet is his miracles. Mr. Wajdi's main purpose seems to be how to deny the extraordinary aspects of the Prophet's biography. In fact, each aspect of the Prophet's life is so perfect, unique and beautiful that no explanation is possible except to acknowledge that he was no ordinary man, but rather, a messenger of Almighty Allah; the greatest of His messengers, one who combines in his person all the excellent qualities of Allah's messengers.

Indeed, Muhammad (ﷺ) was more than that. In every matter relating to earthly life, be it the welfare of mankind and the struggle for it, or fortitude and steadfastness in the pursuit of truth, or disregard for worldly gains or making peace deals with sworn enemies or magnanimity in times of hardness, whatever the field, he acted in the best possible way inconceivable for any person other than a prophet. His was the noblest conduct. That is the perfection of Prophethood. That is his greatest miracle.

The Denial of Miracles – a Sign of Perverted Faith

In the whole of human history there has never been a society without prophets. Some call them Avtār (Sanskrit), some call them Wakhshoor (Old Persian), Apostolos (Greek) or Shaleekh (Hebrew).[1]

The Qur'an has mentioned the most famous of them. The Torah and the Injīl (New Testament) mentioned others. So too have other nations remembered their holy men. There is no gainsaying the fact that those prophets of Allah were the best of men, blameless, possessing the best possible human qualities and unimpeachable moral conduct. None can match them in virtue, piety and excellence of character. They left indelible imprints on human history. Indeed, the most eloquent proof of Muhammad (ﷺ)'s Prophethood is his extraordinary success, unparalleled by any other human in existence.

To deny the miracle of the final Prophet and Messenger of Allah ﷺ is not merely unjust, but is evidence of a malicious and perverted mindset.

1 Qamoos-ul-Kitāb P. 435.

As in the Indian sub-continent, there emerged later in the Arab world a number of writers who came under the influence of the West, to some extant, but not its mental slave, most of whom were connected with Arab universities. One notable example was Muhammad Kudri Bek who wrote the four-volume *Muhādarāt Fi Tareekh-il-Umam -il-Islamiyyah,* the first half of the first volume being a biography of the Prophet (ﷺ). His other book *Noor-ul-Yaqeen Fi Seerat Sayyed -il-Mursaleen* is a devoted and detailed biography of the Prophet (ﷺ). Similarly, Dr. Hasan Ibrahim Hasan devoted a part of his *Tareekh -ul-Islam* to the Prophet's biography. These authors represented ideas and philosophies similar to Allama Shibli's.

Significant Arabic biographies of Modern Times

As a rejoinder to the Orientalists, there emerged in the Muslim world a new generation of writers who, following the Islamic methodology of research, wrote a number of biographies in different languages. Some Arab authors, following Ibn Qayyim's methodology, took their material from acceptable Ahādeeth and inferred points of law while writing their biographies. There are two notable books in this series, both bearing the title of *Fiqh-us-Seerah,* one by Shaikh Muhammad Ghazālī, and the other by Shaikh Muhammad Sa'eed Ramadān Būtī. Dr. Mustafa Sabā'ī's *As-Seerah An-Nabawiyyah: Duroos wa 'Ibar* lists points of wisdom, not points of law or rulings.

Lately, thanks to the efforts of hardworking students of Hadith many important works of *Muhadditheen* have been published. There is a scholars who published their valuable research works, there was a general awakening among the Muslims and they felt they should rely on the Qur'an and authentic Hadith and reliable accounts found in books of history and biographies. When Shaikh Ghazālī's *Fiqh-us-Seerah* became popular, Shaikh Nāsiruddin al-Albānī convinced him of the need to reference and document the Ahādeeth he had quoted in his book according to the standard set by the *Muhadditheen.*

Shaikh Ghazāli agreed, however, when Shaikh Al-Albāni started his inquiry, Shaikh Ghazālī felt considerably disturbed. He gave permission to publish the new edition with Al-Albānī's research work, a token of his academic integrity, but at the same time he tried to defend himself in the face of Al-Albānī's criticism.

Shaikh Al-Albānī continued his work and then turned to research Tirmidhi's *Ash-Shamā'il-ul-Muhammadiyyah,* and, later on, Ibn Khatheer's *As-Seerat-un-Nabawiyyah,* a great work of the great Hadith scholar, commentator of the Qur'an and historian. In his inquiries, he had already reached the Ahādith relating to the Prophet's Night Journey and Ascent to heaven when he passed away. His research work was published under the title of *Sahih As-Seerah An-Nabawiya,* which covers events of the Messenger's life up to his ascent to heaven.

In the Indian sub-Continent, biographical literature had already evolved and passed through these stages. Shibli's biography was followed by Abdur-Rauf Danapuri's biography *'Asahh-us-Siyar'* published in 1932 in Urdu. He relied mostly on basic biographies and tried his best to take those narrations which met the standard set by Hadith scholars. Though he did not grade the narrations he selected, nor provide a list of his references, in general his referencing is correct.

Among such books in Arabic language, Muhammad Abu Zuhrah's *Khatam An-Nabiyyeen,* Shaikh Muhammad 'Isa Darooza's Seerat *Rasoolullah Sallalaho 'alaihi wa Sallam: Suwar Muqtabasah Minal-Qur'an-il-Kareem wa Tahleelāt wa Dirāsāt Qurāniyyah,* and Shaikh Abul-Hasan Ali Nadwi's *As-Seerat-un-Nabawiyyah* are the most distinguished ones.

More recently, a number of books based on authentic narrations have been published. The best among them are *Ar-Raheeq Al-Makhtoom* by Shaikh Safi-ur-Rahmān Mubarakpuri, *As-Seerat an-Nabawiyyah* by Dr. Ali As-Salābi, *As-Seerat-un-Nabawiyyah Kamā Jā'at fil-Ahādith As-Sahihah* by Muhammad Suyāni, *As-Seerat-un-Nabawiyyah fi-dau-il-Masadir-il-Asliyyah* by Dr. Mahdi Rizqullah, and *As-Seerat-un-Nabawiyyah -us-Sahihah* by Dr. Diyā'-ul-'Umrī.

Apart from these, there is a constant flow of books based on authentic narrations. There are also books on some selected topics relating to Seerah, for example, Dr. Akram Diyā' 'Umrī's *Al-Mujtama'-ul-Madanī*.

Authentic Ahādith and Historical Narrators

Dr. 'Umri wrote in the preface of his book *As-Seerat-un-Nabawiyyah-us-Sahihah:*

وَقَدْ ظَهَرَ جَلِيًّا أَنَّ الِاعْتِمَادَ عَلٰى صَحِيحِ الرِّوَايَاتِ وَ حَسَنِهَا يَكْفُلُ تَوْضِيحَ الْأَبْعَادِ التَّارِيخِيَّةِ لِلسِّيرَةِ النَّبَوِيَّةِ دُونَ حَاجَةٍ إِلَى الضَّعِيفِ مِنَ الرِّوَايَاتِ .

"It has become clear that relying on those narrations which are authentic *(Sahih)* and acceptable *(Hasan)* is enough to demonstrate the historical dimensions of the Prophet's biography, there being no need to use weak *(Da'eef)* Ahādeeth."[1]

Dr. 'Umri distinguishes between authentic Ahādeeth and authentic historical narrations. He says:

شَرْطُ الصَّحِيحِ مِنَ الْحَدِيثِ هُوَ أَنْ يَّرْوِيَهُ الْعَدْلُ الضَّابِطُ عَنِ الْعَدْلِ الضَّابِطِ إِلٰى مُنْتَهَاهُ مِنْ غَيْرِ شُذُوذٍ وَّلَا عِلَّةٍ فَشَرْطُ الرِّوَايَةِ التَّارِيخِيَّةِ الصَّحِيحَةِ أَنَّ كُلَّ رُوَاتِهَا الْمُتَعَاقِبِينَ ــ إِلٰى شَاهِدِ الْعِيَانِ ــ مُتَدَيِّنُونَ تَدَيُّنًا صَحِيحًا وَّعِنْدَهُمْ مَّلَكَةُ الْحِفْظِ الَّتِي تَمْنَعُ وُقُوعَهُمْ فِي الْأَوْهَامِ وَالتَّخْلِيطِ ......

"The condition for a Hadith to be authentic is that it is narrated by an upright *('Adl)* and accurate *(Dābit)* narrator from (another) upright and accurate narrator up to the last of the chain of narration, there being no *Shudhoodh* (non-conformity to similar Ahādeeth, narrated on the same topic, whose chains are stronger) and no *'Illah* (hidden defects). As for an authentic historical narration, the condition is that all its narrators should be consecutive up to the eye-witness - religious in the right sense, possessing the gift of memory that prevents them from fancies and confusion."[2]

1 As-Seerat-un-Nabawiyyah Lil-'Umri: 1/19.

2 Op.cit. 1/39.

As for Dr. 'Umri's condition of 'religiosity,' instead of uprightness and accuracy (*'Adl* and *Dābit*) for an historical narrator, Hadith scholars say on the basis of their observation and experience that a religious man may also mouth a lie (unwittingly). Imam Muslim has elaborated this point in the detailed preface of his collection of authentic Ahādith. He says that 'Abdullah bin Mubārak asked his teacher Imam Sufyān Thaurī about a pious man of his times, 'Abbād bin Kathīr, whether he should tell people not to accept Ahādith from him because he narrates abnormal things. He replied: "Why not?" Ibn Mubārak said, "From then onward, in any sitting when the name of 'Abbad was mentioned, I would praise him for his piety and at the same time tell people not to accept Ahādeeth from him."

Imam Abdullah bin Mubarak also said that when he went to Imam Shu'bah, he said: 'He is 'Abbād bin Kathīr. Keep away from him.'

Imam Muslim also quoted Yahya bin Sa'eed Qattān as having said:

لَمْ تَر أَهْلَ الْخَيْرِ فِي شَيْءٍ أَكْذَبَ مِنْهُمْ فِي الْحَدِيثِ .

"You will never see pious men lying more than in the matter of Ahādeeth." He used to say:

يَجْرِي الْكَذِبُ عَلٰى لِسَانِهِمْ وَلَا يَتَعَمَّدُونَ الْكَذِبَ .

'Their mouth lies though they do not intend to do so.'[1]

Among the possible causes of this anomaly are: lack of skill in scrutinizing narrations, inclination towards odd things in a bid to 'soften' hearts according to their own fancies, naivety, and love for abstinence and worship rather than for academic research.

Laxity in Writing the Messenger's Biography

There can be no rules better than those laid down by *Muhadditheen* to evaluate Ahādeeth. They meet the demands of sound wisdom and objectivity. Hadith scholars divided Trustworthy *(Thiqah)* narrators into two grades. They then divided Truthful *(Sadooq)* narrators into two: *Sadooq La Ba'sa Bihi* (truthful narrators whose reliability is

1 Sahih Muslim: preface P.38 and 40.

slightly tainted because of occasional mistakes) and *Sadooq Yahimu* (truthful narrators with occasional delusions).

Below them are those who narrated only a few Ahādeeth (and hence many scholars did not care to make inquiries about them) and who have no defect in them requiring the rejection of their Ahādeeth.

If he has a corroborator *(Mutābi')*, he is called *Maqbool* (Acceptable). In case he has no corroborator, he is called *Layyin-ul-Hadith* (Feeble). This is the lowest degree of reliability.

Next to them are *Mastoor* (Concealed), *Da'eef* (Weak), *Majhool* (Unknown), *Matrook-ul-Hadith* (Abandoned), *Kadh'dhāb* (Liar) and *Wad'dā'* (Fabricator). They are the people whose statements may not be attributed in any way to the Prophet. When Hadith scholars accept a Hadith, they also mention the levels of its narrators as well as the grades of their narrations as a matter of precaution.[1]

Some cautious biographers of modern times have suggested that, while writing a biography, it was necessary to be very cautious about Ahādeeth from which points of law may be inferred; on the other hand, laxity could be permitted with regards to Ahādeeth which related to building, town planning, excavation of canals, acts of valour on battlefields, and so on.[2]

However, this argument is incorrect. The history of the Prophet's lifetime is no ordinary history; it is the biography of the greatest man on earth, the ultimate example of human perfection. No laxity can be allowed to tarnish the records of this amazing person. No word, action, or even inference can be attributed to the Prophet Muhammad (ﷺ) unless its authenticity has been verified without a shadow of a doubt to mar it.

Caution and balance in Recording Biographical Facts

It should be noted that the Muhadditheen kept a perfect balance in recording Ahādith. They strictly followed the rules and saw to it that

1 For levels of narrators, see Taqreeb-ut-Tahdheeb, Author's Preface, P. 24-25.

2 As-Seerat-un-Nabawiyyah lil-'Umri: 1/40.

no incorrect piece of information was attributed to the Prophet (ﷺ); on the other hand, they also ensured that no part of any reliable narrations were lost.

To expound this point further, a quote from an excerpt from Hafiz Ibn Hajar's manuscript *Al-'Ujāb fi Bayān-il-Asbāb* (as reported by Dr. Akram Diyā' Umri from a copy of the manuscript found in the library of the Islamic University of Madinah). Ibn Hajar says:

فِي طُرُقِ هٰذِهِ الْقِصَّةِ الْقَوِيُّ وَالضَّعِيفُ، وَلَا سَبِيلَ إِلٰى رَدِّ الْجَمِيعِ فَإِنَّهُ يُنَادٰى عَلٰى مَنْ أَطْلَقَهُ بِقِلَّةِ الْاِطِّلَاعِ وَالْإِقْدَامِ عَلٰى رَدِّ مَا لَا يَعْلَمُهُ، لٰكِنِ الْأَوْلٰى أَنْ يُنْظَرَ إِلٰى مَا اخْتَلَفَتْ فِيهِ بِالزِّيَادَةِ وَالنَّقْصِ، فَيُؤْخَذَ بِمَا اجْتَمَعَتْ عَلَيْهِ، وَيُؤْخَذَ مِنَ الْمُخْتَلَفِ مَا قَوِيَ، وَيُطْرَحَ مَا ضَعُفَ وَمَا اضْطَرَبَ، فَإِنَّ الْاِضْطِرَابَ إِذَا بَعُدَ بِهِ الْجَمْعُ بَيْنَ الْمُخْتَلَفِ، وَلَمْ يَتَرَجَّحْ شَيْءٌ مِّنْهُ، الْتَحَقَ بِالضَّعِيفِ الْمَرْدُودِ.

"Concerning this event, there are strong as well as weak channels. There is no way to reject them all for, if anyone who does so, he will be squarely blamed for lack of knowledge and for rejecting a thing of which he has no knowledge. It would be better if we look at different narrations containing more or less information and accept those parts on which there is consensus. As for the parts on which there is disagreement, we should take from it that which is strong (with respect to the chain of transmission) and reject that which is weak *(Da'eef)* and confused *(Mudtarib)* because when it becomes difficult to reconcile the conflicting narrations and give preference to any because of the confusion, then that, too, is counted among the weak and the rejected."[1]

Weak Ahādith Fill Missing Links

With respect to "filling in the gaps (اكمال الفراغ)", the author of *As-Seerat-un-Nabawiyyah-as-Sahihah* writes:

1 As-Seerat-un-Nabawiyyah Lil 'Umrī: 1/41,40.

أَمَّا الرِّوَايَاتُ الضَّعِيفَةُ الَّتِي لَا تَقْوَى أَوْ تَعْتَضِدُ فَيُمْكِنُ الْإِفَادَةُ مِنْهَا فِي إِكْمَالِ الْفَرَاغِ الَّذِي لَا تَسُدُّهُ الرِّوَايَاتُ الصَّحِيحَةُ وَالْحَسَنَةُ عَلَى أَلَّا تَتَعَلَّقَ بِجَانِبٍ عَقْدِيٍّ أَوْ شَرْعِيٍّ ......

"If there is no way to strengthen a weak *(Da'eef)* narration (by means of other corroborating Ahādith), we may make use of them to fill in the gaps which Authentic *(Sahih)* and Good *(Hasan)* Ahādith cannot, provided they are not connected with dogmatic beliefs or the canonical law."[1]

The most important thing to note in this connection is the word 'gap (فراغ).' What does it mean? The word must be defined, and its limits determined lest many weak narrations, such as those in Waqidī, which provide details one way or the other, will find their way into biographies. Indeed, they are already present in the writings of many authors. The ambiguity surrounding this word will open the door to all types of narrations creeping into biographies of the Prophet Muhammad (ﷺ).

If the 'gaps' refer to the missing links in the chain of events, links which aid towards a better understanding of the biography, the sequence of events, or to overcome other difficulties such as reconciling between divergent Ahādeeth, then there is no harm in including them for clarification and with the necessary references.

Hadith scholars, commentators of the Qur'an and jurists sometimes do need to find missing links in connection with the historical background of Qur'ānic Verses, in addition to the Seerah. Hadith scholars have already worked hard on some available narrations which do not come up to the level required by *Muhadditheen* but which help to fill in the gaps in the chain of events. Hadith scholars have already labored hard on such narrations, collected them, found other corroborating Ahādeeth, and verified their texts or parts of their texts by rational or traditional means. Through their relentless efforts, most of the missing links have been found.

To keep the Prophet's biography safe from incorrect narrations and to find the essential missing links, it is acceptable to use Ahādeeth of lower than the standard level which Hadith scholars have found to be

1 As-Seraat-un-Nabawiyyah Lil-'Umrī: 1/40.

worthy of consideration, providing that the grades of each respective narration is clearly mentioned.

Hafiz Ibn Hajar worked extensively in this field; for example, he takes note of such Disconnected *(Mursal)* Ahādeeth as do not come in conflict with authentic Ahādeeth and to which all biographers agree. It is imperative that, when quoting them, the levels of their narrators and the grades of those Ahādeeth according to the Science of Validation *(Al-Jarh wat-Ta'deel)* are mentioned.

Biography: Sources and Levels of Accuracy

Now that a review has been conducted on the works of biographers over different periods of Muslim history and all the issues relating to verifying and authenticating Ahādeeth, it is clear how modern writers ever work in this field and what methodology and basic rules they have to follow.

The most authentic and eternal source of the Prophet's biography is the Qur'ān. The Prophet's whole life was Qur'an in action, and through it, mankind can gather brief outlines of the important events of his life.

The second source of information about the Messenger's life is the Ahādeeth. From the very first day, the Companions evolved an elaborate, strong and impeccable system of preserving Ahādeeth, both by memorizing and writing them. Penning down Ahādeeth began during the era of the Prophet ﷺ himself. It was done with the permission or at the instruction of the Prophet ﷺ himself by the Companions and later on continued by their successors *(Tābi'een)* and the successors of the successors *(Atbā' ut-Tabi'een)*.

The process of rejecting irresponsible or spurious narrations was also initiated by the Companions themselves. They laid down very strict rules to verify the soundness of statements attributed to the Prophet. After them, during the succeeding generations, those rules became still more stringent.

The earliest Muhadditheen were the *Tābi'een* and *Atbā' ut-Tabi'een*. Their students went further afield in search of Ahādeeth, took Ahādeeth from every scholar they came across, and benefited from different books, sheets, and compilations of Ahādeeth collected and arranged by their teachers. In turn, they presented what they learnt in different forms of compilations: *Al-Musannaf, Al-Musnad, Sahih,* and *Sunan*. These are the books now in the hands of the *Ummah,* a priceless heritage.

The Ahādeeth relating to the Prophet's biography were arranged in different genres: *Maghāzī* (military campaigns), *Siyar* (biography), *Shamā'il* (physical characterstics), *Khasā'il* (moral qualities), *Dalā'il-un-Nabuwwah* (miracles). The early books on this subject are considered to be basic and valuable sources for anyone attempting to write a biography of the Prophet Muhammad (ﷺ).

Another unique branch of history founded by the Muslims was the history of individuals *(Tareekh-ur-Rijāl)*. Muslim historians also described cities, locations and the influential people who lived or frequented those areas.

Old and modern geographers, as well as the cartographers of modern times, also provided valuable works which are indispensable to biographers, enabling them to identify the exact locations of important events.

Similarly, the literary works of both prose and poetry dating back to pre-Islamic as well as post-Islamic times aid biographers in establishing the backgrounds and atmospheres for numerous historical incidents.

Finally, Divinely inspired revelations such as the Torah, the Bible, and religious books of other nations, in whatever forms they exist today, contain significant prophecies of the coming of a final Prophet to guide mankind. Although the exact details and complete texts cannot be relied upon completely, they do include descriptions of the coming Prophet's physical characteristics, his achievements and his moral qualities. In this way, the books of past nations remain a source of information for any writer undertaking a biography of the Messenger of Allah, Muhammad (ﷺ).

Review of Hostile Literature

Over the last few centuries, many books have been written against the Prophet (ﷺ) and his mission. This inimical, hostile literature should be subjected to close scientific analysis and inquiry. In fact, the contents of these hostile books have opened new ways for writers and brought to the limelight every enlightening aspect of the Prophet's life.

The Prophet's entire life is a model for the Muslims. Muslim jurists, Hadith scholars, and many others derived lessons and points of law from the Prophet's life. Every future biographer has to take note of their writings and make use of them. While producing this Seerat Encyclopedia we will consider all these sources.

In the undertaking of examining the life of the Prophet Muhammad (ﷺ) within this work, all Ahādeeth labeled as authentic are done so according to the standards set by the venerable Muhadditheen. To fill in gaps and complete missing links, only those Ahādith, of a lesser grade, which have been considered worthy of attention by Hadith scholars, will be used. Their level of accuracy and degree of soundness will be clearly referenced.

We pray to Allah, the Blessed, the Lofty, to help us produce this encyclopedia in a format which inspires its readers, fills their hearts with faith in Him and His messenger, warms their souls, edifies them morally, gives them strength of will, goads them on to action, and brings them closer to Him and His messenger.

The Prophet's life is a model for us to follow. By following his way, a believer can reach the highest grade of spiritual bliss. For a spiritual pilgrim, there are many ways to reach Allah; but the only right way is the way of the Messenger of Allah ﷺ, the way which we can know only from a study of his life. Our destination is the one to which his way leads. A destination which his way does not lead us to is not the right one. It is not wanted. Any rest camp on such a way is full of dangers. The 'Shining Path' *(Al-Mahajjat-ul-Baidā')* is the one which has the footprints of the Prophet. Hadith scholars have all along been trying to lead us on to this 'Shining Path'.

﴿وَأَنَّ هَٰذَا صِرَٰطِي مُسْتَقِيمًا فَٱتَّبِعُوهُ ۖ وَلَا تَتَّبِعُوا۟ ٱلسُّبُلَ فَتَفَرَّقَ بِكُمْ عَن سَبِيلِهِۦ ۚ ذَٰلِكُمْ
وَصَّىٰكُم بِهِۦ لَعَلَّكُمْ تَتَّقُونَ ﴿١٥٣﴾﴾

"And verily, this (i.e. Allah's Commandments mentioned in the

above two Verses) is my straight path, so follow it. And follow not (other) ways, for they will separate you away from His path. This He has ordained for you that you may become pious."[1]

The Prophet ﷺ said:

قَدْ تَرَكْتُكُمْ عَلَى الْبَيْضَاءِ، لَيْلُهَا كَنَهَارِهَا، لَا يَزِيغُ عَنْهَا بَعْدِي إِلَّا هَالِكٌ

"I am leaving you on a shining (path). Its night is (as brilliant) as its day. After me no one will leave it except the one who is (going) to perish."[2]

اَللّٰهُمَّ! وَفِّقْنَا لِمَا تُحِبُّ وَتَرْضٰى وَ اجْعَلْ آخِرَتَنَا خَيْرًا مِّنَ الْأُولٰى. اَللّٰهُمَّ! إِنَّا نَسْأَلُكَ حُبَّكَ وَ حُبَّ مَنْ يُّحِبُّكَ وَ حُبَّ عَمَلٍ صَالِحٍ يُّقَرِّبُنَا إِلَيْكَ.

O Allah, help us to do what pleases You, make our afterlife better than our worldly life. O Allah, we seek Your love and the love of those who love You, and the love of deeds of virtue which bring us closer to You. Amen.

اَللّٰهُمَّ! صَلِّ عَلٰى مُحَمَّدٍ وَّ عَلٰى اٰلِ مُحَمَّدٍ كَمَا صَلَّيْتَ عَلٰى إِبْرَاهِيمَ وَعَلٰى اٰلِ إِبْرَاهِيمَ إِنَّكَ حَمِيدٌ مَّجِيدٌ. اَللّٰهُمَّ! بَارِكْ عَلٰى مُحَمَّدٍ وَّعَلٰى اٰلِ مُحَمَّدٍ كَمَا بَارَكْتَ عَلٰى إِبْرَاهِيمَ وَعَلٰى اٰلِ إِبْرَاهِيمَ إِنَّكَ حَمِيدٌ مَّجِيدٌ.

Prof. Muhammad Yahya
Senior Research Scholar,
Darussalam, Lahore.
July, 2013

1 Al-An'ām 6: 153.
2 Sunan Ibn Mājah: 43.

وَمُبَشِّرًا بِرَسُولٍ

يَأْتِي مِنْ بَعْدِي اسْمُهُ

أَحْمَدُ

"And giving glad tidings
of a messenger to come after me,
whose name shall be Ahmad (the praised one).
(As-Saff 61:6)

Chapter - 1

Geographical & Historical Background of the

Arabian Peninsula

The location of Arabia and physical, geographic and historical facts of its different regions in pre- and post-Islamic times.

In This Chapter

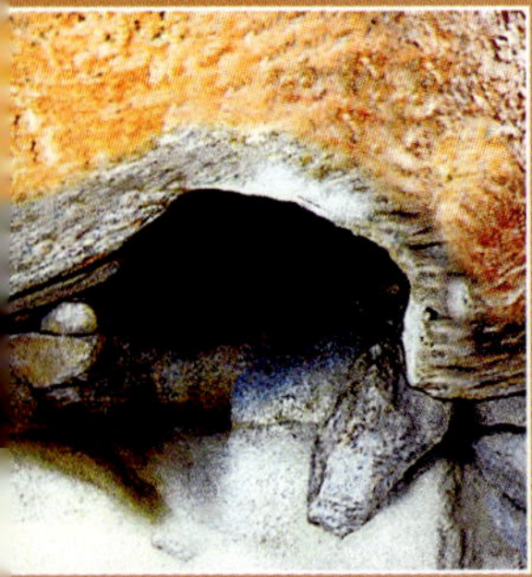

Describes the physical geography of Arabian Peninsula: its climate, mountains, deserts, rivers, rocky areas, vegetation and animals, minerals, and the lifestyle of the Arabs.

In addition, while describing the physical division of Arabian Peninsula, it gives a complete description of Tihama, Bahrain, Oman, Nejd, Hejaz, and Yemen, the social and political conditions prevailing there and the pre-Islamic events influencing them.

Under the main headings of Makkah, Madinah, and Ta'if and Badr, the chapter provides valuable information about Makkah (i.e. Bakkah) and Madinah (Yathrib), as they occur in Qur'an, and the merits of Makkah and its Sacred Precincts, Arafat, Mina, Muzdalifa, Jabal Hira, and Jabal Thawr.

1

Physical Geography of the Arabian Peninsula

Island and Peninsula

An island is a piece of land from where water has sunk down or ebbed. The Arabs say: جزر الماء عن الارض Jazar-al-Mā'o 'An-il-'Ard (water receded from the land)[1].

Technically, the word 'island' (جزيرة) is used to mean a piece of dry land surrounded on all its sides by water; for example, the islands of Cyprus, Sicily, Cuba or Java. A piece of dry land surrounded by water on its three

1 Al-Mu'jam-ul-Waseet: see under' Jazara'.

sides, with its fourth side connected with a large piece of land, is called a 'peninsula.' Arabia is considered to be a peninsula because it is surrounded on its three sides (in the east, west and south) by water; only in the north it is linked with dry land. In Arabic, it is called the (جزيرة العرب) 'Island of Arabia'; however, it is more correctly known as the شبه جزيرة العرب (Arabian Peninsula).

Ahadeeth refer to it as Jazeerat-ul-Arab (جزيرة العرب) or Haazi-hil-Jazeera (هٰذه الجزيرة) ("this island"). A Hadeeth narrated by Ibn Abbas says:

اَخْرِجُوا الْـمُشْرِكِينَ مِنْ جَزِيرَةِ الْعَرَبِ

"Expel pagans from the Arabian Peninsula."[1]

Another Hadeeth says:

«إِنَّ الشَّيْطَنَ قَدْ أَيِسَ أَنْ يَعْبُدَهُ الْمُصَلُّونَ فِي جَزِيرَةِ الْعَرَبِ وَلٰكِنْ فِي التَّحْرِيشِ بَيْنَهُمْ»

"Surely the Devil has given up all hope that those who pray will ever worship him in the Arabian Peninsula, but he will keep inciting them against one another."[2]

Imam As-Soyooti also quoted a weak *(Da'eef)* Hadeeth:

«لَقَدْ طَهَّرَ اللّٰهُ أَهْلَ هٰذِهِ الْجَزِيرَةِ مِنَ الشِّرْكِ إِنْ لَّمْ تُضِلَّهُمُ النُّجُومُ»

"Allah has cleared 'this island' (i.e. Arabian Peninsula) of polytheism (Shirk) if belief in stars does not mislead them".[3]

Maqdasi and Yaqut Hamawi refer to it as جزيرة العرب (the Arabian Peninsula).

Hisham Kalbi, using his own chain of narration, quoted Ibn Abbas as having said: "The Arabs divided the island (i.e. the Arabian Peninsula) into five parts: Tihama (تهامه), Hijaz (حجاز), Nejd (نجد), 'Urood (عروض) and Yemen."

Kalbi goes on to say: "Arabia is called an island because it is surrounded all around with rivers and seas." He continued to say that its limits reach up to the Euphrates, the rural areas of Iraq, Basra, Ubullah, Abadan (Iran),

1 Sahih-ul-Bukhāri: 3053.
2 Sahih Muslim: 2812.
3 As-Silsilat al-Hadith ad-Dha'ifa: 4316.

Kazimah (Kuwait), Qateef (Saudi Arabia), Hajar (هجر) (Bahrain), Qatar, Oman (عُمان), Shahr (شحر) (Hadhramaut), Abyan, Aden, Jaza'ir Dahlak, Jaza'ir Farasan (Saudi Arabia), Jedda, the coast of Makkah, the coast of Madinah, the coast of Tur (Sinai), Khaleej Ailah (Elat) (Gulf of Aqaba), Qulzum Misr (Gulf of Suez), the Nile River, Sea of Egypt and Syria (the Mediterranean), Palestine, Ashkelon (seaport in SW Palestine), Sur (Tyre, Lebanon), Beirut, the coast of Homs (حمص), and the coast of Qinnasreen (Syria).[1]

Etymology of the Word 'Arab'

Why was this part of the world called Arabia? There are different theories. Linguists, genealogists, and geographers have all tried to explain it, each in their own ways.

1. According to genealogists, the first man to settle this part of the world was Ya'rub bin Qahtān. He was the progenitor of the people of Yemen. Hence, the land and its inhabitants were named after him. However, this opinion does not appear to be correct. Were it so, obviously his own homeland, Yemen, the southern part of the peninsula, would have been named after him first, rather than the northern part of the peninsula; although, according to historians, it was the latter which was named Arab first.

2. Linguists say that the word *'Arab'* was derived from the Arabic word 'Irab (عِرب) meaning 'eloquence.' Since the inhabitants of this part of the world were proud of their eloquence, they considered other people to be quite stupid and ignorant, unable to express themselves eloquently like them. Thus, they called themselves *'Arab'* and the rest of the world *'Ajam* (عجم), an Arabic word meaning 'dumb.'

3. Geographers give yet another explanation. According to them, the word is derived from *'Arabah* (عَرَبَه) meaning: 'dry, barren land without water and vegetation.' In Hebrew, too, *'Arabah* conveys the same meaning.[2] Arab poets have also used this word in the same sense.

1 Mu'jam-ul-Buldan: see under 'Jazeerat-ul-Arab'.

2 Mu'jam-ul-Buldan: see under 'Arabah'; and Al-Mufassal Fi Tareekh-il-Arab Qabl-al-Islam: 1/14-19.

The Prophet's uncle, Abu Tālib bin 'Abdul-Muttalib, while saying a few verses in praise of his dear nephew, Muhammad (ﷺ), used the same word to refer to Makkah:

وَعَرَبَةُ دَارٌ لَّا يُحِلُّ حَرَامَهَا   مِنَ النَّاسِ إِلَّا اللَّوْذَعِيُّ الْحُلَاحِلُ

"*Arabah* is a house (i.e. place) whose sanctity may be eased off only by a chieftain of quick wit and good speech."

This leads us to guess that the word *'Arabah'* was initially used to refer to Makkah, the most important place in the barren desert of the Arabian Peninsula, and later to the entire peninsula.

However, some people maintain that Ishmael's (Ismail's) offspring who had settled at a place called *'Arabah'* in Tihama (تهامه), came later on to be known as Arabs, a word derived from the name of the place of their settlement.[1]

Location of Arabia

The Arabian Peninsula lies in the southwest of Asia. To its east lie the Arabian Gulf (Persian Gulf) and the Gulf of Oman, to its west the Red sea, to its south the Gulf of Aden and the Arabian Sea. The latter is, in fact, north-western extension of the Indian Ocean.

Beyond the Arabian/Persian Gulf lies Iran and, further beyond, Afghanistan and Turkestan (Central Asia). A large part of all these three regions was generally known in the past as Khorasān. To the west of modern Iran lie Turkey, Iraq and the Arabian Gulf, to the north-east of it Turkmenistan, to the north Azerbaijan, Armenia and the Caspian Sea, to the east of it Afghanistan and Pakistan, and to the south of it the Gulf of

1 Mu'jam-ul-Buldān: See under 'Arabah'.

Oman.

The total area of Iran is 1,648,000 sq km. Beyond Khorasan, the Turkic regions lying across the River Amu (جيحون Jaihūn or Oxus) were known as *Ma Warā'-un-Nahr* (ماوراء النهر), a name given to those regions by the Arab historians of old. The word *Nahr* (نهر) referred to the River Oxus. Today Turkestan (Central Asia) is divided into Uzbekistan, Tajikistan, Kyrgyzstan, Kazakhstan, and Turkmenistan. Across the Gulf of Oman lies Baluchistan, known in the olden times as Makran, and now divided between Pakistan and Iran.

Close to Makran, in the times of the Prophet ﷺ, were Sind and the Indian sub-Continent

An-Nafud Great Desert

The Natural Division of the Arabian Peninsula and the neighbouring countries

Map.1

(India and Pakistan), the western coast of the latter providing a convenient place to carry on maritime trade with the Arabs through the Arabian Sea and the Indian Ocean.

To the south of the Gulf of Aden lies the Horn of Africa (Somalia), so named because it looks like a horn sticking out into the Indian Ocean. To the west of Red Sea lie Egypt, Sudan, Eritrea, Djibouti, and Ethiopia. Though Christianity has been a dominant religion in Ethiopia but the north-eastern Africa as a whole is a Muslim majority area.

To the north of the Arabian Peninsula lie Iraq and Jordan, with the Syrian Desert stretching deep into the latter two. To the west of Jordan lie the Jordan River, the Dead Sea, and Palestine; while to the south of it lie Saudi Arabia and Gulf of Aqaba. To the east of it lie Iraq and to the north Syria. Several companions of the Prophet lie buried in Jordan. In the past Jordan was traditionally a part of *ash-Shām* (Syria).

The site of the Battle of Mu'ta, near Al-Karak, is also located in Jordan. Its area totals 90740 sq. km.

To the north of Syria and Iraq lies Turkey which, during the era of the Prophet ﷺ, was a part of the Byzantine or Roman Empire known to Arabs generally as ar-Rūm (الروم). Geographers wrangle among themselves over the northern limits of Arabia, where it ends and where the territory of Syria (الشام) begins. The general opinion is that the territory of Arabia in the north is bound by the River Euphrates. Viewed from this angle, since it is surrounded approximately on all its four sides with water, it may well be called an island. The Arabian peninsula, from northwest to southeast is 2200 km long and 1200 km wide. Its total area, allowing for the controversy over its northern boundary, measures 1,000,000 to 1,300,000 sq mi.[1]

1 'Asr-un-Nabuwa Li'l-Ka'bi PP 7,8; and Makkah Wal-Madinah Fil Jāhilia Wa 'Ahd-ir-Rasūl, P.13

Safe from External Invasion

Most of Arabia is a vast, barren desert where geography diluted alien military power since time immemorial. Nature made it safe from foreign invaders. For an external foe there was no hope of survival; the inhospitable sea of sands promised little economic gain. No reckless adventurer could keep hold of it for long.

It was for these reasons that the inhabitants deep in the desert could live, free and independent, since ancient times. On the eve of the dawn of Islam, there were two great powers around the Arabs, the Romans (the Byzantine Empire) and the Persians (Iran) but, except for a few peripheral areas to the north or around the coastline, neither could subjugate the Arabs or force them to pay taxes.

As for the territories on the margins of Arabia, the Ethiopians used to launch attacks on Yemen through the Straits of Bab-el-Mandab. During the Prophet's era, Yemen was under Iranian occupation while the Arab rulers of Oman, Bahrain and Hirah (حيره) owed allegiance to the Iranian kings and paid them taxes. Likewise, the Ghassanid Arabs of Busra ash-Sham paid tribute to the Romans. The Battle of Tabūk was, in fact, caused as a matter of the Romans trying to safeguard their occupied territories.

A Dead Volcano of Harrah Rāhat

Jabal al-Baida' and Jabal al-Aqar in Harrah Kheybar

Rocky Regions

The rocky regions of Arabia were formed by lava flowing from volcanoes. There were occasional eruptions even after the Prophet's era. For example, a volcano erupted in Hejaz in 654 AH (1256 CE) and for weeks on end it continued spewing lava which covered a wide area. Some of the famous rocky regions of Arabia are Harrah Waqim and Harrah Wabrah (to the east and west of Madinah), Harrah Kheybar, Harrah Rāhat (between Makkah and Madinah), Harrat-ul-Hijaz, Harrah Kishb, Harrah Bani Sulaim, and Harrah al-Kara'.[1]

Deserts of Arabia

A large part of Arabia is covered with deserts. Four of them are the largest: An-Nafud Al-Kabīr, Ad-Dahnā', Al-Jafūrah, and Ar-Rub' Al-Khali (the Empty Quarter), the last being the largest.

An-Nafud al-Kabīr: This desert begins in the north, from al-Jauf (the name of the northern Saudi region or province) and ends up at Hā'il in the south. Its historical city, Dūmat al-Jandal, is about 1200 km away

A Sand dune of An-Nafūd al-Kabīr

1 Makkah Wal-Madinah Fil Jāhiliya wa 'Ahd-ir-Rasūl PP. 15, 16; and Atlas At-Tarīkh-ul-Arabi Al-Islami, P. 33.

from Riyadh and about 250 km away from Jordanian border. The capital of al-Jauf region is Sakākah. an-Nafud al-Kabīr (area: 64630 sq km) is 342 km wide, at the maximum, from east to west and about 572 km wide from north to south. Towards its eastern end, its width keeps diminishing both in the north and the south till it remains no wider than 128 km. This gives the desert a triangular shape. The winds are strong and keep moving the sand dunes, some of them reaching up to a height of 450 ft. The historic city of Dūmat Al-Jandal is sited in the northwest of an-Nafud al-Kabīr.

Ad-Dahnā'

Ad-Dahnā': Like a thin arc, it sits between an-Nafud al-Kabīr and ar-Rub' al-Khāli (the Empty Quarter). Its area is approximately 40789 sq. km. It is flanked by Jabal Tuwaiq on its western side and by as-Sammān (الصمان) plateau on its eastern side. It is 1200 km long and 20 to 60 km wide. There is yet another sandy arc like it on the western side of Jabal Tuwaiq. It is called Nafud Ad-Dahi.[1] It may well be counted as a desert of Nejd. Here sits the town of Laila (ليلى) on the highway leading from Riyadh to Najrān and Abha.

Al-Jafūrah: This desert, also below an-Nafud, runs along the coast in the form of a narrow strip, east of the As-Sammān plateau. This desert strip starts from Jubail and goes up to the Empty Quarter.[2]

Ar-Rub' al-Khali: One of the great deserts of the world, it stretches over an area of 600,000 sq. km. It is 1200 km long from east to west and 640 km wide at the most. When its sands are dug up, there gush forth streams of cool water. It has been named ar-Rub' al-Khali (The Empty Quarter) because it covers one-fourth of the area of the peninsula and is totally empty of all life, human or animal. The southern part of this desert is also called Al-Ahqāf.

1 Atlas Al-Mamlaka Al-Arabia As-Saudia, P. 37.

2 Masalik-wal-Mamalik Li'l- Al-Astakhari, P.P 27, 28; 'Asr-un-Nabuwa Lil-Ka'bi P.P 9, 10; Atlas Al-Mamlaka Al-Arabia As-Saudia Wal-'Alām P. 16

Famous Deserts of Arabia
Complete Desert
Portial Desert
International Border
International Border
Syrian Desert
Turayf
'Ar'ar
Al Jawf
Sakākah
DUMAT AL JANDAL
Iraq
KUWAIT
Ar-Ruq'i
Al-Khafji
IRAN
Great Nafūd Desert
Nafud-as-Suwairat
Ha'il
Jubayl
Arabian Gulf
Buraydah
Dammam
Bahrain
Nafud-al-'Urayq
Nafud-as-Sirr
Qatar
Al Riyadh
Madina
Munawwarah
Al Kharj
Ad-Dahna
As-Sammān
Salwah
Batha'
Nejad
Al-Jafūrah
U.A.E.
Nafud-as-Surrah
Nafud-ad-Dahy
Jabal Tuwayq
'Irq Subay'
Shubaitah
Makkah
Mukarramah
Laila
Ta'if
SAUDI ARABIA
Rub' al Khali
(The Empty Quarter)
الليث
Bāhah
Qunfidhah
Kharkhair
OMAN
Abhā
Najrān
Sharaurah
Red Sea
Jāzān
(Jizan)
Wuday'ah
At-Tuwal
Hadharmawt
YEMEN
Eritrea
Aden
Arabian Sea
Ethiopia

Map.2

Famous Mountains of Arabia

Jibal As-Sarāt: Known also as Jibal As-Sarwāt, it is the longest mountainous range of Arabia. It runs along the coast of the Red Sea and extends up to the east of the lower regions of Tihāma. Its average height is approximately 2,000 m.

Some of the famous mountains of this range are:

Jabal Uhud: It lies to the north of Madinah, five and a half kilometers away from the Prophet's Mosque. Today the city of Madinah has expanded and people have settled around the mountain. It is counted as lying within the Haram (حرم), sacred precincts of Madinah, because the limits of the Haram reach up to Mt. Thawr in the north. From east to west, it is nearly 6 km long. To the south of it lie the graves of the martyrs of the Battle of Uhud.

Jabal Thawr: To the south of Makkah, about three miles away from the Sacred Mosque (المسجد الحرام), is the summit of Jabal As-Sarāt called Thawr where the Prophet ﷺ and his companion Abu Bakr رضي الله عنه spent three nights in its cave. Mt. Thawr is 759 m. high. The surface of the summit is about 30 sq. m. Cave Thaur has two openings, the smaller one being half a meter wide and the larger one on the other side about one meter wide. The cave is approximately 4 m long and 2.5 m wide.[1]

Jabal an-Nūr (Jabal Hira'): This mountain is located about 4 km east of Makkah. It rises to an altitude of 639 m above sea level. The famous cave of Hira', where the Prophet received the first revelation, is located inside Jabal an-Nūr. The cave of Hira' is by the side of the mountain where about 0.5 m thick, 1.75 m wide and 3 to 4 m long rocky planks are propped against the mountain side in a way that makes the mouth of the cave look like an isosceles triangle whose both sides are 2.5 m long each and the base about 1 m long. The cave is about two or two-and-a quarter m long. The front mouth of the cave is wider, and the rear mouth is only a narrow opening.[2]

Jabal Radwa: Beside Mt. Radwa (رضوىٰ), a part of Jibal As-Sarāt, west of Madinah, the Battle of Buwāt took place in Rabīʿ al-Awwal, 2 AH. The name of this 1814 m high mountain occurs in Arabic poetry. Abu

1 Fi Manzil-il-Wah'yi by Muhammad Husain Heykal.
2 Atlas Sīrat-i-Nabawi, P.115.

Tay'yib Ahmad bin Husain Ju'fi Mutanabbi, in his elegy on the death of Muhammad bin Ishāq Tanūkhi, says:

مَا كُنْتُ آمُلُ قَبْلَ نَعْشِكَ أَنْ أَرٰى   رَضْوٰى عَلٰى أَيْدِي الرِّجَالِ تَسِيرُ

(Before I saw your dead body, I had never hoped to see Mt. Radwa moving on the hands of people).[1]

To the southwest of Makkah, a few peaks of Jibal As-Sarat rise up to a height of over 2500 m. Later, this mountainous range rises to its highest altitude in southern 'Asīr and Yemen. To the west of San'a one peak reaches up to a height of 3760 m. Jibal As-Sarat is called Jibal Madyan in the north, Jibal 'Aseer in the south, and Jibal Hijaz in the middle.[2]

Al-Jabal al-Akhdar

Al-Jabal al-Akhdar: This Mountain in the eastern part of Oman runs all along the coast of the Gulf of Oman. Its highest peak is 3018 m high.[3]

Jabal Tuqaiq

Jabal Tubaiq: Sits on the border of Saudi Arabia and Jordan.

Jibal Aja wa Salma:

Mountains Aja and Salma are located south of the Nafud desert, inside the region of Hā'il. They join up in the southwest and are collectively called Jibal Shamar. According to Zamakhshari, Aja and Salma are two mountains which lie on the left side of Samīra' while Abu Obaid Sakūni called these mountains, west of Faid, Mountains of Tayy

1 Diwān-ul-Mutannabi, P. 71.
2 Atlas As-Sīrat-un-Nabawiya P.17.
3 Atlas Al-Mamlaka Al-Arabia As-Saudia Wal-'Alām P.10.

Jabal Tuwaiq

(Jibal Tayy). These mountains are named after Aja and his beloved Salma. Both were killed in this area by Salma's brothers.[1]

Jabal Qatan: It is located near 'Uqlat-us-Suqūr, in the north of Madinah-al-Qasīm highway. There is also a town of the same name on the southern side of the mountain. Once there was a spring of Banu Asad. Here in Muharram, 4 AH, the expedition of Abu Salma Makhzūmi took place. The expedition (سريّه) was sent as the news of Tulaihah bin Khuwailid Asadi preparing to fight the Muslims reached Madinah but his men fled as the Muslim fighters arrived.[2]

Jabal Tuwaiq: It may be rightly called the backbone of Nejd. It is 1,000 km long from Khashm Jazrah, east of Riyadh, to Khashm Khatmah near the border of the Empty Quarter. Its rocky plateau is low compared to that of as-Sammān, east of Ad-Dahnā'.

Jabal Buhrān: It is a mountain located on the confluence of the Wadi (valley) of Hajar (formerly called As-Sa'ira) and Rābigh or "Murr." It lies at a distance of 90 km east of Rābigh. Here the Holy Battle of Buhrān took place in Jamād Al-Ūla, 3 AH. The wadi of Rābigh was formerly known as Marr Unaib.[3]

1 Mu'jam-ul-Buldān: See under 'Aja'.
2 Atlas Sīrat-i-Nabawi, P.253; and Atlas Mamlakat-il-Arabia As-Saudia, P. 189.
3 Mu'jam-ul-Ma'ālim Al-Jughrafiyyah Fis-Sīrat-in-Nabawiya, P. 40.

Wadi al-Abyadh

Lifestyle of the Desert Arabs

Since most of the land is barren desert, the Arabs living inland have, since time immemorial, looked to cattle-raising as their chief occupation and a means of survival. Ever in search of water and grass, the Bedouin kept moving along with their camels, goats and sheep. They never built permanent homes, but rather used tents built of camel or goat hair, which were easy to carry wherever they went. In reference to their nomadic homes, they were called Ahl Al-Wabar (people of tents made of hair or furs of camels and goats).

Important Valleys and Places

The internal regions of the Peninsula are extremely hot. The mountains are mostly dry and barren, without permanent bodies of water flowing throughout every season of the year. However, there are many temporary rivulets or streams (called Wadi) fed with rainwater. The most well-known of them are:

Sarhān Wadi: In the north of Arabia, on the border with Jordan, there is a Wadi called Sarhān Wadi. It is, in fact, a lowland area, 300 km long and 50 to 70 km wide, fed with several small rainwater streams.

Water of Wadi al-Bātin

Tributaries of Euphrates: In the northeast of the Peninsula, there are a number of Wadis whose waters fall into the Euphrates. The most important of them are Wadi 'Al-Abyad, Wadi 'Ar'ar and Wadi Al-Khaur.

Wadi al-Bātin: It is in the north of Dahnā' desert. It flows along the frontier of Kuwait and falls into the Arabian Gulf.

Wadi ad-Dawāsir

Wadi ad-Dawāsir: Three large streams, Ranyah, Bīshah and Tathlīth, flow down the eastern slopes of Jibal As-Sarat. Later, they join up to make a Wadi called Ad-Dawāsir. It is variously known as 'Aqīq Al-Yamāmah and 'Aqīq Tamrah. There is also a small settlement called Tamrah. Wadi ad-Dawasir occasionally floods. The water of the Wadi reaches up to the Empty Quarter and then dries up.

A view of Dhat Atlah

Dhat Atlah: It is located in 'Ard Shām (modern Jordan). Today it is called Tala' or Dahal. It is 25 km south of Ghor as-Sāfi. It is the place where the Prophet ﷺ sent a military expedition *(Sariyyah)* under the command of Ka'b bin 'Umair Ghifāri in 8 AH. Ka'b was wounded but escaped while all his companions, fourteen in number, were martyred. This expedition led to a second one, *Ghazwah Mu'tah,* launched the following month.[1]

Nahr ad-Disa (Tabuk)

Remains of Dūmat al-Jandal Fort

Tabūk: During the era of the Prophet ﷺ, it was a region of the tribe of Banu Qudā'ah who were under the domination of the Romans. It is 778 km north of Madinah and connected with the latter via Taimā' and Kheybar. It is the northernmost city of Saudi Arabia and the site of a large military base. To the north of it lies the Jordanian town of Ma'an, 238 km away. A beautiful mosque now stands on the place where the Prophet ﷺ had pitched his camp during the Battle of Tabūk. It was also the site of an important station of Hijāz railways built in 1312 AH/1894 CE.[2]

Dūmat Al-Jandal: It was home to the tribe of Kalb bin Wabrah, a branch of Banu Qudā'ah. Here was also the altar of the pagan idol named *Wadd.*

1 Mu'jam-ul-Ma'ālim Al-Gughrafiyyah fis Sīrat-in-Nabawia PP. 30,31. naderatieh. maktoobblog.com.

2 Op.cit. PP 59, 60.

It is a town of Al-Jauf, a province of Saudi Arabia, and now called Dūmat al-Jandal. Here are also found the ruins of Marid Fort of Ukaidar al-Kindi. It lies about 60 km off Sakākah, the capital town of al-Jauf, and about 450 km off Taimā'. The place is named after Dūm or Dūman, the son of Ishmael (Ismā'īl).[1]

Bark Al-Ghimād (Al-Bark): It is a seaport town about 600 km south of Makkah and currently known as al-Bark. Here is also a Wadi of the same name. It lies 14 km north of the town of Dhahban *(Asīr)*.[2] Abu Bakr ﵁ arrived here when he set out for migration to Abyssinia (Ethiopia) but later went back to Makkah at the persuasion of Ibn Daghna.

Vegetation of Arabia

Most of the Arabian Peninsula is rocky and sandy, although the coastal areas are blessed with green valleys. The southwestern region of Yemen has long been known for its greenery; even before the time of the Prophet Muhammad (ﷺ). Situated on the coasts of both the Red Sea and the Arabian Sea, Yemen is known for its lush vegetation.

Yemen and 'Asīr are known for their fine coffee. Mukha, a port of Yemen, has been known for trade in coffee and Lauban (a fragrant aromatic resin, also called gum benzoin). There was a brisk trade in Lauban and other aromatics as far back as two thousand years ago. Exports of these items followed the famous route known as the Incense Road, from southern Arabia to the Mediterranean countries.

A Greek historian writes: "The Greeks fumigated their houses and temples and the Romans the graves of their priests with incense. During the reigns of the

1 Op.cit. p 127.
2 Op.cit, P. 42; and Atlas Al-Mamlaka Al-Arabia As-Saudia.

Lauban

Ptolemies of Egypt and the Romans, the Egyptians used to buy it from Arab traders who visited their land via the Red Sea. The Arabs would buy, in turn, gems and other precious stones to adorn their towns and places of worship."[1]

Lauban grows even now in Mahrah (eastern Yemen) but the people have turned now to the cultivation of indigo, which is relatively more useful. The tree that produces it is called Haweer (حوير) and its dye is called indigo. Tamarind, acacia, jujube (botanical name: ziziphus spina), and euphorbia (a kind of myrobalan) trees are also found. Wheat, barley, maize and millet are the important food crops. Alfalfa, a common feed of livestock, grows in the shade of date trees and is widely cultivated.

Grapes were also harvested in the Peninsula, but they were far outweighed by dates in importance and value. Dates and milk were the staple food of Arabs. Coconuts also grew in Zufār (ظفار) and other places. In the green areas of the Peninsula, other fruits including apples, pomegranates, raisin, peaches, figs, bananas and watermelons were also found. These fruits are still found in plenty there.[2]

1 Sanājat-ut-Tarab Fi Taqad'dumāt-il-Arab li-Ibn Naufal At-Tarabulasi.
2 Husn-ul-Muhadarah Li's-Sayūti. 254/2.

Tā'if is famous for its roses and pomegranates, Al-Kharj for its watermelons (called Jihh in Nejd, Habhab in Hijaz and Debshi in the north), and Buraimi (United Arab Emirates) for mangoes.

Animals

Many kinds of animals are found in the Peninsula. Among those found on land are camels, horses, cows, goats, sheep, deer, donkeys, mules and stags.

Camels: A camel was a very useful animal in Arabia. It was called 'the ship of the desert,' for in the days when there were no cars and paved roads, it was impossible to cross vast stretches of sands without a camel. A red camel was the most treasured possession of an Arab. Camels were considered the embodiment of real wealth. Blood money and indemnity for bodily injury were also determined in terms of camels.

Apart from milk, camels are also a source of other useful commodities such as flesh, hides and wool. Their dung was used as fuel. Occasionally, they were used to plough fields and draw water from wells. The general word for a camel in Arabic is *Ibil;* that for mount, *Dhulūl* or *Rikab;* the one which feeds on Arak leaves *Arika* (pl. *Awarik*); and the one of pure breed *Aseel* (pl. *Asa'il*). Those of Oman are called *'umaniyyat*. Among the she-camels used by the Prophet ﷺ were *as-Samra', al-'Arees, al-Hina'* and *ash-Shaqra'*. *As-Samra'* was the mount of Ayesha ﵂ and Al-'Arees that of Umm Salamah ﵂. *Al-Qaswa'* was the name of the she-camel the Prophet ﷺ mounted while migrating to Madinah, and *Al-Jad'ā'* the she-camel he mounted while delivering the Farewell Hajj Sermon. *Sahri,* which belonged to Abu Jahl, fell to the lot of the Prophet ﷺ as a part of the spoils of war.[1]

1 Urdu Encyclopedia of Islam: 13/66; for more detail about Prophet (ﷺ) animals see Subol Al-Huda war-Rashād: 11/418-422.

Horses: Horses were important for Arabs due to their various qualities. Certain types of horses were highly prized by the Arabs.

The Messenger of Allah (ﷺ) mentioned some of them:

«خَيْرُ الْخَيْلِ الْأَدْهَمُ، الْأَقْرَحُ، الْمُحَجَّلُ، الْأَرْثَمُ، طَلْقُ الْيَدِ الْيُمْنٰى، فَإِنْ لَّمْ يَكُنْ أَدْهَمَ، فَكُمَيْتٌ عَلٰى هٰذِهِ الشِّيَةِ»

"The best horse is the one which is black with a small white mark (blaze) on its forehead, whiteness in four legs, white nose and upper lip, the right foreleg not white. In case the horse is not black, then a blackish red one possessing these qualities (*Kumait* كميت) is also good."[1]

A Hadeeth says: "Blessedness is in horses which are red."[2]

The Prophet ﷺ disliked a *Shikal* horse, a colored horse with a white right foreleg and left hind leg or, conversely, white left foreleg and right hind leg.[3]

Sheep and Goats: The Bedouin used to raise cattle as well as sheep, the latter was often the center point of important dishes in Arab feasts. Butter was made from milk of ewes and she-goats. The Prophet ﷺ grazed cattle for Banu Sa'd in his childhood. He said:

«اِتَّخِذُوا الْغَنَمَ فَإِنَّهَا بَرَكَةٌ»

"Raise sheep and cattle. They are blessed."[4]

We find names of some of the she-goats belonging to the Prophet ﷺ in his biographies: *'Ajawah, Barakah, Qamrah, Ghaunah,* and *Zamzam*.

Different Animals: Apes, rabbits and porcupines are also found in the Arabian Peninsula. Among its varied fauna are scorpions, spiders and locusts, birds of prey like hawks and eagles, small birds like hoopoes, nightingales, parrots, house-martins, wood-pecker, Bayer weavers (a sweet-voiced weaverbird with a crown on head), and tall, red-legged cranes. The

1 Sunan Ibn Majah: 2789.
2 Sunan Abu Dawood: 2545.
3 Sahih Muslim: 1875.
4 Al-Jami' us-Sagheer: 2806.

pigeons of Makkah are known the world over.[1]

Of late, ostriches have become extinct in the Arabian Peninsula although the shells of their eggs are occasionally found in desert and the names of some places bear the word *Na'ām* (Arabic for ostrich). Sometimes whales swim up to the Persian Gulf from the Indian Ocean. We know from a Hadīth that the Companions lived on the meat of a huge fish for as many as eighteen days during the Battle of Sīf Al-Bahr. That huge fish was most probably a whale. When a rib of that fish was fixed in the earth, a whole camel together with its rider passed from under the arc of the rib.[2]

Minerals of Arabia

The Bible refers frequently to the gold, silver and gems of the Arabs. *"Uphar"* or *"Ophir"*, a place in central Arabia, was famous for its pure gold when the Children of Israel were at the pinnacle of their power. The Queen of Sheba's gifts to Solomon included gold, precious stones and fragrances. The Bible describes the event in great detail:

"Now when the Queen of Sheba heard the fame of Solomon, she came to Jerusalem to test him with hard questions, having a very great retinue and camels bearing spices and very much gold and precious stones...... then she gave the king a hundred and twenty talents of gold, and a very great quantity of spices and precious stones; there were no spices such as those which the Queen of Sheba gave to King Solomon. Moreover the servants of Hiram and the servants of Solomon who brought gold from Ophir, brought algum wood and precious stones.[3] Bahrain and Oman have been famous since the earliest days for their matchless pearls. Similarly, the Yemeni carnelian has been popular to this day.

1 'Asr-un-Nabuwa Lil-Ka'bi P. 19-18; Urdu Encyclopedia of Islam: 68-65/13.

2 Sahīh-Bukhari: 4359.

3 Bible: 2 Chronicles 9:1-10 and 1 Kings 10:1-11.

2

Physical and Political Division of Arabian Peninsula

Geographers have divided the Arabian Peninsula into five physical parts:

1. Tihamāh 2. Urūd 3. Nejd
4. Yemen 5. Hijaz

Shauqi Abu Khalīl, a famous Arab research scholar, in his Atlas As-Sīrat an-Nabawiyyah, considers Jibal as-Sarāt, not Hijaz, the fifth part of the Arabian Peninsula. He writes: It stretches from Gulf of 'Aqaba to Yemen. In the north it is called Jibal Madyan (Midian), in the south Jibal 'Asīr, and in the middle Hijaz where Makkah and Madinah are located.[1]

1 Atlas As-Sīrat an-Nabawiyyah, P. 17.

Remains of Kingdom of Tadmur (Syria)

Allāmah Istakhri has included three more regions in the Arabian Peninsula:

1. The desert of Iraq *(Badiyāt al-Iraq)*
2. The desert of the Peninsula *(Badiyāt al-Jazīrah),*
3. The desert of Syria *(Badiyāt ash-Shām).*[1]

Badiyāt al-Iraq is also called *Badiyāt as-Samavah*. Moreover, Istakhri takes *Badiyāt al-Jazīrah* to mean the desert region of Central *al-Jazīrah* which lies to the north of the Euphrates.

Badiyāt as-Shām, or the Desert of Syria, is a vast desert area covering the southeastern part of Syria, the northeastern part of Jordan and the western part of Iraq.[2] The city of Tudmur (Palmyra) of modern Syria was the capital town of a great Arab empire in the third century of the Christian era and was called *'Arūs as-Sahrā'* (the bride of the desert).

1 Masālik-ul-Mamālik Lil-Istakhri, P. 20, 21.
2 Atlas-ul- 'Alām, P. 12.

Aden (Yemen)

Hudaidah Seaport

Seaport of Jeddah

Seaport of Yanbu

1. Tihāmah

Tihāmah is a low-lying coastal belt running along the coast of the Red Sea and the southern coast of Arabia. Some geographers have included Makkah within Tihāmah. The famous ports of Tihāmah are Yanbu, Jeddah, Hudaidah, and Aden. In the sea, close to the coast, are found coral reefs which make it difficult to build many seaports along the coast.

Tihāmah is derived from *Taham* (تهم) which means extreme heat and dropping of wind. The region is also called *al-Ghaur* which means 'depression or low-lying area.' Here the heat is unbearable.

A beautiful view of Yanbu

Boundaries of Tihāmah

Scholars differ over the limits of Tihāmah.

Allama Asma'ī says: In the direction of Hijaz, Tihamah ends up at Madārij al-Araj, which is a big town of Bilād Hudhail in the valley of Tā'if. In the direction of Nejd, Tihāmah begins from Dhat 'Irq. According to 'Ammārah bin 'Aqīl Yarbu'i, the area from the sea up to Harrah Banu Sulaim and Harrah Laila is called Tihāmah and *al-Ghaur*. Mada'ini says: Whoso passes through *Wajrah* (a place on the highway from Makkah to Basrah), Ghamrah and Tā'if and then arrives at Makkah has already entered Tihāmah.[1]

The name 'Tihāmah' is found in the inscriptions of South Arabia. Its width is not uniform but varies from place to place. It is very narrow at places such as Qunfudha and Luhayyah, while in Yemen, its surface rises up to 2000 ft. above sea level. Its width varies from thirty miles (48 km) to fifty miles (80 km).

In May and September the temperature of Tihāmah is 35 to 43 degrees C. In summer, some rare rain showers lower the temperature. In winter, the temperature ranges from 25 to 35 degrees C, dipping sometimes even to 14 degree C. In southern Yemen, the oases of Maifa'ah and Lahij are extremely fertile.[2] Maifa'ah is a town in the Shabwah province of Yemen. It is 474 km east of San'a' on the coast of Arabian Sea.[3]

1 Mu 'jam-ul-Buldān: see under 'Tihāmah'.
2 Urdu Encyclopedia of Islam: 6/ 851-855.
3 Wikipedia (Encyclopedia).

Dhat 'Irq *(Nakhlah Shāmiyyah)*: This is the Mīqāt for the Hajj pilgrims coming from Iraq. It is located near Autas, on the border of Nejd and Tihāmah. It lies at a distance of 90 km from Makkah.[1]

Wadi Idam *(al-Hamd)*: It is a Wadi of Jibal Tihāmah *(Hijaz)*. Near Madinah, it is called Al-Qanāt. Higher up, near Sadd, it is called ash-Shazāt. Further down ash-Shaztāt up to the sea, it is called Idam.

In the valley of Idam there are settlements of the tribes of Ashja' and Juhainah.[2] Wadi Idam is currently called Wadi al-Hamd. It begins from the southeast of Harrah Kheybar, passes near Madinah, takes in Wadi Aqīq and other Wadis, and finally Wadi-ul-Qura *(al-Jazal)* joins up with it.

Wadi Idam

Here Wadi al-'Ees, flowing from the southwest, joins up with al-Hamd, on the bank of which lies the town of al'-Ees, 90 km east of the coastal town of Amlaj.

Wadi al-'Ees

In Ramadan 1 AH, the expeditionary force of Sīf-ul-Bahr, under the command of Hamza (the Prophet's companion), passed through al-'Ees.

From then onward al-Hamd flows westward till it reaches south of Al-Wajh and falls into the sea (Red Sea). In the same place are found the relics of the ancient Greek temple, Kasr Karīm, which served as a maritime base for the trading ships of Greece. Wadi al-Hamd is about 900km long.[3] In Ramadan of the year 8 AH, the Prophet ﷺ sent Abu Qatādah to Batn Idam which lies at a distance of 58 km from Madinah.[4]

1 Atlas Al-Hadith, p. 181.
2 Mu'jam-ul-Buldān see under 'Idam'.
3 Makkah Wal-Madinah Fil-Jāhiliah Wa 'Ahd-ir-Rasūl, P. 22.
4 Atlas As-Sīrat-an-Nabawiyyah, P. 392.

2. 'Urūd

'Urūd is the name given to that part of the Arabian Peninsula which extends from the eastern part of Nejd and the frontier of Iraq up to the Persian Gulf and the coast of Oman. It is so named because, running along the Gulf coast, it assumes a rectangular shape and sits right between Persia and Yemen plus other parts of Arabia.[1] It contains both high and low lands, mountains and Wadis. 'Urūd includes Bahrain and Oman.

Bahrain

Al-Bakri writes: Bahrain lies on the western coast of the Persian Gulf. To the west of it lies Yamāmah and to the north of it Basrah (Iraq) while its southern part is linked with Oman.[2]

In the olden times, the state of Bahrain included the eastern part of modern day Saudi Arabia and the peninsula of Qatar. Its capital town was Darain, which was located on the peninsula of Tarūt, east of Saudi city of al-Qatīf. Tarūt is a tiny peninsula of Saudi Arabia in the Arabian Gulf (Persian Gulf). Some of the towns of Tarūt Peninsula are Darain, Sanabis, and ar-Rabī'ah. The fort of Tarūt is sited in the middle of it. It was built in 921 AH (1515 CE).[3]

Today the Kingdom of Bahrain is a group of Bahrain and several other smaller islands, between Saudi Arabia and Qatar, in the Arabian Gulf. The largest island was called Awal or Uwal in ancient reference works but is now called Bahrain. Its capital is Manama.[4] The ancient Bahrain was home to Banu 'Abdul-Qais, a tribe of Adnān. Some

1 Mu'jam-ul-Baldān: see under 'Urood.
2 Al-Masālik Wal-Mamālik Li-Abi Obaid Al-Bakri: 1/285.
3 Wikipedia (Encyclopedia).
4 Atlas As-Sīrat-an-Nabawiyyah P. 30.

branches of Banu Rabī'ah also settled here.[1]

'Atīq bin Ghaith al-Baladi writes in *Mu'jam al-Ma'ālim al-Jughrāfiyyah:*

Tarūt Fort

Al-Bahrain was the name of the coast of Nejd stretching from Qatar to Kuwait. Hajar (هجَر), now called al-Hafuf, was an important town of the region. The region was formerly known as al-Hasa and later, during the Ottoman period, came to be called al-Ahsa' while the word al-Bahrain began to be used to refer to the larger island lying to the east of the coast. It was formerly known as Awal and is currently called al-Bahrain. After the founding of the kingdom of Saudi Arabia, al-Ahsa was renamed *al-Manteqat-ush-Sharqiyyah* (The Eastern Region). Dammam is the capital of that region.[2]

Bahrain – Islam, Zoroastrianism, and Judaism: Until the sixth century CE Bahrain had been under the control of Iran. In 6 AH (628 CE) the ruler of Bahrain, Mundhir bin Sāwa, responding to the call of the Prophetﷺ, accepted along with most of his subjects the faith of Islam.

However, a considerable number of native Zoroastrians (fire-worshippers) and Jews kept to their old faiths. Consequently, the *Jizyah* tax was imposed on them, according to the law of Islam.[3]

In the third century AH, the call of the founder of the Karmatian creed, Hamdān (Karmat) bin Ash'ath, made headway with the Zoroastrians of Bahrain.[4] The Karmatians are a branch of the esoteric sect of the Muslims. This creed was founded by Zoroastrians, Mazdakites,

1 Tarīkh Ibn Khaldūn: 2/346.
2 Mu'jam Al-Ma'ālim Al-Jughrafiyyah Fis-Sīrat-in-Nabawiyyah, P. 4140.
3 At-Tabaqāt Li-Ibn Sa'd: 1/ 263; and Mausū'a As-Sīrat-un-Nabawiya Ash-Sharīfa (Murat'taba Alf'baiya), P. 140.
4 Al-Bidāya Wan-Nahāya: 65,66/11.

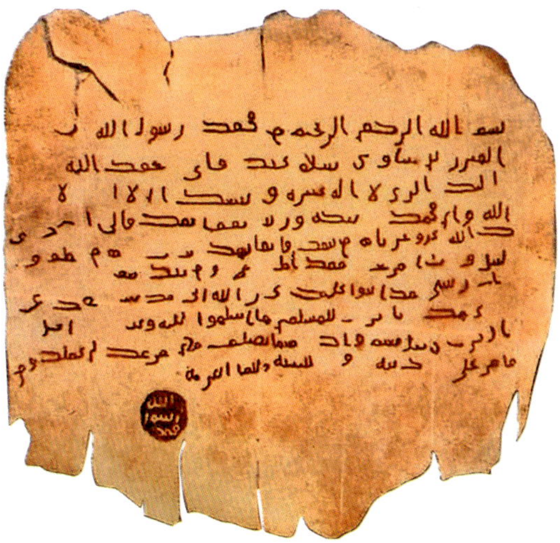

The Prophet's letter of the ruler of Bahrain

Jews and atheists to weaken the Islamic faith.

The beliefs of Karmatians are a heterogeneous medley of alien beliefs repugnant to Islam like those of fire-worshippers, Jews and philosophers. They claimed to be related to the family of the Prophet and propagated that the Qur'ān and Sunnah have both esoteric and exoteric meanings, the former meaning known only to their imams, whom they considered as innocent of sins as the prophets of Allah. They believed that the Muslims should follow the imams only.

They also believed that Ali﵁, like Jesus, would return to the earth. The Karmatians believed in the duality of Godhead. They annulled religious duties like obligatory prayers, Zakat, fasting and Hajj and allowed marriage between consanguineous couples.

This so-called religious movement started first in southern Iran and thence grew in strength gradually and spread beyond the borders of Iran and reached Iraq, Syria, Palestine and Bahrain till they became strong enough to establish a state of their own. In 317 AH (929 CE) they attacked Makkah, pillaged the land, and carried away the sacred Black Stone (حجر اسود) to Bahrain. Later, in 339AH (951 CE), during the reign of the 'Abbasid Caliph Mutee'Lillah, the Black Stone was retrieved and put in its original place in the Holy House of Makkah. Ultimately, the Karmatian state was overthrown in 470 AH (1077 CE) but their teachings remain to this day in Iran, Palestine and Yemen.[1]

1 Mau Sū'at-ul- Adyān P. 404, 405; Al-Mausū'at-ul-Mu'Yassara Fil-Adyān Wal-Madhā'hib: 1/ 378-382.

Oman

This part of the Arabian Peninsula is situated on the coast of the Arabian Sea and the Gulf of Oman. It is bordered in the east by the Gulf, in the west by the Empty Quarter (Saudi Arabia), in the north by 92100 sq. km territory of United Arab Emirates, in the south by Arabian Sea, and in the Southwest by Hadramaut (Yemen). Its area is 310,000 sq km.[1] In ancient times, Oman was famed for its swift-running horses and donkeys. In those days Suhar was an important trade centre. Allāma Maqdasi called it an equal of Egypt and Aden with respect to international trade and termed Oman and Siraf, a town 380 km off Bunder Abbas (Iran) and devastated by Earthquake in 977 CE, as the 'doorway of China' because from here ships sailed to china.[2]

Dibba, another port of Oman, was also an important centre of trade in the olden days. Now it is called Dibba al-Hasan. It is located near the border of United Arab Emirates, in the Omani territory extending upto the straits of Hormuz (also called Ormuz). It was here where Hudhaifa bin Mohassan ؓ, a companion of the Prophet ﷺ, defeated Dhut-Tāj Laqīt, a pretender to prophet hood, during the caliphate of Abu Bakr Siddiq ؓ in 12 AH/ 633 CE.[3]

1 Atlas-ul-'Alām, P. 16 and 66. Encyclopedia Britannica: see under 'Arabia'.
2 Ahsan-ut-Taqāsīm P. 35 and 426.
3 Oman, Sir Donald Hawley, P. 35.

Daba

Masqat

Jabal Shammar

Wadi Hanīfah

Wadi ar-Rummah

3.Nejd

Literally, the Arabic word 'Nejd' means: highland, tableland, plateau. The Arabian region of Nejd is so called because it is on an elevated plane as compared to other regions. It lies 750 to 1500 m above sea level.[1] Hudhail, a tribe of Adnān, and people of Hijaz called it Nujud.[2]

Boundaries of Nejd and its geographic division

Nejd is surrounded on its three sides by barren deserts. So its geography kept it relatively safe from foreign invasions and alien influences. To the north of it lie the deserts of Syria, Iraq and Jordan. To the west of it is Hijaz, to the east the desert of Dahnā', and to the south of it the territory of Yamāmah. Yamāmah is flanked in the south by the Empty Quarter.

According to Istakhri, sometimes Nejd is taken to mean that part of Arabian Peninsula which stretches from Yamāmah to Yathrib (Madinah) and from Basrah to Bahrain.[3] Yaqūt Hamawi, the geographer, quotes: Nejd extends from Khandaq Kisra (Trench of Shapur in Iraq) to Harrah (Bani Sulaim).

1 Al-Mausā'a Al-Arabia Al-Muyassara: 2/1824; Lisan-ul-Arab: see under 'Nejd'.
2 Mu'jam-ul-Buldān: see under 'Nejd'.
3 Masālik Al-Mamālik Lil-Istakhri: 1/14.

It is also said that Nejd refers to a vast land area whose highlands (the Upper Nejd) are Tihāmah (including Hijaz) and Yemen while its lowlands (the Lower Nejd) are Iraq and Syria.[1]

It is an acknowledged fact that Nejd means 'highland'. This is also evident from compound names, of which Nejd is a component word. According to Allāma Asma'ī, names of many places contain the word 'Nejd' like Nejd Barq (name of a wadi of Yamāmah), *Nejd-ul-Wadhdh* (the region of Hudhail), *Nejd 'Uqab, Nejd Aja, Nejd Shara, Nejd Khal* (Iraq), *Nejd 'Ufr, Nejd Kabkab* (near Arafāt), *Nejd Marī'*.[2]

To the north of Nejd lies the desert of Nufud and in the middle is located Mountain of Tuwaiq. It is cris-crossed by several Wadis (streams), the most important of which are *Wadi ar-Rummah* and *Wadi Hanīfah*. It is home to many tribes, the well-known among them being 'Anzah, 'Otaibah, Harb and Matīr. Jabal Shammar, al-Qasīm, Sudair (Wadi Faqi), Washm, 'Arid, al-Kharj, al-Harīq, al-Aflaj, and Wadi ad-Dawasir--- all lie within the territory of Nejd. Al-Kharj is a very fertile region.[3]

Arab poets have praised Nejd for its fertility and good climate. A Bedouin poet says:

أَلَا حَبَّذَا نَجْدٌ وَّطِيبُ تُرَابِهَا   وَغِلْظَةُ دُنْيَا أَهْلِ نَجْدٍ وَّلِينُهَا

How fine is Nejd and how fragrant its soil, How fine is the roughness of people of Nejd in worldly matters and the greenery thereof.[4]

Sā'idah bin J'ayyah Huzali, while recollecting his travels in Nejd Sharā, says:

تَحَمَّلْنَ مِنْ ذَاتِ السُّلَيْمِ كَأَنَّهَا   سَفَائِنُ يَمٍّ تَنْتَحِيهَا دَبُورُهَا

مُيَمِّمَةً نَّجْدَ الشَّرٰى لَا تَرِيمُهُ   وَكَانَتْ طَرِيقًا لَّا تَزَالُ تَسِيرُهَا

Mounts full of riders come from Banu Sulaim like ships driven by

1 Mu'jam-ul-Buldān: see under 'Nejd'.
2 Op.cit.
3 Al-Mausū'a Al-Arabia Al-Muyassara: 2/1824.
4 Az-Zahra Li-Ibn Dawūd Al-Asbahāni: 1/104; Mu'jam-ul-Buldān: see under 'Nejd'.

westerly winds, bound for Nejd Sharā, not swerving therefrom, moving along one way continuously.[1]

Upper and Lower Nejd

Arab geographers name the region adjacent to Hijaz and Tihāmah as Upper Nejd and the region sprawling in the direction of Iraq as Lower Nejd. In the sixth century of the Christian Era, historians tell us, there were forests and fruit trees in Nejd, particularly Ash-Sharabbah and Wajrah south of Wadi Ar-Rummah and northeast of Makkah, regions famed for abundance of fruit trees.[2]

Imortant Places of Nejd

Tayy Mountains and Ha'il: The Ta'yy mountains consist of Aja and Salma Mountains. It is the native place of Hatim Ta'yy, an Arab chieftain of ancient times whose name is a proverb for generosity and hospitality. Ha'il, the beautiful city of Nejd, is sited here. It is known for its dates, *Halwat-ul-Jabal*. Other important towns of the Saudi province of Ha'il are Jubbah, Baq'ā', Ghazalah, Hulaifa, As-Sulaima, As-Sab'an and Al-Miyah. Ha'il is the capital city of the province and located on the bank of a stream (Wadi Ha'il) flowing down from Jabal Aja.[3]

1 Mu'jam-ul-Buldān: see under 'Nejd'.
2 Al-Mufassal Fi Tarīkh-il-Arab Qabl-al-Islam: 1/182.
3 Tarīkh-e-Nejd by Mahmūd Shukri, P. 19, 20.

Ruins of Hatam Tā'is Citadel

Al-Qasīm: It is the central part of Nejd, lying between Washm and Tayy Mountains (Jabal Shammr). The stream (Wadi Ar-Rummah) flowing down from Harrah Kheybar passes through the middle of the province of Al-Qasīm. Buraidah is the capital town of the province. To the west of Al-Qasīm, Mt. Tamiyah rises to a height of 1286 m. The region is distinguished for its date harvest. Important places of Al-Qasīm are:

بُرَيْدَه ، عُنَيزَه ، الرَّسْ ، المِذْنَب ، البُكَيْرِيَّه ، عُقْلَةُ الصُّقُورِ، نَقِرَه، قُبَّه ، الخَبْرَاء .

Buraidah, ʻUnaizah, Ar-Ras, Al-Midhnab, Al-Bukairiyyah, ʻUqlat-us-Suqūr, Naqirah, Qubbah, Al-Khabra'.

The dwelling-place of Ashāb-ur-Rass: Qur'ān refers to Ashāb-ur-Rass (the people of the well) along with the people of Noah, 'Ād and Thamūd in Al-Furqān (Verse 38) and Qāf (Verse 12). They rejected Allah's messengers and were destroyed. Historians tell us that they were so named because they threw down their messenger into a well. Some commentators say that Ashāb-ur-Rass and Ashāb-ul-Ukhdūd (people of the ditch) are the same people. It is also said that it was the name of a settlement in Yamāmah called Falaj (or Falaj-ul-Aflāj). According to another opinion, it is the dwelling-place of one of the clans of Thamūd.[1] Today Falaj is called al-

1 Atlas-ul-Qur'ān by Shauqi Abu Khalīl, P.220.

Don
Volga R.
Ural R.
Ukraine
Russia
Ital
Azov
Kuban
Crimea
Black Sea
Georgia
Arran
Derbent
Tbilisi
Caspian Sea
Baku
Armenia
Turkey
Azerbaijan
Asia Minor
Van Lake
Tariz
Lake of Orumiyeh (Urmia)
Rey
Mosul
Aleppo
Cyprus
Mediterranean Sea
Damascus
Euphrates R.
Tigris R.
Esfahan
Yazd
Sistan
Syrian Desert
Persia
Kerman
Ubullah
Shiraz
Aqabah
Sinai
An Nafūd Desert
Arabian Gulf (Persian Gulf)
Madian
Najd
Makran
Ar-Rass
Madinah Munawwarah (Yathrib)
Al Riyadh
Al Yamamah
Gulf of Oman
Muscat
Egypt
Red Sea
Oman
Hijaz
Falj
Nubian Desert
Jeddah
Makkah Mukarramah
ARABIA
Al Rub' al Khāli (The Empty Quarter)
Asir
Salalah
Hadramawt
Arabian Sea
San'ā
Sudan
Massawa
Yemen
Al Mukalla
Aden
Aseb
Gulf of Aden
Socotra
Berbera
Horn of Africa
Indian Ocean
Ethiopia
0
200
400
600
800
1000
km
Buraydah
Al Zulfi
Al Bakiriyah
Al Qasim
Al-Khabra'
Unayzah
Sadīr
Ar Rass
Al Majma'ah
Shaqra'
Raghbah
Thamamah
Najd
Jubaylah
Dir'iyah
Ad Dawadimi
Riyadh
Al Yamamah
'Afif
Yamāmah
Al Kharj
Najad (Nejad)
Al Hillah
Tropic of Cancer
ad Adhay
Al Aflaj
(Falj)
Laila
Al Badi'
Possible Area of Ashāb-ar-Rass
(1) Ar-Rass (Najd)
(2) Falj (Yamāmah)
(3) Azerbaijan
(4) Arran
(5) A settlement of Hadramawt

Map 3

Aflāj.

Ruins of the ancient town of ar-Rass

There is a town named ar-Rass, nearly 70 km southwest of Buraidah, in the province of al-Qaseem, Nejd.[1] Though Yaqūt Hamawi, the author of *Mu'jam-ul-Buldan,* said that ar-Ras was a settlement of Yamāmah, he also quoted Ibn Duraid as having said that ar-Rass and ar-Rusais were the two Wadis or the two towns of Nejd.[2] Since Yamāmah is also counted as lying within the boundaries of Nejd, it looks probable that ar-Rass of modernday al-Qaseem (Nejd) is the same old town of ar-Rass considered by some scholars a settlement of Yamāmah.

'Ārid-ul-Yamamah: *Nejd-ul 'Ārid ('Ārid-ul-Yamāmah)* consists of 120 km-long Wadi Hanifah *(Al-'Ird)* and Yamāmah. Here, later on, Dir'iyah was settled when the Saudi Kingdom was founded.

Location of Yamāmah: Yamāmah is flanked in the east by UAE and Bahrain, in the north and west by original Nejd, and in the south by the Empty Quarter. Some scholars include Yamāmah within 'Urood but most include it within Nejd. Yaqūt Hamawi, the famous geographer, wrote: "It is included within Nejd and its central town is Hajr (حَجْر)."[3] Today the town of Yamamah is sited in the northwestern suburb of Al-Kharj, nearly 80 km off Riyadh.

Ruins of Yamamah (al-Kharj)

1 Atlas Al-Mamlaka Al-Arabia As-Saudia Wal 'Ālam, P. 14 and 17.

2 Mu'jam-ul-Buldān: see under 'Ar-Rass'.

3 Mu'jam-ul-Buldān: see under 'Yamamah'.

Thamamah bin Uthāl, Ruler of Yamāmah

It was this region ruled by Thamamah bin Uthāl when the Prophet ﷺ started his prophetic mission.[1] His conversion to Islam makes an interesting story. He was a pagan and an ally of Quraish. In 7 AH he set out for Umrah. The companions of the Prophet arrested him and bound him to a pillar of the Prophet's Mosque. The Prophet ﷺ inquired of him about his intention. He replied:

[إِنْ تَقْتُلْنِي تَقْتُلْ ذَا دَمٍ، وَإِنْ تُنْعِمْ تُنْعِمْ عَلَى شَاكِرٍ]

> "If you kill me, my blood shall not go in vain (that is, my blood shall be avenged) and if you do me a favour, then you shall favour a grateful person."

The next day the Prophet ﷺ asked him again: "Thamamah, what do you think now?" He replied: The same as I said before. The third day, the Prophet ﷺ asked him again: "Thamamah, how do you see it now?" He replied: The same as before. Then the Prophet ﷺ told the companions to unbind him. When the rope had been unfastened, Thamamah went straight to a garden near the Prophet's Mosque, took a bath, came back to the Prophet, and embraced Islam, saying:

[أَشْهَدُ أَنْ لَّا إِلٰهَ إِلَّا اللّٰهُ وَأَشْهَدُ أَنَّ مُحَمَّدًا رَّسُولُ اللّٰهِ]

> "I bear witness that there is no true god except Allah and I bear witness that Muhammad is the Messenger of Allah."

Then he said:

[يَا مُحَمَّدُ! وَاللّٰهِ! مَاكَانَ عَلَى الْأَرْضِ وَجْهٌ أَبْغَضَ إِلَيَّ مِنْ وَّجْهِكَ، فَقَدْ أَصْبَحَ وَجْهُكَ أَحَبَّ الْوُجُوهِ إِلَيَّ، وَاللّٰهِ! مَاكَانَ مِنْ دِينٍ أَبْغَضَ إِلَيَّ مِنْ دِينِكَ، فَأَصْبَحَ دِينُكَ أَحَبَّ الدِّينِ إِلَيَّ، وَاللّٰهِ! مَاكَانَ مِنْ بَلَدٍ أَبْغَضَ إِلَيَّ مِنْ بَلَدِكَ، فَأَصْبَحَ بَلَدُكَ أَحَبَّ الْبِلَادِ إِلَيَّ]

> "O Muhammad, by Allah, no face was more hateful to me in the world than yours but (now) your face has become to me the dearest of all faces. By Allah, no religion was more hateful to me

1 Tareekh Ibn Khaldūn: 2/348.

than your religion but (now) your religion has become to me the dearest of all religions. By Allah, no town was more hateful to me than your town but (now) your town has become to me the dearest of all the towns."

Later on, Thamamah ﷺ went off to perform 'Umrah. When he arrived at Makkah, the people started saying: Thamamah has become a proselyte. He retorted: 'No. I believe in Muhammad ﷺ now. From onward, no grain of wheat will reach Makkah without the Prophet's leave.'[1]

Today a settlement called Thamamah (ثمامه), 60 km north of Riyadh, and the Wadi of Thamamah evoke the memory of the Prophet's companion, Thamamah ﷺ.

Zarqā' Al-Yamāmah

Why was Yamāmah so named?

Yaqoot Hamawi says that Yamāmah was the dwelling-place of the ancient tribes of Tasm and Jadees. Formerly, it was called *Jaww*. It was ruled by 'Amleeq bin Habash bin Hailas who belonged to the tribe of Banu Tasm. He was a very ill-natured, cruel tyrant. He ordered that any girl just married should first be sent to him. The chieftain of Jadees tribe, Aswad bin Ghifār, had a sister called Afeerah bint Ghifār. On the eve of her marriage, following the tradition, she was sent to 'Amleeq. At this wild, beastly act, she reproached her brother and her tribesmen and cried for help. Thereupon, they rose up and killed all the nobles of Banu Tasm.

A man of Banu Tasm, Riāh bin Murrah, escaped to Tubba' of Yemen

Cemetery of the martyrs of the Battle of Yamamah

1 Sahīh Bukhāri 4372; and Sahīh Muslim: 1764.

Wadi an-Nakhīl, al-Hanākiyah

(Hassān bin Tubba‘) and appealed to him for help. Hassan set out with a large force but when he reached near "Jaww", Riāh bin Murrah said to the king: 'Stay here, please. One of my sisters has been married into the tribe of Bani Jadees. Her name is Yamāmah. She is blessed with miraculous eyesight. She can espy a man from a distance of one day and one night. I am afraid, she may espy us and inform her people'. Thereupon, Tubba‘ stopped and asked a man to go up the mountain to have a look around and observe the situation. When the man climbed up, his shoe lace split up. As he knelt to mend it, Yamāmah noticed him and informed her people but they laughed it away.

Later on, the Yemeni contingent attacked Banu Jadees, routed them, and arrested Yamāmah. When, at the bidding of Tubba‘, her eyes were gouged out, they discovered that her eye sockets were full of antimony. It is said that she was the first to use antimony. Anyhow, at the order of Tubba‘, she was hanged to death at the gateway of "Jaww". Later, at his bidding, the region was named after her: Yamāmah.[1]

1 Mu'jam-ul-Buldan: see under 'Yamamah'.

Later on, the people remembered her as Zarqā'-al-Yamāmah (the blue-eyed woman of Yamāmah). Tasm and Jadees were succeeded by Banu Hanifah as rulers of Yamāmah. Banu Hanifah are an offshoot of Banu Bakr bin Wa'il who belong to the Adnani branch of the Arabs. They trace their lineage to Hanifah bin Luhaim bin Sa'b bin Ali bin Bakr bin Wa'il. They dwelt in Yamāmah. From them came Haudha (هوذة) bin Ali to whom the Prophetﷺ wrote a letter exhorting him to accept the Islamic faith.[1] It should be noted that Musailamah the Liar, son of Thamāmah bin Kuthay'yir bin Habeeb, also belonged to this tribe.[2]

Musailamah made pretension to prophethood during the last days of the Prophetﷺ.[3] Abu Bakr Siddiq sent an expeditionary force to stamp out this heretical movement. Musailamah was slain by Wahshi bin Harb in the ensuing battle.[4] The site of the battle of Yamāmah lies 40 km northwest of Riyadh and is now called al-Jubailah. At al-Jubailah there are also graves of the Prophet's companions who fell martyrs while fighting the apostates in that battle.

Dariyyah: Here, in Muharram, 5 AH, the military expedition of Qurata' was sent under the command of Muhammad bin Muslamah. The Qurata' tribe was a branch of the clan of Banu Bakr bin Kilāb Qaisi. Dariyyah (ضريّة) is the name of a pasture ground in the middle of Nejd. Today the town of Dariyyah is 165 km off Rabadha

Dariyyah or Rabadha

1 Nihayat-ul-Arab, P. 223.
2 Tareekh Ibn Khaldūn: 2/348.
3 Fat'h-ul-Bari: 7/464.
4 Sahīh-ul-Bukhāri: 4072.

and 247 km off All-Hanakiyah in the east, 135 km south of Al-Batrā' (on Al-Hanākiyah-'Unaizah highway) and 90 km north of Al-'Afeef.[1]

Dhat-ur-Riqā': It is the name of a mountain of Nejd, so named because of its variegated colouring from red, black and white patches (رقاع). Jabal Dhat-ur-Riqā' is 100 km northeast of Madinah, 15Km south of Al-Hanakiyāh. Here, in Muharram, 5 AH, the Battle of Dhat-ur-Riqa' took place. But some people give another reason. They say that the Muslim soldiers wounded their feet walking. So they wrapped their wounded feet with rags called *Riqa'* in Arabic. Hence the name of their holy battle (Ghazwa).

The forty-years long battle of Basus

In the ancient times Nejd was home to the extinct Arabs *(Al-Arab Al-Ba`idah)*. Later, the Qahtani tribes from the southern part of Arabian Peninsula and, later, the tribes of Adnan from Hijaz came to settle here.[2]

Bakr bin Wa'il, one of the tribes of Adnan, also settled in Nejd. Banu Bakr are considered the most eloquent of the Arabs. They were related to Banu Taghlīb. Once a chieftain of the latter, Kulaib bin Rabee'ah Taghlibi, was slain by a man of Banu Bakr named Jasas bin Murrah Shaibani. This led to a bloody battle between the two tribes, a battle which raged for as long as forty years. It is called in the annals of Arabia the *Battle of Basoos*.[3]

Nejd is the home of some of the greatest Arab poets. Muhalhal, the brother of Kulaib bin Rabee'ah Taghlibi and the pioneer of Arab poetry, was born in Nejd. He can be rightly called the Originator of Arab poetry. The greatest of the pre-Islamic Arab poets was, of course, Imra-ul-Qais bin Hujr bin Harith. He belonged to the tribe of Kindah of Nejd.[4]

Islamic mission in Nejd

All through the lifetime of the Prophet ﷺ, relations between the Muslims and the tribes of Nejd remained tense. In the tenth year of his prophetic

1 Atlas Seerat an-Nabawiyyah, P.285; Atlas Al-Mamlaka Al-Arabia As-Saudia, plate 9.
2 Ulema-o-Nejd Khilal Thamania Quroon: 1/8,9.
3 Al-Jamhara Li-Ibn Hazm P. 305.
4 Al-Kāmil Li Ibn-il-Athīr 1/608-609; Imta'-ul-Ama' Lil-Muqreezi: 1/49.

mission, before his migration, on the eve of the annual Hajj, as well as in the trade fairs of the pagan Arabs, the Prophet ﷺ contacted men from about fifteen tribes in a bid to solicit their help and asked them to support him and his mission. The rudest of them all were Banu Haneefah of Nejd.[1]Later, in Rabee-ul-Awwal of 4 AH, the tragedy of Bi'r Ma'una occurred in Nejd when 70 reciters of the Qur'ān were slain by treachery.[2]

In 7 AH the Prophet ﷺ wrote a letter to Haudhah bin Ali Hanafi, the Christian king of Banu Haneefah and poet and orator, asking him to accept Islam. He wrote back: "… If you give me some powers, I will accept your authority."[3]

Though, of course, the tribes of Nejd converted to Islam after the Conquest of Makkah but heresy and apostasy broke out even during the lifetime of the Prophet ﷺ. The Prophet ﷺ sent an expeditionary force under the command of Abu Qatādah رضي الله عنه to crush the heresy.[4]

1 Al-Muntazam: 2/138; Tareekh Ibn Khaldūn: 2/347.
2 See Sahīh-ul-Bukhāri: 4090.
3 At-Tabaqat Li-Ibn Sa'd: 1/262.
4 Sahīh-ul-Bukhāri: 4338; and Fat'h-ul-Bari: 8/70.

4.Yemen

Yemen, which lies in the southwest of the Arabian Peninsula, has always been an independent state. It is the most civilized part of the Peninsula and home to the Arab tribes of Qahtān.

Archaeological finds and inscriptions reveal that the people of Yemen were next to none in terms of civilization, arts, and sciences. That is why it is called *al-Yaman as-Sa'eedah* (the Happy Yemen) or *al-Yaman al-Ghaniyyah* (the fertile Yemen).[1]

Yemen: how it came to be so named

Ibn Abbas ﷺ, explaining the etymology of the word Yemen, says: "The Arabs spread out widely over the different parts of the peninsula. Some turned right. So their region was named Yemen after the direction they went off. (*Yameen* is Arabic for right-hand side. The root word is *Yumn* (يُمن) which is Arabic for blessedness or blessing. Hence the right-hand side is considered to be blessed). According to another opinion, when Makkah

1 Qissa wa Tareekh-ul-Hadārāt Al-Arabia: 15/28.

(with respect to one facing east) became too populous and crowded, those who lived on the right side of Makkah with respect to one facing east gathered in Yemen, which is on the extreme right side of Makkah. Hence the name.[1]

Abdullah bin Abbas' explanation is fine. He says: There is a sea (The Red Sea) west of Makkah. Nejd is in front of it, Yemen on the right of it, and Syria on the left of it. By virtue of the region of Yemen being on the right hand side of Makkah, it got the name of Yemen. That is the reason why a corner *(Rukn)* of Kaaba (Ka'bah) is called *Rukn Yamāni*.

The ancient Arabs called it *al-Arab as-Sa'eedah* (the happy or blessed Arab) or *al-Yaman al-Khadra'* (The green Yemen).[2] According to Ibn Yaqoob Hamadani, the region is called 'The green Yemen' *(al-Yaman al-Khadra')* because there are trees, fruits and harvests of crops in plenty.[3]

Ancient Sabaean relics mention Yemen as *"Yamanaat"* or *"Yamanat"* meaning: blessedness. That is why Roman writers referred to it as Arabia Felix which means *al-Arabia as-Sa'eedah* or *al-Arabia al-Khairiyyah*.[4]

Expansion of Yemen

This green land is bounded in the south by Gulf of Aden and the Arabian Sea, in the west by the Red Sea, in the north by Hijaz, Nejd and the Empty Quarter, and in the east by Oman. The present-day Yemen extends over an area of 527,000 sq km.[5] Its boundary in the north extends to Saudi areas of Najran, al-Wadi'ah, about 460 km north of al-Mukalla, and *Urooq-ul-Mawarid* (Empty Quarter), and in the east up to Habrūt (Sultanate of Oman). Najran-o-Yemen of the past is now a part of Saudi Arabia.[6]

The borders of Yemen have always been fluid, changing across different periods of its history. Hamadani defines its limits as extending

1 Mu'jam-ul-Buldan: see under 'Yemen'.
2 'Asr-un-Nabuwa Lil-Ka'bi, P. 19.
3 Sifat-o-Jazeerat-il-Arab, P.90.
4 Qissa Wa Tareekh-ul-Hadarat Al-Arabia: 15/ 25.
5 Atlas Al-'Alam, P. 16 and 96.
6 Atlas Al-Mamlaka Al-Arabia As-Saudia Wal 'Alam, P. 30,31.

Map.4

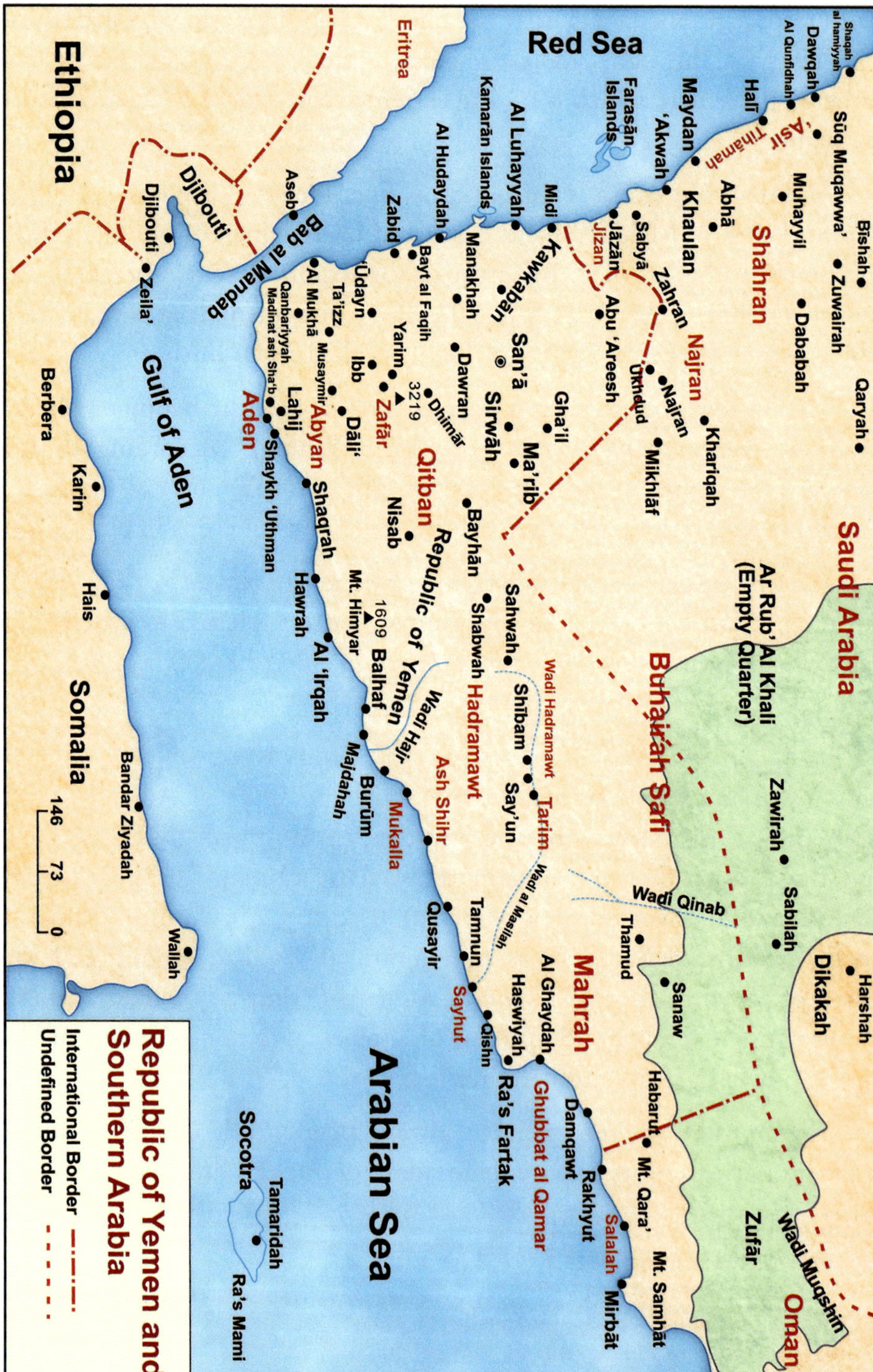
Republic of Yemen and Southern Arabia
International Border
Undefined Border
Red Sea
Arabian Sea
Gulf of Aden
Bab al Mandab
Ethiopia
Eritrea
Djibouti
Somalia
Saudi Arabia
Oman
Ar Rub' Al Khali (Empty Quarter)
Buhairah Safi
Republic of Yemen
Shahran
Najran
Hadramawt
Mahrah
Qitban
Abyan
Aden
Zafār
Ash Shihr
Mukalla
Sayhut
Tarim
Salalah
Ghubbat al Qamar
Wadi Hadramawt
Wadi Hajr
Wadi Qinab
Wadi al Masilah
Wadi Muqshim
Tihāmah
'Asir
Jīzan
Shaqah al hamiyyah
Dawqah
Al Qunfidhah
Halī
Sūq Muqawwa'
Muhayyil
Abhā
Bīshah
Zuwairah
Dababah
Qaryah
Maydan
'Akwah
Khaulan
Farasān Islands
Kamarān Islands
Al Luhayyah
Al Hudaydah
Midi
Sabyā
Jāzān
Zahran
Abu 'Areesh
Kawkabān
Manakhah
San'ā
Bayt al Faqih
Zabid
Asseb
Ukhdud
Najran
Khariqah
Mikhlāf
Gha'il
Sirwāh
Ma'rib
Dawran
Dhimār
Yarim
3219
'Udayn
Ibb
Ta'izz
Al Mukhā
Musaymir
Qanbariyyah
Madinat ash Sha'b
Lahij
Dāli'
Shaykh 'Uthman
Shaqrah
Nisab
Bayhān
Shabwah
Sahwah
Shibam
Say'un
Mt. Himyar
1609
Hawrah
Al 'Irqah
Balhaf
Majdahah
Burūm
Qusayir
Tamnun
Qishn
Haswiyah
Al Ghaydah
Ra's Fartak
Damqawt
Rakhyut
Mirbāt
Mt. Qara'
Mt. Samhāt
Habarut
Thamud
Zawirah
Sabilah
Sanaw
Dikakah
Harshah
Zufār
Zeila'
Berbera
Karin
Hais
Bandar Ziyadah
Wallah
Socotra
Tamaridah
Ra's Mami
146 73 0

Miqat yalamlam (as-Sadiyah)

from the border of Oman and Yebreen to the border of Yamāmah, then from Al-Hujairah, Tathleeth and Jurash up to Tihāmah, then finally up to Mt. Kudummul near Hamidah.[1] Tathleeth and Hamidah are presently located in the Saudi province of 'Aseer. Tathleeth is approximately 200 km north of the Yemeni border.

Ancient Arab geographer Ibn Hauqal counts two-thirds of the Arabian Peninsula as falling within Yemen. According to him, Tihāmah, Nejd-o-Yemen, Oman, Mahrah, Hadramaut, San'ā, Aden, and all other districts of Yemen lie within Yemen. He defines its northern limits as extending from Sirrain to Yalamlam (the Miqat for the Hajj pilgrims of Yemen) and Tā'if. Then he stretches forth these boundaries from Nejd-o-Yemen to the Persian Gulf.[2]

Districts of Yemen

During the reign of the Abbasids, Yemen was a vast, sprawling province of the Arabian Peninsula. Ahmed bin Ishaq Ya'qoobi (d. 292 AH) says that Yemen had 84 districts (i.e. administrative regions), the most important of them being:

ذِمَار، جُرَش، صَعْدَه، الحِجْر، المَعافِر، السَّكُون، مَأرِب، حَضُور، جَيْشان، بَيْش، السّاعِد،
زَبِيد، لَحْج، أَبْيَن، حَضْرَمَوْت، عَنْس، بني عامر، مَأذَن، حُمْلان، خَوْلان، السَّرْو،
الدَّثِينَه، كُبَيْبَه، تَباله، عَدَن، المَنْدَب، غَلافِقَه،الحَمِضَه اور السِّرَّيْن .

Dimar, Jurash, Sa'dah, al-Hijr, al-Ma'āfir, as-Sakoon, Ma'rib, Hazoor, Jaishān, Beysh, As-Sā'id, Zabeed, Lahj, Abyan, Hadhramaut, 'Ans, Bani 'Āmir, Ma'dhan, Humlan, Khaulan, As-S'arv, ad-Datheenah, Kubaibah, and Tabālah. And the districts

1 Sifat-o-Jazeerat-il-Arab, P. 90.
2 Taqweem-ul-Buldan, P. 80.

adjoining the sea coast were 'Aden, al-Mandab, Ghalāfiqah, al-Hamidah, and Sirrain.[1]

Tradesmen of Yemen

Greek historian Strabo, describing the Yemen of his days, writes that the southern Arabia (Yemen) is the richest part of the Arabian Peninsula. The natives dress well. Utensils of gold and silver are found in abundance. They decorate their houses with elephant tusks, gold, silver and precious stones. The secret of their wealth lies in their trade.

The Yemeni traders used to carry the produce of Arabia and India in caravans to the west or by sea to Babylon. Their ships plied the Indian Ocean. They used to go to "Obees" in large ships through the Tigris and make large gains by selling this merchandise to Media (northwestern Iran), Armenia, and other neighbouring lands.[2]

Merits of Yemenites

Yemen is a blessed, thriving country, both materially and spiritually. There are words in praise of Yemen in both Qur'ān and Hadeeth.

1 Tareekh-ul-Yaqoobi: 1/172, 173.
2 Qissa Wa Tareekh-ul-Hadarat Al-Arabia: 15/ 35.

References in Qur'ān:

﴿ يَـٰٓأَيُّهَا ٱلَّذِينَ ءَامَنُوا۟ مَن يَرْتَدَّ مِنكُمْ عَن دِينِهِۦ فَسَوْفَ يَأْتِى ٱللَّهُ بِقَوْمٍ يُحِبُّهُمْ وَيُحِبُّونَهُۥٓ أَذِلَّةٍ عَلَى ٱلْمُؤْمِنِينَ أَعِزَّةٍ عَلَى ٱلْكَـٰفِرِينَ يُجَـٰهِدُونَ فِى سَبِيلِ ٱللَّهِ وَلَا يَخَافُونَ لَوْمَةَ لَآئِمٍ ۚ ﴾

"O You who believe! Whoever from among you turns back from his religion (Islam), Allah will bring a people whom He will love and they will love Him; humble towards the believers, stern towards disbelievers, fighting in the way of Allah and never fear the blame of the blamers."[1]

When the companions asked the Prophet ﷺ as to who those people are, about whom Allah said: 'Whom He loves and who love Him', he replied:

«هٰؤُلَاءِ قَوْمٌ مِّنَ الْيَمَنِ، ثُمَّ مِنْ كِنْدَةَ، ثُمَّ مِنَ السَّكُونِ، ثُمَّ مِنْ تُجَيْبٍ»

"Those people belong to Yemen, then to Banu Kinda, then to Banu Sakoon (bin Ashras bin Thaur) and then to Banu Tujaib".[2]

Allah says in Surat Al-Hajj:

﴿ وَأَذِّن فِى ٱلنَّاسِ بِٱلْحَجِّ ﴾

"And proclaim unto mankind the Pilgrimage."[3]

Commenting on this Verse, Abdullah bin Abbas رضي الله عنهما says: When Allah bade Ibrāhīm (Abraham) to tell mankind to make pilgrimage to the House of Allah, he climbed up Mt. Abu Qubais (which was closest to the House of Allah), inserted his fingers into his ears, and proclaimed: 'Allah has imposed upon you as a duty to perform Hajj. So respond to the call of Allah.' To his call responded every person who was (dormant or yet unborn) in the backs of males and in the wombs of women. The first to respond to this call were the people of Yemen.[4]

1 Qur'ān: Al-Ma'idah, 5: 54.

2 Tafseer Ibn Abi Hatim: Al-Ma'idah (5): 54; Al-Mu'jam Al-Ausat Li At-Tabarani 1/380. Hadeeth 1392. Its chain of narration is Hasan (good). See Majma'-uz-Zawa'id 7/ 16, Hadeeth 10977; As-Silsalah As-Saheeha: 7/1103-1106.

3 Qur'ān: Al-Hajj, 22: 27.

4 Tafseer Ibn Abi Hatim, Tafseer Al-Baghawi: Al-Hajj, 22: 26, 27.

References in Hadeeth:

Ibn Mas'ud says that once the Prophet ﷺ remarked:

« الْإِيمَانُ هٰهُنَا - وَأَشَارَ بِيَدِهِ إِلَى الْيَمَنِ»

"The faith is here - and he pointed with his hand in the direction of Yemen."[1]

The Messenger of Allah (ﷺ) said:

«أَتَاكُمْ أَهْلُ الْيَمَنِ، هُمْ أَرَقُّ أَفْئِدَةً، وَأَلْيَنُ قُلُوبًا، الْإِيمَانُ يَمَانٍ، وَالْحِكْمَةُ يَمَانِيَةٌ»

"The people of Yemen have come to you. They are soft and tender of heart. Faith is Yemeni and wisdom is Yemeni."[2]

Important places of Yemen

San'a: This city is not only the heart of Yemen but also the cradle of one of the most ancient civilizations. Its old name was Uzāl. It is one of the oldest towns on the face of the earth. It is said that it was settled by Sām (Shem), the son of Nūh (Noah).[3]

When the Ethiopians occupied San'a, they were struck with wonder when they saw that the town had been built of rocks and they cried out: "هذه صنعه" 'This is workmanship (San'ah)'. So the town came to be known as San'a.[4]

When in the year 525 of the Christian Era (CE), the

Acient palace of a yemenite Chieftain, San'ā

1 Sahīh-ul-Bukhāri: 4387; Sahīh Muslim: 51.
2 Saeeh-ul-Bukhari: 4388; Sahheeh Muslim: 52.
3 Sifat Jazeerat-il-Arab, P. 102, 103.
4 Mu'jam-ul-Buldan: see under 'San'a'.

Christian king Aksūm defeated the last Hamyari king of Yemen, Dhu Nuwās, he appointed a Christian governor for Yemen. The latter took San'a as his capital.[1] San'a and its fort, Ghamadan, were raised to the status of capital during 537-548 CE.[2] San'a remains the capital of Yemen to this day. It is 2196 m above sea level. The province of San'a includes the districts of Imran, al-Jauf, Hauth, Mahweet, Reehah, Kaukaban and Haraz.[3]

San'a has a pleasant, temperate climate. Allama Zakariyyah bin Muhammad Qazwini writes: 'San'a is a masterpiece of architecture. It is a city of pleasant climate, sweet water, clean earth, with few ailments. Flies, mosquitoes and other (noxious) insects are rare. A sick man comes to San'a and gets well and cured. Camels with ailments are brought to the meadows of San'a. As soon as they graze its grass, they are healed. Its salubrious climate prevents abandoned meat from rotting for as long as a week.' Allama Hamdani says that the residents of San'a enjoy the pleasures of summer and winter, each twice in a single year.[4]

An Arab poet, Abu Muhammad Yazeedi Nahvi Basri says in praise of San'a:

قُلْتُ وَنَفْسِي جَمٌّ تَأَوُّهُهَا   تَصْبُو إِلٰى أَهْلِهَا وَأَنْدَهِهَا

سُقْيًا لِّصَنْعَاءَ لَا أَرٰى بَلَدًا   أَوْطَنَهُ الْمُوطِنُونَ يُشْبِهُهَا

"My heart sighs, longing to see my land. I consoled my heart and said: may blessings rain down on San'a. I never saw a settlement the like of San'a."[5]

The valleys of San'a were very fertile. If you looked in any direction, you would see fruit trees reaching up to the horizon.

The palace of Ghamadan was a masterpiece of architecture. It was built by Liyashrakh bin Yahsab, a Tubba' ruler. The palace was square in form, red on one side, white on the other, yellow on the third, and

1 Qissa Wa Tareekh-ul-Hadarat Al-Arabia: 15/ 32 and 34.
2 Wikipedia (Encyclopedia).
3 Al-munjid Fil 'Alam, p. 348.
4 Athar-ul-Bilād wa Akhbar-ul-Ibād, P. 50.
5 Mu'jam-ul-Buldan: see under 'San'a'.

A mountain village of Haraz - Yemen

green on the fourth. Inside it there was yet another palace. It had seven storeys. Each storey was forty cubits (about 60 ft.) high. As the sun rose, the palace cast a shadow as long as three miles. Liyashrakh bin Yahsab built on its top storey a meeting hall made of coloured marble, the roof of which was a one-piece marble. Each pillar had the image of a lion. As the wind blew, the images gave a sound like the roaring of lions.

At night, as the Ghamadan palace was lit with lamps, it glittered like flashes of lightning one sees from behind the clouds. It is said that as the Tubba' king lit up lamps to sit there, its brilliance could be seen by travellers several days journey away. There is a mountain of alum (potassium-aluminum sulfate) near San'a. Water flows down all over its sides from its summit and, before it reaches the ground, the alum content of the water sets.[1] It is a high-quality alum called *"Shabb Yamani"*.[2]

Hadharamaut: It is also one of the oldest regions of Yemen. To the west of it is Aden, to the east of it is Oman, to the south of it is the Arabian Sea, and to the north of it Nufud-ud-Dahna'. The long coast of Hadhramaut lies on the Arabian Sea. Its area is approximately 4500 sq km.[3]

Historians call it variously as Hazrmaut or Hazarmaveth but most of them refer to it as Hadhramaut. Literally, the name means: 'city of death',

1 Athar-ul-Bilad Wa Akhbar-ul-Ibad, P. 51,52.
2 Urdu Lughat: see under 'Shabb'.
3 Tareekh Hadhramaut As-Siasi Lli-Salah Al-Bikri, P. 1,2.

Wadi Dharwān (Yemen)

because the popular belief among the Greeks was that it was a valley of death. According to ancient inscriptions of South Arabia, its name was also Hadhramaut.[1]

Torah refers to it as 'Hazarmaveth'.[2] This name also carries the same meaning.

According to Salah al-Bakri, Hadhramaut was known in ancient times as *'Ahqāf'*. Some historians say that Amir bin Qahtan was the first man to enter Ahqāf. Whenever he took the field, slaughter and carnage on a large scale followed in his wake. So wherever he went, people would say: *Hadaramaut* حَضَرَ مَوْت (death has come). Thus his nickname 'Hadramaut' or 'Hadhramaut' became so widely known that the region where he lived also became known as Hadhramaut.[3]

The region had been the site of many great Arab empires of old. That was the land of the 'Ād, Aqyals of Tubba', and kings of 'Himyars, Kindahs, and Ma'eens. During the era of the Prophet Muhammad (ﷺ), the kings who ruled Hadhramaut were called "'Abahila". The Prophet sent Wa'il bin Hujr ؓ with a letter addressed to Aqyāl (kings) and 'Abāhila and made him the governor of Hadhramaut.[4]

In Hadhramaut there is a place called 'Qabr Hūd' (The Grave of (prophet) Hūd عليه السلام). There are different opinions about it but most historians say that Hadhramaut was the place where prophet Hūd عليه السلام was buried.[5] Hamdani, a historian of the fourth century AH, says that prophet Hūd عليه السلام was buried in the lower ranges of the Ahqāf valley, in a cave on a red hillock.[6]There are many relics in Hadhramaut known as Dar 'Ād (home of the tribe of 'Ād).

1 Al-Mufassal Fi Tareekh-il-Arab Qabl-al-Islam: 2/130.
2 Tareekh Hadramaut As-Siasi, P.30.
3 Op.cit. P.30 .
4 Taj-ul-Uroos: see under 'Abhal'.
5 Jami'-ul-Hadīth by As-Sayūti: 29/315.
6 Sifat-o-Jazeerat-il-Arab, P. 170.

A beautiful view of San'ā

Islam in Hadhramaut: The inhabitants of Hadhramaut were pagans and the idol they worshipped was called Marhab.[1] When Allah gave Muhammad bin Abdullah (ﷺ) the prophetic mission, the people of Hadhramaut were filled with love for Islam and they sent a delegation to the Prophet ﷺ under the leadership of Wa'il bin Hujr Hadhrami Qahtani. When Wa'il bin Hujār came to Madinah, the Prophet ﷺ received him warmly and prayed for him.[2]

Similarly, in 10 AH, Ash'ath bin Qais, the chief of Kindah tribe, leading a 70-men delegation, came to see the Prophet ﷺ who received him with honour. He accepted Islam. But he renounced the Islamic faith after the death of the Prophet ﷺ and was arrested. When he was brought to Abu Bakr رضي الله عنه, he repented and again became a Muslim. He died in Kūfah. His funeral prayer was led by Hasan رضي الله عنه.[3] It was the same day when Hasan رضي الله عنه and Mu'awiah رضي الله عنه made compromise.

Ma'rib and Saba (Sheba): Ma'rib is a historic city, 70 km east of San'a, the capital of Yemen. It was the capital of the kingdom of Sheba (Arabic: Saba) which was founded around 1000 BC. It was ruled by Queen Bilqees who later became a believer (Muslim) and married Prophet Solomon عليه السلام. During the heyday of its glory (650 BC – 115 BC) the kingdom of Saba extended as far as Abyssinia (modern Ethiopia and Eritrea). Saba also built

1 Mu'jam-ul-Buldān: see under 'Marhab'; and Al-Muhabbar by Ibn Habib, P. 318.
2 'Aun-ul-Ma'bood 2/413, under Hadīth: 723.
3 Tareekh Dimashq Al-Kabeer 9/93; At-Ta'deel Wat-Tajreeh: 1/388; Mu'jam-ul-Buldān: see under 'Hadramaut', .

a large dam, which was destroyed during the period 570-542 CE. Today Ma'rib is the capital of the province of Al-Baida'[1]

Shibām and Tareem: The historic cities of Al-Bahr-us-Safi, Shibām and Tareem lie on the bank of Wadi Hadhramaut which is 150 km north of the ports of Al-Mukalla and Ash-Shahr. The former (Al-Mukalla) is 500 km northeast of Aden while the latter (As-Shahr) is 65 km east of Al-Mukalla.

Shibam was settled by the tribesmen of Shaboh.[2]About 40 km east of Shibam is another historic city, Tareem, which is 735 km east of San'a. It is known as 'the city of mosques'.

Najran: It is another historic city of ancient Yemen. It lies about 250 km north of San'a. Now it is a part of Saudi Arabia. Najran is a green region and was once upon a time a transit point of trade caravans.[3]

According to Yaqut Hamawi, it was named after Najran bin Zaidan bin Saba bin Yashjub bin Ya'rub bin Qahtan, the person who pioneered this settlement.[4]

In 9 AH (630 CE) a delegation of the Christians of Najran came to the Prophet ﷺ. The delegation consisted of sixty persons, twenty-four of them were the nobles of Najran. Three of them were the chiefs: one 'Aqib (Abdul-Maseeh) who was like a ruler, the second a Sayyed, named Aiham or Shurahbeel, who was responsible for their cultural and political

1 Al-Munjid Fil-'Alām: see under 'Ma'arib' and 'Saba'.

2 Mu'jam-ul-Buldān: see under 'Shaboh'.

3 Al-mufassal Fi Tareekh-il-Arab qabal-al-Islam: 2/507.

4 Mu'jam-ul-Buldān: see under 'Najran'.

Pillars of the throne of Queen bilqis - Ma'rib

affairs, and the third a bishop (named Abu Hārithah bin 'Alqamah) who was their spiritual and religious leader. They wanted to debate with the Prophet ﷺ some points of religion. Thereupon, Allah revealed some Verses (Al-Imran: Verses 33-36) denying the divinity of Jesus and challenging them to Mubāhala (invoking Allah's curse on the liar) in case they did not accept the Unity of God. They agreed to pay Jizyah (a small tax imposed on non-Muslims living in a Muslim state, exempting them from military service).[1]

Tareem (Hadhramaut)

Oasisaf Najran

Famous Wadis of Yemen

Wadi Najran: It flows in Najran, north of Yemen. It dries up into the Empty Quarter, south of Mt. Tuwaiq.

A view of River Hujr

River Hujr: South of Hadhramaut, it is the only river of the Arabian Peninsula which flows round the year but it is not more than 100 km long.

Wadi Hadhramaut

Wadi Hadhramaut: It lies in the northeast of Hadhramaut. As the streams flowing down from the north and the south join it, it is called Wadi Al-Maseelah which falls into the Arabian Sea near Saihoot, a town in Mahrah, the eastern province of Yemen. Saihoot lies on the coast of the Arabian Sea, 522 km off Mukalla and 1318 km off San'a. Boats are also built here.[2]

Shibām (wadi Hadhramaut)

1 Ar-raheeq-ul-Makhtum, PP. 453, 454; and As-Seerat-un-Nabawiya by Abi Shahbah 2/546-548.
2 Al-Ma'rafa: Wikipedia (Encyclopedia).

Hudhoor-un-Nabi Shu'aib Yemen

5-Hijaz

To the Muslims, Hijaz (حجاز) is the most important region, spiritually, economically and culturally. From here the sun of Islam rose. Here are Islam's holiest places: Makkah, the birth-place of the Prophet ﷺ and the place where Qur'ān was revealed the first time, and Madinah where the Prophet was buried.

Hijaz is bordered in the east by Nejd, in the west by Tihāmah, in the north by Syria, and in the south by Yemen. Hijaz is, in fact, a mountainous range called Jibal Sarat which begins from southern Syria (River Yarmūk) and ends up in Najran (border of Yemen). There are a number of valleys here which turn into rivulets during the rainy season. It is called Hijaz because it is a barrier (Arabic: Hajiz حاجز) between Nejd and Tihamah.[1]

Hijaz, from east to west, is 350 mi (560 km) wide. Tihāmah is popularly considered to be a part of Hijaz while some scholars include even Tabūk and Palestine within the borders of Hijaz. The mountainous range of Jibal Sarat is said to be the backbone of the Arabian Peninsula. Some of its summits, as we move towards Yemen, are quite high where it snows in winter.

1 Tareekh-ul-Islam by Hasan Ibrāhīm: 1/10.

High mountains of Hijaz

The well-known summit *"Hudhoor-un-Nabi Shu'aib"* west of San'a is 3760 m high.[1] But this mountainous range drops down in height, relatively, as it approaches Makkah, then again begins rising higher up as it moves towards Tā'if. Jabal Kara, between Makkah and Tā'if, is 2000 m high.[2]Likewise, Jabal Radwa, between Madinah and Yanbu', is 1814 m high. Still another summit of Jibal Sarat, between Al-Baha and Tā'if, is 2595 m high. Still another summit of Jibal Sarat, in the northwest of Abha, rises to a height of 2910 m.[3]

Presently, Hijaz has been divided into several provinces: Tabūk, Madinah, Makkah, Al-Bahah, 'Aseer and Jazan, while a part of it has been included within the province of Najran.[4]The largest coastal city of Hijaz is Jeddah (or Jiddah) which serves as a port for Makkah. The second largest seaport town is Yanbu' which serves Madinah.[5]

In praise of the people of Hijaz

The Prophet ﷺ said in praise of the natives of Hijaz:

«غِلَظُ الْقُلُوبِ وَالْجَفَاءُ فِي الْمَشْرِقِ وَ الإِيمَانُ فِي أَهْلِ الْحِجَازِ»

"Hardness of heart and rudeness are in the people of the east while faith is in the people of Hijaz."[6]

Main historic cities of Hijaz are Makkah, Madinah, and Tā'if.

1 Atlas Al-Mamlaka Al-Arabia As-Saudia Wal-'Alam P. 17, 19.
2 Makkah Wal-Madinah Fil-Jahilia Wa 'Ahd-ir-Rasool, P.20, 21.
3 Atlas Mamlaka Al-Arabia As-Saudia Wal-'Alam, P. 17, 19.
4 Op.cit., P. 15,17,19.
5 Tareek Ardh-ul-Qur'ān (Kamil): 1/81.
6 Sahīh Muslim; 53.

Makkah

Makkah, a city sited on dry and barren mountains, was founded by Prophet Abraham ﷺ (Arabic: Ibrāhīm). According to Sayyad Suleman Nadvi "This city is the foundation of an old prophet (Abraham), the refuge of a young prophet (Ishmael/Ismā'īl), and the birth-place of an orphan prophet (Muhammad)ﷺ."[1] May Allah bless them all.

Makkah lies at latitude 21 degrees 25 minutes N and longitude 39 degrees 49 minutes E. It is nearly 300 m above sea level. It lies in Wadi Ibrāhīm (the Valley of Abraham) surrounded on all sides by mountains. To the west of Makkah is Mt. Qu'aiqi'an to the southeast is Mt. Thaur, and to the south of it Mt. Kudayy. To the east of it is 420 m high Mt. Abu Qubais, the one nearest to the House of God. Behind it is Mt. Khandamah.[2]

1 Tareekh Ardh-ul-Qur'an (Kamil): 1/81.
2 Al-Munjid Fil-'Alam, P. 21.

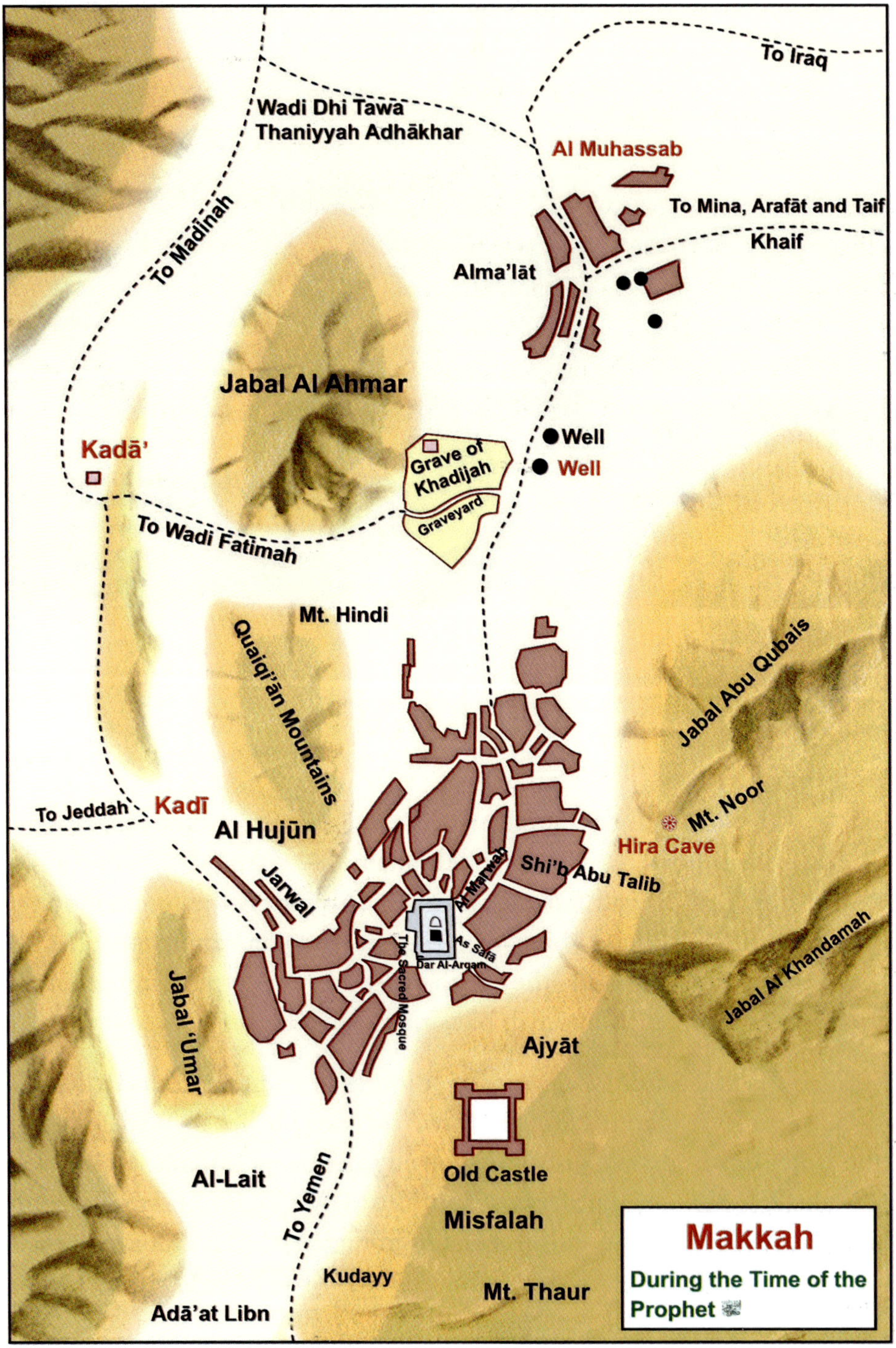
To Iraq
Wadi Dhi Tawa
Thaniyyah Adhākhar
Al Muhassab
To Mina, Arafāt and Taif
Khaif
To Madinah
Alma'lāt
Jabal Al Ahmar
Well
Well
Kadā'
Grave of Khadijah
Graveyard
To Wadi Fatimah
Mt. Hindi
Quaiqi'ān Mountains
Jabal Abu Qubais
To Jeddah
Kadī
Al Hujūn
Mt. Noor
Hira Cave
Jarwal
Al Marwah
Shi'b Abu Talib
As Safa
Dar Al-Arqam
The Sacred Mosque
Jabal Al Khandamah
Jabal 'Umar
Ajyāt
Old Castle
Al-Lait
To Yemen
Misfalah
Kudayy
Mt. Thaur
Adā'at Libn
Makkah
During the Time of the Prophet

Map.5

In the northwest of Makkah stands Mt. Al-Hajūn. It was from the direction of the Kada' ridge (presently *Ree'al-Hajūn*), that the Prophet ﷺ entered the city on the eve of the Conquest of Makkah. Mt. Hira, in the northeast of Makkah, is 642 m above sea level while Mt. Thaur, 728 m high, is 4.123 km off the House of Allah. The settlement of Makkah is stretched lengthwise like a crescent.

The southern part of the Valley of Makkah is called Bathā' (بطحاء) Quraish or just Bathā'. The low-lying settlement, below the Sacred Mosque (المسجد الحرام), is called *Masfalah* while the upper part is called *Mu'allat* or *Al-Mu'alla*. To the east lies Shi'b Ali (Shi'b Abi Tālib) which is connected with Makkah via *"Aqabah"* (meaning 'ridge'). It was called in the pre-Islamic age of Ignorance as Shi'b Bani Hashim.[1]

Mt. Al-Hujūn

Jabal Kada'

Mt. Qu'aiqi'an

Jabal Abu Qubais

The name 'Makkah'

As to the literal meaning of Makkah, there are different opinions:

The word is derived from Makak which means: to put an end to. Since Makkah puts an end to sins, the city was named Makkah.

1 Tareekh-ul-Arab Fil-Jahilia, P, 349, 350; Mu'jam-ul-Buldan: see under 'Makkah'.

The word means: to attract, to absorb. The city is so named because it attracts people from all over the world.

Makkah means 'a place of little water'. Since there is a paucity of water there, it is called Makkah.[1]

Names of Makkah

This holy city has fifty names.[2] The Qur'ān mentions some of its names like *Makkah, Bakkah, Qaryah, Umm-ul-Qura* and *Al-Balad-ul-Ameen*.

"Bakkah" in Surah Āl-'Imrān

﴿إِنَّ أَوَّلَ بَيْتٍ وُضِعَ لِلنَّاسِ لَلَّذِي بِبَكَّةَ مُبَارَكًا وَهُدًى لِّلْعَالَمِينَ﴾

"Surely, the first House of worship appointed for mankind was that at Bakkah, full of blessing, and a guidance for Al-Ālamīn mankind and Jinn."[3]

"Umm-ul-Qura" (ام القرىٰ) in Sura Al-An'am

1 At-Tafseer-ul-Kabeer Li'r-Razi: Āl-'Imrān, 3: 96.
2 Shifa'-ul-Gharam: 1/48-53.
3 Āl-'Imrān, 3:96.

The Qur'ān refers to Makkah as Umm-ul-Qura' (the mother of the settlements or towns) in the following Verse:

﴿وَلِتُنذِرَ أُمَّ ٱلْقُرَىٰ وَمَنْ حَوْلَهَا﴾

"That you may warn the Mother of Towns and those around her."[1]

"Qaryah" (قرية) in Surah An-Nahl

﴿وَضَرَبَ ٱللَّهُ مَثَلًا قَرْيَةً كَانَتْ ءَامِنَةً مُّطْمَئِنَّةً﴾

"And Allah puts forward the example of a township (قرية) *that dwelt secure and well-content."*[2]

"Makkah" in Surah Al-Fat'h

﴿وَهُوَ ٱلَّذِى كَفَّ أَيْدِيَهُمْ عَنكُمْ وَأَيْدِيَكُمْ عَنْهُم بِبَطْنِ مَكَّةَ مِنۢ بَعْدِ أَنْ أَظْفَرَكُمْ عَلَيْهِمْ﴾

"And He it is Who withheld their hands from you and your hands from them in the midst of Makkah, after He had made you victors over them."[3] *(Here is a hint at the peaceful Conquest of Makkah).*

"Al-Balad" (البلد) in Surah Al-Balad

Allah swore by this city (Al-Balad):

﴿لَآ أُقْسِمُ بِهَٰذَا ٱلْبَلَدِ﴾

"I swear by this city."[4]

Here the city refers to Makkah.

"Al-Balad-ul-Ameen" in Surah At-Teen:

﴿وَٱلتِّينِ وَٱلزَّيْتُونِ ۝١ وَطُورِ سِينِينَ ۝٢ وَهَٰذَا ٱلْبَلَدِ ٱلْأَمِينِ﴾

"By the fig, and the olive. By Mount Sinai, and by this city of security (Makkah)."[5]

Writing about the history and etymology of Makkah, Sayyed Suleman Nadvi says: "The word Arab was coined in the tenth century BC. The

1 Al-An'am, 6:92.
2 An-Nahl, 16:112.
3 Al-Fat'h, 48:24.
4 Al-Balad, 90:1.
5 At:Teen, 95:1-3.

word Hijaz came later. Its another name is "Makaraba" which we find in the writings of Ptolemy in the second century CE. It is for this reason that Torah (hebrew) refers to it as *"Madbar"* meaning 'desert'. The Qur'ān called it (in the words of Abraham) 'a land without vegetation' because it had no name by then..... The word Arab also means, literally: desert. Hence, *Madbar* (desert), land without vegetation, and Arab are synonymous words. Therefore, Torah's statement "Ishmeal settled in a desert" means that he settled in Arabia.[1]

Ibn Abbas, the Prophet's companion, says: The area from Fajj to Tan'eem is called Makkah and the area from the House of Allah to Batha' is called Bakkah. Imam Shu'bah, quoting Ibrāhīm Nakh'ī, says: "Bakkah is the name of the House of Allah and the Mosque". That is also the opinion of Imam Zuhri. According to 'Ikramah and Maimoon bin Mehran, the word Bakkah applies to the House of Allah and the surrounding area. The area outside is Makkah. But Abu Malik, Abu Salih, Ibrāhīm Nakh'i, Atiyyah 'Aufi, and Muqatil bin Hay'yan say that only the House of Allah *(Baitullah)* is Bakkah and the rest of the city is Makkah.[2]Around Bakkah, the House of Allah, is that specific place where the rite of circumambulation may be performed. The area outside the Sacred Mosque is not Bakkah but Makkah.[3]

Superiority of Makkah

Allah has exalted Makkah above all other cities and conferred on it a superiority he gave to no city, a fact frequently mentioned in Qur'ān. That Makkah is superior in the sight of Allah is also clear from the words the Prophet ﷺ spoke while addressing Makkah before he left for Madinah:

«وَاللّٰهِ! إِنَّكِ لَخَيْرُ أَرْضِ اللّٰهِ وَأَحَبُّ أَرْضِ اللّٰهِ إِلَى اللّٰهِ وَلَوْلَا أَنِّي أُخْرِجْتُ مِنْكِ مَا خَرَجْتُ»

"By Allah, you are the best land and the one dearest to Allah. If I had not been turned out of it, I would not leave it."[4]

1 Tareekh Ard-il-Qur'ān (Kamil): 2/37.
2 Tafseer Ibn Kathīr: Āl 'Imrān, 3: 96.
3 Tafseer-ut-Tabari: Āl 'Imrān, 3:96.
4 Al-Mustadrak lil-Hakim: 3/7, Hadīth: 4270.

Its greatest merit is that here the House of Allah is sited, the first house exclusively built for the worship of Allah. Around it is the Sacred Mosque where one prayer is better than a prayer said elsewhere, as Jabir (ﷺ) narrated from the Messenger of Allah (ﷺ):

«صَلَاةٌ فِي مَسْجِدِي هٰذَا أَفْضَلُ مِنْ أَلْفِ صَلَاةٍ فِيمَا سِوَاهُ إِلَّا الْمَسْجِدَ الْحَرَامَ، وَ صَلَاةٌ فِي الْمَسْجِدِ الْحَرَامِ أَفْضَلُ مِنْ مِّائَةِ أَلْفِ صَلَاةٍ»

"A prayer in this mosque of mine is better than one thousand prayers elsewhere except the Sacrosanct Mosque, and a prayer in the Sacred Mosque is better than one hundred thousand prayers."[1]

Sanctity of Makkah

Makkah is called *'Al-Balad-ul-Haram'* (the sacrosanct or inviolable land or sanctuary or the sanctum). According to a Hadith, Makkah has been a sanctuary since the creation of the universe. Abu Hurairah relates that when Allah gave the Prophet ﷺ victory over the Makkans, he extolled Allah and said: Allah barred the elephants from reaching Makkah but He gave His Messenger and the believers control over Makkah. No one was allowed to violate the sanctity of Makkah before me nor will anyone be ever allowed to do so after me. It was allowed for me only briefly. [Beware!] let no bird or animal of prey be threatened and made to run away. Let no thorny tree be cut off. Let no thing lying (on ground etc.) be picked up except by the announcer. He may pick it up. One, whose kinsman is killed, may choose the better (of the two courses: slaying of the killer or blood money). (That is, he may choose whatever he thinks it to be better for him). Abbas ﷺ pleaded: 'O Messenger of Allah ﷺ, exempt *Idhkhar* (a kind of sweet-smelling grass) because we use it in our homes and on grave sites'. He said: "Yes, *Idhkhar* is exempted."[2]

Limits of Haram (the Sanctuary)

Abraham (Ibrāhīm عليه السلام) was the first person to define the limits of

1 Musnad Ahmad: 3/343.
2 Sahīh-ul-Bukhāri: 2434; Sahıh Muslim: 1355.

Hudood-e-Haram (wadi Tan'eem)

the Sanctuary (the sacred precincts) by Allah's leave. He put up boundary stones defining the limits of the Sanctuary, according to the instruction given to him by Archangel Gabriel. They remained unchanged until Qusayy renewed them. Then in the year of the Conquest of Makkah, the Prophetﷺ charged Tameem bin Asad Khuzā'i to reconstruct them. Since then no change was made in them till 'Umar bin Khattābرضي الله عنه appointed four men from Quraish who renewed those stones.[1]

Makkah and the area around it, all are sacrosanct but the sacred precincts are not at the same distance from Ka'bah. The limits have been clearly marked on all the highways leading to Makkah. Here are the details:

1. In the west, on Jiddah Road, Shumaisi (formerly known as Huddaibiyyah) is the limit. It is 22 km away from Makkah.
2. In the south, on the way from Tihamah to Yemen, the place called Ada'at-o-Libn (أضاءة لِبن) is the limit. Ada`at means: earth, while Libn is the name of a hill 12 km off Makkah.
3. In the east, the western edge of Wadi 'Uranah (عُرَنَة) which is 15 km off Makkah.
4. In the northeast, a settlement called *Shara'i'-ul-Mujahideen* on the road to Ji'irranah (جِعِرَّانَة). It is 16 km away from Makkah. The settlement is named after those Mujahideen who were with king Abdul-Azīz Al-Saud in the conquest of Hijaz.[2]

1 Akhbar Makkah Li'l-Azraqi: 2/684.
2 Wikipedia (Encyclopedia)

5. In the north, the place called Tan'eem (تنعيم) which lies 7 km off Makkah on *Tareeq-ul-Madinah (Tareeq-ul-Hijrah)*.[1]

Today the city of Makkah is expanding beyond these limits.

Mount Thaur

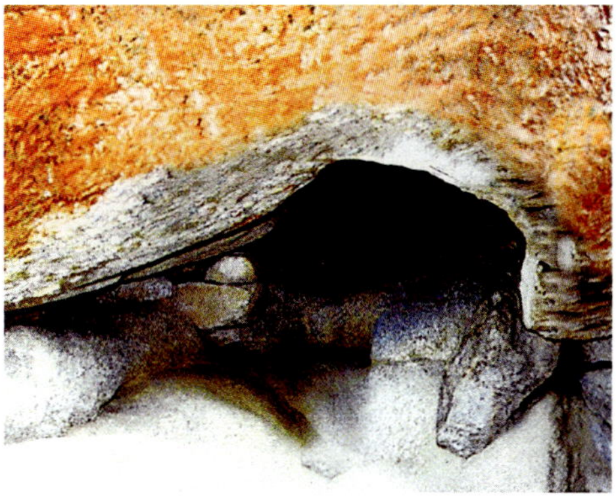

The cave of Thaur

Famous Wadis (rivelets), Mountains and Places of Makkah

Mount Thaur (جبل ثور)

It is nearly 3 km off the old Makkah. Here is the cave of *Thaur* where the Prophet ﷺ and Abu Bakr ﷺ stayed three nights on their way to Madinah. The cave is 18 spans long (4.014 m) and 11 spans across (2.053 m). One mouth of the cave is two-thirds of a span (15.2 cm) wide and the other five spans (1.15 m) wide.[2]

Mount Hira (جبل حرا)

It is also called Jabal Nūr. It is about 4 km away from the Sacred Mosque. It is located in the northeast of Makkah, on the left-hand side of Mina-Arafāt highway. The cave of Hira is in one of the sides of the mountain, about 60 m below its summit. About half a meter thick, 1.75 m wide (max.) and 3-4 m long gray planks of stones of varying sizes are propped against the mountain in a way that gives the mouth of the cave the look of an isosceles triangle, each side of which is 2.5 m long and the base 1 m

1 Tareekh Makkah Mukarrama, P.19
2 Travelogue Ibn Jubayr Al-Andalusi, P. 54

The cave of Hira

Jabal Noor (Mount Hira)

long. Inside, the cave is 2 - 2.5 m long, its height diminishing gradually as it proceeds further along.[1]

Arafāt (عرفات) or Arafah (عرفه)

Southeast of Makkah, at the foot of Jabal ar-Rahmāt, lies the plain of Arafāt (عرفات) or Arafah (عرفة) where the Hajj pilgrims spend the day, the fundamental rite of Hajj. The Prophet ﷺ stayed here on 9 Zul Hajjah from the time the sun crossed the meridian until sunset. The plain is about 22 km away from Makkah.

The boundary of the Arafāt plain extends from wadi 'Uranah, Thaubah and Nimrah plain to Zul-Majaz and the last stopping-place of Maziman. Among the famous places included within the Arafat plain are wadi Nimrah and Jabal ar-Rahmah.

There are several opinions as to why the plain of Arafāt has been so named. For example, a narration from Ali (رضي الله عنه) as quoted in Musannaf Abd ur-Razzaq says: Allah, the Exalted, sent Gabriel to Prophet Abraham عليه السلام. Both performed Hajj together. When Abraham came to Arafāt, he said: *"qad 'arafto"* (I have recognized it) because he had already visited this place before. So the plain is called Arafah (عرفة). Other narrations attributed to Ibn Abbas رضي الله عنهما, Ata bin Abi Ribah and Abu Mijlaz رحمه الله give the same account.[2]

Imam Razi quotes eight opinions explaining why it has been so named. One of them says: When Allah sent Adam and Eve to the earth, they met

1 An-Hazoor ke Naqshi-i-Qadam Pa (Haram-i-Makkah): 3/152.
2 Al-Musannaf li-Abdur-Razzaq: 5/ 96; Tafseer Ibn Kathīr: Al-Baqarah, 2:198.

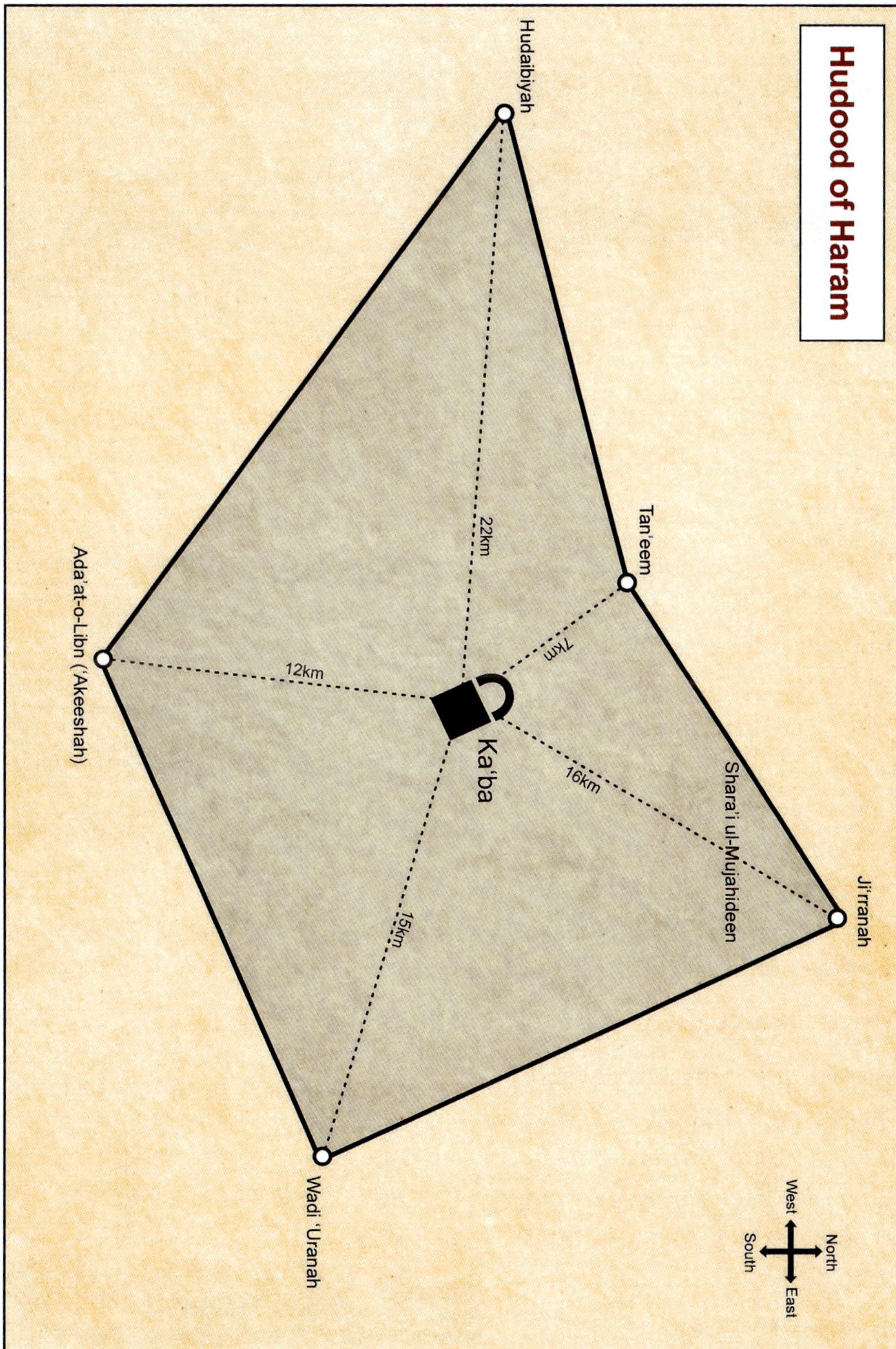
Hudood of Haram
Hudaibiyah
Tan'eem
Ji'rranah
Shara'i ul-Mujahideen
Ka'ba
22km
7km
12km
16km
15km
Ada'at-o-Libn ('Akeeshah)
Wadi 'Uranah
West
North
South
East

Map.6

Jabal ar-Rahmah (Arafāt)

in the plain of Arafāt after years but they recognized each other. That is why the plain is called *Arafah* (Arabic for recognition).[1]

Mina (مِنٰى)

Masjid-e-Khaif

The pilgrims are obliged to stay here on the night of Arafāt until sunrise, return to Mina on the Day of Sacrifice *(Yaum-un-Nahr)*, stay here the remaining *tashreeq* days, including their nights. Here the pilgrims strike *Jamarāt* with pebbles. The boundary of Mina extends from the edge of Wadi Muhassir to the valley close to the last *Jamarāh* in the direction of Makkah. It is called *Jamarah Aqabah*.[2]

Muzdalafah (مزدلفه)

Al-Mash'ar Al-Haram Mosque

Muzdalafah is the place where pilgrims are obliged to stay, after returning from Arafāt, the night between Arafāt and 9th and 10th of Zu'lhijja. It is located between Arafāt and

1 At-Tafseer-ul-Kabeer Li'r-Razi: Al-Baqarah, 2:198.
2 Mu'Jam-ul-Buldan; see under 'Mina'.

the two narrow mountainous paths of wadi Muhassir. Muzdalafah is also called *Jam'un* (جمعٌ) because pilgrims gather here. Close to it is *Al-Mash'ar-ul-Harām*, a hilly place. Qur'ān refers to it:

﴿فَإِذَآ أَفَضۡتُم مِّنۡ عَرَفَٰتٖ فَٱذۡكُرُواْ ٱللَّهَ عِندَ ٱلۡمَشۡعَرِ ٱلۡحَرَامِۖ﴾

"Then when you leave Arafāt, remember Allah (by glorifying His Praises, i.e. prayers and invocations."[1]

Wadi Muhassir

Pilgrims are obliged to cross this place quickly. It is the name of a valley between Mina and Muzdalafah but it is not a part of either of them. It is also called Wadi Muhallal (وادی مُهلّل). Pilgrims walk fast through this place while saying *Takbeer (Allah-o-Akbar)*. That was also the tradition of the Prophet ﷺ. It is the place where the 'Owners of the Elephants' were punished by Allah. About such places where Allah punished rebellious folks, the Prophet's instruction is:

"Do not enter the homes (region) of people who were chastised by Allah except while weeping. If you cannot weep, don't enter them lest you should suffer that punishment which was their lot."[2]

Wadi Nakhlah *(Nakhlah ash-Shāmiyyah, Nakhlah al-Yamāniyyah)*
Two Wadis of Banu Hudhail are called *Nakhlah: Nakhlah ash-Shāmiyyah (Batn Nakhlah)* and *Nakhlah al-Yamāniyyah*. Their confluence is about 43

1 Tareekh Makkah Al-Mukarrama, P. 123, 124; Mu'jam-ul-Buldan: see under 'Muzdalafah'.
2 Sahīh-ul-Bukhāri: 4702; and Sahīh Muslim: 2980.

Wadi Nakhla ash-Shāmiyyah

km off Makkah in the northeast near *Batn Murr* and *Saboohah* (a branch of *Nakhlah al-Yamāniyyah*). *Nakhlah al-Yamāniyyah* flows down *Qarn-ul-Manāzil* known also as *Qarn-uth-Tha'alib. Qarn-ul-Manāzil* is 80 km east of Makkah. *Nakhlah-ash-Shāmiyyah* joins wadi Fatimah (near *Ar-Rayyān*) which crosses the Jeddah-Makkah highway and runs down to Tihamah. *Nakhlah al-Yamāniyyah*, generally known as *Wadi Nakhlah*, joins *Nakhlah-ash-Shāmiyyah* a few kilometers north of *Az-Zeema*. On his way back from Tā'if, the Prophet ﷺ stayed in *Nakhlah* where Jinn listened to him as he recited the Qur'ān. Sayyad Maudoodi writes: That place was either *Az-Zeemah* or *as-Sail al-Kabeer*. Both these places are in Wadi Nakhlah. There is a distance of about 35 km between them". In Rajab, 2 AH, the Expedition of Abdullah bin Jah'sh took place, one of the causes leading to the Battle of Badr.

Wadi Hunain ***(Sharā'i')*:** This wadi (rivulet), about 30 km east of Makkah, is counted among the Wadis of Makkah. Nowadays it is called Ash-Sharā'i' but its upper part is called Hunain to this day. Its water flows down via *Wadi Al-Mughammas* into *Sail 'Uranah*. As we travel from Makkah to Ta'if via *Tareeq-ul-Yamāniyyah*, we come to Wadi ash-Sharā'i', 28 km off *Masjid al-Harām* (the Sacred Mosque of Makkah). Ash-Sharā'i' is the name of a stream and a settlement. The Wadi is named after them. This stream was formerly known as *al-Mushash*. It was here where Queen Zubaidah built a canal, named after her (*Nahr Zubaidah* or Zubaidah Canal), running up to Makkah. The canal dried up later. Today the word Hunain is known only to a few persons here.[1]

Wadi Hunain (Sharā'i')

Al-Abtah (الابطح): It is the site where Qusayy (Chief of Quraish), Khuza'ah

1 Mu'jam al-Ma'alim Al-Jughrafiyyah Fis-Seerat-in-Nabawiyyah, P.107.

and Bakr fought during the pre-Islamic Age. The area right from the bend of Wadi Makkah up to Al-Hajoon is called al-Abtah. From there onward to the Sacred Mosque, the area is called al-Bathā'. Both, are included within *Al-Mu'alla*. In Makkah there are several ridges whose waters join together in Abtah. The road from the bend of Makkah up to *Ree'-ul-Hajoon* is called *Shari'-ul-Abtah*. The pilgrims going from the Sacred Mosque to Mina pass by this road.[1]

Al-Bathā' (البطحاء): The word Bathā' is applied to any Wadi through which flood waters pass, leaving the earth sandy, but scholars use this word to refer to that part which lies between Al-Hajoon and the Sacred Mosque of Makkah. That included *Al-Ghazah* and *Sooq-ul-Lail*. It is also called Bathā' Makkah. There are no remains of it now. There was also once an area called Bathā' Quraish near Mt. Thaur.[2]

Wadi 'Uranah and Nimrah Mosque

Wadi 'Uranah: It is close to Nimrah Mosque (Arafah Mosque). It is said that if the wall of Nimrah Mosque facing Ka'bah topples down, it will fall into this Wadi. It is also said that this wall and the oratory (place of worship of the prayer-leader) are located in Arafah but, in fact, they are outside it. In Wadi 'Uranah, before Arafat, there are fourteen wide bridges within a one-kilometer area. In Muharram, 4 AH, the Expedition of Abdullah bin 'Unais took place near 'Uranah. The Wadi of 'Uranah is, in fact, a large stream which rises in Mughammas and passes, west of Arafāt, by Nimrah Mosque. A little further down, it is joined by Wadi Nu'mān. From there onwards it is called Wadi 'Uranah which flows down south of Makkah and thence in the direction of the west till, when it has reached a place 30 miles

1 Mu'jam-ul-Ma'alim Al-Jughrafia Fis-Seerat-in-Nabawiyyah, P. 13, 14 .
2 Op.cit., P. 46.

south of Jeddah, falls into the sea.[1]

Masjid-e-'Ayshah (Tan'eem)

Batn Sarif

Thaniyyat-o-Ghazāl

Ar-Rajee' (الرجيع): It is the name of a spring which is now called al-Watiyyah (الوطيه). It flows down the slope of Harrah Bani Jābir, north of the stream named Shāmiyyah Ibn Hamadi, about 70 km north of Makkah. Wadi shāmiyyah is the lower part of al-Hada Wadi *(Hada Ash-Shamr)*. There is a town here called Shāmiyyah. Al-Watiyyah lies 8 km east of 'Asfan. Al-Watiyyah is so named because here the Prophet's she-camel set her foot. Its root وَطِئَ means 'trampled the earth'. Wadi Shāmiyyah, flowing on the right-hand side of Makkah-'Usfan Road, reaches upwards Dhahban and falls down into the sea. It was this place where the tribes of Adal and Qārah slew the Prophet's companions, Marthad bin Abi Marthad and his comrades-in-arms, in the Tragedy of Rajee' (Safar, 4 AH).[2]

Dajanan (ضجنان) *(Bahrat-ul-Muhsiniyyah)*: Its name occurs in the Hadeeth describing the Prophet's Night Journey *(Hadeeth-ul-isrā')*. Dajanan is a rocky area 54 km north of Makkah. The Madinah Highway *(Tareeq-ul-Madinah)* passes through it. Today it is known as *Bahrat-ul-Muhsiniyyah*.[3]

Amaj: It is an agricultural valley beside the main road, 100 km north of Makkah. The town of Amaj is two miles away south of Khulais. When the

1 Op.cit. P. 205.
2 Op.cit. p. 138.
3 Op.cit. P183.

Prophet ﷺ migrated to Madinah, he passed through this area. In those days it was settled by Banu Kinanah but now Banu Harb live here.[1] Amaj and Ghurrān are two Wadis which rise in Harrah Bani Sulaim and fall into the sea.[2]

Batn Sarif: A Wadi which rises near Ji'rranah and flows down 12 km north of Makkah. Here the Mother of the Believers, Maimoonah bint Harith رضي الله عنها, died in 38 AH and was buried here.[3]

Marr-uz-Zahrān (Wadi Fātimah): It is a large Wadi of Hijaz and is fed by *Nakhlatain* (the two *Nakhlas* mentioned earlier). It runs 22 km north of Makkah and falls, approx. 20 km south of Jeddah, into the sea. Here are the settlements of Hadā' حداء (or Hadah حدا), Bahrah and Al-Jamoom. It is now called Wadi Fatimah.[4]

Al-Baidā' *(Thaniyyat-ut-Tan'eem)*: The name of this valley occurs in the Hadeeth relating to the Prophet's Night Journey (to Jerusalem). Here the road from Madinah descends into Wadi Fakh of Makkah. There is also the Mosque of Ayeshah here where pilgrims put on Ihram (two seamless woolen or linen sheets), providing they have some excuse justifying it. Thaniyyat-ut-Tan'eem is also called *Al-Makān-ul-Umrah* or *Umrat-ut-Tan'eem*. Today nobody knows it by the name of Al-Baidā'. Wadi at-Tan'eem crosses this valley and falls into Wadi Yā'jaj which, in turn, falls into Wadi

Wadi Ghurrān

Wadi Fatimah

Wadi Amaj

1 Op.cit.. P 32; and Mu'jam Mas-Ta'jama: 3/956.
2 Mu'jam-ul-Buldān: see under 'Amaj'.
3 Atlas Al-Hadīth An-Nabawi, P. 72.
4 Mu'jam Al-Ma'alim Al-Jughrāfiyyah Fis-Seerat-in-Nabawiyyah, P.288; and Atlas Al-Mamlaka Al-Arabiia As-Saudia, Plate 12.

Marr-uz-Zahrān.[1]

Fakh: A large[2] wadi between at-Tan'eem and the Inviolable Mosque. It is also called az-Zāhir. Here Bilāl ﷺ had a fever and he mentioned it in one of his verses.

Thaniyyat-o-Ghazāl: It is the name of a valley north of 'Usfān. On the other side of it is Wadi Ghurrān.

Thaniyyat-o-Laft (al-Fait): Lying opposite *Thaniyyat-o-Ghazāl,* this valley is called now *Thaniyyat-ul-Fait.* It is over 30 km north of Khulais. Now sand dunes have blocked its passage.

Ghurrān: It is a large Wadi between Amaj and 'Usfān. We come across it 87 km off Makkah on way to Madinah. It is near Thaniyyat-o-Ghazāl.[3]

Ghadeer Khumm *(al-Ghurabah)*: Eight kilometers east of al-Juhfah, its modern name is Al-Ghurabah. Here are the settlements of the tribesmen of Khuza'ah and Kinanah. The Prophet ﷺ addressed the Yemeni delegation beside Ghadeer Khumm.[4]

---

1 Mu'jam-ul-Ma'alim Al-Gughrafiyyah Fis-Seerat-in-Nabawiya, P. 55 ,54.
2 Op.cit., P.234.
3 Op.cit P. 225.
4 Mu'jam-ul-Buldān: see under 'Khum'; and Atlas Al-Hadīth-in-Nabawi, P. 285.

Ghadeer Khumm (al-Ghurabah)

Madinah

Madinah is the city of the Prophet ﷺ. The Prophet himself gave it this name. Its old name was Yathrib. Now it is the capital of the province of the same name. Together with Makkah, the twin cities are called *Al-Haramain ash-Shareefain* (the two highly honourable places). In a Hadeeth reported by Abu Musa Ash'ari رضي الله عنه, the Prophet (ﷺ) says:

"I dreamt that I was leaving Makkah for a place full of date-palms. I thought that perhaps it was Yamāmah or Hajar (هَجَر) but it is Madinah, that is, Yathrib (يثرب)."[5]

According to Abul-Qasim Zujaji, a man named Yathrib bin Qāyinah or Qaniyah, a descendant of Shem, son of Noah عليه السلام, laid the foundation of this city which later came to be named after him.[6]

Ptolemy's geography refers to it as Jathripa. Probably it was also called 'Madinah Yathrib' because Stephen of Byzantium wrote it as Medinta

5 Sahīh-ul-Bukhāri, 3622; and Sahīh Muslim: 2272.

6 Al-Mufassal Fi Tareekh-il-Arab Qabl-al-Islam: 4/128.

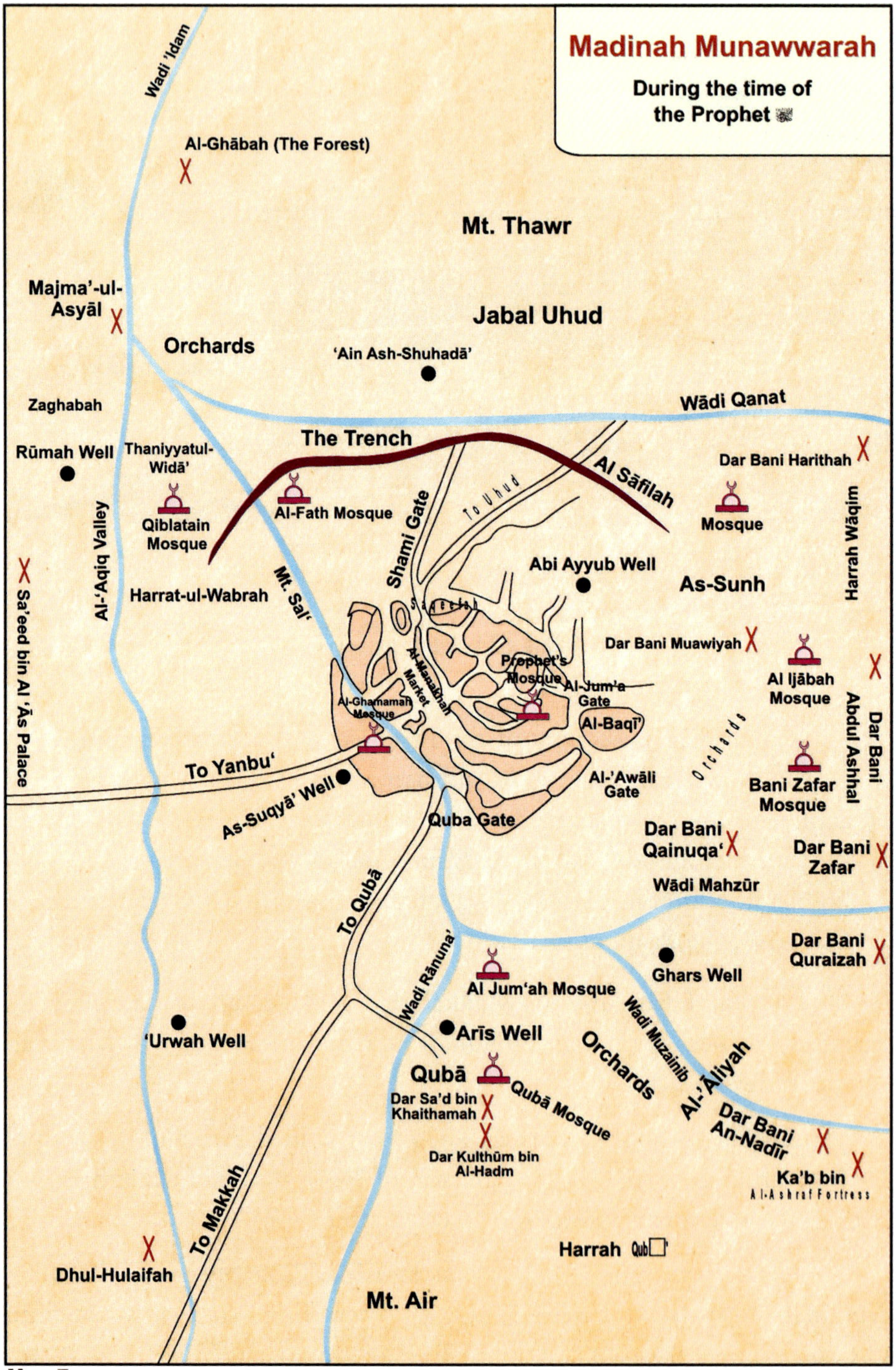

Madinah Munawwarah
During the time of the Prophet ﷺ
Wadi 'Idam
Al-Ghābah (The Forest)
Mt. Thawr
Majma'-ul-Asyāl
Jabal Uhud
Orchards
'Ain Ash-Shuhadā'
Zaghabah
Wādi Qanat
The Trench
Rūmah Well
Thaniyyatul-Widā'
Al Sāfilah
Dar Bani Harithah
Qiblatain Mosque
Al-Fath Mosque
Shami Gate
To Uhud
Mosque
Harrah Wāqim
Al-'Aqiq Valley
Sa'eed bin Al 'Ās Palace
Harrat-ul-Wabrah
Mt. Sal'
Abi Ayyub Well
As-Sunh
Dar Bani Muawiyah
Prophet's Mosque
Al-Jum'a Gate
Al Ijābah Mosque
Al-Ghamamah Mosque
Al-Baqi'
Dar Bani Abdul Ashhal
Orchards
To Yanbu'
As-Suqyā' Well
Al-'Awāli Gate
Bani Zafar Mosque
Quba Gate
Dar Bani Qainuqa'
Dar Bani Zafar
To Qubā
Wādi Mahzūr
Wadi Rānuna'
Al Jum'ah Mosque
Ghars Well
Dar Bani Quraizah
'Urwah Well
Arīs Well
Orchards
Wadi Muzainib
Al-'Āliyah
Qubā
Qubā Mosque
Dar Sa'd bin Khaithamah
Dar Bani An-Nadīr
Dar Kulthūm bin Al-Hadm
Ka'b bin Al-Ashraf Fortress
To Makkah
Dhul-Hulaifah
Harrah
Mt. Air

Map.7

which may be an abbreviation of Madinah Yathrib. In the parlance of southern Arabia, it was called 'Bikr' as the ancient inscriptions discovered in Ma'een (Yemen) mention. After the Migration, it was called Madinat-un-Nabi which was shortened by usage to just Madinah. The Prophet ﷺ gave the city some more names: *Tabah* and *Taibah*.[1] Both the words mean 'pure, clean'. The city was so named because it was cleansed of idolatry. Maybe, the name was changed because, literally, Yathrib means: reproach, corruption, evil, etc.

Yathrib and Madinah in the Qur'ān

Both the names, Yathrib and Madinah, occur in the Qur'ān.

In the Battle of Trench, when the Quraish of Makkah and other pagan tribes of Arabia attacked Madinah, the hypocrites did not help the Muslims, sat back in their homes and even tried to discourage the Muslims and dishearten them. The Qur'ān refers to it in the following Verse:

﴿ وَإِذْ قَالَت طَّآئِفَةٌ مِّنْهُمْ يَـٰٓأَهْلَ يَثْرِبَ لَا مُقَامَ لَكُمْ فَٱرْجِعُوا۟ ﴾

"And when a party of them said: "O people of Yathrib! there is no stand (possible) for you against the enemy attack!, therefore go back."[2]

Allah condemns the Hypocrites who deliberately lagged behind and did not take part in the Battle of Tabūk:

﴿ وَمِمَّنْ حَوْلَكُم مِّنَ ٱلْأَعْرَابِ مُنَـٰفِقُونَ ۖ وَمِنْ أَهْلِ ٱلْمَدِينَةِ ۖ مَرَدُوا۟ عَلَى ٱلنِّفَاقِ ﴾

"And among the bedouins around you, some are hypocrites, and so are some among the people of Al-Madinah who persist in hypocrisy."[3]

﴿ مَا كَانَ لِأَهْلِ ٱلْمَدِينَةِ وَمَنْ حَوْلَهُم مِّنَ ٱلْأَعْرَابِ أَن يَتَخَلَّفُوا۟ عَن رَّسُولِ ٱللَّهِ ﴾

"It was not becoming of the people of Al-Madinah and the bedouins of the neighbourhood to remain behind Allah's Messenger."[4]

Allah warns the hypocrites who plotted against the Muslims:

1 Atlas Seerat Nabawi, P. 154; and Al-Mufassal Fi tareekh-il-Arab Qabl-al-Islam 4/ 130 and Urdu Encyclopedia of Islam: 20/228.
2 Al-Ahzāb, 33:13.
3 At-Taubah, 9:101.
4 At-Taubah, 9:120.

﴿لَّئِن لَّمْ يَنتَهِ ٱلْمُنَٰفِقُونَ وَٱلَّذِينَ فِى قُلُوبِهِم مَّرَضٌ وَٱلْمُرْجِفُونَ فِى ٱلْمَدِينَةِ لَنُغْرِيَنَّكَ بِهِمْ
ثُمَّ لَا يُجَاوِرُونَكَ فِيهَآ إِلَّا قَلِيلًا﴾

"If the hypocrites, and those in whose hearts is a disease, and those who spread false news among the people in Al-Madinah stop not, We shall certainly let you overpower them, then they will not be able to stay in it as your neighbors but a little while."[1]

On way back home from the Battle of Banu Mustalaq, the chief of the hypocrites, Abdullah bin Ubayy, said words disparaging the Muslims. The Qur'ān condemns him and his associates:

﴿يَقُولُونَ لَئِن رَّجَعْنَآ إِلَى ٱلْمَدِينَةِ لَيُخْرِجَنَّ ٱلْأَعَزُّ مِنْهَا ٱلْأَذَلَّ ۚ وَلِلَّهِ ٱلْعِزَّةُ وَلِرَسُولِهِۦ
وَلِلْمُؤْمِنِينَ وَلَٰكِنَّ ٱلْمُنَٰفِقِينَ لَا يَعْلَمُونَ﴾

"They (hypocrites) say: 'If we return to Al-Madinah, indeed the more honourable will expel therefrom the mean. But honour, power and glory belong to Allah, and to His Messenger, and to the believers, but the hypocrites know not."[2]

For more information about the merits of Madinah, see the chapter of 'Merits of Madinah' next to 'Migration to Madinah' (Vol. 04).

Location of Madinah

Madinah lies in longitude 39 degrees 50 minutes East and in latitude 24 degrees 32 minutes North, north of the Tropic of Cancer. It is nearly 427 km north of Makkah'[3] 209 km east of Yanbu', and 600 m above sea level. Jabal Uhud is 4

1 Al-Ahzāb, 33:60.
2 Al-Munāfiqūn, 63:8.
3 Atlas Al-mamlaka Al-Arabia As-Saudia, P. 142.

km north of Madinah. Quba in the south, and Jabal 'Aeyr (عَير) 6 km off in the southwest. To the west of the city is Harrah Wabrah and to the east Harrah Wāqim. These Harrahs are vast planes full of black and burnt rocks spreading over several miles.[1]

Madinah: Streams, Wadis and Produce

In Madinah there are more than twenty-four springs, the most important of them being *"Ain-uz-Zarqā'"*. Around the city are a number of Wadis (rain-filled streams). Apart from Wadi Al-Aqeeq, the following Wadis are worthy of note: Rānoonā', Mahzoor, Bat'hān, Al-Qanāt, Muzainab (or Muzaineeb), and Naqma.

Wadi Qanāt: This Wadi starts from south of Mahd-uz-Zahb and runs in eastern Hijaz up to the middle of Harrat-un-Nar (presently called Harrah Kheybar) covering a large area. It is 200 km long. It is joined by ar-Rabazah, Rahrahān, and ash-Shuqran flowing down from the east. Wadi Qanāt, passing through Madinah and Uhud, joins Bat'hān and Aqeeq-ul-Madinah to make another Wadi called 'Idam (اضم). When Wadi Qanāt used to flow down from the direction of Nejd, its water would pass by Madinah for as long as one month.[2]

Wadi Qanāt

Wadi Rānoonā'

Wadi Rānoonā': It rises in the south from Mt. 'Aeyr and, passing by Harrah Quba', falls into wadi Bat'hān south of Al-Ghamām Mosque. The name of this wadi is not known to many. Anyhow, here, the Friday Mosque *(Masjid-ul-Jum'ah)* is quite well-known because it was the

1 Urdu Encyclopedia of Islam: 20/228.
2 Mu'jam-ul-Ma'alim Al-Jughrafiyyah Fi's-Seerat-in-Nabawiyyah, P. 257, 258.

mosque, in the settlement of Bani Sālim bin 'Auf, where the Prophet ﷺ led the Friday prayer during the Migration to Madinah. It was the first Friday congregation prayer offered in Madinah.[1]

Ain-uz-Zarqā

Wadi Bat'hān (بطحان)**:** It used to flow down from the direction of al-Harrah ash-Sharqiyyah, pass by west of the Prophet's Mosque, and join Wadi-al-Ateeq north of Jamādāt. Between Wadi Bat'hān and Wadi āl-Aqeeq lies Thaniyyāt-ul-Wabrah (Harrah-al-Gharbiyyah).[2]

Wadi Bat'hān

Bat'han is, in fact, formed by the confluence of the two other wadis, Mahzoor and Muzainib, besides which the Jewish tribes of Banu Quraizah and Banu Nadeer were settled respectively.

Wadi ar-Rummah: This wadi lies northeast of Madinah, near Harrah Fadak. It emerges al-Qaseem in the east. It is over 950 km long.

Wadi as-Safrā' (الصفراء)**:** It is one of the wadis of Hijaz lying on Tareeq-ul-Hājj (the route of pilgrims). There are many date-palm gardens here. The Prophet passed by it more than once. Here there is also a settlement named as-Safrā'. It rises in Mt. Waraqān, flows down by al-Musaijeed (old al-Munsarif المنصرف), and goes up to Yanbu'. Formerly, it was the dwelling place of the tribes of Juhainah, Ansar, Banu Fihr, Nahd and Radwa. Now it is known as Wadi Yalyal.[3]

Wadi-al-Qura (وادى القُرىٰ)**:** This important Wadi lies between Tabūk and Kheybar, on the old trade route going to Syria. It is now known as Wadi al-

1 Mu'jam Al-Ma'alim Al-Jughrafiyyah Fi's- Seerat-in-Nabawiyyah, P. 135.

2 Atlas Hadīth-un-nabawi, P. 70.

3 Mu'jam-ul-Buldan: see under 'As-Safrā', Mu'jam Ma'sta'jam: 3/836.

Wadi-al-Qura

Wadi as-Safrā'

Wadri ar-Rummah

'Ulā or Daidān. It falls into Wadi al-Jizl which joins Wadi al-Hamd. North of it is the town of al-'Ulā. Wadi as-Salsalah coming down from the right-hand side of al-'Ula also meets al-Jizl. Abul-a'la Maudoodi writes: Most probably, al-'Ulā is the place referred to as Wadi-ul-Qura in Hadeeths and books of history. Madā'in Salih is at a distance of about 30 miles from al-'Ulā.[1] After the Battle of Kheybar (Muharram, 7 AH), the Prophet ﷺ went to Wadi-ul-Qura and invited the Jews of that region to the fold of Islam. They were defeated in the ensuing two-day battle and surrendered.[2] Wadi-al-Qura' (al-'Ulā') is 350 km north of Madinah.

Wadi-al-Ghamrah: It is a tributary of Wadi al-Hamd. It rises in Harrah Kheybar, north of Kheybar. The town of Ghamrah, known formerly as *Al-Ghamr* or *Ghamr Marzooq*, is 195 km north of Madinah, on Kheybar-Taima' highway. In Rabee'-ul-Awwal, 6 AH, the Prophet ﷺ sent 'Ukashah bin Mihsan Asadi ﷺ to Ghamr Marzooq, a well of Banu Asad. It is called the Expedition of Ghamr.[3]

Wadi al-Aqeeq (وادى العقيق)**:** This Wadi flows exactly west of Madinah.

1 Safarnama 'Ard-il-Qur'ān (Kamil), 1/206.
2 Atlas Seerat-an-Nabawiyyah, P. 331 and Urdu Encyclopedia of Islam 22/566.
3 Atlas Seerat-an-Nabawiyyah, P. 292.

Wadi Buwāt

Wadi al-Aqeeq

Wadi-al-Ghamrah

Al-Aqeeq originally rises 140 km south of Madinah, and is fed by water from Jibāl Quds and Harrat-ul-Hijāz. The upper part of it is known as Wadi-an-Naqee'. When it reaches between Jabal 'Ayr (عير) and Hamrā'-ul-Asad, it is called al-Hasa and, further beyond Zul-Hulaifah, it is called al-Aqeeq. Harrat-ul-Wabrah lies between this Wadi and Madinah. In the north it joins Wadi al-Hamd (old اضم Idam). In the south of Madinah, Mt. 'Ayr is on the right bank of Wadi-al-Aqeeq. According to a Hadeeth reported by both Bukhāri and Muslim, al-Aqeeq is a blessed wadi where an angel asked the Prophet ﷺ to offer a prayer *(Salat)*. In this very Wadi, Bi'r Rūmah and Bi'r 'Urwah were sited. The place where the waters of the wadis of Mahzoor, Muzainib, Qanāt and Bat'hān join Wadi-al-Aqeeq is called *Majma'-al-Asyāl*. Another Wadi-al-Aqeeq rises in the neighbourhood of Tā'if, flows in the direction of the north, and falls into the swampy *Tās-ul-Uqool* (طاس العقول) between Makkah and Madinah.[1]

Wadi Buwāt (وادى بواط): This Wadi in the northwest of Madinah rises in Mt. Buwāt (now called *Jibal-ul-Ajrad*), passes east of Mt. Radwa, and flows down to *Yanbu'l-Nakhl*. Here the Battle of Buwāt took place in Rabee'-ul-Awwal, 2 AH. A town of the name of Buwāt is sited in Wadi-ul-Hamd, 42 km off Madinah, on the Kheybar Road.

In these wadis, there are a number of orchards and farmlands. The water of Madinah is light, cool, and sweet. Dates, pomegranates and grapes grow in abundance in the east of Madinah. In the south, in the black soil of Qubā', Awālī, and Aqeeq, wheat, barley, pomegranates, fruits and flowers of various hues grow.[2]

Yathrib and its inhabitants

Yāqūt Hamawi writes: "Those who pioneered farming and date-palm plantation were the descendants of 'Amlāq (عملاق) bin Arfakh'shad bin Sām bin Nūh عليه السلام. (Sām is Arabic for Shem and Nūh for Noah). They were called Amāleeq (عماليق).[3]Moses عليه السلام, accompanied by a few Israelites, performed Hajj and later went to Yathrib. There he noted

1 Urdu Encyclopedia of Islam: 13/414; Mu'jam Al-Ma'alim Al-Jughrafiyah Fi's Seerat-in-Nabawiyyah, P. 213.

2 Jughrafia shib'hi jazeerat-il-Arab li-Umar Radha Kahala, P. 147-137.

3 Mu'jam-ul-buldan: see under 'Madinah'.

some qualities of the town including that it was the town of the last Prophet of Allah as prophesied in Torah. Some of those who were with him decided to stay there. That place came to be called later on as Sūq Bani Qainuqā'. According to Ibn Zabala[1], Moses sent a military contingent to Hijaz to crush the rebellion of Amāleeq. Prophet David (Dāwūd) عليه السلام also launched an attack on the tribes of Sa'l and Fālij.[2]

How the Jews came to Yathrib

Most historians agree that the Jews of Yathrib were the descendants of those Israelites who migrated from Palestine and settled in Yathrib. Some of them were those who had fled from Palestine when Nebuchadnezzar attacked their country (585-86 BC). Later, when the Romans persecuted them in 70 CE and 135 CE, other Jewish tribes (Banu Quraizah, their kinsmen Banu Hadl and, later on, Banu Nadeer) migrated to Hijaz and settled in the valleys of Yathrib, Mahzoor and Muzainib.[3] Banu Qainuqā', who dwelt in the north of Mahzoor valley were the descendants of Prophet Joseph (Yusuf, عليه السلام). Abdullah bin Salām رضي الله عنه, the famed Companion who was a Rabbinical scholar, belonged to this very tribe.

1 Ibn Zabala (d. 180 AH/ 796 CE): His full name is Abdul-Hasan Muhammad bin Hasan bin Zabala Madani. Hadīth scholars declared him to be a liar. See taqreeb-ut-tahzeeb, P. 836;

2 Wafa'-ul-Wafa li's-Samhūdi: 1/157-159.

3 See Wafa'-ul-Wafa li's-Samhudi: 1/160, 161.

Fort of Ka'b bin Ashraf

The Jews had many 'Ātāms (singular 'utum اطم fort-like high-rise buildings) between Madinah and Qubā'. A well in Banu Nadeer's fort-like dwelling in Qubā' shared the same name of 'Quba'; the Jewish tribe of Banu Nadeer was led by a chief named Ka'b ibn Ashraf. According to Ibn Najjar, the 'Ātām of the Jews of Yathrib numbered fifty-nine, in all.[1] Fairs and bazaars were often held in front of those 'Ātām.

Hebrew was the mother tongue of the Jews, but as they settled in Yathrib, they gradually learnt Arabic and began using it in their daily life. Hebrew remained their religious and spiritual language. In addition to the Jews, there were also a few Christians in Madinah.

The Arab tribes of 'Aus lived in the south and east of Madinah, while those of Khazraj lived in the central and northern area. The Jews often pitted these two tribes one against the other in order to exploit them and divert their attention from the Jews themselves.

The most important marketplace of Madinah was Sūq Bani Qainuqā', famous for trade in gold and silver Jewellery, clothing and other goods.[2]

---

1 Op.cit., 1/164, 165.

2 At-Tarateeb-ul-Idaria: 1/97.

'Aus and Khazraj Control Yathrib

When the 'Aus and Khazraj migrated to Yathrib, they found that its entire economy was controlled by the Jews. They made peace treaties with the Jews and lived together in peace for some time until the Jews reneged on their pledges and extended and entrenched their control over Yathrib. In response to this challenge of superior power, the 'Aus and Khazraj enlisted the help of their kinsmen, attacked the Jews and overpowered them.[1]

While the 'Aus and Khazraj were under the domination of the Jews and feared that they would soon be forced to go into exile, they chose Mālik bin 'Ajlān Khazraji as their chief. During that time, the ruler of the Jews of Yathrib was one named Fityaun.

Fityaun was a cruel tyrant whose tyranny knew no bounds. He forced every bride from the tribes of 'Aus and Khazraj to spend a night with him before she could go to her husband. Mālik bin Ajlān's sister was married to a man of his tribe. One day, while Mālik was sitting with his fellow tribesmen, his sister passed by, lowering her skirt. Angry and ashamed, Mālik rushed home and rebuked his sister for her behaviour. She retorted, "If I am sent to a stranger who will do to me what he will do, that is still worse!"

His sense of honour affected, Mālik took his sword, disguised himself as a woman, and went along with his sister to Fityaun's palace as the evening fell. There he lay in wait until he was able to seize the opportunity to slay the tyrant.

Mālik bin Ajlān later turned to Abu Jubailah, the king of Ghassan, for help against the Jews. Abu Jubailah came with a large force, slew the chiefs of the Jews of Yathrib, and gave honour and power to the 'Aus and Khazraj.[2]

Ibn Qutaibah writes that the people of Yathrib went to Tubba' Al-Asghar, the king of Yemen, and complained to him against the tyranny

1 Al-Mufassal Fi Tareekh-il-Arab Qabl-al-Islam: 4/ 129, 130.

2 Wafa'-ul-Wafa li's-Samhudi: 1/178 - 180.

of the Jews. In response, Tubba' attacked Yathrib, seized 350 Jews, bound them, and slew them. He intended to lay waste the town of Yathrib as well, until an ancient Jewish man said, 'O king, do not rage! You cannot destroy this settlement because it is the refuge of a Prophet from the family of Ishmael (Ismā'īl) عليه السلام who will be born in Makkah.'

On hearing this prophesy, Tubba' changed his mind and stayed his hand. He then went to Makkah along with the old Jewish scholar who had spoken, put a covering over the Ka'bah, and entertained the people.[1]

Sacred Precincts of Madinah

The Prophet Muhammad's ﷺ migration to Madinah elevated it in status and instantly made it the second most honoured and sacred city in the world, after Makkah. Madinah and its surrounding areas were declared inviolable and sacrosanct, as proven by various authentic Ahādeeth.

End of Haram for Madinah

Abdullah bin Zaid bin 'Āsim رضي الله عنه narrated that the Messenger of Allah ﷺ said:

"Abraham عليه السلام made Makkah a sanctum and prayed (to Allah) for that. I have also made Madinah a sanctum just as Abraham made Makkah a sanctum. I prayed (to Allah) to bless its Mudd (مُدّ) and Sā' (صاع) (the two dry measures of corn) just as Abraham prayed for Makkah."[2]

Both Bukhāri and Muslim

1 Al-Ma'arif li-Ibn Qutaibhah, P. 276.
2 Sahīh-ul-Bukhāri: 2129.

report from Ali bin Abi Tālib ﷺ that the Prophet ﷺ said:

"Madinah is inviolable from Mt. 'Ayr (عير) to Thawr (ثور). Whoso innovates or gives shelter to an innovator, he is under the curse of Allah, His angels, and all the people. Allah will not accept from him on the Day of Resurrection any act, obligatory or voluntary."[1]

Madinah After the Prophet's Passing

After the death of the Messenger of Allah (ﷺ), his successor, the Caliph Abu Bakr Siddiq ﷺ, kept Madinah as the capital of the Islamic State. It remained so from 11 AH to 36 AH.

The second caliph, Umar ﷺ, established a central treasury, expanded the Prophet's mosque, and built outposts, rest houses, and water ponds at every stopover along the route from Makkah to Madinah.

A hand written Quran attributed to Uthman ﷺ

Uthman bin Affan ﷺ further expanded the Prophet's mosque, fixed carved stones in the entire mosque, and reinforced the pillars with lead.

It was from within this very mosque that Uthman ﷺ dispatched copies of the authorized version of the Qur'ān to every part of the Islamic empire. These copies had already been authorized during the caliphate of Abu Bakr ﷺ.

When Ali bin Abi Tālib ﷺ went back to Kufah after the Battle of Camel, he established Kufah as the seat of the caliphate instead of Madinah. It was moved later to Damascus when Hasan ibn Ali ﷺ made a settlement with Mu'āwiyah ibn Abi Sufyān ﷺ and gave up his claim to the caliphate.

Madinah slowly changed from capital city of the Islamic State to little more than a provincial town; however, it always retained its academic

1 Sahīh-ul-Bukhāri: 1870 and Sahīh Muslim: 1370.

and spiritual importance. Al-Hasan ibn Ali رضي الله عنهما returned to Madinah after giving up his claim to the caliphate; the Messenger of Allah's grave is located in Madinah, an honour which no part of the world can compete with. The Mothers of the Believers, the Prophet's son Ibrāhīm, the Prophet's daughters, the first three Caliphs, several other Companions, male and female, Imam Mālik, and other Tabi'een and Atbā' At-Tābi'een - all are buried in Madinah.

Madinah during the Ottoman and Saudi Eras

Throughout the various dynasties that ruled during the Muslim history, Madinah always remained an integral part of the Muslim empire. The Ummayad, Abbasid, Ubaidi (Fatimid)W, Zangi, Ayyubi, and Ottoman rulers all paid homage to Madinah at some time during their reigns; *Khalifah* Waleed bin Abdul Malik, *Khalifah* Mahdi Abbasi, Mameluke king, Sultan Ashraf Qayetbai, and Ottoman Caliph Abdul-Majeed I all ensured that extension work on the Masjid an-Nabawi continued. The Turks completed the Damascus-Madinah railway in 1908 which was destroyed during the First World War. The Shareef of Makkah,

Madinah Munawwarah During the Ottoman Caliphate

Al-Husain, founded his kingdom in Hijaz. The founder of the Saudi kingdom, King Abdul-Azīz Āl-Sa'ud, seized control of Hijaz in 1924, declared himself the king of Nejd and Hijaz and restored law, order and security in the country.

A new era of economic prosperity began in 1930 with the discovery and export of oil. The current prosperity of Madinah owes itself to the efforts of King Faisal bin 'Abdul-'Azīz and his heirs, King Khalid, King Fahd and king Abdullah. They spent hundreds of thousands of sterling pounds on the extension and adornment of the Prophet's Mosque, and established the foundation of the internationally renowned Islamic University of Madinah.

Interestingly, Madinah's local population includes large numbers of Muslims whose ancestry traces back to the Indian sub-Continent, Bukhara (Turkestan) and Syria.[1]

1 Urdu Encyclopedia of Islam: 20/238-244.

A Beautiful view of Tā'if City

Tā'if and Badr

Tā'if (طائف): Tā'if, located on Mt. Ghazwān southeast of Makkah, is one of the oldest towns of Arabia. Tā'if had a reputation in the past for tanning hides, so much so that it earned the epithet of *'Balad ad-Dibāgh'* (the city of tanning).[1]

The inhabitants of Tā'if, unlike those of Hijāz, were also skilled craftsmen and known for their workmanship in wood and iron.[2] Tā'if is known for its mild climate and greenery; orchards of fruit trees abound, with grapes, raisins, bananas and pomegranates as the main crops. In winter, on the summit of Mt. Ghazwān, water freezes.

Tā'if is 65 km off Makkah and 1630 meters above sea level. Tā'if is considered to be a cold region in Saudi Arabia. For the Makkans, it has always been a summer resort, and even now it is the summer capital of Saudi Arabia.[3] Where once Laat, the idol of Banu Thaqeef, was worshipped, there now stands an impressive guest house. A residential quarter (neighbourhood) of Tā'if named *Ash-Shuhadā'* (Arabic for martyrs) evokes

1 Sifat-o-Jazeerat-il-Arab, P. 233.
2 Al-Mufassal Fi Tareekh-il-Arab Qabl-al-Islam: 4/153.
3 Al-Munjid Fi'l-A'lām, P. 354.

the memory of the martyrs of the Battle of Tā'if (8 AH).[1]

Tā'if is surrounded by a number of wadis: Al-Qayyim, Khushrab, Al-Mahram, Al-Maween, Liy'yah, and Wajj.

Okaz: It is an oasis located in a wadi north of Tā'if. Wadi Sharib and Wadi Al-'Arj join together nearby. At a place called 'Uthaidā', a famous bazaar called the 'Suq of Okaz' was held. It was also the seat of the Battle of Fujār. 'Uthaidā' is now called al-Hawiyyah, which is an important town 35 km off Tā'if on the Riyadh Road. The airport of Tā'if is also situated in Al-Hawiyyah.[2]Okaz was sited northeast of the modern town of Al-Hawiyyah.

Banu Thaqeef in Tā'if

Area of Banu Thaqeef

Initially, Tā'if was called Wajj, named after Wajj bin Abdul-Hayy, a chief of the Amalekites. The Amalekites are related to Amlāq (Amleeq) bin Arfakhshad bin Sam bin Nūh. They were pure Arabs (Arab 'Āribah), whose home was Babel (Babylon) until it was seized by Persia, an event forcing them to scatter far and wide across the Arabian Peninsula and Syria. From their descendants came the kings of Iraq and Al-Jazeerah, as well as the Jabirs of Syria and the Pharaohs of Egypt. Tabari says: "The Amalekites were Arabs and they spoke Arabic."[3]Later, the Adnani tribe Banu 'Adwān bin 'Amr bin Qais bin 'Ailan took over.

Ibn Abbas ﷺ said: *Thaqeef* (Qasiyy bin Munabbih bin Bakr bin Hawazin) and *Nakha'* (Jasr) were maternal cousins who had set out in

1 Al-Mufassal Fi Tareekh-il-Arab Qabl-al-Islam: 4/152.
2 Mu'jam-ul-Buldan: See under 'Okaz'; Atlas-ul-Hadīth, P. 274; and Mu'jam-ul-Ma'alim Al-Jughrāfiyah Fi-Seerat-in-Nabawiyyah, P. 215.
3 Al-Bidāya Wan-Nihāya 1/119; and Al-A'lam: 5/88.

search of pasture-grounds. At some point, they quarreled with an official of the king of Yemen; a brawl ensued and they killed the official. They fled, choosing to migrate in different direction.

Area of Banu Thaqeef

Nakha' went off to Yemen, and Qasiyy to Umm al-Qura where he came across a childless Jewess who adopted him as her son. On the eve of her death, she gave him a few dinars and a branch of grapevine. Qasiyy took those things and went off to Wajj. There, using a trick which a slave girl of 'Amir bin Zarb 'Adwāni had taught him, he took refuge with the latter. Later on, 'Amir gave him his daughter in marriage. Afterwards, when it was realized that Qasiyy had achieved all of this through trickery, he was nicknamed *'Thaqeef'* (smart and clever).

The descendants of Thaqeef thrived in Wajj until they expelled Banu 'Adwān from Tā'if, the latter of which went to Tihāmah. Later, rich fugitive of Banu Sadaf,[1] who had killed his cousin, came to Wajj and proposed to the people to build a wall to defend themselves from the marauding Arab tribes. With his help, Banu Thaqeef built a wall and made Wajj look like a fortress; since a wall encircled Wajj, people began calling it by the name Tā'if.'[2]

When the Islamic era began, *Banu Thaqeef* was divided into two groups: Banu Mālik and Ahlāf. The name Ahlāf applied to the following six tribes of Quraish: Abd ad-Dār, Ka'b, Jumah, Sahm, Makhzūm, and Adī. A clan of Thaqeef was also called Ahlāf. In a battle, Ahlaf drove Banu Mālik into

1 There are three tribes bearing the name of Banu Sadaf: 1. Sadaf bin Aslam, a Qahtani tribe of Hadramaut. 2. Sadaf bin Amr, a Himyari tribe. 3. Sadaf bin Malik, a branch of Kindah, a tribe of Qahtani extraction – (Mu'jam Qaba'il-il-Arab 2/637).

2 Mu'jam Ma'sta'Jama: 1/64 - 67.

Wadi Lahb, behind Tā'if; as a result, Banu Mālik allied with Daus and Khath'am against Ahlāf.[1]

The famous persona Hajjaj bin Yusuf Thaqafi belonged to this very city. Muhammad bin Qasim Thaqafi, the conqueror of Sind, was the son of a cousin of Hajjāj bin Yusuf Thaqafi.[2]Earlier, during the reign of Umar āl-Farooq ﷺ, the Muslim commander Abu 'Ubaid bin Mas'ūd Thaqafi ﷺ (d. 13AH/634 CE) came from this area; he fell as a martyr in the Battle of *Jisr* (13 AH) while fighting the Persians.[3]

Famous wadis of Tā'if

Shuh'tah (شوحطة) (Khaybāt Banu Sa'd): The foster mother of the Messenger of Allah (ﷺ), Haleemah ﷺ, belonged to the tribe of Banu Sa'd, whose settlement lay 70 km southeast of Tā'if.

Abdur-Rahman Abd writes in his travelogue: "We had travelled for a distance of about 20 km from Tā'if when we crossed the Yemen Road

1 Al-Kamil li-Ibn-il-Athīr: 1/ 542, 543.
2 Urdu Encyclopedia of Islam: 19/345.
3 Usd-ul-Ghāba: 5/37; and Al-Bidāya Wan-Nihaya: 7/121.

Area of Banu Sa'd where the Prophet (ﷺ) was brought up

and turned to the road on the right-hand side...the region of Banu Sa'd stretches for several miles. That part of it which relates to Haleemah Sa'diyyah is called Khaybāt. The name of her specific settlement is ash-Shahtah. On arriving in Khaybat, we got down at a place called as-Sahn. As we walked along, we came to the end of the metalled road. Ahead of us was now a dirt track. There we saw a sign: Banu Sa'd".[1]

Wadi Mahram

Meeqat Qarn al-Manāzil

Wadi Liyyah

Abdul-Malik Mujahid, the Managing Director of Darussalam, writes in his travelogue: "The name of Haleemah's hamlet is Shūh'tah. Some write it as Shah'tah. However, the correct name is Shūh'tah. It is 160 km off Makkah by road. The unpaved road from Shiqsān on the Yemen Road to this place must be about 15 to 20 km long. Brother Saif-ur-Rahmān pointed to a distant valley, exclaiming: 'There!

1 Anhuzoor Ke Naqsh-i-Qadam Paa (Haram-e-Arafāt): 4/65.

That is the hamlet of Sayyedah Haleemah‎ﷺ. The car took a round from the right-hand side and climbed up a high mound. On the thither side of it we could see the Shūhtah hamlet about two furlongs away. The car kept on climbing. Down the mound there was a cemetery and some dry farmlands. At the foot a hillock in front of us, we noticed a few traces suggesting that there had been a human settlement here once. It was not more than 15 to 20 acres wide. There are marks of stones. There are four small walls. As we walked up the hillock on the other side, we were shown two or three places and told that those were the dwelling-places of the tribesmen of Haleemah. Some Pakistani had scrawled in white: Haleemah's House. The rooms were very small."[1]

Wadi Mahram (وادی محرم): It is now the Mīqāt (میقات) for the pilgrims coming from Tā'if, about 10 km off Tā'if on the new Makkah Highway. Nearby rises Wadi Mahram, flows northward and, as it approaches *as-Sail al-Kabeer*, joins Wadi *Nakhlah ash-Shāmiyyah*.

Another Miqāt named Qarn Al-Manāzil is the location where the Prophet (ﷺ) put on his *Ihrām* for *'Umrah* when returning from the Battle of Tā'if to Makkah. Heykal in his book, *Manzil al-Wahy*, identifies Qarn al-Manāzil with the present *as-Sail al-Kabeer*.

Wadi Liyyah: It is one of the large wadis of Tā'if. It rises in Jabal as-Sarāt located southwest of Tā'if, from where the territory of Banu Huzail and Banu Thaqeef begins, turns eastward, and then runs on 15 km away southeast of Tā'if. There it is intersected by the territory of Banu Sa'd and the highway leading to Yemen.[2]

1 "Zia-e-Hadīth", March 2011.
2 Mu'jam-ul-Ma'alim Al-Jughrāfiyah Fi's Seerat-in-Nabawiyyah, P. 274.

Badr

The Battle of Badr took place on 17 Ramadān, 2 AH. It was the first full-fledged battle that the Muslims fought against the disbelievers of Quraish, whom they defeated with a resounding victory.

Badr was formerly a watering-place for Banu Ghifār, but later changed into the name of a stream. Trade caravans coming from Syria and Egypt along a route close to the eastern coast of the Red Sea would pass through it and use it as a watering-hole.

With the expansion of the Muslim empire, it became a main transit route for the Hajj pilgrims. Today, Badr is a large town which is situated in the lower Wadi as-Safrā' *(Wadi as-Sareer)*. The distance between Madinah and Badr is 155 km and the distance between Makkah and Badr is 310 km.

It is at a distance of 75 km from the seacoast. Close to Badr was a jetty named al-Jār. When it fell into ruinous disrepair, the present town of ar-Rā'is was established and now supplies fish from the sea to Badr.

Southwest of Badr, about 5 km away, is another place called *al-Ghazlān*, where there is a hub of routes leading to Makkah, Jeddah and Yanbu'.[1]

In the pre-Islamic Age of Ignorance, an annual eight-day fair was held in Badr starting from 1 Dhul-Qa'dah. Badr is an oval-shaped 5.5 ml long and 4.5 ml wide plain surrounded by high mountains. At both of its edges (in the west and the southeast) are *al-'Udwat ad-Dunyā* (the near side of the valley) and *al-'Udwat al-Quswa* (the farther side) mentioned in *Sūrah al-Anfāl*. Between them, in the southwest, is a low mountain (Jabal Asfal), from the summit of which one may clearly see the Red Sea.

On the mound where the Prophet ﷺ had pitched his camp at Badr, a mosque named *Masjid al-'Areesh (Masjid Ghamāmah)* has been built. At the end of the small oasis of Badr there is a cemetery and beside it a walled compound where the martyrs of the Battle of Badr are buried.[2]

1 Op.cit, PP. 41. 42 and Atlas Al-Mamlaka Al-Arabia As-Saudia.

2 An'Hazoor Ke Naqsh-i-Qadam Paa (Haram-e-Madinah): 2/41-42.

Cemetery of Badr

Al-'Udwat ad-Danyā

Masjid al-'Areesh

Al-'Udwat-al-Quswa

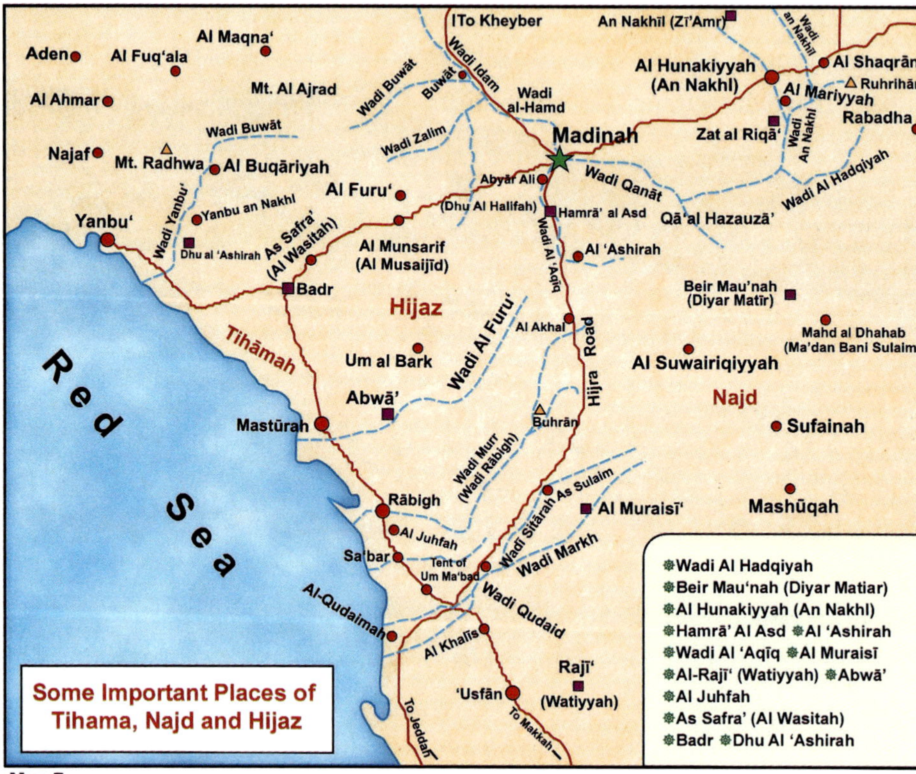

Map.7

Some Important Places of Tihāmah, Nejd and Hijāz

Munsarif: It is now called *Al-Musaijeed*, named after the Prophet's place of prostration. Its relics are still extant. It is located 80 km off Madinah, on the road to Makkah. On his way to Badr in 2 AH, the Prophet Muhammad (ﷺ) reached Munsarif, and then leaving the Makkah highway on his left side, he travelled to *as-Safr*ā*'* via *Nāziyah*.[1]

Bi'r Ma'oonah: Bi'r Ma'oonah is presently called *Diyār Mateer*. It lies at the foot of Jibal Ubla, a range of black mountains close to *Harrāt*

1 Mu'jam Al-Ma'alim Al-Jughrafiyah fi's-Seerat-in-Nabawiyyah, P. 303.

al-Hijaz, southwest of *Mahd adh-Dhahab* (Ma'dan Bani Sulaim). In the time of the Messenger (ﷺ), the region was also named after Bi'r Ma'oonah. It was here that Banu Sulaim slew seventy reciters of the Qur'ān *(Qurrā')* in Safar, 4 AH.[1]

Wadi Qudaid

Qudaid (قديد): A fertile wadi of Hijāz and Tihamah, it rises in Harrah Dharah. The upper part is called *Sitārah* and the lower part is known as *Qudaid*. This Wadi intersects the Makkah-Madinah Highway at about 120 km and falls into the sea in the neighbourhood of *al-Qudaimah*. The Prophet (ﷺ) passed through Qudaid during his Hijrah to Madinah and on his way to the Battle of Muraisee'. The settlements of Harb and Banu Sulaim were located here.[2]

Wadi al-Muraisee

Al-Muraisee' (المريسيع): It is a rivulet, a branch of the stream Horah (حوره), which is a tributary of wadi Sitārah (Qudaid); it is the location of the Battle of Bani Mustalaq in 5 AH. Today, Banu Sulaim have replaced Banu Mustalaq *(Khuzā'i)* and are settled here.

Wadi al-Munsarif

Al-Muraisee', about 80 km away from the sea, is in Jibal Tihāmah (Hijaz).[3] The settlement of as-Sulaim on the modern Makkah-Madinah road is located east of wadi Sitārah, about 250 km south of Madinah.

1 Op.cit. ,PP. 52,53.
2 Op.cit, P. 249.
3 Op.cit., P. 290.

A View of Kheyber

Al-Abwa' (Al-Khuraibah)

Qa' al-Hadudā (Qarqarat al-Kudr)

Dhu-'Amr: The Battle of Ghatfān took place here in *Rabee' al-Awwal*, 3 AH. According to old historians, Dhu-'Amr was about 15 km north of *Al-Hunākiyyah* and close to an-Nakheel, which is the name of both a wadi and a settlement. *Al-Hunākiyyah* is about 90 km away on Ar-Riyadh Road. Dhu-'Amr is no longer known by most.[1]

Qarqarat al-Kudr: Located east of Madinah, it is a round-shaped lowland where several wadis meet and is currently called *Qa' al-Hadūdā'*. While travelling about fifty to fifty-five kilometers from Madinah to *al-Hunākiyyah*, one comes across a place called as-Suwaidarah. To the south of it lies the wide expanse of the waters of *al-Hadūdā'* reaching up to *Mahd-adh-Dhahab*.[2] In the Battle of Saweeq (*Dhul-Hijja*, 2 AH), the Prophet (ﷺ) chased Abu Sufyān's contingent as far as Qarqarat Al-Kudr.

Al-Abwā'(al-Khuraibah): A wadi of Hijaz Tihamiah formed by the confluence of *wadi al-*

1 Op.cit., P. 33; Atlas Al-Mamlaka Al-Arabia As-Saudia, Lauhah: 9.

2 Mu'jam Al-Ma'alim Al-Jughrafiyah, P. 251; and Atlas Al-Mamlaka Al-Arabia As-Saudia, Lauhah: 9, 10.

Rabadhah

Fadak (al-Hā'it)

Far' and *wadi al-Qāhah (Wadi an-Nakhl)*, it flows past the ruins of Waddān (which are on its left side) and falls into the sea in the neighbourhood of the town of Mastūrah. Its modern-day name is wadi Al-Khuraibah, although scholars of the past know it by the name of al-Abwā.'[1]The town of al-Abwā', as it stands today, is about 30 to 35 km east of *Mastūrah*; it is the location where the Prophet's mother, Aminah, died.

Kheybar: Kheybar is 165 km north of Madinah; those travelling to Taima' will cross through it. Several wadis join here, making the area lush and green. It is known for its rich date crops and said to be 'the countryside of Hijāz'. Hassān bin Thābit, the famous poet, praised this region:

فَإِنَّا وَمَنْ يُهْدِي الْقَصَائِدَ نَحْوَنَا كَمُسْتَبْضِعٍ تَمْرًا إِلَى أَهْلِ خَيْبَرَا

"We and the man reading to us his verses *(Qaseedahs)* are like one selling dates to the people of Kheybar."[2]

These days the tribe of Anazah have made Kheybar their home, with its primary town being that of Ash-Shareef.[3]

Fadak (al-Hā'it الحائط): Fadak is a town, 115 km east of Kheybar, in a wadi which flows down to wadi ar-Rumma. Now known as al-Hā'it, the people of Fadak surrendered to the Messenger of Allah (ﷺ) after the conquest of Kheybar (6 AH).[4]Fadak lies about 35 km west of a town

1 Mu'jam Al-Ma'alim Al-Jughrafiyah Fi-Seerat-in-Nabawiyyah, P. 14.
2 Diwan Hassan bin Thabit Al-Ansari, P. 109.
3 Mu'jam-ul-Ma'alim al-Jughrafiyah fi's Sīrat-in-Nabawia, P. 118.
4 Op.cit., P 235; and Atlas Al-Mamlaka Al-Arabia As-Saudia, Lauhah: 9.

Wadi Al-'Is

called *al-Haleefah As-Sufla* on al-Qaseem Road.

Khaimah Umm Ma'bad: On their Hijrah to Madinah, Allah's Messenger (ﷺ) and Abu Bakr passed by the tent of a woman named Umm Ma'bad Khuzāiyyah, with whose permission the Prophet milked her goat to have fresh milk to drink. The spot has been memorialized and retains its own name: the Tent *(Khaimah)* of Umm Ma'bad. It is situated on the northern edge of Wadi Qudaid in the direction of the coast, with Thaniyyah al-Mushallal in the north of it.[1]

Rabadhah: The famous Companion Abu Dharr Al-Ghifāri is buried here. It was located on the Pilgrims Highway *(Darb Zubeydah)* but destroyed in 319 AH by the Qarmathians *(Qaramitah)*. It is now known as Birkah Abu Sulaim, and the name Rabadhah is unknown to the locals. It lies about 80 km southeast of al-Hunākiyyah and 150 km north of *Mahd adh-Dhahab*.

Mushallal: It is a valley in the north of Qudaid. Harrah Mushallal, where the idol of the Quraish Manat was kept, can be seen from the town of Sa'bar which lies between Rabigh and Al-Qudaimah. There was once a stream called Ghassān in Mushallal but it is unknown now.[2]

Thaniyyat Al-Murrah: While migrating to Madinah, the Prophet (ﷺ) passed through this area. It was between al-Kharrār and Liqf; it is known to this day by its old name. It lies between Ghadeer Khumm and Al-Fura'.[3]

Al-'Is (العيص): It is the wadi of Banu Juhainah, between Madinah and the sea. In *Ramadan* 1 AH, the Expedition of Hamzah took place in its neighbourhood. It flows down from the direction of Jabal al-Ajrad and

1 Mu'jam-ul-Ma'alim al-Jughrafiyah Fi-Sīrat-in-Nabawiyyah, P. 119,120.
2 Op.cit., P. 298.
3 Op.cit., P. 289.

Kharrar and meets wadi 'Idam (al-Hamd) from its left side. The town of Al-'Is is the central town of the emirate, with schools, a police post and a Sharia court. al-'Is is nearly 180 km northwest of Madinah and 80 km east of the coastal town of Amlaj.

al-Asāfir الاصافر (as-Suffur): On his way to Badr, the Prophet Muhammad (ﷺ) passed through the valley of Dhafirān (ذفران) and then through the valley of al-Asāfir, after which he descended to a settlement named ad-Dabbah. Today al-Asāfir is called as-Suffur.[1]

Ad-Dabbah: It is difficult to identify ad-Dabbah or determine its exact location today. If one comes from the direction of Madinah and goes down the ridges of Asāfir or ās-Suffur, one would come face to face with a town named al-Birkah. On one side of it there is a "Dabbah" which may well be the same Dabbah which is mentioned in the Prophet's biographies. However, it should be noted that the people of Hijaz call a round, level sand dune a Dabbah. In any case, the town now, which is known as ad-Dabbah lies south of Badr, in the direction of the Ka'ba. The natives of Badr say that it is the same ad-Dabbah as mentioned in Seerah literature.[2]

Wadi al-Kharrar (al-Juhfah)

Wadi Autās (وادى اوطاس): The name of this wadi occurs in the accounts of the Battle of Hunayn (*Shawwal*, 8 AH). A statement of Duraid bin Sammah led some people to believe that Autas lies in Wadi Hunayn, although in actuality it is at a distance from it. Autas was a plain which the pilgrims from Iraq would cross on their way to Makkah. When they had reached Birkah Zubeydah *(Birkat al-'Aqeeq)*, they used to descend into Wadi 'Aqeeq. From there they would reach Autas in an

1 Op.cit., P. 125.
2 Op.cit., P. 125.

Wadi Tabālah

hour, as Autas is an extremity of *Aqeeq al-Yusra*. There they would climb up the incline of the Harrah and make for the Mīqāt customs-post in the north of the town of 'Asheerah and about 160 km northeast of Makkah. When the Hujjāj (pilgrims) reached Autas from Makkah, they would take two different routes. Those bound for Basrah would go right while those heading for Kufah and Baghdad would turn left.[1]

Al-Kharrār (Ghadeer Khumm): It is a wadi also called Wadi Al-Juhfah or Ghadeer Khumm, close to the town of *Al-Kharrar*, which lies about 25 km east of *Rābigh*. While migrating to Madinah, the Prophet ﷺ went to Thaniyyāt Al-Murrah via Kharrār.[2]

Tabālah: It is a large wadi lying 200 km southeast of Tā'if. It flows around the outskirts of Al-Bāha, through Sūrat Ghāmid, Balaqran and Balajrash, turns eastward and falls into Wadi Beshah. The natives of Beshah are called Shahrān.[3]

1 Op.cit., PP. 34,35.
2 Op.cit., P. 112.
3 Op.cit., P.56.

Chapter - 2

Peoples and Tribes

of the Arabian Peninsula

Division of the Arab Peoples;
Hūd, Sālih, Ibrāhīm and Ismā'īl A History of these prophets and their People Deterring Examples from the History of the People of Lūt and Shu'aib

مَا كَانَ مُحَمَّدٌ أَبَآ أَحَدٍ مِّن رِّجَالِكُمْ وَلَٰكِن رَّسُولَ ٱللَّهِ وَخَاتَمَ ٱلنَّبِيِّـۧنَ وَكَانَ ٱللَّهُ بِكُلِّ شَىْءٍ عَلِيمًا

"Muhammad is not the father of any of your men, but he is the Messenger of Allah and the last (end) of the Prophets. And Allah is Ever All-Knower of everything."
Al-Ahzāb: 33:40.

In This Chapter

Describes the people of the Arabian Peninsula have been divided into three classes: The extinct Arabs (Arab Bā'idah), the pure Arabs (Arab 'Āribah), and the immigrant or domiciled Arabs (Arab Musta'ribah).

This chapter covers the history of these three types of Arabs. It gives an account of those Arab nations which are now extinct, and relates the tale of their prophets Hūd and Sālih (عليه السلام), their call to their people to worship One, True God, and how their people opposed them and perished.

This chapter also describes in detail the history of Arab 'Āribah; that is, the offspring of Qahtān, their various clans and tribes and how they spread across Arabia.

Under the third category, Arab Musta'ribah, we describe Ibrāhīm's migration from Iraq to Palestine, the settlement of his wife and son, Ismā'īl (عليه السلام), in the barren valley of Makkah and how their offspring multiplied and divided into tribes and spread across the Peninsula.

The chapter closes with deterring examples from the history of the rebellious people of Lūt and Shu'aib (عليه السلام).

Three Categories of the Arabs

Most historians divide the Arabs into three categories: the extinct Arabs, pure Arabs, and domiciled Arabs.[1] Ibn Khaldūn divided the Arabs, from their earliest known origins until his times, into four categories: pure Arabs, domiciled Arabs, Arabs subordinate to Arabs (Al-Arab at-Tābi'ah lil-Arab) and alien or non-Arab Arabs (Arab Musta'jimah).[2]

On the contrary, Ibn Kathir divides them into two categories: pure Arabs and domiciled Arabs. In his view, the extinct Arabs are the true, original Arabs (Arab 'Āribah). According to him, various tribes from amongst the ancient people, such as 'Ād, Thamūd, Tasm, Jadees, Amalekites, Umaim, Jurhum and Qahtān, were unable to retain their separate identities. They intermarried and mingled with other tribes, resulting in new clans and identities.

Furthermore, Ibn Kathir's view is that the second type of Arabs are the Musta'ribah, which includes the progeny of Ishmael (Ismā'il).[3]

However, the majority of historians and biographers of the Prophet Muhammad (ﷺ) classify the Arabs into three categories: nonexistent (extinct) Arabs, pure Arabs, and alien (immigrant) Arabs.[4]

1 Al-Mufassal Fi Tareekh-il-Arab Qabl-al-Islam: 294/1.
2 Tareekh Ibn Khaldūn: 2/20-23.
3 Al-Bidaya Wan-Nihaya: 2/145.
4 Tareekh Quraish by Dr. Husain Mu'nis, P. 18.

Extinct Arabs

The term "extinct Arabs" refers to the earliest known Arabs to have existed. Though their bloodlines have perished, their names and fragments of their history have been passed on from generation to generation; their names were known to the people during the era of the Messenger of Allah (ﷺ). Amongst those perished tribes whose names were known to the Arabs were like 'Ād, Thamūd, Amalekites (عماليق), Tasm (طسم), Jadees, Umaim, 'Abīl of Yathrib and Jurhum.

The Qur'ān also refers to those people who had lived in Arabia in the remote past, and mentions their conduct as a warning to succeeding generations.

As with all mankind around the world, Allah sent prophets and messengers to the ancient Arabs; however, only a few of them answered the call of their prophets, and the vast majority of them spurned them. They would made a jest of them, called them mad, sorcerers, liars, exploiters working to serve their own interests and ostentations. They tortured their followers, some of their leaders and even killed some of the prophets.

Ultimately, the wrath of Allah came upon them and they were utterly destroyed. Some remnants of their settlements survive to this day as deterring examples for the coming generations.

Map.8

The Tribe of ʿĀd

The oldest and most powerful people to come after Prophet Nūh (Noah) ﷺ were the tribesmen of ʿĀd, who gained greatness and splendor in Arabia.

'Ād's Lineage

Dr Jawwād Ali writes: This is how the genealogy of 'Ād is traced: 'Ād bin Uz[1] bin Iram bin Sām bin Nūh ﷺ. The name 'Ād had become for Arabs a proverb for oldness, a synonym for antiquity. When they saw a very old thing, they would say: "انه عادى" (It belongs to the times of 'Ād). If they see an old house and did not know of his owner, they would exclaim: "انه بناء عادى" (This house belongs to the people of 'Ād).[2]

The Qur'ān mentions the people of Noah (Nūh) ﷺ and the tribes of 'Ād and Thamūd as being of the ancient peoples:

﴿ أَلَمْ يَأْتِكُمْ نَبَؤُا۟ ٱلَّذِينَ مِن قَبْلِكُمْ قَوْمِ نُوحٍ وَعَادٍ وَثَمُودَ ۛ وَٱلَّذِينَ مِنۢ بَعْدِهِمْ ﴾

"Has not the news reached you of those before you, the people of Nūh (Noah), and 'Ād, and Thamūd? and those after them?"[3]

The Era of 'Ād

Surah Al-A'rāf calls 'Ād the successors of the people of Noah. This suggests that the resettlement of Syria and Arabia and the prosperity of the progeny of Shem (سام) was initiated during the time of 'Ād. The Verse also gives some idea about their age, as well as confirms the opinion that the earlier Semites and 'Ād were the same people with two names. That is why Qur'ān calls them the

1 The name of 'Ād in the Bible is Uz. Say'yed Suleman Nadvi thinks that the Arabs used to say 'Ād bin Iram but when they heard the Jews saying Uz bin Iram, the Arabs combined both the names and said 'Ād bin Uz bin Iram although. 'Ād and Uz are the same person. – (tareekh 'ard-ul-Quran (kamil): 1/106.

2 Al-Mufassal fi Tareekh-il-Arab Qabl-al-Islam: 1/308, 309.

3 Ibrāhīm: 14:9.

earlier (or the first) 'Ād. Evidence suggests that their period was somewhere around 3000 BC.

According to modern historians, the period of the known prosperity of Banu Shem (Semites) is 2200 BC-2000 BC. This was also the period when the Semites attacked Babylon (Babel) and Egypt; they reached the zenith of their power and perished well before Musa (Moses). The proof for this is in the Qur'ān, which relates that the man who was a secret believer in Musa's message said Pharaoh's court:

﴿يَٰقَوْمِ إِنِّيٓ أَخَافُ عَلَيْكُم مِّثْلَ يَوْمِ ٱلْأَحْزَابِ ۝٣٠ مِثْلَ دَأْبِ قَوْمِ نُوحٍ وَعَادٍ وَثَمُودَ وَٱلَّذِينَ مِنۢ بَعْدِهِمْ﴾

"O my people! verily, I fear for you a fate like that day (of disaster) of the Confederates (of old)! Like the fate of the poeple of Nūh (Noah), and 'Ād, and Thamūd and those who came after them." Al-Mu'min (40): 30, 31.[1]

The Earlier 'Ād and Later 'Ād

Muslim historians divide the tribesmen of 'Ād into two: the first 'Ād ('Ād al-'Ūla) and the second 'Ād ('Ād Thāniyah). This division is based on the evidence from Qur'ān which says:

﴿وَأَنَّهُۥٓ أَهْلَكَ عَادًا ٱلْأُولَىٰ﴾

"And that He (Allah) destroyed the former (tribe of) 'Ād."[2]

When the first tribe of 'Ād perished due to their irreverent and unrepentant sinning and pagan beliefs, the believers among them who had escaped the divine punishment left their land. These believers travelled great distances, and resettled in areas somewhat similar to their original habitat. They progressed and prospered and, later, when they too strayed from the straight path, they were also destroyed. The later tribe of 'Ād have also been mentioned with reference to their native land.

Commentators of Qur'ān and historians, old and new, taking the

1 Tareekh ard-il-Qur'ān (Kamil): 1/106, 107.
2 An-Najm: 53:50.

Ruins of the city of early 'Ād

Qur'ānic term 'the earlier 'Ād' as a guideline, tried to identify 'the later 'Ād' in various ways. Historians repeatedly call them the second 'Ād.[1]

Ibn Kathir states that the 'Ād of Iram refers to 'Ād 'Ūla' (the earlier 'Ād.[2]) Baidawi hypothesizes that 'Ād of Iram refers to the folk of Prophet Hud عليه السلام, while Mas'udi infers that the 'Ād of Iram are the 'second 'Ād.;[3] Sayyad Tantawi believes that the 'first 'Ād' were the people of Prophet Hud عليه السلام, and the 'second 'Ād were the tribe of Thamūd. Between them was an interval of one hundred years.[4] This last opinion was shared by Abdur-Rahman bin Nasir Sa'di, who also says that the 'second 'Ād' refers to Thamūd.[5]

The 'Ād of Iram

In light of the recent discoveries, inscriptions, opinions of non-Arab

1 Al-Mufassal fi Tareekh-il-Arab Qabl-al-Islam: 1/301.
2 See Al-Bidāya Wan-Nihāya: 1/117.
3 Tafseer Al-Baidawi: Al-Fajr: 89:7; Murooj-uz-Zahab: 2/44.
4 Tafseer-ul-Waseet -Muhammad Say'yad Tantavi; Al-A'raf: 7:65.
5 Taiseer-ul-Lateef-ul-Mannan fi Khulasat-i-Tafseer-il-Qur'ān, Qissat-i-Sālīh: 1/347.

Ruins of the 'Ād of Iram

contemporary historians, and detailed study of the history and civilizations of different peoples, the correct opinion seems to be that of Ibn Kathir and Ibn Khaldūn – that is, that the term 'former 'Ād' refers to the 'Ād of Iram.

It appears most likely that after the Deluge of Nūh's flood, the progeny of Shem, son of Nūh, settled in the neighbourhood of the land devastated by the flood. This land happened to be next to the valley of the Tigris and Euphrates Rivers, stretching from Iraq to Syria, Palestine, and northern Arabia.

According to genealogists, 'Ād (or Uz عوض) tribesmen were the children of Iram bin Sām (Shem) bin Nūh عليه السلام. Thus, the inference can be made that the first people of 'Ād were those closest in time and lineage to Iram ibn Sam ibn Nūh. Indeed, Yaqūt Hamawi says: "According to historians, Syria is named after Sam, son of Nūh."[1]

Another ancient name of Syria is Iram, also known as Aram and Aaram, so named after Nūh's grandson, Iram. He and his descendants settled and remained in this area. It should be noted that wherever the Urdu version of the Old Testament mentions Aram, the English text refers to it as Syria. In other words, the names Aaram and Syria have referred to the same land since the most ancient of times.

It is reasonable to believe that wherever the Aramaic-Semitic families settled, those areas came to be named Iram or Aram. The Torah mentions Mesopotamia (the region between Euphrates and Tigris), which is present-

1 Mu'jam-ul-Buldan: see under 'Sham'.

day Iraq, as 'Aram Nahra'im' or 'Padan Aram' (Arabic: "Feddan Aram"). Syria has been called 'Aram' or 'Aram Dimashq'. In fact, the whole of northern Arabia has also been referred to as "Aram."[1]

Another strong evidence that supports this theory is that most of the ancient inscriptions found in Babylon (Iraq), Ashur (Al-Jazeerah), Syria, Canaan (Palestine), Phoenicia (Lebanon) and northern Arabia were written in Aramaic, or full of Aramaic words.[2]

Arab geographers, too, support this view. Yaqūt Hamawi writes, "There is a mountain named Jash Iram near Mt.Tayy. On the heights of that mountain are the settlements of 'Ād and Iram with graven images."[3]

Dr. Jawwad Ali says:"'Ād and Iram. The conjunction 'and' (وَ) may be an error of the scribe. The pre-Islamic poets, Tarafah Wāilī, Nabighah[4], Zuhair bin Abi Salma Muzanī Mudri, the humorous poets, Tufail bin Auf Ghanvi and Mutammim bin Nuwairah, his brother Mālik bin Nuwairah and Umayyah bin Abi Salt --- all of them, while referring to the settlements of 'Ād, mention places which lie in the northern parts of Arab lands."

In 1932, Horsefield, working under the Archaeology Department of Jordan, undertook excavations at Mt. Rum, 25 miles east of Aqaba. Horsefield, Savignac and H. W. Gladon studied the inscriptions found

1 See: Holy Bible: Genesis 10:22, 23 and 46:15 and kings 1:20:1-43, 22:1-31.
2 Encyclopedia Britannica.
3 Mu'jam-ul-Buldan: see under 'Jash'.
4 Ibn Athir wrote his name as Nabigha Ja'di. Ibn Sa'd says that Nabigha belonged to the tribe of Adi bin Najar. A group of poets is also nicknamed 'Nabigha'. – (At-Tabaqat by Ibn Sa'd: 1/99, Tareekh At-Tabari: 2/8; Al-Kamil by Ibn Athir: 1/548).

Jabal Rum (Jordan)

there and gave their opinion which confirms that this was the very region of Iram to which the Qur'ān refers in the context of 'Ād.[1]

Jeron Gate - Damascus

Dr. Jawwad Ali goes on to say: "The 'Ād (Oaditae) mentioned by Ptolemy are those 'Ād tribesmen who lived around Hisma (حِسْمَى) in the northwestern parts of the Arabian Peninsula (Upper Hijaz). Mauritus, a well-known archaeologist, also says that the place named Aramaua in Ptolemy's geography is Iram or Many-columned Iram which is known today as Ram."[2]

Ibn Khaldūn, Mas'ūdī and other Arab historians, quoting other scholars, say that Dimashq (Damascus) is "Iram," known also as "Many-columned Iram," as Dimashq was the most important place of the people of Iram. According to a statement of Mas'ūdī, this city was built by Jeron bin Sa'd bin 'Ād and he named it Iram. A door of the city of Dimashq retains to this day his name: Bāb Jeron.[3]

A clay tablet found in Ebla, Syria

During 1964-1975, the excavations carried out by Italian archeologists near the town of Tal Merdeekh revealed the relics of the ancient town of 'Abeel (Ebla) mentioned in the Egyptian and Accadian inscriptions. From these excavations nearly fifteen thousand tablets with inscriptions written in Eblaite (a Semitic language) in cuneiform script were discovered. Those Eblaite tablets contained names of Adam, Eve,

1 Al-Mufassal Fi Tareekh-il-Arab Qabl-al-Islam: 1/306, 307.
2 Op.cit, 1/305.
3 Tareekh Ibn Khaldun: 2/25 .

Abraham (Ibrāhīm), Ishmael (Ismā'īl), Asurael, Michael (Michaya), Essau, Saul (Talūt), David, Sinai, Jerusalem, Jopa (Yafa), Ur, Sodom and Gomorrah. The rulers of Ebla were called Mālikon or Mālikom (kings), and one of them was named Ibra'im. Many of the words of the Eblaite language have become integrated in Arabic – some examples are the words Kutub (books), Mālik (king), Yad (hand), Qamh (wheat), Jazar (carrot), Teen (figs), Mi'ah (hundred).

It was also discovered from those tablets that the city of Aleppo (called Halab in Arabic) was called Armi in those days, a hint that Aleppo, like other Aramaic towns in that region, was a town of 'Ād Iram.

The Eblaites thrived in 2500 BC, but later diminished in power. From 1850 BC to 1600 BC, they recovered and rose in stature. In 1750 BC, Hammurabi and, later, the Hittite king Mursili I destroyed them completely.[1]

The Remnants of 'Ād of Iram

In the light of these evidences, it can be concluded that the term of 'Ād of Iram does indeed refer to the descendants of Iram ibn Shem. Thus, they are those to whom the Qur'ān refers to as 'Âd Iram in Surah Al-Fajr (Verses 6 – 7) and 'Âd al-'Ûla in Surah An-Najm (Verse 50).

Thamád, a branch of the descendants of Iram, moved away from their original land and settled a little further south (Al-Hijr, northern Arabia). They thrived and prospered and, finally, perished. A part of the remaining Aramaeans remained settled in the regions of Syria, and again they rose as

1 Atlas Tareekh-ul-Arab Al-Islami, P. 9; and Wikipedia (Encyclopedia).

Remains of the ancient city of Ebla - Syria

Aramaeans in the thirteenth century BC. Their language had an important position among the Semitic languages.1

A section of them made their way to the fertile regions in the south of the Arabian Peninsula, occupied those regions and rose once again as a powerful society.

Iram, the Garden of Shaddād

Some commentators of Qur'ān interpret "Iram" as referring to a unique garden built by Shaddād as a rival to Paradise itself.[2]The man who built it called it "Iram."[3]Yaqūt Hamawi, while portraying this earthly paradise, sites it in Yemen, between Hadramaut and San'a.[4]

The evidence for 'Ād the First and 'Ād the Second lies in that though historians and geographers could not definitively identify the regions they belonged to, they always quoted two different narrations when writing about the native land of the tribe of 'Ād.

According to one narration, they lived in Syria and the northern parts of the Arabian Peninsula and, according to another, they lived in southern Arabia. The closest approximation to the truth appears to be that the 'Ād tribesmen thrived and gained power in both the regions, each during a different period of history, only to be destroyed later on for their disbelief and sinning.

Ruins of the Garden of Shaddād

1 Atlas-ul-Qur'ān (Urdu), P. 57.
2 Athaar-ul-Bilad Wa Akhbar-ul-'Ibad, P. 15, 16.
3 Tareekh Ibn Khaldun, Al-Muqaddama (preface to prolegomena): 1/14.
4 Mu'jam-ul-Buldan: see under 'Iram'.

Curved sand hills of al-Ahqāf (Empty Quarter)

Land of 'Ād the Second

The Qur'ān relates that the prophet sent by Allah to guide 'Ād in Ahqaf warned them against sinning. Modern maps of the Arabian Peninsula site Ahqaf between the Empty Quarter and Hadramaut. According to some historians, 'Ād occupied those parts of Arabia which were richest in those times. Their regions stretched from the north of Hijaz to Hadramaut and Yemen. Allah's words:

﴿ وَٱذْكُرْ أَخَا عَادٍ إِذْ أَنذَرَ قَوْمَهُۥ بِٱلْأَحْقَافِ ﴾

"And remember the brother of 'Ād when he warned his people in Al-Ahqāf"[1] suggest that Ahqaf was the central or main settlement of 'Ād.

The Region of Ahqāf

According to most commentators of the Qur'ān and various historians, Ahqāf lies somewhere in southwest Arabia. There are a few differing opinions; Mujāhid is reported to have said that the word Ahqāfin

﴿ أَنذَرَ قَوْمَهُۥ بِٱلْأَحْقَافِ ﴾

"When he warned his people in Al-Ahqaf" refers to Hishaf (soft rocks

1 Al-Ahqāf: 46:21.

on a plain ground) in the region of *Hisma*.[1]

Yaqūt Hamawī, quoting Ibn Ishāq, says that Ahqāf lies between Oman and Hadramaut, and quotes Qatādah that it lies near Shihr (شحر) (a coastal town in south Yemen), and quotes Dahhāk that Ahqāf is the name of a mountain in Syria.[2]

Sayyed Suleman Nadvi writes: "Ahqāf means 'desert'. It is found in south Arabia as well as north Arabia. Therefore, there is no reason to specify the southern desert (Yemen) as the place where the Prophet of 'Ād was sent."[3]

It should also be noted that sand dunes (Ahqaf) are not a particular feature of the southern desert (Empty Quarter) for they are found in the northern desert as well (Nafud and the desert of Syria).

The word Ahqaf is not applied to any desert or sand dune, but only to those sand dunes or sand hills which are oblong and curved.

Lisan-al-Arab defines the word very clearly:

اَلْأَحْقَافُ: وَهِيَ جَمْعُ حِقْفٍ، وَهُوَ مَا اسْتَطَالَ وَاعْوَجَّ مِنَ الرَّمْلِ الْعَظِيمِ، وَلَا يَبْلُغُ أَنْ يَكُونَ جَبَلًا.

"Hiqf (plural: Ahqaf) means a sand hill which is long and curved."[4]

Ma'wardi is more explicit:

اَلْحِقْفُ مِنَ الرَّمْلِ: اَلْمُعْوَجُّ ...... وَقَدِ احْقَوْقَفَ الرَّمْلُ إِذَا طَالَ وَاعْوَجَّ.

"Ahqaf is the plural of Hiqf, meaning a large formation of sand which is very long and curved and which does attain to (the size of) a hill."[5]

Such long, curved sand hills are found nowhere in the Arabian Peninsula, Syria or Iraq except along the southern edge of the Empty Quarter. To this day the southern area of Arabia is known as Al-Ahqaf. These unique sand

1 Tafseer-ul-Qurtubi: Al-Ahqāf: 46:21.
2 Mu'jam-ul-Buldan: see under 'Ahqaf'.
3 Tareekh ard-il-Qur'ān (Kamil): 1/134.
4 Lisan-ul-Arab: see under 'Hiqf'.
5 Tafseer-ul-Ma'wardi: Al-Ahqāf: 26:21.

A camel caravan passing through *al-rub al-khali* (Empty Quarter)

hills exist on either side of the Yemeni-Saudi border, on either side of the Saudi-Omani border, and in the United Arab Emirates, in the form of a strip running from west to east. This strip is 1200 km long and 50 to 300 km across. These sand hills start 150 km off Sana'a in Yemen, extend over both sides of Omani-Saudi border and reach up to a point 100 km short of al-'Ain in the United Arab Emirates. A part of this strip (150 km long) is in Yemen, a part (600 km) on either side the joint Yemeni-Saudi Arabian border, a part (200 km) on either side of the Oman-Saudi Arabian border, 300 km further down inside Saudi Arabia, and the rest (50 km) inside the United Arab Emirates.

Each sand hill there is one-half to one km wide and 50 to 150 m high. Some of those curved sand hills are hundreds of kilometers long, compact, without break.

It should be noted that these curved sand hills look like hard rocks or cliffs but, in fact, they are made up of very soft sands and, stranger still, by virtue of their peculiar formation and their inherent chemicals, they retain their shapes in the face of violent storms.

According to geologists, Al-Ahqāf contains a large quantity of underground water. This is due to the rain-waters brought by the monsoons in the mountain ranges of Yemen and Oman that go into the well-known valleys of *Rahoot* and *'Arabah* and then into the sand hills in this southern part of the Peninsula. In the intervening lowlands between these high sand

Water found in Empty Quarter

hills, where water is nearer to the surface of the earth or exists in the form of streams, people have been living for centuries and maintaining farms. These regions feature an abundance of oases and flocks of cattle.

The following Verses of the Qur'ān relate what Prophet Hud عليه السلام said to his people, the tribesmen of 'Ād:

﴿ أَتَبْنُونَ بِكُلِّ رِيعٍ ءَايَةً تَعْبَثُونَ ﴿١٢٨﴾ وَتَتَّخِذُونَ مَصَانِعَ لَعَلَّكُمْ تَخْلُدُونَ ﴿١٢٩﴾ وَإِذَا بَطَشْتُم
بَطَشْتُمْ جَبَّارِينَ ﴿١٣٠﴾ فَاتَّقُوا اللَّهَ وَأَطِيعُونِ ﴿١٣١﴾ وَاتَّقُوا الَّذِي أَمَدَّكُم بِمَا تَعْلَمُونَ ﴿١٣٢﴾ أَمَدَّكُم بِأَنْعَامٍ
وَبَنِينَ ﴿١٣٣﴾ وَجَنَّاتٍ وَعُيُونٍ ﴾

"Do you build high palaces on every high place, while you do not live in them? And do you get for yourselves palaces (fine buildings) as if you will live therein forever? And when you seize (somebody), seize you (him) as tyrants?. So fear Allāh, keep your duty to Him, and obey me. And keep your duty to Him, fear Him Who has aided you with all (good things) that you know. He has aided you with cattle and children. And gardens and springs."[1]

﴿ فَلَمَّا رَأَوْهُ عَارِضًا مُّسْتَقْبِلَ أَوْدِيَتِهِمْ قَالُوا هَٰذَا عَارِضٌ مُّمْطِرُنَا ۚ بَلْ هُوَ مَا اسْتَعْجَلْتُم بِهِ ۖ رِيحٌ فِيهَا
عَذَابٌ أَلِيمٌ ﴿٢٤﴾ تُدَمِّرُ كُلَّ شَيْءٍ بِأَمْرِ رَبِّهَا فَأَصْبَحُوا لَا يُرَىٰ إِلَّا مَسَاكِنُهُمْ ﴾

"Then, when they saw it as a dense cloud coming towards their valleys, they said: "This is a cloud bringing us rain!" Nay, but it is that (torment)

1 Ash-Shu'ara': 26:128-134.

which you were asking to be hastened – a wind wherein is a painful torment! Destroying everything by the Command of its Lord! So they became such that nothing could be seen except their dwellings! Thus do We recompense the people who are Mujrimūn (criminals, sinners, polytheists, disbelievers)!"[1]

Surah *Al-Hāqqah* gives another graphic account of their utter destruction, and of the carnage wreaked by a cold, violent storm (*Sarsar* صر صر):

﴿ وَأَمَّا عَادٌ فَأُهْلِكُوا بِرِيحٍ صَرْصَرٍ عَاتِيَةٍ (٦) سَخَّرَهَا عَلَيْهِمْ سَبْعَ لَيَالٍ وَثَمَانِيَةَ أَيَّامٍ حُسُومًا
فَتَرَى الْقَوْمَ فِيهَا صَرْعَىٰ كَأَنَّهُمْ أَعْجَازُ نَخْلٍ خَاوِيَةٍ (٧) فَهَلْ تَرَىٰ لَهُم مِّن بَاقِيَةٍ (٨) ﴾

"And as for `Ād, – they were destroyed by a furious violent wind! Which Allāh imposed on them for seven nights and eight days in succession, so that you could see men lying overthrown (destroyed), as if they were hollow trunks of date palms! Do you see any remnants of them?"[2]

﴿ فَأَرْسَلْنَا عَلَيْهِمْ رِيحًا صَرْصَرًا فِي أَيَّامٍ نَّحِسَاتٍ لِّنُذِيقَهُمْ عَذَابَ الْخِزْيِ فِي الْحَيَاةِ الدُّنْيَا ۖ وَلَعَذَابُ
الْآخِرَةِ أَخْزَىٰ ۖ وَهُمْ لَا يُنصَرُونَ (١٦) ﴾

"So, We sent upon them a furious wind in days of evil omen (for them) that We might give them a taste of disgracing torment in this present worldly life. But surely the torment of the Hereafter will be more disgracing, and they will never be helped."[3]

The following Verses describe the situation of 'Ād in more detail:

﴿ وَإِلَىٰ عَادٍ أَخَاهُمْ هُودًا ۗ قَالَ يَا قَوْمِ اعْبُدُوا اللَّهَ مَا لَكُم مِّنْ إِلَٰهٍ غَيْرُهُ ۚ أَفَلَا تَتَّقُونَ (٦٥) قَالَ الْمَلَأُ
الَّذِينَ كَفَرُوا مِن قَوْمِهِ إِنَّا لَنَرَاكَ فِي سَفَاهَةٍ وَإِنَّا لَنَظُنُّكَ مِنَ الْكَاذِبِينَ (٦٦) قَالَ
يَا قَوْمِ لَيْسَ بِي سَفَاهَةٌ وَلَٰكِنِّي رَسُولٌ مِّن رَّبِّ الْعَالَمِينَ (٦٧) أُبَلِّغُكُمْ رِسَالَاتِ رَبِّي وَأَنَا لَكُمْ
نَاصِحٌ أَمِينٌ (٦٨) أَوَعَجِبْتُمْ أَن جَاءَكُمْ ذِكْرٌ مِّن رَّبِّكُمْ عَلَىٰ رَجُلٍ مِّنكُمْ لِيُنذِرَكُمْ ۚ وَاذْكُرُوا
إِذْ جَعَلَكُمْ خُلَفَاءَ مِن بَعْدِ قَوْمِ نُوحٍ وَزَادَكُمْ فِي الْخَلْقِ بَسْطَةً ۖ فَاذْكُرُوا آلَاءَ اللَّهِ لَعَلَّكُمْ
تُفْلِحُونَ (٦٩) ﴾

1 Al-Ahqāf: 46:24-25.
2 Al-Haqqa: 69: 6-8.
3 Hamim As-Sajdah (or Fussilat): 41: 16.

"And to 'Ād (people, We sent) their brother Hūd. He said: ``O my people! Worship Allāh! You have no other Ilāh (God) but Him. (Lā ilāha illallāh: none has the right to be worshipped but Allāh.) Will you not fear (Allāh)?" The leaders of those who disbelieved among his people said: ``Verily, we see you in foolishness, and verily, we think you are one of the liars." (Hūd) said: ``O my people! There is no foolishness in me, but (I am) a Messenger from the Lord of the 'Ālamīn (mankind, jinn and all that exists)! ``I convey to you the Messages of my Lord, and I am a trustworthy adviser (or well-wisher) for you. ``Do you wonder that there has come to you a Reminder (and an advice) from your Lord through a man from amongst you to warn you? And remember that He made you successors after the people of Nūh (Noah) and increased you amply in stature. So remember the graces (bestowed upon you) from Allāh so that you may be successful."[1]

﴿كَذَّبَتْ عَادٌ ٱلْمُرْسَلِينَ ﴿١٢٣﴾ إِذْ قَالَ لَهُمْ أَخُوهُمْ هُودٌ أَلَا تَتَّقُونَ﴾

"'Ād (people) denied the Messengers. When their brother Hūd said to them: "Will you not fear Allāh and obey Him?"[2]

﴿وَٱذْكُرْ أَخَا عَادٍ إِذْ أَنذَرَ قَوْمَهُۥ بِٱلْأَحْقَافِ وَقَدْ خَلَتِ ٱلنُّذُرُ مِنۢ بَيْنِ يَدَيْهِ وَمِنْ خَلْفِهِۦٓ أَلَّا تَعْبُدُوٓا۟ إِلَّا ٱللَّهَ إِنِّىٓ أَخَافُ عَلَيْكُمْ عَذَابَ يَوْمٍ عَظِيمٍ﴾

"And remember (Hūd) the brother of 'Ād, when he warned his people in Al-Ahqāf (the curved sand-hills in the southern part of Arabian Peninsula). And surely, there have passed away warners before him and after him (saying): "Worship none but Allāh; truly, I fear for you the torment of a mighty Day (i.e. the Day of Resurrection)."[3]

﴿وَتِلْكَ عَادٌ ۖ جَحَدُوا۟ بِـَٔايَـٰتِ رَبِّهِمْ وَعَصَوْا۟ رُسُلَهُۥ وَٱتَّبَعُوٓا۟ أَمْرَ كُلِّ جَبَّارٍ عَنِيدٍ﴾

"Such were ' Ād (people). They rejected the Ayāt (proofs, evidences, verses, lessons, signs, revelations, etc.) of their Lord and disobeyed His Messengers, and followed the command of every proud, obstinate (oppressor of the

1 Al-A'raf: 7:65-69.
2 Ash-Shu'ara: 26:123-124.
3 Al-Ahqāf: 46:21.

truth from their leaders)."[1]

The Ruins of ʻĀd People excavated from al-Ahqāf

These Verses mention various pieces of information that point to the reason for the destruction of ʻĀd. The tribesmen of ʻĀd gained power and prosperity several times during their existence, yet when their prophet came to them, they denied him repeatedly. Prophet Hūd ﷺ reminded them of the blessings of Allah upon them and that He made them successors of Noah's folk, multiplied them in the land, and gave them strength. These blessings related to the initial period of their history when they were very prosperous, tall in stature, and strongly built.

Prophet Hūd ﷺ was not the only prophet whom they had rejected; Allah had sent to them other warners as well, whom the people of ʻĀd rebelled against as well. In their arrogance, the tribesmen of ʻĀd denied the divine blessings showered upon them, and consistently ignored the pleading of their prophets.

In conclusion, it can be said that the first tribe *(ʻĀd Ūla)*, the *ʻĀd of Iram*, dwelt in northern Arabia and Syria.[2] These people were the first generation of ʻĀd, who thrived and reached the zenith of their power and were eventually destroyed on account of their disbelief. As for the second generation of ʻĀd, the later ʻĀd *(ʻĀd Ukhra),* they were those who lived inside the Peninsula, in Yemen, near Hadramaut, beside the Ahqāf (sand dunes).

A Hadith (Musnad Ahmad 3/482) with a Hasan (good) chain of

1 Hūd: 11:59.
2 Al-Maʻarif li-Ibn Qutaiba, P.14

Settlement of 'Ād (Hadhramout)

A grave attributed to Prophet Hūd

narration relates that Harith bin Hassān Bakrī and 'Alā' bin Hadramī(رضي الله عنه) set out to see the Prophet. The Hadith goes on to say: "I (Hārith) said: I seek the refuge of Allah and His Prophet from becoming like the envoy of 'Ād." The Prophet (ﷺ) asked him: "What is the matter of 'Ād's envoy?"He (ﷺ) already knew the answer, but asked the question to see what answer Hārith would give. Harith continued, "I said: "When 'Ād were afflicted with famine, they sent Qail bin Anazah to Mu'āwiyah bin Bakr in Makkah and asked him to pray for rain. Their envoy, Qail, stayed with Mu'āwiyah for a month. During this time he was entertained by two female singers. When a month had passed, he went out, very depressed and sad, and as he prayed for rain for the people of 'Ād, two clouds appeared. He chose the dark one. Then he heard a voice, saying: "Take this! It is burnt ash. It will not leave a single one of 'Ād."

A Hadith collected by Tirmidhi relates the same story.

This narration supports the story that these were the people who were doomed by 'a fatal wind' *(ar-Reeh al-'Aqeem)*.[1]

An inscription relating to this tribe was discovered in 1834 at Hisn Ghurab, a place near Aden. According to this inscription, their kings would punish their wicked men according to the law of Hud. This, or a similar inscription was discovered during the caliphate of Mu'āwiyah ibn Abi Sufyān(رضي الله عنهما). That inscription, read by the contemporary archeologists, confirms the view that Hūd عليه السلام was sent as a prophet to the later 'Ād. According to Rev. Forester, this inscription dates to a period eighteen

1 Jami' At-Tirmidhi: 3273.

hundred years before Jesus.

Several commentators of the Qur'ān and historians quote a narration from Ali bin Abi Talib ﷺ saying that Hud's grave is sited on a red-colored mound, the head of it shaded by a casuarina tree (a kind of oak).[1]This narration has a weak chain of transmission but, according to a popular saying, Hud's grave is sited at a place in Hadramaut, about 200 km north of the coastal town of al-Mukallah. However, there is also a claim that Prophet Hūd عليه السلام was buried in Palestine.

Of the two assertions, it is most likely that Prophet Hūd عليه السلام was buried in Hadramaut, as it corresponds to the evidence that he عليه السلام was sent to the people of 'Ād who were located in Yemen.

In Hadramaut there are many relics named Dār 'Ād (the home of 'Ād) by the natives of the area.[2]It can be thus inferred that a people with a great civilization lived thousands of years ago beside the Ahqāf.

In 1843, a soldier from Bavaria (Germany) travelled to the southern edge of that region, near Hadramaut. He stated that if one stood on the northern height of Hadramaut and viewed this desert, it would look a thousand feet lower, interspersed with several white sandy patches, the sands of which are as fine as powder. If something fell within those sands, it would continue to sink and never be recovered.[3]

It may be that this man had arrived in the very region where the dwelling-place of the 'Ād tribesmen had been destroyed by a barren (fatal) wind. The Qur'ān relates:

﴿وَفِي عَادٍ إِذْ أَرْسَلْنَا عَلَيْهِمُ الرِّيحَ الْعَقِيمَ ﴿٤١﴾ مَا تَذَرُ مِن شَيْءٍ أَتَتْ عَلَيْهِ إِلَّا جَعَلَتْهُ كَالرَّمِيمِ﴾

"And in `Ād (there is also a sign) when We sent against them the barren wind; It spared nothing that it reached, but blew it into broken spreads of rotten ruins."[4]

1 Tareekh 'Ard-il-Qur'ān (Kamil): 1/32; and Historical Geography of Arabia, P. 90, 91.

2 Al-Mufassal Fi Tareekh-il-Arab Qabl-al-Islam: 1/304, 305; and Al-Bidaya Wan-Nihaya: 1/113.

3 Arabia and the Isles, Harold Ingrams, London, 1946.

4 Adh-Dhariyat: 51:`41-42.

Religion of 'Ād

Both eras of the tribesmen of 'Ād, those of Iram and otherwise, were idol-worshipers. According to Arab historians, their chief idols were three: *Sadā* (صدا), *Samood* (صمود), and *Hibā'* (هبا)' (or *Harā'* هراء). They were the first people to renew the worship of idols after the Deluge of Nūh (Noah). Amongst other things, these Arab people also worshipped the moon.[1]

Prophet Hūd عليه السلام

The Qur'ān mentions the first tribe of 'Ād *('Ād Ūla)* only briefly. As for the 'Ād tribesmen who lived in the southern part of the Arabian Peninsula, the Qur'ān describes them and their conduct frequently in considerable detail. The Qur'ān tells us that when they trespassed all limits, Allah appointed one of their own tribe as a prophet to guide them. His name was Hūd عليه السلام. Allah mentions him after the story of Noah عليه السلام:

﴿وَإِلَىٰ عَادٍ أَخَاهُمْ هُودًا ۗ قَالَ يَٰقَوْمِ ٱعْبُدُوا۟ ٱللَّهَ مَا لَكُم مِّنْ إِلَٰهٍ غَيْرُهُۥٓ ۚ أَفَلَا تَتَّقُونَ﴾

"And to 'Ād (people, We sent) their brother Hūd. He said: ``O my people! Worship Allāh! You have no other Ilāh (God) but Him. (Lā ilāha illallāh: none has the right to be worshipped but Allāh.) Will you not fear (Allāh)?"[2]

Hostility Towards Hūd

Prophet Hūd عليه السلام preached and exhorted his people to worship Allah alone, obey Him, and seek His forgiveness. He warned them that, in case they did not obey his call, they would be doomed in this world and the next. However, they retorted, claiming:

﴿إِنَّا لَنَرَىٰكَ فِى سَفَاهَةٍ﴾

"We surely see you in foolishness."3

In essence, they dismissed the belief in One True God as insanity and idolatry as rational and wise! Furthermore, they denied that Hud was a prophet sent by Allah; in response, Hūd عليه السلام said,

1 Tareekh-ut-Tabari: 1/150; and Al-Bidaya Wan-Nihaya: 1/113.

2 Al-A'raf: 7:65.

3 Al-A'raf: 7:66.

﴿ يَٰقَوۡمِ لَيۡسَ بِي سَفَاهَةٞ وَلَٰكِنِّي رَسُولٞ مِّن رَّبِّ ٱلۡعَٰلَمِينَ ﴾

"O my people! There is no foolishness in me, but (I am) a Messenger from the Lord of the 'Ālamīn (mankind, jinn and all that exists)!"[1]

Rejection

Not only did Hūd's people reject his prophethood, they also denied the resurrection of the dead, dismissing it as something unreasonable and impossible. In their denial of Hud's message, they asserted that a human being can never be a messenger of God:

﴿ وَقَالَ ٱلۡمَلَأُ مِن قَوۡمِهِ ٱلَّذِينَ كَفَرُواْ وَكَذَّبُواْ بِلِقَآءِ ٱلۡأٓخِرَةِ وَأَتۡرَفۡنَٰهُمۡ فِي ٱلۡحَيَوٰةِ ٱلدُّنۡيَا مَا هَٰذَآ إِلَّا بَشَرٞ مِّثۡلُكُمۡ يَأۡكُلُ مِمَّا تَأۡكُلُونَ مِنۡهُ وَيَشۡرَبُ مِمَّا تَشۡرَبُونَ ٣٣ وَلَئِنۡ أَطَعۡتُم بَشَرٗا مِّثۡلَكُمۡ إِنَّكُمۡ إِذٗا لَّخَٰسِرُونَ ٣٤ أَيَعِدُكُمۡ أَنَّكُمۡ إِذَا مِتُّمۡ وَكُنتُمۡ تُرَابٗا وَعِظَٰمًا أَنَّكُم مُّخۡرَجُونَ ﴾

"And the chiefs of his people who disbelieved and denied the Meeting in the Hereafter, and whom We had given the luxuries and comforts of this life, said: "He is no more than a human being like you, he eats of that which you eat, and drinks of what you drink. If you were to obey a human being like yourselves, then verily, you indeed would be losers. Does he promise you that when you have died and have become dust and bones, you shall come out alive (resurrected)?"[2]

When Hūd's folks spurned his call, he proclaimed his innocence of the sin of idolatry:

﴿ إِنِّيٓ أُشۡهِدُ ٱللَّهَ وَٱشۡهَدُوٓاْ أَنِّي بَرِيٓءٞ مِّمَّا تُشۡرِكُونَ ٥٤ مِن دُونِهِۦۖ فَكِيدُونِي جَمِيعٗا ثُمَّ لَا تُنظِرُونِ ﴾

"All that we say is that some of our gods (false deities) have seized you with evil (madness)." He said: I call Allāh to witness and bear you witness that I am free from that which you ascribe as partners in worship, with Him (Allāh). So plot against me, all of you, and give me no respite."[3]

1 Al-A'raf: 7:67.
2 Al-Muminun: 23:33-35.
3 Hūd: 11:54-55.

Punishment

Hūd's folk persisted in their rebellion. Exhausted and weary, he turned to Allah for help:

﴿ قَالَ رَبِّ ٱنصُرْنِي بِمَا كَذَّبُونِ ﴿٣٩﴾ قَالَ عَمَّا قَلِيلٍ لَّيُصْبِحُنَّ نَٰدِمِينَ ﴿٤٠﴾ فَأَخَذَتْهُمُ ٱلصَّيْحَةُ بِٱلْحَقِّ
فَجَعَلْنَٰهُمْ غُثَآءً ۚ فَبُعْدًا لِّلْقَوْمِ ٱلظَّٰلِمِينَ ﴾

" He said: "O my Lord! Help me because they deny me." (Allāh) said: "In a little while, they are sure to be regretful." So, As-Saihah (torment—awful cry) overtook them in truth (with justice), and We made them as rubbish of dead plants. So, away with the people who are Zālimūn (polytheists, wrongdoers, disbelievers in the Oneness of Allāh, disobedient to His Messengers)."[1]

Allah sent clouds over the valley wherein they lived, and the people of Hud were gleeful, thinking that these were rain clouds sent to nourish them. However, these were not harbingers of beneficial rain, but portents of widespread death and destruction, just as Hūd (عليه السلام) had promised:

﴿ فَلَمَّا رَأَوْهُ عَارِضًا مُّسْتَقْبِلَ أَوْدِيَتِهِمْ قَالُوا۟ هَٰذَا عَارِضٌ مُّمْطِرُنَا ۚ بَلْ هُوَ مَا ٱسْتَعْجَلْتُم بِهِۦ ۖ رِيحٌ فِيهَا عَذَابٌ
أَلِيمٌ ﴿٢٤﴾ تُدَمِّرُ كُلَّ شَىْءٍۭ بِأَمْرِ رَبِّهَا فَأَصْبَحُوا۟ لَا يُرَىٰٓ إِلَّا مَسَٰكِنُهُمْ ۚ كَذَٰلِكَ نَجْزِى ٱلْقَوْمَ ٱلْمُجْرِمِينَ ﴾

"Then, when they saw it as a dense cloud coming towards their valleys, they said: "This is a cloud bringing us rain!" Nay, but it is that (torment)

1 Al-Muminun: 23:39-41.

which you were asking to be hastened – a wind wherein is a painful torment! Destroying everything by the Command of its Lord! So they became such that nothing could be seen except their dwellings! Thus do We recompense the people who are Mujrimūn (criminals, sinners, polytheists, disbelievers)!"[1]

The entire civilization of 'Ād was destroyed, except for Hūd and those individual believes who followed him.

﴿ وَلَمَّا جَآءَ أَمْرُنَا نَجَّيْنَا هُودًا وَٱلَّذِينَ ءَامَنُوا۟ مَعَهُۥ بِرَحْمَةٍ مِّنَّا وَنَجَّيْنَٰهُم مِّنْ عَذَابٍ غَلِيظٍ ﴾

"And when Our Commandment came, We saved Hūd and those who believed with him by a mercy from Us, and We saved them from a severe torment."[2]

Thus, they were destroyed by a violent storm which kept blowing continuously for seven nights and eight days. This is the storm described in Surah *al-Hāqqah*, which destroyed them completely.

﴿ وَأَمَّا عَادٌ فَأُهْلِكُوا۟ بِرِيحٍ صَرْصَرٍ عَاتِيَةٍ ﴿٦﴾ سَخَّرَهَا عَلَيْهِمْ سَبْعَ لَيَالٍ وَثَمَٰنِيَةَ أَيَّامٍ حُسُومًا فَتَرَى ٱلْقَوْمَ فِيهَا صَرْعَىٰ كَأَنَّهُمْ أَعْجَازُ نَخْلٍ خَاوِيَةٍ ﴿٧﴾ فَهَلْ تَرَىٰ لَهُم مِّنۢ بَاقِيَةٍ ﴾

"And as for `Ād, – they were destroyed by a furious violent wind! Which Allāh imposed on them for seven nights and eight days in succession, so that you could see men lying overthrown (destroyed), as if they were hollow trunks of date palms! Do you see any remnants of them?"[3]

1 Al-Ahqāf: 46:24-25.
2 Hūd: 11:58.
3 Al-Hāqqah: 69:6-8.

Thamūd

Thamūd was another famous, ancient tribe of Arabia. Like the people of 'Ād, the sire of this tribe, Thamūd, was one of the descendants of Iram, son of Shem, son of Noah عليه السلام.

Their story mirrors that of 'Ād: in their days of prosperity, they rebelled against Allah and transgressed the limits He had placed upon them. Allah sent His prophet, Sālīh عليه السلام, to guide them just as He had sent Hūd عليه السلام to guide the people of 'Ād. Historians have pieced together the lineage of Sālih عليه السلام from various sources, tracing it as such: Sālih son of Obaid son of Asf son of Māsikh son of Obaid son of Khādar son of Thamūd son of Jāthir ('Ābir) son of Iram son of Shem son of Noah.[1]

1 Tareekh-ut-Tabari: 1/158; see also Al-Bidaya Wan Nihaya: 1/123.

The Era of Thamūd

These people are counted amongst the extinct Arab tribes *(al-Arab al-Bā'idah)*. It is difficult to determine the exact period in history during which they lived, although accounts from the Revealed Books relate that they had already perished before Prophet Abraham ﷺ started his mission. Like 'Ād, they, too, were the descendants of Shem, son of Noah ﷺ and, therefore, their political heirs. Allah says:

﴿وَاذْكُرُوا إِذْ جَعَلَكُمْ خُلَفَاءَ مِنْ بَعْدِ﴾

"And remember when He made you successors after 'Ād (people)."[1]

Dwellings of Thamūd

Bi'r Thamūd (well of Thamūd)

The tribesmen of Thamūd lived in al-Hijr (الحجر), in houses hewn from the mountains themselves. The Qur'ān describes their dwellings in the following Verses:

﴿وَلَقَدْ كَذَّبَ أَصْحَابُ الْحِجْرِ الْمُرْسَلِينَ ﴿٨٠﴾ وَآتَيْنَاهُمْ آيَاتِنَا فَكَانُوا عَنْهَا مُعْرِضِينَ ﴿٨١﴾ وَكَانُوا يَنْحِتُونَ مِنَ الْجِبَالِ بُيُوتًا آمِنِينَ﴾

"And verily, the Dwellers of Al-Hijr (the rocky tract) denied the Messengers. And We gave them Our Signs, but they were averse to them. And they used to hew out dwellings from the mountains, (feeling themselves) secure."[2]

Al-Hijr was the central town of the tribesmen of Thamūd. Relics of this town have been found a little further away from al-'Ulā, a place northwest of Madinah.

When the Prophet Muhammad (ﷺ), on his way to Tabūk, passed by Al-Hijr, he covered his head with a sheet of cloth, quickened his beast of carriage, and said to his companions: "Do not enter the homes (i.e. the

1 A'raf: 7:74.
2 Al-Hijr: 15:80-82.

territory) of those who were doomed except in a state of crying and, in case you cannot cry, do not enter them lest you might be doomed like them."[1]

A Verse of the Qur'ān seems to suggest that *Wadi al-Qura* was the place where Thamūd lived:

﴿وَثَمُودَ ٱلَّذِينَ جَابُوا۟ ٱلصَّخْرَ بِٱلْوَادِ﴾

"And (how your Lord dealt with) Thamūd (people) who hewed out rocks in the valley (to make dwellings)?"[2]

According to the commentators of the Qur'ān, 'the valley' *(Bi'l-wād)* refers to Wadi al-Qura where their dwellings were sited.[3]

Various geographers and historians have visited this location. Muhammad Asim Al-Haddād, who accompanied Sayyed 'Abul- 'A'la Maudoodi, on a visit to that place, said: "The doors of the dwellings were hewn out of rocks and bore graven images of animals (horses, falcons, etc.). There is also an inscription above the door of a house. In some houses there were also shelves and other places to store things. No house has a

1 Sahih Al-Bukhari: 4419, 4702; and Sahih Muslim: 2980.
2 Al-Fajr: 84:9.
3 Ttafseer-ul-Qurtubi: Al-Fajr: 89:9.

Panorama picture of Alula

threshold."[1]

There is also a well named Bi'r Thamūd.[2]The inscriptions found there suggest that the tribesmen of Thamūd lived in al-'Ulā and its surrounding areas, and in the region between Hijaz and Jordan.

Some inscriptions prove that Thamūd had occupied a number of places including Ha'il, Tabūk, Taimā', Madā'in Sāleh and Hijaz while some inscriptions also showed that they ranged as far as Ta'if and al-Wajh, a coastal town of Hijaz. According to some inscriptions and relics, they also dwelt in areas of Yemen.

Some scholars have opined that Thamūd was, in fact, the second 'Ād, due to the evidence that some of the sub-branches of Thamūd settled down in areas as far-flung as southern Arabia (Yemen).[3]

From Rābigh to 'Aqabah, and from Madinah and Kheybar, to Taimā' and Tabook, the entire region is full of the relics relating to Thamūd. In the south up to Kheybar and in the north up to 50 km deep inside Jordan, there are cleft mountains, a sign that the earthquake which struck this

1 Safarnama Ard-ul-Qur'ān, P. 202, 210.
2 Al-Mufassal Fi Tareekh-il-Arab Qabl-al-Islam: 1/324.
3 Op.cit. 1/328, 329.

region in ancient times affected an entire area about 500 km long and about 150 km wide.[1]

Al-Hijr and Madā'in Sāleh

Today, al-Hijr is called Mada'in Sālih. However, this name has no factual basis and indeed is confused with another area which has been known as Mada'in Sāleh.

Sa'd bin Abdullah bin Junaidal, quoting a modern research scholar, Hamd al-Jāsir, writes: "These days, people give to al-Hijr valley, which lies north of the town of al-'Ulā, the name of Madā'in Sāleh. This is a serious misunderstanding, however. Here are some facts:

1. Al-Hijr is the name of a valley of a people who lived in pre-Islamic times and were doomed by Allah. Due to the severity of their destruction, the Prophet Muhammad (ﷺ) forbade Muslims to drink even the water of that place.
2. About 55 km south of the town of al-'Ulā, there are relics of some old houses which are now called al-Mābiyāt. This is a new name; in truth, it was called Madinah Sāleh around the seventh century AH and, later, came to be known as Madā'in Sāleh.

Before the seventh century AH, it was most likely called *ar-Ruhbah*; this name occurs frequently in travelogues and dictionaries. Sometime later, like ar-Ruhbah, the name Madinah Sāleh or Madā'in Sāleh fell into oblivion

1 An-Hazoor ke Naqsh-i-Qadam paa (Haram-i-Madinah): 2/117.

Ruins of the stone like structures of the people of Thamūd

Ruins of al-Mābiyāt (Thamūd Area)

and the place came to be known as the valley of al-'Atas. Ibn Batūtah, who visited this place during his travels in the eight century AH, refers to this area in his travelogue by this name. In other books written by Arabs and non-Arabs, this place was variously known as Wadi Daidān, Dadān and Dādān. Yaqūt Hamawi writes: Ar-Ruhbah is a settlement near Wadi-ul-Qura, between Madinah and Syria.[1]

Wadi Daidān (the valley of Daidān), in which Madinah Sāleh (also known as Mada'in Sāleh) is sited, is not adjacent to Wadi Al-Hijr but well away from it.

Cause of Misunderstanding

The pre-Islamic relics of Wadi al-Hijr, north of al-'Ulā, and those belonging to the early days of Islam in the south of al-'Ulā became mixed up and confused with the passage of time.

Mada'in Sāleh, which lies south of al-'Ulā, is named after a pious man, named Sālīh, of Banu Abbas. He was the founder of this town. This town remained populated till the fourth century AH. On the other hand, the inhabitants of Al-Hijr were called the people of Sāleh *(Qaum Sāleh)*. There was also a well called Bi'r Nāqah, and a place here called Masjid Sāleh.

Due to the closeness in location as well as in name, and the abundance of relics proving the existence of past civilizations, al-Hijr has incorrectly been confused with Madā'in Sāleh.

The oldest book in which this error was found is the Arabic translation of a Turkish book entitled *Bahjat Al-Manāzil* or *Nahjat Al-Manāzil*. The name of the Turkish writer is Muhammad Adeeb, who was a chronicler of the Ottoman empire, as mentioned in *Idāh al-Maknoon* (ايضاح المكنون)[2]. According to him, Al-Hijr was known as Madā'in Sāleh, Qura Sāleh, and

1 Mu'jam-ul-Buldan: see under 'Ruhba'.
2 See Eedah-ul-Maknoon Fi'dh-dhail 'Ala Kashf-iz-Zunoon: 2/696.

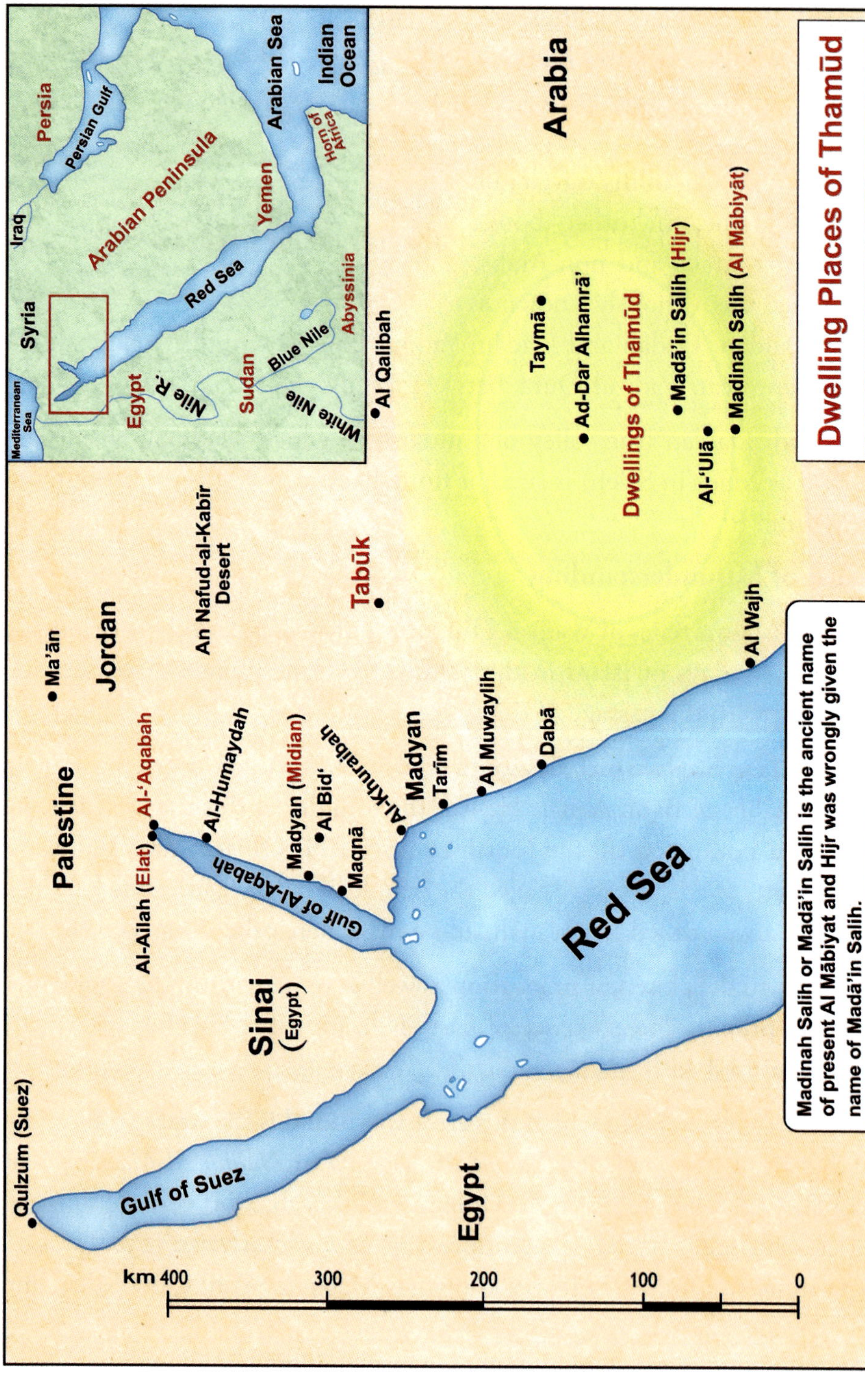
Dwelling Places of Thamūd
Madinah Salih or Madā'in Salih is the ancient name of present Al Mābiyat and Hijr was wrongly given the name of Madā'in Salih.
Arabia
Dwellings of Thamūd
Taymā
Ad-Dar Alhamrā'
Madā'in Sālih (Hijr)
Al-'Ulā
Madinah Salih (Al Mābiyāt)
Al Qalibah
Tabūk
Al Wajh
Dabā
Al Muwaylih
Tarīm
Madyan
Al-Khuraibah
Madyan (Midian)
Al Bid'
Maqnā
Al-Humaydah
Al-'Aqabah
Al-Ailah (Elat)
Gulf of Al-Aqabah
Red Sea
Palestine
Jordan
Ma'ān
An Nafud-al-Kabīr Desert
Sinai (Egypt)
Egypt
Gulf of Suez
Qulzum (Suez)
km 400 300 200 100 0
Mediterranean Sea
Syria
Iraq
Persia
Persian Gulf
Arabian Peninsula
Yemen
Red Sea
Arabian Sea
Indian Ocean
Horn of Africa
Abyssinia
Blue Nile
White Nile
Nile R.
Sudan
Egypt

'Adāl. The first man to confuse one with the other, calling the place south of al-'Ulā (Madā'in Sāleh) the al-Hijr of Thamūd, was a Spanish (Andlucian) traveler named al-Balwi, who in 738 AH had travelled along with the Hajj pilgrims of al-Kark from the direction of Syria.[1]

From the research done by Hamd al-Jāsir, it can be known that in the past al-Hijr and Mada'in Sāleh were the names of two separate places. As time passed, people forgot the name of Mada'in Sāleh situated south of al-'Ulā, and instead began to refer to al-Hijr by the same name. Further confirmation came from British traveler Doughty, who stated that al-Hijr and Mada'in Sāleh were two separate places.[2]

Religion of Thamūd

The people of Thamūd were pagans, who worshipped a number of deities besides Allah – and in some cases, even excluding Him (Allah the Exalted)! Ancient inscriptions reveal the names of their idols, with some of the most famous of them being: Wadd, Yaghūth, Shams, Manāf, Manāt, Ba'lah or Ba'l, Hubal, Qain, Ilāh, Ala, Alahi, al-Lat, and Zu-shara[3]

Of these idols, Wadd and Yaghūth had already been worshipped by the people of Nūh (Noah) before the Arabs. Later on, these idols and those of the people of Nūh were worshipped by other pagans, in addition to the Arabs.

The Qur'ān mentions the names of the most famous idols:

﴿وَقَالُوا۟ لَا تَذَرُنَّ ءَالِهَتَكُمْ وَلَا تَذَرُنَّ وَدًّا وَلَا سُوَاعًا وَلَا يَغُوثَ وَيَعُوقَ وَنَسْرًا﴾

"And they have said: `You shall not leave your gods, nor shall you leave Wadd, nor Suwā`, nor Yaghūth, nor Ya`ūq, nor Nasr ' (these are the names of their idols)."[4]

The Phoenicians worshipped Ba'l in the belief that it was a god of fertility.[5]

1 Mu'jam-ul-Amkinah Al-Warid Dhikruha Fi'l-Qur'ān Al-Kareem Li-Sa'd bin Abdullah bin Junaidal, P. 118-120.
2 Al-Mufassal Fi tareekh-il-Arab Qabl-al-Islam: 1/326.
3 Op.cit., P. 1/329-331.
4 Nūh: 71:23.
5 Al-Munjid Fi'l A'lam: P. 130.

Arabia Petra

Prophet Sālih ﵇ and the Miraculous She-Camel

When the tribesmen of Thamūd became entrenched in the swampy beliefs of idolatry, Allah sent a prophet named Sālih to guide them. In the tradition of all the previous prophets, he called his people to the pure worship of the One True God. However, aside from a few men from the poorest segment of society, none heeded his call. The powerful and affluent derided him:

﴿ قَالَ ٱلْمَلَأُ ٱلَّذِينَ ٱسْتَكْبَرُوا۟ مِن قَوْمِهِۦ لِلَّذِينَ ٱسْتُضْعِفُوا۟ لِمَنْ ءَامَنَ مِنْهُمْ أَتَعْلَمُونَ
أَنَّ صَٰلِحًا مُّرْسَلٌ مِّن رَّبِّهِۦ ۚ قَالُوٓا۟ إِنَّا بِمَآ أُرْسِلَ بِهِۦ مُؤْمِنُونَ ﴿٧٥﴾ قَالَ ٱلَّذِينَ
ٱسْتَكْبَرُوٓا۟ إِنَّا بِٱلَّذِىٓ ءَامَنتُم بِهِۦ كَٰفِرُونَ ﴾

> *"The leaders of those who were arrogant among his people said to those who were counted weak – to such of them as believed: ``Know you that Sāleh is one sent from his Lord." They said: ``We indeed believe in that with which he has been sent. Those who were arrogant said: ``Verily, we disbelieve in that which you believe in."*[1]

Sālih's people accused him of being bewitched, and challenged him to produce evidence that would prove the truth of his claims. Allah sent a miraculous she-camel to be the token of Sālih's truthfulness, but in their arrogance, the evil people of Sāleh's tribe profaned it.

1 Al-A'rāf: 7:75-76.

﴿ قَالَ هَٰذِهِۦ نَاقَةٌ لَّهَا شِرْبٌ وَلَكُمْ شِرْبُ يَوْمٍ مَّعْلُومٍ ﴿١٥٥﴾ وَلَا تَمَسُّوهَا بِسُوٓءٍ فَيَأْخُذَكُمْ عَذَابُ يَوْمٍ عَظِيمٍ ﴿١٥٦﴾ فَعَقَرُوهَا فَأَصْبَحُوا۟ نَٰدِمِينَ ﴾

"He said: "Here is a she-camel: it has a right to drink (water), and you have a right to drink (water) (each) on a day, known. And touch her not with harm, lest the torment of a Great Day should seize you. But they killed her, and then they became regretful."[1]

Thamūd's transgression of all limits resulted in their terrible punishment. Sāleh warned them,

﴿ تَمَتَّعُوا۟ فِى دَارِكُمْ ثَلَٰثَةَ أَيَّامٍ ﴾

"Enjoy yourselves in your homes for three days!"[2]

The Doom of Thamūd

The people of Thamūd not only denied the blessings of Allah, but they deliberately disobeyed Him and destroyed the she-camel that had been sent as a miracle to them. Their actions brought about Allah's Wrath and a severe Punishment, which has been described in various places in the Qur'ān:

﴿ فَأَخَذَتْهُمُ ٱلصَّيْحَةُ مُصْبِحِينَ ﴿٨٣﴾ فَمَآ أَغْنَىٰ عَنْهُم مَّا كَانُوا۟ يَكْسِبُونَ ﴾

"But As-Saihah (torment—awful cry) overtook them in the early morning (of the fourth day of their promised punishment days). And all that they used to earn availed them not."[3]

﴿ إِنَّآ أَرْسَلْنَا عَلَيْهِمْ صَيْحَةً وَٰحِدَةً فَكَانُوا۟ كَهَشِيمِ ٱلْمُحْتَظِرِ ﴾

"Verily, We sent against them a single Saihah (torment – awful cry), and they became like the stubble of a fold-builder."[4]

In His Mercy, however, Allah saved Sāleh and those who believed in him.

﴿ وَأَنجَيْنَا ٱلَّذِينَ ءَامَنُوا۟ وَكَانُوا۟ يَتَّقُونَ ﴾

"And We saved those who believed, and used to fear Allah, and keep their duty to Him."[5]

1 Ash-Shu'ara': 26:155 - 157.
2 Hūd: 11:65.
3 Al-Hijr: 15:83-84.
4 Al-Qamar: 54:31.
5 An-Naml: 27:53.

Thamūd the Second

Those who were saved from the Punishment of Allah, such as Sāleh ﷺ and his followers, are known in history as Thamūd the Second.

Sayyed Suleman Nadwi writes:

"The name of Thamūd the Second is found in the inscriptions of Assyria as well as in the history of the Romans. Thamūd is mentioned among the Arab tribes ruled by Sargon II, king of Assyria (722 BC-705 BC). Their names are found in the inscriptions commemorating his victory."

The Greek historian Dydoros named Thamūd as Thamūdeni. Ptolemy referred to them as Thamūditae. The Greek author Uranus stated that the tribesmen of Thamūd were settled beside Nabateans.

During the reign of Roman emperor Justinian (527 CE-565 CE), 300 Thamūdi Arabs served in the Roman army. They were known for their long spears and camels. Most of their territory had already been seized by the Midianis and the rest occupied by the Nabateans. Thus, when the Romans occupied Arabia Petra[1] shortly before the birth of Christ, they escaped to their northern neighbors and sided with them out of hostility to the Nabateans.

When Islam came, there was no trace left of Thamūd in Arabia. Their territory was resettled by the tribes of Juhainah and Baliyy, and by the Jews.[2]

1 The Jordanian town of Petra evokes the memory of Arabia Petra.

2 Tareekh 'Ard-il- Qur'ān (Kamil): 160 – 159 /1; Al-Musassal Fi Tareekh-il-Arab Qabl-al-Islam: 325/1.

Tasm and Jadees

Tasm and Jadees were two tribes who, like ʿĀd and Thamūd, thrived and prospered by the Grace of Allah; however, they became ungrateful to their Lord and turned to idolatry. Their fate became the same as that of their predecessors: they were doomed to extinction.

A settlement of Tasm and Jadees

Genealogists describe the lineage of Lauz (لاوذ), the sire of Tasm and Jadees: Lauz, son of Iram, son of Shem, son of Noah عليه السلام. Tasm and Jadees were brothers whose offspring were settled in Yemen.

The punishment of their sins came in the form of mutual hostility. It is said that Banu Jadees, exasperated by the tyranny of their ruler Amlooq (or Amleeq) who was from the tribe of Tasm, decided to massacre Banu Tasm. A man of the latter tribe, named Rabah bin Murrah, escaped the massacre, fled to Hassān bin Tubbaʿ, and appealed to him for help. He invaded Banu Jadees and destroyed them.[1] This is the same story as that of Zarqā' al-Yamāmah, mentioned previously in this volume.

Hajr Yamāmah was a thriving settlement of Tasm and Jadees. After the two tribes were destroyed, they left behind splendid mansions and amazing gardens. Later, one-and-half miles away from Hajr, a new settlement was established. Its name was Bādiyah, the settlement of Banu Yarbū ʿ bin Thaʿlabah bin ad-Du'l bin Haneefah.[2]

1 Al-Mufassal Fi tareekh-ul-Arab Qabl-al-Islam 1/334-339; and Wafa'-ul-Wafa Is-Samhūdi: 1/183-186.

2 Urdu Encyclopedia of Islam: 3/870.

A view of Yamāmah

Banu Jurhum

Banu Jurhum were another prominent tribe who played a part in the history of the Arabian peninsula.

Hamdani states that there were two Jurhums; the earlier Jurhums were related to the earlier Semites, while the later Jurhums (Jurhum the Second) were Qahtānis. The former Jurhums, who were contemporaries of 'Ād and Thamūd, became extinct.[1]

The second generation of Banu Jurhum were the descendants of Jurhum, a son of Qahtān. Jurhum's other brother, Ya'rub bin Qahtān, was the ruler of Yemen while Jurhum bin Qahtān was the ruler of Hijaz. The Hijazi tribe of Jurhum were to become the in-laws of Prophet Ismā'īl (Ishmael)عليه السلام.[2]Ismā'īl's second wife was the daughter of Madād Jurhumi, who bore him twelve sons.[3]However, two of those sons became famous - Nābit and Qeydār.

After the death of Prophet Ismā'īlعليه السلام, his son Nābit became the custodian of the Ka'bah. However, it is also said that it was Qeydar who became the custodian of the Ka'bah first and, later, his brother Nābit took over the position. Most of Ismā'īl's sons went further afield in search of livelihood, although some of them stayed near to the Ka'bah. When Nābit died, most of Ismā'īl's children had left the surrounding areas, and those left behind were few in number and much younger in age.

Madād (the Second) bin 'Amr Jurhami undertook the custodianship of the Ka'bah. Sameeda' bin Hūbar, an Amelekite, quarreled with Madād

1 Al-Ikeel Lil-Hamadani: 1/78.
2 Sahih-ul-Bukhari: 3364.
3 Tareekh-ul-Ya'qubi: 1/190.

over the custody of Ka'bah, but Madād succeeded in winning. Sameeda' then left for Syria, and consequently, the rule of Makkah and the custody of the Ka'bah remained in the hands of Madād until he died.

The children of Ismā'īl (Banu Ismā'īl) were dominant wherever they went. However, they also accepted the rule of Banu Jurhum, their maternal kinsmen who also held Banu Ismā'īl in great regard.

During the time of Banu Jurhum, the custody of the Ka'bah remained in the hands of Banu Ismā'īl, as the tribesmen of Jurhum greatly respected the descendants of Ismā'īl and acknowledged their high status as the sons of prophets.

Nabit bin Ismā'īl was succeeded by Ameen, Yashjub bin Ameen, Humaisa', and finally by 'Udad. During this period, Banu Jurhum began to adopt corrupt and evil practices, which 'Udad despised. The last king of Banu Jurhum was Hārith bin Madād Thāni bin 'Amr, a scion of Madād Jurhum. His period of rule was one of the worst, as the tyranny of Banu Jurhum knew no bounds. Eventually, Allah decreed that they be afflicted by an invasion of ants and they were all destroyed during the lifetime of 'Udad.[1]

1 Tareekh-ul-Ya'qūbi: 1/190-191.

Ruins of Banu Jurhum

'Arab Āaribah

(The Pure Arabs)

The 'Arab 'Āaribah,' or pure Arabs, are tribes descended from Sabā bin Yashjub bin Ya'rub bin Qahtān. In reference to their ancestor, they are called Qahtāni Arabs.

Most scholars trace Qahtān's lineage to Iram bin Sām bin Nūh عليه السلام, while some others to 'Ābir bin Shālekh bin Arfakhshad bin Sām bin Nūh عليه السلام. Ibn Hajar gives more weight to the opinion which says that the Qahtān tribesmen are the offspring of Ismā'īl.

Qahtān is also called Abul-Yaman (the father of Yemen), due to the fact that Yemen was the birthplace of the Qahtāni Arabs. The two tribes of Himyar and Kahlān, who were descended from the two sons of Saba bin Yashjub bin Ya'rub bin Qahtān, of the same names, became well known.

Banu Himyar branched off into several tribes, the most famous being Zaid al-Jamhūr, Qudā'ah, and Saksak.

The following are the famous branches of Banu Kahlān:

Hamadān, Anmār, Tayy, Khuzā'ah, Madhhij, Kindah, Lakhm and Judhām, Azd, Aus, Khazraj, and Jafnah.

The majority of those from the Kahlāni tribes left Yemen and scattered over different parts of the Peninsula, sometimes before Sail Iram (the Flood of Iram), when the Romans occupied Egypt and Syria and took control of the maritime trade routes of the Yemenis. On the other hand, the Himyari tribes did not leave Yemen.

A settlement of Mā'rib where 'Arab Āribah lived

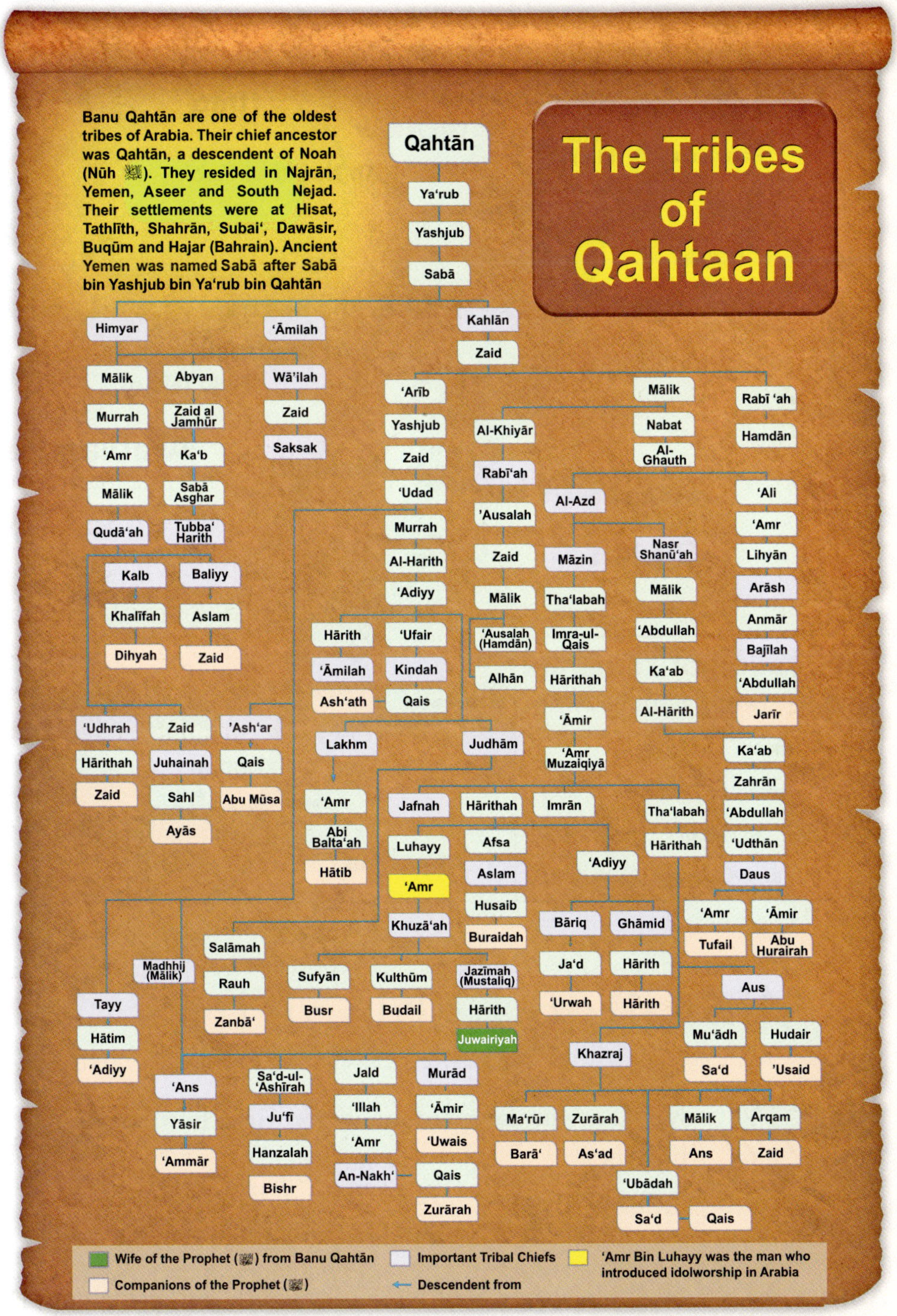

Source: Atlas-ut-Tārīkhī Li-Seerat-ir-Rasool; Mu'jam Qabā'il-il-Arab; Asad-ul-Ghābah; Mujam Masta'jama; Kitāb-ush-Shajart-un-Nabawiyyah; Sabā'ik-dh-Dhahab.

Map.11

Migrating Kahlani Tribes

The Kahlānis who migrated are divided into four famous branches:

1. Azd 2. Lakhm and Judhām 3. Banu Tayy 4. Banu Kindah.

Azd

Azd was the son of Al-Ghauth, son of Nabt (or Nābit), son of Mālik, son of Zaid, son of Kahlān. Azd had six sons: Māzan, Nasr, Abdullah, 'Amr,

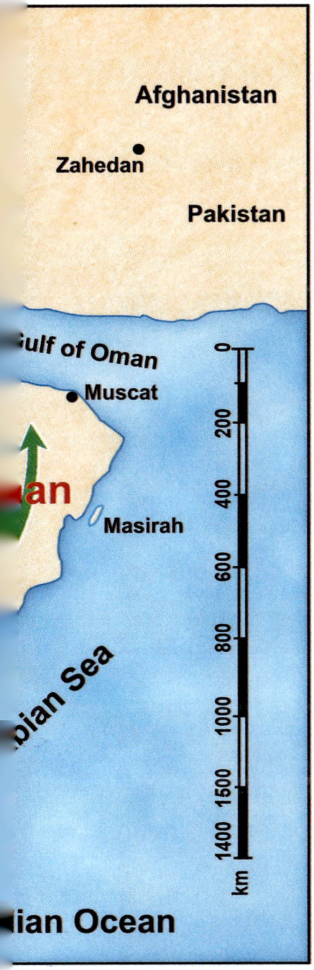

al-Hin' and al-Hārith.[1]

(A) Māzan bin Azd

Banu Māzan bin Azd left their native place on the advice of their chieftain, Imran bin 'Amr Muzaiqiya bin 'Āmir Mā'-as-Samā'. Initially, they roamed within the borders of Yemen but later moved towards the north until their various branches settled in different areas.

The details of the migration of the four sons of 'Amr Muzaiqiya – Tha'labah Bahlūl, the ancestor of the Ansar of Madinah; Hāritha, the ancestor of Banu Khuzā'ah; Imran (Azd Oman); and Jafnah (the family of Ghassān), and their offspring are as follows:

Tha'labah bin 'Amr Muzaiqiya

He moved with his family to Hijaz and stayed between Tha'labiyyah and Dhi Qār. Later, his children moved to Yathrib (Madinah) and settled there. According to the majority of genealogists, Aus and Khazraj have descended from Hārithah bin Tha'labah bin 'Amr.[2]

Aus and Khazraj

The Arab tribes of Aus and Khazraj are the descendants of Hārithh bin Tha'laba Bahlūl bin 'Amr Muzaiqiya bin 'Āmir Mā'-as-Samā' bin Hārithah al-Ghatreef. Those of the genealogists who consider them to be Azdi-Qahtāni trace the upper part of their lineage in the following way: Hārithah al-Ghatreef bin Imra-al-Qais bin Tha'labah bin Māzan (bin 'Abdullah) bin Azd. Qailah was the mother of Aus and Khazraj, the sons of Harithah. For this reason, the latter are also called Banu Qailah. According to Ibn Kalbi and Yaqūt, Aus and Khazraj were known collectively as Khazraj in the Age of Paganism. The ancestor of Banu Khazraj, Khazraj bin Hārithah, was called Khazraj al-Akbar.

1 Sabā'ik-uz-Zahab, P. 270.
2 Ar-Raheeq-ul-Makhtūm, P. 16-17.

Sub-tribes of Banu Aus

1. Banu Hārithah bin Hārith bin Khazraj al-Asghar bin 'Amr (Nabeet) bin Mālik bin Aus. Their dwelling place, *al-Maseer*, was in Dar Bani Abdul-Ash'hal, near Harrah Sharqiyyah. Later, they moved northwest and built a dwelling-place called ar-Rayyan. Barā' bin 'Āzib رضي الله عنه, a Prophet's companion, belonged to this very tribe.

2. Banu Abdul Ash'hal bin Jusham bin Hārithah bin Hārith bin Khazraj al-Asghar. They too, were settled near Harrah Sharqiyyah (Harrah Wāqim). The name of the settlement was Wāqim. When Banu Harithah quarreled with them and settled west of Mash'had Hamzah (the place where Hamzah رضي الله عنه, the Prophet's uncle and companion, was martyred), Banu Abdul-Ash'hal settled in al-Maseer. Dar Bani Abdul-Ash'hal was near to the present site of Shaikhain where the Prophet ﷺ had pitched his camp on the Day of Uhud. Banu Za'ūrā' bin Jusham were also their kinsmen. Sa'd bin Mu'ādh (the chief of Aus) and Usaid bin Hudair حضير, the Prophet's companions, belonged to Banu Abdul-Ash'hal. Banu Harithah, Abdul-Ash'hal, Banu Za'ura' and Banu Zafar were called "Nabeet".

Harrah Waqim (near Madinah)

3. Banu Zafar (Ka'b) bin Khazraj Al-Asghar. They lived in the neighbourhood of Abdul-Ash'hal, east of Baqee'. Thābit bin Qais رضي الله عنه

, a companion of the Prophet Muhammad ﷺ, belonged to this tribe. The Prophet ﷺ gave him the title of *Hāsir* (one without armour and without head covering), due to his participating in the battle of Uhud.

4. Banu 'Amr bin 'Auf bin Mālik bin Aus. They lived in Qubā, and their house was called *"ash-Shunaif"*. The Prophet's companion, 'Āsim bin Thābit bin Abul-Aqlah ﷺ belonged to this tribe, as did the companion Kulthūm bin Hadm bin Imra-al-Qais ﷺ, at whose place the Prophet ﷺ had stopped at initially.

5. Banu Mu'āwiyah bin Mālik bin 'Auf bin 'Amr bin 'Auf bin Mālik bin Aus: They were settled behind Baqee' al-Gharqad, the well-known cemetery of Madinah, in a residential district of the same name. The Ijabah Mosque was built in that area. The Prophet's companions, Abdullah bin Abdullah bin Thabit bin Qais and Subai' bin Hātib bin Qais ﷺ, belonged to this tribe.

The Ijabah Mosque

6. Banu Umayyah bin Zaid bin Qais bin 'Āmir bin Murrah bin Mālik bin Aus: A rivulet named Mudhainib flowed through their settlement. The dwelling-place of their kinsmen, Banu Wa'il bin Zaid, was called *"al-Mauja"*.

Sub-tribes of Banu Khazraj

1. Banu Hārith bin Khazraj al-Akbar bin Hārithah: They dwelt in 'Awāli, east of Wadi Bat'hān. Jusham and Zaid, the twin sons of Hārith bin Khazraj, dwelt in a residential district named as-Sunh. To this tribe belonged the Prophet's companion Abdullah bin Zaid bin Abd-Rabbihi ﷺ who heard in a dream the words of the *Adhaan* (call to prayer) that Muslims use until today.

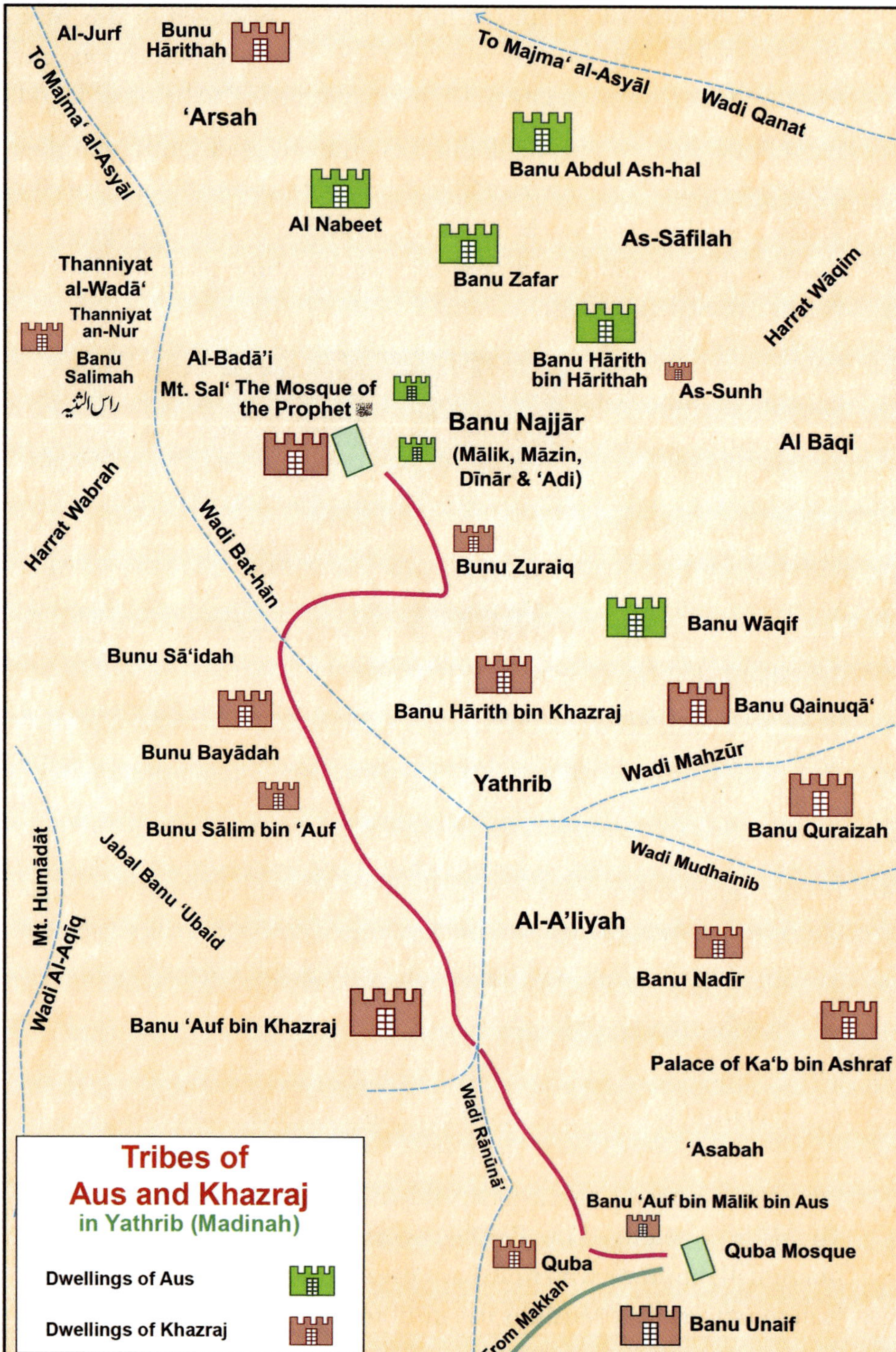

Al-Jurf
Bunu Hārithah
To Majma' al-Asyāl
'Arsah
To Majma' al-Asyāl
Wadi Qanat
Banu Abdul Ash-hal
Al Nabeet
As-Sāfilah
Banu Zafar
Thanniyat al-Wadā'
Thanniyat an-Nur
Harrat Wāqim
Banu Hārith bin Hārithah
As-Sunh
Banu Salimah
راس الثنيه
Al-Badā'i
Mt. Sal'
The Mosque of the Prophet ﷺ
Banu Najjār (Mālik, Māzin, Dīnār & 'Adi)
Al Bāqi
Harrat Wabrah
Wadi Bat-hān
Bunu Zuraiq
Banu Wāqif
Bunu Sā'idah
Banu Hārith bin Khazraj
Banu Qainuqā'
Bunu Bayādah
Wadi Mahzūr
Yathrib
Banu Quraizah
Bunu Sālim bin 'Auf
Mt. Humādāt
Jabal Banu 'Ubaid
Wadi Mudhainib
Al-A'liyah
Wadi Al-Aqiq
Banu Nadīr
Banu 'Auf bin Khazraj
Palace of Ka'b bin Ashraf
Wadi Rānūnā'
'Asabah
Tribes of Aus and Khazraj in Yathrib (Madinah)
Banu 'Auf bin Mālik bin Aus
Quba
Quba Mosque
Dwellings of Aus
From Makkah
Dwellings of Khazraj
Banu Unaif

Map.12

2. Sālim and Ghanm, the sons of 'Auf bin 'Amr bin 'Auf bin Khazraj al-Akbar. They lived in Dar Bani Sālim in Wadi Ranoonā', near Harrah Gharbiyyah, where the Friday Mosque (Masjid Jum'ah) was sited. To this tribe belonged Ubādah bin Sāmit ﵁, a companion of the Prophet ﷺ. The dwelling-place of Banu Sālim was named *"al-Muzdalaf"*. It was Hārith bin Khuzaimah ﵁ of the tribe of Banu Salim who looked for and found the she-camel of the Prophet ﷺ during the Battle of Tabūk.

Masjid Jum'ah (Friday Mosque)

Bani Harām Mosque

Wadi Bathān

3. Banu Hubla (Mālik) bin Sālim: This branch of Banu Sālim was settled in a place between Qubā' and Dar Bani Hārith bin Khazraj al-Akbar. The house known as Muzahim, in Dar Bani Hubla, belonged to the chief of the Hypocrites, Abdullah bin Ubayy ibn Salool. Many Companions ﵃ who participated in the Battle of Badr, including Abdullah ibn Abdullah ibn Ubayy, and Aus bin Khauli ﵄, belonged to this tribe.

4. Banu Salimah bin Sa'd, a branch of Banu Jushm bin Khazraj al-Akbar: They were settled between the Qiblatain Mosque and Utum Bani Harām. The name of their settlement was Dar Khurba, which the Messenger of Allah (ﷺ) renamed Sulhah. Abul-Yasar Ka'b bin 'Amr Salimi ﵁, who arrested the Prophet's uncle Abbas ﵁ in the Battle of Badr, belonged to Bani Salimah. The orchards and farmlands of Banu Salimah and Banu Haram were located between Qiblatain Mosque and al-Kharbah Mosque.

5. Banu 'Ubaid bin 'Adi bin Ghanm: A sub-branch of Banu Salimah, they were settled near al-Kharbah Mosque. The residence of their chief, Barā' bin Ma'rūr ﵁, a Companion, was called al-Ashannaq. Jābir bin Abdullah bin Ri'ab ﵁, a Companion of the Prophet ﷺ, belonged to this tribe.
6. Bani Harām bin Ka'b bin 'Adi: They also belonged to Banu Salimah. They dwelt between the Cemetery of Bani Salimah and Madhad. Jābir bin Adbullah bin 'Amr Ansari, a companion of the Prophet, belonged to this tribe. The Prophet said a prayer in Bani Haram as-Sagheer Mosque. They had another mosque, Bani Haram al-Kabeer, near Mt. Sal'.
7. Banu Mālik bin Ghadb bin Jusham bin Khazraj al-Akbar. They were sub-divided into five branches: Banu Bayādah wa Zuraiq, Banu Habeeb, Banu 'Adharah, Banu Allain, and Banu Ajda'. They dwelt near Masjid Jum'ah, between Dar Bani Sālim and Wadi Bathān. They had nineteen residences. The Companions Salimah bin Sakhr bin Salmān, Ziyad bin Labeed bin Sinān Badri, and Dhakwan bin Abd Qais bin Khaldah ﵃ belonged to Banu Mālik, Banu Bayādah and Banu Zuraiq, respectively.
8. Banu Sā'idah bin Ka'b bin Khazraj al-Akbar's two branches, Banu 'Amr and Banu Tha'labah were settled in Dar Bani Sā'idah which was situated between the Madinah marketplace and the residential quarter named Bani Damrah. Abu Dujānah ﵁, a Companion of

Saqeefah Bani Sā'idah (Madinah)

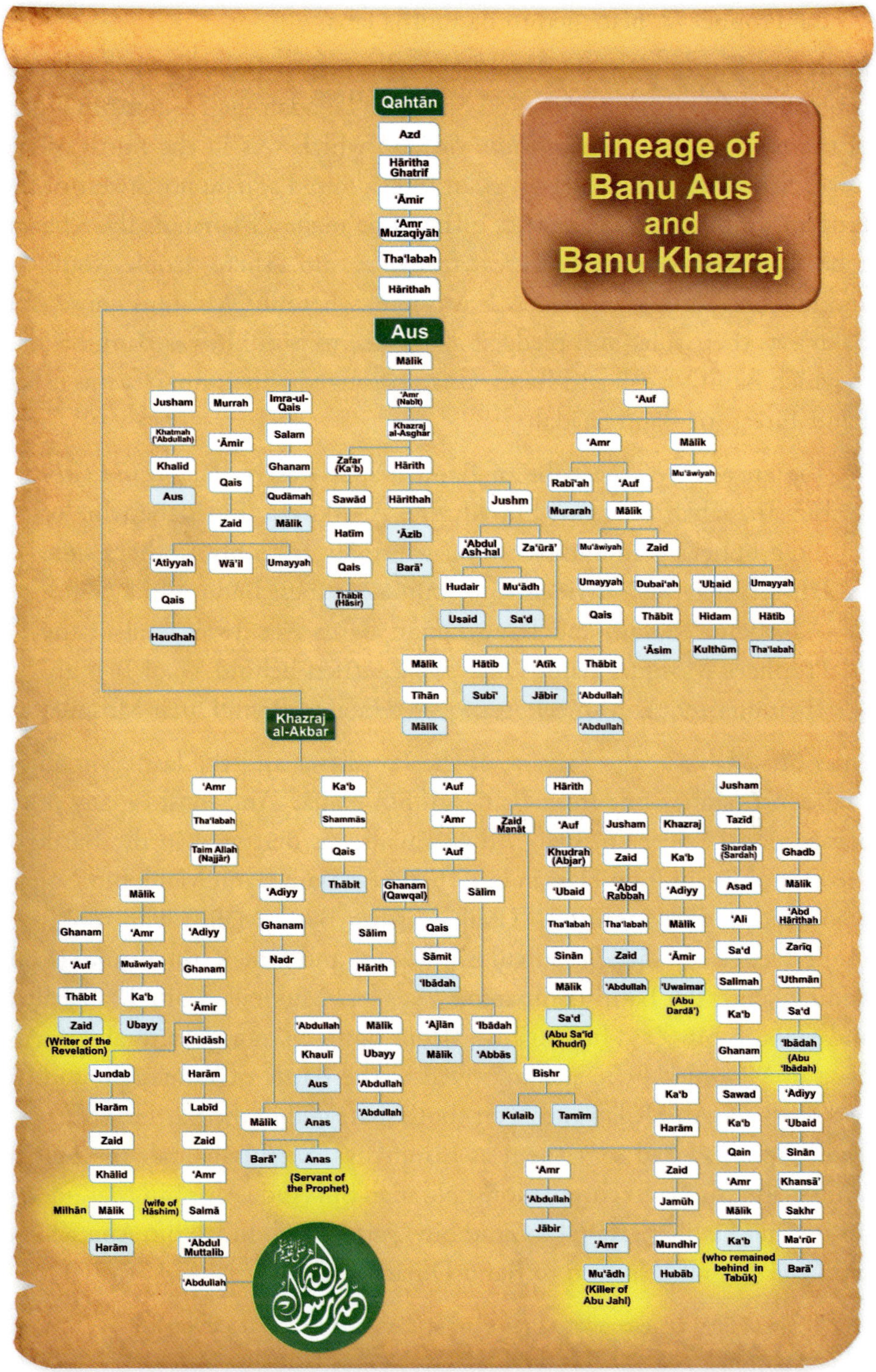
Lineage of Banu Aus and Banu Khazraj
Qahtān
Azd
Hāritha Ghatrif
'Āmir
'Amr Muzaqiyāh
Tha'labah
Hārithah
Aus
Mālik
Jusham
Murrah
Imra-ul-Qais
'Amr (Nabit)
'Auf
Khatmah ('Abdullah)
'Āmir
Salam
Khazraj al-Asghar
'Amr
Mālik
Khalid
Qais
Ghanam
Zafar (Ka'b)
Hārith
Mu'āwiyah
Rabī'ah
'Auf
Aus
Zaid
Qudāmah
Sawād
Hārithah
Jushm
Murarah
Mālik
Mālik
Hatīm
'Āzib
'Abdul Ash-hal
Za'ūrā'
Mu'āwiyah
Zaid
'Atiyyah
Wā'il
Umayyah
Qais
Barā'
Hudair
Mu'ādh
Umayyah
Dubai'ah
'Ubaid
Umayyah
Qais
Thābit (Hāsir)
Usaid
Sa'd
Qais
Thābit
Hidam
Hātib
Haudhah
'Āsim
Kulthūm
Tha'labah
Mālik
Hātib
'Atīk
Thābit
Tihān
Subī'
Jābir
'Abdullah
Mālik
'Abdullah
Khazraj al-Akbar
'Amr
Ka'b
'Auf
Hārith
Jusham
Tha'labah
Shammās
'Amr
Zaid Manāt
'Auf
Jusham
Khazraj
Tazīd
Taim Allah (Najjār)
Qais
'Auf
Khudrah (Abjar)
Zaid
Ka'b
Shardah (Sardah)
Ghadb
Mālik
'Adiyy
Thābit
Ghanam (Qawqal)
Sālim
'Ubaid
'Abd Rabbah
'Adiyy
Asad
Mālik
Ghanam
'Amr
'Adiyy
Ghanam
Sālim
Qais
Tha'labah
Tha'labah
Mālik
'Ali
'Abd Hārithah
'Auf
Muāwiyah
Ghanam
Nadr
Hārith
Sāmit
Sinān
Zaid
'Āmir
Sa'd
Zarīq
Thābit
Ka'b
'Āmir
'Ibādah
Mālik
'Abdullah
'Uwaimar (Abu Dardā')
Salimah
'Uthmān
Zaid (Writer of the Revelation)
Ubayy
Khidāsh
'Abdullah
Mālik
'Ajlān
'Ibādah
Sa'd (Abu Sa'īd Khudrī)
Ka'b
Sa'd
Khaulī
Ubayy
Mālik
'Abbās
Ghanam
'Ibādah (Abu 'Ibādah)
Jundab
Harām
Aus
'Abdullah
Bishr
Ka'b
Sawad
'Adiyy
Harām
Labīd
'Abdullah
Kulaib
Tamīm
Harām
Ka'b
'Ubaid
Zaid
Zaid
Mālik
Anas
Qain
Sinān
Khālid
'Amr
Barā'
Anas (Servant of the Prophet)
'Amr
Zaid
'Amr
Khansā'
Milhān
Mālik
(wife of Hāshim)
Salmā
'Abdullah
Jamūh
Mālik
Sakhr
Harām
'Abdul Muttalib
Jābir
'Amr
Mundhir
Ka'b (who remained behind in Tabūk)
Ma'rūr
'Abdullah
Mu'ādh (Killer of Abu Jahl)
Hubāb
Barā'

the Prophet ﷺ, belonged to Banu Tha'laba.

Banu Abi Khuzaimah bin Tha'labah, a branch of Banu Sā'idah, was the tribe of the Prophet's companion Sa'd bin 'Ubadah ﷺ. He lived in a part of the town called *Saqeefah Bani Sa'idah* which was in the north of the town. Saqeefah Bani Sa'idah was, in fact, a raised square northwest of the Prophet's mosque in the district of Banu Sa'idah, a branch of the Khazraj tribe. It served as a shady retreat from the sun. There people would sit and talk and settle their issues. It was here where the Muslims chose Abu Bakr ﷺ as their ruler and pledged allegiance to him.[1] It was Banu Sā'idah to which Banu Waqsh and Banu 'Unaq belonged. Their quarter was called Banu Tareef (or Banu Sa'idah).

9. The ancestor of the tribe of Banu Najjār was Najjār *(Taimullah)* bin Tha'labah bin 'Amr bin Khazraj Al-Akbar. This is the tribe of the Prophet's grandfather, Abdul-Muttalib, from his mother's side. Banu Najjār were divided into four sub-tribes: Banu Mālik, Banu 'Adi, Banu Māzan, and Banu Dīnār. Banu 'Adi dwelt west of the Prophet's Mosque. Banu Dīnār were settled behind Wadi Bathan. Their quarter, Al-Muneef, was located behind Banu Dīnār Mosque.

Anas bin Mālik ﷺ, the Servant of the Prophet ﷺ and the last companion to die in Basrah, came from Bani 'Adī bin Najjār. And so did many other companions: Saleet bin Qais 'Adwi ﷺ who was martyred in the Battle of the Day of Jisr in Iraq; Hassān bin Thābit ﷺ (from Banu Mālik bin Najjār) who lived in Fāri'; Sahl bin 'Utaik ﷺ (from Banu Mālik) who took part in the Pledge of 'Aqabah; Suhail bin Rāfi' ﷺ and Suhail bin 'Amr ﷺ (from Banu Mālik); the Badri companion Qais bin Mukhallad bin Tha'labah ﷺ and Habeeb bin Zaid bin 'Āsim ﷺ (from Banu Māzan); Hārithah bin Abi Sa'sa'ah Māzani ﷺ (who was martyred in the Battle of Yamāmah) and his two brothers, Abu Kilāb and Ja'far (both martyred in the Battle of Mu'tah). The Prophet ﷺ had sent them as his envoys to Musailamah the Liar in Yamāmah. The Badri companions, Nu'mān bin Abd, 'Amr bin Mas'ūd and his brother Dahhāk, Ka'b bin Zaid bin Qais and Abdullah bin Abu Khālid bin Qais ﷺ – all belonged to Banu Dīnār.[2]

1 Mu'jam-ul-Buldan: see under 'Saqīfa banī Sa'idah; Wikipedia (Encyclopedia).
2 A summary of Wafa'-ul-Wafa li'-Samhūdi: 1/190-214.

The Bloody Battle of Bu'āth

In the era before Islam, the area of Yathrib (Madinah) and its surrounding districts were occupied by three main groups: the tribes of 'Aus and Khazraj, and the Jews. While the former two were pagans, the latter were a distinct minority who felt the precariousness of their situation in a foreign land. In an effort to deflect attention from their growing population and their increasing control over businesses and commodities, the Jews bent their efforts into manipulating the 'Aus and Khazraj, pitting them against each other and engaged in ongoing conflicts for over 120 years.

Of these numerous battles, the more famous were: the Battle of Sumair, the Battle of Ka'b bin 'Amr, the Battle of Yaum as-Sarārah, the Battle of Yaum ad-Deek, and the Battle of Bu'āth. In most of these battles, the Khazraj had the upper hand. Eventually, 'Aus allied with the Jews of Banu Quraizah. This tactic failed, however, when the Khazraj threatened to fight the Jews, who then withdrew their support from 'Aus and announced their neutrality. As a further measure, the Khazraj demanded a ransom from Jews, which resulted fourty young men of the Jewish tribes being distributed amongst the different tribes of al-Khazraj as hostages. Once again, the Khazraj tribes banded together and launched a joint attack on 'Aus; in the ensuing battle, many men of the 'Aus tribe were killed.

According to Abul-Faraj Isfahani, a man of 'Aus slew an ally of Khazraj. When the deceased man's family demanded retribution or blood money, the tribe of 'Aus refused to accede to either. Predictably, this led to war between the 'Aus and Khazraj yet again.

The battle that took place in the seventh year of the Prophetic mission (617 CE), in a place called Bu'āth in the territory of Banu Quraizah, northwest of the 'Awāli Oasis.[1] The commander of the 'Aus forces was Hudair bin Simāk, the father of Usaid bin Hudair, who was a Companion). His adversary and counterpart on the enemy side was 'Amr bin Nu'mān; those under 'Amr's command were mainly from Khazraj, but also included some bedouin men from Banu Juhainah. On the opposite side, all the tribes of 'Aus were arrayed for battle, except Banu Hārithah, who had been driven out by Abdul-Ash'hal. Initially, the battle swayed in favour of the Khazraj and the warriors of 'Aus were forced to fall back. However, they quickly regained their ground and forced their opponents to flee the field. With the commanders of both sides killed, the battle's conclusion was indecisive. As a result, an uneasy truce was drawn up and remained in force until the advent of Islam, which brought the 'Aus and Khazraj together, ended their age-old hostility, and turned them into brothers in faith.[2]

Origins of Aus and Khazraj

The 'Aus and Khazraj are most notably recognized due to their being amongst the Ansār; that is, the residents of Madinah who pledged their allegiance and aid to Prophet Muhammad ﷺ, earning the title of Ansār or 'the Helpers.'

Their origins, however, remain a question over which genealogists wrangle and question. In general, most historians and genealogists state that the 'Aus and Khazraj originated from Yemen, descending from Qahtān, who is considered to have been the father of all pure Arabs (Arab Muta'arribah or Arab 'Aribah).

Al-Hafiz Ibn Hajar Al-'Asqalāni (d. 852 AH) wrote a discourse on the topic during his commentary of Sahih-ul-Bukhari, in a chapter entitled

1 Mu'jam-ul-Ma'alim Al-Jughrafiyah Fi's-Seerat-in-Nabawiyyah, P. 47.

2 Wafa'-ul-Wafa li's-Samhūdi: 1/215-218; Urdu Daira' Ma'arif Islamia (Urdu Encyclopedia of Islam: 4/623.

Nisbat Al-Yemen Ila Ismā'īl. He said, "There is controversy over the lineage of Qahtān. Most of the scholars hold that Qahtān was the son of 'Abir bin Shalekh bin Arfakhshad bin Sām bin Nūh or one of the offspring of Hūd ﷺ(the prophet) or his nephew. It is also said that he was the first person to speak Arabic and that he is the sire (remotest ancestor) of pure Arabs *(Arab Mut'arribah)* while Prophet Ismā'īl is the sire or remotest ancestor of the domiciled Arabs *(Arab Musta'ribah).*" However, Zubayr bin Bakkār disagrees and states that Qahtān himself was a descendant of Ismā'īl, his lineage being: Qahtān bin Humaisa' bin Taim bin Nabat bin Ismā'īl.[1]It is also clear from the story of Hajar (the mother of Ismā'īl) as narrated by Abu Hurairah, for he said, while addressing the Ansār:

فَتِلْكَ أُمُّكُمْ يَا بَنِي مَاءِ السَّمَاءِ!

"That is your mother, o children of the water of the sky!"[2]

Abu Hātim Ibn Hibbān, while commenting on this statement, writes: "All the offspring of Hajar are called بنى ماء السماء or 'Children of the water of the sky' because Ismā'īl ﷺ, the son of Hajar, was nourished and nurtured by the Zamzam water which came down from heaven.[3]

Have Banu Qahtān descended from Ismā'īl?

Ibn Hajar theorizes, "That the family of Qahtān descended from Ismā'īl has, in my view, more weight because the number of ancestors in between the major Ansari Companions is almost the same as that of the ancestors between the major Quraishi Companions and Adnan." Ibn Hajar goes on to quote more than ten different statements relating to the ancestral line from Adnan to Ismā'īl, listing four or five to forty (ancestral) links.[4]

Hafiz Ibn Hajar also writes: "According to the Hadith of Salama bin Akwa', the Prophet ﷺ, while addressing the Yemeni tribe of Banu Aslam Khuzā'ī Qahtānī, said that they were from (i.e. the offspring of) Banu Ismā'īl."

Ibn Abdul-Barr Qurtubi wrote in the narration of Qa'qa' bin Abi

1 Fat'h-ul-Bari: 6/657.
2 Sahih-ul-Bukhari: 3358.
3 Sahih Ibn Hibbān (Al-Ihsan): 7/496.
4 Fat'h-ul-Bari: 6/657-659.

Hadrad[1] that the Prophet Muhammad (ﷺ) said to a group of Banu Aslam and Khuza'ah while they were competing in archery: "O children of Ismā'īl, shoot the arrows!"

Some say that he may have called all of them Banu Ismā'īl (children of Ismā'īl) due to the fact that most of them were from Banu Khuzā'ah. Hamdāni disagrees. He says that the Prophet's ﷺ calling Banu Aslam and Banu Khuzā'ah by the name of Banu Ismā'īl is no proof that they were the children of Ismā'īl from their father's side; rather, they could be the children of Ismā'īl from their mother's side, as the Qahtānis and Adnānis had intermingled by marriage. Thus, the offspring of Qahtān may be the children of Ismā'īl from their mother's side.

Another proof the Yemenites being the children of Ismā'īl is the following verses of Ibn Mundhir bin 'Amr bin Harām[2], the grandfather of Hassān bin Thābit (the Companion):

وَرِثْنَا مِنَ الْبَهْلُولِ عَمْرِو بْنِ عَامِرٍ　　وَ حَارِثَةَ الْغِطْرِيفِ مَجْدًا مُؤَثَّلَا

مَآثِرَ مِنْ آلِ نَبْتِ ابْنِ مَالِكٍ　　وَنَبْتِ ابْنِ إِسْمٰعِيلَ مَا إِنْ تَحَوَّلَا

(We inherited true nobility from Bahlool (Tha'labah), 'Amr bin 'Āmir and Hārithah al-Ghitreef.

If we make a change (Tahawwul) and link lineage with Nabt bin Mālik[3] and Nabt bin Ismā'īl, we are then the inheritors of both.)[4]

Sayyed Suleman Nadwi's arguments

Sayyed Suleman Nadwi, a well-known research scholar and historian, has carried out much sustained research work on the pedigree of the Arab tribes. He rejects the opinions of Hishām bin Muhammad bin Sā'ib Kalbi and Ibn Hishām, and supports Ibn Hajar's view that Aus and Khazraj are the offspring of Prophet Ismā'īl عليه السلام. To support his contention, he

1 According to some scholars, his name was Qa'qa' bin Abdullah bin Abi Hadrad Aslami. Bukhari counts him among the Companions.

2 According to Usd-ul-Ghaba (2/7) and Al-Isabah (2/55), the name of Hassan's grandfather is Mundhir bin Harām bin 'Amr.

3 He was Nabt bin Mālik Qahtāni and a grandfather of Azd bin Ghauth.-(Saba'ik-udh-Dha'hab, P 118).

4 Fat'h-ul-Bari: 6/659.

advances the following cogent arguments:

Imam Bukhari records that Abu Hurairah ﷺ narrated the story of Hajar, the mother of Ismā'īl ﷺ, to an assembly of the Ansar, and concluded with the words, "O the sons of the water of the sky, that was your mother."

All the genealogists are unanimous that 'Aus and Khazraj have a common lineage with Ghassān. Moreover, 'Aus and Khazraj themselves assert the same. Therefore, the proofs of Ghassanids being of Nabti extraction (as descendants of Ismā'īl) apply exactly to 'Aus and Khazraj and prove that they, too, are of Nabti extraction.

Yet another proof of Aus and Khazraj being descended from Ismā'īl is that there were extremely strong ties of kinship between them and the Quraish, and that they regularly visited Makkah to perform Hajj every year.

Mundhar bin Harām (the grandfather of Hassān bin Thābit),[1]who lived in the pre-Islamic times and was from the tribe of Khazraj, traced his lineage (in the aforementioned verses) to Nābit bin Ismā'īl and was boastful of it.

'Amr (Muzaiqiyā) bin 'Āmir bin Hārithah was the ancestor of both Ghassan as well as 'Aus and Khazraj. Ghassān went away to Syria while 'Aus and Khazraj settled down in Yathrib (Hijaz).[2]

Harithah bin 'Amr Muzaiqiya

The offspring of Khuzā'ah bin 'Amr bin Luhayy bin Hārithah, a branch of Banu Hārithah bin 'Amr Muzaiqiya, were called Banu Khuza'ah. Initially, this tribe roamed the land of Hijaz, pitched their camps at *Marr-az-Zahran*, and finally seized the Haram (Holy Sanctum) in Makkah.

They drove out Banu Jurham and settled in Makkah. One of their men, 'Amr ibn Luhayy, was responsible for introducing idolaltry in Makkah, and polluting the purity and sanctity of the Ka'bah by bringing those idols within the Ka'bah itself.

---

1 In Usdulghābah and al-Isābah the name of Hassān's grandfather is given as "Mundhar bin Harām bin 'Amr" but not "Ibn Mundhar".

2 Tareekh Ard-il-Qur'ān (Kamil): 2/65-66 .

Wadi Mar Az-Zahrān (Wadi Fatima)

The wife of the Prophet Muhammad ﷺ, Juwairiyyah ﵩ, belonged to Banu Mustalaq *(Jazeemah)*, a branch of this tribe. The other branches of Banu Hārithah were Aslam, Bāriq and Ghāmid. Buraidah bin Husaib Aslamī, a famous Companion, belonged to Banu Aslam.

'Imrān bin 'Amr Muzaiqiyā

'Imrān and his offspring settled in Oman, and consequently, became known as Azd Oman.1

Jafnah bin 'Amr Muzaiqiyā (Family of Ghassān)

The people of Jafnah headed towards Syria and settled there along with their children. They are called Ghassān because their Azdi ancestors, before they had migrated to Syria, had sojourned beside a stream named Ghassān at Mushallal (Tihāmah) or in Yemen. According to some others, Māzan bin Azd, the remotest ancestor of Ghassānis, was called Ghassān.[2]

Genealogists say that Ghassanis are Qahtānis, just as the 'Aus and Khazraj are. However, Abu Tahir Maqdasi writes in *Al-Bad'u Wal-Akhbar*: "Mundhir bin Harām, a pre-Islamic poet and grandfather of Hassān bin Thābit ﵁ (the Companion), traces their lineage (that is, the lineage of 'Aus and Khazraj) to Ghassan, to Nabit bin Mālik, and then up to Nabt bin

1 Muhādarat Tareekh-il-Umam Al-Islamiyyah: 1/15.

2 Mu'jam Qaba'il-il-Arab: 3/884; Muhadarat

Ismā'īl bin Ibrāhīm."

Sayyed Suleman Nadwi, while declaring them to be Adnānis, also advances as proof the fact that the family of Ghassān spoke a variant of Arabic peculiar to the north of Arabia and wrote the Nabatean script. Were they Qahtānis, both their language and script would be Himyari.[1]

(B) Nasr (Shanū'ah) bin Azd

The tribes relating to this clan stayed in Tihāmah and were called Azd Shanū'ah.[2] From among the progeny of Nasr Shanū'ah, Banu Daus earned a strong reputation. The Companion named Abu Harariah and Tufail bin 'Amr ad-Dausi belonged to this tribe.

Lakhm and Judhām

From among the offspring of Zaid bin Kahlān, 'Adī bin Hārith bin Murrah bin Udad bin Zaid had four sons: Lakhm (Mālik), Judhām, 'Āmilah (Hārith) and 'Ufair. The settlements of Lakhm were in Syria and Palestine, while those of Judhām were from Madyan up to Tabūk. At the time of their conversion to Islam and afterwards, Banu Lakhm were scattered across Egypt, al-Maghrib (Morocco), Golan (Syria) and Palestine. The Ghassanid dynasty of Iraq, and that of Banu 'Abbād of Morocco and Andalusia were descendants of these tribes. In pre-Islamic times, they were known to have worshipped the planet Jupiter and an idol named Uqaisar.

Banu Tayy

They are the progeny of Tayy (Julhamah) bin Udad bin Zaid bin Yashjub bin 'Areeb bin Zaid bin Kahlān. This tribe, after Banu Azd had left their native place, headed north and settled permanently around Mt. Ajā and Mt. Salma, until the two mountains came to be known by the name of Tayy.

The famous Arab chieftain, Hātim Tai, who is known to this day for generosity so great that his name was a synonym for the quality, belonged to this tribe. His son, 'Adi bin Hatim, became a Muslim and was one of

1 Tareekh ard-il-Qur'ān (Kamil): 2/60-61.
2 Muhadarat Tareekh-il-Umam-il-Islamiyyah: 1/15..

the great companions of the Prophet Muhammad ﷺ.

Banu Kindah

They are the offspring of 'Afeer bin 'Adi bin Hārith bin Murrah bin Udad bin Zaid bin Yashjub, a brother of Lakhm and Judhām. They encamped first in Bahrain (modern al-Ahsā') but were forced to move on to Hadramaut. However, they were unable to find security there and eventually settled in Nejd, where they founded a great state.

Famous tribes of Banu Himyar

The following three tribes of Banu Himyar became more famous than others: 1.Banu Qudā'a 2.Banu Saksak 3. Zaid A-Jamhoor.

Banu Qudā'ah

Among the descendants of Mālik bin Himyar, the tribesmen of Quda'ah are famous (although its Himyarite descendency is disputable). They left Yemen, their native locality, and settled in the desert of Samawah, inside the territory of Iraq. During the time of the Messenger Muhammad (ﷺ), the following branches of Qudā'ah were famous: Baliyy, Kalb, 'Udhrah, and Juhainah.

Banu Saksak

The offspring of Saksak, the son of Zaid bin Wā'ilah (Wā'il) bin Himyar, came to be called Sakasik. Saksak was the king of Yemen, whose title was Muqa'qi' al-'Umud (one who travels very often). He died in Iraq and was buried in Yemen.[1] A branch of Banu Kindah was also called Humais As-Saksak.[2]

Zaid Al-Jamhoor

Their lineage is as follows: Zaid Al-Jamhoor bin Sahl bin 'Amr bin Qais bin Mu'āwiyah bin Jusham bin Abd Shams bin Wa'il bin Al-Ghauth bin Qatan bin 'Uraib bin Abyan bin Himyar.

---

1 Mu'jam-ul-Buldān: see under 'As-Sakasik'; Mu'jam Qaba'il-il-Arab: 2/527; Al-A'lam: 3/105.

2 For details about these tribes, see Qalb-o-Jazeerah-il-Arab, P. 231-236; Muhadarat Tareekh-il-Umam-il-Islamia: 1/15-16.

Domiciled Arabs

(Arab Musta'ribah)

The third largest group of Arabs, after the extinct Arabs (Arab al-Bā'idah) and the pure Arabs (Arab 'Āribah), are the domiciled Arabs (Arab Musta'ribah).

The domiciled Arabs are the offspring of the Prophets Ibrāhīm (Abraham) and Ismā'īl (Ishmael) عليهما السلام. Originally, Ismā'īl عليه السلام spoke Syriac-Hebrew; however, when he settled in Makkah, he and his children spoke Arabic. For this reason, the offspring of Ibrāhīm are known as 'domiciled Arabs' – Arab Musta'ribah.

Aramaic Arabic

There is another opinion, however. Shauqi Abu Khaleel, a research scholar of Syria, contends that Ibrāhīm and Ismā'īl عليهما السلام were native speakers of Arabic. He writes: "All talk about Domiciled Arabs is a self-coined story. This is an old concoction which has come down to us from historians of old. The truth is that the age of Abraham and Ishmael عليهما السلام is the age of Arabic. It has nothing to do with Syriac or Hebrew. During the time of Abraham, there

An ancient arab tribe is traveling through desert

was only one language (mother tongue) in this region. The people of the Arabian Peninsula had been speaking the same (Arabic) language before they migrated to the Fertile Crescent. Different variants (or dialects) of that language like Canaanite, Aramaic or Amorite had not yet came into existence. The Aramaic tribes with whom Abraham was connected spoke the same language which the Canaanites and Amorites of Palestine spoke. It was very close to the mother tongue (Arabic-Aramaic).... Abraham and Ishmael عليهما السلام were related to Arab-Aramaic tribes who had settled in this region centuries before the Israelites and Jews came into existence.... The terms "Semite" and "non-Semite" have no historical significance. The mischievous term "Semite" was first introduced by a German scholar, A.L. Schlūtser, in his book 'Catalogue of Torah and Eastern literature' (published in 1781 CE) in support of the Jewish claims."[1]

The age of the Domiciled Arabs (Arab Musta'ribah) begins with Ibrāhīm and Ismā'īl عليهما السلام. In order to understand the later history of these Arabs, it is important to know the biographies of these two Prophets.

1 Atlas-ul-Qur'ān, P. 44-47.

1. Abraham, عليه السلام The Father of Prophets

The lineage of Prophet Ibrāhīm, as related in the Bible, is as follows:

Abraham son of Tareh (Azar) son of Nahor son of Sharogh son of Argua son of Falegh son of 'Abir son of Shalekh son of Arfakhshad son of Sam (Shem) son of Nūh (Noah).[1] (The Urdu version of the Bible gives his father's name as Tareh.)

Ibrāhīm's Father

Allah says: "

﴿وَإِذْ قَالَ إِبْرَٰهِيمُ لِأَبِيهِ ءَازَرَ أَتَتَّخِذُ أَصْنَامًا ءَالِهَةً﴾

"And (remember) when (Abraham) said to his father Āzar: Do you take idols as āliha (gods)?"[2]

1 Al-Ma'arif li-Ibn Qutaiba, P 15; Holy Bible: Genesis 11: 10-27.
2 Al-An'am: 6:74.

Ziggurat of Ur in south of Iraq in Province of Dhi Qar

Ibn Abbas ﷺ and the majority of genealogists say that Ibrāhīm's father's real name was Tareh.[1] Ibn Jarir At-Tabari said, "In my opinion, his name was Azar but he could have had two names."[2] In other words, the name 'Azar' could have been a second name, or a nickname, for the man named Tareh.

However, The Qur'ān explicitly states that Azar was the father of Ibrāhīm ﷺ. Moreover according to a tradition narrated by Abu Hurairah ﷺ, the Prophet Muhammad (ﷺ) said: "Ibrāhīm will see his father Azar on the Day of Resurrection, while his (Azar's) face will be covered with darkness and dust."[3] Both the Qur'ān and Sunnah agree that the name of Ibrāhīm's father was Azar.

Ibrāhīm's Birthplace

It is widely believed that Prophet Ibrāhīm ﷺ was born in Ur, a town in Babel (Iraq). However, he was in fact born in the small town of Kūtha, northeast of Babel (Babylon). Ibrāhīm's relocation to Ur took place after he had been saved from Nimrod's fire; from Ur he migrated to Harran, and later to Palestine.[4]

Babylon (Kūtha) birth place of Prophet Ibrāhīm

Kūtha is 40 km off the city of Bābil (Babylon). Mu'jam Al-Buldan describes Kūtha in the following words:

"This town is located on the bank of Kūtha Canal. It is named after a man, named Kūtha, from Banu Arfakhshad bin Sam bin Nūh ﷺ. He was the grandfather of Ibrāhīm's mother, who was named Būna bint Karnaba bin Kūtha. Kūtha was the first canal dug out from the Euphrates. 'Ubaida Salmāni, a famous Tabi'ee, is reported to have heard Ali ﷺ saying: 'We are the Nabateans of Kūtha.' A narration of Ibn Abbas ﷺ also says: 'We, the Quraish, are a branch of the Nabateans of Kūtha.'

1 Al-Bidaya Wan-Nihaya: 1/134.
2 Tafseer-ut-Tabari: Al-An'am: 6:74.
3 Sahih-ul-Bukhari:3350.
4 Atlas Seerat Nabawiyyah (Darussalam), P. 43.

During the era of 'Umar Farooq رضي الله عنه, after the conquest of Qādisiyyah, Zuhra bin Hawiyyah رضي الله عنه (a Companion) attacked Kūtha on the order of Sa'd bin Abi Waqqās رضي الله عنه (a Companion), slew the ruler of the area, and seized control of the town. According to the local tradition, that was the place where Nimrod and his countrymen flung Abraham عليه السلام into a raging fire. Sa'd رضي الله عنه travelled from Babel to Kūtha to see the town himself, invoked blessings on Prophet Abraham عليه السلام`, and recited the following Verse of Qur'ān:

﴿وَتِلْكَ ٱلْأَيَّامُ نُدَاوِلُهَا بَيْنَ ٱلنَّاسِ﴾

"And so are the days (good and not so good), that We give to men by turns." Āl 'Imrān (3): 140.[1]

Resemblance between Ibrāhīm عليه السلام and Muhammad (ﷺ)

Abdullah bin Abbas رضي الله عنهما quotes the Prophet ﷺ as having said:

"To know (the personal appearance of) Ibrāhīm, look at your companion (Muhammad). As for Moses, he was a man of curly hair and light brownish complexion riding a red camel with a halter made of palm-leaves, as if I am seeing him going down the lowland of a valley."[2]

Dialogue with a Pagan Father

Prophet Ibrāhīm's father was not only an idol-worshipper, but in fact used to carve them himself. Thus, Ibrāhīm عليه السلام first focused on calling Azar to the worship of the One True God. Ibrāhīm عليه السلام spoke to his father with both affection and wisdom; however, Azar responded harshly and even threatened him. Allah says:

﴿إِذْ قَالَ لِأَبِيهِ يَٰٓأَبَتِ لِمَ تَعْبُدُ مَا لَا يَسْمَعُ وَلَا يُبْصِرُ وَلَا يُغْنِى عَنكَ شَيْـًٔا ﴿٤٢﴾ يَٰٓأَبَتِ إِنِّى قَدْ جَآءَنِى
مِنَ ٱلْعِلْمِ مَا لَمْ يَأْتِكَ فَٱتَّبِعْنِىٓ أَهْدِكَ صِرَٰطًا سَوِيًّا ﴿٤٣﴾ يَٰٓأَبَتِ لَا تَعْبُدِ ٱلشَّيْطَٰنَ ۖ إِنَّ ٱلشَّيْطَٰنَ كَانَ
لِلرَّحْمَٰنِ عَصِيًّا ﴿٤٤﴾ يَٰٓأَبَتِ إِنِّىٓ أَخَافُ أَن يَمَسَّكَ عَذَابٌ مِّنَ ٱلرَّحْمَٰنِ فَتَكُونَ لِلشَّيْطَٰنِ وَلِيًّا ﴿٤٥﴾
قَالَ أَرَاغِبٌ أَنتَ عَنْ ءَالِهَتِى يَٰٓإِبْرَٰهِيمُ ۖ لَئِن لَّمْ تَنتَهِ لَأَرْجُمَنَّكَ ۖ وَٱهْجُرْنِى مَلِيًّا ﴿٤٦﴾ قَالَ سَلَٰمٌ
عَلَيْكَ ۖ سَأَسْتَغْفِرُ لَكَ رَبِّىٓ ۖ إِنَّهُۥ كَانَ بِى حَفِيًّا ﴿٤٧﴾ وَأَعْتَزِلُكُمْ وَمَا تَدْعُونَ مِن دُونِ ٱللَّهِ
وَأَدْعُوا۟ رَبِّى عَسَىٰٓ أَلَّآ أَكُونَ بِدُعَآءِ رَبِّى شَقِيًّا﴾

1 Op.cit., P. 43,44; Mu'jam-ul-Buldan: see under 'Kūtha'.
2 Sahih-ul-Bukhari: 3355.

"When he said to his father: "O my father! Why do you worship that which hears not, sees not and cannot avail you in anything? O my father! Verily, there has come to me of the knowledge that which came not to you. So follow me, I will guide you to a Straight Path. O my father! Worship not Shaitān (Satan). Verily, Shaitān (Satan) has been a rebel against the Most Gracious (Allāh). O my father! Verily, I fear lest torment from the Most Gracious (Allāh) should overtake you, so that you become a companion of Shaitān (Satan) (in the Hell-fire). He (the father) said: "Do you reject my gods, O Ibrāhīm (Abraham)? If you stop not (this), I will indeed stone you. So get away from me safely (before I punish you). Ibrāhīm (Abraham) said: "Peace be on you! I will ask forgiveness of my Lord for you. Verily, He is to me Ever Most Gracious And I shall turn away from you and from those whom you invoke besides Allāh. And I shall call upon my Lord and I hope that I shall not be unblest in my invocation to my Lord."[1]

Ibrāhīm's Belief in God

Allah gave Ibrāhīm عليه السلام the gift of wisdom. By observing the movement of heavenly bodies and their orbits, Ibrāhīm عليه السلام realized that those who worshipped astronomical objects were in grave error; these constructs did not deserve anyone's worship, but rather, their Creator was the One Who deserved to be worshipped by all.

The Qur'ān vividly describes Ibrāhīm's journey of truth:

﴿ وَكَذَٰلِكَ نُرِيٓ إِبۡرَٰهِيمَ مَلَكُوتَ ٱلسَّمَٰوَٰتِ وَٱلۡأَرۡضِ وَلِيَكُونَ مِنَ ٱلۡمُوقِنِينَ ٧٥ فَلَمَّا جَنَّ عَلَيۡهِ
ٱلَّيۡلُ رَءَا كَوۡكَبٗاۖ قَالَ هَٰذَا رَبِّيۖ فَلَمَّآ أَفَلَ قَالَ لَآ أُحِبُّ ٱلۡأٓفِلِينَ ٧٦ فَلَمَّا رَءَا ٱلۡقَمَرَ بَازِغٗا قَالَ
هَٰذَا رَبِّيۖ فَلَمَّآ أَفَلَ قَالَ لَئِن لَّمۡ يَهۡدِنِي رَبِّي لَأَكُونَنَّ مِنَ ٱلۡقَوۡمِ ٱلضَّآلِّينَ ٧٧ فَلَمَّا رَءَا ٱلشَّمۡسَ
بَازِغَةٗ قَالَ هَٰذَا رَبِّي هَٰذَآ أَكۡبَرُۖ فَلَمَّآ أَفَلَتۡ قَالَ يَٰقَوۡمِ إِنِّي بَرِيٓءٞ مِّمَّا تُشۡرِكُونَ ٧٨ إِنِّي وَجَّهۡتُ
وَجۡهِيَ لِلَّذِي فَطَرَ ٱلسَّمَٰوَٰتِ وَٱلۡأَرۡضَ حَنِيفٗاۖ وَمَآ أَنَا۠ مِنَ ٱلۡمُشۡرِكِينَ ﴾

"Thus did we show Ibrāhīm (Abraham) the kingdom of the heavens and the earth that he be one of those who have Faith with certainty. When the night covered him over with darkness he saw a star. He said: ``This is my lord." But when it set, he said: ``I like not those that set. When he saw the moon rising up, he said: ``This is my lord." But when it set, he said:

1 Maryam: 19:42-48.

"Unless my Lord guides me, I shall surely be among the people who went astray. When he saw the sun rising up, he said: "This is my lord. This is greater." But when it set, he said: "O my people! I am indeed free from all that you join as partners (in worship with Allāh). Verily, I have turned my face towards Him Who has created the heavens and the earth Hanīfa (Islamic Monotheism, i.e. worshipping none but Allāh Alone), and I am not of Al-Mushrikūn."[1]

Ibrāhīm, the Iconoclast

Ibrahim mosque in al-Kheel

The people of Bābil were idol-worshippers. Though Ibrāhīm عليه السلام spoke to them of the folly of their beliefs, they persisted in denying his calls to the truth. One day, Ibrāhīm عليه السلام took advantage of their day of celebration to drive home the truth and prove the helplessness of their own deities. While his people were out of the town celebrating, he smashed their idols and proved his point.

﴿فَجَعَلَهُمْ جُذَاذًا إِلَّا كَبِيرًا لَّهُمْ لَعَلَّهُمْ إِلَيْهِ يَرْجِعُونَ ﴿٥٨﴾ قَالُوا مَن فَعَلَ هَٰذَا بِآلِهَتِنَا
إِنَّهُ لَمِنَ الظَّالِمِينَ ﴿٥٩﴾ قَالُوا سَمِعْنَا فَتًى يَذْكُرُهُمْ يُقَالُ لَهُ إِبْرَاهِيمُ ﴿٦٠﴾ قَالُوا فَأْتُوا بِهِ عَلَىٰ
أَعْيُنِ النَّاسِ لَعَلَّهُمْ يَشْهَدُونَ ﴿٦١﴾ قَالُوا أَأَنتَ فَعَلْتَ هَٰذَا بِآلِهَتِنَا يَا إِبْرَاهِيمُ ﴿٦٢﴾ قَالَ بَلْ
فَعَلَهُ كَبِيرُهُمْ هَٰذَا فَاسْأَلُوهُمْ إِن كَانُوا يَنطِقُونَ ﴿٦٣﴾ فَرَجَعُوا إِلَىٰ أَنفُسِهِمْ فَقَالُوا
إِنَّكُمْ أَنتُمُ الظَّالِمُونَ ﴿٦٤﴾ ثُمَّ نُكِسُوا عَلَىٰ رُءُوسِهِمْ لَقَدْ عَلِمْتَ مَا هَٰؤُلَاءِ يَنطِقُونَ ﴿٦٥﴾
قَالَ أَفَتَعْبُدُونَ مِن دُونِ اللَّهِ مَا لَا يَنفَعُكُمْ شَيْئًا وَلَا يَضُرُّكُمْ ﴿٦٦﴾ أُفٍّ لَّكُمْ وَلِمَا
تَعْبُدُونَ مِن دُونِ اللَّهِ أَفَلَا تَعْقِلُونَ﴾

"So he broke them to pieces, (all) except the biggest of them, that they

1 Al-An'am: 6:75-79.

might turn to it. They said: "Who has done this to our ālihah (gods)? He must indeed be one of the Zālimūn (wrongdoers). They said: "We heard a young man talking against them, who is called Ibrāhīm (Abraham). They said: "Then bring him before the eyes of the people, that they may testify. They said: "Are you the one who has done this to our gods, O Ibrāhīm (Abraham)? [Ibrāhīm (Abraham)] said: "Nay, this one, the biggest of them (idols) did it. Ask them, if they can speak!" So they turned to themselves and said: "Verily, you are the Zālimūn (polytheists and wrongdoers). Then they turned to themselves (their first thought and said): "Indeed you [Ibrāhīm (Abraham)] know well that these (idols) speak not!" [Ibrāhīm (Abraham)] said: "Do you then worship besides Allāh, things that can neither profit you nor harm you? Fie upon you, and upon that which you worship besides Allāh! Have you then no sense?"[1]

Nimrod's Fire

Ruins of Harran Turkey

In anger, and unable to find a suitable reply to Ibrāhīm's questioning, the pagans decided to punish Ibrāhīm عليه السلام and make him a deterring example for others who dared to question their false religion.

However, Allah caused their scheme to fail and saved Ibrāhīm.

﴿قَالُوا۟ حَرِّقُوهُ وَٱنصُرُوٓا۟ ءَالِهَتَكُمْ إِن كُنتُمْ فَٰعِلِينَ ﴿٦٨﴾ قُلْنَا يَٰنَارُ كُونِى بَرْدًا وَسَلَٰمًا عَلَىٰٓ إِبْرَٰهِيمَ ﴿٦٩﴾ وَأَرَادُوا۟ بِهِۦ كَيْدًا فَجَعَلْنَٰهُمُ ٱلْأَخْسَرِينَ﴾

"They said: "Burn him and help your ālihah (gods), if you will be doing." We (Allāh) said: "O fire! Be you coolness and safety for Ibrāhīm (Abraham)!" And they wanted to harm him, but We made them the worst losers."[2]

1 Al-Anbiya': 21:58-67.
2 Al-Anbiya': 21:68-70.

Map.14

Migration to Ur, Harran and Palestine

After the incident with the fire, Ibrāhīm ﷺ left his home and went to a place called Ur of Chaldea, on the right bank of the Euphrates. There he sojourned awhile with his wife, Sarah, and his nephew, Prophet Lūt ﷺ.

Ibrāhīm ﷺ then left Ur to go to Harran (Turkey), continuously preaching the creed of monotheism, and then went to Palestine via Aleppo (Syria). Palestine became the center for his missionary work.[1]

1 Atlas-ul-Qur'ān (Urdu). P. 74, 80.

Journey to Egypt

Though Ibrāhīm now resided in Palestine, he also visited Egypt with his wife, Sarah, to propagate his faith. However, the king of Egypt at the time was a ruthless and greedy tyrant. When he learned that Sarah was a woman of dazzling beauty, he decided to deceive Ibrāhīm and pretend that he was interested in monotheism. In truth, he intended only to lure Sarah into his clutches.

Before he could attack her, however, Sarah prayed to her Lord for protection, and immediately, the king's hands were paralyzed. He attempted to attack her twice more, and each time, Sarah was protected by Allah.

In the end, the king feared that Sarah and Ibrāhīm were employing witchcraft, and in an effort to placate them, he gave Sarah a slave girl named Hajirah (Hagar). Sarah then gave Hajirah as a gift to Ibrāhīm, who then married her.[1]

It is generally believed that Hajirah was a slave girl; however, Suleman Mansūrpuri's research claims that she was not a bondwoman but rather, a free woman and a princess.[2]

The Divine Plan

Ibrāhīm left Egypt, with Sarah and Hajirah in two, and returned to Palestine. There, Hajirah fell pregnant and gave birth to Ibrāhīm's firstborn son, Ismā'īl. Sarah, who was still barren and childless, felt deep sorrow and the pangs of jealousy.

Allah inspired Ibrāhīm with the order to take Hajirah (Hagar)

1 Sahih-ul-Bukhari: 2217, 3358.

2 See Rahmatun-lil-'Ālameen: 2/38-41.

and his son Ismā'īl, and have them relocate to another area.

A Hadith in Sahih Al-Bukhari relates the tale, wherein Ibrāhīm ﷷ took his infant son and his wife to a barren desert. Though this was where the Ka'bah was to be built later on, at the time there was only a large raised mound. Other than that, the entire area was entirely desolate, lacking in both food and water.

Without a word, Ibrāhīm ﷷ gave his wife a bag of dates and a water-skin, and began to walk away. Shocked and surprised, Hajirah (Hagar) ran after him, pleading, "O Ibrāhīm, are you leaving us here in this wilderness?" No matter how much she asked, he would not answer; indeed, he did not even turn to look at her.Eventually, she realized, "Did Allah command you to leave us here?" Ibrāhīm finally answered. "Yes." With that, Hajirah left Ibrāhīm and returned to where he had left her, saying, "If it is so, Allah will never abandon us."

Ibrāhīm kept walking until his family was out of sight. Then he turned his face in the direction of the House of Allah, and supplicated to his Lord:

﴿رَّبَّنَآ إِنِّيٓ أَسۡكَنتُ مِن ذُرِّيَّتِي بِوَادٍ غَيۡرِ ذِي زَرۡعٍ عِندَ بَيۡتِكَ ٱلۡمُحَرَّمِ رَبَّنَا لِيُقِيمُواْ ٱلصَّلَوٰةَ فَٱجۡعَلۡ أَفۡـِٔدَةٗ مِّنَ ٱلنَّاسِ تَهۡوِيٓ إِلَيۡهِمۡ وَٱرۡزُقۡهُم مِّنَ ٱلثَّمَرَٰتِ لَعَلَّهُمۡ يَشۡكُرُونَ﴾

"O our Lord! I have made some of my offspring to dwell in an uncultivable valley by Your Sacred House (the Ka'bah at Makkah) in order, O our Lord, that they may perform As-Salāt (the prayers). So, fill some hearts among men with love towards them, and (O Allāh) provide them with fruits so that they may give thanks."[1]

The Well of Zamzam

In the empty desert, the sun beat down mercilessly upon Hajirah (هاجره) and baby Ismā'īl. Very soon, the water-skin became dry and Hajirah had no more milk left in her breasts to feed her infant son. Only water could help them survive. As Ismā'īl's tiny stomach contracted in hunger, his wails filled the desert air. Hajirah (Hagar) herself was parched and weak, but her son's cries motivated her to continuously search for water. Increasingly

1 Ibrāhīm: 14:37.

desperate, she ran up a hill, which would later be known as the mountain of Safā (صفا), and scoured the surrounding area with her eyes in search of even one other human being. It was in vain. Unwilling to give up, Hajirah descended the hill, ran across the lowland, and climbed the next hill, Marwah (مروه). Once again, there was no one in sight, and no source of water as far as the eyes could see. Restless, desperate, and heartbroken at her son's need, Hajirah ran up and down over Safā and Marwah seven times.

The Prophet Muhammad (ﷺ) related that this excruciating journey between the two hills is the basis of the rite of *Sa'y* (سعى) during both *Hajj* and *'Umrah*. On Hajar's seventh round, as she reached the peak of Marwah, the Archangel Jibreel arrived and dug his wing into the ground. From that hole, water gushed forth, pure, clear, and miraculous. This was the water of *Zamzam*, a blessed gift to Hajirah (Hagar), and Ismā'īl, and all mankind.

In amazement, Hajirah (Hagar) ran to the water and, in fear that it would dry up or go to waste, dug around the water-source, forming the shape of a well. In joy and gratitude, she thanked Allah and began to feed her son Ismā'īl.

The Messenger of Allah (ﷺ), commenting on this momentous event, remarked:

«يَرْحَمُ اللّٰهُ أُمَّ إِسْمٰعِيلَ، لَوْ تَرَكَتْ زَمْزَمَ - أَوْ قَالَ: لَوْلَمْ تَغْرِفْ مِنْ زَمْزَمَ - لَكَانَتْ زَمْزَمُ عَيْنًا مَّعِينًا»

> "May Allah have mercy on the mother of Ismā'īl! Had she let Zamzam (continue to flow) or, had she not taken a handful of the water, Zamzam would be a flowing stream."

The angel Jibreel informed Hajar, "Do not ever fear for your life. Here is the (site of the) House of Allah which this child and his father will build. Allah does not let His slaves perish in vain."

Arrival of Banu Jurhum

Days passed, and Hajirah (Hagar) and Ismā'īl survived and thrived off

Source of Zamzam

of the well of Zamzam. However, they were still terribly alone in the vast desert, and Hajirah began to long for human company. Allah swiftly answered her prayers.

One day, a few men from the tribe of Banu Jurhum passed through the desert. They crossed Kudā' (the upper part of Makkah) and pitched their camp in the lowland of the Makkah valley. There, they observed swarms of birds hovering above nearby, a clear sign of a source of water. What surprised them, however, was that they had crossed through the valley of Makkah many times before, and had never found any trace of water. Curious, they sent two of their men to follow the birds. Once the two men confirmed the existence of the water source, they returned to their campsite and informed their tribesmen of this strange occurrence. Together, the group went back to the well of Zamzam, and found Hajirah sitting next to it.

They asked her, "Will you allow us to pitch our camp in your neighbourhood?"

Hajirah replied, "Yes but you will have no control of the water (that is, you will not own it)." The men of Banu Jurhum accepted this condition.

Ibn Abbas ؓ narrated that the Prophet Muhammad (ﷺ) said, "Now Ismā'īl's mother had neighbors. She liked the presence of humans nearby."

The tribesmen of Banu Jurhum set up their camp in Makkah, and sent word to other men of their tribes to join them there. Soon, the valley of Makkah became well-populated, and Ismā'īl grew up with the people of Banu Jurhum.[1]

1 Sahih-ul-Bukhrai: 3364.

2. A Prophet's Dream

Prophet Ibrāhīm ﵇ used to visit Makkah erratically, reuniting with his wife Hajirah (Hagar) and his son Ismā'īl. One day, he dreamt that he was sacrificing young Ismā'īl, who was his only son at the time. However, Ibrāhīm ﵇ was a Prophet, and understood that the dream was, in fact, a command from Allah. Ismā'īl ﵇ was only seven years old at the time.[1]

Though Ismā'īl ﵇ was such a young boy, Ibrāhīm ﵇ shared his dream with his son.

﴿ فَلَمَّا بَلَغَ مَعَهُ ٱلسَّعۡيَ قَالَ يَٰبُنَيَّ إِنِّيٓ أَرَىٰ فِي ٱلۡمَنَامِ أَنِّيٓ أَذۡبَحُكَ فَٱنظُرۡ مَاذَا تَرَىٰۚ قَالَ يَٰٓأَبَتِ ٱفۡعَلۡ مَا تُؤۡمَرُۖ سَتَجِدُنِيٓ إِن شَآءَ ٱللَّهُ مِنَ ٱلصَّٰبِرِينَ ﴾

" And, when he (his son) was old enough to walk with him, he said: "O my son! I have seen in a dream that I am slaughtering you (offering you

1 Mustadrik Hakim part 1 page: 466.

Jamarat is the place where the Devil tried to misguide Ibrahim ﵇. Pilgrims throw stones at the pillars

in sacrifice to Allāh). So look what you think!" He said: "O my father! Do that which you are commanded, In shā' Allāh (if Allāh wills), you shall find me of As-Sābirūn (the patient)."[1]

The Devil's Trick

Prophet Ibrāhīm took Ismā'īl with him on a walk, towards the destination where he intended to carry out Allah's command. However, as they were crossing the area now known as Mina, they were waylaid by a man who questioned them, "Where are you headed?" Ibrāhīm عليه السلام responded, "I have some business at hand that I am going to attend to." The man's answer then revealed his true nature – this was no human being, but rather Iblees himself. "Do you want to slaughter Ismā'īl?" he questioned Ibrāhīm عليه السلام. Ibrāhīm عليه السلام made it clear that this was an order from Allah that he would not disobey. *Iblees* continued to wheedle with Ibrāhīm عليه السلام, attempting to dissuade him from his task, until *Jibreel* came to Ibrāhīm عليه السلام with the order to pelt *Iblees* with stones.[2]

This occurred two more times, with Ibrāhīm عليه السلام throwing stones at Iblees until he finally gave up. This story forms the basis for the *Hajj* rite of *Ramy Al-Jamarāt* (رمى الجمرات).

1 As-Saffat: 37:102.
2 Musnad Ahmed Hadith: 279.

The place of Sacrifice in Mina

The Great Sacrifice

Prophet Ibrāhīm and Ismā'īl arrived at their destination. Once again, Ibrāhīm made clear to Ismā'īl what he was going to do. Ismā'īl responded with firm faith, "Do what Allah has commanded, for good is only in carrying out His commandments." He then said, "Do not tell my mother, lest she be overwhelmed with sorrow. Oh my father, when you put the knife to my neck, turn your face away so that you are not moved by regret or pity."

Ibrāhīm عليه السلام lay his only son down, gently turned his face away, and lay the knife over Ismā'īl's throat. However, the blade did not slice the skin. He tried once more, and again the knife failed to do its duty. Ibrāhīm عليه السلام honed the knife on a stone several times over, and attempted to sacrifice his son for the third time. It did not work.[1]

Trembling at the emotional agony, Ibrāhīm was swiftly relieved by a call from his Lord:

﴿فَلَمَّآ أَسْلَمَا وَتَلَّهُۥ لِلْجَبِينِ ﴿١٠٣﴾ وَنَٰدَيْنَٰهُ أَن يَٰٓإِبْرَٰهِيمُ ﴿١٠٤﴾ قَدْ صَدَّقْتَ ٱلرُّءْيَآ ۚ إِنَّا كَذَٰلِكَ نَجْزِى ٱلْمُحْسِنِينَ ﴿١٠٥﴾ إِنَّ هَٰذَا لَهُوَ ٱلْبَلَٰٓؤُا۟ ٱلْمُبِينُ ﴿١٠٦﴾ وَفَدَيْنَٰهُ بِذِبْحٍ عَظِيمٍ﴾

"Then, when they had both submitted themselves (to the Will of Allāh), and he had laid him prostrate on his forehead (or on the side of his forehead for slaughtering); We called out to him: "O Ibrāhīm (Abraham)! You have fulfilled the dream!" Verily, thus do We reward the Muhsinūn (good-doers.). Verily, that indeed was the manifest trial. And We ransomed him with a great sacrifice (i.e. – a ram); "[2]

Sacrifice of Ismā'īl or Ishāq?

The story of the sacrifice is related thus in the Qur'ān:

﴿فَلَمَّا بَلَغَ مَعَهُ ٱلسَّعْىَ قَالَ يَٰبُنَىَّ إِنِّىٓ أَرَىٰ فِى ٱلْمَنَامِ أَنِّىٓ أَذْبَحُكَ فَٱنظُرْ مَاذَا تَرَىٰ ۚ قَالَ يَٰٓأَبَتِ ٱفْعَلْ مَا تُؤْمَرُ ۖ سَتَجِدُنِىٓ إِن شَآءَ ٱللَّهُ مِنَ ٱلصَّٰبِرِينَ ﴿١٠٢﴾ فَلَمَّآ أَسْلَمَا وَتَلَّهُۥ لِلْجَبِينِ ﴿١٠٣﴾ وَنَٰدَيْنَٰهُ أَن يَٰٓإِبْرَٰهِيمُ ﴿١٠٤﴾ قَدْ صَدَّقْتَ ٱلرُّءْيَآ ۚ إِنَّا كَذَٰلِكَ نَجْزِى ٱلْمُحْسِنِينَ ﴿١٠٥﴾ إِنَّ هَٰذَا لَهُوَ ٱلْبَلَٰٓؤُا۟ ٱلْمُبِينُ ﴿١٠٦﴾ وَفَدَيْنَٰهُ بِذِبْحٍ عَظِيمٍ ﴿١٠٧﴾ وَتَرَكْنَا عَلَيْهِ فِى ٱلْءَاخِرِينَ ﴿١٠٨﴾ سَلَٰمٌ عَلَىٰٓ إِبْرَٰهِيمَ﴾

1 [Weak] Al-Mustadrak li'l-Hākim: 555/2, 556, Hadith: 4040.
2 As-Sāffāt: 37:107-103.

"And, when he (his son) was old enough to walk with him, he said: "O my son! I have seen in a dream that I am slaughtering you (offering you in sacrifice to Allāh). So look what you think!" He said: "O my father! Do that which you are commanded, In shā' Allāh (if Allāh wills), you shall find me of As-Sābirūn (the patient). Then, when they had both submitted themselves (to the Will of Allāh), and he had laid him prostrate on his forehead (or on the side of his forehead for slaughtering); We called out to him: "O Ibrāhīm (Abraham)! You have fulfilled the dream!" Verily, thus do We reward the Muhsinūn (good-doers.). Verily, that indeed was the manifest trial. And We ransomed him with a great sacrifice (i.e – a ram); And We left for him (a goodly remembrance) among the later generations. Salām (peace) be upon Ibrāhīm (Abraham)!."[1]

However, evidence from the Bible proves that this replacement of Is'hāq for Ismā'īl is a contradiction within the Bible itself. One chapter of the Bible states that Ibrāhīm's only son was Is'hāq, not Ismā'īl, at the time of the sacrifice; however, another section says that Ismā'īl was born to Ibrāhīm thirteen or fourteen years before Is'hāq.

The first Biblical excerpt is as follows:

"After these things God tested Abraham, and said to him, "Abraham!". And he said, "Here am I." He said, "Take your son, your only son Isaac, whom you love, and go to the land of Mori'ah, and offer him there as a burnt offering upon one of the mountains of which I shall tell you." So Abraham rose early in the morning, saddled his donkey and took two of his young men with him, and his son Isaac; and he cut the wood for the burnt offering, and arose and went to the place of which God had told him. On the third day Abraham lifted up his eyes and saw the place afar off. Then Abraham said to his young men, "Stay here with the donkey; I and the lad will go yonder and worship, and come again to you." And Abraham took the wood of the burnt offering, and laid it on Isaac his son; and he took in his hand the fire and the knife. So they went both of them together. And Isaac said to his father Abraham, "My father!" And he said, "Here am I, my son." He said, "Behold, the fire and the wood; but where is the

1 As-Saffat: 37:109-102.

lamb for a burnt offering?" Abraham said, "God will provide himself the lamb for a burnt offering, my son." So they went both of them together. When they came to the place of which God had told him, Abraham built an altar there, and laid the wood in order, and bound Isaac his son, and laid him on the altar, upon the wood.

Then Abraham put forth his hand and took the knife to slay his son. But the angel of the Lord called to him from heaven, and said "Abraham, Abraham!" And he said, "Here am I." He said, "Do not lay your hand on the lad or do anything to him, for now I know that you fear God, seeing you have not withheld your son, your only son, from me."[1]

The second Biblical narration states:

"Now Sar'ai, Abram's wife, bore him no children. She had an Egyptian maid whose name was Hagar; and Sar'ai said to Abram, "Behold now, the Lord has prevented me from bearing children; go in to my maid; it may be that I shall obtain children by her." And Abram hearkened to the voice of Sar'ai. So, after Abram had dwelt ten years in the land of Canaan, Sar'ai, Abram's wife, took Hagar the Egyptian, her maid, and gave her to Abram her husband as a wife. And he went in to Hagar, and she conceived; and when she saw that she had conceived, she looked with contempt on her mistress."[2]

Verse 11 of the same chapter says:

"And the angel of the Lord said to her, "Behold, you are with child, and shall bear a son; you shall call his name Ishmael; because the Lord has given heed to your affliction."

According to Bible, Ibrāhīm was eighty-six years old when Ishmael was born.

"Abram was eighty-six years old when Hagar bore Ishmael to Abram."[3]

1 Bible: (Genesis) 22: 1-12.
2 Bible: (Genesis) 16: 1-4.
3 Bible: (Genesis) 16:16.

When Isaac was born, Abraham was one hundred years old.

> "Abraham was a hundred years old when his son Isaac was born to him."[1]

When God gave Abraham the good tidings of the birth of Isaac, He said:

> "And God said to Abraham, "As for Sar'ai your wife, you shall not call her name Sar'ai, but Sarah shall be her name. I will bless her, and moreover I will give you a son by her; I will bless her, and she shall be a mother of nations; kings of peoples shall come from her." Then Abraham fell on his face and laughed, and said to himself, "Shall a child be born to a man who is a hundred years old? Shall Sarah, who is ninety years old, bear a child?" And Abraham said to God, "O that Ishmael might live in my sight!" God said, "No, but Sarah your wife shall bear you a son, and you shall call his name Isaac. I will establish my covenant with him as an everlasting covenant for his descendants after him."[2]

Imam Ibn Al-Qayyim, in *Zād al-Ma'ād*, gives twenty categorical arguments to prove that Ismā'īl, not Ish'āq, was sacrificed.[3]

Ismā'īl's Marriage

Ismā'īl ﷺ grew up amongst the children of Banu Jurhum, learning their customs and speaking their language, Arabic. Both his character and his physical looks attracted much admiration and attention, and when he came of age, the men of Banu Jurhum married him to one of their women.

Time passed, and Hajar, Ismā'īl's mother, died. Ibrāhīm ﷺ returned to Makkah after a long period of time to visit his son, but did not find Ismā'īl ﷺ at home. Ismā'īl's wife informed Ibrāhīm ﷺ that he had gone out in search of sustenance. Ibrāhīm ﷺ began to question his daughter-in-law with regards to her husband, his treatment of her, and how they lived. She began to complain, saying that they lived a difficult life with many hard days and little food.

1 Bible: (Genesis) 21:5.
2 Bible: (Genesis): 17:15-19.
3 Zād-ul-Ma'ād: 1/71-75.

Ibrāhīm عليه السلام took his leave, and told her, "When your husband comes home, give him my salūtation and tell him to change the threshold of his home."

When Ismā'īl عليه السلام returned, he sensed something and asked his wife, "Has anyone visited you?" She replied, "Yes, an old man of such and such description came and asked me about you and I informed him and he asked about our state of living and I told him that we were living in a hardship and poverty.'"

On that Ismā'īl عليه السلام asked, : "Did he advise you about anything?"

She said, "Yes, he told me to convey his salūtation to you and to tell you to change the threshold of your gate."

Ismā'īl عليه السلام said, "It was my father and he has ordered me to divorce you. Go back to your family."

Ismā'īl divorced his first wife, and later remarried into the tribe of Banu Jurhum. After some time had passed, Ibrāhīm عليه السلام returned to Makkah and again visited his son's home, only to find that Ismā'īl عليه السلام was absent. He then posed the same questions to his new daughter-in-law that he had asked of the first wife.

Ismā'īl's wife thanked and praised Allah for her husband, their easy lifestyle, and their food. Ibrāhīm عليه السلام asked her what it was that they lived on, and she answered, "Meat and water." Thereupon, Ibrāhīm عليه السلام supplicated, "O Allah, bless their meat and water."

The Prophet Muhammad (ﷺ) commented, "In those days, they had no food grain. If they had grain to eat, he would surely pray to Allah to bless it as well."

Ibrāhīm عليه السلام told his son's wife to convey his salūtations to her husband, and to retain the threshold of his home. When Ismā'īl عليه السلام returned, he sensed something once again and asked his wife if any visitors had come by.

She responded in the affirmative, saying that an old, good-looking man had called on him and asked her about their living. "What did you tell him?" Ismā'īl عليه السلام asked. She told him that they lived an easy life, for

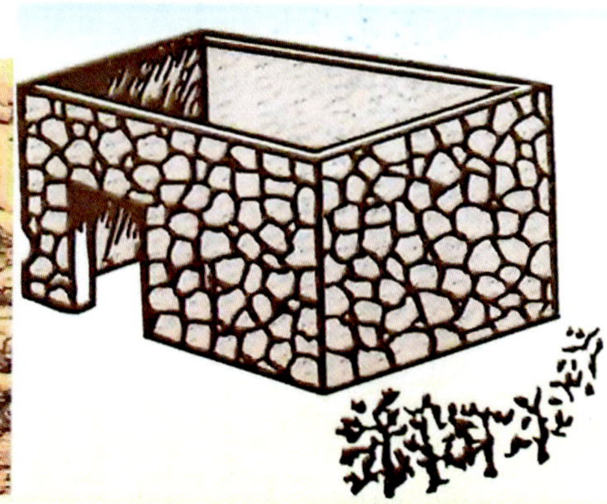

which she was grateful to Allah. "What advice did the man give you?" Ismā'īl عليه السلام inquired. "He conveyed his greetings, and told you to retain the threshold of your home."

Ismā'īl عليه السلام informed her, "That was my father. You are the threshold of my home, and he told me to remain married to you."

Construction of the Ka'bah

Prophet Ibrāhīm عليه السلام continued to visit Makkah periodically. One day he returned to Makkah and found his son Ismā'īl عليه السلام, sitting next to the well of ZamZam, in the shade of a large tree, making arrows. For the first time in many years, father and son were reunited. However, as prophets, there

was a greater purpose to their meeting.

Ibrāhīm ﷺ informed his son Ismā'īl that Allah had commanded him to build a great monument, one that would be known as the House of Allah – the Ka'bah. The location of this building was a raised mound, which had been present even before Ismā'īl and his mother Hajar first arrived in Makkah.

Together, Ibrāhīm and Ismā'īl raised the foundations of the Ka'bah. Ismā'īl would gather rocks and boulders, and Ibrāhīm would lay them in place, building the House of Allah. When the walls were raised and Ibrāhīm needed to reach higher, Ismā'īl brought a large rock upon which Ibrāhīm stood. This rock is now known as Maqām Ibrāhīm.

While they built the Ka'bah, both Ibrāhīm and Ismā'īl circumambulated the rising House, reciting the following supplication:

﴿رَبَّنَا تَقَبَّلْ مِنَّآ إِنَّكَ أَنتَ ٱلسَّمِيعُ ٱلْعَلِيمُ﴾

"Our Lord! Accept from us (this Service). Surely, You are the All-Hearer, the All-Knower." Al-Baqarah: 2:127.[1]

Station of Ibrāhīm (Maqām Ibrāhīm, Haram Ka'bah)

1 Sahih-ul-Bukhāri: 3364.

The Monastery in ancient city of Petra, Jordan

3.The Nabateans

Twelve sons were born to Ismā'īl (Ishmael) عليه السلام from his wife, Bint Madād. Their names were: Nābat or Nabāyūt (spelt variously as Nabt, Nabth, Nabāyūth), Qeydār, Obaiel, Mabsham, Mashma', Doma (Dūma), Meesha, Hadar or Hadad, Taima, Yathur, Nafees, and Qeydman.

They dwelt in Makkah and lived on trade with Yemen, Egypt and Syria. Later, they spread across other parts of the Arabian Peninsula and abroad. Of all his sons, only Nabat and Qeydar were remembered in history.[1] Note that Ishāq (Isaac), the half-brother of Ismā'īl, also had twelve sons.

1 Qalb-o-Jazeerat-il-Arab, P. 230. After Nābat bin Ismā'īl, Banu Jurhum got the custody of the House of Allah though its management remained in the hands of Banu Ismā'īl who were held in esteem by them.

The tribes of Banu Adnan

Banu 'Adnan are Arab Musta'ribah i.e. outsiders who became Arabs. They are descendants of Ismā'īl ﷺ. It is said that there are 40 links between Adnan and Hazrat Ismā'īl. Hazrat Ismā'īl had 12 sons. Out of them Qaidāss descendants inhabited in Hijaz and their settlements spread in Tihāmah and Najad . Later on they reached Irāq, Aljazeerah and other areas.

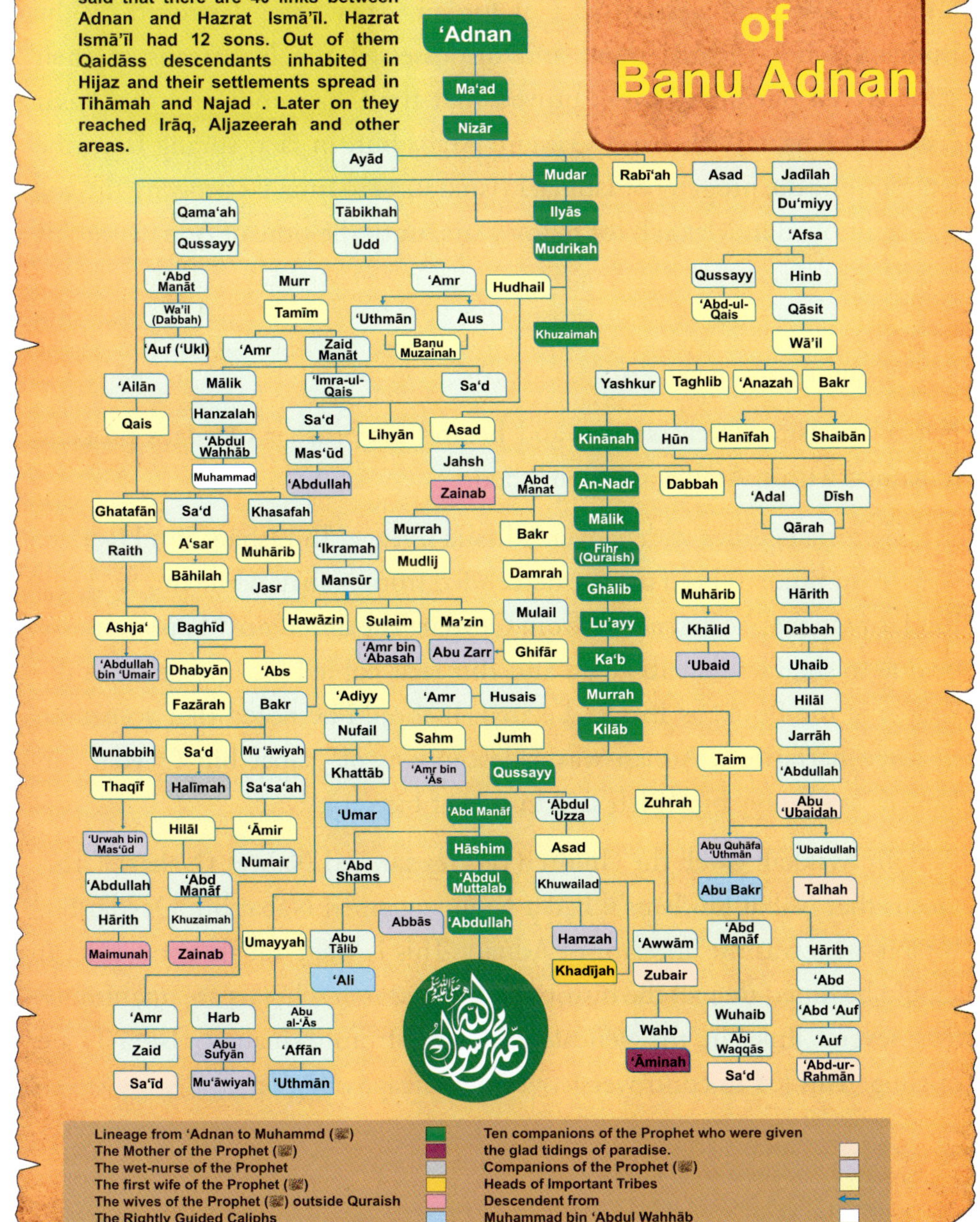

Ascendancy of the Nabateans

The progeny of Nabt or Nābat are called Nabateans. They gained ascendancy in northern Hijaz, established a strong government, and subjected other peoples and states around them. Petra was their capital city; its ruins are found in the southwestern part of Jordan. They were destroyed by the Romans, who defeated them and dispossessed the Nabateans of their state.Sayyed Suleman Nadwi proved that the Ghassanids and the Ansār ('Aus and Khazraj) were not Qahtāni Arabs but, in fact, sprang from the remnants of the progeny of Ishmael (Ismā'īl)عليه السلام.[1] Ismā'īl's progeny thrived and multiplied in Makkah for many years, until the time of Adnan and his son Ma'add (معدّ).

Adnānis
Descendants of Qeydar, or Nabateans?

Nabat was Ismā'īl's eldest son, and he and his brother Qeydār's progeny remained within Arabia and flourished.

Historians differ widely over Adnān's lineage. Ibn Ishāq, Ibn Hishām, and Imām Bukhāri hold that he descended from Nābat, while Ibn Sa'd and Ibn Jarir say that he descended from Qeydār. The difference of opinion may be due to the fact that Ibn Sa'd and Ibn Jarir copied his lineage from the People of the Book, as Ibn Sa'd stated. It should be noted that according to some narrations, Adnān was a descendant of Nābat bin Qeydār bin Ismā'īl, as Qusayy bin Kilab said in one of his verses:

"In Makkah dwell the children of Qeydār and Nabeet (Nabat)." This means that Nābat bin Ismā'īl had a nephew named Nābat bin Qeydār bin Ismā'īl, who was the ancestor of Adnān. This is what Tabari also wrote. It should be noted that all the historians and research scholars are unanimous that several links in the genealogical tree, from Adnan to Ismā'īl, are missing. This led to controversy over the lineage of Adnān.[2]

---

1 Tareekh Ard-il-Qur'ān (Kāmil): 2/60-69.

2 As-Seerah Li-Ibn Ishāq: 1/17; As-Seerah Li-Ibn Hisham: 1/34; At-Tabaqat li-Ibn Sa'd: 1/56; Tareekh Tabari: 2/28; At-Tareekh-ul-Kabeer: 1/5.

Tribes of Banu Adnān

Adnān belongs to the twenty-first generation of the Prophet Muhammad's family tree. According to some narrations, while relating his pedigree, the Messenger of Allah (ﷺ) would pause at Adnān and say that the genealogists erred when they went further back.[1]

According to a group of scholars, there are forty generations between Adnan and Ibrāhīm. A narration says that Ma'add, a son of Adnan, was a contemporary of Nebuchadnezzar, the king of Babel (Babylon). This is the opinion of Qadi Suleman Mansurpuri; however, the intervening generations from the Prophet ﷺ back to his age are too few to make it likely. Allah knows best.

Imām Ibn Qutaibah says that Ma'add bin Adnān had eight sons. Four of them were famous; those men being: Qudā'ah, Nizār, Qanas, and Iyād. Qudā'ah was the progenitor of Himyari tribes. The kings of Hīrah were the descendants of Qanas. Iyād left no tribe worthy of mention. Nizār was the most famous of them.[2]He had four sons: Iyād, Anmār, Rabee'ah and Mudar.[3]

The latter two tribes became very well known: From Rabee'ah came Abdul-Qais, and from them Bakr and Taghlib, and from Bakr came Banu Hanīfah and Banu 'Ajl. All of them left their names in Arab history.

Tribes of Qais

The descendants of Mudar sub-divided further into two large tribes: Qais (bin) 'Ailān bin Mudar and Ilyās bin Mudar.

1 Tareekh-ut-Tabari: 2/28-32; Al-A'lam: 4/218; As-Silsala Ad-Da'eefa: 1/228-229, Hadith: 111.

2 Al-Ma'arif li-Ibn Qutaiba, P. 29.

3 Al-Ansab Li's-Sam'āni: 1/23; Ar-Raud-ul-Unf: 1/160.

Qays 'Ailān divided further into several sub-tribes such as Banu Māzan, Banu Sulaim, Banu Hawāzan and Banu Ghatfān. From Banu Ghatfān came other sub-tribes: 'Abs, Dhabyān, Ghaniyy (Banu A'sar) and Ashja'. Haleemah ﷺ, the Prophet's foster-mother, belonged to the tribe of Sa'd bin Bakr bin Hawāzan, while the Mothers of the Believers, Maimoonah bint Hārith and Zainab bint Khuzaimah, belonged to Banu Hilāl, a branch of Hawāzan. Banu 'Abs and Banu Dhabyān also belonged to Qais 'Ailān. Banu Fazārah is a branch of Banu Dhabyan while 'Adwān and Bāhilah are also the sub-tribes of Qais 'Ailan. The tribes of Ra'l, Dhakwān and 'Usayyah are branches of Banu Sulaim.[1]

The Messenger of Allah (ﷺ) sent seventy reciters of Qur'ān to these tribes (of Banu Sulaim) for religious instruction. However, their tribesmen ambushed and killed these Qurrā,' whereupon the Prophet (ﷺ) invoked Allah's punishment upon them for an entire month. According to another narration, he did so for forty days.[2]

Division of Mudari Tribes

Banu Tamim, Banu Mudrika, and Banu Khuzaimah: Ilyas bin Mudar's son Mudrikah and the latter's son, Khuzaimah, were among the ancestors of the Prophet (ﷺ).

Tābikhah bin Ilyās bin Mudar is the progenitor of the famous tribe of Tamim bin Murr, while Mudrikah bin Ilyās that of Hudhail bin Mudrikah, Banu Asad bin Khuzaimah and Kinānah bin Khuzaimah.

Abu Dharr Al-Ghifāri, a famous Companion of the Messenger of Allah, belonged to Bakr bin Abd Manāt bin Kinanah.

Apart from Kinānah and Asad, Khuzaimah had another son named Hoon. Banu Asad and Qarah, along with the Prophet ﷺ, group under Khuzaimah, 'Adl bin Hoon bin Khuzaimah and Deesh bin Hoon bin Khuzaimah together are called Qarah (or 'Adl wa Qarah). Zaynab bint Jah'sh, the Mother of the Believers, belonged to Banu Asad. Mudrikah groups Banu Hudhail along with the Prophet ﷺ. Abdullah bin Mas'ud, a famous Companion, is a notable figure from this tribe. Banu Tamim and

1 Mukhtasar Seerat-ur-Rasool (Urdu), P. 27-28.

2 Sahih-ul-Bukhari: 1300, 2801.

Muzainah group along with the Prophet ﷺ under Ilyas.

Kinanah: Banu Kinānah bin Khuzaimah bin Mudrikah bin Ilyās bin Mudar is the name of a large Arab tribe who dwelt during the early days of Islam around Makkah, in the areas stretching from Tihāmah, southwest of Makkah, to the northeast of the city. They derived their importance from the twin facts: they were large in numbers and the Prophet's tribe of Quraish links a few generations up the family tree with the tribe of Kinānah. Fihr (Quraish) were the great grand-children of Kinanah.

Since Banu Kinanah lived in the neighbourhood of the House of Allah, theirs had been an important role in the pre-Islamic times. For example, Qusayy, a chieftain of Quraish, bought the government (control) of Makkah from Banu Khuzā'ah. Later, when a quarrel broke out over it, an elder of Kinānah, Ya'mar bin 'Auf, was chosen to decide the issue finally. He gave a judgment, in the light of the proofs, in favour of Quraish, another branch of Kinānah. For this ruling, he was given the title of Ash-shaddākh and, according to Ibn Hishām, also the title of Ash-shuddākh, because he 'crushed' the quarrel by his judgment.[1]

Banu Kinanah includes, besides Quraish, Banu Bakr, Banu Mudlaj, Banu Laith, Banu Damrah, and Banu Hārith (who also include Ahābeesh). Abu Dharr Al-Ghifāri رضي الله عنه, a Companion, belonged to Banu Damrah.

Quraish and its branches

The tribe of Quraish is a branch of Banu Kinanah. This tribe is the offspring of Fihr (Quraish) bin Mālik bin Nadar bin Kinanah, who was the tenth ancestor of the Prophet ﷺ.

Quraish themselves sub-divided into several branches, the most famous being Hārith, Muhārib, Ghālib, Jumah, Sahm, 'Āmir, 'Adi, Makhzoom, Taim, Kilāb, Zuhrah, Asad, Hāshim, and 'Umayyah.

Banu Ghālib, Banu Muhārib and Banu Hārith: Ghālib, Muhārib, and Hārith were the three sons of Fihr. Of all the children of Ghālib, Lu'ayy was conspicuous. Among his children, Banu Ka'b and Banu 'Āmir became famous. Saudāh bint Zam'ah رضي الله عنها, the Mother of the Believers, belonged

1 Urdu Encyclopedia of Islam: 17/411-412; As-Seerah li-Ibn Hisham: 1/124.

to Banu 'Āmir. Abu Obaidah bin Jarrāh ﷺ belonged to Banu Hārith bin Fihr while Darār bin Khattāb ﷺ, a Badri companion, belonged to Banu Muhārib. Ka'b was the seventh ancestor of the Prophet (ﷺ).

Banu 'Adi, Banu Sahm and Banu Jumah: Ka'b bin Lu'ayy had three sons: 'Adī, Murrah and Husais. The second caliph of the Muslims, Umar ibn Al-Khattāb ﷺ, also belonged to Banu 'Adī. Among the offspring of Husais, Banu Sahm and Banu Jumah became famous. 'Amr bin 'Ās and Abdullah bin Hudhāfah ﷺ (the Companions) belonged to Banu Sahm. Umar's lineage connects, in the eighth generation, with the Prophet ﷺ at Ka'b bin Lu'ayy. In the civic administration of Makkah, the departments of diplomacy and settlement of lawsuits belonged to Banu 'Adi. Umar ﷺ had also the honour to look after those departments. Umar's cousin, Zaid bin 'Amr bin Naufal, was a follower of Abraham's religion. His son, Sa'eed bin Zaid ﷺ, was one of *al-'Asharah al-Mubash'sharāh* (the ten Companions promised Paradise by the Prophet Muhammad).

Banu Taim, Banu Yaqzah and Banu Kilāb: Murrah bin Ka'b had three sons: Kilāb, Taim and Yaqzah. Kilāb's son, Qusayy, was great– great–great grandfather of the Prophet (ﷺ). The offspring of the second son, Zuhrah, came to be called Banu Zuhrah. The Prophet's mother, Aminah, and his well-known Companions, Sa'd bin Abi Waqqās and Abdur-Rahmān bin 'Auf ﷺ, belonged to Banu Zuhrah. From among Banu Taim, Abu Bakr Siddiq, the first Caliph, and Talhah bin 'Ubaidullah ﷺ (Companion) rose to prominence. Their ancestral line joins the Prophet ﷺ in the seventh generation at Murrah. Among the descendants of Yaqzah bin Murrah's son Makhzoom were Umm Salamah, the Mother of the Believers, Khalid bin Waleed, Arqam ﷺ bin Abi Arqam and Abu Jahl ('Amr) bin Hishām.

Banu Hāshim, Banu Abd-ud-Dār and Banu Asad: Qusayy bin Kilāb had four sons: Abdul-Uzza, Abd Manāf, Abd-ud-Dār and Abd (Abd Qusayy). Abd Manāf was the grand ancestor of the Prophet ﷺ. Banu Abd-ud-Dār had the offices of *Siqāyah* and *Rifādah*.[1] Abdul-Uzza's son was Asad. The Prophet's first wife, Khadijah bint Khuwaylid ﷺ bin Asad, belonged to Banu Asad. Zubair bin 'Awwām ﷺ, a prominent Companion, was the

1 As-Seerat-un-Nabawiyyah li-Ibn Kathir, P. 30,31.

nephew of Khadijah.

Banu Abd Shams and Banu Umayyah: Abd Manāf bin Qusayy had four sons: Abd-Shams, Naufal, Hāshim, and Al-Muttalib. Two of his offspring, Banu Abd-Shams and Banu Hashim, became more famous. The offspring of Umayyah, the son of Abd Shams, came to be called Banu Umayyah. Abul-'Ās, 'Ās, and Harb were the prominent persons of Banu Umayyah. The third caliph of Islam, Uthmān bin Affān, Abu Sufyān, and Mu'āwiyah ﷺ belonged to Banu Umayyah. Umayyah was the real nephew of Hāshim while 'Uthmān bin Affān's father, Affān bin Abil-'Ās bin Umayyah, and Abu Sufyān bin Harb bin Umayyah were cousins. 'Uthmān's mother, Arwa, was the daughter of the Prophet's paternal aunt, Umm Hakeem Bayda' bint Abdul-Muttalib.[1]

Sa'eed bin 'Ās bin Sa'eed bin 'Ās bin Umayyyah ﷺ, another Companion, was born the same year when the Prophet ﷺ migrated to Madinah. His father, 'Ās, was slain by Ali ﷺ in the Battle of Badr.[2]

The Messenger of Allah (ﷺ) said: "Allah chose Ismā'īl from among the children of Ismā'īl, chose Kinanah from among the children of Ishmael, chose Quraish from among the progeny of Kinanah, chose Banu Hāshim from among the Quraish, and,

Dwelling place of Banu Thaqif

1 Atlas Seerat-i-Nabawi, P. 57.
2 Usd-ul-Ghabah: 2/328.

finally, chose me from among Banu Hāshim."[1]

Harrah Banu Sulaim

Banu Naufal and Banu Muttalib:

'Adi bin Khiyār bin 'Adi bin Naufal (a famous Companion) was a descendant of Naufal bin Abd Manaf while the Companions, Qais bin Mukhrimah, Qāsim bin Mukhrimah, and Ubaidah bin Hārith, who was martyred in the Battle of Badr, were the grandsons of Muttalib bin Abd-Manaf. Muttalib was older than both of his brothers, Hāshim and 'Abd-Shams. Their mother was 'Ātikah bint Murrah bin Hilāl. After Hāshim he was charged with the duty to supply water to pilgrims and keep the House of Allah clean. He went to Yemen on a trade journey and died there in *Radmān*. [2]

Banu Adnān Across Arabia

The progeny of Adnān multiplied and spread across Arabia, searching for food, water, and suitable areas of residence. Several sub-tribes of Abdul-Qais and Bakr bin Wā'il (from Banu Rabee'ah) and Banu Tamim, a branch of Banu Tābikhah bin Ilyās bin Mudar, moved to Bahrain *(al-Ahsā')* and settled in eastern Arabia.

Banu Haneefah bin Sa'b bin Ali bin Bakr went to Yamāmah and settled down in Hajar (حجر), the central area thereof. The remaining branches of Bakr bin Wā'il pitched their camps all over the areas stretching from Yamāmah to Bahrain, along the coasts of Kāzimah (modern Kuwait), and up to Sawād al-Iraq, Ubullah and Hait (Iraq).

1 Sahih Muslim: 2276; Jami' At-Tirmidhi: 3605.

2 Muhadarat Tareekh-il-Umam Al-Islamiyyah: 1/17-19; See also Mu'jam Qaba'il-il-Arab and Al-Jamharah Li-Ibn Hazm .

Banu Taghlib bin Wā'il settled in Jazeerah Furatiyah (al-Jazeerah) while some of their branches settled along with Banu Bakr. Banu Tamim spread as far as Nejd, Basrah, Yamāmah and 'Udhaib, near Kūfah.

Banu Sulaim, a sub-tribe of Banu Qais, pitched their camps near Yathrib (Madinah). Their settlement started from Wadi al-Qura up to Kheybar and, running east of Madinah, extended to the two mountains adjacent to Harrah Banu Sulaim.

Banu Thaqeef found home in Ta'if while Banu Hawāzan dwelt around Wadi Autas, east of Makkah. Banu Thaqeef are, in fact, a branch of Banu Hawāzan. Their progenitor was Thaqeef bin Munabbih bin Bakr bin Hawāzan.

Banu Asad established themselves east of Taima' (the Tabūk province) and west of Kūfah. In between them and Taima', Buhtar, a clan of Banu Tayy, was already established. The settlement of Banu Asad was five days journey from Kufah. Banu Dhabyan domiciled near Taimā' and around Haurān (Syria).

There remained in Tihāmah the families of Banu Kinānah. Those among them who were Qurashi dwelt in and around Makkah. They remained scattered till Qusayy bin Kilāb united the Quraish and gave them honour and prestige.[1]

1 At-Tabaqāt Li-Ibn Sa'd: 1/81-83; As-Seerah Li-Ibn Hisham: 1/106; Tareekh-ut-Tabari: 2/14.

Dwelling place of Banu Kinanah

Lot's cave - Sodom (Jordan)

The People of Lūt

Ancestry

Prophet Lūt (Lot) عليه السلام was the son of Hārān, and the nephew of Ibrāhim عليه السلام. Hārān was the youngest son of Tareh (Tarekh), and was brother to Ibrāhim عليه السلام. He died before his father at Ur.[1] Ibrāhīm, Hārān and Nāhor were brothers.[2]

Lūt عليه السلام believed in Ibrāhīm's message of monotheism, accompanied him on the migration from Iraq to Harrān (Turkey). From there, he went to Palestine and pitched his camp at a hill east of Jerusalem (Beit El). Lūt عليه السلام was accompanied by his wife. They arrived in Egypt during the time of the shepherd kings; however, they found the conditions there unsuitable and

1 Qamoos-ul-Kitab, P 316; Ar-Raud-ul-Unf: 1/40.

2 Al-Bidaya Wa'n-Nihaya: 1/132.

returned to Palestine.[1]

Lūt's Message

Lūt ﷺ was commanded by Allah, though Ibrāhīm ﷺ, to move from Hebron (al-Khaleel) in Palestine to Sodom, a town in Ghaur Zughar. There, he settled down and made it his mission to spread the message of *Tawheed* to the people of the region. Sodom and its surrounding areas are located south of the Dead Sea. The people of Sodom were known to be crude and violent, known in particular for their highway robbery and public lewdness.[2]

Reaction to the Message

The people of Sodom were amongst the most depraved people of their time. Not only were they violent criminals who robbed anyone who crossed their roads, but their evilness extended to their sexual behaviour. Rather than engaging in normal, heterosexual relationships, the men of Sodom abandoned their women and instead gratified their lust with other males. Prophet Lūt ﷺ called these people to believe in the Unity of God *(Tawheed)* and to reform their behaviour in accordance to purity of morals. However, Lūt's people spurned his call and mocked him constantly.

Allah mentions the story of Lūt ﷺ several times in the Qur'ān.

﴿وَلُوطًا إِذْ قَالَ لِقَوْمِهِۦٓ أَتَأْتُونَ ٱلْفَٰحِشَةَ مَا سَبَقَكُم بِهَا مِنْ أَحَدٍ مِّنَ ٱلْعَٰلَمِينَ ٨٠
إِنَّكُمْ لَتَأْتُونَ ٱلرِّجَالَ شَهْوَةً مِّن دُونِ ٱلنِّسَآءِ ۚ بَلْ أَنتُمْ قَوْمٌ مُّسْرِفُونَ﴾

"And (remember) Lūt (Lot), when he said to his people: ``Do you commit the worst sin such as none preceding you has committed in the 'Ālamīn (mankind and jinn)? Verily, you practise your lusts on men instead of women. Nay, but you are a people transgressing beyond bounds (by committing great sins)."[3]

At another place Allah says:

---

1 Bible: (Genesis), chapter: 11-13; Atlas-ul-Qur'ān (Urdu), P. 104-106.

2 See Al-Bidāya Wan-Nihāya: 1/144.

3 Al-A'raf: 7:80-81.

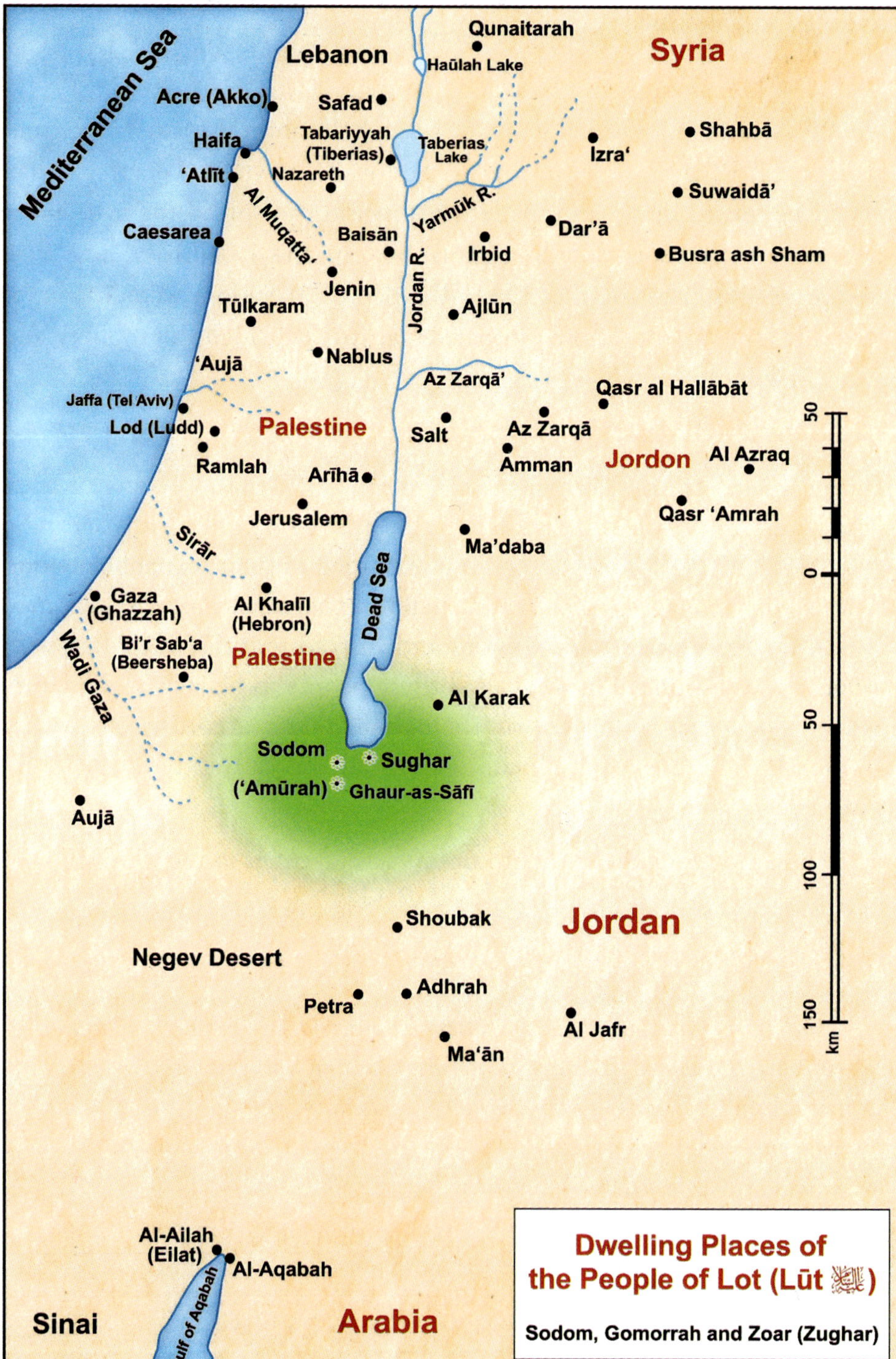
Mediterranean Sea
Lebanon
Qunaitarah
Haūlah Lake
Syria
Acre (Akko)
Safad
Haifa
Tabariyyah (Tiberias)
Taberias Lake
Shahbā
'Atlīt
Nazareth
Izra'
Suwaidā'
Al Muqatta'
Yarmūk R.
Caesarea
Baisān
Dar'ā
Irbid
Busra ash Sham
Jenin
Jordan R.
Tūlkaram
Ajlūn
'Aujā
Nablus
Az Zarqā'
Qasr al Hallābāt
Jaffa (Tel Aviv)
Lod (Ludd)
Palestine
Salt
Az Zarqā
Ramlah
Amman
Jordon
Al Azraq
Arīhā
Jerusalem
Qasr 'Amrah
Sirār
Ma'daba
Dead Sea
Gaza (Ghazzah)
Al Khalīl (Hebron)
Bi'r Sab'a (Beersheba)
Palestine
Wadi Gaza
Al Karak
Sodom
Sughar
('Amūrah)
Ghaur-as-Sāfī
Aujā
Shoubak
Jordan
Negev Desert
Adhrah
Petra
Al Jafr
Ma'ān
50
0
50
100
150
km
Al-Ailah (Eilat)
Al-Aqabah
Gulf of Aqabah
Sinai
Arabia
Dwelling Places of the People of Lot (Lūt)
Sodom, Gomorrah and Zoar (Zughar)

Map.16

﴿كَذَّبَتْ قَوْمُ لُوطٍ ٱلْمُرْسَلِينَ ﴿١٦٠﴾ إِذْ قَالَ لَهُمْ أَخُوهُمْ لُوطٌ أَلَا تَتَّقُونَ ﴿١٦١﴾ إِنِّى لَكُمْ رَسُولٌ أَمِينٌ ﴿١٦٢﴾
فَٱتَّقُوا۟ ٱللَّهَ وَأَطِيعُونِ ﴿١٦٣﴾ وَمَآ أَسْـَٔلُكُمْ عَلَيْهِ مِنْ أَجْرٍ ۖ إِنْ أَجْرِىَ إِلَّا عَلَىٰ رَبِّ ٱلْعَـٰلَمِينَ﴾

"The people of Lūt (Lot) (–who dwelt in the towns of Sodom in Palestine) denied the Messengers. When their brother Lūt (Lot) said to them: "Will you not fear Allāh and obey Him? Verily, I am a trustworthy Messenger to you. So fear Allāh, keep your duty to Him, and obey me. No reward do I ask of you for it (my Message of Islāmic Monotheism); my reward is only from the Lord of the 'Ālamīn (mankind, jinn and all that exists)."[4]

Despite Lūt's great concern, his people refused to believe in him and instead plotted to drive him out of the town. The folk cared not a jot for their messenger nor believed in him but rather planned to drive him out of the town.

﴿فَمَا كَانَ جَوَابَ قَوْمِهِۦٓ إِلَّآ أَن قَالُوٓا۟ أَخْرِجُوٓا۟ ءَالَ لُوطٍ مِّن قَرْيَتِكُمْ ۖ إِنَّهُمْ أُنَاسٌ يَتَطَهَّرُونَ﴾

"There was no other answer given by his people except that they said: "Drive out the family of Lūt (Lot) from your city. Verily, these are men who want to be clean and pure!"[5]

4 Ash-Shu'ara': 26:160-164.
5 An-Naml: 27:56.

The area south of Dead Sea where people of Lot were doomed to extinction by a hail of rocks and stones

The Punishment

Lūt warned his people that they would meet a terrible fate if they persisted in their sinning and refused to repent. They continued to mock him, and challenged him:

﴿ٱئْتِنَا بِعَذَابِ ٱللَّهِ إِن كُنتَ مِنَ ٱلصَّٰدِقِينَ﴾

"Bring Allah's torment upon us if you are one of the truthful!" [1]

Finally, Allah decreed that they had transgressed His limits too far, and imposed His divine punishment upon them all, including Lūt's disobedient wife.

﴿فَلَمَّا جَآءَ أَمْرُنَا جَعَلْنَا عَٰلِيَهَا سَافِلَهَا وَأَمْطَرْنَا عَلَيْهَا حِجَارَةً مِّن سِجِّيلٍ مَّنضُودٍ ﴿٨٢﴾
مُّسَوَّمَةً عِندَ رَبِّكَ ۖ وَمَا هِيَ مِنَ ٱلظَّٰلِمِينَ بِبَعِيدٍ﴾

"So when Our Commandment came, We turned (the towns of Sodom in Palestine) upside down, and rained on them stones of baked clay, in a well-arranged manner one after another; Marked from your Lord; and they are not ever far from the Zālimūn (polytheists, evildoers)." [2]

Thus were the folk of Lūt doomed to extinction by a hail of rocks and stones. Sayyed Abul-'A'la Maudoodi writes in his travelogue, "We reached a place called al-Lisān on the eastern coast of the Dead Sea. Nearby, to the south, lies that part of the Dead Sea which is said to be the site of Sodom and other townships destroyed by Allah. Therefore, also the Dead Sea is also called the Lot Sea (بحرلوط). As one looks around the Dead Sea, one feels even today that a formidable doom has split up the earth and pounded it at several places."[3]

1 Al-'Ankabut: 29:29.
2 Hūd: 11:82-83.
3 Safarnama Ard-il-Qur'ān, P. 236.

Banu Qatūrā: The People of Shu'aib

Shu'aib عليه السلام was a prophet sent to the people of Madyan (Midian). Madyan is the name of a tribe, the offspring of Prophet Ibrāhīm's son, Madyan, from his third wife, Qatūrā. The people of Madyan were named Banu Qatūrā after their ancestress.

The people of Madyan were Arabs whose settlements lay south of the port of *Ailah*, all along the eastern coast of the Gulf of Aqaba and the Red Sea, and stretched as far east as Tabūk. *Ailah* (ايله) was a Jewish town,[1] named after Ailah bint Madyan.[2] Presently, the town is a part of Israel and called Eilat.

The territory of the Madyanites reached up to the last part of Hijaz, next to Jordan. During the times of the Prophet ﷺ, travellers from Hijaz

1 Al-Bidāya Wan-Nihāya: 173/1.
2 Mu'jam-ul-Buldan: see under 'Aila'.

The area of al-Bad'a where the people of Shu'aib were settled

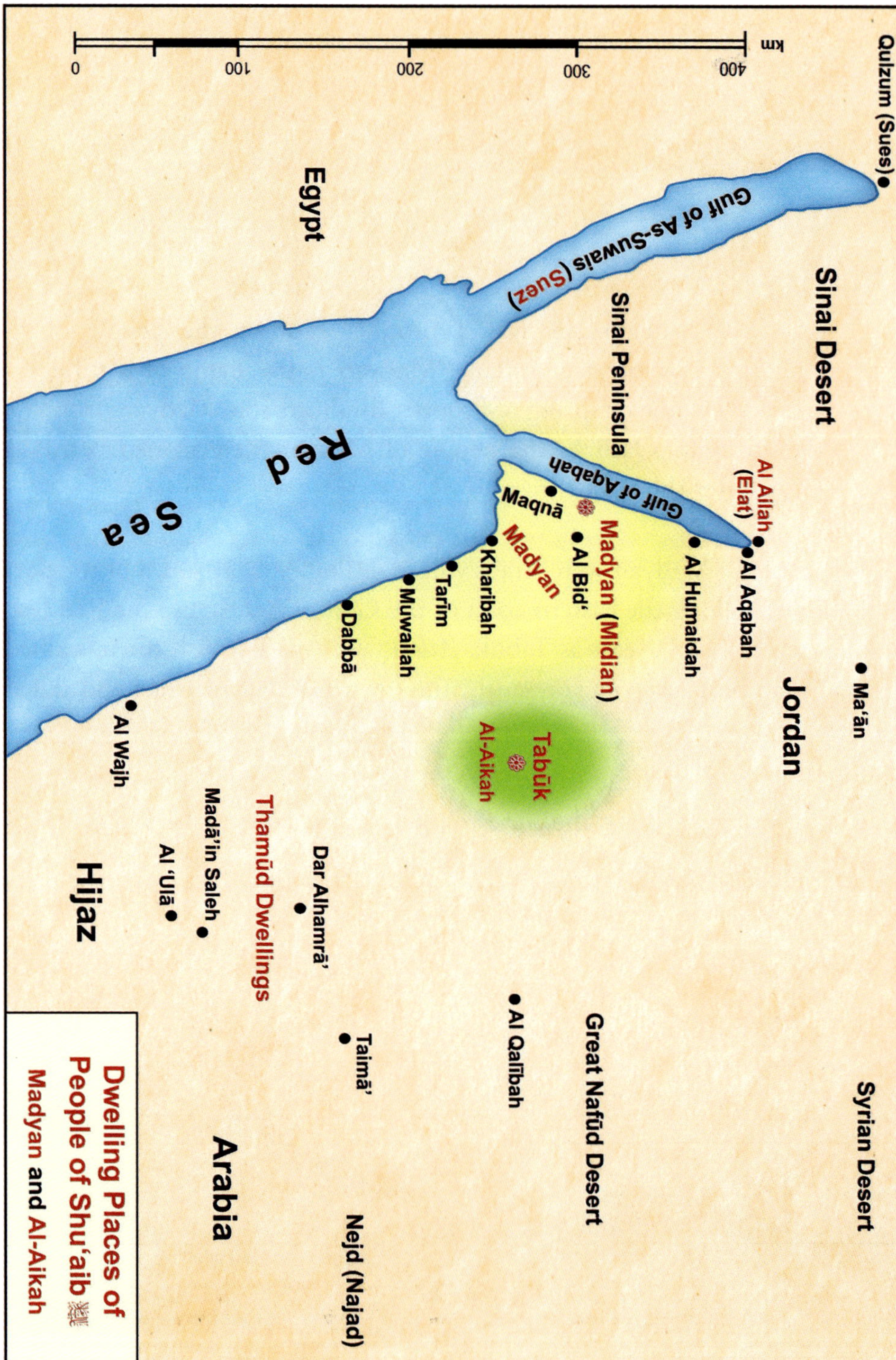
Dwelling Places of People of Shu'aib ﷺ
Madyan and Al-Aikah
km
0
100
200
300
400
Qulzum (Sues)
Gulf of As-Suwais (Suez)
Sinai Desert
Sinai Peninsula
Egypt
Red Sea
Gulf of Aqabah
Al Ailah (Elat)
Al Aqabah
Al Humaidah
Maqnā
Madyan (Midian)
Al Bid'
Madyan
Kharibah
Tarīm
Muwailah
Dabbā
Al Wajh
Ma'ān
Jordan
Tabūk
Al-Aikah
Thamūd Dwellings
Dar Alhamrā'
Madā'in Saleh
Al 'Ulā
Hijaz
Al Qalībah
Great Nafūd Desert
Syrian Desert
Taimā'
Nejd (Najad)
Arabia

Map.17

passed through the relics of Madyan on their way to Syria, Palestine and Egypt. The Qur'ān refers to this trade route as *Imam-e-Mubeen* (open and clear way).[1] This route passed through the territories of both the people of Lūt and the people of Madyan. Today, in the territory of Madyan there are many townships like al-Humaidah, Miqna, Al-Khuraibah, Tareem, Muwailah, and Dabā.[2]

People of Aikah (اصحاب الايكه)

Most historians take both the inhabitants of Madyan and those of Aikah as a single people with two names. According to them, they are named Madyan after their ancestor and named Aikah for its geographical features. Some scholars, however, hold the view that they are two different peoples with a single prophet; that is, Shu'aib ﷺ was appointed a prophet for Madyan first and for Aikah later.[3]

Allah says:

﴿ كَذَّبَ أَصْحَٰبُ لْـَٔيْكَةِ ٱلْمُرْسَلِينَ ﴿١٧٦﴾ إِذْ قَالَ لَهُمْ شُعَيْبٌ أَلَا تَتَّقُونَ ﴾

"The dwellers of Al-Aikah [near Madyan (Midian)] denied the Messengers. When Shu'aib said to them: "Will you not fear Allāh and obey Him?"[4]

Ibn Kathir says, "The correct opinion is that the people of Aikah refer to the people of Madyan. Prophet Shu'aib ﷺ belonged to those tribesmen. Here, unlike the chapter of *al-A'rāf*, Allah did not say 'their (that is, the Midianites') brother' but here the reference is made to *Aikah* (woods) which those people worshipped.

Aikah is the name of a tree or, according to another opinion, the word means 'woods dense with trees.' Here the point to note is that Allah said only "The dwellers of Al-Aikah [near Madyan (Midian)] denied the Messengers. When Shu'aib said …" but did not say when 'their brother Shu'aib said.' This is a veiled hint that Shu'aib ﷺ was also a prophet for the people of the woods (Aikah) although he was their brother and belonged to the same

1 See Al-Hijr: 15:79.
2 Atlas-ul-Qur'ān (Urdu), P. 128.
3 Al-Muntazam: 1/324.
4 Ash-Shu'ara': 26:176-177.

tribe. Some people failed to perceive this hidden hint and thought that the people of al-Aikah and of Madyan were two different peoples. That is, they thought that Shu'aib was sent to two separate communities. Some even think that he was sent to three communities.[1]

A Hadith terms Shu'aib *Khateeb Al-Anbiyā'* (the orator-prophet) for his oratory skills and for the rhetorical language he used in the course of his sermons.[2]

The people of Madyan were pagans and thieves, who terrorized passing travellers and worshipped a tree named Aikah. When they conducted business, they were extremely dishonest and cheated their customers; when they would weigh their goods, they would charge their customers more money for less weight. On the other hand, if they were the ones making purchases, they would demand extra weight and refuse to pay fully. Allah appointed one of their own men a prophet to guide them.

Shu'aib's Mission

Prophet Shu'aib's charge was, as with every other prophet, to call his people to the worship of the One True God, and to be just in their transactions.

1 Tafseer Ibn Kathir: Ash-Shu'ara': 26:176-180.
2 Al-Mustadrak Li'l-Hakim: 2/568.

Settlements of the people of Shu'aib (Al-Bad'a)

﴿وَإِلَىٰ مَدْيَنَ أَخَاهُمْ شُعَيْبًا ۚ قَالَ يَٰقَوْمِ ٱعْبُدُوا۟ ٱللَّهَ مَا لَكُم مِّنْ إِلَٰهٍ غَيْرُهُۥ ۖ وَلَا تَنقُصُوا۟
ٱلْمِكْيَالَ وَٱلْمِيزَانَ ۚ إِنِّىٓ أَرَىٰكُم بِخَيْرٍ وَإِنِّىٓ أَخَافُ عَلَيْكُمْ عَذَابَ يَوْمٍ مُّحِيطٍ﴾

"And to the Madyan (Midian) people (We sent) their brother Shu'aib. He said: ``O my people! Worship Allāh, you have no other ilāh (god) but Him, and give not short measure or weight. I see you in prosperity and verily, I fear for you the torment of a Day encompassing."[1]

Shu'aib ﷺ wished his people well, reminded them of the blessings of their Lord, and exhorted them to worship Him alone, and stop cheating in their weighing and measuring.

The people of Madyan, however, reacted the same way as the people of Lūt – they rejected his teachings and threatened him with stoning and exile.

﴿قَالَ ٱلْمَلَأُ ٱلَّذِينَ ٱسْتَكْبَرُوا۟ مِن قَوْمِهِۦ لَنُخْرِجَنَّكَ يَٰشُعَيْبُ وَٱلَّذِينَ ءَامَنُوا۟ مَعَكَ مِن قَرْيَتِنَآ أَوْ لَتَعُودُنَّ
فِى مِلَّتِنَا ۚ﴾

"The chiefs of those who were arrogant among his people said: ``We shall certainly drive you out, O Shu'aib, and those who have believed with you from our town, or else you (all) shall return to our religion."[2]

1 Hūd: 11:84.
2 Al-A'raf: 7:88.

Finally, in despair, Shu'aib ﷺ said,

﴿ وَيَٰقَوۡمِ ٱعۡمَلُواْ عَلَىٰ مَكَانَتِكُمۡ إِنِّي عَٰمِلٞۖ سَوۡفَ تَعۡلَمُونَ مَن يَأۡتِيهِ عَذَابٞ يُخۡزِيهِ وَمَنۡ هُوَ كَٰذِبٞۖ وَٱرۡتَقِبُوٓاْ إِنِّي مَعَكُمۡ رَقِيبٞ ﴾

"And O my people! Act according to your ability and way, and I am acting (on my way). You will come to know who it is on whom descends the torment that will cover him with ignominy, and who is a liar! And watch you! Verily, I too am watching with you."[1]

Various forms of Chastisement

Allah said of them:

﴿ وَلَمَّا جَآءَ أَمۡرُنَا نَجَّيۡنَا شُعَيۡبٗا وَٱلَّذِينَ ءَامَنُواْ مَعَهُۥ بِرَحۡمَةٖ مِّنَّا وَأَخَذَتِ ٱلَّذِينَ ظَلَمُواْ ٱلصَّيۡحَةُ فَأَصۡبَحُواْ فِي دِيَٰرِهِمۡ جَٰثِمِينَ ﴾

"And when Our Commandment came, We saved Shu'aib and those who believed with him by a mercy from Us. And As-Saihah (torment–awful cry) seized the wrongdoers, and they lay (dead) prostrate in their homes."[2]

In this Verse, the word used for to describe the punishment of Madyan is *"as-Sai'hatu"* الصيحة (awful or tremendous cry) while in al-A'raf (7: 91) the word is *'Ar-Raj'fatu'* الرجفة (earthquake) and, in *ash-Shu'arā'* (26: 189), the word is *'Adhabu Yaum-iz-Zullah* عذاب يوم الظله (day of shadow or gloom). When brought together, it is understood that the people of Madyan were punished in various ways.

First, the people of Madyan were made to suffer intense heat for seven days. On the last day, clouds began to gather over them, and they rejoiced, thinking that it was coming to shade them and save them from the grueling heat. Instead, Allah rained fire and burning coals upon them, followed by an earthquake. On the heels of these punishments was a terrible cry from the heavens, which ripped the souls from their bodies.

﴿ إِنَّهُۥ كَانَ عَذَابَ يَوۡمٍ عَظِيمٍ ﴾

"Surely, that was the torment of a Great Day."[3]

1 Hūd: 11:93.

2 Hūd: 11:94.

3 Tafseer Ibn Kathir: Ash-Shu'ara', 26:185-191

Chapter - 3

Domains and Kingdoms

of the Arabian Peninsula

Accounts of Pre-Islamic Domains And Kingdoms, The Queen of Sheba, Nebuchadnezzar's Incursion Into Hijaz, Custody of The Ka'bah, Distribution of Power Among Qusayy's Sons, And Events of Makkah

لقد جاءكم

رسول من أنفسكم

عزيز عليه ما عنتم حريص عليكم

بالمؤمنين رءوف رحيم

"Verily, there has come to you a Messenger, (Muhammad ﷺ) from amongst yourselves. It grieves him that you should receive any injury or difficulty. He (Muhammad ﷺ) is anxious over you; for the believers full of pity, kind and merciful." At-Tawbah: 9:128

In This Chapter

Gives a brief account of the Arab regimes and monarchies that existed prior to the Prophet Muhammad's era. It covers the kingdoms of Yemen, the state of Ma'een, the kingdom of Saba and its religion, Queen Bilqees, the kingdom of Qitban, the kingdom of Himyar, the construction of Ma'rib dam and its eventual destruction, Tubba' king As'ad Abu Karb's conversion to Islam in the Age of Paganism, occupation of Yemen by Abyssinians and later by Persians, the Lakhmi kingdom of Hirah, and the victory of Arabs in the Battle of Zi Qār.

It also deals with the Ghassani kingdom of Syria, the kingdom of Oman, the rule of Kindah, Nebuchadnezzar's attack on Hijaz and the capture of Ma'dd bin Adnan, Banu Jurhum's expulsion from Makkah and Banu Khuzā'ah's domination, Qusayy's return and custody of Ka'ba, distribution of powers among Qusayy's sons, the regime of Makkah, the tribal chieftains and other related topics.

Types of Arab Rulers

At the time that Islam came to the Arabian Peninsula, three types of rulers controlled its various regions.

1. Crowned kings: These kings were not independent but rather, were under the domination of any of the two contemporary superpowers, the Romans and the Persians, and paid them tributes in exchange for their continued reign.

   The crowned kings at the time included the kings of Bahrain, kings of Oman, the Ghassanid kings (Syria), and the Hīrah kings (Iraq).

2. Tribal rulers and chieftains: In their internal affairs, they behaved like and were treated like crowned kings; however, they were in fact fully independent, did not owe allegiance to either the Romans or the Persians, and did not pay any tributes to those empires.

3. Governors: The Persian emperors nominated governors in Yemen who would rule on behalf of the Persian Empire.

At the time, there also existed the kingdom of Kindah in central Arabia. It lasted from 425 CE to 550 CE and, at the height of its power, stretched from Yemen to Dūmat al-Jandal in the north.

Kingdoms of Yemen

The Yemeni people, and in particular the Sabaeans, are recorded as the oldest and most ancient race of the pure Arabs *(Arab Al-'Aribah)*. Their names occur in ancient inscriptions discovered in Ur (Iraq), dating back to two thousand and five hundred years BC.

Sabā, both as a people and as a state, is named after Abd Shams Sabā who was, according to genealogists, the great grandson of Qahtān.

In ancient Yemen, four kingdoms were founded, one after the other: Ma'een, Sabā, Qitbān, and Himyar.

Kingdom of Ma'een

The first organized, well-ordered kingdom in the history of Yemen was that of Ma'een. It was established around 1600 BC in Ahqāf-Yemen (al-Jauf valley), with Hadramaut to the east and Sabā in the southwest.

A headstone of Ma'een era

In the heyday of its glory, this kingdom extended from Gulf of Aden to Hijaz. The kingdom was named after its capital town, Ma'een (or *al-Qarn*), which was northeast of San'a. Among its relics is the temple of Ishtār, a major goddess. In the seventh century BC, the dominion of Ma'een was replaced by the kingdom of Sabā.[1]

Kingdom of Sabā

The state of Sabā was named after Abd Shams Sabā who was, according to genealogists, a great grandson of Qahtān. His full name was Sabā bin Yashjub bin Ya'rub bin Qahtān. The history of Sabā falls into two epochs:

1. **Makārabs of Sabā**
2. **Kings of Sabā.**

Makārabs of Saba (1000 BC – 650 BC): 'Makārab' or 'Makrab' was the title of the kings of Sabā. It was a composite word, consisting of the word 'rab.' In the Sabaean language, 'rab' meant 'big' or 'king'

1 Al-Munjid Fi'l A'lām; P 538; Qissa Wa Tarikh Al-Hadarat-il-Arabia: 15/29.

The Throne of the Makarabs of Sabā - Sarwāh

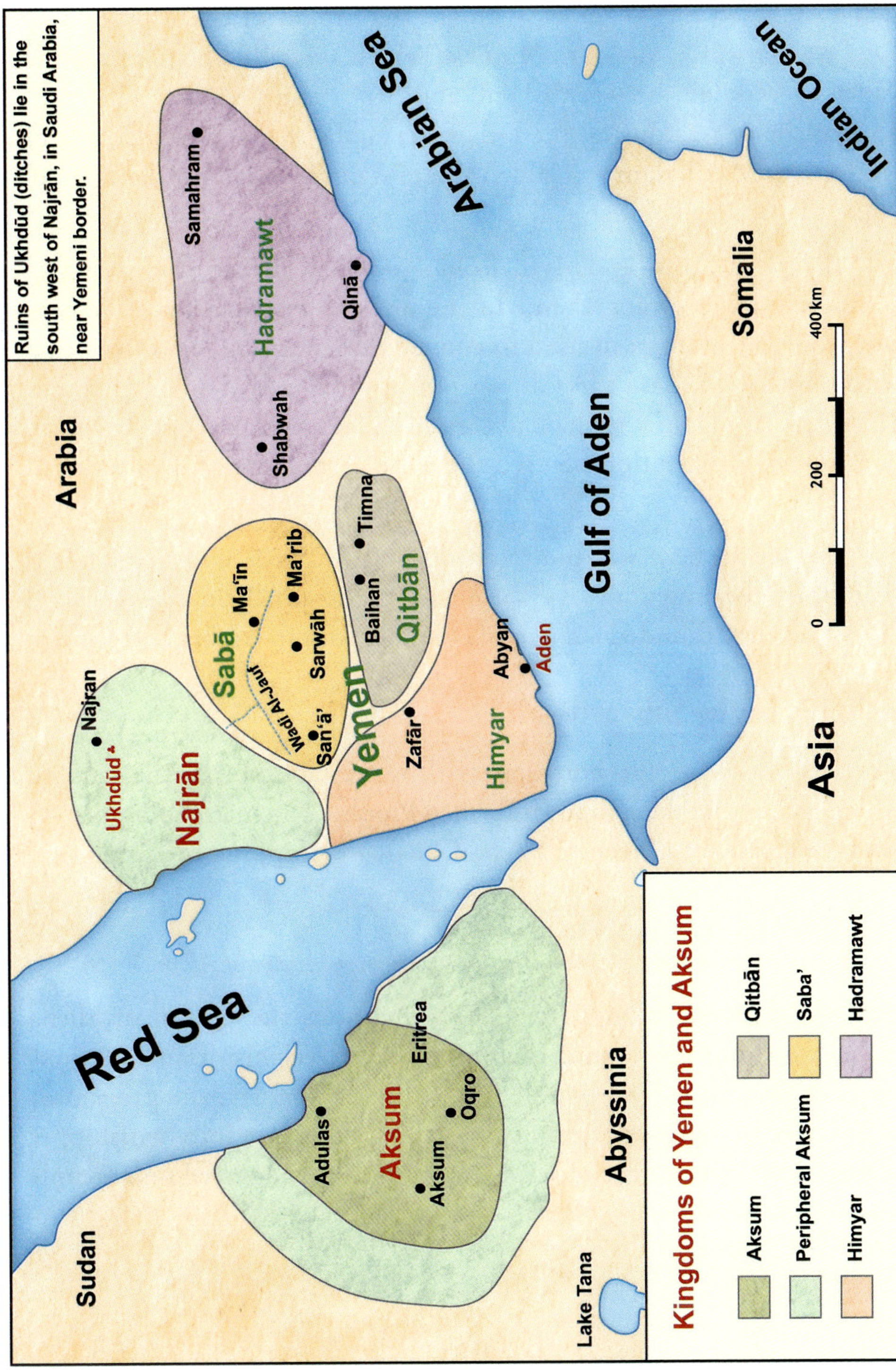
Ruins of Ukhdūd (ditches) lie in the south west of Najrān, in Saudi Arabia, near Yemeni border.
Arabia
Arabian Sea
Indian Ocean
Samahram
Hadramawt
Qinā
Shabwah
Timna
Qitbān
Baihan
Ma'rib
Ma'īn
Sarwāh
Sabā
Wadi Al-Jauf
San'ā'
Yemen
Najran
Ukhdūd
Najrān
Zafār
Himyar
Abyan
Aden
Gulf of Aden
Somalia
Asia
0
200
400 km
Red Sea
Sudan
Lake Tana
Abyssinia
Eritrea
Adulas
Oqro
Aksum
Aksum
Kingdoms of Yemen and Aksum
Aksum
Peripheral Aksum
Himyar
Qitbān
Saba'
Hadramawt

Map.18

while Makārab meant 'priestly king.' The capital of the Makārabs of Sabā was Sarwāh (صرواح), the ruins of which are still to be found in the valley of Wākifāh, between Ma'rib and San'ā, and presently known as Khuraibah. It was during the era of Makārabs that the foundation of the famous Ma'rib dam was laid. The Arabs of Hijāz call the dam 'Sudd' while the Arabs of Yemen call it "'Arim."

The word 'Arim is derived from *'Arman*, which in the dialect of southern Arabic means 'dam.' In the ancient inscriptions of Yemen, this word has often been used to convey that meaning. An inscription dating back to 542 or 543 CE was put up by the Abyssinian governor of Yemen, Abrahah, after he had carried the reparation work on Ma'rib dam. In that inscription he used the word 'Arman repeatedly to mean 'dam.'[1]

The Ma'rib dam was built around 800 BC. It is said that around that time, the kingdom of Sabā increased so much in strength and glory that they founded a chain of colonies both in Arabia and abroad.

Religion of the Sabaeans

The Sabaeans were sun-worshippers. This is established by the Qur'ān, which relates that the hoopoe informed Prophet Sulemān (Solomon) عليه السلام about Bilqees, the Queen of Sheba (Saba), worshipping the sun:

﴿ وَجَدتُّهَا وَقَوْمَهَا يَسْجُدُونَ لِلشَّمْسِ مِن دُونِ ٱللَّهِ ﴾

"I found her and her people worshipping the sun instead of Allah."[2]

Targum, a Jewish religious text, also mentions the Queen of Sheba (Saba) worshipping the sun. Theophrastus, a Greek historian, mentions heaps of incense in 'the Temple of the Sun.' Moreover, the progenitor of the tribe of Sabā was 'Abd Shams' which translates into 'worshipper of sun.' In the early days of Islam, an inscription engraved on a temple was found. It read:

1 Tafheem-ul-Qur'ān: 4/192.
2 An-Naml: 27:24.

In the Name of Allah. This is what (king) Shammar Yar'ush built for the sun goddess.[1]

Sabaean Moon-god Temple, Marib, Yemen

Queen Bilqees surrendered to Sulemān ﷺ and accepted the Islamic faith[2] but generations later, her people left the pure faith of *Tawheed* and returned to their worship of the sun. Historical evidence suggests that there were some men in ancient Yemen who believed in the Unity of God.

Some inscriptions dating back to about 650 BC were found in several places in Yemen. They name that deity as *Mālikan Dhusamawa* (ملكن ذُسموى) (king of heavens). Another inscription dating back to 378 CE mentions a temple built in the name of 'the god of heavens': *"Ilah Dhū Samawa."* (الٰه ذوسموى) Later, another inscription dated 465 CE contains the words: *"Bi-Nasr Wa Rida Ilahan Ba'l Sameen Wa Ardeen"* (بنصرو ردا الٰهن بعل سمين وارضين) – this translated to, "with the help and support of God who owns the heavens and the earth."

Still another inscription dated 458 CE refers to that god as Rahman (The Beneficent): *"Bi-Rida Rahman-an"*(بردا رحمنن); that is, 'with the support of the Beneficent.'[3]

1 Tarikh Ard-il-Qur'ān (Kamil): 1/214-215; Mulook-ul-Ard, P. 110.
2 An-Naml: 27:44.
3 Tafheem-ul-Qur'ān: 4/194.

Ruins of the Dam of Ma'rib

The Dam of Ma'rib and its Destruction

The famous Ma'rib Dam built by the Sabaeans was situated in the valley of Uzainah, east of the town of Ma'rib.[1] The Qur'ān refers to the Sabaeans and their dam:

﴿لَقَدْ كَانَ لِسَبَإٍ فِي مَسْكَنِهِمْ ءَايَةٌ جَنَّتَانِ عَن يَمِينٍ وَشِمَالٍ كُلُوا مِن رِّزْقِ رَبِّكُمْ وَاشْكُرُوا لَهُ
بَلْدَةٌ طَيِّبَةٌ وَرَبٌّ غَفُورٌ ﴿١٥﴾ فَأَعْرَضُوا فَأَرْسَلْنَا عَلَيْهِمْ سَيْلَ الْعَرِمِ وَبَدَّلْنَاهُم بِجَنَّتَيْهِمْ جَنَّتَيْنِ ذَوَاتَيْ
أُكُلٍ خَمْطٍ وَأَثْلٍ وَشَيْءٍ مِّن سِدْرٍ قَلِيلٍ ﴿١٦﴾ ذَٰلِكَ جَزَيْنَاهُم بِمَا كَفَرُوا وَهَلْ نُجَازِي إِلَّا الْكَفُورَ
﴿١٧﴾ وَجَعَلْنَا بَيْنَهُمْ وَبَيْنَ الْقُرَى الَّتِي بَارَكْنَا فِيهَا قُرًى ظَاهِرَةً وَقَدَّرْنَا فِيهَا السَّيْرَ سِيرُوا فِيهَا
لَيَالِيَ وَأَيَّامًا ءَامِنِينَ ﴿١٨﴾ فَقَالُوا رَبَّنَا بَاعِدْ بَيْنَ أَسْفَارِنَا وَظَلَمُوا أَنفُسَهُمْ فَجَعَلْنَاهُمْ أَحَادِيثَ
وَمَزَّقْنَاهُمْ كُلَّ مُمَزَّقٍ إِنَّ فِي ذَٰلِكَ لَءَايَاتٍ لِّكُلِّ صَبَّارٍ شَكُورٍ﴾

"Indeed there was for Saba' (Sheba) a sign in their dwelling place – two gardens on the right hand and on the left; (and it was said to them:) "Eat of the provision of your Lord, and be grateful to Him." A fair land and an Oft-Forgiving Lord! But they turned away (from the obedience of Allāh), so We sent against them Sail Al-'Arim (flood released from the dam), and We converted their two gardens into gardens producing bitter bad fruit, and tamarisks, and some few lote trees. Like this We requited them because they were ungrateful disbelievers. And never do We requite in such a way except

1 Atlas Al-Qur'ān (Urdu), P. 173; Al-Munjid Fi'l-A'lam, P. 510 .

those who are ungrateful (disbelievers). And We placed, between them and the towns which We had blessed, towns easy to be seen, and We made the stages (of journey) between them easy (saying): "Travel in them safely both by night and day." But they said: "Our Lord! Make the stages between our journey longer," and they wronged themselves; so We made them as tales (in the land), and We dispersed them all totally. Verily, in this are indeed signs for every steadfast, grateful (person)."[1]

Rise and Fall of Sabā (Sheba)

Abul-A'la Maududi writes: 'The Sabaeans rose for two reasons: agriculture and trade. They developed agriculture by means of an advanced irrigation system, the like of which was not found anywhere in the world in those times save Babel (Babylon). There was no river in their land, so they tapped the abundant rain water flowing down the hills.

By building a chain of dams over rain-filled streams, they collected water into pools or reservoirs, dug out a network of irrigation canals from there to cover the whole land. This ingenious system of irrigation made the whole country green and verdant.

As the Qur'ān says, gardens could be seen everywhere. With a great deal of rain water which they distributed through an elaborate network of canals over the entire land, the whole country became lush, green and verdant as far as one could see. The largest reservoir of water was

1 Saba': 34:15-19.

Ruins of Ma'rib

Map.19

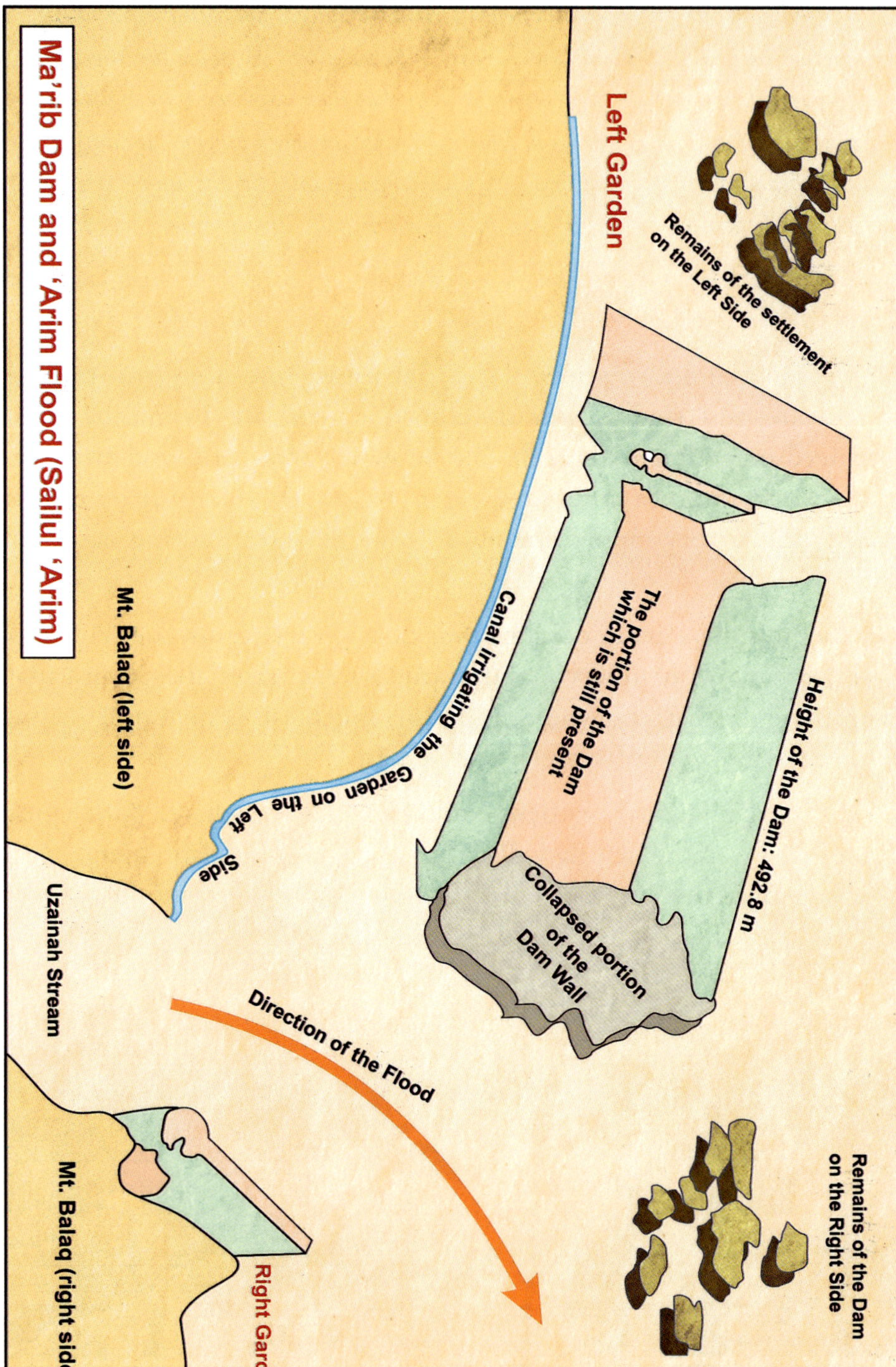

Ma'rib Dam and 'Arim Flood (Sailul 'Arim)

the tank made by building a dam over the river between the Balaq Mountains near the town of Ma'rib.

However, they displeased Allah and so He destroyed the great dam in the middle of the fifth century CE. A torrent of water gushed forth, breaking down all the smaller dams, one after the other, that came in its way till the entire irrigation system collapsed beyond hope of repair.

A headstone attributed to Umm 'Amr Ma'dikarab (Ma'rib)

For more than a thousand years the people of Sheba remained a medium of trade between East and West. On the one hand, their seaports received varied merchandise from diverse countries: silk from China, spices from Indonesia and Malabar, textiles and swords from India, negro slaves, apes, feathers of ostriches and tusks of elephants from East Africa. On the other hand, they re-exported those merchandise to Egypt and Syria to be carried further beyond to Rome and Greece. Moreover, there was an ample produce in their land of frankincense, aloes, ambergris, musk, myrrh, cinnamon, and other aromatics which they exported to Egypt, Syria, Rome and Greece.

There were two routes of this thriving trade: maritime and overland. For a thousand years the maritime route was controlled by the Sabaeans because they knew best the seasonal winds of the Red Sea, the undersea reefs and rocks, and the places of safe mooring. No other people could navigate this dangerous sea. The Sabaeans would carry their merchandise by sea to the ports of Jordan and Egypt. The land routes from Aden and Hadramaut linked up at Ma'rib whence a highway went up to Petra via Makkah, Jeddah, Yathrib, al-'Ulā', Tabūk, and Ailah. Another route went up to Egypt and still another to Syria. Along this trade route, as the Qur'ān tells us, the Sabaeans had built a chain of colonies right from Yemen to the borders of Syria. All along this route their trade caravans would ply their wares day and night. Relics of those

colonies exist to this day and excavations continue to reveal inscriptions written in Sabaean and Himyari languages.'[1]

Sayyed Suleman Nadwi writes: 'There are two mountains named Balaq, on the right and left, south of the town of Ma'rib. In between the two mountains there is the valley of Uzainah. The water flowing down the mountains collects in the valley of Uzainah and turns the valley into a river.

Around 800 BC, the Sabaeans built a dam, called the Ma'rib Dam, between those two mountains. Inscriptions found in the parts of the dam still extant bear the names of the founders of the dam (the Makāribs of Sabā). They have been deciphered and translated as the names of Yatha' Amr Bayyin, Samah'ali Yanuf, Karb Ail Bayyin, Zamar 'Ali and Yada' Il.

This dam was built over a long period of time by the kings of Yemen. This great irrigation system changed an area of 200 sq miles of the desert into a flourishing agricultural area where fruits of various kinds and sweet-smelling trees grew in abundance. The Ma'rib Dam was destroyed sometimes between 542 CE and 570 CE.'[2]

Kings of Sabā (650 BC – 115 BC): During this period the kings of Saba (Sheba) assumed the title of Mālik (king) and made Ma'rib their capital city. Ma'rib was also known as 'Sabā.' The royal palace was named Salheen, the remains of which are found 60 miles east of San'a.[3]

Until recently Ma'rib was the capital of the province of Baidā', 130 miles southeast of San'ā, the capital of Yemen. Presently, Ma'rib is itself a province.

1 Tafheem-ul-Qur'ān: 4/197-198.
2 Tarikh Ard-il-Qur'ān (Kamil): 1/202; Al-Munjid Fi'l A'lām P. 510; Al-Mufassal Fi Ttarikh-il-Arab Qabl-al-Islam: 2/285.
3 Tarikh Ard-il-Qur'ān (Kamil): 1/188-196.

The Kingdom of Qitbān (or Qatbān)

The ancestor of Banu Qitbān was Qitbān bin Radman bin Wa'il bin Ghauth Himyari.[1] This Yemeni kingdom continued to exist in the valley of Baihān, southeast of Sabā, from 500 BC to 200 CE.

References to it have been found in the ancient inscriptions of southern Arabia and in Greek and Roman literature. Its capital was Timna', which was situated along the trade route passing through Hadramaut and the kingdoms of Saba and Ma'een. The people, Banu 'Amm, were named after their chief idol, 'Amm. Their rulers were called Makrab.[2]

Coins of the Kingdom of Qitban

The Kingdom of Himyar

Banu Himyar belonged to the family of Sabā. They dwelt in western Yemen, in the areas close to the Red Sea and the Arabian Sea. Their rulers were called 'Dhu' (chief) who lived in Raidān Fort, next to the capital, Zufār. The relics of Zufār are found on a round hill near the town of Yareem, south of San'ā.

After the destruction of Sabā (Sheba), the Himyars extended their territory to Ma'rib. Up until that time, they bore the title of 'King of Sheba', and 'Dhu Raidān.' During that period, a part of the kingdom began to be called Yamnat or Yamnāt. Gradually, the whole land came to be called Yemen, which stretched from 'Aseer to Aden and from Bab-al-Mandab to Hadramaut.

Words like 'Himyar' and 'the land of Himyars' are found in some of the inscriptions of the Abyssinians. Greek historians mentioned the word 'Himyar' for the first time in 20 BC. The word 'Himyar' may be a derivative

Coins of Himyar era

1 Al-Mufassal Fi Tarikh-il-Arab Qabl-al-Islam: 2/173.
2 Urdu Islamic Encyclopedia: 16/1/266; Wikipedia (Encyclopedia).

from the Arabic and Abyssinian word 'Humr' (red). Since the Arabs call the Abyssinians Aswad and Saudan (black), it is assumed that the Abyssinians may well have called the Arabs humr (that is, fair or reddish-complexioned). An inscription of Abrahah, the Abyssinian conqueror of Yemen, bears the words: "The Abyssinian king came with the Himyari army." In other words, both black and white platoons arrived.

Domination of Abyssinians

Coins of the King Udhainah's era

The history of the Himyari kings of Sabā begins from late second century BC (115 BC), or the middle of the first century BC. The first generation of the Himyars ruled from the first century BC to the closing years of the third century CE. Their title was *"Mālik Sabā wa Dhu Raidān,"* 'the King of Saba and the chief of Raidān.'

The Aksumi Abyssinians of Sabaean extraction began attacking Yemen during the second century CE; however, Tubba' the Great Harith ar-Raish (Shammar Yahra'ish: 280-315 CE) drove them out of Hadramaut and became the first king to rule both Yemen and Hardramaut.

From 340 to 375 CE, the Aksumi Abyssinians occupied the land from Aksum to Yemen (Himyar) and Hadramaut. During this period, the king Udhainah and his successors called themselves the 'Kings of Aksūm, Himyar, Raidān, Ethiopia, Sheba (Sabā) and Zaila Zaila '(Northern Somalia).[1]

Second Generation of Himyar (Tabābi'ah)

The second generation of Himyar kings were entitled "Kings of Sheba, Dhu Raidan and Hadramaut." The Arabs called them *"Tubba'"* (plural:

1 Synopsis of Tarikh Ard-il-Qur'ān (Kamil): 1/221-228. Zaila' is currently situated in Somalia, on the Gulf of Aden coast.

Tabābia'h). It could be that Tubba' is another version of the Arabic word Matbū' (the one who is obeyed and followed), although recent research has proved that it was an Abyssinian word meaning 'able, and powerful'. The first Tubba' was Kalikarb or, according to the ancient inscriptions, Mālik Yakrab, who expelled Aksumis in 375 CE and took control of Yemen and Hadramaut.[1]

Tubba' As'ad Abu Karb's Conversion to Islam

Of all the Tubba' kings, three were most famous: Tubba' the Great Harith ar-Raish (280 CE – 315 CE), Tubba' the Middle As'ad Abu Karb bin Kalikarb (400 CE – 425 CE), and Tubba' the Small Hassan bin Tubba' (425 CE-455 CE).[2] Tubba' As'ad Abu Karb converted to Judaism.

Samhudi writes: "When the Tubba' the First, Taban As'ad Abu Karb bin Kalikarb, passed through Madinah (Yathrib), he was accompanied by four hundred scholars. They decided to stay in that town. Tubba' As'ad asked them why they wanted to stay there. They replied: "We knew from our books that the last and the greatest Prophet of Allah, whose name is Ahmad or Muhammad, will migrate to this town. Thus, we wish to stay here so that we may have a chance to see him."

The Tubba' built homes for them all and wrote a letter declaring his conversion to Islam and also wrote the following verses:

شَهِدْتُ عَلٰى أَحْمَدَ أَنَّهُ   رَسُولٌ مِّنَ اللّٰهِ بَارِئُ النَّسَمِ

فَلَوْ مُدَّ عُمْرِي إِلٰى عُمْرِهِ   لَكُنْتُ وَزِيرًا لَّهُ وَ ابْنَ عَمِّ

(I bear witness that Ahmad is the Messenger of Allah, the Creator. If I lived to see him, I would be his helper and his kinsman).

He sealed the letter with gold, and gave it to the most senior scholar, and said, "If you live long enough to see him, give it to him and, in case you do not see him, let it be delivered by your son or grandson."

1 Tarikh Ard-il-Qur'ān (Kamil): 1/228-229.

2 Op.cit., 1/230-231.

The Tubba' also built a house for the coming prophet. Time passed, and eventually, the house fell to the lot of Abu Ayyūb al- Ansāri, who was a descendant of that scholar.[1]

Imam Ahmad quoted a Marfū' (traceable) Hadeeth on the authority of Sahl bin Sa'd Ansāri:

«لَا تَسُبُّوا تُبَّعًا فَإِنَّهُ قَدْ كَانَ أَسْلَمَ»

"Do not reproach Tubba', for he accepted the Islamic faith."[2]

Towards the end of the first era of the Tubba' reign, the Roman army took control of Aden, Yemen's largest seaport. With their help, and by taking advantage of the discord between Himyars and Hamdan, they occupied Yemen for the first time in 340 CE; this occupation continued until the year 375 CE.

Yemen regained its freedom, but the Ma'rib dam began to slowly crack until it collapsed completely during (542 CE – 570 CE).[3] The collapse caused the great flood which the Qur'ān calls *Sail al-'Arim*.[4] The terrible flood destroyed the settlements and displaced the tribes.

Re-occupation of Yemen by Abyssinians

Coins of Abrahah

The Caesar of Rome instigated the king of Abyssinia, who owed allegiance to the former, to invade Yemen; Caesar then supplied him with a naval fleet for that purpose. In 525 CE, a force of seventy thousand Abyssinain soldiers, under the command of Aryāt, invaded Yemen and occupied it. For some time, Aryat ruled Yemen as a governor on behalf of the Abyssinian king, but was eventually assassinated by one of his deputy commanders, Abrahah Ashram (Ashram: having slit nose) who

1 Wafa'-ul-Wafa Li's-Samhudi: 1/188-189.
2 Musnad Ahmad 5/340; As-Silsala As-Sahiha: 2423.
3 Al-Munjid Fi'l A'lām, P 510; Al-Mufassal Fi Tarikh-il-Arab Qabl-al-Islam: 2/285.
4 Saba': 34:16.

took control of the land. Abrahah perished in the Year of the Elephant and was succeeded by his two sons, Yaksūm and Masrooq, as rulers of Yemen.

Iranian Occupation of Yemen

A few years later, the Yemenis, under the command of Ma'dikarab, son of Saif Dhi Yazan Himyari, revolted against the Abyssinians and drove them out of their land in 575 CE. However, Ma'dikarab retained some Abyssinians to serve him and to adorn royal festive processions. This worked against him, unfortunately, as these retainers later ambushed and slew him.

A Beautiful Mosque of Shabām (Yemen)

Saif Dhi Yazan went to Khosrau Anushiravan, the king of Persia, in appeal for aid. He told the Persian ruler, "The crows have pillaged our land!" Khosrau asked, "What crows are they, Abyssinian or Indian?" Saif replied, "These crows have come from Abyssinia."

Khosrau refused the implied offer, saying, "We have no desire to occupy the distant land of yours. In your land there is nothing save camels and sheep." He bade farewell to Saif Dhi Yazan with a gift of ten thousand dirhams and a robe of honour. As Saif left the court, he distributed the money among the slaves, bondswomen and the courtiers. When Khosrau came to know of it, he called Saif back and asked him why he wasted away the royal gift. He answered, "What use was your gift of gold and silver to me? The land from which I have come has mountains of gold and silver. What I need is something else." Khosrau considered this answer, and requested Saif to stay for a few more days.

The Persian king took counsel with his ministers. They counseled him to send the prisoners as an army with Saif; should they be killed, it would be considered merely as a punishment for their crimes. Khosrau approved of this advice, and sent eight hundred murderers under the command of Wahraz, a veteran army officer, to Saif Dhi Yazan. The force landed at the coast of Hadramaut and was later joined by a group of Yemenis. Abrahah's son, Masrooq, came out to confront the invaders, but was slain by the commander Wahraz. The Abyssinian soldiers fled the field and Yemen became the province of Persia, under the command of Wahraz as the first Persian governor of Yemen. The last Persian governor Bādhān became a Muslim in 628 CE. With his conversion, Yemen became free from the control of Persia and came under the Muslim rule.[1]

Story of the Owners of the Garden: The locale of this event mentioned in the Qur'ānic Chapter of Al-Qalam: 68:17-33 was Darwan, a place near San'a. Sa'eed bin Jubair said: They were the dwellers of Darwan, the name of a settlement six miles off San'a.

Some commentators say that they were the People of the Book and the natives of Ethiopia. They inherited this garden from their father who was a pious man. Out of the produce of the garden, he would take enough to cover the cost of farming and maintain himself and his family for a year. The rest he spent in charity. When he died, his sons stopped giving alms, saying that they could get rich quickly if they gave no alms. Consequently, they were punished by Allah, their garden destroyed, and they became paupers.[2]

1 Muhadarat Tarikh-il-Umam Al-Islamiyyah 1/29-30; Ghalaba-e-Rome by Maulana Zafar Ali Khan, P. 16-18.

2 Tafseer-ut-Tabari: Al-Qalam: 68:17-33.

Ancient-inscriptions-and-writings-in-Najran

The People of the Trench

Imam Muslim and Imam Ahmad quoted, on the authority of the Prophet's Companion Suhaib رضي الله عنه, a Hadeeth describing a very strange event relating to Najrān. Suhaib رضي الله عنه narrated that the Messenger of Allah (ﷺ) said:

"Among those who came before you there lived a king who had a sorcerer. As the sorcerer grew old, he said to the king: 'I have grown old, so send some young boy to me so that I may teach him magic.' The king then sent a boy to him so that he might train him (in magic).

On his way to the sorcerer, the boy met a monk and sat with him. The boy listened to the monk's speech and was impressed by it, so whenever he went to the sorcerer, he would first pass by the monk and sit with him. However, when he came to the sorcerer, the sorcerer would beat him for being late.

The boy complained about it to the monk and the monk said to him: 'When you feel afraid of the sorcerer, say: "My family made me late." And when you feel afraid of your family, say: "The sorcerer made me late."'

Najran .. largest historical museum tells the story appeared in the Quran

It so happened that there came a huge beast of prey and it blocked the way of the people. The young boy said: "Today I shall find out whether the sorcerer or the monk is superior." He picked up a stone and said: "O Allah, if the affairs of the monk are dearer to You than the affairs of the sorcerer, bring death to this animal so that the people will be able to move about freely." He threw the stone at the monster and killed it, and the people were able to pass freely.

The boy then went to monk and told him what had happened. The monk said: "My son, today you are better than me. Your affairs have reached a stage where I think that you will be soon put to the test, and in case you are put to the test do not reveal my identity."

With the permission of Allah, the young man began to heal the blind and those suffering from leprosy and he began to cure people of all kinds of illness. When a companion of the king, who had become blind, heard about him, he came to him with numerous gifts and said: "If you heal me, all these things here will be yours." The boy told him, "I myself do not heal anyone; it is Allah Who heals. If you believe in Allah, I shall also pray to Allah to heal you."

The courtier believed in Allah , and Allah healed him. The man then went to the king and sat by his side as he used to sit before. The king said to him: "Who restored your eyesight?" The man answered, "My Lord."

The king demanded, "Do you have any Lord other than me?"

The man responded, "My Lord and your Lord is Allah!"

Furious, the king imprisoned the courtier and tortured him until he revealed the identity of the boy. The boy was then summoned and the king said to him: “O boy, it has been conveyed to me that you have become so proficient in your magic that you heal the blind and those suffering from leprosy and you do such and such things.”

Thereupon, the boy said: “I do not heal anyone; it is Allah Who heals.”

Angry once more, the king imprisoned him as well and tortured him to reveal who it was who taught him about Allah. Under great pain, the boy divulged the monk’s identity, and the monk, too, was summoned before the king. The king told the monk, “Turn back from your religion!” However, the monk refused to do so. The king ordered a saw to be brought, and he placed it in the middle of the monk’s head and cut it until it fell apart. Then the courtier of the king was brought and it was said to him, “Turn back from your religion!” but he refused to do so. So the saw was placed in the middle of his head and it was cut until it fell apart. The boy was brought to the king and it was said to him: “Turn back from your religion.” He refused to do so and he was handed over to a group of the king’s soldiers.

The king commanded, “Take him to such and such a mountain; make him climb that mountain and when you reach its top ask him to renounce his faith; but if he refuses to do so, then throw him down the mountain!”

They took the boy and made him climb the mountain and he said اَللّٰهُمَّ! اكْفِنِيهِمْ بِمَا شِئْتَ “O Allah, save me from them however You will.” The mountain began to shake and they all fell down, and the boy came walking back to the king.

The king said to him: “What has happened to your companions?” The boy said: “Allah has saved me from them.”

The king handed the boy over to more of his soldiers and commanded, “Take him and carry him away in a small boat and when you reach the middle of the ocean ask him to renounce his religion, but if he does not renounce his religion throw him into the water.”

So they took the boy into the ocean and he said:

اَللّٰهُمَّ! اكْفِنِيهِمْ بِمَا شِئْتَ “O Allah, save me from them and what they

The site of the Trenches (Saudi Arabia)

want to do." It was not long before the boat overturned and they were drowned, but the boy came walking back to the king. The king said to him: "What has happened to your companions?" The boy answered, "Allah has saved me from them." Then the boy said to the king, "You will not be able to kill me until you do what I ask you to do." The king asked, "What is that?" The boy said: "You should gather people in a plain and crucify me on the trunk of a tree. Then take an arrow from my quiver and say: "In the name of Allah, the Lord of the boy"; then shoot an arrow. And if you do that, then you will be able to kill me."

So the king called the people to an open plain and crucified the boy on the trunk of a tree. He took an arrow from his quiver, placed the arrow in the bow and then said: باسم الله رب الغلام "In the name of Allah, the Lord of the boy." He then shot an arrow and it hit the boy on his temple. The boy placed his hands upon the temple where the arrow had hit him, and he died.

The people who witnessed this all declared, "We believe in the Lord of this boy, we believe in the Lord of this boy, we believe in the Lord of this boy!" Some people came to the king and said to him: "Do you realize that what you feared has happened? All the people now believe in the Lord of the boy!"

The king commanded ditches to be dug at the entry-points of the roads. When these ditches were dug, and fires were lit in them it was said to the people: "He who does not turn back from the boy's religion will be thrown in the fire!"

The people rushed to jump into the fire, each vying with the other to be the first to jump into the fire. A woman arrived with her infant child, and she hesitated to jump into the fire. Her child then spoke: "O mother, be patient, for you are following the Truth."[1]

Ibn Ishāq, writing in his Seerah, narrates this story in a different way. He says that the people of Najrān had accepted the faith of the boy (that is, Christianity which was until then free from tampering and other strands of paganism). Dhu Nawas then came to them along with his forces and gave them the choice to become Jews or be killed, but the people preferred death to Judaism. Thereupon, he threw them into the fire, slew them, and mutilated their bodies. As many as twenty thousands of them were killed.

The following Verses of the Qur'ān refer to the story of the people of the ditch:

﴿ قُتِلَ أَصْحَٰبُ ٱلْأُخْدُودِ ﴿٤﴾ ٱلنَّارِ ذَاتِ ٱلْوَقُودِ ﴿٥﴾ إِذْ هُمْ عَلَيْهَا قُعُودٌ ﴿٦﴾ وَهُمْ عَلَىٰ مَا يَفْعَلُونَ بِٱلْمُؤْمِنِينَ
شُهُودٌ ﴿٧﴾ وَمَا نَقَمُوا۟ مِنْهُمْ إِلَّآ أَن يُؤْمِنُوا۟ بِٱللَّهِ ٱلْعَزِيزِ ٱلْحَمِيدِ ﴿٨﴾ ٱلَّذِى لَهُۥ مُلْكُ ٱلسَّمَٰوَٰتِ
وَٱلْأَرْضِ ۚ وَٱللَّهُ عَلَىٰ كُلِّ شَىْءٍ شَهِيدٌ ﴾

"Destroyed were the owners of the ditch of the fuel-fed fire, when they sat by it, and were themselves the witnesses of what they did to the believers. They had naught against them save that they believed in Allah, the Mighty, the Owner of Praise, Him unto Whom belongs the sovereignty of the heavens and the earth; and Allah is of all things the Witness." - Al-Buruj (85): 4-9.[2]

Ibn Ishāq, Ibn Hishām and other historians identify that king with Dhu Nawas and say that the reason the "people of the ditch" were killed was their refusal to accept Judaism. However, in the light of various Ahadeeth, their opinion does not appear to be correct; the king who slew the people of the ditch was a pagan who claimed godship for himself, while Dhu Nawas was a Jew.

---

1 Sahih Muslim: 3005; Musnad Ahmad: 6/16-18.

2 As-Seerah by Ibn Ishāq: 1/36-37; As-Seerah by Ibn Hishām: 1/34-36.

Remains of the palace of Ardeshir Sassanid

Lakhmi kingdom of Hirah (Iraq)

Iranian, Greek and Sassanid occupation of Iraq

Iraq and its adjoining territories had been under the occupation of the Persians since the time of the Achaemenid king Cyrus the Great *(Dhul-Qarnain)* (557 BC-529 BC), until Alexander of Macedonia defeated Darius (Dara) the Third and destroyed the Persian power with the concomitant break-up of the Achaemenid empire.

When Alexander the Great died in 323 BC, the Asian part of his empire fell to the Seleucids. The founder of the Seleucid dynasty was Seleucus, a general of Alexander the Great. They founded the capital of their empire at Seleucia, on the western bank of the Tigris.

From 171 BC to 226 CE, it was ruled by the Parthians of northern Iran. During this period, the Qahtāni tribes left their habitations and settled in and around the lush and green border areas of Iraq. They were followed by a wave of Adnāni immigrants (Mudar, Rabee'ah, and Banu Bakr) who forced entry into the area and settled in a part of *Jazeerah Furātiyyah (Al-Jazeerah)*.

Coins of Ardeshir III

In 226 CE Artaxerxes (Ardeshir) founded the Sassanid kingdom in Iran. When he subjugated the Arabs living along the frontiers of his kingdom, the Qudā'ah tribesmen moved further on to Syria, while the Arab inhabitants of Hīrah and Anbar accepted his sovereignty and agreed to pay tributes.[1]

Anbar is a town 55 km west of Baghdad on the bank of the river Euphrates; it was in this town where Nebuchadnezzar kept the Jewish prisoners. Today, the western province of Iraq is called Anbar.[2] Artaxerxes (Ardeshir) the Third, Anushiravan (Nosherwan or Khosrau the First), Ormuz (Hormuz) the Fourth and Khosrau Parvez (Khosrau/ Chosroes the Second) were the famous kings of the Sassanid dynasty. (Persion 'Khosrau' is rendered as Kisra كسرىٰ in Arabic.) Their capital town Madā'in was situated on the eastern bank of the Tigris, opposite Salukia (Saluqia/ Seleucia). Prophet Muhammad ﷺ was born during the reign of Anushiravan the Just (Nosherwan 'Ādil) (d. 579 CE).

Coin of Seleucid Empire

1 Muhadarat Tarikh-il-Umam Al-Islamia: 1/30-31.
2 Mu'jam-ul-Buldan: See under 'Anbār', Al-Munjid Fi'l-A'lām, P. 72.

The Dependent Kingdom of Hirah

Tomb of Artaxerxes I
Longimanus King of Persia original

During the reign of Artaxerxes the First, the regions of Hirah and *Badiyāt-al-Iraq* (Samāwah Desert) and the tribes of Rabee'ah and Mudar living in al-Jazeerah were ruled by *Jazeemat-al-Waddah*.

Artaxerxes felt that it was difficult to control the unruly Arab tribes directly or stop them from plundering along the frontiers, so he appointed Jazeemah, one of their own men, as their ruler. Through him, he hoped to keep the undisciplined tribes quiet, as well as able to seek their help in the event of need against the Romans. The Persian rulers would always keep a military contingent with the kings of Hirah, to keep the nomads in check and crush them in case they revolted.

Lakhmi Rulers of Hīrah

Jazeemah died in 268 CE and was succeeded by 'Amr bin 'Adi bin Nasr Lakhmi, a contemporary of the Sassanid king Shapur. The Lakhmi tribesmen ruled Hirah until the reign of Qabād bin Feroz. It was during the reign of Qabād that the heresy of Muzdak started. Muzdak was a freethinker and propagated a creed of libertinism, and was supported by Qabad and many of his subjects.

Qabād wrote to the king of Hīrah, Mundhir bin Mā'-us-Samā', to embrace the new creed but he refused. Thereupon, Qabād removed him and replaced him by a Muzdakite named Harith bin 'Amr bin Hujr Kindi.

Qabād was followed by Khosrau Nosherwan as emperor of Persia. He hated the Muzdaki creed and persecuted the Muzdekites, slew a large number of them, and reinstated Mundhir as the ruler of Hīrah.

Battle of Dhi Qār

Hīrah remained under the rule of Mundhir bin Mā'-us-Samā' and his family until Nu'mān bin Mundhir (d. 15 years before hijra/608 CE). A man named Zaid bin 'Adi bin Zaid Ibādī (590 CE) made a false complaint to Khosrau Parvez (Chosroes) against Nu'mān bin Mundhir; in exasperation, the Kisra summoned Nu'mān to hold him to account. Nu'mān went to Hāni bin Mas'ūd, a chieftain of Banu Shaibān Himyari Qahtāni, and entrusted him with his family and wealth before going to Khosrau's court. The latter sent Nu'mān to prison, where he died. Zaid bin 'Adi, who initiated the complaint against Nu'mān, was the person who pioneered Arabic writings in Chosroes court.

When Chosroes had sent Nu'mān to prison, he installed Ayās bin Qabeesah Tāi as the ruler of Hirah. He also ordered Ayās to demand Nu'mān's trust from Hāni ibn Mas'ud. However, Hāni was a man of honour and refused to give up Nu'mān's family and wealth. Finally, he declared war against Ayās, who arrived with Persian reinforcements. A fierce battle took place at Dhi Qār, and the Persians were routed by the Arab forces. The victory of Banu Shaibān marked the first Arab victory over the Persians. This event took place a little after the Prophet Muhammad ﷺ started his mission.

Chosroes nominated a Persian ruler over Hīrah after Ayās, but the Lakhmīs regained control when Mundhir bin Ma'rur took the reins of power in 632 CE. However, only eight months later the Muslim *Mujāhideen*, under the command of Khālid bin Waleed رضي الله عنه, entered Hirah and put an end to the Lakhmi rule for ever.[1] Within a span of two or three years the whole of Iraq became a part of the Muslim empire.

1 Tarikh-ut-Tabari: 1/609; Al-Kamil Fi't-Tarikh: 1/379; Mohadarat Tarikh-il-Umam Al-Islamiyyah: 1/30; Al-Munjid Fi Al-a'lām, P. 257; Urdu Encyclopedia of Islam: 10/55.

Detail from a Ghassanid mosaic in a Church at Mount Nebo Jordan, bearing the inscription "Arethas son of Al-Arethas," a Ghassanid King

The Ghassanids of Syria

During the time when the migration of Arab tribes was at its peak, several sub-tribes of Khuzā'ah entered Syria. They belonged to Bani Saleeh bin Hulwān; one of their branches was Banu Daj'am bin Saleeh who later came to be known as Daja'imah.

The Romans made them rulers of Syria; the purpose of this strategy being that they would help stop the marauding Arab tribes from pillaging and robbing, as well as to use them against the Persians.

Ghassanids Rulers of Busra ash-Sham

The Dajā'imah's rule spanned the entire of the second century CE. After they were vanquished by the Ghassanids, the Romans accepted the latter as rulers over the Arab inhabitants of Syrian territories (the southeastern part of modern Syria and Jordan).

The Ghassanid state included many cities including Tadmur, Raqeem (Petra), Amman, and Ma'an. Their capital city was Busra (Busra ash-Sham). As agents of the Romans, their rule over the Syrian territories continued. The Ghassānids, most of whom had become Christian, always supported the Romans in their battles against the Persians.

Hārith bin Jablah (d. 569 CE) was a brave and magnanimous king, who was succeeded by Mundhir, whom the Romans crowned as the new king of the Ghassanids. During the era of the Prophet Muhammad (ﷺ), it was Hārith bin abu-Shamar Ghassani who ruled them. He resided in Ghutah (Damascus) when the Prophet's emissary Shujā' bin Wahb Asadi delivered him the Prophet's letter.

During that same time period, the ruler of Balqa', Shurahbeel bin Amr Ghassani, slew the Prophet's emissary, Harith bin 'Umair Azdi, an event that led to the Battle of Mutah. Then, in 15 AH/ 636 CE,

The Prophet's ﷺ letter to Abu Shamar Ghassani

during the caliphate of Umar, the Battle of Yarmūk took place and the last Ghassanid ruler, Jablah bin Aiham bin Jablah Ghassani (d. 20 AH/ 641 CE) became a Muslim.

Proud and unable to bring himself to accept the Islamic ideal of equality of humans, he renounced the Islamic faith during the reign of Umar al-Farooq, and went to the Roman emperor.[1]

It is said that once Jablah, accompanied by Umar al-Farooq, was circumambulating Ka'bah when, by chance, a Fazārī man stepped over his sheet of cloth. In rage, Jablah slapped the man and disfigured his nose. The Fazārī complained to Umar who, in turn, demanded retribution. Jablah said: 'How can it be? I am a king and that one is a lowly man.' Umar told him that Islam decreed that all men were equal. He retorted: "I thought Islam would improve me in station.' He also warned Umar that he might turn back to Christianity. Umar informed him: 'If you abandon the faith, you will be slain.' Thereupon, Jablah asked Umar to respite him one night. His request was granted, but that night, he fled, along with his retinue and soldiers to Syria and from there to Constantinople. The Caesar welcomed him warmly. Later, Jablah repented his action but died in the state of disbelief.[2]

1 Muhadarat Tarikh-il-Umam Al-Islamiyyah: 1/35;Ttarikh Ard-il-Qur'ān (Kamil): 2/62-64.
2 Al-Bidāya Wan-Nihāya: 8/65-69.

A view of the Wadi Yarmuk

Kingdom of Oman

Two or three generations before the birth of the Messenger of Allah, Banu Mustakbir had established a vast empire in Oman, although they owed allegiance to the Sassanid kings of Persia. One of their rulers, Julanda bin Mustakbir, is a famous figure in Arabic literature. During the Prophet's era, Oman was jointly ruled by the two sons of Julanda: Jaifar and his younger brother Abd. The former was the king, while the latter helped him in the affairs of the state. Their capital was Suhār, a town on the coast of Gulf of Oman, which is 225 km northwest of Muscat, the present capital of the Sultanate of Oman.

Response of the Rulers to Islam

When Jaifar and Abd responded to the Prophet's call and accepted the Islamic faith, the Prophet ﷺ appointed his companion 'Amr bin al-'Ās رضي الله عنه as his envoy to the royal court of Oman.[1] The people of Oman swiftly converted to Islam.[2]

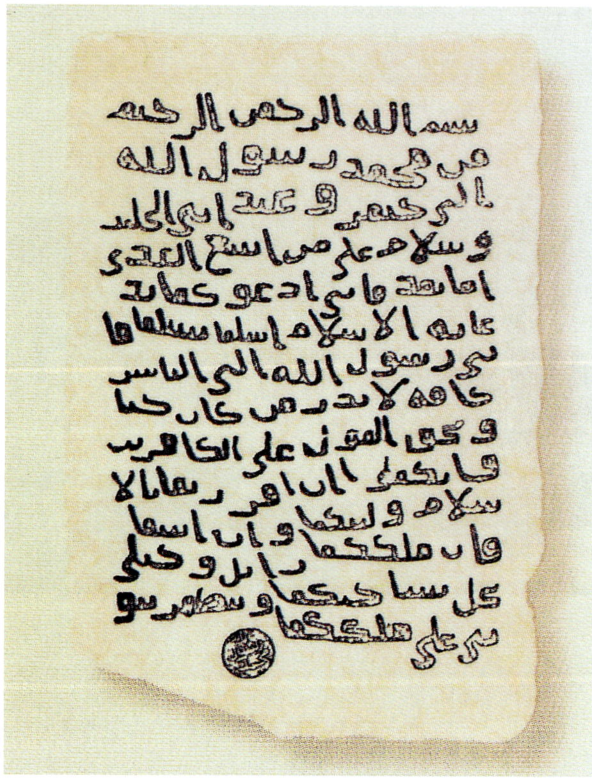
بسم الله الرحمن الرحيم
من محمد رسول الله
الى جيفر و عبد ابني الجلندى

Letter of the Prophet ﷺ to Jaifar & Abd (King of Oman)

Laqeet bin Mālik Azdi Zu'at-Tāj made claims to Prophethood during the caliphate Abu Bakr as-Siddeeq رضي الله عنه. His title, *"Zu'at-Taj"* (owner of the crown) was a title which he or his father received from the Persian kings.

In Oman, a Persian military governor (Aswār) called Bastajān lived at a place called Dimā. In addition to Azd, the tribes of Thamālah and Hadān also dwelt in Oman. A letter of the Prophet ﷺ addressed to them has been found.

During the Umayyad rule, the people of Oman adopted the Khāriji creed and became powerful enough to defeat the forces sent by Hajjaj bin Yusuf. Later, the Umayyad forces defeated the Julanda family and they fled to the island of Zanzibar (East Africa).[3]

1 Al-Watha'iq As-Siasiyyah, P. 46.
2 Mausoo'ah Al-'Alam-il-Islami, P. 130.
3 Histoire Des Arabes, cl. Huart: 2/257-258.

Remains of the ancient Fort of the Kingdom of Kindah

The Kingdom of Kindah

The Arab state of Kindah, which was founded in Nejd in 425 CE, survived until the year 550 CE. The Kindas claimed to be the equal of the Mundhirs, the kings of Hirah. Kindah was a great Qahtāni tribe which was named after Thaur (Kindah) bin 'Ufair bin Adi bin Hārith bin Murrah bin Udad. He was nicknamed Kindah for disobeying his father. It is divided into three major branches: Mu'awiyah bin Kindah, as-Sakūn, and Saksak.[1]

Hujr bin 'Amr, who was entitled 'Ākil-ul-Murār Himyari,' was a descendant of Thaur (Kindah) bin 'Ufair of Banu Kahlān, and was a step-brother of King Hassān bin Tubba'. When Hassān had invaded the interior of Arabia and subdued a number of tribes, he made Hujr bin 'Amr a ruler over the subdued tribes.

1 Mu'jam Qabā'il-il-Arab: 3/998; Al-Mufassal Fi Tarikh-il-Arab Qabal-al-Islam: 3/315.

Map. 18

Battle of Kulāb

Hujr bin 'Amr was the founder of the kingdom of Kindah; he was succeeded by his son, 'Amr bin Hujr, who was in turn succeeded by Harith bin 'Amr. The latter ruled Hirah for some time during the reign of King Qabad, but lost his power when Nosherwan (or Anusherwan) gained control of the throne in 531 CE.

tate of Kindah: Its capital was (Al-Fau) now a on the main road. Caravans coming from Sheba, , Qataban, Hadramawt and Himyar passed h this place. 'Imra' Al-Qais, played an important the state of Kindah.

History Society at the University of Riyadh started ing on the site of Al-fau since 1972, and discovered arket, the palace, the temple and a big residential

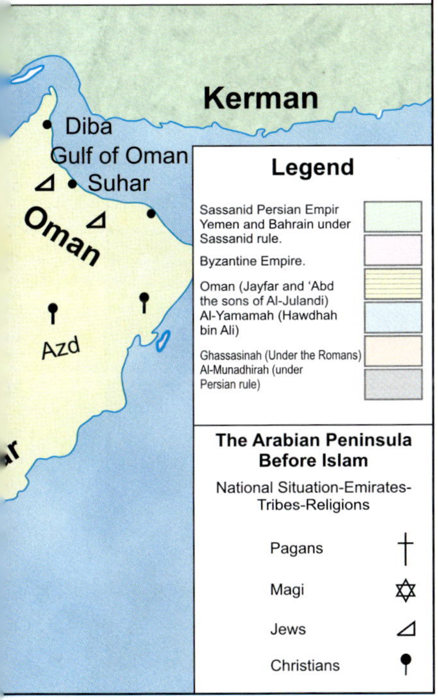

In 528 CE Harith split up his kingdom among his four sons: Hujr, Shurahbīl, Ma'dikarab and Salamah. Hujr ruled over the tribe of Banu Asad; Shurahbīl over the tribes of Banu Bakr, Hanzalah, 'Amr bin Tameem and Ribab; Salamah over the tribes of Banu Taghlib and Namr bin Qasit; and Ma'dikarab over the tribes of Sa'd bin Zaid Manāt, Banu Qais and Banu Kināhah.

After some time, their disputes grew to such a level that they turned to battle. This battle was known as the Battle of Kulāb. Shurahbīl was killed during this military expedition, while Hujr did not take part in it.

In 540 CE Banu Kalb Qudā'i slew Hārith bin 'Amr. His son, Hujr, continued to rule over Banu Asad Adnani. In 550 CE Hujr was ambushed and killed by Banu Asad. Thereupon, his son Imra-ul-Qais fled to Caesar in Constantinople to seek his help, but was disappointed. Indeed, Caesar had him murdered in Angora (modern Ankara)[1] in 560 CE.[2]

1 Ankara (formerly known as Angora or Ankyra) a town in the northwest of Anatolia, has been the capital of Turkey since 1341 AH/ 1923 CE. It was conquered by Persian Khusrau Parvez in the beginning of seventh century CE, by the Muslim fighters in 33 AH/654 CE, again by Haroon ar-Rasheed in 190 AH/ 806 CE, and finally by Sultan Alep Arsalan Saljuqi in 464 AH/ 1071 CE. He defeated the Roman king Diogenes Romanos and annexed Anatolia, including Ankara, to the Muslim empire. In the Battle of Angora (804 AH/ 1402 CE), Ameer Taimur defeated Ottoman Sultan Bayazeed the First (Yildiram) and imprisoned him. (Mu'jam-ul-Buldan: see under 'Ankara'; Al-Munjid fi'l-A'lam, P. 78; Al-Mausoo'a Al-Arabia Al-Muyassara 248/1; Urdu Encyclopedia of Islam: 450/3; Oxford English Reference Dictionary.

2 Tarikh Ibn Khaldun: 2/316-320; Al-Kamil Li-Ibn-il-Atheer: 1/315-316; Al-Arab Qabl-al-Islam: 1/216-218; Mu'jam Qaba'il-il-Arab: 2/515-516.

Ruins of Al-Fao, the capital of the Kingdom of Kindah

AL-Fao: Capital of Kindah

Al-Fao, the capital of Kindah, is now called al-Qaryah. It was situated on the trade route of caravans going northeast from Sabā (Sheba), Ma'een, Qitbān, Hadramaut and Himyar. This state stretched from Dumat-al-Jandal in the north to the Empty Quarter in the south.

In 1972, an archaeological team from the University of Riyadh began excavation work and found remains of a market-place, palace, temple and houses.[1] Al-Fao lies 120 km northeast of Najran.[2]

1 Atlas Seerat Nabawiyyah, P. 66.

2 Al-Mufassal Fi Tarikh-il-Arab Qabl-al-Islam: 1/178.

The Arab Kingdom of Tadmur

The ancient city of Tadmur (Palmyra) was known as the 'Bride of the Desert.' According to popular legend, it was built by King Suleman عليه السلام with the help of the Jinn. It was at this location that a strong Arab state was founded in the first century of the Christian Era. Later, it reached the zenith of its power during the reign of Udhainah (Odenathus) the Second and Queen Zenubiya (Zeynab). Under the tutelary authority of the Roman king Gallienus, Odenathus became the ruler over all the eastern territories of the Roman Empire, and received the title of Augustus by the Roman court. After his murder sometime between 266 -267 CE, Queen Zenubiya conquered Egypt and extended her domain further still.

The temple of Baal Shaman - Palmyra (Tadmur)

Destruction of Tadmur by Romans

After the conquest of Egypt, Tadmur revolted against Rome, but was defeated in 270 CE and laid the arms. In 272 CE it took up arms once again, but this time the Roman ruler Orlean attacked Tadmur, arrested Queen Zenubiya, sent her to Rome, and destroyed the city.

Among the remains of the destroyed city is the famous temple of Baal. During the three and a half centuries of Roman hegemony, Christianity became popular in Tadmur. Indeed, Christianity became widespread in the whole of Syria during this era, until it became a part of the Muslim Empire during the reign of caliph Umar al-Farooq رضي الله عنه.[1]

1 Encyclopedia Tarikh-i-'Alam: 2/64-65; Atlas al-Futoohat al-Islamiyyah, P. 116. 179, 186; Urdu Encyclopedia of Islam: 5/572-573.

Emirate of Hijaz

The settlement of the town of Makkah was established at the time of Ismā'īl (عليه السلام). He lived for 137 years[1] and spent his entire life as the leader of Makkah and the custodian of the House of Allah. Upon his death, two of his sons, Nabit (Nabaioth) and Qaidār (Kedar) became the leaders of Makkah, one after the other. After them, their maternal grandfather, Madad bin Amr Jurhumi, became the chief of Makkah. Thus, the leadership of Makkah was transferred to Banu Jurhum.[2]

Nebuchadnezzar Invades

Banu Jurhum had already weakened in power before Nebuchadnezzar emerged on the horizon of Iraq. Now it was the tribe of Adnān that was ascendant in Makkah; the evidence for this being that when the Arabs fought Nebuchadnezzar in Dhat 'Irq, the man commanding the Arab forces was not from the tribe of Banu Jurhum.[3]

Coin of Nebuchadnezzar II

When Nebuchadnezzar II launched a second invasion in 586 BC, Banu Adnan fled to Yemen. This was the time of the Israeli prophet Jeremiah عليه السلام, who accompanied Adnān's

1 Bible: (Genesis) 25:17

2 Qalb-o-Jazeerat-il-Arab, P.230. Ibn Hishām mentions only Nabit (Naba'ioth) among the sons of Ishmael as having inherited the custody of Ka'ba.

3 Op.cit., P.230

Area of Marr-uz-Zahrān

Banu Khuzā'ah in Makkah

Towards the end of their prominence in Makkah, Banu Jurhum began to display unacceptable and criminal behaviour. They treated the pilgrims unfairly and embezzled the funds belonging to the Ka'bah and its upkeep.

When Banu Khuzā'ah, led by Amr bin Luhayy, encamped at Marr-uz-Zahrān, they took advantage of the situation and, with the help of a Mudari Adnāni tribe (Banu Bakr bin abd-Manāf bin Kinānah) declared a war against Banu Jurhum, expelled them from Makkah, and took control of it. This event took place sometime around the middle of the second century CE.[2]

Hiding the Well of Zamzam

Angry at their deceit, Banu Jurhum spitefully sealed off the well of Zamzam, burying with it many priceless mementoes and historical treasures. In fact, they removed every mark of the well's location.

According to Mas'ūdi, the Persians used to send gifts and jewels for the Ka'bah. For example, Sasān

1 Al-Kamil Li-Ibn-il-Athir: 1/206-207; Ar-Raud-ul-Unf: 1/33.
2 Qalb-o-Jazeerat-il-Arab, P.231-232.

bin Bābak had sent two deer made of gold, jewels, swords and a lot of gold as gifts to the House of Allah.

Muhammad bin Ishāq relates 'Amr bin Hārith bin Madād Jurhumi[1] removed the two golden deer and the Black Stone from the House of Allah and buried them in the Zamzam well before he moved along with his tribe, Banu Jurhum, to Yemen.[2]

Banu Jurhum were deeply upset at their expulsion from Makkah and their loss of power. 'Amr expressed his profound grief in his verses:

كَأَنْ لَّمْ يَكُنْ بَيْنَ الْحَجُونِ إِلَى الصَّفَا　　أَنِيسٌ وَّ لَمْ يَسْمُرْ بِمَكَّةَ سَامِرُ

بَلٰى نَحْنُ كُنَّا أَهْلَهَا فَأَزَالَنَا　　صُرُوفُ اللَّيَالِي وَالْجُدُودُ الْعَوَاثِرُ

(It feels there is no close friend between Hajoon and Safa,
Nor any partner in nightly conversation at Makkah.
Surely, we are its inhabitants but the vicissitudes of time and bad luck uprooted us.)[3]

Prophet Ismā'īl ﷺ lived around the time of 1800 BC. Thus, it is inferred that Banu Jurhum ruled over Makkah for about two thousand years.

The Mudari Tribesmen in Makkah

Banu Khuza'ah ruled over Makkah alone, refusing to share power with Banu Bakr. However, three of the important positions of power were occupied by the Mudari tribesmen.

1. Carrying the pilgrims from Arafāt to Muzdalifah and giving them permission to leave Mina on *Yaum an-Nafar*, that is, the 13th of *Dhul Hijjah*. This honour went to Ilyās bin Mudar's family, Banu Ghauth bin Murr, who were called Soofah. No pilgrim was allowed to throw pebbles at *Jamarāt* on the 13th of *Dhul Hijjah* unless a specified man from the *Soofah* had not performed this

1 He is not the same Madad Jurhumi as mentioned in the story of Ishmael.
2 Murooj-uz-Zahab: 1/250.
3 As-Seerah Li-Ibn Hishām: 1/114-115.

rite first. When the pilgrims had finished throwing pebbles at the *Jamarāt* and wanted to leave Mina, the Soofah men would stand in a circle on both sides of Aqabah, the sole passageway of Mina, and did not allow anyone to pass through unless they had done so first. With the end of Soofah's hegemony, this honour went to an Adnāni family, Banu Sa'd bin Zaid Manāt Tameemi.

2. Arranging pilgrims' departure from Muzdalifah to Mina on the morning of 10th *Dhul Hijjah*. This office went to Banu 'Adwān.

3. Advancing or delaying the Sacred Months, an act which they considered honourable. This office went to Banu Fuqaim bin 'Adi, a branch of Banu Kinanah.[1]

Dispersion of Adnāni Tribes

Banu Khuzā'ah ruled over Makkah for nearly three hundred years.[2] It was during this time that the Adnāni tribes left Makkah and Hijaz, and dispersed to areas such as Nejd, Iraq and Bahrain. Only a few branches of Quraish, most of whom were bedouins, remained in Makkah. These were a few families of Banu Kinānah, who had no say in the government of Makkah or the custody of Ka'bah. This state of affairs continued until the emergence of Qusayy bin Kilāb.[3]

Qusayy bin Kilāb Returns to Makkah

Qusayy bin Kilāb was an infant when his father died; after his death, Qusayy's mother married a man named Rabee'ah bin Harām of the Tribe of Banu 'Udhrah. This tribe lived at borders of Syria, and so Qusayy's mother took him with her when she left to settle there.

When Qusayy grew older, he returned to Makkah, where Hulail bin Hubashiyyah Khuzā'i was the ruler at the time. Qusayy asked for the hand of Hulail's daughter, Hubba (حُبّى); Hulail accepted the offer and married his daughter to Qusayy.[4]

1 As-Seerah Li-Ibn Hishām: 1/44, 119-122.
2 Mu'jam-ul-Buldan: see under 'Makkah'.
3 Muhadarat Tarikh-il-Umam Al-Islamia: 1/36.
4 As-Seerah Li-Ibn Hishām: 1/117-118.

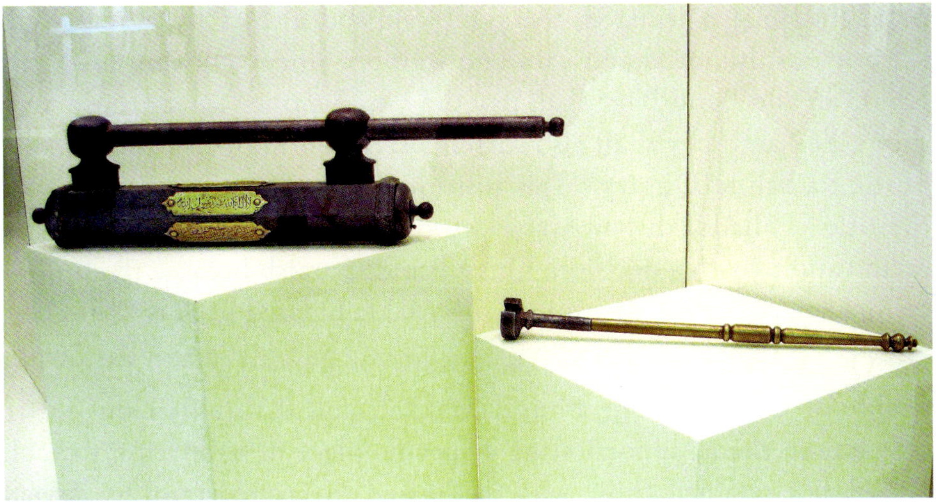

Custody of the Ka'bah

When Hulail died, Qusayy challenged the authority of Soofah with the support of the Quraish and Banu Kinānah. They claimed that they had a greater right to the custody of the Ka'bah, and other related offices, than the Soofah did.

This led to an armed struggle between the two groups, in which Qusayy overcame the people of Soofah and took over the positions of power. During this time, both Banu Khuzā'ah and Banu Bakr stayed away from Qusayy; suspecting a rebellion against him, Qusayy challenged them as well. A fierce battle took place during which large numbers of men were slain, from both sides. Eventually, there was a plea for truce.

Ancient key and Lock of Ka'bah

A man from Banu Bakr, Ya'mar bin 'Auf, was appointed as an arbiter. His ruling was that Qusayy, not Banu Khuzā'ah, had a greater right to the custody of the Ka'bah and the rule of

Makkah. He also declared, "All the blood spilled by Qusayy, I declare it to be unsubstantial and vain and stamp it under my feet; however, Khuzā'ah and Banu Bakr shall pay the blood money for all those men they killed and they shall also surrender, unconditionally, the custody of the Ka'bah to Qusayy." This historic decision conferred on Ya'mar the title of Shaddākh (an Arabic word meaning: One who lets blood go in vain).[1] By this decision, Qusayy and Quraish became the leaders of Makkah. Qusayy's dominion over Makkah dated back to 440 CE.[2]

Qusayy administered Makkah in his own way. He called back the people of Quraish from around Makkah and distributed the entire city among them, apportioning a specific place of habitation to each family, but retained those who readjusted the sacred months as well as the families of Safwān Jumahi, Banu 'Adwān and Banu Murrah bin 'Auf. He kept them in their former positions, as it was the belief of the people to consider those particular duties to it to be a part of their religion which did not allow for change or amendment.[3]

Construction of Dar an-Nadwah

Qusayy built a house, called Dar an-Nadwah, north of the Ka'bah. Its entrance door opened in the direction of the mosque. It served as a parliament seat for the Quraish, where important affairs were debated and decided; it was one of Qusayy's landmark achievements, which helped preserved the unity of the Quraish, who now had an avenue in which to settle their quarrels peacefully.[4]

In his capacity as the chief, Qusayy had the following prerogatives:

1. Presidency of Dar an-Nadwah. He presided over the meetings of Dar an-Nadwah where the Quraish would hold consultations and discuss important issues. The house also served as a venue for weddings.

2. *Liwā'* (flag bearing). The flag of battle was unfurled and borne

1 As-Seerah Li-Ibn Hishām: 1/123-124.
2 Qalb-o-lazeerat-ir-Arab, P. 232.
3 As-Seerah Li-Ibn Hishām: 1/125, Muhadarat Tareekh-il-Umam Al-Islamiyyah: 1:36.
4 Op.cit., 1/124,125,130; Muhadarat Tarikh-il-Umam Al-Islamiyyah: 1/36,37.

by Qusayy during the battle.

3. *Hijābah* (guardianship of the Ka'bah). Qusayy alone held the key to the Ka'bah and had the only authority to open its doors.

4. *Siqāyah* (slaking the thirst of pilgrims). Qusayy was responsible for the tanks filled with water for visiting pilgrims. Dates and raisins would also be put into the tanks to sweeten the water.

5. *Rifādah* (feeding the pilgrims). To feed pilgrims, Qusayy levied a tax on the Quraish. The money thus collected was spent on preparing meals for the pilgrims.[1]

Distribution of Offices

Despite being the most powerful man of the Quraysh at the time, Qusayy was obviously unable to fulfill every responsibility personally. He chose several of his sons to take control of certain offices of power in his stead.

1 As-Sīrah Li-Ibn-Hishām: 1/124-125 and 130; Mohadarat Tarīkh-il-Umam Al-Islāmiyyah: 1/36-37.

Qusayy's eldest son was Abd ad-Dār; although his second son, Abd Manāf, had already attained honour and prestige during his father's lifetime, Qusayy transferred all his powers to Abd ad-Dār in his will. abd Ad-Dār thus become the heir to the presidency of *Dar an-Nadwah*, the *Hijābah*, *the Liwā'*, the *Siqāyah*, and *Rifadah*.

After Qusayy's death, his sons carried out their father's will faithfully; however, upon Abd Manaf's death, his sons then quarreled with their cousins (the son of Abd Ad-Dar) over the offices of power.

This split the Quraish into two antagonizing groups, which could have led towards armed battle. However, the two groups reconciled and agreed to a redistribution of power.

As a result, *Siqāyah* and *Rifādah* were given to Abd-Manāf while the presidency of *Dār an-Nadwah, Liwā'* (flag) and *Hijābah* were handed over to Banu Abd ad-Dār. In Abd-Manāf's stead, his son Hashim received the offices of *Siqāyah* and *Rifādah*. On Hashim's death, his brother Muttalib succeeded him. When Muttalib died, this office went to his nephew Abdul-Muttalib bin Hashim, the grandfather of the Prophet ﷺ. He was succeeded by his sons. When the era of Islam began, Abbās bin Abdul-Muttalib رضي الله عنه, the Prophet's uncle, held this high position.[1]

Distribution of Positions in Makkah

The civic government of Makkah before Islam had fourteen positions distributed among ten officials who were chosen from among the ten tribes of Quraish. Those positions, and those who held them, were as follows:

Religious Services

1. *Siqāyah* (supplying pilgrims with water and receiving them): Abbās bin Abdul-Muttalib رضي الله عنه (Banu Hashim).

1 As-Sīrah Li-Ibn Hishām: 1/129, 132, 135-137, 142, 178, 179; Mohādarāt Tarīkh-il-Umam Al-Islāmiyyah: 1/37.

2. *Rifādah* (monetary assistance to pilgrims): Hārith bin 'Amir (Banu Naufal)
3. *'Imārah* (populating the House of Allah): Abbās bin Abdul-Muttalib ﷺ (Banu Hāshim)
4. *Sidānah* (keeping the key of the Ka'bah and its custody): Uthmān bin Talha ﷺ (Banu Abd ad-Dār).
5. *'Isār* (custody of arrows kept beside idols for soothsaying and fortunetelling): Safwān bin Umayyah ﷺ (Banu Jumah).
6. *Amwāl Muhajjarah* (Administering properties and votive offerings dedicated to idols): Hārith bin Qais ﷺ (Banu Sahm)

Judicial Services

7. *Dār an-Nadwah (administering judicial and consultative affairs: Uthmān bin Talha ﷺ (Banu Abd ad-Dār)*
8. *Mushwarah (Shura or counseling): Yazeed bin Zam'ah Asadi ﷺ (Banu Asad)*
9. *Ashnaq (administering blood-money and penalties): Abu Bakr Siddīq ﷺ (Banu Taim)*
10. *Hukumah (deciding Law suits): Hārith bin Qais ﷺ (Banu Sahm)*

Wartime Services

11. *'Uqāb (standard-bearing): Abu Sufyān ﷺ (Banu Umayyah)*
12. *Qubbah (administering military camp): Khalid bin Waleed ﷺ (Banu Makhzūm)*
13. *A'innah (commanding the cavalry): Khalid bin Waleed ﷺ (Banu Makhzum)*
14. *Sifārah (di*plomatic affairs): Umar bin Khattāb ﷺ (Banu 'Adi)[1]

1 Ar-Rahīq-ul-Makhtūm, P. 40,41; Tarīkh Ard-ul-Qur'ān (Kāmil): 80-79/2; At-Tabaqāt-li-Ibn-Sa'd:73-66/1.

Arab Chieftains

The Arab tribes settled around the state of Hirah were considered to be subsidiaries of Hirah, while those living in *Badiat ash-Shām* were supposed to be under the suzerainty of Ghassanid rulers. However, the dominion of the Ghassanids over the Arab tribes was nominal and had no actual merit. Aside from Hirah and those within the immediate vicinity of *Badiat ash-Shām*, the Arab tribes living in the desert were independent and fought any attempts at control from outward forces.

The Tribal System

The tribal system of government followed a certain hierarchy, and in particular was based upon chieftainship. Every tribe had a chieftain whose position over his people and the power he wielded over his people was similar to that of a king ruling his subjects.

In truth, the very entity of a tribe was founded upon tribal loyalty and a common interest in the defense and protection of the tribal territory. The chief of the tribe was sovereign; in peace or war, all tribesmen were compelled to obey their chief and submit to his decision in all matters. No matter what happened, none could disobey him.

Some chieftains were so powerful that if one lost his temper, his clansmen would unsheathe their swords to please him without even knowing the cause of his anger.

Because the tribal system was also based upon familial ties, there were often conflicts for power amongst brothers and cousins. Thus, it was a necessary characteristic for a tribal chief to be magnanimous, liberal, lenient, generous, and ever ready to receive guests, in addition to always being ready to defend bravely the tribe's honour.

In short, a tribal chieftain was desired to be the quintessence of virtue, the cynosure of all those around him, especially for the poets who were the voluble spokesmen and critiques for the tribes.

Chieftains' Powers

In proportion to their duties, the tribal chieftains exercised certain powers and rights to the exclusion of other tribesmen. One poet summarized these special rights thus:

لَكَ الْمِرْبَاعُ مِنْهَا وَالصَّفَايَا وَحُكْمُكَ وَالنَّشِيطَةُ وَالْفُضُولُ

(For you (O chief) are one-fourth *(Mirbā')* of the spoils of war, the choicest part, and the one you decide to be yours *(Safāyā)*, and what comes to you on the way *(Nasheetah)*, and the remainder after division *(Fudool)*.

Mirbā': One-fourth of the booty

Safāyā (singular: *Sifiyy*): Part which a chief chooses for himself before the booty is distributed.

Nasheetah: Part of booty which falls to a chief's lot before the booty reaches the tribe.

Fudool: Remainder after booty has been distributed equally among tribesmen and cannot be further distributed among them equally.

These portions of the war-booty gathered during military excursions were the especial allowance of the tribal chieftains alone.[1]

1 Ar-Raud-ul-Unf: 4/78; Ar-Raheeq-ul-Makhtum, P. 42.

Chapter - 4

Pre-Islamic Religions

of the Arabian Peninsula

A distorted version of the faith of Ibrâhîm, idol-worship, Judaism, Christianity, Zoroastrianism, and Sabianism

ربنا وابعث فيهم رسولا منهم

يتلوا عليهم ءايتك ويعلمهم

الكتب والحكمة ويزكيهم

إنك أنت العزيز الحكيم

"Our Lord! And send amongst them a Messenger of their own, who shall recite to them Your Verses and instruct them in the Book and the wisdom, and purify them. Surely, You are the All-Mighty, the All-Wise."
Al-Baqarah: 2:129.

In This Chapter

Describes the idol-worship initiated by 'Amr bin Luhayy, the names of idols and their altars in the Arabian Peninsula, and the various pagan customs. It also throws light on the innovations which disfigured the pure faith of Prophet Ibrāhīm عليه السلام.

The chapter gives information about Judaism, Christianity, Zoroastrianism, Sabianism and their followers and how those faiths came to Arabian Peninsula and where their centers were located.

Judaisr

Christianit

Zoroastrianisr

Sabianisr

Idol Worship in Arabia

Prophet Ismāʻīl ﷺ preached the monotheistic creed of his father. The people of Makkah listened to him, obeyed him and worshipped Allah alone. However, as time passed, they forgot and neglected parts of the pure religion, although the faith they professed did contain some remnants of that creed. This lasted until the chieftain of Banu Khuzāʻah, ʻAmr bin Luhayy, emerged on the scene.

Beginning of Idolatry in Arabia

ʻAmr bin Luhayy travelled to Syria where he saw people worshipping idols. When he asked them about, they told him that they prayed to the idols for rain and to seek their help against their foes. Intrigued, ʻAmr ibn Luhayy asked them for an idol, which they gave him as a gift. He brought to Makkah with him an idol named Hubal, placed it in the Kaʻbah, and called the people to worship it. Interested and excited by this new way, the Makkans began to worship Hubal; soon, the people of Hijāz followed in the footsteps of the Makkans.[1]

In addition to Hubal, several other idols became known as the most famous deities of Arabia. Manāt, Lāt, and ʻUzza were located in Ta'if and Wadi Nakhlah, and worshipped by the Arabs. The evil of idolatry did not stop with these four idols; instead, the number of idols multiplied until every area of the Hijaz had its own local idol. It is said that ʻAmr ibn Luhayy had a companion Jinn who convinced him to begin the worship of idols. He told ʻAmr that the idols of the folk of Noah (Wadd, Suwāʻ, Yaghūth, Yaʻūq and Nasr) lay buried in Jeddah. ʻAmr bin Luhayy went to Jeddah,

1. Akhbar-o-Makkah Li'l Azraqi: 1/117; Al-Mufassal Fi Tareekh-il-Arab Qabl-al-Islam: 6/77 .

Idol sites in Arabia
Idols and Images of the Arabs
1 Suwā‘ 2 Al-Uzza 3 Al-Lāt 4 Manāt
5 Nasr 6 Wadd 7 Ya‘ūq 8 Yaghūth,
Idols which are not mentioned in the Quran
9 Hubal 10 Dhul-Khalasah 11 Dhu-sh-Shara
12 Dhul-Kaffain 13 Isaf & Nāilah 14 Al Jalsad
Mediterranean Sea
Alexandria
Cairo
El Faiyum
Egypt
Nile R.
Nubian Desert
Sudan
Sinai
Al Ailah
Al Aqabah
Midian
Dead Sea
Tabūk
Daumatul Jandal
Great Nafūd Desert
Yanbu
Hijaz
Rabigh
Madinah
Jaddah (Jedda)
Makkah
At-Taif
Nejd
Asīr
Red Sea
Massawa
Abyssinia
Jizan (Jāzān)
Aseb
Bab al-Mandab
Al Mukha (Mucha)
Al Hudaidah
San‘ā’
Najrān
Aden
Yemen
Hadramawt
Tarīm
Al Mukalla
Gulf of Aden
Horn of Africa
Empty Quarter
Arabian Peninsula
Iraq
Kazimah
Al Ahsā
Darain
Arabian Gulf (Persian Gulf)
Bushehr
Shiraz
Persia (Iran)
Zahedan
Daba
Suhār
Gulf of Oman
Muscat
Oman
Masīrah
Zafār
Arabian Sea
Indian Ocean
0 200 400 600 800 1000 km

Map. 19

dug them out from under the earth and brought them to Tihamah. When the Hajj season arrived, he gave those idols to various tribes who then carried them to their regions.

Idolatry became so widespread that eventually, every household of every tribe had its own idol to worship. Even the Ka'bah, the House of Allah, was not spared – on the day of the Conquest of Makkah, there were three hundred and sixty idols inside and around the House of Allah.[1]

Ruins of Ka'bah Yamāniyyah in Tabālah

Idols of Arabia

'Isāf and Nā'ilah: These idols had human figures. 'Amr bin Luhayy kept them beside the Zamzam well, where people circumambulated them and offered animal sacrifices. One story relates that 'Isāf was a man and Nā'ilah was a woman. This couple committed adultery inside the Ka'bah itself. When they were found, they had been turned into stone, and the people of Makkah placed them on the hills of Safā and Marwah as a deterring example. Later on, 'Amr ibn Luhayy began worshipping them in the Haram.[2]

Uqaisar: Uqaisar was an idol worshipped by the tribes of Qudā'ah, Lakhm, Judhām, 'Amilah, and Ghat'fān. Its altar was on a plateau (Mashārif) in Syria. According to Hishām, the tribesmen of Qudā'ah, Lakhm, Judhām and the Syrians used to go there on pilgrimage and shave their heads beside it.[3]

1. Akhbar-o-Makkah Li'l-Azraqi 1/120-121; Ighath'ath-ul-Lahfan: 2/269.
2. Al-Mufassal Fi Tareekh-il-Arab Qabal-al-Islam: 6/266-268; Ighathath-ul-Lahfan: 2/264.
3. Ighathath-ul-lahfan: 2/265; Mu'jam-ul-Buldān. See under 'Uqaisar'.

Al-Jalsad: Al-Jalsad was the idol of the Kindah tribesmen in Hadramaut. Its custodians and caretakers were Banu Shukāmah bin Shabeeb Kindi. They had consecrated a pasture-ground to the idol where animals to be sacrificed in its name grazed. The idol, with the figure of a huge human being, had been carved in white stone.[1] Ukaidar, the king of Dūmat-ul-Jandal, belonged to Banu Shukāmah tribe and accepted Islam when he received a letter from the Prophet Muhammad (ﷺ).[2]

Dhu'l Khalasah: This idol was situated in Tabālah, a place between Makkah and Yemen, in a house of the same name during the Age of Paganism. It was worshipped by the tribesmen of Daus, Khath'am, and Bajeelah and known as the "Ka'bah Yamāniyyah" or "Ka'bah Shāmiyyah." The Prophet's Companion Jareer bin Abdullah Bajalī ؓ destroyed it after the Conquest of Makkah.[3] Allah's Messenger (ﷺ) said: "The (Day of) Resurrection shall not come until the women of Daus have not shaken their buttocks around Dhu'l Khalsa."[4]

Dhu'sh-Shara: It was the idol of the Daus and Azd tribes, although the Nabateans also worshipped a pair of deities named Dhu'sh-Shara and Harees. It was worshipped in the area of 'Aseer. Shara was a hill in Tihāmah, and was also the name of a hill in Jordan, where Dhu'sh-Shara was worshipped as well.[5]

Dhu'l-Kaffain: It was the idol of 'Amr bin Hamamah, the chief of the tribe of Daus. Tufail bin Amr ad-Dausi ؓ, the Prophet's companion, took permission from the Messenger of Allah after the Conquest of Makkah to set it on fire.[6]

Suwā': In Surah Nūh, the Qur'ān mentions Suwā', along with Wadd, Yaghooth, Ya'ūq and Nasr, as the five idols worshipped by the people of prophet Nūh (Noah). In pre-Islamic Arabia, people worshipped this idol at a place called Ruhāt, near Yanbu', west of Yathrib. In Dumat Al-Jundal, the tribe of Huzail also worshipped it. Suwā' had the figure

---

1. Nihayat-ul-Arab, P. 280-281; Al-A'lam: 3/171.
2. Mu'jam-ul-Buldān. See under 'Al-Jalsad'.
3. Sahīh-ul-Bukhāri: 2823, and 4357; Sahīh Ibn Hibban (Ibn Majah): 15/150; As-Seerah li-Ibn-Hishām: 1/86.
4. Sahīh-ul-Bukhāri: 7116; Sahīh Muslim: 2906.
5. Atlas Sīrat Nabawiyyah, P. 60; Urdu Encyclopedia of Islam: 10/44-45.
6. Ighathath-ul-Lahfan: 2/265; Atlas Sīrat Nabawiyyah, P. 60.

of a woman.[1]

Daizanān: It is the dual of Daizan meaning "competition, rivalry." Daizanān were two idols fixed to the gateway of Hīrah (Iraq) by Juzaimat Al-Abrash or Munzir Al-Akbar. Anyone entering the city was required to prostrate to the idol, the purpose being to test the visitor's loyalty.[2]

'Ā'im: According to Allama Yaqūt, Kalbi said that 'Ā'im was the name of the idol of "Azd Sarāt."[3]

Al-'Uzza: It is the feminine of the superlative of 'Azeez (the masculine being A'azz). Its altar was under an acacia tree in Wadi Nakhla and it was worshipped by Banu Kinānah. There was also an idol of 'Uzz in the Inviolable Place of Worship in Makkah. It was destroyed after the Conquest of Makkah, smashed by Khalid bin Waleed رضي الله عنه.[4]

Al-Lāt: This idol was worshipped in Tā'if by Banu Thaqeef. Lāt was the name of a man who gave to pilgrims a preparation of barley flour mixed with water. Long after he had died, Amr ibn Luhayy suggested to the people that they make an idol of him and worship it. The Quraish would pray to Lāt and 'Uzza before going to bed and swore by them.[5]

1. Al-Mufassal Fi Tareekh-il-Arab Qabl-al-Islam: 6/257-259; Atlas Sīrat Nabawiyyah: P. 59.
2. Tareekh-ut-Tabāri: 1/440; Llisan-ul-Arab: see under 'Dazan'.
3. Ighathath-ul-Lahfan: 2/266; Mu'jam-ul-Buldān: see under 'As'im'.
4. Lisan-ul-Arab. See under 'Azaza'; Al-Mufassal Fi Tareekh-il-Arab Qabal-al-Islam: 6/235.
5. Musnad Ahmad: 222/4 and 362/5; Tafseer Ibn Katheer, An-Najm (19 :(53; Jawami' As-Seerah Li-Ibn Hazm. P. 257.

A square cliff was chiseled to make the image of Lāt. Banu Mu'attib (or Banu 'Itab) were in charge of this idol, and they raised a building over it. The Quraish and other tribes venerated the idol and circumambulated it. After the conquest of Ta'if, Mugheera bin Shu'bah Thaqafi, a Companion of the Prophet (ﷺ) broke it down. Today, where once the altar of Al-Lāt stood, rises the minaret of the great mosque of Ta'if.[1]

Manāt: Manāt was one of the most ancient idols of Arabia, located at Mushallal near Qudaid on the Red Sea coast.[2] Lāt, Manat and 'Uzza were the three greatest idols of the pagan Arabs. The trio are mentioned in the Qur'anic chapter of an-Najm. Worship of Manāt was also initiated by Amr bin Luhayy, and all the Arabs, especially the Aus and Khazraj, revered it highly. Banu Azd and Ghassān visited its shrine as pilgrims, while Aus and Khazraj removed their ihram beside Manāt after the pilgrimage. On the way to the Conquest of Makkah, Ali bin Abi Talib destroyed this idol at the command of the Messenger of Allah (ﷺ).[3]

Nasr: The idol 'Nasr,' which was named after the vulture (Nasr) whose shape it took[4], was worshipped by the tribe of Dhi'l Kalā' in Yemen, near Najrān. Najrān is now a province of Saudi Arabia by the frontier of Yemen.

Hubal: The idol's original name was Hub'al, which was later Arabicized to "Hubal." The root-word of the name was Ba'l or Baal, an idol worshipped by the Syrians. Ba'labakk (Baalbek), an ancient city in Lebanon, was also named after it. Literally, Ba'l means 'power' but it is used figuratively to mean 'master,' and is why the Qur'ān uses it to mean 'husband.'

The Quraish discovered this idol, which had a human figure and was chiseled from red carnelian. It was also missing a right hand, which the Quraish then replaced with one made of gold.

Hubal was placed within the Ka'bah, and the Quraish would throw their divining dice in front of it when seeking to discover the future. The people of Quraish would praise Hubal with the cry "'Ulu

1. As-Seerah Li-Ibn Hishām 186/4; Al-Mufassal Fi Ttareekh-il-Arab Qabl-al-Islam: 229-227/6.
2. Sahīh-ul-Bukhāri: 1643 and 1790.
3. Al-Mufassal Fi Ttareekh-il-Arab Qabl-al-Islam: 6/246-249.
4. Op.cit., 6/263.

Hubal!" ("long live Hubal") during times of war. It was destroyed by Ali on the eve of the Conquest of Makkah.[1]

Wadd: Wadd was situated in Dumat al-Jandal and worshipped by Banu Kalb and the Quraish. It was destroyed by Khālid bin Waleed ﷺ on the eve of the Battle of Tabūk.[2]

Ya'ūq: Ya'ūq was one of the five idols buried in Jeddah. Its name means "One who holds back calamity." It had the form of a horse and was located in Yemen at a place called Arhab, two nights journey from San'a, in the direction of Makkah. Its devotees were Banu Hamdān and Khaulān.[3]

Yaghuth: Sited in Akmah-u-Mazhaj (Yemen) it was worshipped by Banu Mazhaj and Hamdān. An'am, a branch of the tribe of Tayy, Murād and Banu Ghutaif were also its devotees. Its name meant "One who responds to petition," and it had the form of a lion.[4]

Rites of Arab Idol Worship

The rites and ceremonies of Arab idolatry were the inventions of Amr bin Luhayy, which the Arabs accepted as "amendments" to the original religious system of Prophet Ibrāhīm عليه السلام.

Some of their rites and customs were as follows.

1. The pagan Arabs would sit beside their idols as custodians or keepers, seek their protection, cry to them loudly and supplicate fervently in the vain hope that they would intercede with Allah on their behalf and have their need or wish fulfilled.

2. They used to go on pilgrimage to the sites of idols, go round them, stand before them in awe and reverence, and bow and prostrate to them.

3. They made offerings, vows and animal sacrifices for their idols. Animals were slaughtered at the altars of idols; or elsewhere, but

1. Ar-Rahīq-ul-Makhtūm, P. 45; Al-Mufassal Fi Tareekh-il-Arab Qabl-al-Islam: 6/250-253.
2. Ar-Rahīq-ul-Makhtūm, P. 46; Al-Mufassal Fi Islam: 6/255-257.
3. Mu'jam-ul-Buldān. See under 'Ya'uq; Al-Mufassal Fi Tareekh-il-Arab Qabl-al-Islam: 6/262-263.
4. Mu'jam-ul-Buldān. See under 'Yaghuth'; Al-Mufassal Fi Tareekh-il-Arab Qabl-al-Islam: 6/260-262.

always in the name of an idol. Allah prohibited both kinds of animal sacrifices:

﴿وَمَا ذُبِحَ عَلَى ٱلنُّصُبِ﴾

"And that which is sacrificed (slaughtered) on An-Nusub (stone-altars)." [1]

﴿وَلَا تَأْكُلُوا۟ مِمَّا لَمْ يُذْكَرِ ٱسْمُ ٱللَّهِ عَلَيْهِ﴾

"And eat not (O believers) of that (meat) on which Allāh's Name has not been pronounced." [2]

4. To grow closer to their idols and earn their pleasure, the pagans would apportion a part of their farm produce and cattle to their idols. They would also apportion a part of their property to Allah, but would re-allocate this part to the idols if they felt like it. However, they would never give an idol's share of property for the Sake of Allah, no matter the circumstances.

﴿وَجَعَلُوا۟ لِلَّهِ مِمَّا ذَرَأَ مِنَ ٱلْحَرْثِ وَٱلْأَنْعَـٰمِ نَصِيبًا فَقَالُوا۟ هَـٰذَا لِلَّهِ بِزَعْمِهِمْ
وَهَـٰذَا لِشُرَكَآئِنَا ۖ فَمَا كَانَ لِشُرَكَآئِهِمْ فَلَا يَصِلُ إِلَى ٱللَّهِ ۖ وَمَا كَانَ لِلَّهِ
فَهُوَ يَصِلُ إِلَىٰ شُرَكَآئِهِمْ ۗ سَآءَ مَا يَحْكُمُونَ﴾

"And they assign to Allāh a share of the tilth and cattle which He has created, and they say: ``This is for Allāh" according to their claim, ``and this is for our (Allāh's so-called) partners." But the share of their (Allāh's so-called) ``partners" reaches not Allāh, while the share of Allāh reaches their (Allāh's so-called) ``partners"! Evil is the way they judge!" [3]

5. Another pagan practice to grow closer to Allah was that they made some vows, not sanctioned by Allah, concerning their crops and cattle.

﴿وَقَالُوا۟ هَـٰذِهِۦٓ أَنْعَـٰمٌ وَحَرْثٌ حِجْرٌ لَّا يَطْعَمُهَآ إِلَّا مَن نَّشَآءُ بِزَعْمِهِمْ وَأَنْعَـٰمٌ حُرِّمَتْ
ظُهُورُهَا وَأَنْعَـٰمٌ لَّا يَذْكُرُونَ ٱسْمَ ٱللَّهِ عَلَيْهَا ٱفْتِرَآءً عَلَيْهِ ۚ﴾

"And according to their claim, they say that such and such cattle and crops

1. Al-Ma'idah: 5:3.
2. Al-An'am: 6:121.
3. Al-An'am: 6:136.

are forbidden, and none should eat of them except those whom we allow. And (they say) there are cattle forbidden to be used for burden (or any other work), and cattle on which (at slaughtering) the Name of Allāh is not pronounced; lying against Him (Allāh). He will recompense them for what they used to fabricate." [1]

6. The pagans did the same in case of *Baheera, Sa'iba, Wasilah*, and *Hām*.

Bahirah and Sā'ibah: Ibn Ishaq said that a Bahirah is the calf born to a *Sā'ibah*. *Sā'ibah* was the she-camel which gave birth to ten female calves (baby camels) with no male baby in between. The pagans would set her free, would not ride her nor cut the hairs nor drink her milk except for their guests. If this she-camel (the *Sā'ibah*) gave birth to another female baby, that infant's ear was pierced and set free like her mother. None would ride her nor cut her hair nor would anyone drink her milk except the guests. This female offspring of the Sā'ibah was known as Bahirah.

Wasilah: This name was applied to a she-goat which gave birth to female twins five times over (that is, ten female kids) with no male kid in between. She was called *Wasilah* because she 'connected' all the female kids. After that, if the *wasilah* goat gave birth to more kids, their flesh was eaten by men only. It was forbidden to women. In the event that she gave birth to a dead kid, its flesh was allowed to both men and women.

Hām: Name of a he-camel which begat ten female baby camels, there being no male baby in between. None would ride it or cut its hair. He would be left with the pack of camels for coupling.

Allah condemns these pagan customs:

﴿مَا جَعَلَ ٱللَّهُ مِنۢ بَحِيرَةٖ وَلَا سَآئِبَةٖ وَلَا وَصِيلَةٖ وَلَا حَامٖ وَلَٰكِنَّ ٱلَّذِينَ كَفَرُواْ يَفۡتَرُونَ عَلَى ٱللَّهِ ٱلۡكَذِبَۖ وَأَكۡثَرُهُمۡ لَا يَعۡقِلُونَ﴾

"Allāh has not instituted things like Bahīrah or a Sā'ibah or a Wasīlah or a Hām (all these animals were liberated in honour of idols as practised by

1. Al-An'am: 6:138.

pagan Arabs in the pre-Islamic period). But those who disbelieve invent lies against Allāh, and most of them have no understanding." [1]

Another Verse says:

﴿ وَقَالُوا۟ مَا فِى بُطُونِ هَٰذِهِ ٱلْأَنْعَٰمِ خَالِصَةٌ لِّذُكُورِنَا وَمُحَرَّمٌ عَلَىٰٓ أَزْوَٰجِنَا ۖ وَإِن يَكُن مَّيْتَةً فَهُمْ فِيهِ شُرَكَآءُ ۚ سَيَجْزِيهِمْ وَصْفَهُمْ ۚ إِنَّهُۥ حَكِيمٌ عَلِيمٌ ﴾

"And they say: ``What is in the bellies of such and such cattle (milk or foetus) is for our males alone, and forbidden to our females (girls and women), but if it is born dead, then all have shares therein." He will punish them for their attribution (of such false orders to Allāh). Verily, He is All-Wise, All-Knower." [2]

The Prophet Muhammad (ﷺ) said: "Amr bin Luhayy was the first person who released animals in the name of idols." Sa'eed bin Musayyab, a prominent Tabi'ee, said: "The milk of these animals was reserved for their idols."[3]

The pagan Arabs would carry out these practices in a misguided effort to win the favour of Allah. They had the ridiculous belief that these idols were a medium between them and Allah, and that the idols would intercede with Him on their behalf. The Qur'ān refers to their pretences:

﴿ مَا نَعْبُدُهُمْ إِلَّا لِيُقَرِّبُونَآ إِلَى ٱللَّهِ زُلْفَىٰٓ ﴾

"We worship them only that they may bring us near to Allah." [4]

﴿ هَٰٓؤُلَآءِ شُفَعَٰٓؤُنَا عِندَ ٱللَّهِ ۚ ﴾

"And they say: These are our intercessors with Allah." [5]

1. Al-Maidah: 5:103.
2. Al-An'am: 6:139.
3. Sahīh-ul-Bukhāri: 4623.
4. Az-Zumar: 39:3.
5 Yunus: 10:18.

Remains of Banu Quraizah - Khayber

The Jews of Arabia

The Jews came to Arabian Peninsula as immigrants in two successive waves. They came first in 722 BC when Sargon II, king of Assyria, attacked and dismantled their northern kingdom of Samaria, forcing the Jews to leave their homeland.

Again in 587 BC, the king of Babylon, Nebuchadnezzar II, attacked their southern kingdom, Judea, and destroyed the Temple of Jerusalem. Nearly one hundred thousand Jews were driven out of Palestine and forced to live in exile in Iraq. Others made their way to the northern areas of Hijaz.

The Jews in Yathrib

When the Roman forces, led by Titus, attacked Palestine in 70 CE, pillaged the land and destroyed the Temple of Solomon, several Jewish tribes fled from Palestine and came to Hijaz. They settled in Yathrib,

Khaybar, and Taima'. Those Jewish immigrants introduced Judaism to the native Arabs.

The most prominent Jewish tribes in Arabia at the beginning of Islam were Banu Nadir, Banu Mustalaq, Banu Quraizah, and Banu Qainuqā'.[1] Samhudi stated that the earlier and the later Jewish immigrants totaled more than twenty tribes.[2]

Judaism in Yemen

Judaism also flourished in Yemen, thanks to the conversion of Tubba' (king) of Yemen, Tubān As'ad Abu Karb. According to Ibn Hishām, when Tuban As'ad had finished his expedition in the east, he passed through Yathrib on his way back home.

In Yathrib, he came across two Jewish scholars who influenced him deeply. The king accepted Judaism and, through him, the Jewish faith began and thrived in Yemen. Abu Karb's son, Yusuf Dhu Nawās, was even more enthusiastic than his father. Filled with religious zeal, he attacked the Christians of Najrān and forced them to convert to Judaism. When they refused, he ordered a trench to be dug out and all the Christians, old and young, men and women, be thrown into the fire-filled trench. It is said that the number of those burnt to death were somewhere between twenty thousand and forty thousand.[3]

1. Qalb-o-Jazeerat-il-Arab, P. 251.
2. Wafa'-ul-Wafa li's-Samhudi: 1/165.
3. As-Seerah Li-Ibn Hishām: 1/20-36.

Some historians disagree with this version of the story and argue that Dhu Nawas has been told to be a Jew, while, according to the Qurān the king who martyred the People of the Trenches was a pagan.[1]

The Managing Director of Darussalam, Abdul Malik Mujāhid, writes in his Travelogue of Najrān: "When we entered the area of the People of the Trenches, we saw grey-coloured hills in front of us. It must be an area of 10sq. Km. After covering about half a kilometer, those ridges began to appear where the incident of the people of the trenches took place. There were small rooms made of big stones, in which some walls were just a few feet high. The earth was dented and some places were like dunes. The trenches had been dug in an area of one kilometer by 300 metres to the right of the trenches a big circular hollow ground was to be seen where many hundred people could sit to see the scene. Probably here the king and the high officials were sitting and seeing the oppressed being martyred."[2]

1. See the story of the Owners of the Trench under 'Kingdoms of Yemen' in this book.
2. Monthly Zia-e-Hadith (September 2011).

Ruins of Akhdood - Najran

Ruins of najran church

Christianity in Arabia

Christianity came to the Arab lands through Abyssinian occupiers and Roman conquerors. The Abyssinians occupied Yemen the first time in 340 CE and this occupation continued till 375 CE. During this time, the evangelists continued their missionary work.

During the Abyssinian occupation of Yemen, a very devout Christian man by the name of Famyūn, arrived in Najrān and started preaching the Gospel. The people of Najrān were impressed by him and became Christians.[1] Tubba' Abd-Kaleel was the only ruler of Yemen who became a Christian; most of the other Tubba' kings were Jews, while a

1. As-Seerah Li-Ibn Hishām: 1/31-34.

few of them were star-worshippers.[1]

When the Abyssians re-occupied Yemen in 525 CE and Abrahah Ashram took over the reins of the government of Yemen, he worked with great zeal for the propagation of the Christian faith. He built a church in San'ā', and planned to destroy the Ka'bah in Makkah in an effort to force the Arabs to come to San'ā' for Hajj instead. However, Allah destroyed his invading forces and made him a deterring example for others.[2]

Christianity became widespread among the family of Ghassān and the tribes of Banu Taghlib and Banu Tayy, who lived close to the Roman territories. Some Arab kings of Hīrah also accepted Christianity.[3]

1. Tareekh Ard-il-Qur'ān (Kamil): 234/1.
2. See the commentaries on Surah 'Al-Feel' (The Elephant) and the chapter 'Ām-ul-Feel of this book.
3. Ar-Rahīq Al-Makhtūm, P. 53.

The place of al-Qullays where Abraha built his cathedral - San'ā

A Zoroastrian Fire Temple in central Iran

Zoroastrianism and Sabaism in Arabia

Zoroastrianism

The Zoroastrian faith flourished mostly among those Arabs who lived in the neighborhood of Persians, such as some parts of Iraq, Bahrain (Al-Ahsā'), Hijr and the coastal areas of the Arabian Gulf. It made no headway in Yemen except during the Persian rule, but even then, without any significance.[1]

Sabaism (Sabeanism)

The Sabeans were star-worshippers. Excavations of archaeological sites in Iraq revealed inscriptions which suggest that the people of Prophet Ibrāhīm عليه السلام, the Chaldeans, were Sabeans. The people of Syria and Yemen were also followers of this astrological faith, although it gradually faded with the emergence and dominance of Judaism and Christianity. Some tribes which lived close to the Zoroastrians retained

1. Ar-Rahīq-ul-Makhtūm, P. 54.

this religion in Iraq and along the Persian Gulf coast.[1]

For further information about the Zoroastrians and Sabeans and their beliefs, see 'The Neighbors of Arabs, their Kingdoms and Religions.'

1. Tareekh Ard-ul-Qur'ān (Kamil): 2/193-208; Ar-Rahīq-ul-Makhtūm, P. 54.

Temple of Sabeans in Basrah - Iraq

Customs of the Pagan Arabs

Though the Quraish had become pagans in belief and practice, there remained within their culture some remnants of the pure Abrahamic faith. For example, they honoured and greatly revered the House of Allah, regularly circumambulating the Ka'bah, and performed *Hajj*, *'Umrah*, and sacrifice of animals. However, they polluted these originally pure practices with many pagan innovations.

Hums

The Quraishi tribesmen believed that since they were the offspring of Abraham, custodians and defenders of the Ka'bah, nobody could match them and that no one deserved the same rights that they did. For this reason, they called themselves *'Hums'* (brave and zealous), and said that it was beneath their high station to leave the precincts of the Holy Sanctuary *(Al-Masjid Al-Harām)*.Thus, they would not go to *Arafât* during *Hajj,* nor did they perform the *Ifâdah* (a kind of Hajj); rather, they would remain in Muzdalifah and perform the *Ifadah* from there.[1] Allah disapproved of this innovative practice:

﴿ ثُمَّ أَفِيضُوا۟ مِنْ حَيْثُ أَفَاضَ ٱلنَّاسُ ﴾

"Then depart from the place whence all the people depart." [2]

The term Hums also encompassed the descendants of those Arabs who

1. A pilgrim is obliged to leave the plain of 'Arafāt on the Day of 'Arafāt for Muzdalifa after sunset, shorten the Maghrib and Isha' prayer and offer them both jointly, spend the night at Muzdalifa, and offer the following Fajr prayer at Muzdalifa-all these acts are called Ifadah. – (Mu'jam lughat-il-Fuqaha;, P. 79).
2. Al-Baqarah, (2): 199, As-Seerah Li-Ibn Hishām: 1/199; Sahīh-ul-Bukhāri: 1665; Sahīh Muslim: 1219.

lived outside or inside the precincts of the Sanctuary. The rules applying to the Quraish also applied to them; those things permitted for Quraish were allowed to them, and the things prohibited for Quraish were likewise prohibited for them.[1]

The status of Hums also imposed upon them the prohibition to make cheese or butter while he was in the state of *Ihram*. Likewise, they could neither enter a dwelling-place (tent) made of hair nor benefit by its shade. However, they were allowed to benefit by the shade of a tent made of leather.[2]

Another law stipulated that if the pilgrims living outside the precincts of the Sanctuary brought food and drinks with them, it was not permissible for them to eat it.[3]

The Quraish had imposed as a duty on those living outside the limits of the Sanctuary to perform their first *Tawāf* (circumambulation) around the Ka'bah in clothes supplied by the *Hums*. In case such clothes could not be had, the men would go around the Ka'bah in the nude while women would take off their clothes and put on a small, loose shirt and recite the following verse while going round the Ka'bah:

اَلْيَوْمَ يَبْدُو بَعْضُهُ أَوْ كُلُّهُ   وَمَا بَدَا مِنْهُ فَلَا أُحِلُّهُ

"Today a part or whole of body is bare. As for the part which is

1. As-Seerah Li-Ibn Hishām: 1/199.
2. Op.cit. 1/202.
3. Op.cit., P. 1/202.

bare, I shall not make it permissible for others."

Allah put an end to this behaviour:

﴿يَٰبَنِيٓ ءَادَمَ خُذُواْ زِينَتَكُمۡ عِندَ كُلِّ مَسۡجِدٖ﴾

"O Children of Adam! Take your adornment (by wearing your clean clothes) while praying." [1]

If a respectable person brought his own clothing from outside the precincts of the Sanctuary and circumambulated the Ka'bah wearing those clothes, he would then discard of those clothes. Neither he would wear them again nor allow anyone else to wear them.[2]

While in the state of *Ihrām*, the Quraish would not enter their houses by their front door but make large holes in the backs of their houses for entrance and exit. In their eyes, this odd custom was an act of piety; however, the following Qur'ānic Verses forbade this practice.

﴿وَلَيۡسَ ٱلۡبِرُّ بِأَن تَأۡتُواْ ٱلۡبُيُوتَ مِن ظُهُورِهَا وَلَٰكِنَّ ٱلۡبِرَّ مَنِ ٱتَّقَىٰۗ وَأۡتُواْ ٱلۡبُيُوتَ مِنۡ أَبۡوَٰبِهَاۚ وَٱتَّقُواْ ٱللَّهَ لَعَلَّكُمۡ تُفۡلِحُونَ﴾

"It is not Al-Birr (piety, righteousness) that you enter the houses from the back, but Al-Birr (is the quality of the one) who fears Allâh. So, enter houses through their (proper) doors, and fear Allâh that you may be successful." [3]

This was the religion of the pagan Arabs – strange customs and baseless superstitions.[4]

Divining, Fortune-telling, Omens and Gambling

The pagan Arabs were steeped in superstitious "magical" practices. Amongst these beliefs were the use of divining arrows, known as *Azlām*, to forecast the future and the unknown. The word *Azlam* is the plural of *Zalm*, meaning 'an arrow without feathers.'

1. Al-A'raf: 7:31.
2. Op.cit., P. 1/202-203; Sahīh-ul-Bukhāri: 1665.
3. Al-Baqarah: 2:189.
4. Ar-Rahīq-ul-Makhtūm: P. 51-52.

Ancient game board

They used three types of divining arrows: One with the word 'yes,' and the other with the word 'no' written on it. These were most commonly used with regards to marriage or making journeys. The divining arrows were also used for matters such as digging a new well or settling a debt of blood-money.

When the pagan Arabs doubted a person's lineage, they would give him one hundred dirhams and a camel and take him to the idol Hubal. The camel and the money were given over to the priest. The priest would then shuffle all the three arrows and shake them violently and then draw one. If the arrow said 'He is one of you,' the person was declared to be a respectable member of the tribe. If the arrow drawn said 'He is from someone other than you,' he was considered an ally. If it said 'connected,' the person retained his station. He was considered neither belonging to the tribe nor an ally.[1]

The pagan system of gambling was also based on arrows. The gamblers would slaughter a camel and divide its flesh into ten or twenty-eight portions. The gamblers would then draw arrows; if the arrow had the mark of a winner, the person would take his share. If the arrow had no mark, he would pay the price.

Fortune-telling was another popular pastime of the pagan Arabs, and the people in general were great believers in their priests, soothsayers, and astrologers. Some priests claimed that they had a jinni

1. As-Seerah li-Ibn Ishaq: 1/85-86; As-Seerah li-Ibn Hishām: 1/152-153; Fat'h-ul-Bāri: 8/351.

in their service, who told them of future events. Others claimed that they had special gifts which helped them discover where a particular event took place and how. The astrologers claimed that by calculating the movements and timings of the stars and planets, they were able to predict the future.[1] Many of the pagan Arabs believed that the stars influenced life on earth, and would consult the astrologers regarding important natural occurrences (such as rainfall) or significant events (the outcomes of battles).[2]

Islam has strictly forbidden all Muslims from consulting or listening to such priests, fortune-tellers, and astrologers. The Messenger of Allah (ﷺ) said:

«مَنْ أَتٰى عَرَّافًا فَسَأَلَهُ عَنْ شَيْءٍ لَّمْ تُقْبَلْ لَّهُ صَلَاةُ أَرْبَعِينَ لَيْلَةً»

"Whosoever goes to a soothsayer and inquires of him about something, his prayer shall not be accepted for forty nights."[3]

Another Hadeeth relates:

«مَنْ أَتٰى كَاهِنًا أَوْعَرَّافًا فَصَدَّقَهُ بِمَا يَقُولُ، فَقَدْ كَفَرَ بِمَا أُنْزِلَ عَلٰى مُحَمَّدٍ ﷺ»

"Whosoever goes to a fortuneteller or a soothsayer and believes him, he has indeed denied that which has been revealed to Muhammad (ﷺ)."[4]

Imrān bin Husain (رضي الله عنه) reported that the Messenger of Allah (ﷺ) said:

«لَيْسَ مِنَّا مَنْ تَطَيَّرَ أَوْ تُطُيِّرَ لَهُ، أَوْتَكَهَّنَ أَوْتُكُهِّنَ لَهُ أَوْ سَحَرَ أَوْ سُحِرَلَهُ، وَمَنْ أَتٰى كَاهِنًا فَصَدَّقَهُ بِمَا يَقُولُ فَقَدْ كَفَرَ بِمَا أُنْزِلَ عَلٰى مُحَمَّدٍ ﷺ»

"Not from us is he who believes in evil omen or for whom evil omen is predicted, or for whom divines the unknown or he who divines the unknown for him, or he who casts spell or he who casts spell for him. And whoso goes to a soothsayer (fortuneteller)

1. Mer'at-ul-Mafātīh: 2/248.
2. Shar'h-un-Nawawi 'Ala Sahīh Muslim: 2/79-80.
3. Sahīh Muslim: 2230.
4. Musnad Ahmad: 2/429.

and believes in what he says has indeed denied what has been revealed to Muhammad (ﷺ)."[1]

As part of their obsession with the future, the pagan Arabs would also seek out information through the flight of birds and movement of animals. For example, they approached a bird or deer and make it fly or run and if it flew or ran to the right side, it would be considered a sign of good luck. If it veered to the left, they would take it as a bad omen. Similarly, if a bird or animal crossed their path, they took it as something foreboding evil. For this purpose the pagans also used to hang the ankle-bone of a rabbit, and they took some particular days, months, animals, houses and women as ominous, and considered diseases to be contagious. They also believed that, unless murder was not avenged, the soul of the murdered roamed about in the wilderness in the form of an owl, crying plaintively: 'I am thirsty' and 'Give me a drink' and that only when his blood had been avenged would the spirit rest.[2]

The pure faith of Islam wiped out these false beliefs and ignorant superstitions.

1. Sahīh At-Targhīb Wat-Tarhīb Li'l-Albāni: 3041.
2. Fat'h-ul-Bāri: 7/323 and 10/297; Ar-Rahīq-ul-Makhtūm, P. 51.

Chapter - 5

The Culture, Trade, and Customs

of the Arabian Peninsula

Pre-Islamic wedding customs, relations between men and women, tribal consciousness, trade fairs, evolution of Arabic prose and poetry, and different dialects of Arabic language

وَإِنَّكَ لَعَلَىٰ خُلُقٍ عَظِيمٍ

"And verily, you O Muhammad are on
an excellent (standard of) character."
Al-Qalam: 68:4

In This Chapter

Deals with the social conditions prevailing in pagan Arabia, the various modes of marriage, tribal bigotry, trade fairs, some high moral qualities of the Arabs, and Arabic language and literature.

It also reviews the various branches of Arabic language, the difference between northern and southern Arabic, the different periods of Arabic development, how and why it developed, natural oratory gifts of the Arabs, and their different dialects. The chapter also gives a glimpse of Arab orator Qus bin Sa'idah, the Arab poets of different ages, and a selection of verses of Imra-ul-Qais, Prince of Kinda. In short, this chapter is a rich mosaic of information for the general reader.

Social Relations in the Arabian Peninsula

In the elite high class of the nobles, women in Arabian society were generally respected and had a degree of independence not allowed to those women of lower classes. A Quraishi noblewoman was often intelligent and powerful; she wielded some measure of influence over men, who would listen to and obey her. Indeed, such a woman would merit the defense of her tribe's men, who would draw their swords to defend her honour. Nonetheless, a man was still considered the undisputable head of the family. His word was decisive and final. Amongst the noblemen, wedlock was the only way for males and females to join together and that could take place only under the aegis and watchful eyes of a woman's legal guardian.

Four Types of Pagan Marriages

Among the lower strata of the society, men and women built ties of intimate relations in a way which could only be described as adultery and lewdness.

'Ā'ishah, the Mother of the Believers, related that four types of marriage were prevalent in pre-Islamic Arabia.

The first type was that which continues to exist today; that a man would ask the legal guardian of a woman for her hand in marriage. If the guardian and the woman agreed, the man would pay the *Mahr* (bridal gift) and marry the woman.

The second type was that when a woman was cleansed of her menses, her husband would call another man to cohabit with her. The husband would not go near his own wife until she had fallen pregnant from the other man. Once it was clear that she had conceived, her husband would return to her and become intimate with her once more. The intent of this practice was for the child to be of noble descent (via the second man). This form of "marriage" was called 'marriage of *'Istibdā'* استبضاع (known in the Hindu religion as *Ni'og*).[1]

The third form of "marriage" was that a group of not more than ten men would all sleep with the same woman. When the woman fell pregnant and delivered, she would call for all the men she had been intimate with. None of them were exempted from attending. The woman would then tell the men, "You are all aware of this matter." She would point to one man – whomever she chose – and declared that her child was his offspring. The chosen man was obligated to acknowledge the child as his own.

The fourth type of relationship was, basically, prostitution. To indicate her availability, a woman would place a flag at the doorstep of her home, and many different men would have intimate relations with her. When she would fall pregnant and deliver the child, an expert in determining parentage of children would be called. The expert would take note of the men who had visited the prostitute, and based on the apparent physical features of the child, would determine who the father of the child was. The man who was picked had no choice but to acknowledge the child.

The Messenger of Allah ﷺ abrogated each one of these forms of "marriage" except for the first, which still exists today.[2]

Other Forms of Intimate Relations

Cohabitation took place in other forms as well. In Arabia's tribal society, battles took place extremely often – and to the victor went the spoils. The victorious tribe of a battle would seize the women of the defeated tribe and keep them as slave-girls, to use as they wished. Children born to these women lived in a state of limbo: they were neither legitimate nor free.

1. Mannu Dharam Shastar, P. 212.
2. Sahīh-ul-Bukhāri: 5127.

Pagan Arabia placed no limit to the number of wives one man could have.[1] Men would often marry two women who were blood sisters; it was allowed for a man to marry his step-mother after his father's death[2]. Man alone had the unrestricted right to divorce.[3]

Adultery was common and prevalent in every level of society, with few exceptions. Only those men and women who had great personal dignity ever refrained from committing this type of lewdness.

Nonetheless, adultery was no source of shame, for majority, in pagan Arabia. This is demonstrated by an incident reported in Sunan Abu Dawud, which relates that a man once stood up and said, 'O Messenger of Allahﷺ, such and such man is my son. I committed adultery with his mother during the Age of Ignorance.'

The Messenger of Allah ﷺ replied, "Such claims are baseless in Islam. The Age of Ignorance is over and everything relating to it has gone. From now on, a child shall be attributed to the man whose wife or bondwoman gives birth to it, and the adulterer shall be stoned."[4]

On the eve of the Conquest of Makkah, Sa'd bin Abi Waqqas and 'Abd bin Zam'ah ﷺ disputed over the son of Zam'ah's slave-woman. They went to the Prophet ﷺ, and Sa'd ﷺ said: 'He (the boy) is my nephew. My brother took a pledge from me concerning him.'

'Abd bin Zam'ah ﷺ objected. 'He is my brother. He is the son of my father's slave woman. He was born on his bed.'

The Prophet ﷺ said, "O 'Abd bin Zam'ah, he is your brother. The child belongs to the man on whose bed he is born, but an adulterer shall be stoned."[5]

Female Infanticide

The Arabs were well-known to have a great love for children, both male and female. Their poetry contained many verses attesting to their devotion to their children.

1. Sunan Abi Dāwūd: 2241,2242.
2. As-Sunan Al-Kubrā Li'l-Baihaqi: 7/163.
3. Sunan Abi Dāwūd: 2195.
4. Sunan Abi Dāwūd: 2274.
5. Sahīh-ul-Bukhāri: 2053.

إِنَّمَا أَوْلَادُنَا بَيْنَنَا أَكْبَادُنَا تَمْشِي عَلَى الْأَرْضِ

"Our children among us are our livers walking on earth."

At the same time, some pagan Arabs considered the birth of daughters to be both shameful and disgraceful. They would bury their own daughters alive rather than suffer the ignominy.[1] Others would kill their children out of fear for poverty, in the disgraceful belief that daughters were a waste of resources. But it is difficult to say that this cruelty was prevalent because the Arabs were more in need of their issue, comparatively, for their safety from their enemy, and they realized it well.[2]

Tribal Racism

The Arab social system was based on tribal consciousness and tribal partisanship. The oft-repeated motto was (أُنْصُرْ أَخَاكَ ظَالِمًا أَوْ مَظْلُومًا) "Help your brother, whether he be the oppressor or oppressed.[3] In their practice, this meant that they would support their fellow tribesman no matter what he did to others.

Allah's Messenger ﷺ re-interpreted these words for Muslims – to help one's brother when he was the oppressor meant stopping him from oppressing others. Arab tribes often fought each other for position, power and prestige; each one wanted to surpass his rival. Most of their battles were rooted in ancient tribal rivalries. The most notable examples of tribal rivalry were the long-standing grudges between the Aus and the Khazraj, the Abs and Dhabyān, and the Bakr and Taghlib.

In addition to their rivalries, the pagan Arabs also placed great importance on tribal alliances. As well, fighting would usually stop during the Sacred Months, which was a mercy to the common people who struggled for their livelihood.[4]

1. An-Nahl: 16:58-59.
2. Bani Israel/Isrā':17:31.
3. This is not just an Arab proverb but it has become now a Hadeeth for the Prophet ﷺ himself said these words. See Sahīh-ul-Bukhāri: 2443, 2444.
4. Sahīh-ul-Bukhāri: 4376; Fat'h-ul-Bāri: 8/114. see also Ar-Rahīq-ul-Makhtūm, P. 57.

Dūmat al-Jandal

Famous Annual Fairs and Bazaars

Dūmat al-Jandal: From the first to the fifteenth of *Rabee' al-Awwal,* a great bazaar was held in the area of Dūmat al-Jandal. After the fifteenth, trade activity became less hectic but continued until the end of the month. The tribes of Banu Jadeelah and Banu Kalb lived in this region.

Mushaqqar: This market was held near Hijr in Bahrain (modern Ahsa') from the beginning of *Jamād al-Ākhirah* to the end of the same month. The Persians used to bring their merchandise for sale. The tribes of Abd al-Qais and Tameem lived in the territory nearby.

Suhār (صُحار)**:** This was a five-day fair beginning on the 1st of *Rajab*. It was held in Oman (عُمان).

Dabā: This market was also held on the coast of Oman on the last day of *Rajab*. Tradesmen from Sindh, India, China and other countries of

Ruins of Sūq Okaz

East and West would come and take part in it.

Shihr (شِحر): This bazaar was held at Mahrah (Hadramaut) at the foot of the hill where the grave of Prophet Hūd عليه السلام is said to be located. The tribesmen of Banu Muhārib dwelt in the neighbourhood. The fair began in the middle of the month of *Sha'bān*.

Sūq 'Aden (Aden Bazaar): It was a ten-day bazaar beginning from 1st of *Ramadān*.

Sūq San'ā': This bazaar was held from the middle of *Ramadān* and continued until the end of the month.

Rābiyah: This market was held in Hadramaut, near the territory of the Kindah tribe. It ran concurrently with the Okaz bazaar, from the middle of *Dhul Qa'dah* to the end of the month.

Okaz ('Ukāz): The fair of Okaz was one of the largest and most popular events of the Arabs. It was held near 'Arafāt, and several tribes regularly took part in this bazaar, including Quraish, Ghatfān, Hawāzin, Banu Aslam, Khuzā'ah, 'Uql, and Mustaliq.

Ruins of Suhār Oman

During the fair, poets would recite their *Qasā'id* (ballads), orators would deliver their speeches, and rulers would proclaim their decrees, while Shaikhs would settle the provisions of their treaties. This bazaar started from the middle of *Dhul Qa'dah* and continued till the end of the month.

Dhul-Majāz: This bazaar was held near Okaz, from the 1st of Dhul Hijjah to the 8th of *Dhul Hijjah (Yaum Tarwiyah)*. After that, people would depart for Mina. Another bazaar named Majinnah was also held north of Dhul-Majāz.

Natāt (نطاة)**:** This market was held in Kheybar from the 10th of *Muharram* to the end of the month.

Hajr (حجر)**:** This market was held in Yamāmah from the 10th of *Muharram* to the end of the month.[1]

1. Al-Azminah Wa'l-Amkinah Li'l-Marzūqi: 170-161/2.

Ruins of Dabā

Virtues of the Arabs

Although it is true that the pagan Arabs had many vile and outrageous customs which transgressed both common sense and Allah's boundaries, they also displayed various excellent characteristics.

Generosity

Generosity was a characteristic which played a huge role in Arab society. It was a quality both admired and envied; individuals and tribes alike would vie with each other in displays of hospitality. It is said that half of Arabian poetry revolved around the theme of generosity. In times of severe winter and starvation, if a guest knocked on the door of a poor Arab with no possession save a camel to support him and his family, he would rise up and slaughter his camel for the guest. There are many examples of this admirable quality of the Arabs, from both the pre-Islamic era as well as the modern day. Hātem at-Ṭā'iy, an Arab poet from the age of Jahiliyyah, was famous for his many displays and expressions of munificence, such that his name became a proverb for benevolence.

The noblemen of the Arabs would volunteer to pay the blood-money and bear others' financial burdens to stop further bloodshed and collateral destruction. This would be done not out of love for life and abhorrence of violence, but as a means of outshining other tribal chiefs.

The Arabs would drink heavily and pride themselves on their intoxication, which would cause them to be more generous. They would call the grapevine *"al-Karam"* and wine *"Bint al-Karam,"* which was a play on words, as the Arabic word for generosity was *"Karam."*

The poet Antarah bin 'Amr bin Shaddād 'Absi said in his *Mu'allaqah,*

فَإِذَا شَرِبْتُ فَإِنَّنِي مُسْتَهْلِكٌ مَالِي، وَعِرْضِي وَافِرٌ لَّمْ يُكْلَمِ

وَإِذَا صَحَوْتُ فَمَا أُقَصِّرُ عَنْ نَّدَى وَكَمَا عَلِمْتِ شَمَائِلِي وَ تَكَرُّمِي

"When I am drunk, I lavish my money, but my honour remains safe, untarnished. When I come to myself, I am not lax in generosity, as you (o my beloved!) know my morals and generosity.[1]

When they gambled, many times it was not to make money, but to give away in charity to help the needy and the poor. It was in reference to this that the Qur'anic Verse which forbade alcohol and gambling referred to their perceived benefit:

﴿وَإِثْمُهُمَآ أَكْبَرُ مِن نَّفْعِهِمَا﴾

"But the sin of them is greater than their benefit."[2]

Fulfilling Oaths

The fulfillment of oaths and promises were considered a great virtue. An honourable pagan Arab would keep his word, whatever the circumstances were. He would be willing to sacrifice his life, that of his household, and his property in order to fulfill a vow. Examples of

1. As-Sab'-ul-Mu'àllaqāt: Mu'allaqa 'Antara bin Shaddād.
2. Al-Baqarah: 2:219.

how important it was for them to fulfill their oaths and promises can be seen in the stories of Hāni bin Mas'ūd Shaibāni, Samu'āl (Samuel) bin 'Ādiyā, and Hājib bin Zurarah.[1]

Honour and Determination

The Arabs prized their dignity and honour over all else and could not bear oppression. They would guard their reputations fiercely, and never hesitated to take up arms for the sake of their self-respect. They were willing to sacrifice their lives and families in the name of honour. The Arabs were also known for their determination. Once they made up their mind about something, considering it a means of dignity, they would strive hard to achieve their goals. Nothing could deter them from carrying out their plans.

Clemency and Honesty

Gentleness, clemency, and forbearance were virtues in the sight of the Arabs of *jāhiliyyah* (ignorance), but they were quite rare amongst hot-tempered Arabs. As for honesty, it was ingrained within the Arabs. They lived in the desert, relatively cut off from civilization, and were thus sheltered from the tainted sophistication and political deceits of more developed societies. As a result, the Arabs in general were a simple folk who were, for the most part, truthful, honest, straightforward, frank and simple. The advent of Islam focused and channeled the energy and virtues of the Arabs into positive and constructive goals; it provided for them a high and noble ideal which made them suitable for leading mankind.[2]

1. See the story of Hāni bin Mas'ūd in "Victory of Arabs in the Battle of Zi Qār" under "Lakhmi kingdom of Hīra (Iraq)".
2. Ar-Rahīq-ul-Makhtūm, P. 58-60.

Arabic Language and Literature

The literature of any community or society mirrors the collective thoughts and emotions of those people. To understand a people, the most descriptive source is their own literature. In an effort to understand the Arabs, one must turn to their own works of prose and poetry as well.

ARABIC: The Mother of Semitic Languages

Arabic is one of the Semitic languages[1] spoken by the prominent Arab tribes of the Arabian Peninsula.

Sayyed Suleman Nadwi states that "Arabia was the original home of Banu Sām (the progeny of Shem). Therefore, whatever name the Semitic language may have, geographically it should be called Arabic though, of course, it may be called Aramaic in the national sense. Since the most prominent Semitic tribe was Banu Iram bin Sām whose remains are found in Arabia, Iraq and Syria, the Aramaic language may well have been the first branch of Arabic. Prophet Ibrāhīm عليه السلام spoke Aramaic Arabic. That is also the opinion of Reverend Gabriel

A tablet of Aramaic Script

1. Semitic languages refer to the languages spoken by the different tribes of the descendants of Sam (Shem) son of Noah عليه السلام.

Farwahi, a Maronite Christian and professor of Syriac and Arabic languages: "Aramaic was the language of Abraham, the ancestor of the Hebrews." This proves that Ismāʿīl's ancestral language was not Hebrew but Aramaic Arabic.[1]

In any case, since he lived amongst Banu Jurhum for a great deal of time, he mastered the pure Arabic language.[2]

A tablet of Sabaean Language

Theodore Noeldeke, the European Orientalist, says: "The Aramaic language was spoken in Iraq and Syria. Moreover, its traces have been found even in Egypt and Iran."

Sabaean, Himyari and Abyssinian were the languages of southern Arabia. Sabaean had long since become extinct, but the Himyari and Abyssinian languages continued to be spoken at the beginning of the Islamic era. Himyari was the language of the People of the Trenches *(Ashāb Al-Ukhdūd)* while Abyssinian that of the Owners of the Elephants *(Ashāb Al-Feel)*.

ʿArim (meaning dam), a word of Sabaean-Himyari language,

1. Tarīkh Ard-ul-Qur'ān (Kāmil): 2/98-99.
2. Fat'h-ul-Bāri: 6/488.

A tablet of Himyari Language

occurs in the Qur'an while many words of the Abyssinian language, current among the Christian Arabs, are also found in the Qur'an. For example,

Nifāq (Hypocrisy), *Suhūf* (books), *Burhān* (Evidence), *Marj* (Meadow), *Mā'idah* (Table Spread), *Mishkāt* (Lamp), *Surah, Hawāri* (apostle), *Istabraq* (Silk), *Waraq* (Leaf).

A tablet of Abyssinian Language

Note the difference in the meanings of some of the words of Northern and Southern Arabic:

Word	Northern Arabic	Southern Arabic
Dhu ذو	owner (e.g. *Dhu'l Hijjah*)	king (e.g. Dhu-Raidan)
Bait بيت	house *(Baitullah)*	Fort
Hadar حضر	settled population, civilized region	town

The Nabataen language, which was spoken by the people of Hijr, is very close to the Arabic of the Qur'an. The Nabataen script is also close to the ancient Arabic script, and similar to the Kufi style of writing. The tribes of northern Arabia spoke the same words with a different accent or pronounced them differently or spoke them with different vowel marks. For example:

1. Banu Tameem changed the initial *Hamza* (ء) into the letter *'Ain* (ع): *'Aslam* (عسلم) for *Aslam* (اسلم). They also used the letter *Gaf* (گ) which is non-existent in Arabic, as, for example, *Gabr* (گبر) instead of *Jabr* (جبر).
2. Banu Qudā'ah changed the letter *Ya* (ي) into *Jeem* (ج). Example:

Tameemaj for Tameemi

3. Banu Sa'd used *Nun* (ن) for *'Ain* (ع). Example: *Anta* (أنطى) for *A'ta* (أعطى).
4. Quraish and Asad tribesmen use *Fathah* or *Dammah* over *Ya* to indicate present tense. Other tribes used *Kasrah* for the same purpose. They said *Yif'alo* (يِفعَل) instead of *Yaf'alo* (يَفعُل).
5. The Rabee'ah and Mudar tribesmen added the letter *Sheen* to the letter *Kaf* (ك) used for the feminine of the second person. For example *'Alaikish* (عَلَيكِش) for *'Alaiki* (عَلَيكِ).[1]

Periods of Arabic Literature

Arabic literature has been divided into five periods:

1. **Age of Ignorance (Pre-Islamic):** This period stretches for about 150 years, that is, up to the Islamic times.
2. **Early Islamic Era (Umayyad Dynasty):** This period began at the emergence of Islam to the point that the Abbasids took power, that is, up to the end of 132 AH/ 750 CE.
3. **Abbasid Dynasty:** This period began at the establishment of the Abbasid empire and ended with the Tartar invasion of Baghdad and its eventual destruction, up to 656 AH/ 1258 CE. The Tartars are one of the Turanian tribes who were initially settled in Mongolia, north of China, and later, under the leadership of Genghis Khan, spread across wide areas of Central and Western Asia and Eastern Europe.
4. **Turkish Era:** This period began at the destruction of Baghdad and ended with the beginning of the *Nuhzah Jadeedah* (نهضة جديدة ---modern movement), by the year 1220 AH/1805 CE. The Turkish states included the Seljuks, the Mameluke kingdom of Egypt and Syria, the Tartari states of Asia, and the Ottoman Empire spanning the three continents of Asia, Europe and Africa.
5. **Modern Movement *(Nuhzah Jadeedah)*:** This period begins

1. Tarīkh Ard-ul-Qur'ān (Kāmil): 2/103.

from the beginning of the rule of Muhammad Ali Pasha of Egypt (1220 AH/1805 CE) and continues to our times.

Characteristic Features of Arabic Language

Arabic is one of the oldest languages in the world, and the richest in vocabulary. It is the sweetest language in speech, the most elegant in style, stunning in effect and widest in its coverage of emotions and feelings.

Arabic was the language of an illiterate (Ummi) people; the Arabs knew neither the Greek sciences nor the arts and crafts of China. They passed away from this world but left a legacy, their rich language, which continued across centuries, generation after generation, and suited every age and every clime. Were it without a life-giving soul of its own, it would have long since perished like its other coeval languages.

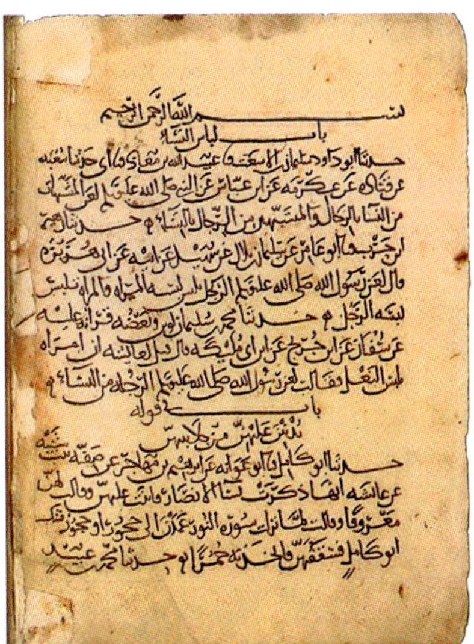

A page of Hand written Sunan Abu Dawood

A page from a beautifuly Designed Quran

Development of Arabic

Arabic developed for a number of reasons which were non-existent in the case of other languages. For example, its inherent capacity to coin new words giving a range of meanings, inflection of words, set principles governing derivatives, use of figures of speech, allusion and metonymy, and profusion of synonyms, in addition to rules of *Qalb, Ibdal, Naht* and *Ta'reeb*. Finally, the Qur'ān was revealed in Arabic, the most important reason of its survival over the ages.

Adnāni Arabic

According to major scholars of language studies, the formal Arabic language that exists today, which is used in the Qur'ān and *Ahādeeth*, is a mixture of the languages of those tribes who lived in the Arabian Peninsula. It is mainly 'Adnāni Arabic.

Variety of Dialects

As a people, Arabs are a mixture of two major tribes: Banu Qahtān and Banu 'Adnān, who in turn are made up of several sub-tribes and groups. The dialects of those tribes were united on fundamental rules but differed on subsidiary and minor ones. In Yemen, the Himyari language was once dominant but later faded and became extinct. However, some Himyari words merged with the 'Adnāni language and thus survived.

On the other hand, the 'Adnāni language (which later on transformed into the Mudari language) dominated over other languages. In fact, it even dominated the Himyari language in its own native place.

Arab Orators

The pagan Arabs were illiterate, warlike and bellicose. Their battles and disputes continued for years. Each tribe would incite its people to fight and take revenge on the others, and to that end, they hired the services of an orator, glib of tongue. At other times, when a battle was about to break out, the orators would stand up and advise caution, remind people of the horrors of war, and try to calm them down and urge reconciliation. The themes of their orations were varied, but in general, they would dwell on the merits of their tribes, boast of their lineage, and brag about the valour and virtue of their ancestors.

Orators were many, but the most famous of them were Qus bin Sā'idah Iyadi, Ka'b bin 'Lu'ayy, Dhu'l-Isba' Harthān bin Muhrith, Qais bin Kharijah bin Sinān Dhabyāni, Khuwailad bin 'Amr Ghatfāni, and Aktham bin Saifi. Ka'b bin Lu'ayy was the great grandfather of the Prophet ﷺ.

Qus bin Sā'idah Iyadi:

Qus bin Sā'idah Iyadi has been acknowledged as one of the greatest Arab orators in history. His name became a synonym for eloquence, wisdom and good advice. He was also monotheist and believed in the resurrection of the dead and the Hereafter. He urged the Arabs to shun idol-worship and believe in the Unity of God. These were his favourite themes and the focus of his poetry in fairs and public gatherings.

It is said that he was the first person to stand up on a high ground to deliver his orations and the first to use the words *Amma Ba'd* (meaning 'but after that').[1] He was also the first man to lean on a sword or staff while delivering his sermons. People would go to him to settle their disputes, and he would give wise and correct judgement.

Once he went to the Byzantine ruler. The Caesar asked him: 'What is the highest wisdom'? 'To know oneself,' he replied. Caesar asked: 'What is the highest knowledge?' Qus replied: 'To keep to the limit of one's knowledge.' Caesar asked another question: 'What is the greatest valour?' Qus answered: 'To preserve one's honour.' Finally, Caesar asked him: 'What is the greatest wealth?' He replied: 'The one spent to fulfill duties and rights'.

The Prophet(ﷺ), before he started his prophetic mission, once saw Qus seated on a dull grey camel, delivering his oration in the Okaz bazaar. He was impressed by the beauty of his oration and his opinions, praised him for his unique qualities. Qus lived for a long time, but he died a little before the Prophet started his mission.

His words were balanced, refined, and free from over exaggeration. His style was moving and effective. His rhymed prose (سجع - *Saj'*)[2] was

1. According to Hāfiz Ibn Hajar, it is highly controversial as to who used these words first. Prophet Jacob عليه السلام, Prophet David عليه السلام, Ya'rab bin Qahtān, Ka'b bin Lu'i, Sahbān bin Wā'il and Qus bin Sā'idah – each of them is credited with this honour. – (Fat'h-ul-Bārī: 520/2).
2. *Saj'* is a form of prose in which each sentence ends with a rhymed word. - (Al-Mu'jam-ul-Wasīt: See under '*Saj'*'; Wikipedia (Encyclopedia).

marked by short pauses and dominated his relaxed, leisurely style of oration.

Ahmad bin Ali bin Ahmad bin Abdullah Qalqashandi, in his book Sub'h al-'Asha, quotes one of the sermons he delivered in the Okaz bazaar:

[أَيُّهَا النَّاسُ! اِسْمَعُوا وَعُوا، مَنْ عَاشَ مَاتَ، وَمَنْ مَّاتَ فَاتَ، وَكُلُّ مَا هُوَ آتٍ آتٍ، لَيْلٌ دَاجٍ وَّنَهَارٌ سَاجٍ، وَسَمَاءٌ ذَاتُ أَبْرَاجٍ، وَ نُجُومٌ تَزْهَرُ، وَبِحَارٌ تَزْخَرُ، وَجِبَالٌ مُّرْسَاةٌ، وَأَرْضٌ مُّدْحَاةٌ، وَأَنْهَارٌ مُّجْرَاةٌ، إِنَّ فِي السَّمَاءِ لَخَبَرًا، وَإِنَّ فِي الْأَرْضِ لَعِبَرًا، مَابَالُ النَّاسِ يَذْهَبُونَ وَلَا يَرْجِعُونَ، أَرَضُوا فَأَقَامُوا أَمْ تُرِكُوا فَنَامُوا؟ يُقْسِمُ قُسٌّ بِاللّٰهِ قَسَمًا لَّا إِثْمَ فِيهِ! إِنَّ لِلّٰهِ دِينًا هُوَ أَرْضٰى لَكُمْ وَ أَفْضَلُ مِنْ دِينِكُمُ الَّذِي أَنْتُمْ عَلَيْهِ، إِنَّكُمْ لَتَأْتُونَ مِنَ الْأَمْرِ مُنْكَرًا]

'O people! Listen and remember. He who lives must die and he who dies is gone. That which is going to take place must take place. Night is dark and day still. The sky is full of Zodiacal signs and stars shine. The sea waves are rolling and mountains are firmly fixed. The earth is spread and rivers are flowing. Doubtless, the sky has a sign (pointing to the existence of the Creator) and there are lessons in the earth. What about men who depart but never return? Do they like to stay in where they are or have they been abandoned to sleep? Qus swears an oath in which there is no sin. Allah offers a faith which He prefers to yours, one which is better than yours. No doubt, you are committing an abomination."

It is said that Qus, after delivering this sermon, recited the following verses.

فِي الذَّاهِبِينَ الْأَوَّلِي مِنَ الْقُرُونِ لَنَا بَصَائِرُ

"Surely, in those who have passed away before us, there are lessons for us."

لَمَّا رَأَيْتُ مَوَارِدًا لِّلْمَوْتِ لَيْسَ لَهَا مَصَادِرُ

"When I saw that death has doors of entrance but no door of

exit;

وَرَأَيْتُ قَوْمِي نَحْوَهَا تَمْضِي الْأَكَابِرُ وَالْأَصَاغِرُ

I noted that all my people, big and small, are going towards death."

لَا يَرْجِعُ الْمَاضِي إِلَيَّ وَلَا مِنَ الْبَاقِينَ غَابِرُ

"None who has gone away comes back to me and none who remains will ever stay."[1]

Arab Poetry

The Arabs were poets by nature. Their nomadic lifestyle and their illiteracy meant that their history was not written down on paper and stored in a safe place; rather, their history, their values, and their emotions were kept alive through orally transmitted verse.

Arab poets have been divided and classified into four categories based on their chronology.

1. **Poets of *Jāhiliyyah*** (جاهليّين)**:** Refers to the poets of the Age of Ignorance.
2. ***Mukhadrameen*** (مخضرمين)**:** Poets whose life spans bridge the age of *Jāhiliyyah* and that of Islam.
3. **Poets of Islamic Age** (اسلاميين)**:** Those poets who grew up in Islamic milieu and retained the purity of Arabic. They are the poets of the Umayyad period.
4. **Modern Poets** (مولّدين)**:** Although they were of pure Arab extraction but they emerged during a period when the language had been defiled by the mixing together of Arabs and non-Arabs. Under this class come all the poets from the Abbasid period up to our present times.

Imra'ul Qais, Prince of Kindah

His title was *al-Malik ad-Daleel* (الملک الضّليل - the Wandering Prince), his surname Abul-Hārith, and his full name Hundaj bin

1. Subh-ul-A'shā: 255/1.

Hujr Kindi. He was a famous poet of Yemen (South Arabia) and the forerunner of the poets of the Age of Ignorance. His ancestors were the noblemen and kings of the tribe of Kindah. His mother's name was Fatimah bint Rabee'ah, a sister of Kulaib and Muhalhil Taghlibi. His father, Hujr, was the last king of Banu Kindah.

Imra'ul Qais grew up in Nejd among Banu Asad, the subjects of his father, and lived a luxurious lifestyle like that of any other prince. He spent his time in idle pursuits, drinking, love affairs, and writing romantic poetry which sometimes verged on the explicit and the obscene. He cared little for those things which could qualify him to rule and administer a state.

His father, the king, tried hard to prevent him from losing himself in frivolity, but Imra'ul Qais ignored him. Eventually, his father lost patience with him and threw him out, whereupon he was immediately beset by those who wanted to take advantage of him.

Ruins of the fort of Abul-Hārith

One day while he was carousing with his companions, he received the news of his father's death. Banu Asad had revolted against the king and killed him, due to his cruelty and habit of overtaxing his subjects. Fearing that his reaction to the news might upset his shallow companions, Imra'ul Qais showed no outward emotion, but remained silent before saying, "My father wasted my youth, and now that I have grown up, he laid on me the burden of avenging his blood. Today is the day of drinking, tomorrow the day of action."

To avenge his father's blood, he made preparations and, with the help of some tribes, launched attacks on Banu Asad's tribesmen and slew many of them. However, this did not slake his thirst for revenge.

There was animosity between Mundhir, the king of Hīrah, and the family of Imra'ul Qais dating back to the days when the Mundhir dynasty and Kaiqubād, the king of Persia, had fallen out. Imra'l Qais' grandfather, Hārith, had opposed the Mundhir kings in order to become the deputy ruler over Hīrah and a viceroy of the Persian emperor.

Now, Mundhir had rallied the tribes of Iyād, Bahrā' and Tanūkh against Imra'ul Qais. In the meanwhile, Nausherwan, the Persian emperor, also dispatched a cavalry of mounted soldiers in support of Mundhir. Obviously, Imra'ul Qais could not fight them all and, consequently, his supporters scattered.

He then sought refuge with several tribes, one after the other, until he reached Samuel bin 'Adiyā (d. 65 years before Hijra/ c.560 CE). Samuel kept Imra'ul Qais, his daughter, his armour, and his weapons in trust and the prince asked him to write a letter to Hārith bin Abi Shammar Ghassāni to help him reach the court of Caesar. He arrived at the Byzantine court and requested him for help to fight his enemies. Caesar prepared a legion of soldiers for him but before Imra'ul Qais could leave Constantinople, Caesar had a second thought, recalled the soldiers, and sent him a poisoned cloak. When Imra'ul-Qais put it on, his body broke out in blisters. The sickness became worse and he died when he reached Angora (modern Ankara) and there he was buried.

Imra'ul Qais' Poetry: Imra'ul Qais is said to be one of the earliest and the greatest of Arab poets, although other poets such Abu Dawood Iyādi and Muhalhil, his maternal uncle, had preceded him. Imra'ul Qais was the first poet to introduce themes which were novel in his time. He asks his companions to stay a while beside ruins and weep over the homes of the loved ones gone by. He was the first to compare women to deer, wild cows and eggs, and to use the term *Qaid al-Awābid* (قيد الاوابد) in praise of the horse. He made the initial erotic part of a *Qasīda (Tashbeeb)*[1] plaintive and melancholic. He is the innovator

1. Erotic part of a *Qasīda* in praise of one's beloved.

of unique metaphors. Eroticism, waywardness of youth, vicissitudes of life, and indifference of friends in times of hardships – these are the most dominant themes of his poetry. Some of his erotic sonnets are explicitly obscene and lewd. Wisdom, nobility and a feeling of kingly authority are only a few of things mentioned in his poetry.

فَظَلَّ الْعَذَارَى يَرْتَمِينَ بِلَحْمِهَا وَشَحْمٍ كَهُدَّابِ الدِّمَقْسِ الْمُفَتَّلِ

"The virgin girls began throwing at each other the flesh and fat of the she-camel which were like nooses of twined silk."

وَلَوْ أَنَّ مَا أَسْعَى لِأَدْنَى مَعِيشَةٍ كَفَانِي وَلَمْ أَطْلُبْ قَلِيلٌ مِّنَ الْمَالِ

وَلٰكِنَّمَا أَسْعَى لِمَجْدٍ مُّؤَثَّلٍ وَقَدْ يُدْرِكُ الْمَجْدَ الْمُؤَثَّلَ أَمْثَالِي

"Had I aspired for simple living, a little money would suffice me: I would not ask for more. But I aspire for lasting glory, and men like me get lasting glory."

Imra'ul Qais' expressions were rough, like that of a bedouin. He used crude and coarse words, although the introductory parts of his Qasidas are full of meaning. His verses were plaintive, amatory and easy to understand. He set fine examples for the following generations of poets. He says in praise of his beloved:

وَإِذْ هِيَ تَمْشِي كَمَشْيِ النَّزِيفِ يَصْرَعُهُ بِالْكَثِيبِ الْبُهُرْ

بَرَهْرَهَةٌ رُّخْصَةٌ رُّودَةٌ كَخُرْعُوبَةِ الْبَانَةِ الْمُنْفَطِرِ

"She walked like one drained of blood, gasping for breath, treading sand hills with faltering steps.[1] She has a soft body, young and delicate, like a branch of willow tree which has just sprouted."[2]

1 He likens the gait of his beloved to that of a man who has lost a lot of blood and become too weak to walk, especially across sand dunes.

2. Tarīkh-i-Adab-i-Arabi (Urdu), PP. 14, 17, 21, 42, 64-67,130-137. See also Ash-Shi'r Wash-Shu'arā' Li-Ibn Qutaiba, P. 23-37.

Chapter - 6

Neighbours of the Arabs,

Their Kingdoms and Religions

A review of the people before the Prophet's era, their religions, kingdoms and social, economic and political conditions

ٱلَّذِينَ يَتَّبِعُونَ

ٱلرَّسُولَ ٱلنَّبِىَّ ٱلْأُمِّىَّ

ٱلَّذِى يَجِدُونَهُۥ مَكْتُوبًا عِندَهُمْ

فِى ٱلتَّوْرَىٰةِ وَٱلْإِنجِيلِ

"Those who follow the Messenger, the Prophet who can neither read nor write, whom they find written with them in the Taurāt (Torāh) and the Injīl (Gospel)."

Al-A'raf 7:157

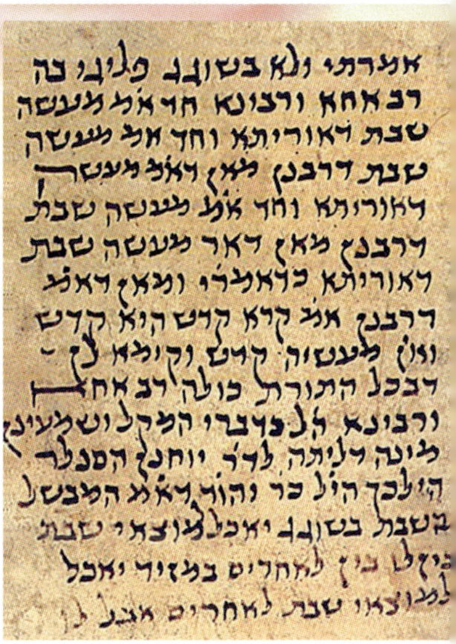

In This Chapter

Muhammad, the Messenger of Allah (ﷺ) was, without a doubt, the greatest man in history. His teachings had far-reaching effects. He revolutionized the entire world. In order to understand his life and mission, it is imperative to have full knowledge of the conditions of the world during his times and those before his birth. Without such a detailed study it would be difficult to realize the full dimensions of Allah's Messenger's teachings, their effects worldwide, and the impact of his personality on Arabia and other lands beyond Arabia's shores.

To that end, this chapter looks at the civilized nations of his age, their religions, their kingdoms and their social, economic and political conditions. Such a study is sure to bring into the right perspective the relative need, importance, and the universality of the Prophet's revolutionary mission.

Ruins of Persepolis

Kingdom of Iran

In ancient times, the people of the world were divided into two major races. One race was that of the Semites, who were settled in the valleys of the Tigris and the Euphrates, and the other was that of the Aryans who lived in Central Asia. Around 5000 BC, the Aryans lived like nomads, wandering from place to place, with some tribes settling around the Caspian Sea. Around 2000 BC, they split up into two large groups. One group migrated to the south and southeast and settled in regions which later on came to be known as Iran and India. The other group made their way to Greece, Germany, Italy and other countries which now make up Europe. Some tribes from the first group also settled in mountains and valleys east of Tigris and Euphrates. This region was named Iran.[1]

1 Qadīm Tahzīben Aur Mazāhib, P. 104.

One branch of the Aryans settled in western Iran, the central region of Medea near the Zagros Mountains. They were called Medes. The other branch crossed over Khurasan and arrived in southern Iran (Pars or Fars). They were called Parsi.[1]

Pars, Fars and Iran Shahr

In the southwest of Iran was a region named Persis, named after the tribe that had settled there. Plaoutus, a famous Roman writer, used the word Persia in one of his writings. The word Pars or Persia used for Iran is derived from a Greek-Roman title, Persae, which was used in ancient Iran for the kings of Achaemenid dynasty.

The one of column at the entrance gate of Persepolis ancient city at Shiraz , Iran

Persia (or Pars) is Iran of today. During the Islamic era, the word 'Fars' or 'Faris' applied to this region. Similarly, the word Al-Furs often used in Arabic literature is used for all the people of Iran. It is synonymous with the Arabic word *al-'Ajam* (foreigners).

The name 'Iran,' which was derived from the word 'Aryana,' is sometimes used for southern Iran, sometimes for the whole of Iran and sometimes for the central part of the Sassanid kingdom. The Sassanid kings called themselves the 'kings of Iran and Aneeran.'[2]

Writing on Iran Shahr, Yaqūt Hamawi said: "Iraq (Bilād Iraq), Fars, Jibāl and Khurasān – all are collectively called 'Iran Shahr' (the country of Iran) while according to al-Asma'ī, Ard Iraq (that is, Iraq) was called *'Dil Iran Shahr'* (literally, the heart of Iran Shahr). In his

1 Urdu Encyclopedia of Islam: 3/635.
2 Urdu Encyclopedia of Islam: 3/627.

opinion, the Arabs arabicized the middle word, Iran, and called it Iraq. On the other hand, the Persians of the post-Islamic era claimed that 'Iran' was the name of Arfakhshad bin Sām bin Nūh. In other words, according to them, Iran Shahr meant the 'Land of Arfakhshad'.[1]

Mythology gives a different account. It is said that Hoshang, the son of Kiumerth (کیو مرث), named his country Iran. When his son, Pars, was enthroned, his country was called 'the country of Pars.' In the Islamic era, Firdausi's Shahnama revived the myths of this ancient land and the name of Iran became popular again.

This word is also found in the writings of Abul-Fadhl bin Mulla Mubarak, vol. 1: 'Shah Abbas Safawi (1587 CE – 1629 CE), king of the land of Iran.'

Coin of Pahlavi Era

1 Mu'jam-ul-Buldān: See under 'Iran'.

In any case, Arab historians continued calling Iran 'the country of Fars.' It was only in 1935 that 'Iran' became the official name of the country, and the same is used in Arabic and other languages.[1]

The Iranian Empire

During the times of Pars bin Hoshang, the king of ancient Iran, the Iranian empire was very extensive. It included Baluchistan, Kech, Mekran, Kirman, Ghaur, Bamyan, Kabulistan, Sistan, Zablistan (Afghanistan), Khorasan, *Ma Wara-un-Nahr* (Transoxiana), Resht, Isfahan, Mazandaran, Astrabad, Gorgan (Jurjan), Faris, Laristan, Khuzistan, Punjab, Kurdistan, Sherwan (Azerbaijan), Babel (Babylon), Mosul (Iraq), and Diyār Bakr (Turkey).[2]

Jamshed, Afrasiyab, Rustam and Sohrab

Jamshed or Jem is an important figure in the early history of Iran. His kingdom came to an end at the hands of Dahhak, but a man from the family of Jamshed, with the help of Kaveh the Ironsmith, defeated the tyrant Dahhak and re-conquered Iran. Later on, the kingdom of Iran split into two parts. Menuchehr took over the territory up to the bank of river Oxus, while the territory beyond the Oxus *(Ma-Wara-an-Nahr)* fell to the lot of Afrasiyab. The territory of the latter was called Turan (Turkistan). This event most likely took place sometime between 2500 BC and 2200 BC.

The Persian Empire declined and shrank in size until it was reduced to the central province of Fars. This was followed by the era of the

1 Urdu Encyclopedia of Islam: 3/627-628.
2 Urdu Encyclopedia of Islam: 3/627.

Ruins of Imperial Treasury at Persepolis, Iran

Naqsh e Rostam [Pasargadae (Istakhar) Iran]

Kayāni kings: Kaikubad, Kaikaus, Kaikhosrau, Lahrasap, Gashtasap and Asfandyar. Rustam, the son of Zal bin Sam, was a famous wrestler of this age. Rustam's son, Sohrab, was in the service of the king of Turan. He was accidentally killed by his father during the Iran-Turan war. They both were unaware of each other's identity during the fierce duel.[1]

Cyrus the Great or Dhu'l-Qarnain

Gurash (Korash) was a young man of the Achaemenid dynasty of Pars. He has been called several different names: Cyrus by Greeks, Khoras or Korash by Hebrews, and Qūrush by Arabs. In Old Persian he is called Khurs, and in modern Persian as Korash Kabīr or Korosh Buzurg.[2]

In 549 BC Cyrus, the king of Persia, conquered Medea and became the king of all Iran. He was the founder of the Achaemenid dynasty. In 546 BC, Cyrus occupied Lydia (Asia Minor) and in 538 BC his forces entered Babel, the main city of Chaldea (Iraq). Iraq remained a part of the Iranian empire until the beginning of the Islamic era. Abul-Kalam

1 Husn-ul-Lughāt (Persian): See under 'Rustam and Sohrāb'.

2. Ashab-i-Kahf aur Ya'jūj Maj'ūj by Abul-Kalām Azād, P. 32; Bible: Daniel 1:21; Gawan Encyclopedia (Persian), P. 368-369.

Azad and Abul-A'la Maududi, the two modern commentators of the Qur'ān, say that it is Cyrus, the monotheist king of Iran, to whom the Qur'ān refers to as Dhu'l-Qarnain. Cyrus allowed the Jews, whom Nebuchadnezzar had driven out of Palestine and forced them to live in exile in Iraq, to return to Palestine. Later, Cyrus's son, Cambyses (529 BC - 521 BC) invaded Egypt and annexed it to the Persian Empire.

Writing on Dhu'l-Qarnain, Abul-Kalam Azad goes on to say: "Alexander the Great was a great conqueror. He conquered many countries and built up a vast, extensive empire in both east and west. This naturally led many commentators of the Qur'ān to guess that Alexander could well be the Dhu'l-Qarnain of the Qur'ān. Imam Razi also took Alexander as Dhu'l-Qarnain. This is gravely incorrect. Judged from any angle, Alexander could not possibly be Dhu'l-Qarnain as mentioned in the Qur'ān. He was not a monotheist, nor a just king, nor generous and magnanimous towards the conquered nations nor he built any barrier as was reported in the Qur'ān. On the other hand, the Companions and the pious predecessors are reported to have interpreted Allah's Statement قلنا يا ذا القرنين "We said: O Dhu'l-Qarnain" as proof that he was a prophet. Among the later generations, Ibn Taymiyyah and Ibn Katheer are two prominent scholars who supported this interpretation. As for Cyrus, he was a Zoroastrian ruler, a prophet, and the first king of Achaemenid dynasty. According to Greek historian Zenophen, he was not only a king but a humanitarian, supporter and a kind father-figure to nations in general. With one stroke of his pen, he abrogated all the cruel law of the Assyrian and Babylonian kings. The Book of Isaiah says about him: God says that 'Cyrus is my shepherd' and 'He is my Messiah.' Jeremiah had forecast that he would deliver the children of Israel from

Tomb of Cyrus the Great

Iranian Khorasan is divided into three provinces nowadays i.e. Northern Khorasan, Radhavi Khorasan and Southern Khorasan. Capital of Radhavi Khorasan is Mashhad where Imam Ali Raza is lying buried.
Khorasan
Boundary of Ancient Khorasan
Iranian Khorasan
International Boundary
River
China (Eastern Turkestan)
Jamu & Kashmir
Hindustan
Pakistan
Kabul
Ghazni
Bamiyan
Afghanistan
Baluchistan
Arabian Sea
Makran
Helmand R.
Lake Helmand
Sistan
Gulf of Oman
Kazakhstan
Khujand
Tajikistan
Termiz
Balkh
Zarafshan R.
Samarqand
Syr Daryo
Turkestan
Khorasan
Hari Rud
Herat
Merv
Uzbekistan
Bukhara
Amu Daryo
Aral Sea
Turkmenistan
Iranian Khorasan
Iran (Persia)
Kazakhstan
Caspian Sea
Tehran
Rey
Pasargadae
Ecbatana (Hamadan)
Chechnya
Russia
Georgia
Armenia
Azerbaijan
Azerbaijan
Turkey
Iraq
Kuwait
Saudi Arabia
Bahrain
Qatar
Persian Gulf
United Arab Emirates
Oman
Oman
0
500
km

Map. 20

the tyranny of the Babylonians.

Archeologists have found among the ruins of Astakhar an image of Cyrus, carved in stone, with the wings of a falcon on both his sides and two horns on his head like those of a lamb. Daniel had also seen in a dream a lamb with two horns and Gabriel interpreted to him his dream, saying that the two horns represented the twin kingdoms of Medea and Persia. It should be noted that Dhu'l-Qarnain also means 'the one with two horns.'

From the words of the Qur'ān, it is quite clear that Dhu'l-Qarnain was a believer in Allah and the Hereafter, that he obeyed the commandments of Allah and believed that all his achievements were by the grace of Allah. These attributes can also be applied to Cyrus. The Qur'ān also mentions Dhu'l-Qarnain's exploits in both the East and the West; Cyrus was famous for having conquered both eastern and western territories. Moreover, according to Herodotus and Zenophon, Cyrus took measures to stop the raids of Scythians, a Mongoloid people (assumed to be Gog and Magog) while there is no evidence of Alexander taking such preventive measures. This seems to suggest that the Barrier of Gog and Magog was built by Cyrus. As well, there is a river in Caucasia which was called Gorish (modern name: Kur), and named in Roman inscriptions as Cyrus. European travellers such as Anthony Jenkenson (1557 CE) refer to this river as Cyrus in their writings, while Armenian inscriptions call the barrier Phak Kurai (Door of Kur). Kur is a variant of the name Gorish, and many consider these facts to be strong evidence that the Cyrus of Iranian history is the man named Dhu'l-Qarnain in the Qur'ān.[1]

Babylon great walls

1. Summary of Ashāb-ul-Kahf Aur Ya'jūj Wa Ma'jūj.

The Rule of the Achaemenids

Cyrus was known far and wide to be a wise and just king but, his successors were not. How they ruled can best be understood through events recorded by historians.

Cambyses and Darius

The Greek historian Herodotus narrates a strange event from the reign of Cambyses.

"One day Cambyses asked one of his courtiers, Peraxapus, about the public opinion regarding him. Peraxapus replied, "All the people are full of praise for Your Majesty except that Your Majesty drinks too much." On hearing this answer, Cambyses became furious and said, 'Look, there is your son standing. I will shoot an arrow. If it strikes him right in his heart, then the public is wrong. But if I miss the target, they are right and the alcohol has deranged my senses.' Then he picked up an arrow and shot at the target. The arrow struck Peraxapus' son in the chest and he collapsed.

Coin of Darius I

Cambyses then ordered for the son's chest to be cut open. When the wound was examined, it was found that the arrow had struck the son at the center of his heart. Cambyses was exhilarated and remarked, "This proves that the Iranian public is mad!" The now-grieving courtier said timidly, 'Indeed, such a clear shot is possible for none except Your Majesty.'

Cambyses was succeeded by Darius I, who conquered Gandhara (north Punjab and the Frontier province of Pakistan), Thrace, Macedonia, and Greece but, later in the Battle of Marathon (490 BC) suffered defeat at the hands of the Greeks. However, Darius I built a canal linking the Nile with the Red Sea, a remarkable achievement, for it opened a sea route from the Mediterranean Sea to the Persian Gulf via the Nile.[1] Darius I was followed by Xerxes, Artaxerxes Darazdast, Darius II, Artaxerxes II, Artaxerxes III, and Darius III.

Punishment by Boat

The Iranian kings would punish anyone who dared to insult or mock them. Many of these punishments were outrageous and shockingly cruel, such as burying the criminals alive while inside a wall, flaying off a man's skin while he was still alive, or nailing him down on planks. However, the punishment by boat was one of the most horrific and terrible of all the punishments which were met out.

The Achaemenid king Artaxerxes III's younger brother Korosh revolted against him and a fierce fight took place between the two forces. In the course of the battle, Korosh came up to the king and attacked him, but was killed by a soldier named Mehrdad. The king, of course, attributed this feat of bravery to himself.

One day Mehrdad got drunk and angry, and began to shout: 'The king pretends to be a hero. He brags that he slew Korosh when in fact,

1. Jawan Encyclopedia (Persian), P. 371.

Ruins of Persepolis the Capital of Achaemenid Empire

it was I who killed him.' When the king came to know of Mehrdad's announcement, he became furious and ordered the soldier to be given the punishment of boats.

Two boats were built, one fitting over the other. In one of them Mehrdad was laid, while the other was fixed over it. His fore limbs, feet and his mouth were kept out of the boat. He was then force-fed until he was full, and administered a laxative. His face was covered with honey which attracted swarms of ants and other worms which gnawed at his cheeks and lips. In the meantime, the laxative had its effect. The lower boat was filled with the filth. As days passed, worms bred in the stools, eating away at his intestines, heart and kidney. For seventeen long days he wallowed and convulsed in pain until he finally died.[1]

Persepolis *(Takht-i-Jamshed)* was the capital of the Achaemenid kings. Its remains are found in the northeast of Shiraz. Later, the capital was shifted to Susa. The Achaemenid Empire, at the peak of its power, consisted of 21 provinces and 46 nationalities.

End of the Achaemenid Empire

Darius III was the last king of the Achaemenid dynasty. In 330 BC, he was defeated by Alexander the Great and killed. Iran then came under the control of Seleucus, one of Alexander's generals. The Seleucids ruled Iran until 185 BC,[2] when they were replaced by the Parthians whose empire, in their days of glory, stretched over a vast area from the River Indus to the River Euphrates.[3]

The Sassanids

In 226 CE Artaxerxes Babakan defeated Ardwan, the Parthian king, and founded the Sassanid kingdom. Artaxerxes Babkan's grandfather was Sassan, and he claimed to be a descendant of the Achaemenids.

Artaxerxes's son, Shapur I, invaded Asia Minor in 258 CE, occupied

1. Riwāyāt-i-Tamad'dun-i-Qadīm, P. 158-159.
2. Urdu Encyclopedia of Islam: 3/635-636.
3. Oxford English Reference Dictionary.

Antākiyah (Antioch), and took the Roman king Valerian and many of his men as captives. It is said that when Shapur wanted to mount his horse, he would first set his foot on Valerian's neck. When Valerian died, Shapur flayed his skin, stuffed it with chaff, and placed it in Iran's largest fire-temple as a memento.[1] Shapur I was succeeded by Hormuz I, Behram I, Behram II, Behram III, Nersi, Hormuz II, and Azar Nersi.[2]

Coin of Shapur I

Claim to Divinity

The Sassanid kings believed that they were gods in human forms. A Pehlavi inscription found in Hajiabad lists the titles of the Sassanid king Shapur I: "Worshipper of Ormuzd, god personalized, Shapur, emperor of Iran and Beyond Iran, from the race of the Creator, son of the worshipper of Ormuzd, embodiment of divinity, Artakhshtar, emperor of Iran, from the race of the Creator, divine grandson of Shah

1. Jawan Encyclopedia, PP 376-377; Ghalaba-i-Rome, P. 30.
2. Jawan Encyclopedia, P. 377.

A pahlavi inscription found in Hajiabad

Babak castle in Iran

Babak."[1]

Shah Babak refers to the father (Babak) of Artaxerxes Babkan (Artakhshtar), whose grandson was Shapur while Ormuzd was another name for Ahurmuzda, the One God. Shapur named himself and his forefathers as 'embodiments of divinity' and worshippers of Ormuzd.

Hormuz II's son, Shapur II (309 CE-379 CE), called Shapur the Great, took back all those provinces which had been taken away during the rule of Nersi. He also conquered Armenia.

Shapur II was followed by Artaxerxes II, Shapur III, Behram IV and Yezdgerd I. Behram V (420 CE – 440 CE), the son of Yezdgerd I, was defeated by the Romans and forced to sign a peace treaty with them, however he defeated and pushed back the Huns from *Ma-Wara-an-Nahr* (Transouana). Being fond of Hunting wild ass *(Gur Khar)* he was called Behram Gūr. He was followed by Yezdgerd II, Hormuz III, Feroz, Balash and Qubād in succession.[2]

It was during the reign of King Qubād that the Mazdekite movement emerged. In 523 CE, a general massacre of Mazdekites took place.

1. Ghalaba-i-Rome, P. 170.
2. Jawan Encyclopedia, P. 377.

“Nosherwan the “Just

Qubād was succeeded by his son, Khosrau I, known also as Nosherwan the Just (531 CE-579 CE). His minister, Buzurg Mehr (known to Arabs as Buzurjmahr) was a very capable administrator. The Prophet Muhammad (ﷺ) was born during Nosherwan's reign.

During the rule of the Roman king Justinian, three battles took place between the Iranians and the Romans. Nosherwan pillaged the entire land of Syria and forced Justinian's successor, Justin II (565 CE-573 CE) to pay reparations and sign a peace treaty. The famous *Danishgah* (House of Knowledge) of Jundi Shapur was a monument of Nosherwan's era.[1]

Nosherwan was widely known for his justice. However, a closer look at his behaviour shows that this justice was practiced only between his subjects; when it came to the king and his subjects, his 'justice' would take on another form entirely. It was an ill-kept secret that he would often slay nobles and scholars of his own land without cause.[2]

Coin of Nosherwan the Just

One story relates the following:

“The king called a meeting of his counselors and commanded the tax official to read aloud the new tariff. When he had read the list, Khosrau asked his counselors three times as to whether anyone had an objection to it.

One man stood up and respectfully asked as to whether the king wanted to levy a permanent tax on perishable commodities, a system which would prove to be unjust with the passage of time.

The emperor's face darkened and he demanded, “Who are you, you cursed one?” The man who had spoken answered, “I am a scribe.”

Upon hearing this, the king's twisted sense of humor kicked in

1. Al-Munjid Fi'l-A'lam, P. 159; Encyclopedia Tarīkh-i-'Ālam: 2/130; Ghalaba-i-Rome, P. 93.
2. Tarīkh Ibn Khaldūn: 2/205.

and he commanded all the scribes in attendance to stone the man with their pen-pots until he died.

Realizing their fate they should displease the king, other scribes hastily told the king, "Your Majesty, all the taxes you have levied on us are fair and just."[1]

Atrocities of Hormuz IV

With the accession of Hormuz IV to the throne, the days of his predecessor Nosherwan became a distant dream. The new king became a formidable tyrant.

Anyone who came to him with a petition to redress his grievance was beheaded on the spot. In a short time, no less than thirteen thousand men were put to death by the executioner's sword for crimes they did not commit.

These atrocities quickly stirred public resentment and rebellion; the people of Babel, Susa and Kirman soon revolted against the emperor. Taking advantage of this rebellion, the Romans started launching attacks on the western provinces of Iran. A four hundred thousand-strong force of Turkish soldiers also attacked Iran from the other direction, but were routed at the Mazandran Pass by twelve thousand soldiers under the command of Iranian general Bahram Chobeen.[2]

When the same Behram Chobeen was defeated by the Romans on the bank of the Araks River, Hormuz ordered him to come to the royal court in feminine clothing, holding a spinning wheel as a form of humiliation. This was too much to bear; Behram revolted, had

Coin of Hormuz IV

1 Nabee-i-Rahmat, P. 65.

2. Behrām was a lean and thin man and, therefore, nicknamed Chobeen (an adjective derived from the Persian word Chob meaning 'wood') Husn-ul-Lughāt.

Hormuz's messenger crushed to death by an elephant, arrested Hormuz inside the royal palace and slew him.[1]

Reign of Khosrau Parvez

After the murder of Hormuz IV, his son Khosrau Parvez or Khosrau II (589 CE-628 CE) acceded to the throne, but was defeated by Behram and fled to the Romans, where he sought refuge. The Caesar Maurice, hoping to promote goodwill and peace between Persia and Rome, provided Khosrau with an armed force. Khosrau used this gift of soldiers to regain his kingdom, and forced Behram to flee to Turkistan.

Gold coin of Khosrow II.

As a token of gratitude and reverence, Khosrau referred to Maurice as 'father.' When a general named Phocas seized the Roman throne and killed the Caesar Maurice and his family, Khosrau Parvez launched a war against Rome as a way of requiting the favour that Maurice had bestowed on him. This war continued for twenty years and ended with the defeat of Iran.

In keeping with the Sassanid claims to divinity, Khosrau Parvez added the following titles to his name: "Immortal human among the gods, and among humans a god without peer. High is his name. Rises with the sun; light of the eyes of night."[2]

The Sassanid Court

All the wealth and revenue of the state was supposed to be the sole property of the Sassanid kings. The detailed accounts of the royal

1. Ghalaba-i-Rome, P. 97-104.
2. Iran Ba-'Ahd-i-Sassanian, P. 339. The haughty king tore off the Prophet's letter. By his action he earned the wrath of Allah. See the details under 'Prophet writes to kings to accept the Islamic faith'.

court of Mada'in are stunning; the *Bahar-i-Kisra*, (the carpet on which the Iranian kings sat and drank during spring time), the crown of Khosrau, the retinue and the servants of the royal court, wives and concubines, service boys, cooks, trainers of birds and animals, hunting paraphernalia, and royal vessels, are only a part of the total possessions of the Sassanids.[1]

When Yezdgerd III, the last monarch of Iran, fled his capital Mada'in, before the advancing Islamic forces, he was accompanied by one thousand cooks, one thousand singers and one thousand trainers of tigers, in addition to a large number of falcon overseers, servants, retinue and companions. Despite these multitudes of men and servants, he was not content and thought he was pitiable since he needed more than he had already had.[2]

1. Tarīkh-ut-Tabari: 4/178.
2. Tarīkh-i-Iran, P. 498.

Religions and Beliefs of Ancient Iran

Monotheistic Messengers

It is well known that Allah sent Prophets and Messengers to every nation on the face of the earth. With regards to Iran, the religious books of ancient Persia called such men "Wakhshoor" or "Shat Wakhshoor," meaning "Prophet" or "true Prophet."

According to ancient Iranian traditions, the earliest Prophets of Persia were Mah Abad, Azar Abad, Ja Afram, and Jay Abad. Mah Abad preached Unity of God, that is, belief in One God. For thirteen generations, people followed his teachings, but later on strayed from his path.

Kiumerth and Hoshang were also believed to be Wakhshoors, or Prophets, of their time. Some historians say that Kiumerth was the son of Prophet Nūh (Noah). One of the revelatory books of Hoshang was entitled *'Jawedan Khirad,'* which was translated by Hasan bin Sahl into Arabic during the reign of Ma'mūn ar-Rasheed. Hoshang's preachings had a great effect and ushered in an era of justice and fair play.

Hoshang was granted the title of *"Peshdad"* (meaning First Just) by the people who loved and respected him. However, those who denied the Unity of God plotted against him and eventually stoned him to death while he was praying.[1]

When Cyrus the Great (identified by some as Dhu'l-Qarnain) of the Achaemenid dynasty ascended the throne, he brought about a return to monotheism. For that reason, the Iranians called him the

1 Qadīm Mazhabi Tarīkh, P. 98-99.

Shat Wakhshoor of his time. The impact of his teachings lasted about a century and a half. During the reign of Artaxerxes II the Iranians once again relapsed into disbelief and darkness.

Fire-Worship and Zoroastrianism

When and where the children of Adam discovered fire, no one can say with any certainty. One theory is that man first discovered fire when gas or petroleum deposits deep in the earth caught fire accidentally; another theory suggests fire was first obtained when a piece of flint was found. Flint is a grey-coloured stone consisting of pure silicon (silicon dioxide) found in pebbly lumps in chalk or calcium carbonate.[1] It is well-known that some of the earliest tribes of mankind would make a fire by rubbing together certain types of wood; even today, it is a skill utilized by both those who live far away from civilization, and those who make a point of learning these skills.

Flint grey-coloured stone

Fire worship is an ancient tradition in Iran. According to Firdausi, the author of *Shahnama-i-Iran*, fire was discovered in Hoshang's era, through the friction of two stones. Hoshang gave thanks to Allah for this discovery, and the day fire was discovered was declared to be a national holiday called *Jashn Sadah*. As time passed, however, Hoshang's monotheistic teachings were distorted and people began to believe in the sanctity of fire. Firdausi believed that this marked the beginning of fire-worship in Iran.

Although Firdausi's claims regarding the discovery of fire cannot be verified, there is no gainsaying the fact that in Iran, as elsewhere,

1. Oxford English Reference Dictionary.

the original monotheistic teachings of the Messengers of Allah were twisted into different sets of beliefs and practices altogether.

Zoroastrian Fire Temple

Abdullah bin Abbas ﷺ, the Prophet's Companion, said, "When the prophet of the Persians died, the devil decreed for them Zoroastrianism."

The Zoroastrians believed that the world was divided in two: that good was light, and that darkness was evil. Fire, they argued, was the source of light. To grow closer to their angel of light, Yazdan, they built a large fire and worshipped it, declaring this to be a fundamental principle of their faith. The followers of this fire-worshipping faith were called *Magi*.

Hoshaing was followed by Tahmurath Devband as the king of Iran. During the era of this king, a mysterious, fatal disease broke out in the land. Many people died, and to commemorate the memory of their elders, the people built images and effigies in their homes. This slowly led to idol-worship.

Jamshed's Pretension to Divinity

King Jamshed began his reign as an iconoclast – he destroyed most of the popular idols of Iran, but later fell victim to paganism himself by declaring himself "god of the earth." He had statues and images of himself made and distributed amongst his subjects, who were commanded to worship him. Whomsoever refused to do so and denied his 'godhood' were tortured severely; many were flung into fires and burned alive.

A Sabeans Temple

Dahhak, who seized the throne from Jamshed, was also a cruel man and a pagan. Firdausi called him a disciple of the Devil and a lover of magic, who initiated star-worship in his era.

Adherents of Sabaism (star-worshippers) kept images of seven stars or planets in their temples called *'Paikaristan Shaidan'* built for the worship of Kewan (Saturn), Hormuz (Jupiter), Behram (Mars), Sun, Naheed (Venus), Teer (Mercury) and moon.[1]

Zoroaster: Reformer or Prophet?

Zoroaster, or Zardasht, was born in Urmia, a city of Medea (northwest Iran), around 660 BC. The Persian word "Zartasht" or "Zardasht" literally means "worshipper of God." According to Prof. Jackson, he was born in the Medean tribe of Magi. He died in 583 BC or, according to a popular tradition of the Magi, was taken up to heaven in lightning and thunder.

He founded a monotheistic creed known as Zoroastrianism, which was heavily distorted and deformed with the passage of time. It spread until it found its way into Bakhtar (northern Afghanistan).

King Darius Gushtasap became a follower of this faith, and gradually this faith spread all over the country. Shahrastani writes: "When Zoroaster grew to the age of thirty years, Allah made him a

1 Riwāyāt-i-Tamaddun-i-Qadīm, P. 162.

prophet for all mankind."

Zoroaster told people to keep away from worshipping idols and called them to the worship of Ormuzd (Lord of wisdom). In his times, Mithraism was a powerful force in the land.

An inscription on the palace of Ardashir II

Zoroaster was forced to first preach his new doctrine secretly, and oppose Mithraism and the cult of bull-worship for ten years. In ancient India and Persia, Mithra was believed to be the god of light.

Before Zoroaster, the Iranian Magi worshipped Mithra as a sun-god, mentioning his name as a witness in oath-taking ceremonies and signing legal documents. They would sacrifice oxen in his name.[1]

By the time the reign of Achaemenid king Artaxerxes II began, the religion of Zoroaster had already been distorted and mixed with Mithraism. An evidence for this is an inscription found on the northern

1. Encyclopedia of World Religions, P. 74.

View to the Zoroastrian temples ruins and the Tower of Silence in Yazd, Iran.

wall of the royal palace sited in Persepolis *(Takht-e-Jamshed):* "May Ormuzd and god Mithra perpetuate my name, my country and my great achievements to the last day of the world."[1]

Ormuzd, One God

Magianism was a polytheistic faith. The Magi worshipped multiple gods, but among those gods, there was one who held a central position. He was known as "Ahuramazda," and was considered to be the chief deity.

Zoroaster opposed the worship of all deities, and preached the worship of only one God, Ahuramazda. "Gat Ha" is a collection of hymns, said to be the composition of Zoroaster, and which contain the core beliefs of Zoroastrianism.

The Gat Ha states that Ahuramazda is the Creator of heaven and earth, the source of light and darkness, and the One Who changes light into darkness and darkness into light. He Alone is All-Powerful, the law-maker, the focus of Nature. He is the Judge of the world and the Founder of ethics and morals.[2]

Ahuramazda was variously called Ormuzd, Hormuzd and Hormuz.[3]

Yazdan: god of virtue

The Persian word 'Yazdan' is the plural of 'Yazd,' meaning 'angel' or 'god.' In the singular, however, the word 'Yazdān' means 'god' or 'god of virtue.'[4] The word Aezd also means 'god' or 'angel'.

Yazdan was said to be the leader of a group of angels whom Ahuramazda has created to manage the affairs of the world and confront the forces of Ahriman (Devil). Belief in the twin gods, Yazdan and Ahriman, is known as Dualism.

1. Hazārah Ha'i Gum Shudah: 1/330.
2. Encyclopedia of Worlds Religions, P. 1165.
3. Al-Ma'jam-ul-Wasīt: see under 'Hormuz'.
4. Farhang Fārsi: See under 'Yezd'.

Ahriman, god of evil

In ancient Persia, Ahriman was called the god of evil and worshipped as such. The Zoroastrians, who believed in the duality of gods, called him the 'evil spirit.' They believed that the only way to escape his wrath was to worship him.

Zoroaster taught his people that Ahriman was the chief of devils. In Zend Avesta, his name is Angra Mainyu (the fatal demon). Zoroastrians believe that Ahuramazda (Ormuzd) will put an end to him on the Day of Resurrection.

The Doctrine of Free Will

Abdullah bin Umar ﷺ reported that the Messenger of Allah (ﷺ) said:

"Those who assert free will *(Qadariyyah)* are the Magi of this *Ummah*. Do not visit them when they fall sick and do not attend their funeral prayer when they die."(Abu Dāwūd: 4691)

Maulana Umar Farooq Sa'eedi, commenting on this Hadīth of abu Dāwūd (4691), writes: The Magi believe in two gods. One of them was Yazdān who, they say, is the Creator of good, while the other, Ahriman, is the creator of evil. In the same way, those who deny pre-destination attribute the good to Allah, and attribute evil to someone other than Allah, although Allah is the creator of all things. He has no partners in creation and none is superior to Him.

Allah is All-Wise and, according to His divine plan, He has created evil and the devil. All human actions are governed by and subject to His will. However, will does not always mean agreement or consent or approval, because will and approval are two different things. True, every event takes place by His will. No good or bad work is possible without the divine will. Yet it does not necessarily follow that Allah likes it or approves of it. Allah likes only those things which He has commanded His slaves to do. Other works are not liked by Him, although those deeds, too, take place by His will."[1]

1. Sunan Abi Dāwūd (Urdu), Darussalam, 4/561.

Festival of Mehrjan

The festival of Mehrjan, also known as Mithragan, was a Mithran festival held on the sixteenth day of the autumn season in ancient Iran. It was the greatest festival for the Persians, next to the feast of Nauroz. In this month the Persians would not engage in farming or cattle-raising. They would take rest and offer animal sacrifices and drink an intoxicant made from a herb called *Soom*. The word *Mehrajān*, now used widely in Arabic for all types of fairs and celebrations, is an Arabicized version of the Persian word *Mehrgān*.

Anaheeta

Anaheeta was the Persian goddess of rivers, seas, and greenery. Ancient Persians used to make offerings of pomegranates, fresh tree branches and calves to her in temples devoted to her worship. She was the Persian equivalent of the Semitic Ishtar. Although Zoroaster forbade the worship of all deities except Ahuramazda (Ormuzd), it is said that Anaheeta was the angel of Ormuzd. If Zoroaster had truly been a messenger of God, it can only be that his concept of the Angel Mika'eel was disfigured by later generations, who renamed this angel as their former goddess Anaheeta. The result was that during the reign of Artaxerxes II (404 BC-359 BC) there was a revival of the cult of the worship of this deity and her images were to be seen everywhere in the country.

The Sassanid inscriptions refer to Anaheeta as Anaheed Banu and Ardawisur Banu. In the Medean city of Ecbatana (modern Hamadan), there once stood a temple devoted to her worship, said to be the most magnificent temple in the world. It was adorned with slabs of gold and silver, until it was destroyed by Alexander of Macedonia and the Seleucid kings.

In many parts of Caucasia, Azerbaijan, Afghanistan, Iran and other parts of central Asia, one comes across scores of bridges, castles and forts named after "Dukhtar", such as Pul-i-Dukhtar, Qal'a-i-Dukhtar, Āb-i-Dukhtar. Dukhtar was another name for Anaheeta.

Sarosha and Behram

Zoroastrians believed that Sarosha was an angel whose duty was to hear the words of Ormuzd and communicate them to people. They also believe that no religious ceremony was complete without his presence.

Behram was the god of victory in ancient Persia. His nearest Indian equivalent is Indar, the god of war. Fire made in the name of Behram was, in their belief, the most sacred fire, a combination of sixteen types of flames. Five kings of the Sassanid dynasty were named Behram.

According to the Persian mythology, Behram assumed many forms: bear, predatory bird, ox, camel, young warrior holding a golden sword, and so on. Every twentieth day of a month was earmarked for Behram.

Manicheism

Mani, the founder of the Manichean doctrine, was born in 215 CE in Babel. He was of Iranian extraction and, during his early age, a leader of the Zoroastrian faith. Later, he tried to reconcile the three (apparently conflicting) faiths – ancient Magaism, Buddhism and Christianity – and invented a new faith, Manicheism, named after him. In fact, his religious system is based on the dualism of the pre-Zoroaster age.

An old inscription of Manicheism

Yaqūbi, in his commentary on the teachings of Mani, writes:

"Mani, son of Hammād, emerged during the reign of the Sassanid king Shapur I, son of Artaxerxes. He declared Shapur's faith (Zoroastrianism) null and void and preached Dualism. Mani believed that there are two eternal forces in the universe: light and darkness. In the same way, there are also two creators, the creator of good *(Yazdān)*

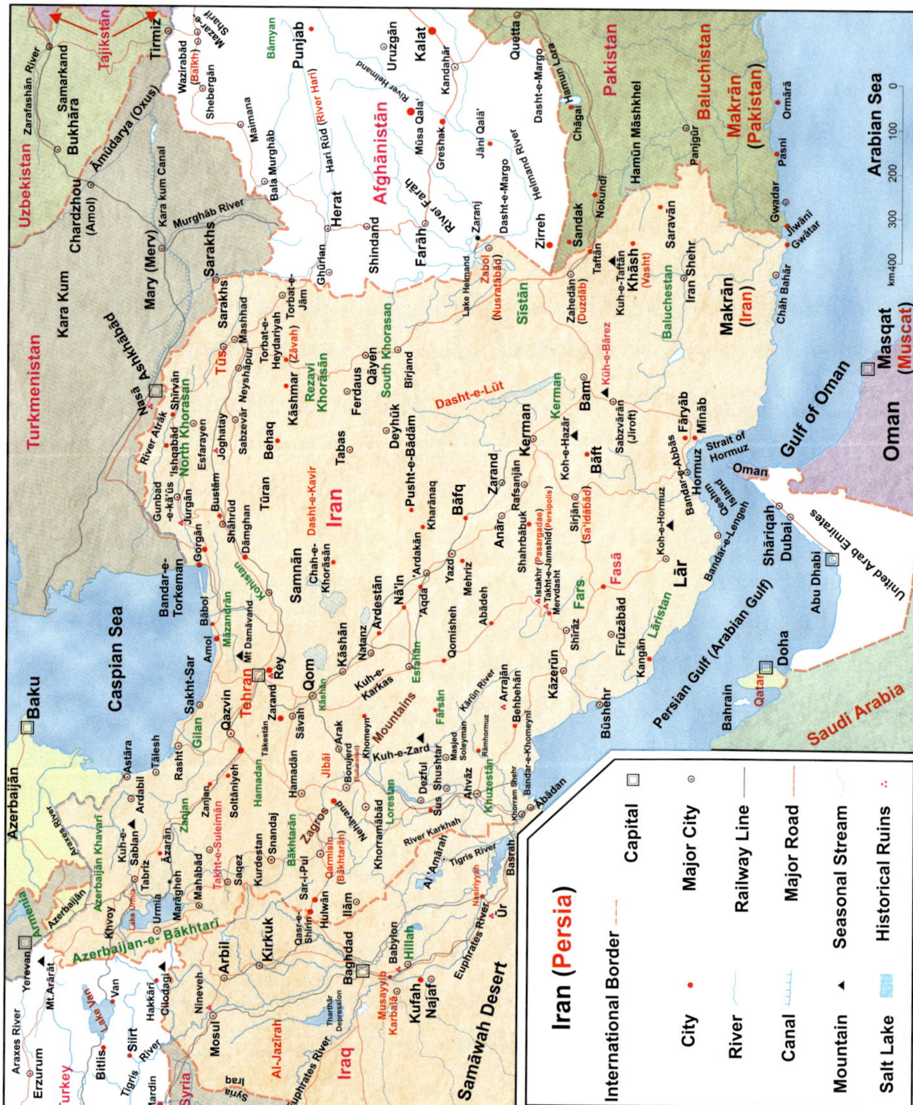

Map. 22

and the creator of evil *(Ahriman)*."[1]

Influenced by the monasticism of Buddhism and other religions, Mani preached a life of self-renunciation, self-abnegation, asceticism and celibacy. He also discouraged procreation in the fond hope that a reduced population would also reduce evil. His teachings earned him hostility from Zoroastrians, a majority, who followed Zoroaster who encouraged procreation and the

1. Riwāyāt-i-Tamad'un-i-Qadīm, P. 169.

multiplication of human race. The followers of Mani prayed four times a day, opposed idolatry, and preached against lying, thieving, killing, greed, hypocrisy and sorcery. They fasted seven days a month. Mani also invented a new script for his books, the most well-known being Shapurkan (named after Shapur). He wrote in gold and silver and bound his books also in gold. When his books were put to torch, the precious metals melted and dripped from them. He was also a great artist and painter. The Uighur Turks of central Asia also became his followers and kept long to this faith.

Although Shapur I became a follower of Mani but the latter could make no headway in the face of fierce opposition by *Mubad-i-Mubadan* (the chief priest of the fire-worshippers). Afraid of Mubad, he fled to India. When he went back to Persia, king Behram I tortured him to death. The king could only kill Mani, not his beliefs, which survived for long and influenced other religious systems. Christian hermits and Muslim Sufis (mystics) were also influenced by Mani who preached a life of self-abnegation and the renouncing of worldly ties. Poets like Abul-'Atāhiyah, Abul-'Alā Ma'arri and Omar Khayyam were also influenced by Mani's pessimism.[1] During the Umayyad and Abbasid eras, there were several men who professed the Islamic faith publicly but secretly believed in the philosophy of Mani. The followers of Mani were considered to be unbelievers, free thinkers and atheists. According to *Sahib-ul-Fihrist,* Ja'd bin Dirham, Bash'shar bin Burd and Ibn-uz-Zayyāt were the followers of Mani. To track down the followers of Mani, Caliph Mansur set up a separate department, the head of which was called *Sahib-uz-Zanādiqah.*[2]

Mazdak and Mazdakism

This heretical movement emerged during the reign of Sassanid king Qubad (487 CE - 531 CE). Initially Qubad joined this heresy but, in the face of fierce opposition of Zoroastrian high priests and his own son Nosherwan, abandoned it shortly after. Mazdak taught that all the evils can be traced back to have their origin in envy, anger and

1. Op.cit., P. 171.
2. Op.cit., P. 171-172.

avarice. These three vices, so he argued, stand in the way of equality of humans, a thing approved and ordained by God. He preached that, in order to keep humans away from avarice, envy and anger, all the things that humans need should be declared a common property of humans and distributed equally among them all. According to him, all possessions of all types should be distributed equally among them. He went even further and, like Plato, called for women to be jointly shared by all. His movement spread quickly and took root among masses till a time came when people would enter anybody's house they wished and seize his possessions and women.[1] There was also a touch of monasticism in Mazdak's religion.

An engraved sign on Zoroastrian Temple

King Qubad's son, Khosrau (Nosherwan), viewed the teachings of Mazdak as a dangerous movement, destructive to society and state. He was dead opposed to his ideas of communism and sexual libertinism. When the prince grew up and had a say in the state affairs, he forced king Qubad to exterminate Mazdakites. A genocide followed and the adherents of this cult were killed by thousands. Nosherwan sentenced Mazdak to be buried alive and ordered an official ban on the religion. Nosherwan imprisoned his own son, Noshzad, because he was leaning to the creed of Trinity. The prince broke jail but was killed later while fighting the royal army. As a reward for his services, the fire-priests gave him the title of *Nosheen Rawan* (eternal spirit) which gradually changed into *Nosherwan*.

Nizam-ul-Mulk Tūsi writes in his book *'Siyāsat Nama'*: "Mazdak's teachings also crept into some Muslim sects. Muqanna'(d. 163 AH),

1. Nabee-e-Rahmat, P. 48.

Babak (d. 224 AH) and Muhammad Ali Shalamghani (322 AH), who revolted against the Abbasid rule, called for collective ownership of property and women like Mazdak. The esoteric sect *(Bātiniyyah)* has also some ingredients of Mazdakism in them.[1]

In the nineteenth century Karl Marx, a German Jew called for communism, a system similar to that of Mazdak, socialism being only a transitional stage. For this reason Iqbal in his poem *"Iblees Ki Majlis-i-Shura"* (the advisory council of the Satan) calls Karl Marx, through an adviser of the Satan, the embodiment of the spirit of Mazdak and then makes the Satan define communism (Mazdakism) himself: "Mazdakism is not the challenge of the future. It is Islam".[2]

Sun-worship in Iran

Like other religions, Zoroastrianism, too, could not remain immune from innovations and extraneous elements creeping into it. Sun-worship was also added to the teachings attributed to Zoroaster. Since the sun was a source of heat and energy, people started worshipping it and made it a part of the Zoroastrian faith.

Christensen, the author of 'Iran under the Sassanids' says: "State officials were obliged to worship the sun four times a day. Moon and fire were also worshipped. They had obligatory prayers specific to each human activity including sleeping, awakening, washing, eating and drinking, sneezing, hair cutting, nail clipping, relieving nature, igniting the candle, and so on. People were told to keep the temple-fire burning and never let fire and water join together, keep metals free from rusting because metals, in their sight, were sacred."[3]

Yazdgerd, the last king of Iran, swore once, saying: "I swear by the sun, the greatest deity." He bade the ex-Christians who had renounced Christianity to worship the sun to prove their sincerity.[4]

---

1. Riwāyāt-i-Tamaddun-i-Qadīm, P. 172-173.
2. Kulliāt-i-Iqbāl (Armughān-i-Hijāz), P. 654-656.
3. Iran ba-'Ahd-i-Sassanian, P. 155.
4. Op.cit., P. 186-187.

The Tomb of Jonah (Nabi-Yunus), on the ruins of Nineveh, vintage engraved illustration. Magasin Pittoresque 1876.

Iraq (Babel and Nineveh)

Area of Iraq

Mesopotamia (also called the land of the Euphrates and the Tigris) or the plane of Iraq extends from the southern slopes of Armenia plateau (southeastern Turkey) to the Persian Gulf, an area of about six hundred miles. This relates to the times when the ancient city of Ur was situated near the Gulf. The earth accumulated by the action of the flood waters of the Tigris and the Euphrates over thousands of years pushed back the Gulf coast sixty miles further south. From east to west, Iraq lies between Zagros mountains (Iran) to *Badiat-ush-Sham.*

In ancient times this region was home to the great nations of the world. It was divided into two parts. The northern part was called Assyria

Mount Ararat (Turkey)

while the southern part was called Bābel (Babylon). Among the chief cities of Assyria were Nineveh, Khorsabad and Arbela (modern Irbeel). The chief cities of Babel were a city of the same name, Babel, and Cush, Akkad, and in the extreme south, Ur. The Assyrian cities were sited along the bank of Tigris while the Babylonian cities along that of Euphrates or near it.

Prophet Noah and the Deluge

According to the Old Testament, Prophet Noah عليه السلام, who belonged to the eighth generation of Sheeth bin Adam, was appointed a prophet for the people settled in and around Kufa (Iraq). His people worshipped the idols named *Wadd, Suwā', Yagūth, Ya'ūq*, and *Nasr.* For as many as nine hundred and fifty years he preached to his people but in vain. They would not repent and refused to give up idol-worship. So, the Wrath of Allah came and they were drowned by the great flood called the Deluge. Noah عليه السلام and a group of forty believers escaped the flood in a boat Noah عليه السلام had built by the command of Allah. From those fortunate few did the human race multiply and spread. Noah's own son, Kana'an (or Canaan) was also drowned to death. The boat (Noah's ark) came to rest at Mt.Judi, a summit of Ararat mountainous range extending across Turkish-Armenian border. Until the eighth century of

The Ruins of Ur

the Christian era there stood a temple which was called the Temple of the Ark.[1]

It should be noted that Noah's son, Canaan, a disbeliever, was drowned in the Deluge, leaving behind him no offspring. Anyhow, Can'aan bin Sam or Canaan bin Ham, bin Noah propagated. Among the people said to be his offspring were the potentates of *Sham* (Palestine). They are frequently mentioned in the Bible.[2]

According to historical evidence, around the close of the Stone and Bronze Ages the area between the Tigris and the Euphrates (*Bilad-ur-Rafidain* or Mesopotamia) was devastated by a great flood. The relics dating back to those times are found in Jermo (near Sulaimāniyah), Tel Hassūnah (south of Mosul), Tel al-Abeed (near Ur), Urūk (Warkā'), Sherubak (Fārah), and Jamdah Nasr (near Kesh), east of Babel. Archaeologists date the remains of Jermo back to 6500 BC and those of Tel Hassūnah to 5750 BC.[3] The remains of the times of Noah may be any one of them.

Sumerian, Accadian and Amori kingdoms

Nearly four thousand years before Christ there flourished two great civilizations in Iraq, the Sumerian in the south and the Accadian in the north. The Sumerians and the Accadians are supposed to be a Semitic race. In the third millennium BC the Amorites came to Babel from northern Syria and around 1900 BC they established their first kingdom there. Then around 1600 BC the Hittites invaded Babel. They were followed by Kassites who, in turn, were followed around 1100 BC by the Aramaeans who pillaged the land and occupied all the areas along the Euphrates. They were also a Semitic race.

Measurement of time and invention of written script

Initially, the Sumerians had a sexagesimal system of calculation but they soon replaced it by a decimal system. Likewise, they started with

1. Qasas-ul-Qur'ān: 1/63-85.
2. Mu'jam-ul-Buldān: See under 'Canaan'; Sabā'ik-uz-Zahab, P.30; Al-Jamhara li-Ibn Hazm, P. 463; Holy Bible (Genesis) 10: 6-20. Wikipedia (Encyclopedia).
3. Atlas-ul-Qur'ān (Urdu), P. 45.

hieroglyphic writing but soon invented the cuneiform script which was well suited for writing on tablets.

An inscription of King Hammurabi

Hammurabi and the first constitution of history

Hammurabi (C. 1800 BC) was the sixth Amori king of Babel. Some research scholars hold that he was a contemporary of Abraham. He conquered the whole of Iraq and prepared a collection of law said to be the first constitution in the history of mankind. His law had no parallel until the times of the Romans.[1] In fact, the Romans learnt a lot from Hammurabi's collection of law.

Abraham[3] and Nimrod

Ibn Jareer Tabari, while quoting a popular saying that Prophet Abraham عليه السلام was born in Babel (Sawad, southern Iraq), also quoted scholars having stated that he was born at a place called Kūtha (كوثى) in Sawād. He was born during the reign of Nimrod bin Kush (or Nimrod bin Canaan bin Kush) bin Sām bin Nūh (Noah) but some scholars disagree and hold that Nimrod was the title of the king whose real name was Dharhi bin Tahmāsfān.[2]

The Bible also refers to him as Nimrod (For detailed information about Prophet Abraham عليه السلام, refer to *'Arab Musta'ribah*/pure Arabs').

Assyrian kingdom of northern Iraq (Nineveh)

The Assyrian kingdom was founded in the eighteenth century BC, its chief city being Nineveh (near modern Mosul). In the tenth century BC its territories were already extending further both in Iraq and Syria. Their chief idol was named Ashur (Assur) but, later on, they also added to their pantheon another female deity named Ishtar. The first

1. Encyclopedia Tarīkh-i-'Ālam: 2/42-46.
2. Tarīkh At-Tabari: 1/162-163.

An inscription of Sumerian Shalemnasir II

phase of their power began in 933 BC when Assurnaserpal II conquered territories up to the Mediterranean Sea. During his era catapults, strong enough to break down fortresses, and other equipment useful for siege came to be used. The other great Assyrian king was Shalmaneser II who exacted tributes from Sidon and Tyre (the twin coastal cities of Lebanon) as well as from Israel. Shalemnasir III (911 BC - 891 BC) was defeated by Ahab, the king of Israel, and by Hadad Ezar, the king of Syria, in the Battle of Qarqār.[1]

Prophet Jonah

Allah appointed Prophet Jonah يونس عليه السلام to guide the Assyrians. It is said that he lived somewhere between 860 BC and 784 BC. Nineveh, the chief town of Assyria, extended over 60 miles in a circular form. Jonah preached a long time but his folk would not listen to him. In despair and anger he left his people and went first to Syria and from there made for Joppa (or Yafa) and took a boat. But as the boat reached the high sea, a storm blew, forcing the boatmen to cast lots to choose the man to be jettisoned to lighten the boat. Three times they did so, but each time the lot fell to Jonah's name. As he threw himself into the sea, a huge fish (probably, a whale) swallowed him up. In the dark belly of the fish, he prayed to Allah and repented for leaving his people without Allah's leave, saying:

﴿لَّآ إِلَٰهَ إِلَّآ أَنتَ سُبۡحَٰنَكَ إِنِّي كُنتُ مِنَ ٱلظَّٰلِمِينَ﴾

"There is no God save You. Glorified (and Exalted) are You! Surely, I have been of the wrongdoer." al-Anbiyā' (21): 87.

By Allah's Command, the fish spewed him out in a clear place. There he kept lying, shaded by a creeping plant, till Allah bade him to return

1. History of the World, P. 52; Eencyclopedia Tarīkh-i-'Ālam: 2/47-48.

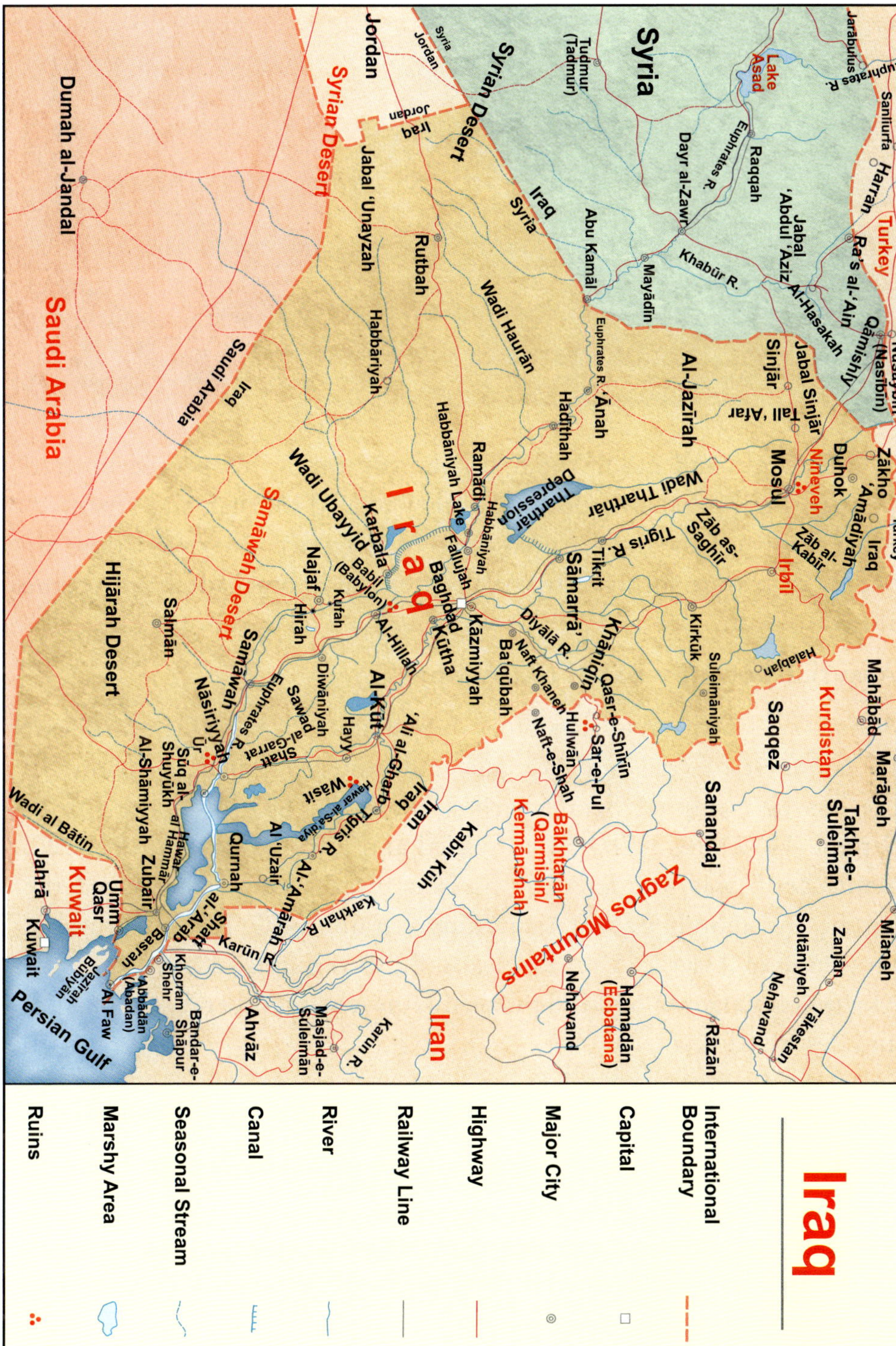
Iraq
International Boundary
Capital
Major City
Highway
Railway Line
River
Canal
Seasonal Stream
Marshy Area
Ruins
Syria
Turkey
Jordan
Saudi Arabia
Kuwait
Iran
Kurdistan
Iraq
Syrian Desert
Samāwah Desert
Hijārah Desert
Zagros Mountains
Persian Gulf
Lake Asad
Euphrates R.
Tigris R.
Khabūr R.
Diyālā R.
Zāb al-Kabīr
Zāb as-Saghīr
Karūn R.
Karkhah R.
Shatt al-'Arab
Wadi Tharthār
Tharthār Depression
Habbāniyah Lake
Wadi Haurān
Wadi Ubayyid
Wadi al Bātin
Baghdad
Babil (Babylon)
Nineveh
Mosul
Irbil
Kirkūk
Sāmarrā'
Tikrit
Ramādi
Fallujah
Karbala
Najaf
Kūfah
Hīrah
Al-Hillah
Kūtha
Kāzmiyyah
Ba'qūbah
Al-Kūt
Wāsit
Nāsiriyyah
Ūr
Samāwah
Basrah
Qurnah
Zubair
Umm Qasr
Al Faw
Kuwait
Jahrā
Rutbah
Hadīthah
'Ānah
Abu Kamāl
Mayādīn
Dayr al-Zawr
Raqqah
Harran
Sanliurfa
Jarābulus
Tudmur (Tadmur)
Nusaybin (Nasībīn)
Qāmishly
Al-Hasakah
Ra's al-'Ain
Sinjār
Jabal Sinjār
Tall 'Afar
Duhok
Zākho
'Amādiyah
Al-Jazīrah
Suleimāniyah
Halabjah
Mahābād
Saqqez
Sanandaj
Marāgeh
Takht-e-Suleiman
Mianeh
Zanjān
Soltāniyeh
Tākestān
Nehavand
Rāzān
Hamadān (Ecbatana)
Bākhtarān (Qarmisin/ Kermānshah)
Qasr-e-Shīrīn
Sar-e-Pul
Hulwān
Khāniqīn
Ahvāz
Khorram Shehr
Abbādān (Abadan)
Bandar-e-Shāpur
Masjad-e-Suleimān
Kabīr Kūh
Dumah al-Jandal
Jabal 'Unayzah
Habbāriyah
Salmān
Al-Shāmiyyah
Sūq al-Shuyūkh
Al-'Amārah
Al 'Uzair
'Ali al-Gharb
Hayy
Diwāniyah
Shatt al-Garraf
Jazīrah Būbiyān

Map. 23

Yafa (Joppa) coast (Palestine)

to his people and guide them. In the meantime his people noticed signs of the approaching doom. So, they turned to Allah and repented. Allah forgave them and restored them to His grace. They were the only people who were forgiven by Allah after the doom had already come close.[1]

Assyrians occupy Babel (Babylon)

A new era of the Assyrian glory began in 745 BC. Tiglath-Pileser III conquered Syria and Armenia and annexed Babel (Babylon) to the Assyrian empire. Sennacherib (704 BC – 681 BC), the son of Sargon II (721 BC - 704 BC) invaded and pillaged Babel in 689 BC. Sennacherib was murdered by his son, Esarhaddon, who seized the throne and rebuilt Babel. Assurbanipal (668 – 627 BC) was the last great king of Assyria. After his death, Babel revolted and, aided by the Medes (Iranians), in 612 BC pillaged Nineveh and other Assyrian cities and destroyed them.[2]

Iraq occupied by Nebuchadnezzar, Alexander and Sassanid

From 729 BC to 625 BC, Babel remained a part of the Assyrian empire. Later, the Chaldean-Aramaeans occupied Babel and later seized the whole of Iraq. Their famous monarch, Nebuchadnezzar, ruled from 605 BC to 561 BC. He destroyed the Temple of Solomon (Jerusalem) in

1. Atlas Al-Qur'ān (Urdu), P. 184-186.
2. History of the World, P. 57-58.

586 BC and also defeated the Egyptians. He annexed the Hebrew state of Judea to Babylonian empire and brought one hundred thousand Jews in chains to Babel. He also built high ramparts around Babel and several magnificent edifices. The terraced gardens called the Hanging Gardens of Babel were built by Nebuchadnezzar. They are counted among the seven Wonders of the Old World.

Two sides of the coin of Abbasid Dynasty

In 538 BC the Iranian Monarch Cyrus (Dhu'l-Qarnain) conquered the whole of Iraq including Babylon (Babel). Iraq remained under Iranian occupation for two centuries until the times of Alexander the Great. In 332 BC Alexander conquered Babel and made it a centre of his empire. After his death, his Asian territories fell to the lot of Seleucids. After them Iraq came under the control of the Parthian (Iranian) kings from 171 BC to 226 CE. The Parthians were followed by the Sassanid of Iran. Then, last of all, came the Arab Muslims who conquered Iraq (636 CE - 637 CE).

Ruins of the city of Babel

Sabaism (Star-Worship)

The correct word for the cult of star-worship is Sabaism but it is erroneously spelt as Sabeanism. Sabeans are star-worshippers. Star-worship is one of the most ancient form of paganism. That was the pagan cult current in Iraq during the lifetime of Prophet Abraham عليه السلام. He opposed this cult and preached the Unity of God. He succeeded but star-worship did not die out entirely but survived in one form or another.

The Sabeans were spread over vast areas including Iran, Iraq and southern Turkey but their main centre was Harran (Turkey) which was known to the ancients as Caria or Carrhe.[1] They spoke Syriac. This sect, according to some scholars, originated in Babel (Babylon) where they learnt Israeli magical lore, Iranian calendar and Iranian words which they added to their own language (Mandaic). But other scholars trace their

A Sabean Temple

1. Jughrafia Khilāfat-i-Mashriqi, P 103/130.

Places of Magians and Sabians
Places of Magians
Places of Sabians
Caspian Sea
Black Sea
Mediterranean Sea
Red Sea
Persian Gulf
Gulf of Oman
Arabian Sea
Indian Ocean
Byzantine (Roman) Empire
Lydia (Turkey)
Asia Minor
Cyprus
Manf
Egypt
Thebes (Luxor)
Sinai
Jerusalem
Sūr (Tyre)
Syria
Damascus
Gassanid Kingdom
Tabūk
Syrian Desert
Ar-Raqqah
Harran
Tigris R.
Al Jazeerah
Baghdad
Euphrates R.
Babylon
Hirah
Ctesiphon
Kingdom of Mundhirs
Dumat Al-Jandal
An Nafūd
Taimā
Al Madinah
Hijaz
Makkah
At-Taif
Najd
Asir
Nubian Desert
Abyssinia
Lake Van
Lake Urmia (Orumiyeh)
Azerbaijan
Derbent
Baku
Media (Iran)
Hamadan
Nehavand
Shush
Ilam
Al-Ahsa
Bahrain
Hajar
Yamāmah
Arabian Peninsula
Empty Quarter
Hadramawt
Isfahān
Persia
Shiraz
Yazd
Sassanid Empire
Turkmenistan
Tūs
Khorasan
Kerman
Suhar
Muscat
Oman
Herat
Afghanistan
Balkh (Fire-temple Naubahar)
Kabul
Sīstan
Helmand R.
Baluchistan
Makran
Pakistan
Indus R.
Sutlag R.
Hindustan (India)
Bombay
0
300
600
900
1200
km

Map. 24

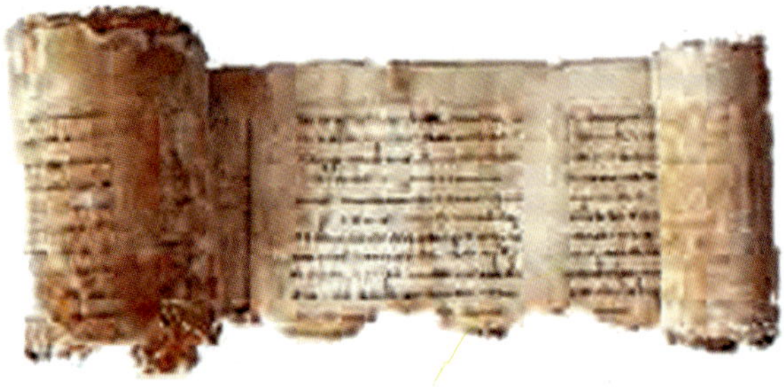

An ancient script of Sabeans

beginnings in Syria and Palestine because their religious book, Haran Gawaitha, says that the Sabean-Mandaean scholars migrated in the first century of the Christian Era (CE) from Palestine to al-Jazeerah (Mesopotamia). Their religious writings have the touch of the Old Testament and their strict moral code and wedding customs are like those of the Jews.[1]

There were two groups of Sabeans during Islamic times:

Mandaeans, also called Subbas. In belief and practice, they were quite close to Christians and Jews. They also practiced baptism.

Sabeans of Harran: an ancient pagan sect. The adherents of this sect did not accept Christ as Messiah عليه السلام. This sect survived for a long time, thanks to many scholars born in this community including Thābit bin Qarah, a distinguished engineer, astronomer and philosopher, Sannan bin Thābit, physician and astrologer, Abu Ishāq bin Hilāl Al-Battani, and Abu Ja'far Khazin.

In 259 AH/ 872 CE, Thābit bin Qarah fell out with his co-religionists. When he was ex-communicated from the Sabean community of Harran, he moved to Baghdad and founded a new branch of Sabean sect. Sometime later, during the reign of Caliph Qāhir Billah, Thābit's son, Sannan, converted to the Islamic faith. In c. 364 AH/ 975 CE. Abu Ishāq bin Hilāl Sabi, the scribe of Caliph Mutee'ulillah and Caliph Tā'i'-ulillah, managed to have a royal decree issued in favour of his brothers in-faith living in Harran, Raqqah, and

1. Encyclopedia of World Religions P. 688.

Diyār Mudar. According to that decree, all the Sabeans, including his co-religionists living in Baghdad, were included among Dhimmis.

There were a lot of Sabeans living in Baghdad and Harran by the beginning of the eleventh century CE but by 424 AH/ 1033 CE there remained only one moon temple, shaped like a citadel, in Harran. The same year it was seized by the Fatimids of Egypt. After the middle of the eleventh century CE we find no trace of Sabeans in Harran although they survived in Baghdad until the end of that century.

Shahrastāni says that all the Sabeans said three prayers. If they touched a dead body, they washed themselves to purify themselves. They were forbidden to eat the flesh of pigs, dogs, birds with claws, and pigeons. The rite of circumcision was non-existent. Divorce took place only with the permission of a Qadi (judge). A man was not allowed to have two wives.[1]

Ruins of the Harran

Sayyed Abul-A'la Maudūdi writes: "In ancient times, there were two groups of the Sabeans. One group followed John the Baptist. They were found in large numbers in Upper Iraq, that is, al-Jazeerah. They practiced the rite of baptism. The other group was that of star-worshippers. They traced their religion to Prophets Sheeth (Seth) and Idrees ﷺ and believed that stars and planets influenced the elements. Their center was Harran but they had branches in different parts of Iraq. This group became famous owing to their achievements in philosophy, science, arts, and medicines. Perhaps they were not known by this name during the time of the revelation of the Qur'ān."[2]

1. Urdu Encyclopedia of Islam: 12/ 3-6.
2. Tafhīm-ul-Qur'ān: Al-Hajj: 22:17.

Syria and Lebanon

In its wider sense the name Syria or Sūriyā (in old Arabic Shām) was applied to the region which lies to the south of Mt. Taurs (southern Turkey), between the eastern Mediterranean Sea and the River Euphrates. Later, the name was applied only to the northeastern part of the aforementioned area. Phoenicia (Lebanon), Palestine and Jordan were excluded from it. The famous cities of ancient Syria were: Damascus Arpad (Tel Arnud), Halab, Antākiyah (Antioch), Qades (Kadesh), Hama, and Tadmur (Palmyra). Damascus is one of the world's oldest cities.

Modern Shām (Syria)

The modern Arab Republic of Syria *(Sūriyā)* is surrounded by the Mediterranean Sea, Lebanon, Turkey, Palestine, Jordan and Iraq. Its capital is Damascus. Modern Syria is divided into thirteen provinces:

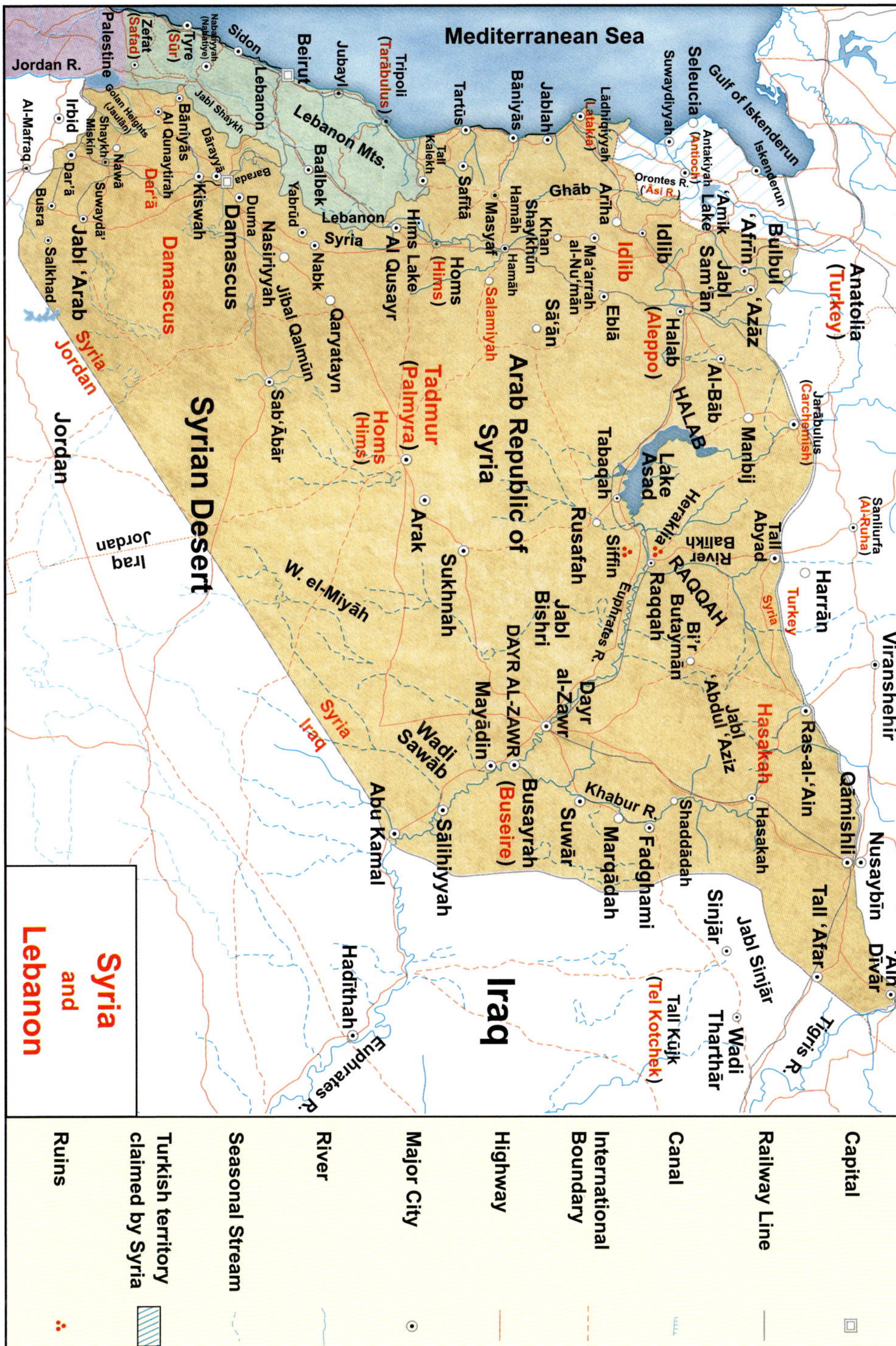
Mediterranean Sea
Gulf of Iskenderun
Iskenderun
Seleucia
Suwaydiyyah
Antakiyah (Antioch)
Orontes R. ('Āsi R.)
'Amik Lake
'Afrīn
Bulbul
Anatolia (Turkey)
Jabl Sam'ān
'Azāz
Idlib
Halab (Aleppo)
Al-Bāb
Manbij
Jarābulus (Carchemish)
Sanliurfa (Al-Ruha)
Harrān
Tall Abyad
Lake Asad
Tabaqah
HALAB
Herakla
River Balīkh
RAQQAH
Raqqah
Siffīn
Rusafah
Euphrates R.
Bi'r Butaymān
Jabl 'Abdul 'Aziz
Viranshehir
Ras-al-'Ain
Hasakah
Qāmishli
Nusaybīn
'Ain Dīvār
Tall 'Afar
Tigris R.
Jabl Sinjār
Sinjār
Wadi Tharthār
Tall Kūjk (Tel Kotchek)
Shaddādah
Fadghami
Marqādah
Khabur R.
Suwār
Busayrah (Buseire)
DAYR AL-ZAWR
Dayr al-Zawr
Jabl Bishri
Mayādīn
Wadi Sawāb
Sālihiyyah
Abu Kamal
Iraq
Hadīthah
Euphrates R.
Arab Republic of Syria
Lādhiqiyyah (Latakia)
Jablah
Bāniyās
Tartūs
Tall Kalekh
Saffitā
Ghāb
Arīha
Ma'arrah al-Nu'mān
Khan Shaykhūn
Hamāh
Ebla
Sā'ān
Masyāf
Salamiyah
Homs (Hims)
Hims Lake
Al Qusayr
Tadmur (Palmyra)
Homs (Hims)
Arak
Sukhnah
W. el-Miyāh
Syrian Desert
Tripoli (Tarābulus)
Jubayl
Beirut
Lebanon Mts.
Baalbek
Lebanon
Syria
Sidon
Tyre (Sūr)
Zefat (Safad)
Jabl Shaykh
Bāniyās
Al Qunaytirah
Dārayyā
Barada
Kiswah
Duma
Damascus
Damascus
Yabrūd
Nabk
Nasiriyyah
Jibal Qalmūn
Qaryatayn
Sab'Ābār
Dar'ā
Dar'ā
Golan Heights (Jaulān)
Shaykh Miskin
Nawā
Suwaydā'
Jabl 'Arab
Busra
Salkhad
Irbid
Al-Mafraq
Palestine
Jordan R.
Jordan
Syria
Jordan
Jordan
Iraq
Syria
Iraq
Syria
Turkey
Syria and Lebanon
Capital
Railway Line
Canal
International Boundary
Highway
Major City
River
Seasonal Stream
Turkish territory claimed by Syria
Ruins

Map. 25

A beautiful view of Damascus

Damascus, Halab, Homs, Latakia, Idlab, Haska, Deir-uz-Zaur, Dar'ā, Suwaidā', Tartūs, Raqqah, and Quneitarah. The plateau of Hauran lies in southern Syria. It should be noted that the Syria of the ancient times is still written *'Shām'* in Urdu, though the Arabs now call it *Sūriyā*. It should also be noted that modern *'Shām'* (Syria) also includes the western part of al-Jazeerah which extends from Abu Kamal (on the bank of the Euphrates) to 'Ain Dewār on the bank of the Tigris and, in the west, up to Jarābulas (Karkamesh).

Shām, Arām, and Sūriyā (Syria)

Dr Sayyed Ridwān Ali Wāsti, a well-known research scholar in 'Daily Ummat', writes: "Since after the First World War the official name of this country is *Sūriyā* (Syria). In ancient Arab history and pre-Islamic poetry, it was known as *'Shām'*. Yaqūt says: According to historians, the country was so named *(Shām)* after Sām, the son of Prophet Noah عليه السلام. (Sām is called Shem in the English version of Torah).[1]

"According to a tradition, after Solomon's death, the state established by the nine Israeli tribes in the northern part of his kingdom was named Shāmeen. Later, the Arab traders of the pre-Islamic times shortened Shāmeen to Shām. The 'Shām' of ancient times covered all the area right from the southern Turkey and the river Euphrates to Al-Areesh west of Gaza and from the Mediterranean Sea to Jabal Tayy north of the Arabian Peninsula. This area also included the Turkish border towns of

1. NIV Study Bible, P. 19.

Masīsah (Masis), Tarsūs, Adāna and Antākiyah. Some commentators of Qur'ān interpret the words "بركنا حوله"(The neighbourhood whereof We have blessed) – Verses of *Sūrah Bani Isrā'īl* or *al-Isrā'* – to cover the whole of Shām including Palestine. In the Verse (رِحْلَةَ الشِّتَاءِ وَالصَّيْفِ) of *Sūrah Quraish*, the summer caravan has also been interpreted to mean the journey to Shām. And it could be that the Hadīth narrated by Būkhari (اللهم بارك لنا في شامنا) "O Allah, bless for us in our Shām"[1] prophesied the conquest of Syria.

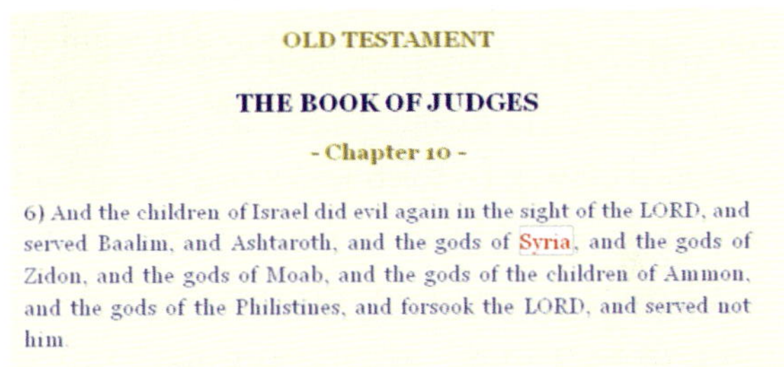
OLD TESTAMENT

THE BOOK OF JUDGES

- Chapter 10 -

6) And the children of Israel did evil again in the sight of the LORD, and served Baalim, and Ashtaroth, and the gods of Syria, and the gods of Zidon, and the gods of Moab, and the gods of the children of Ammon, and the gods of the Philistines, and forsook the LORD, and served not him.

Discription of Syria in Eng. Bible

"*Sūriyā* is the ancient Greek name of *Shām* (Syria). The gospel of Luke supports this view. Its other old name was Aram (or Iram) which was, in fact the name of one of the sons of Sām bin Nūh ﷺ. That is the reason why the Urdu version of the Bible (Old Testament) translates the word *Sūriyā* into Aram, whereas it has been rendered 'Syria' in the English Bible. One feels that the Urdu translators had also with them the Greek version from which the Bible was translated into English. Hence, for this reason, the gospel of Luke (Urdu Bible) retains *Sūriyā*, the original Greek name of *Shām*.

"Yaqūt Hamavi writes under the article *'Sūriya':* "It is the region lying between Khanāsirah (the suburbs of Halab) and Salamyah (the suburbs of Homs). When the Muslims, in the course of their conquest of Syria (Shām), reached Qinnasreen, Heraclius who was in Antakiyah (Antioch) at the time said ruefully: 'O Syria (that is, Sham), greetings to you from the one who says you farewell. He hopes not he will ever come back to you again."[2]

Excavations in 1950 at Tel-es-Salehiya, southeast of Damascus, reveualled a four thousand-year old city centre. The Tel-el-Amarna inscriptions refer to Damascus as Dimashka while the inscriptions of

1. Sahīh-ul-Bukhāri: 1037.
2. Mu'jam-ul-Buldān: see under 'Sūriyā'.

Ramses III (a pharaoh of Egypt) refer to the same city as Darmesek.[1]

Ebla and Phoenicia

A clay tablet discovered from the ancient Syrian city Ebla

Around 4000 BC a trading nation founded a city named Ugarit on the northwestern coast of Syria. Later on, around 3000 BC, the cities of Byblos (now called Jubail) and Ebla (northwest Syria) were settled. From the relics of Ebla archaeologists have retrieved more than fifteen thousand clay slabs with inscriptions written in cuneiform script. These inscriptions give a lot of information about those times.[2] Then, around 1500 BC, other cities emerged on the Lebanese coast: Tyre, Sidon, Tripoli. The region came to be known as Phoenicia, a name derived from a Greek word meaning 'purple', so named because the people of the region dyed their clothes purple at a high price. Hence, the people came to be called Phoenicians. They worshipped an idol named Ba'l. During the tenth century BC, Hiram, son of Abi Ba'l, was the king of Phoenicia. He supplied equipment and good craftsmen to Prophet Solomon عليه السلام when the latter planned to build a mercantile fleet.[3]

After 1000 BC the Phoenicians went up to North Africa and founded new cities like Tripoli (Libya), which they named after a famous city in Lebanon. They also founded in 814 BC the city of Carthage, the remains of which are found in Tunisia. The Phoenicians travelled on further and reached the eastern coast of Spain where they founded a city named Cartagena, a nominal replica of carthage: Another Cartagena exists in Colombia (South America) but that city was founded by the Spaniards about two millennium later.[4]

1. Urdu Encyclopedia of Islam: 9/398.
2. Wikipedia (Encyclopedia).
3. Encyclopedia Tarīkh-i-'Ālam: 2/62.
4. Philips Illustrated Atlas, P. 55, 144.

Aramean kingdom of Damascus

The earliest remains of human settlement found in Syria belong to the Arameans, a Semitic race. Later on, during different periods of history this land was occupied by Accadians, the people of Ur, Hammurabi, and the Pharaohs of Egypt. One of the Pharaohs, Tuthmoses III, conquered Damascus in the fifteenth century BC (1450 BC). It remained under Egyptian occupation for one hundred years. It kept changing hands. The Egyptians were followed by the Hittites, then again by the Egyptians. In the tenth century BC the city was conquered by Prophet David عليه السلام. Later, it became the centre of a powerful Aramean empire which survived till 732 BC. The Bible (Kings 2) says that prophet Elisha (Arabic: Al-Yasa' عليه السلام) told Nu'mān Abras (Naaman the leper), the commander of the royal Aramean forces, to dip into the Jordan river seven times over to cure himself of leprosy. He did so and was cured.

Damascus: From Assyrians to Romans

In 732 BC the Assyrians defeated the Arameans and pillaged the temple and the palace of Damascus. Towards the end of the sixth century BC it was invaded by Nebuchadnezzar, the Chaldean ruler, in 539 BC by Cyrus, the Persian king, and in 332 BC by Alexander the Great, and, after Alexander's death, it was occupied by his generals Ptolemy and Antigonis by turns. Then the Seleucids conquered Damascus and declared it as the capital of their kingdom. In 64 BC Pompeii, the Roman general, annexed Syria to the Roman empire and moved the provincial capital to Antioch.

Egypt and the Nile Valley

Egypt, from north to south, covers a part of the Nile valley stretching from the Nile Delta (Mediterranean Sea) to Aswan and Halfa Valley (Sudan). In the east the land of Egypt reaches up to the coast of the Red Sea and in the west up to Libya. In the northeast it includes the peninsula of Sinai. It was called Kemit (that is, dark or blackish earth) in the ancient Egyptian language.

The valley is five hundred and fifty miles long. In the south it is only about twelve miles wide, on average. Initially, it was divided into two parts: Lower Egypt (Delta) and Upper Egypt (the main valley). Before the reign of King Menes, each part was a separate kingdom. Herodotus called Egypt the 'gift of Nile'.

Mediterranean Sea
0 40 80 120 160 200 km
Tel Aviv
Jaffa (Yāfā)
Jerusalem
Amman
Rosetta (Rashīd)
Lake Burullus
Dumyāt
Lake Manzalah
Port Sa'id
Gaza
Alexandria
Al 'Arish
Palestine
Damanhūr
Al-Mansūrah
Afāris
Al Qantarah
Negev
El-'Alamein
Tantā
Al-Zaqazīq
Suez Canal
Benha
Ismailia
Jordan
Wadi Natrūn
Bitter Lakes
Memphis
Cairo
Giza
Suez
Hulwān
Sinai Peninsula
Tābā
Al-'Aqabah
Birkah Qārūn
Jabl Jalālah al-Bahriyyah
Al Fayyūm
At-Tih Desert
Haql
Gulf of Suez
Abū Zanīmah
Beni Suef
Saudi Arabia
Jabl Jalālah al Qibiliyah
Maghaghah
Jabl (Tūr) Musa (Mt.Sinai)
Midian (Madyan)
Buwaiti
El-Tūr
Mt. Katrinah
El Minya
Jabl Ghārib
Bahriyyah Oasis
Mallawī
Nile River
Rās Muhammad
Tirān Islands
Farafra Oasis
Asyūt
Ghardaqah
Egypt
Jabl Shā'ib
Western Desert
Būr Safājah
Red Sea
Sūhāj
Dishna
Qinā
Quseir
Al Qasr
Nag' Hammādi
Qus
Mūt
Luxor R
Eastern Desert
Dākhilah Oasis
Khārijah
Isna
Mursa 'Alam
Khārijah Oasis
Idfū
Nile River
Bārīs
Kawm Umbu
Jabl Hamatah
Aswān
Aswān High Dam
Al Wadi Al Jadīd
Rās Banās
Egypt and the Nile River
International Boundary
Capital
Peak
River
Major City
Highway
Railway line
Canal
Lake Nāsir
jabl 'Albah
Nile River
Al Wadi al Halfā'
Sudan
Map. 26

Pharaohs and the Pyramids

In ancient Egypt a year consisted of 365 days. This system was most probably put into practice since 2781 BC. Ancient Egyptians used hieroglyphic script which is, in fact, picture-writing. During ancient period of Egyptian history (2900 BC - 2100 BC) the Pharaohs were worshipped as gods both during their lifetimes and after their death. The word Pharoah is, in fact, a combination from two words: per-o, meaning 'great dynasty'. The earliest Pharaohs had eminent architects who built pyramids, palaces and temples with splendid columns.[1]

The largest pyramid is that of king Khofu in Giza. It is 486 ft (148 m) high, made up of nearly twenty-three hundred thousand stone slabs.[2] Dead bodies were preserved by means of special ingredients and spices. Food and other things, a man normally needs in his daily life, were also placed in graves along with mummified bodies because ancient Egyptians believed that death was a journey of soul and that

1. Encyclopedia Tarīkh-i-'Ālam: 2/35-37.
2. History of the World, P.37.

Great Palace of Umayyad Palace at Anjar in Lebanon. It is located about 50km east of Beirut and has led to its designation as a UNESCO World Heritage Site in 1984.

a dead man's body needed sustenance to keep pace with the soul in its new journey.

Egyptian deities and sun-worship

In the early days each city had its own deity. These deities had faces of different animals. Some most famous deities were: Tāh, Atum, Horace, Amon and R'a. Horace, the royal deity of Egypt, had the face of an eagle. Initially, he was called the deity of the sky and later sun-god. Sun-worship began from the city of Heliopolis, a Greek word meaning 'city of sun'. The priests of that city initiated an official religious system and made R'a-worship the official religion.

Intermediate Period (2100 BC – 1580 BC)

The twelfth dynasty of the Egyptian kings conquered Nubia (North Sudan) and also invaded Palestine. During the reign of the fourteenth dynasty foreign invasions began, and around 1650 BC Egypt was occupied by Hyksos (shepherd) kings. Arab historians call them Amalekites, a Semitic people, who came to Egypt from Palestine and Syria. They were the people who introduced horses into Egypt.

Seal of the Hyksos King Apophis

Joseph's arrival in Egypt

Prophet Abraham's grandson, Jacob (Ya'qūb ﷺ), lived in Canaan (Palestine). Jacob ﷺ had twelve sons but he loved his son Joseph (Yūsuf) ﷺ the most. Joseph's step-brothers who envied him threw him into a well. A caravan which passed by the well pulled him up from the well and sold him away in Afāris (later, Tanis), the then capital of Egypt during the reign of Hyksos king Apophis. Afāris (Avaris) is now called Sān-ul-Hajar, a place near Manzalah Lake (Tanis Lake).

Joseph ﷺ was bought by Fotifar (entitled 'Azīz as in the Qur'ān) who, according to a tradition of Abdullah bin Abbās رضي الله عنهما, was an officer of the royal treasury. His wife, Zuleikha, who failed to tempt Joseph عليه السلام, levelled against him a false charge and had him sent to prison where he spent nine or ten years. Joseph عليه السلام had a gift to interpret dreams. He interpreted the dreams for two of his prison mates. The one who was released from captivity came several years later to Joseph عليه السلام asking him to interpret the king's dream. Joseph عليه السلام interpreted the king's dream and the king, elated and highly impressed by his interpretation, called him to the court and appointed him his deputy to run the state affairs and supervise the treasury.

The Ruins of San al-Hajar (Egypt)

Joseph عليه السلام knew from the king's dream that a severe famine was about to strike the land. So he made preparations to store food grains to tide over the famine. His step-brothers also came to him from Canaan to buy food grains. They came a second time with their step-brother Benjamin (Joseph's real brother) because Joseph عليه السلام had told them to do so.

When they came the third time, Joseph عليه السلام disclosed to them who he was. This upset his brothers and they expressed remorse and regret for their past behaviour. Joseph forgave them and recalled his parents and all his brothers to Egypt. The family and their offspring (the Israelites) settled in the region of Goshen, at Bilbīs (now called Saft-ul-Hannah). Thus did the Israelites gain power in Egypt, through Prophet Joseph عليه السلام.[1] Throughout the reign of Hyksos kings they lived in Egypt comfortably. The Hyksos lost power when popular rebellions broke out against them. Eventually, in 1532 BC, 17th dynasty came to power and the Hyksos were forced to leave Egypt for good.[2]

1. Atlas-al-Qur'ān (Urdu), P. 116-119; Tafhīm-ul-Qur'ān: Yūsuf (12): 87; Qasas-ul-Qur'ān: 1/224.
2. Oxford English Reference Dictionary.

New Kingdoms (1580 BC – 332 BC)

Tel-el-Amarna-the ancient capital of Egypt

Akhnaton (1375 BC - 1358 BC) belonged to the eighteenth Egyptian dynasty. During his reign Egypt started losing its overseas possessions. Palestine, Syria and Phoenicia broke away. Akhnaton was followed by two of his son-in-law to the throne. One of them, Tutankhamen, was very famous. His mummified body, with all the other things placed in his grave, was recovered in 1922 CE. They are now in a museum in Cairo.[1]

Moses[3] and the two Pharaohs

With the departure of Hyksos kings, the Israelites found themselves in great hardships. The natives (Copts) persecuted them and enslaved them and subjected them to hard labour. Things became still worse

1. Encyclopedia Tarīkh-i-'Ālam: 2/38-40.

Mt. Tūr where Allah appointed Moses as a Prophet

during the reign of Ramses II for astrologers told him an Israeli child would overthrow him. So, he ordered every male Israeli child to be slain at birth. Anyhow, when Moses عليه السلام was born, Allah saved him miraculously from the sword of Pharaoh's soldiers and got him reared in the royal court.

When Moses عليه السلام grew up, he noticed the tyranny of Pharaoh and the persecution of his own people, the Israelites, and was filled with grief. One day he saw an Egyptian beating an Israeli. He intervened and quite accidentally hit the latter and killed him. Afraid of prosecution, he fled to Midian.

Commentators of the Qur'ān say that Prophet Shu'aib عليه السلام lived in Midian in those times. Shu'aib عليه السلام gave one of his daughter to Moses عليه السلام in marriage. Moses عليه السلام lived with him for ten years and then left for Egypt with his wife. On way to Egypt, in a dark, cold night he saw a fire in the distance. That place was Mt.Tūr (Mt. Sinai or Jabal Mūsa). When he reached there, Allah addressed him, appointed him a prophet, and told him to communicate His message to Pharaoh as well as guide the Israelites. With Moses' intercession, his brother, Aaron عليه السلام, was also appointed a prophet and a deputy to him. When Moses عليه السلام arrived in Egypt, Pharaoh Ramses II had already died and his son, Menephtah was the king of Egypt. His capital was Memphis. He called himself a god.

Exodus

Moses and Aaron عليهما السلام transmitted the message of Allah to the new Egyptian king and also asked him to deliver the Israelites from bondage and let them leave Egypt but he would not listen and continued the persecution of the Israelites. One night Moses عليه السلام led his men out of Egypt. When Pharaoh came to know of it, he followed them with his soldiers. When Moses عليه السلام reached a creek of the Red Sea, Allah divided it into two parts. Moses عليه السلام and his men crossed to the other side of the creek by the dry path between the two parts of the sea but when Pharaoh and all his men tried to cross the sea by the same path, Allah closed the parts of the sea. Pharaoh and his men were all drowned to

An aerial view of Suez canal and the Red Sea where Pharaoh was drowned

death. This event took place in 1224 BC. The place where Pharaoh's army was drowned is known today as *Buhairāt Murrah* (Bitter Lakes). The Suez Canal passes through it.[1]

For more details about the Children of Israel and Moses عليه السلام, see under 'Palestine.'

Iranian and Greek occupation of Egypt

In 526 BC the Achaemenid king, Cambyses, invaded Egypt and annexed it to the Iranian empire. Two hundred years later, Alexander defeated Darius III of Iran in Anatolia, conquered the Syrian coast and Palestine, and marched on to Egypt. There he announced that he had come to free the Egyptians from the bondage of Iran.

When Alexander had occupied Egypt, the hierophants of Egypt conferred on him the title of 'Son of Amon and the heir of the Pharaohs'. Alexander told one of his engineers, Keratis, to build a new city, Alexandria, named after him, on the sea coast, appointed Aqledonis his viceroy in Egypt, and marched on further beyond for the conquest of Asia.[2]

1. Atlas al-Qur'ān (Urdu). P. 139-142.
2. Tarīkh-o-Tahzīb-i-'Ālam, P. 46; Tarīkh-i-Misr, P. 37.

Ptolemy dynasty of Egypt

Coin of Ptolemy II

The Ptolemy dynasty in Egypt was founded in 305 BC by Ptolemy I, a Greek, whom Alexander had appointed the governor of Babel (Babylon). Ptolemy II (285 BC -246 BC), following the ancient tradition of Pharaohs, encouraged marriage between brothers and sisters. In fact, he loved his sister very much and desired to take her as his spouse. Following the precedent he had set, every girl of the ruling family married her ruling brother. Ptolemy XII, the last king of the dynasty, was married to his sister Cleopatra, a marriage arranged by Roman king Julius Caesar, who had occupied Egypt. In 44 BC Caesar was killed. Thereupon, Cleopatra got her husband killed and herself became the absolute ruler of Egypt (47 BC –30 BC). When Julius Caesar's successor, Augustus Caesar, invaded Egypt, Cleopatra got herself stung by a poisonous snake and died. Now Egypt became a province of the Roman empire.[1]

Ptolemy: astronomer and geographer

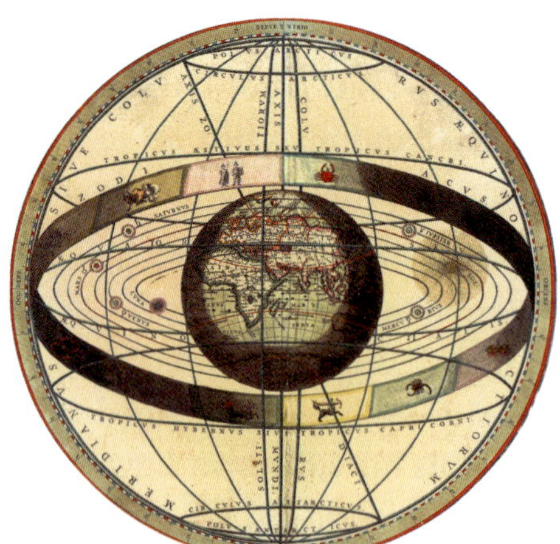

A map of Ptolemy

Ptolemy, the famous astronomer and geographer of Alexandria, was born in the second century CE. He drew a map of the then known world and also wrote a book, Geography, to expound and explain his map. He was the first man to divide the world into longitudes and latitudes, by

1. Encyclopedia Tarīkh-i-'Ālam: 2/106-107.

means of which he located towns and cities. His book on astronomy, Almagest, has been translated into Arabic (المجسطى) which records locations and measurements of 1022 stars and planets.[1]

City of Serapis

The ancient Egyptians were pagans. They worshipped idols and deities, the most famous among them being Osiris and his wife Isis. Serapis was another deity whose great temple was located in Alexandria. The huge idol of Serapis was made by joining together several slabs of gold, silver and other metals. It looked very much like the idol of Jupiter save that it had a basket or bowl on its head, holding in its right hand a snake with three tails and three heads, one of a dog, the other of a lion, and the third of a wolf. The ancient Egyptians took it as the god of the earth and worshipped it till Alexandria became known as the 'City of Serapis'.

Forced conversion to Christianity in Egypt

When the Unity of God as preached by Jesus عليه السلام was tainted with Trinity, it took its roots in Egypt and started spreading. Trinitarians were persecuted in Egypt, as in other parts of the Roman empire, during the reign of Roman ruler Diocletian, a pagan. By a royal decree many Egyptian Christians were put to death. But when Christianity was declared the state religion of the Roman (Byzantine) empire, the Roman emperor, Theodosius I, ordered all the Roman citizens to adopt the Trinitarian version of Christianity. As a result, temples and idols began to be pillaged and destroyed. Theophilus, the archbishop of Alexandria, with an army of his followers attacked

Coin of Theodosius I

1. Tarīkh Ard-ul-Qur'ān (Kāmil): 1/29-30; Oxford English Reference Dictionary.

Ruins of the coptic Temple of Serapis (Alexandria)

the temple of Serapis (Alexandria). In this religious war, thousands on both sides were killed. The temple was torched and, as a result of the fire, the great library attached to the temple was also burnt down to ashes. Some people blame Muslims for burning down the library but Christian historian Edward Gibbon expressed his rage at the Roman Catholics who destroyed that 'great treasure of knowledge'[1] A woman scholar of arts and sciences, Hipathia, was beaten to death before the very image of Mary by the Christians.[2] Later, other Trinitarian groups suffered the same fate.

Most of the Copts of those times belonged to the Jacobite sect considered hostile to the Roman Catholics. For this minor difference two hundred thousand Jacobite Christians were killed in Alexandria alone during the reign of Justinian. Those Egyptians who differed from the Catholic Church were often drowned to death.[3]

1. Qadīm Mazhabi Tarīkh, P. 77-78.
2. Tarīkh-i-Misr by Mufti Hakīm Intizam-ullah Shahabi, P. 39.
3. Qadīm Mazhabi Tarīkh, P. 78-79.

Palestine and Judaism

Ancient Palestine, according to geographic division, was the southwestern part of Syria *(Bilād-ush-Shām)* which stretched, in width, from the Mediterranean Sea to *Bādiyat-ush-Shām* and, in length, from Mt. Hermon (Jabal Sheikh) to B*e'r Sab'*(Beersheba), south of Lot's Sea (Dead Sea).

It was named Palestine because here lived those people whom Herodotus called Philistines. In the Hebrew language, the land west of the Jordan River is called Canaan (Palestine).

Geographically, ancient Palestine was divided into four different parts. The first part is the plain which runs along the sea coast, west of the plateau. The second part consists of the plateau bordered in the north by *Jibāl al-Jalīl* (Galilee hills) or Tabariyyah (Tiberias), in the south by Ephraim hills *(Jibāl Nablus)* and Judea Hills *(Jibāl al-Khalīl)*. The third part is the valley of the Jordan River. In some places, this valley is 100 ft. below the sea level. South of it, the Dead Sea is 1200 ft below the sea level. All these three areas, according to modern

Judea Hills

Ephraim Hills

geographic division, are called Palestine.

The fourth part is the eastern plateau of the Jordan River where the rivers, Yarmūk, Yabuq *(Zarqā')* and Arnon *(Mūjib)* flow. Arameans, Ammonites and Moabites dwelt in this part. Later on, some Israeli tribes like Reuben, Gad and a branch of Manessah also settled in some parts of it.

Jibāl al-Jalīl and city of Tabariyyah

Earliest settlers of Palestine

Since earliest times the tribes speaking Semitic languages started coming to Palestine. The Ammorites arrived here in 2000 BC. Prophet Abraham عليه السلام left his home and came here in 1800 BC. The children of Esau, the eldest son of Isaac عليه السلام, Abraham's son, settled here. Isaac's younger son, Jacob عليه السلام, and his sons dwelt here briefly before they moved to Egypt but, on their return from Egypt, settled here with their kinsmen, offspring of Esau. All the children of Abraham who stayed in Palestine were called Hebrews. In thirteenth century BC people called Philisti or Palestinians also arrived here. The Bible uses the word 'Ibri for the Hebrews.[1] The

1. Holy Bible (Genesis) 39:14.

Ruins of Ashkelon

Ruins of Gath

A headstone of Ekron Kingdom

word 'Ibr or Eber, in the Hebrew language, means: 'from across the land'. Probably the Hebrews were so called because they had come from across the Euphrates or because they were the offspring of Eber, son of Shelah (Shalekh), grandson of Arphaxad and great grandson of Shem (Sām). He was the father of Falaj and Yaqtān.[1] According to the Old Testament, Hebrews include all those peoples who claim their descent from Abraham عليه السلام. For example, Ishmael عليه السلام and the children of both sons of Isaac عليه السلام, Israel (Jacob) and Esau (Edom)[2] as well as the children of Mo'āb and Ammon, sons of Lot عليه السلام. The children of Edom and Lot settled south of the Dead Sea. The Arameans are said to be the children of Abraham's another brother, Nahor. Tribes other than Semites who invaded Palestine were either Horites (Hurrians), who had settled the land of Edom before Edomites, or Hittites and Philistines.[3]

1. Holy Bible (Genesis) 10: 24-25.
2. Esau was nicknamed Edom (red) because, as he came back tired from the woods, he said to Jacob: "Let me eat some of that red pottage, for I am famished!"- Genesis 25: 30.
3. Encyclopedia Tarīkh-i-'Ālam: 2/51.

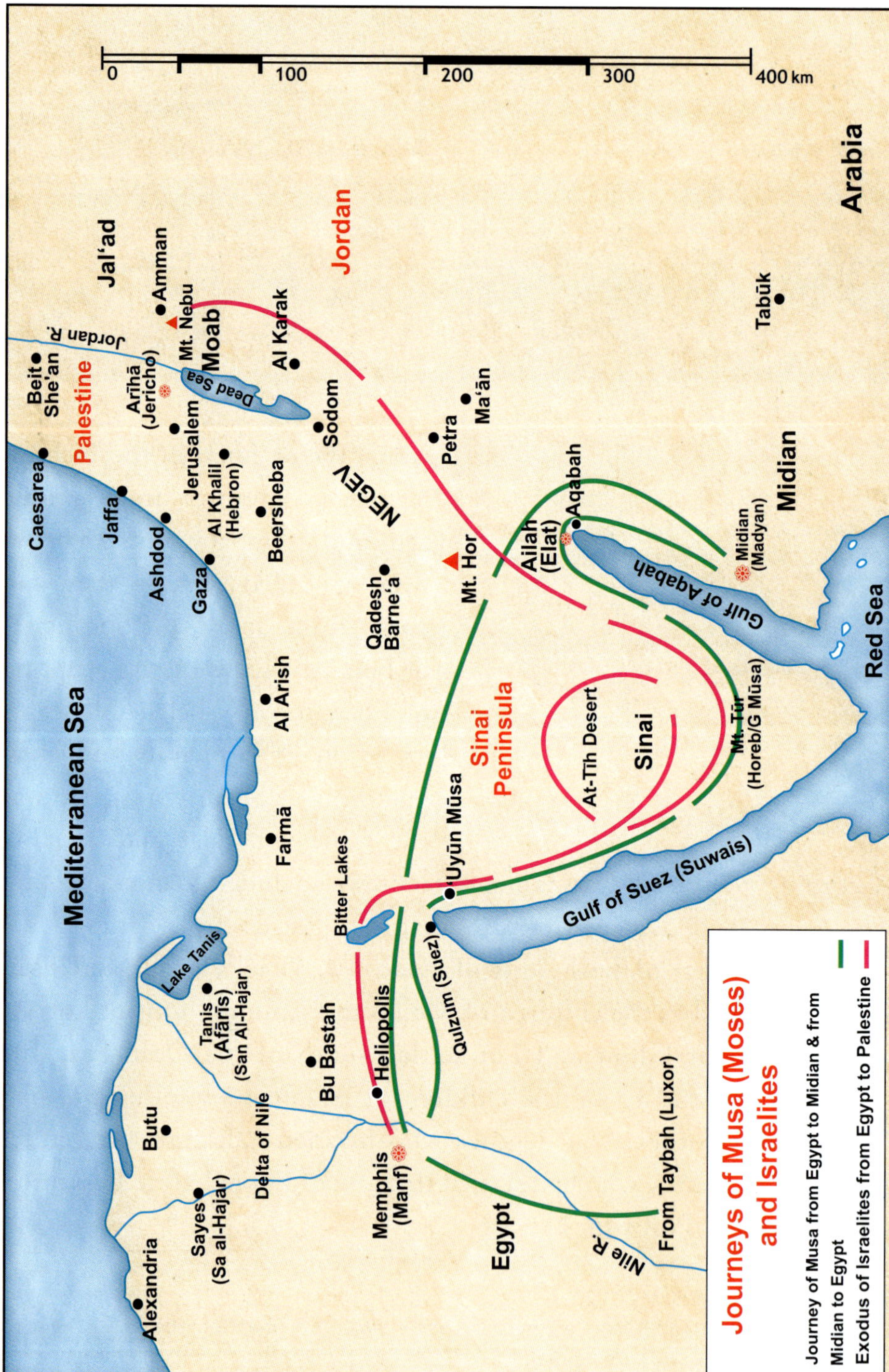
0
100
200
300
400 km
Mediterranean Sea
Jal'ad
Amman
Mt. Nebu
Jordan R.
Beit She'an
Palestine
Arīhā (Jericho)
Dead Sea
Moab
Jordan
Al Karak
Caesarea
Jaffa
Jerusalem
Sodom
Ma'ān
Petra
Al Khalil (Hebron)
Ashdod
Beersheba
NEGEV
Gaza
Qadesh Barne'a
Mt. Hor
Aqabah
Ailah (Elat)
Midian (Madyan)
Midian
Tabūk
Arabia
Gulf of Aqabah
Red Sea
Al Arish
Sinai Peninsula
At-Tīh Desert
Sinai
Mt. Tūr (Horeb/G Mūsa)
Farmā
Uyūn Mūsa
Bitter Lakes
Gulf of Suez (Suwais)
Lake Tanis
Tanis (Afārīs) (San Al-Hajar)
Qulzum (Suez)
Heliopolis
Bu Bastah
Butu
Delta of Nile
Memphis (Manf)
Sayes (Sa al-Hajar)
Alexandria
Egypt
Nile R.
From Taybah (Luxor)
Journeys of Musa (Moses) and Israelites
Journey of Musa from Egypt to Midian & from Midian to Egypt
Exodus of Israelites from Egypt to Palestine

Map.29

Idol-Worship in Canaan (Palestine)

The language current in Canaan in those days was called Hebrew. It was a north-western form of the Semitic language similar to the Phoenician, Moabite and Ammorite dialects. This country was influenced most by the Babylonian civilization. Amulets, charms and other religious practices came here from Egypt. Each region has its own idol called Ba'l which was placed on a hill or some high place. They did not raise any structure for it but, nevertheless, the surrounding areas were deemed sacrosanct. A goddess named Ishtar was also worshipped. Towards the end of the Bronze Age (2100 BC – 1500 BC), Palestine was ruled by the Hyksos kings (the shepherd kings) of Egypt. During the Early Iron Age (1200 BC – 900 BC) the Israelites occupied Mt. Ephraim. The Philistines had been residing here since at least 2000 BC, as the Bible (Gensis 21:34) says that 'Abraham stayed in the land of the Philistines for a long time. They had kept their occupation of the coastal areas where they established five city-states: Ashkelon, Ashdod, Ekron, Gath and Gaza.[1]

Mountains of Moab (Jordan)

Wanderings of Israelites and birth of Judaism

In the thirteenth century BC, Moses عليه السلام got the Israelites freed from the Egyptian bondage. He called them to the worship of Jehovah (Allah). They answered his call and became monotheists.

On his way from Egypt to Palestine, Moses stayed forty nights worshipping Allah at Mt. Sinai (Mt. Horeb) in the desert of Sinai. There he prayed to Allah for a glimpse of His countenance but he could experience only the effects of it. Then he was given Torah written on tablets. During this while the Israelites fell into the trap of Samri, a magician, and took to the worship of a golden calf in the plain of Raha. Aaron عليه السلام tried his best to keep them away from this horrible

1. Op.cit., 2/52.

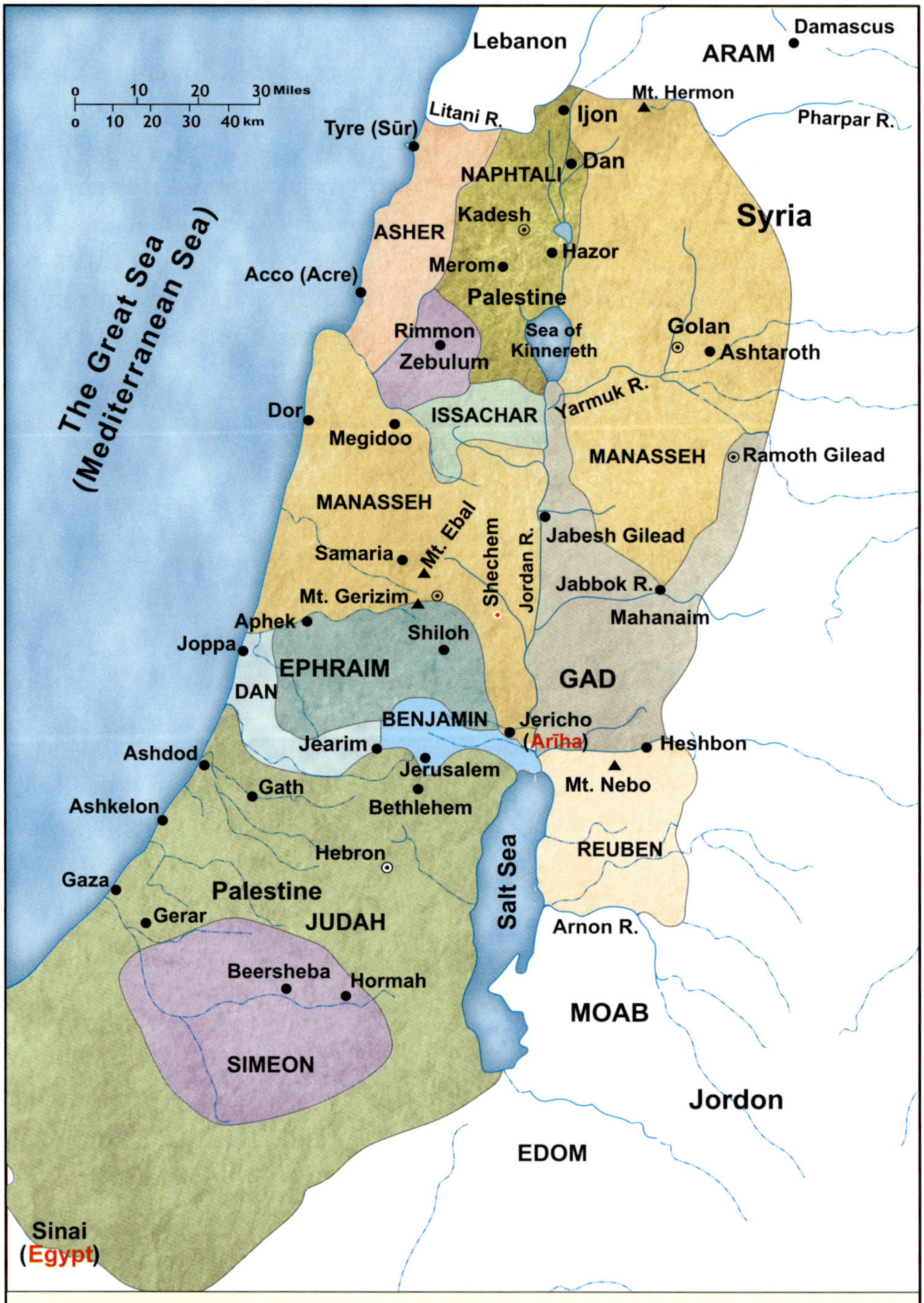

Land of the Twelve Tribes of Jews

Map. 28

sin but they would not listen. So, as a punishment, Allah told them to kill one another, those who did not worship the calf slaying those who did.[1] According to Torah, the numbers of those who were killed totaled seventy thousand Israelites.

Moses, along with the Israelites, departed from Horeb and arrived at Kadesh Barnea. There the Israelites heard that the Canaanites were invincible. Afraid to fight them, they refused to enter Palestine. For their disobedience Allah decreed that they go about the desert wandering for forty long years.[2] To quench their thirst Allah caused twelve streams of water to gush forth from a rock for them, and to feed them Allah sent *Manna* and *quails* (سلوىٰ) from heaven. The Israelites were twelve tribes, in all: Simeon, Judah, Reuben, Benjamin, Dan, Ephraim, Gad, Manasseh, Issachar, Zebulun, Asher and Naphtali. Of these tribes, two of them, Ephraim and Manasseh, were named after the two sons of Prophet Yūsuf (Joseph) عليه السلام while the remaining ten were named after Joseph's brothers. The children of Levi, Joseph's brother, were not counted among those twelve tribes because they were charged to keep the Tabernacle of Testimony (movable tent or sanctuary where the tablets of Torah were kept).[3] According to some commentators, it was the wilderness of Sinai where the wealthy and haughty Korah (قارون),

1. Tafsīr Ibn Kathīr, Al-Baqarah: 2:54.
2. Al-Mā'idah: 5:21-26.
3. Holy Bible (Numbers) 1:53.

with all his treasures, was swallowed up by the earth.[1] And during this time prophet Aaron عليه السلام also died aged 123 years. Later, the Israelites marched on and finally arrived, via Eila (now called Eilath) and Ezion Geber, at Moab (Jordan) and pitched their camps there. Moab is just opposite Areeha (Jericho) of Palestine.

Throughout his long march through the desert of Sinai, over the mountains of Edom and in the planes of Moab, Moses عليه السلام kept preaching and instructing his people. Torah had already been revealed. Now the time to say goodbye to the world was fast approaching. The Old Testament says: Moses عليه السلام, the slave of Allah, died in the plain of Moab, on Mt. Nebo, on the top of Pisgah and buried opposite Beth-peor. He was 120 years old at the time of his death.[2]

Israelites occupy Palestine

Towards the end of the twelfth century BC, after the death of Moses عليه السلام, Joshua عليه السلام became the leader of the Children of Israel. He was the offspring of Ephraim, son of Prophet Joseph عليه السلام. Under his leadership the conquest of Palestine began and its land was distributed among the various tribes of the Israelites and settled by them. That was the age of the Judges (leaders who had the authority to judge and decide matters). It was during this age when the Philistines and the Israelites fought several battles and the former even seized and got off with the Ark of the Covenant (a wooden coffer containing the tablets of Torah and the blessed remnants of Moses and Aaron عليهما السلام). That was the age of Prophet Samuel عليه السلام.

The Israelites asked Samuel عليه السلام to choose a king over them. So, Allah appointed Saul a king over them. He fought the Philistines and took back the Ark of the Covenant. The Philistines were very proud of their strongman and wrestler by the name of Goliath. He was killed by David عليه السلام.[3]

1. Tafsīr-ut-Tabari, Alqasas: 28:81; Qasas-ul-Qur'ān: 427/1; Atlas-ul-Qur'ān (Urdu), P. 145.
2. Holy Bible (Deuteronomy) 34: 1,5-7. These words suggest that they were written after the death of Moses.
3. Al-Baqarah: 2:247–251.

0 10 20 30 Miles
0 10 20 30 40 km
Beirut
Litani R.
Abana R.
Sidon
The Great Sea
(Mediterranean Sea)
Mt. Hermon
Damascus
Pharpar R.
PHOENICIA
Tyre (Sūr)
Dan
Kadesh
ARAM (Syria)
J. Jarmuk
Hazor
Acco
(Acre)
Sea of
Kinnereth
Mt. Carmel
Mt. Tabor
Ashtaroth
Kishon R.
Yarmuk R.
Megiddo
Beth Shan
Ramoth
Gilead
Jordan R.
Samaria
Mt. Ebal
Mahanaim
Shechem
Jabbok R.
Joppa
Shiloh
ISRAEL
Rabbah
(Amman)
Jericho (Arihā)
Heshbon
AMMON
Ashdod
Jerusalem
Mt. Nebo
Gath
Ashkelon
Bethlehem
Gaza
Hebron
(Al.Khalīl)
Raphia
(Rafah)
JUDAH
Arnon R.
JORDAN
PHILISTIA
(Palestine)
Beersheba
MOAB
Zered R.
W. el-Arish
EDOM
WILDERNESS
Kadesh
Barnea
WILDERNESS
Kingdoms
of Israel and Judah

Map. 30

Reign of king David and king Solomon

For seven years, after Saul's death in 1013 BC, his son ruled over the region east of the Jordan River while David عليه السلام ruled over Judea. Prophet David عليه السلام conquered Jerusalem and made it the capital of his kingdom. He also crushed in a short time all the insurgent Philistines and other tribes. He died at age 100 in 973 BC, after a forty-year long rule.[1] He was followed by Prophet Solomon (973 BC – 933 BC). He built the Temple of Jerusalem and many other magnificent buildings. According to Israeli traditions, it took seven long years to build the Temple of Jerusalem. His age is said to be the glorious age, an age of well-being and prosperity.

Valley of the Ants (An-Naml) Ashkelon

David and Solomon عليه السلام were given great gifts by Allah. Iron was made pliable for David عليه السلام. He could cast it any way he liked. Solomon عليه السلام could understand the speech of birds and animals. The wind was also harnessed for him. Besides animals and humans, the Jinn (genii) also obeyed him. The Qur'ān describes the story of Solomon عليه السلام and Queen of Sheba, how she, a sun-worshipper, came to him in submission and became a believer. It is said that the valley of the ants, mentioned in the Qur'ān (Sūrah An-Naml), was somewhere near Ashkelon (Palestine).[2]

Twin kingdoms of Jews: Judea and Samaria

Prophet Solomon عليه السلام was succeeded by his son, Rehoboam, but the Israeli tribes of the north chose Jeroboam as their king. So, the kingdom split into two separate states, the southern state of Judea and the northern state of Samaria (or Israel). The main cities of Judea were Jerusalem (the capital), Hebron (al-Khaleel), Bethlehem, Beersheba

1. NIV study Bible (Old Testament Chronology) gives the years of death of Saul and David as 1010 and 970 BC, respectively.
2. Atlas-ul-Qur'ān (Urdu), P. 170-174.

and Kadesh Barnea. Samaria was the capital of Israel. Jericho (Areeha), Beth Shan (Baisan), Shechem (Nablus), Qadesh, Hasban and Rabbah (Amman) were its main cities. (Samaria was the name of the capital as well as the name of the state which was also called Israel).

Assyrian assault and end of Israel

Jeroboam made Shechem his capital but later moved it to Samaria. For some time Israel paid tribute to the king of Assyria but when Israeli king Hoshea withheld the tribute in 732 BC, he was dethroned. Assyrian king Sargon II laid siege to Samaria (725 BC – 722 BC) and conquered it. He also exiled 27,290 Jews to Ecbatana (Hamadan) and Nineveh and made an end of Israel.[1] Later on Samaria was renamed Sabsathia in Islamic times.

Ruins of Samaria

Nebuchadnezzar invades and destroys Temple of Solomon

Judea survived from 930 BC to 586 BC. In 735 BC Assyrian king Tiglath-Pileser III attacked Judea. Prophet Hosea[2] عليه السلام worked for religious

1. Encyclopedia Tarīkh-i-'Ālam: 2/57.
2. Qāmūs-ul-Kitāb gives different versions of the name: Yusī', Hosī', Hosha' or Hoshī'. It was the name of the successor of Moses عليه السلام. Moses عليه السلام changed it to Yashu' (Joshua) Arabs call him Yūsha'. - (Qamūs-ul-Kitāb, P. 1085).

Model of Temple of Solomon which the Jews want to built at the place of Al-Aqsa Mosque and dome of the rock

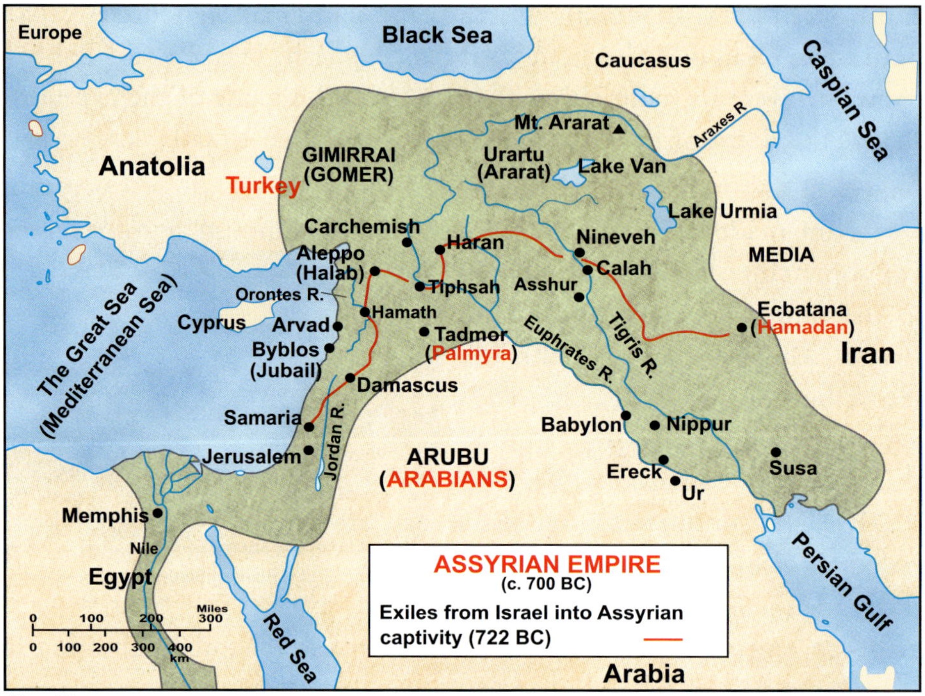
Europe
Black Sea
Caucasus
Caspian Sea
Araxes R
Mt. Ararat
Anatolia
Turkey
GIMIRRAI
(GOMER)
Urartu
(Ararat)
Lake Van
Lake Urmia
Carchemish
Haran
Nineveh
Calah
MEDIA
Aleppo
(Halab)
Tiphsah
Asshur
Orontes R.
Hamath
Ecbatana
(Hamadan)
The Great Sea
(Mediterranean Sea)
Cyprus
Arvad
Tadmor
(Palmyra)
Euphrates R.
Tigris R.
Iran
Byblos
(Jubail)
Damascus
Samaria
Babylon
Nippur
Jerusalem
Jordan R.
ARUBU
(ARABIANS)
Ereck
Ur
Susa
Memphis
Nile
Egypt
Red Sea
Persian Gulf
Arabia
Miles
0 100 200 300
0 100 200 300 400
km
ASSYRIAN EMPIRE
(c. 700 BC)
Exiles from Israel into Assyrian captivity (722 BC)

Map. 31

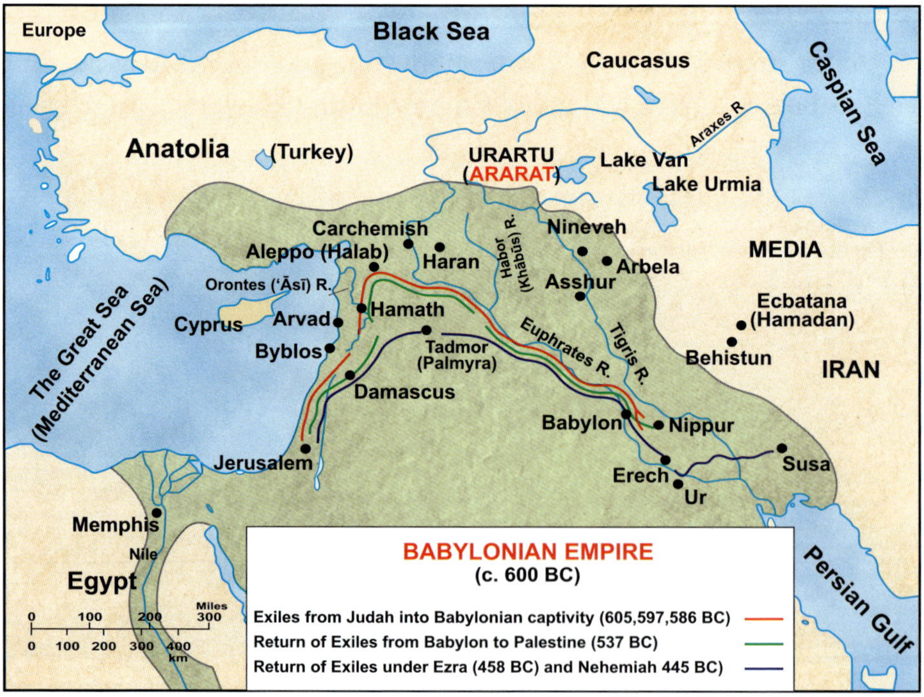
Europe
Black Sea
Caucasus
Caspian Sea
Araxes R
Anatolia
(Turkey)
URARTU
(ARARAT)
Lake Van
Lake Urmia
Carchemish
Aleppo (Halab)
Haran
Habor (Khābūs) R.
Nineveh
Arbela
MEDIA
Asshur
Orontes ('Āsī) R.
Hamath
Ecbatana
(Hamadan)
The Great Sea
(Mediterranean Sea)
Cyprus
Arvad
Tadmor
(Palmyra)
Euphrates R.
Tigris R.
Behistun
IRAN
Byblos
Damascus
Babylon
Nippur
Jerusalem
Erech
Ur
Susa
Memphis
Nile
Egypt
Persian Gulf
Miles
0 100 200 300
0 100 200 300 400
km
BABYLONIAN EMPIRE
(c. 600 BC)
Exiles from Judah into Babylonian captivity (605,597,586 BC)
Return of Exiles from Babylon to Palestine (537 BC)
Return of Exiles under Ezra (458 BC) and Nehemiah 445 BC)

Map. 32

revival and gave the Temple a central position in the land. In 609 BC, Hosea ﷺ fell martyr while fighting the Egyptians. After the Egyptians, the king of Babel, Nebuchadnezzar, invaded Palestine. In 597 BC he took along with him religious leaders including Prophet Ezekiel ﷺ to Babel (Babylon). The last king of Judea was Zedekiah whom Prophet Jeremiah ﷺ had advised not to oppose Nebuchadnezzar but he did not obey him. The result was that Nebuchadnezzar invaded the land and destroyed Jerusalem and the Temple. That was the end of Judea.[1] Nebuchadnezzar also drove away one hundred thousand Jews in chains to Iraq.

Jews' return from Iraq and reconstruction of the Temple

In 538 BC Cyrus (Dhu'l-Qarnain) occupied Jerusalem and allowed the Jews to rebuild the Temple. So, Prophet Nehemiah ﷺ started rebuilding Jerusalem in 537 BC. He also raised ramparts around Jerusalem and enforced the religious law. From 538 BC to 332 BC, that is, for about two hundred years, the Jews remained under the Iranian occupation. In 332 BC Alexander came to Palestine and occupied it. He was followed by the Ptolemy kings. Then, from 198 BC to 168 BC, the Seleucids (Greeks) controlled it. Later, the Jews retook it by war under the leadership of Judas Maccabeus.[2]

Romans occupy Palestine

In 63 BC Palestine came under the influence and rule of the Romans and remained so till 395 CE. In 37 BC a Jewish chieftain named Herod, known in history as Herod the Great, obtained permission from Rome to rule

Ruins of the temple of Augustus in Samaria

1. Encyclopedia Tarīkh-i-'Ālam: 2/57.
2. Encyclopedia Tarīkh-i-'Ālam: 2/49-58.

the land of the Jews. He rebuilt the Temple of Solomon and also built a temple for the Roman king, Augustus, in Samaria. It was during his reign that Jesus ﷺ was born. After his death, his kingdom was divided among his sons. One of his successors, Archelaw, ruled from 4 BC to 6 CE.

John the Baptist's martyrdom

Herod the Great's youngest son, Herod Antipas, became the ruler of Galilee and Peraea (eastern Jordan). He married Artas, the daughter of the Nabatean king. Later he divorced her to marry his half-brother Philip's wife, Herodias. John the Baptist (Prophet Yahya ﷺ) declared this marriage unlawful. This enraged Antipas who beheaded him. But the Jewish historian, Josephus, says that Herod Antipas envied John the Baptist because he was popular among the masses and loved by them. John was beheaded on the Rock in Jerusalem, his head carried away to Damascus. His burial place is said to be beside the Umayyad Mosque.[1]

Second Destruction of Solomon's Temple and Exile of Jews

The Jewish revolt against the Roman rule began in 66 CE. This forced the Romans to take action against them. Roman general Titus invaded Jerusalem in 70 CE and destroyed Jerusalem and the Temple of Solomon. Again in 132 CE the Jews revolted against Roman ruler Hadrian because the Romans had built a temple devoted to the worship of Jupiter at the site of Solomon's Temple. Hadrian stamped out the rebellion and banished the Jews from Palestine.[2] The Jews were banned from visiting Jerusalem except once a year. That was the beginning of the eighteen hundred year-long exile of the Jews i.e. Diaspora.

1. Qāmūs-ul-Kitāb, P. 1090-1162; Atlas-ul-Qur'ān, P. 200.
2. Encyclopedia Tarīkh-i-'Ālam: 2/58-59.

(Roman
Province)
Litani R.
SYRIA
The Great Sea
(Mediterranean Sea)
PHOENICIA
Sidon
Sarpeta
Damascus
Tyre
Jordan R.
Caesarea
GALILEE
Chorazin
Ptolemais (Acco)
Capernaum
Bethsaida
قانا
Tiberias
Sea of Galilee
(Kinnereth)
Gergesa
Mt. Carmel
Nazareth
TETRARCHY OF PHILIP
Gadara
Nain
DECAPOLIS
Caesarea
Pella (Fihl)
SAMARIA
Gerasa
Samaria
Jordan R.
Sychar
Palestine
Philadelphia
(Amman)
Joppa
(Yafa)
Arimathea
Lod
(Ludd)
Ephraim
Jericho
Emmaus (Amwās)
Jerusalem
Jordan
(Al-Quds)
Peraea
Bethlehem
JUDEA
Dead Sea
Hebron
Gaza
Holy Land in the time of Jesus

Map. 33

Judaism and Jewish Bible

Book of Ezekiel

Israeli Prophet Ezekiel was exiled along with the Jews by Nebuchadnezzar to Babylon in 597 BC.[1] Ezekiel wrote a book based on the teachings of other Israeli prophets before him. This book which listed in detail the beliefs and rituals of the Jewish faith, marked the beginning of Judaism. This book, the contents of which were derived from the revelatory books of the earlier prophets, included the law as prescribed by Jehovah (Allah) for the Jews in Deuteronomy.[2]

Ezekiel Bible in the old Latin Version

Jews and the Children of Israel

The title of Prophet Jacob عليه السلام was Israel, and his children are called the Children of Israel (that is, children of Jacob). The word 'Jew' or 'Jews' was not used prior to the book of Prophet Jeremiah. Initially, the word 'Jews' was used for the tribesmen who lived in Judea, the southern kingdom, but later on it was used for all the Jews who had returned from the Babylonian captivity (586 BC – 537 BC) although most of the captives belonged to Judea only. Gradually the term had begun

1. Qāmūs-ul-Kitāb, P. 323.
2. Encyclopedia Tarīkh-i-'Ālam: 2/53.

to be applied to the entire Hebrew race worldwide. Since the times of King Hezekiah (724 BC – 695 BC) the language of Judea had begun to be called Hebrew.[1]

Old Testament Bible

Pages from an early printing of Talmud

Manuscript page from the Book of Daniel

Jews and idol-worship

The Jews could not keep long to the monotheistic creed taught so vigorously by Abraham and Jacob ﷺ. Proximity to pagan nations and the influence of victorious armies who often overran their country introduced many beliefs, customs and rituals alien to their faith. This hard fact is acknowledged by many a fair-minded Jewish historian. For example, a Jewish scholar writes in Jewish Encyclopedia:

"The prophet's fury and rage at the idolatry proves that idolatry had taken root in the hearts of the Jewish masses and that until the return of the exiled Jews from Babel

1. Qāmūs-ul-Kitāb, P. 1187.

it had not been rooted out completely. Superstitions and sorcery had brought in their wake pagan beliefs and customs. There is also proof in Talmud that idolatry had a lot of attraction for the Jews."[1]

Talmud, cherished by the Jews as a very sacred book and sometimes even given precedence over Torah, was current in the sixth century CE. This book is full of foul and offensive language and insolence to God and remarks which make a mockery of universally accepted truths and human reason, a thing which gives us a good idea of the intellectual and moral depravity of the Jewish society of those days.[2]

Talmud is a book of instruction in the Jewish faith and behaviour. Explanatory commentaries on it have been written by Jewish scholars *(rabbis)*. They are of two types: Mishna and Jamara. The former is like the text, the latter its interpretation.[3]

Bible and Talmud

Work on writing, refining, revising and preparing the Old Testament began in 1150 BC. By 130 BC all the books had been included in it. The first five books of Torah were compiled for the first time around 400 BC. Later, other books relating to Jewish history (Joshua, Judges, Samuel, and Kings) were added to it and they, too, gained a religious status.

The early parts of the biographies of Saul and David عليه السلام were taken from the books of Samuel. They were composed in 950 BC. The era of major Israeli prophets was from 750 BC to 550 BC. That was the era of Amos, Hosea, Isaiah, Micah, Jeremiah, and Ezekiel. Their books plus some others were incorporated within Torah around 200 BC. Daniel was included in 164 BC. Psalms of David, Proverbs, and Book of Job were compiled in 586 BC.

1. Jewish Encyclopedia, Vol XII, P. 568-569.
2. See 'Jews in the light of Talmud' By Dr Hilling and its Arabic translation al-Kanz-ul-Marsūd Fi Qawā'id-ul-Talmud' by Dr Yūsuf Hanna.
3. Al-Mau'sū'a Al-Arabia Al-Muyassara: 1/543.

The remaining parts of Old Testament date back to the periods of Iranian and Greek occupation of Palestine. Some books have been condemned by the Jews themselves and dubbed counterfeit or tampered with (Apocrypha). That is, they doubt they are genuine revelations. Those books date back to 180 BC. Talmud, the Jewish book of jurisprudence, was compiled around 500 CE. Mishna, their book of law, was compiled in 200 BC.

Israeli Literature

A page from Targum

Beginning from the times of Moses until 600 CE, the Jews accumulated a large number of books. Not all of them are divine revelations. Some are the products of human efforts. This vast Jewish literature consists of Torah, Kutubīm, Nabi'īm, Targum, Midrash and Talmud. Torah is a Hebrew word meaning 'law'. Essentially, this name applies only to the first five books of the Hebrew Scriptures. They are the Sifr[1] of Genesis (covering the creation, Adam and Eve, Noah, Abraham, Isaac, Ishmael, Jacob and Joseph), Sifr of Exodus (Moses, Pharaoh, Children of Israel, the Law), Sifr of Leviticus (Law, the permitted and the prohibited), Sifr of Numbers (numbers of Israelites at the time of Exodus, battles of Moses, and some commandments and law), and book of Deuteronomy (law and commandments).

In Hebrew, Nabi'īm is the plural of Nabi. In Arabic, it would be Nabiyyīn. Nabi'īm is a collection of the Israeli prophets' sermons and

1. The Arabic word Sifr means: part of Torah or any book. The plural is Asfār. (Al-Qāmūs-ul-Wahīd: See under 'Sifr'.

lamentations with casual references to historical events. The books (Asfār) of Joshua, Judges, Samuel,[1] Chronicles and Kings contain only historical events. Mostly, the word Torah applies to both Torah and Nabi'īm, some of which are also called Kutub'īm.

Targum means 'translation and exposition'. It is a commentary in Aramaic on Torah and Nabi'īm which the rabbis prepared, basing their writings on the oral traditions of the prophets. They were composed over a period stretching from 600 BC to 100 CE.

Midrash is a collection of the sermons of different prophets and scholars. In rank, they are the equivalents of our *Ahadīth*. The Hebrew word 'Midrash' is like the Arabic word *'Dars'*. It means 'instruction'.

Talmud is the Israeli book of jurisprudence. It is based on the earlier books. It is arranged in chapters. Talmud is like the Arabic word *'Tilmīdh'*(تلميذ). It means 'education and knowledge'. Copies of Talmud were prepared, after the destruction of Jerusalem, in the fifth century CE, at the centers of Jewish learning in Tiberias and Babylon.[2]

To the Jews these books are authentic. The Christians acknowledge only Torah, Kutubi'eem and Nabi'īm and call them the Old Testament. The Israeli traditions current among the Muslims (popularly known as *Israeliyyāt*) are mostly borrowed from Targum, Midrash and Talmud.[3]

1. Sifr Samuel is, in fact a book attributed to Prophet Samuel and Sifr of Chronicles is like a diary or daily account of events.
2. Encyclopedia Tarīkh-i-'Ālam: 2/59.
3. Tarīkh Ard-ul-Qur'ān (Kāmil): 1/26,27.

Christ and Christianity

To the Christians, the New Testament is the primary source-book of Christ's life and mission. The New Testament is a collection of the four gospels, Acts of the Apostles, Book of Revelation, and the Epistles of the Apostles and their companions. The information contained therein is insufficient, judged from any aspect. The information given by the different parts of the New Testament is self-contradictory. The biographers of Jesus were faced with a difficult task: which one of these contradictory things to choose and which one to reject. Professor Sajid Mīr's book عیسائیت 'Christianity', based on standard Christian sources, is an important and very valuable research work. There can be no better biography of Jesus according to the Christians' viewpoint. The following information has been taken from the second chapter (Christ and Christianity) of his book.

Jesus, Jeshua, or Joshua means: Jehovah (God) is salvation. In other words, it means that only God is the deliverer.[1] The real name of Jesus was Jeshua or Joshua. He was born in the times when the Children of Israel had already suffered a lot from the destruction, wars and exile brought about by the Assyrians and the Babylonians. It is commonly believed that Jesus was born in 1 CE. When they are told that he was born four or five years earlier, they just gape in wonder. In fact, the Christian calendar was prepared in the sixth century of the Christian Era (CE). A monk named Dionysius Exiguus calculated in 562 CE the year of the birth of Jesus and placed it in the year 754 of the Roman

1. Davis Dictionary of Bible, London: 1972, PP 401-402.

Early printing of the New Testament

calendar. Now we know from history that Herod the Great who ordered genocide of the babies of Bethlehem died in the year 750 of the Roman calendar. This leads us to infer that Jesus' birth must have taken place at least a few months before 750. Most probably he was born in the beginning of the year 749 of the Roman calendar, that is, by the end of 5 BC.[1]

In those turbulent times of their history the Jews were awaiting a deliverer, a messiah who could rescue them from the oppression and slavery, restore their national honour, and boost them up socially and economically. They believed that the coming deliverer would have the special blessings of God. That is why he was called Messiah (Anointed) in Hebrew, Meshiah in Aramaic, مسيح *(Maseeh)* in Arabic and Christos (Christ) in Greek. The age-old custom of the Jews was that they used to rub 'sacred oil' on the heads of their sovereigns and religious chiefs, a mark that they are chosen of God as leaders.[2]

Birth of Jesus (Bible's Version)

As mentioned above there is a lot of controversy over the exact date of the birth of Christ: how many years before the beginning of the Christian calendar did it take place? According to various statements, he was born any time between 4 and 8 BC.[3] The Gospel of Luke says that in the days of Herod, king of Judea "The angel Gabriel was sent from God to a city of Galilee named Nazareth to a virgin betrothed to a man whose name was Joseph, of the house of David, and the virgin's name was Mary."[4]

1. Qāmūs-ul-Kitāb, P. 912.
2. See: In Search of Historic Jesus by L. Roddy and C.E Sellier, New York, P. 3.
3. Jesus in His time, P. 104.
4. Holy Bible (Luke) 1:5 and 1: 26-28. 'Mary' means: devout, pious woman or one chosen of God. – (Jesus in His Time, P. 104).

The angel gave to Joseph,[1] according to Mathew, and to Mary,[2] according to Luke, the glad tidings of the birth of a blessed son, without a father, to be conceived in her of the Holy Spirit.[3] In those times the Roman Caesar, Augustus, had ordered for a general census to be taken. So, Joseph and Mary left Nazareth for Bethlehem where Jesus was born.[4] According to Mathew, some Magi came to honour Jesus while he was still an infant. On hearing from them that the 'King of the Jews' had been born, Herod was alarmed and looked for the child. Since the Magi had left without giving him any more information, he ordered all the infants two years old or less in and around Bethlehem to be slain. But Joseph and Mary had been warned in a dream and they fled to Egypt where they stayed until the death of Herod.[5]

Qur'ān's version of the birth of Jesus

The Muslims revere Jesus عليه السلام greatly and count him among the greatest prophets appointed by Allah for the guidance of mankind.

The Qur'ān states very clearly that he was born of the Virgin Mary (or Maria). It names a whole chapter after her. The chapter of Mary (Maryam) gives some of the details about her and Jesus. In another chapter, the Family of 'Imrān (Āl- 'Imrān), the Qur'ān also gives details

1. Holy Bible: (Mathew) 1:20,21.
2. Holy Bible (Luke) 1:30,31.
3. Holy Bible (Mathew) 1:20.
4. Holy Bible (Luke) 2:1-7.
5. Holy Bible (Mathew) 2: 6-18.

as to how he was born:

﴿ إِذْ قَالَتِ الْمَلَائِكَةُ يَا مَرْيَمُ إِنَّ اللَّهَ يُبَشِّرُكِ بِكَلِمَةٍ مِّنْهُ اسْمُهُ الْمَسِيحُ عِيسَى ابْنُ مَرْيَمَ وَجِيهًا فِي
الدُّنْيَا وَالْآخِرَةِ وَمِنَ الْمُقَرَّبِينَ ﴿٤٥﴾ وَيُكَلِّمُ النَّاسَ فِي الْمَهْدِ وَكَهْلًا وَمِنَ الصَّالِحِينَ ﴿٤٦﴾ قَالَتْ
رَبِّ أَنَّىٰ يَكُونُ لِي وَلَدٌ وَلَمْ يَمْسَسْنِي بَشَرٌ ۖ قَالَ كَذَٰلِكِ اللَّهُ يَخْلُقُ مَا يَشَاءُ ۚ إِذَا قَضَىٰ أَمْرًا فَإِنَّمَا يَقُولُ لَهُ
كُن فَيَكُونُ ﴾

"(Remember) when the angels said: "O Maryam (Mary)! Verily, Allāh gives you the glad tidings of a Word [``Be!" – and he was! i.e. 'Īsā (Jesus) the son of Maryam (Mary)] from Him, his name will be the Messiah 'Īsā (Jesus), the son of Maryam (Mary), held in honour in this world and in the Hereafter, and will be one of those who are near to Allāh." He will speak to the people, in the cradle and in manhood, and he will be one of the righteous."[1]

According to Islamic belief, Jesus' miraculous birth without a father is like that of Adam, created from clay, without father and mother. Allah says:

﴿ إِنَّ مَثَلَ عِيسَىٰ عِندَ اللَّهِ كَمَثَلِ آدَمَ ۖ خَلَقَهُ مِن تُرَابٍ ثُمَّ قَالَ لَهُ كُن فَيَكُونُ ﴾

"Verily, the likeness of 'Īsā (Jesus) before Allāh is the likeness of Adam. He created him from dust, then (He) said to him: ``Be!" – and he was."[2]

Jesus (عليه السلام) begins his ministry

Baptized by John, Jesus (عليه السلام) began his ministry. He was thirty years old. Then, according to Luke, the Holy Spirit descended upon him in bodily form, as a dove.[3] Then Jesus spent forty days in the wilderness, a hard spiritual and physical exercise. There the devil tried to tempt him but he remained steadfast.[4]

Afterwards, Jesus made Galilee the centre of his missionary activity. There he would go round synagogues, teaching and exhorting

1. Āl -'Imrān: 3:45-47.
2. Āl 'Imrān: 3:59.
3. Holy Bible (Luke) 3:21-22.
4. Holy Bible (Mathew) 4:1 – 11; Holy Bible (Mark) 1:12 -13; Holy Bible (Luke) 4:1-13.

people.[1] Apart from Nazareth, a settlement of Galilee, he would also go over to Capernaum for his missionary work. He kept preaching in the different synagogues of Galilee.[2]

Jesus[3] preaches belief in One God

Jesus عليه السلام, like other Messengers of Allah, preached a strict monotheistic creed. He did not change that creed a bit. He only renewed and confirmed the mission of his predecessors.[3]

Allah says:

﴿وَقَفَّيْنَا عَلَىٰٓ ءَاثَٰرِهِم بِعِيسَى ٱبْنِ مَرْيَمَ مُصَدِّقًا لِّمَا بَيْنَ يَدَيْهِ مِنَ ٱلتَّوْرَىٰةِ ۖ وَءَاتَيْنَٰهُ ٱلْإِنجِيلَ
فِيهِ هُدًى وَنُورٌ وَمُصَدِّقًا لِّمَا بَيْنَ يَدَيْهِ مِنَ ٱلتَّوْرَىٰةِ وَهُدًى وَمَوْعِظَةً لِّلْمُتَّقِينَ﴾

"And in their footsteps, We sent 'Īsā (Jesus), son of Maryam (Mary), confirming the Taurāt (Torah) that had come before him, and We gave him the Injīl (Gospel), in which was guidance and light and confirmation of the Taurāt (Torah) that had come before it, a guidance and an admonition for Al-Muttaqūn (the pious)."[4]

1. Holy Bible (Luke) 4:14-16.
2. Holy Bible (Mark) 1:21; Holy Bible (Mathew) 4: 23; Holy Bible (Luke) 4:21-44.
3. Āl-'Imrān: 3:50.
4. Qur'ān: Al-Mā'idah: 5:46.

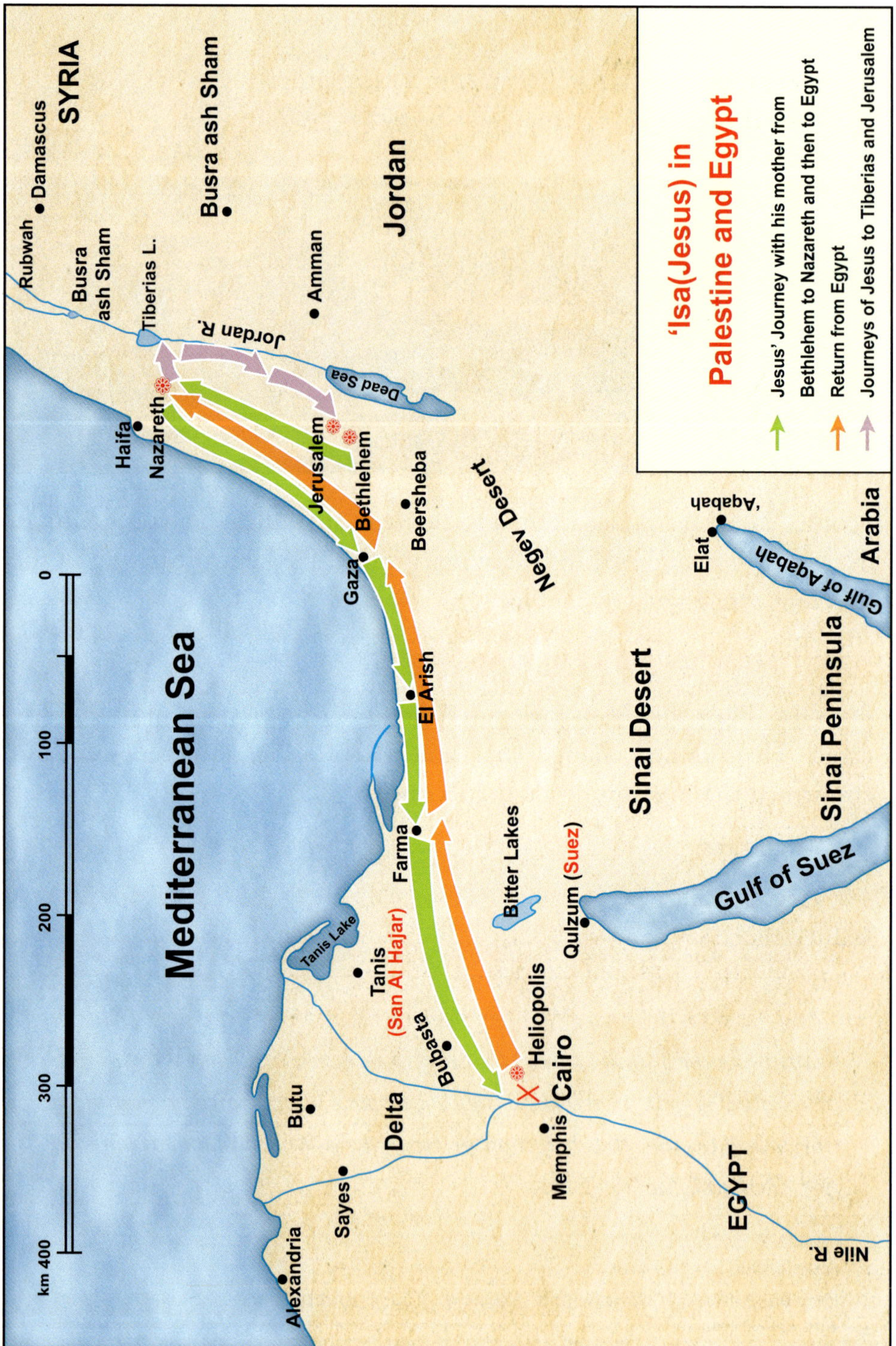
'Isa(Jesus) in Palestine and Egypt
Jesus' Journey with his mother from Bethlehem to Nazareth and then to Egypt
Return from Egypt
Journeys of Jesus to Tiberias and Jerusalem
Mediterranean Sea
km 400
300
200
100
0
SYRIA
Rubwah
Damascus
Busra ash Sham
Busra ash Sham
Tiberias L.
Amman
Jordan
Jordan R.
Dead Sea
Haifa
Nazareth
Jerusalem
Bethlehem
Beersheba
Gaza
Negev Desert
Aqabah
Elat
Arabia
Gulf of Aqabah
El Arish
Farma
Sinai Desert
Sinai Peninsula
Bitter Lakes
Qulzum (Suez)
Gulf of Suez
Tanis Lake
Tanis
(San Al Hajar)
Bubasta
Heliopolis
Cairo
Memphis
Butu
Delta
Sayes
Alexandria
EGYPT
Nile R.

Map. 34

Miracles of Jesus

To strengthen people's belief in him as the prophet of Allah, Jesus عليه السلام performed a number of miracles. The Qur'ān enumerates them:

﴿ أَنِّي قَدْ جِئْتُكُم بِـَٔايَةٍ مِّن رَّبِّكُمْۖ أَنِّيٓ أَخْلُقُ لَكُم مِّنَ ٱلطِّينِ كَهَيْـَٔةِ ٱلطَّيْرِ فَأَنفُخُ فِيهِ
فَيَكُونُ طَيْرَۢا بِإِذْنِ ٱللَّهِۖ وَأُبْرِئُ ٱلْأَكْمَهَ وَٱلْأَبْرَصَ وَأُحْيِ ٱلْمَوْتَىٰ بِإِذْنِ ٱللَّهِۖ وَأُنَبِّئُكُم بِمَا
تَأْكُلُونَ وَمَا تَدَّخِرُونَ فِي بُيُوتِكُمْۚ إِنَّ فِي ذَٰلِكَ لَـَٔايَةً لَّكُمْ إِن كُنتُم مُّؤْمِنِينَ ﴾

"I have come to you with a sign from your Lord, that I design for you out of clay, a figure like that of a bird, and breathe into it, and it becomes a bird by Allāh's Leave; and I heal him who was born blind, and the leper, and I bring the dead to life by Allāh's Leave. And I inform you of what you eat, and what you store in your houses. Surely, in that is a sign for you, if you are believers."[1]

Bible and Miracles of Jesus

The Bible enumerates many of Jesus' miracles. He healed the sick, exorcised demons and evil spirits out of the bodies of humans, cured the lepers and the paralyzed, gave sight to the blind, and speech to the dumb.[2]

His fame spread far and wide "and multitudes of men followed him." From among his followers, Jesus chose twelve disciples called Hawaris by the Qur'ān[3] and 'apostles of Christ' by Christians.[4] The names of those Hawaris or Apostles are: Simon (also called Peter), Andrew (his brother), James, John, Philip, Bartholomew, Mathew, Thomas, James the son of Alphaeus, Simon, Judas (brother of James), and Judas Iscariot. Mathew and Mark mention Thaddaeus instead of Judas (brother of James).[5]

These miracles were enough to convince the Jews that Jesus was the savior they had all along been waiting for. So, they wanted to make him

1. Āl-'Imrān: 3:49.
2. Holy Bible: (Luke) 4:40-41, 5:12-13, 5:18-25.
3. Āl-'Imrān: 3:52; As-Saff: 61:14.
4. Holy Bible (Mathew) 10:1-4; (Luke) 6:13-16.
5. Holy Bible (Mathew) 10:2-4; Holy Bible (Mark) 3:16-19; Holy Bible (Luke) 6:13-16.

their king but he refused, arguing that he was their heavenly (that is, spiritual) leader. Disappointed and disillusioned by his refusal to free them from the Roman yoke as well as tired of his spiritual sermons, the Jews tried to stone him.[1] Later, they changed their plans and wanted to kill him.[2] Now, Jesus, along with his apostles, retired to wilderness.

'Jesus tracked down by 'traitor

According to the current Bible, the Jewish religious scholars issued a decree: 'Anyone who knows where Jesus is should report so that we can arrest him.'[3] Following this announcement, Judas Iscariot (Judes Zaccaria John, according to the Christians who converted to Islam) took thirty coins of silver (from the Jews) and waited for a chance to have Jesus arrested.[4] One day Judas (or Judes) came with some men, appointed by the Jewish scribes, and with soldiers and had him arrested. "Thereupon, all the disciples of Jesus left him and ran away."[5]

After his arrest, Jesus was questioned separately by the Jewish

1. Holy Bible (John) 10:30.
2. Holy Bibe (John) 11:47-53.
3. Holy Bible (John) 11:57.
4. Holy Bible (Mathew) 26: 14-16; Holy Bible (Luke) 22: 3-6.
5. Holy Bible (Mathew) 26: 47-56; Holy Bible (Luke) 22:54.

Golgotha Mountain

scribes[1] and finally brought forth in the supreme council of Jews, Sanhedrin.[2] The Jewish scribes gave him over to Pontius Pilate, the Roman governor, to be executed by him.[3] Anyhow, the Roman governor hesitated to do so because he knew that the Jews had turned against him through envy.[4] But the Jews, in a bid to instigate the governor, charged that Jesus عليه السلام forbade people to pay taxes to the Romans and that he called himself the king of the Jews.[5]

The multitude kept shouting and urging for his execution. They even rejected Pilate's offer to release him to mark the Passover, as was the custom in those days.[6] They agreed to the release of Barabbas, a rebel and a murderer, to mark the Passover rather than Jesus.[7]

Eloi, Eloi, la'ma sabach thani?

Finally, the Pilate delivered Christ to the soldiers to be crucified.[8] Then he was carried away to Golgotha (literally, meaning: field of the skull) and, according to the Gospels, taunted, tortured and crucified.[9] Christ died crying aloud: "Eloi, Eloi, lama sabach thani" that is, my God, my God, why hast Thou forsaken me?[10]

---

1. Holy Bible (John) 18: 13, 24; Holy Bible (Luke) 22:54.
2. Holy Bible (Luke) 22:66.
3. Holy Bible (Mathew) 27:2.
4. Holy Bible (Mathew) 27:18.
5. Holy Bible (Luke) 23:2.
6. Holy Bible (John) 18: 39-40.
7. Holy Bible (Luke)23: 18-19; Holy Bible (John) 18: 40.
8. Holy Bible (Luke) 23: 25; Holy Bible (Mathew) 27:26.
9. Holy Bible (Mathew) 27:32-44; Holy Bible (Mark) 15: 16-26; Holy Bible (Luke) 23: 26-38; Holy Bible (John) 19: 1-24.
10. Holy Bible (Mathew) 27: 46; Holy Bible (Mark) 15: 34.

Qur'ānic Version

The Qur'ān denies strongly the crucifixion of Jesus:

﴿وَمَا قَتَلُوهُ وَمَا صَلَبُوهُ وَلَـٰكِن شُبِّهَ لَهُمْ﴾

"But they killed him not, nor crucified him, but it appeared so to them"[1]

and

﴿بَل رَّفَعَهُ ٱللَّهُ إِلَيْهِ﴾

"But Allah raised him to Himself."[2]

St. Paul and Christian Theology

"Modern Christianity was initially founded by a Jew named Paul (now called St. Paul. He died in 64 CE). The author of 'The Hundred Great Men', Michael Hart, writes of him:

"Jesus died a young man. At the time of his death he had only a few followers (apostles) with him but the Christian theology was basically evolved by St. Paul. Jesus gave a spiritual message. Paul added to it the worship of Jesus. In fact, Paul is the author of a good part of the New Testament."[3]

Origins of Trinity

Christianity, in the very early stage of its history, suffered from the tampering of extremists, the erroneous interpretations of the ignorant, and the pagan beliefs of the Roman Christians.

A Christian scholar says:

"The belief that the one God consists of three constituent elements (three hypostases) had already made its way into the lives and minds of

1. An-Nisā': 4:157.
2. An-Nisā': 4:158. For more details, see Shahādat-ul-Qur'ān by Muhammad Ibrāhīm Sialkoti, and Eesā'iat;Tajzia wa Mutāli'ah by Prof. Sājid Mīr.
3. The Hundred Great Men, P. 37.

the entire Christian community by the end of the fourth century and remained for long as an official and accepted belief of the Christians till it was discovered in the second half of the nineteenth century of the Christian Era that this belief had all along been changing till it took the modern form of Trinity."[1]

Christian or sun-god festival

Narrating an example of how ancient pagan beliefs were included in christianity, a famous christian historian James Houston Baxter writes:

Sun Festival

"Over the years pagan beliefs crept insidiously into Christianity. Those who had forsaken their old idols in favour of the new faith, unwittingly and unconsciously, conferred the supposed qualities and attributes of their old idols on their new saints and martyrs and gave their names to local effigies and images. Thus did the myths relating to their former idols move on to the new martyrs who acquired now a divine or semi-divine status or became landmarks of the devoutness and piety of the Middle Ages. The names of pagan festivals were changed and adopted as Christian festivals till, by 400 CE, the pagan festival of sun-worship became the birthday of Jesus Christ."[2]

The forty writers of Bible

The Christian Bible is the sacred book of the Christians. The word Bible is derived from the Greek word Bublos or Biblus meaning 'a collection of books'. Initially, the Bible was written in two languages, Hebrew and Greek.

1. New Catholic Encyclopedia, Vol. 14, 1967.
2. Rev. James Houston Baxter: The History of Christianity in the Light of Modern knowledge (Glasgow 1929), P. 407.

The Greek Bible

The Hebrew Bible

The Bible was prepared over a period of 1600 years by 40 authors from different parts of the world. The last author was born 1450 years after the death of the first author. The Bible, according to the Roman Catholic Church, consists of 72 books while, according to the Protestant Church, of 66 books. It had been divided into two major parts: Old Testament and New Testament. According to the Catholic Church, the Old Testament consists of 45 books, and the New Testament of 27 books. On the other hand, the Protestant Church says that the Old Testament contains 39 books and the New Testament 27 books. The first five books of Old Testament are collectively called Torah. The Old Testament was (originally) written in Hebrew but some parts of the Book of Daniel and the Book of Ezra were written in Aramaic. The New Testament was, however, written completely in Greek. In 420 CE the Catholic Church got hold of some books which were preserved by an edict of the then reigning Pope. Anyhow, before their preservation they were translated from Hebrew and Greek into Latin. By another decree the Pope forbade anyone to touch them. So, following the Papal decree, nobody has touched them ever since.[1]

Three manuscripts of ancient Bible

1. Three manuscripts of the most ancient Bible are extant now.
2. Vatican manuscript: This manuscript dates back to the fourth century of the Christian Era and has been preserved in Rome (Italy).
3. Sinai manuscript: It also dates back to the fourth century CE and has been preserved in Petersburg (Russia).

1. The Truth of Islam and the Confessions of Science, P. 323-324.

Alexandrian manuscript: It was prepared in the fifth century CE and has been preserved in London.

The books of the New Testament were written after 50 CE. All the four books, Mathew, Mark, Luke and John, were written between 50 CE and 115 CE. Barnabas, a disciple of Jesus, also wrote a gospel which dates back to 55 CE.[1]

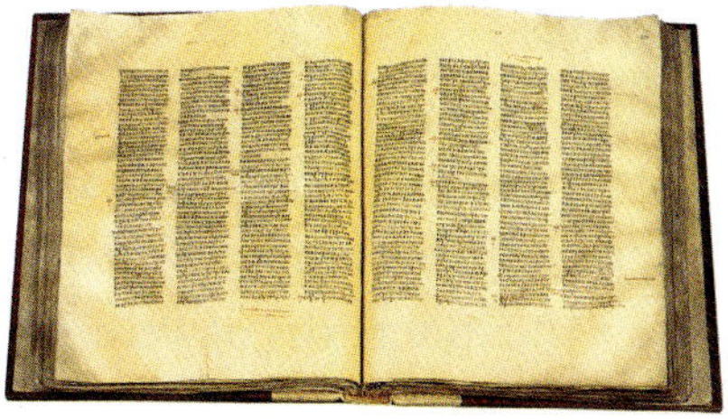

Sinai Manuscript

Vatican Bible

Alexandrian Manuscript

Pope of Rome

In the first century of the Christian Era (CE), Peter, an apostle of Jesus, and Paul (St. Paul), the founder of Christianity, were slain in Rome which became later on the centre of the church hierarchy. Rome is also the site of St. Peter's Church, a sacred place to the Catholics. The chief Christian priests[2] were called bishops. In 341 CE there were five archbishops in the Christian world: In Rome, Constantinople, Jerusalem, Antakiyah (Antioch), and Alexandria. Until 425 CE they were called papas. Later, the word papa or pope was used especially for the archbishop of Rome. When the church of Rome became gradually the only centre of the Christian west, the bishops of Rome started calling themselves the custodians of the graves of St. Peter and St. Paul. Since some words occurring in the gospel of Mathew were interpreted

1. History of Bible (English) by Barkat Masīh.
2. The Indian word 'Pādri' for priest or clergyman is of Portuguese origin. It gives the same meaning as Father.

to mean that Jesus had called his apostle Peter the cornerstone of the church, the bishops of Rome claimed to be the inheritors of Peter. This idea was floated first by Pope Celestine I (422 CE – 432 CE). Thus did the bishop of Rome become the most superior leader (Pope) of christianity.[1]

Islamic view of the Bible

The Christians themselves confess that the Bible has been tampered with and that there are discrepancies and inconsistencies at different places in the texts of the Bible. The Muslims believe that Allah revealed a book named *Ijnīl* (Gospel) to Jesus Christ and it could be that the extant New Testament contains some of the original revelation but it does not follow that the Muslims believe in the current Bible because it is not a collection of original, unaltered books as revealed by Allah. The Jews and Christians tampered with its text, made additions and alterations in it. This hard fact has also been acknowledged by the committee appointed to review the Standard Revised Version. The committee consisted of 32 scholars who were the members of the committee. They included in their report the opinions of an advisory board consisting of fifty representatives of the sects who offered to cooperate with the committee. The committee remarked in the preface to the Bible: "Sometimes some parts appear to have been omitted from the text but none of the manuscripts restored the omitted parts satisfactorily. Therefore, we can only depend on the best possible guesswork of the learned scholars with respect to the most probable reconstruction of the text." The committee added: "Some phrases have been added, giving a clue to important alterations, additions, and tampering."[2]

1. Encyclopedia Tarīkh-i-'Ālam: 2/152.
2. The Truth of Islam and the Confessions of Science, P. 324-326.

Can we have a right idea of the personality and teachings of Jesus from such a Bible with all its omissions, alterations, additions, and tampering?

Islamic view about Jesus

Muslims believe in the mission and ministry of Jesus عليه السلام. He was a true Prophet of Allah. Muslims believe in all the Prophets of Allah. That is the faith of every Muslim. Islam is nothing other than a complete and perfect version of the teachings of all the Prophets of Allah. Qur'ān mentions many Prophets including Jesus عليه السلام and tells us what they said to their people and what they did. *Ahadīth* state very clearly that Jesus, on behalf of other Prophets, will affirm his faith in Islam. Towards the end-time when Allah will judge between people of conflicting faiths and finally give victory to Islam, the only faith acceptable to Allah, Jesus عليه السلام will descend from the heaven just as he went up to it, act by it, execute its commandments, and will dispense perfect justice among those who profess this faith. The impression of Jesus عليه السلام gathered from Qur'ān, authentic Ahadīth and narrations of the Prophet's companions, is much more forceful, beautiful and moving than the one we gather from Christian sources. While this impression confirms some current aspects of Jesus' life among Christians, it rejects some other aspects, especially those which say that he was God incarnate or the son of God or that he was crucified or that any of his apostles betrayed him.

Mary's personality in the Qur'ān

Jesus' mother belonged to a very religious, highly noble, and blessed family, the family of 'Imrān. This family was the chosen of Allah. Mary's mother was a very devoted lady who always sought the pleasure of Allah.[1] She loved Prophets of Allah and saintly men. She named her children after Prophets and their kinsfolk.[2]

One day she vowed to give away her child she had conceived but not yet delivered, to the service of Allah and prayed to Allah to accept her offering. But when she gave birth to a girl, she was dismayed and shocked, crying: O Allah, I have given birth to a girl! But Allah knew

1. Āl-'Imrān: 3:33.
2. Sahīh Muslim: 2135; Musnad Ahmad: 4/252.

whom she had given birth to. She named the girl Mary (Maryam) and prayed for divine protection of her and her offspring from the touch of the devil. Allah answered her prayer, graced her offering with His acceptance, and reared her well.[1]

In the Place of Worship, worshippers quarrelled among themselves over who would take custody of the girl, Mary, daughter of 'Imrān. They cast lots with their pens.[2] And the lot fell to Prophet Zechariah (Zakariyyah) عليه السلام.[3]

It was a very blessed girl. Whenever Prophet Zechariah عليه السلام went to her closet (next to his prayer niche), he found there to his utter surprise fruits of the kind not usual at the season. He asked her: where did you get them from? She replied: 'That is from Allah. He gives whom He wills without limit'. Thereupon, Zechariah عليه السلام, despite his old age and his barren wife, prayed for a son. Allah gave him the glad tidings through His angels that he would soon have a pious and godly son, John the Baptist (Yahya) عليه السلام, a Prophet in his own right.[4]

Allah, the Wise, the Mighty, made this girl independent of the care of others. On the contrary, He made her a source of blessedness for her entire household!

The wonder was in the way she was reared by Allah. Angels would visit her, a token that she had been chosen by Allah for a very high and noble purpose. Allah elevated her above all the womenfolk of the world. The angels would instruct her to obey her Lord, devote herself entirely to His worship, bowing and prostrating with other worshippers.[5]

Miraculous Birth of Christ

The angels gave Mary the glad tidings, by Allah's leave, that she would give birth to a son whose name would be Christ, Jesus, son of Mary and that he would be notable in this world, and close to Allah in the next. He would talk to people in his cradle and in his manhood.[6] Then came the Great Ordeal, the

1. Āl-'Imrān: 3:33-37.
2. Āl-'Imrān: 3:44.
3. Āl-'Imrān: 3:37.
4. Āl-'Imrān: 3:37-39.
5. Āl-'Imrān: 3:42-43.
6. Āl-'Imrān: 3:45.

great test, for a girl of the family of Prophets, a girl born in an environment of devoutness and piety, and reared by a Prophet, a girl who spent her days and nights in the remembrance of the Lord.

One day she left her living place and went east, and screened herself from humans. There came to her, by Allah's command, archangel Gabriel in human form. She said: I seek Allah's refuge from you, if you are a man who fears Allah. (She knew that a pious man would fear Allah at the mention of His great name). He said: 'I am only a messenger of your Lord. I have come here just to give you a faultless son'. She said: How can I ever have a son when no man has touched me nor have I been unchaste. The angel (Gabriel/Holy Spirit) said: 'So will it be. The Lord says: It is easy for Me.'[1]

The Holy Spirit added: 'Allah does as He wills. When He decrees a thing, He says: Be, and it becomes.'[2]

Allah told Mary that He would make the child a great sign for mankind and a mercy from Him, and that is a thing ordained.

﴿فَحَمَلَتْهُ فَانتَبَذَتْ بِهِ مَكَانًا قَصِيًّا ﴿٢٢﴾ فَأَجَاءَهَا الْمَخَاضُ إِلَىٰ جِذْعِ النَّخْلَةِ قَالَتْ يَا لَيْتَنِي
مِتُّ قَبْلَ هَٰذَا وَكُنتُ نَسْيًا مَّنسِيًّا ﴿٢٣﴾ فَنَادَاهَا مِن تَحْتِهَا أَلَّا تَحْزَنِي قَدْ جَعَلَ رَبُّكِ تَحْتَكِ
سَرِيًّا ﴿٢٤﴾ وَهُزِّي إِلَيْكِ بِجِذْعِ النَّخْلَةِ تُسَاقِطْ عَلَيْكِ رُطَبًا جَنِيًّا ﴿٢٥﴾ فَكُلِي وَاشْرَبِي وَقَرِّي عَيْنًا
فَإِمَّا تَرَيِنَّ مِنَ الْبَشَرِ أَحَدًا فَقُولِي إِنِّي نَذَرْتُ لِلرَّحْمَٰنِ صَوْمًا فَلَنْ أُكَلِّمَ الْيَوْمَ إِنسِيًّا﴾

"So she conceived him, and she withdrew with him to a far place (i.e. Bethlehem valley about 4-6 miles from Jerusalem). And the pains of childbirth drove her to the trunk of a date palm. She said: "Would that I had died before this, and had been forgotten and out of sight!" Then [the babe ´Īsā (Jesus) or Jibrāīl (Gabriel)] cried to her from below her, saying: "Grieve not: your Lord has provided a water stream under you. "And shake the trunk of the date palm towards you, it will let fall fresh ripe dates upon you." So eat and drink and be glad. And if you see any human being, say: `Verily, I have vowed a fast to the Most Gracious (Allāh) so I shall not speak to any human being this day."[3]

1. Maryam: 19:16-21.
2. Āl-'Imrān: 3:47.
3. Maryam: 19:22-26.

When Jesus عليه السلام was born, Allah placed a screen (invisible) around him. Bukhari and Muslim narrated a Hadīth: "The devil pokes a finger into the side of every child at its birth, causing it to cry, except Mary and her son. He (the devil) poked his finger but he poked it only into the screen (that is, his finger could not reach Jesus)."[1]

Meeting of two great Prophets

On the Night of Ascent *(Mi'rāg)*, the Prophet ﷺ met with Jesus عليه السلام. He described Jesus عليه السلام in the following words:

«رَبْعَةٌ أَحْمَرُ كَأَنَّمَا خَرَجَ مِنْ دِيمَاسٍ»

> "Of average height, red (-complexioned). It looked as if he had just taken a bath."[2]

The Prophet ﷺ also saw Jesus عليه السلام in a dream while the latter was circumambulating Ka'ba. He described him: "his complexion like grain of wheat, as handsome as a person of that complexion can be, locks of hair hanging down between his shoulders, hair straight and well-kempt, water drops dripping from his head, resting both his hands on the shoulders of two men."[3]

The angels had already told her that her son was no ordinary child. He was noble and blessed. Now she had dates to eat and water to drink. When the angel consoled her, she felt strong enough to face her people.

Infant declares his mother's innocence

These details are enough to rule out any suspicion that Joseph, the carpenter, had anything to do with this miraculous conception. From her conception to the birth of Jesus عليه السلام and from his birth to the time she confronted her people, she remained alone. To prove her innocence, Allah caused the infant Jesus عليه السلام in his cradle to testify to his mother's innocence.

---

1. Sahīh-ul-Bukhāri: 3286, 3431; Sahīh Muslim: 2366.
2. Sahīh-ul-Bukhāri: 3437; Sahīh Muslim: 168.
3. Sahīh-ul-Bukhāri: 3440; Sahīh Muslim: 169.

﴿فَأَتَتۡ بِهِۦ قَوۡمَهَا تَحۡمِلُهُۥۖ قَالُواْ يَٰمَرۡيَمُ لَقَدۡ جِئۡتِ شَيۡـٔٗا فَرِيّٗا (٢٧) يَٰٓأُخۡتَ هَٰرُونَ مَا كَانَ أَبُوكِ
ٱمۡرَأَ سَوۡءٖ وَمَا كَانَتۡ أُمُّكِ بَغِيّٗا (٢٨) فَأَشَارَتۡ إِلَيۡهِۖ قَالُواْ كَيۡفَ نُكَلِّمُ مَن كَانَ فِي ٱلۡمَهۡدِ صَبِيّٗا (٢٩)
قَالَ إِنِّي عَبۡدُ ٱللَّهِ ءَاتَىٰنِيَ ٱلۡكِتَٰبَ وَجَعَلَنِي نَبِيّٗا (٣٠) وَجَعَلَنِي مُبَارَكًا أَيۡنَ مَا كُنتُ وَأَوۡصَٰنِي بِٱلصَّلَوٰةِ
وَٱلزَّكَوٰةِ مَا دُمۡتُ حَيّٗا (٣١) وَبَرَّۢا بِوَٰلِدَتِي وَلَمۡ يَجۡعَلۡنِي جَبَّارٗا شَقِيّٗا (٣٢) وَٱلسَّلَٰمُ عَلَيَّ يَوۡمَ وُلِدتُّ
وَيَوۡمَ أَمُوتُ وَيَوۡمَ أُبۡعَثُ حَيّٗا (٣٣) ذَٰلِكَ عِيسَى ٱبۡنُ مَرۡيَمَۖ قَوۡلَ ٱلۡحَقِّ ٱلَّذِي فِيهِ يَمۡتَرُونَ (٣٤)
مَا كَانَ لِلَّهِ أَن يَتَّخِذَ مِن وَلَدٖۖ سُبۡحَٰنَهُۥٓۚ إِذَا قَضَىٰٓ أَمۡرٗا فَإِنَّمَا يَقُولُ لَهُۥ كُن فَيَكُونُ (٣٥) وَإِنَّ ٱللَّهَ رَبِّي وَرَبُّكُمۡ
فَٱعۡبُدُوهُۚ هَٰذَا صِرَٰطٞ مُّسۡتَقِيمٞ﴾

"Then she brought him (the baby) to her people, carrying him. They said: "O Maryam (Mary)! Indeed you have brought a thing Fariyy (a mighty thing). "O sister (i.e. the like) of Hārūn (Aaron)! Your father was not a man who used to commit adultery, nor your mother was an unchaste woman." Then she pointed to him. They said: "How can we talk to one who is a child in the cradle? ' He [´Īsā (Jesus)] said: "Verily, I am a slave of Allāh, He has given me the Scripture and made me a Prophet; And He has made me blessed wheresoever I be, and has enjoined on me Salāt (prayer) and Zakāt (obligatory charity), as long as I live." And dutiful to my mother, and made me not arrogant, unblest. And Salām (peace) be upon me the day I was born, and the day I die, and the day I shall be raised alive!" Such is ´Īsā (Jesus), son of Maryam (Mary). (It is) a statement of truth about which they doubt (or dispute). It befits not (the Majesty of) Allāh that He should beget a son [this refers to the slander of Christians against Allāh, by saying that ´Īsā (Jesus) is the son of Allāh]. Glorified (and Exalted) is He (above all that they associate with Him). When He decrees a thing, He only says to it: "Be!" and it is. ['Isaā (Jesus) said]: " And verily, Allah is my Lord and your Lord. So worship Him (Alone). That is the Straight Path. (Allah's religion of Islamic Monotheism which He did ordain for all of His Prophets)."[1] (Tafsir At-Tabari)

Miracles of Prophet Jesus عليه السلام

Allah appointed Jesus a prophet for the Children of Israel. He told them:

1. Maryam: 19:27-36.

﴿أَنِّي قَدْ جِئْتُكُم بِآيَةٍ مِّن رَّبِّكُمْ أَنِّي أَخْلُقُ لَكُم مِّنَ الطِّينِ كَهَيْئَةِ الطَّيْرِ فَأَنفُخُ فِيهِ
فَيَكُونُ طَيْرًا بِإِذْنِ اللَّهِ وَأُبْرِئُ الْأَكْمَهَ وَالْأَبْرَصَ وَأُحْيِي الْمَوْتَىٰ بِإِذْنِ اللَّهِ وَأُنَبِّئُكُم بِمَا
تَأْكُلُونَ وَمَا تَدَّخِرُونَ فِي بُيُوتِكُمْ إِنَّ فِي ذَٰلِكَ لَآيَةً لَّكُمْ إِن كُنتُم مُّؤْمِنِينَ ﴿٤٩﴾ وَمُصَدِّقًا لِّمَا
بَيْنَ يَدَيَّ مِنَ التَّوْرَاةِ وَلِأُحِلَّ لَكُم بَعْضَ الَّذِي حُرِّمَ عَلَيْكُمْ وَجِئْتُكُم بِآيَةٍ مِّن
رَّبِّكُمْ فَاتَّقُوا اللَّهَ وَأَطِيعُونِ ﴿٥٠﴾ إِنَّ اللَّهَ رَبِّي وَرَبُّكُمْ فَاعْبُدُوهُ هَٰذَا صِرَاطٌ مُّسْتَقِيمٌ﴾

"I have come to you with a sign from your Lord, that I design for you out of clay, a figure like that of a bird, and breathe into it, and it becomes a bird by Allāh's Leave; and I heal him who was born blind, and the leper, and I bring the dead to life by Allāh's Leave. And I inform you of what you eat, and what you store in your houses. Surely, in that is a sign for you, if you are believers. And I have come confirming that which was before me of the Taurāt (Torah), and to make lawful to you part of what was forbidden to you, and I have come to you with a proof from your Lord. So fear Allāh and obey me. ``Truly, Allāh is my Lord and your Lord, so worship Him (Alone). This is a Straight Path."[1]

The Jews were a haughty and rebellious people. They knew that Mary was a saintly lady. They saw the miracles of Jesus. Yet they denied his mission and doubted his mother's purity and innocence. They denied Jesus was born with the breath of the Holy Spirit. When Jesus grew up, he breathed life into a bird of clay and proved to the doubting Jews that for Allah nothing was impossible. If he could breathe life into an inanimate bird of clay, the breath of the Holy Spirit could very well make a woman conceive, by Allah's leave. He worked many other miracles which were impossible for a human, a proof that he was a true messenger of Allah. He healed the blind, the leper, the sick, and even raised the dead. Yet the Jews refused to believe him.

Allah affirmed the humanity of Christ. Qur'ān says that he was like Adam, made of clay.[2]

When Jesus noticed signs of disbelief among his people, he asked them who could help him in his mission.

---

1. Āl-'Imrān: 3:49-51.
2. Āl-'Imrān: 3:59.

﴿قَالَ ٱلْحَوَارِيُّونَ نَحْنُ أَنصَارُ ٱللَّهِ ءَامَنَّا بِٱللَّهِ وَٱشْهَدْ بِأَنَّا مُسْلِمُونَ ﴿٥٢﴾ رَبَّنَآ ءَامَنَّا
بِمَآ أَنزَلْتَ وَٱتَّبَعْنَا ٱلرَّسُولَ فَٱكْتُبْنَا مَعَ ٱلشَّٰهِدِينَ﴾

"Then when 'Īsā (Jesus) came to know of their disbelief, he said: ``Who will be my helpers in Allāh's Cause?" Al-Hawāriyyūn (the disciples) said: ``We are the helpers of Allāh (i.e., we will strive in His Cause!); we believe in Allāh, and bear witness that we are Muslims (i.e. we submit to Allāh). Our Lord! We believe in what You have sent down, and we follow the Messenger ['Īsā (Jesus)]; so write us down among those who bear witness (to the truth)."[1]

Allah inspired Jesus' disciples to believe in Allah and His messenger and they did.[2]

Table from Heaven

Once his disciples asked Jesus ﷵ to pray to Allah to send them a table spread with food from heaven, not to test him but to acquire peace of mind and heart that comes, after faith, through the visual experience of the power of Allah in action, as Prophet Abraham ﷵ had wished to see the revival of the dead with his own eyes.

﴿إِذْ قَالَ ٱلْحَوَارِيُّونَ يَٰعِيسَى ٱبْنَ مَرْيَمَ هَلْ يَسْتَطِيعُ رَبُّكَ أَن يُنَزِّلَ عَلَيْنَا مَآئِدَةً مِّنَ ٱلسَّمَآءِ
قَالَ ٱتَّقُوا۟ ٱللَّهَ إِن كُنتُم مُّؤْمِنِينَ ﴿١١٢﴾ قَالُوا۟ نُرِيدُ أَن نَّأْكُلَ مِنْهَا وَتَطْمَئِنَّ قُلُوبُنَا وَنَعْلَمَ أَن قَدْ
صَدَقْتَنَا وَنَكُونَ عَلَيْهَا مِنَ ٱلشَّٰهِدِينَ ﴿١١٣﴾ قَالَ عِيسَى ٱبْنُ مَرْيَمَ ٱللَّهُمَّ رَبَّنَآ أَنزِلْ عَلَيْنَا مَآئِدَةً مِّنَ
ٱلسَّمَآءِ تَكُونُ لَنَا عِيدًا لِّأَوَّلِنَا وَءَاخِرِنَا وَءَايَةً مِّنكَ وَٱرْزُقْنَا وَأَنتَ خَيْرُ ٱلرَّٰزِقِينَ ﴿١١٤﴾ قَالَ ٱللَّهُ إِنِّى
مُنَزِّلُهَا عَلَيْكُمْ فَمَن يَكْفُرْ بَعْدُ مِنكُمْ فَإِنِّىٓ أُعَذِّبُهُۥ عَذَابًا لَّآ أُعَذِّبُهُۥٓ أَحَدًا مِّنَ ٱلْعَٰلَمِينَ﴾

"(Remember) when Al-Hawāriyyūn (the disciples) said: ``O 'Īsā (Jesus), son of Maryam (Mary)! Can your Lord send down to us a table spread (with food) from heaven?" 'Īsā (Jesus) said: ``Fear Allāh, if you are indeed believers. They said: ``We wish to eat thereof and to satisfy our hearts (to be stronger in Faith), and to know that you have indeed told us the truth and that we ourselves be its witnesses." 'Īsā (Jesus), son of Maryam (Mary), said: ``O Allāh, our Lord! Send us from the heaven a table spread (with food) that there may be for us – for the first and the last of us – a festival

1. Āl-'Imrān: 3:52-53.
2. Al-Mā'idah: 5:111.

and a sign from You; and provide us with sustenance, for You are the Best of sustainers." Allāh said: ``I am going to send it down to you, but if any of you after that disbelieves, then I will punish him with a torment such as I have not inflicted on anyone among (all) the 'Ālamīn."[1]

None of Christ's disciple betrayed

There are many traditions current among Christians that do not befit the dignity and nobility of Jesus and Mary. Authentic Islamic sources repudiate all such traditions. Similarly, some equally wrong traditions have also made their way into Islamic literature, especially through some Christian scholars who converted to Islam. For example, some traditions say that Jesus' disciples were timid and that they fled away from him when he was arrested by the Roman soldiers. Some other traditions say that one of Jesus' disciples, Judas Iscariot (or, according to Arabic sources, Judas Zechariah John) betrayed Jesus and, as a punishment, Allah made him look like Jesus, and so on. Islam has exposed all these lies. There is evidence in Qur'ān that all the disciples of Jesus remained faithful to him:

﴿وَكُنتُ عَلَيۡهِمۡ شَهِيدٗا مَّا دُمۡتُ فِيهِمۡۖ﴾

"And i was a witness over them while I dwelt amongst them."[2]

Ibn Abi Hātim, and following him, Ibn Kathīr also, writing in their commentaries of Qur'ān, narrated a tradition on the authority of Ibn 'Abbās, a tradition that runs contrary to the current Israeli tradition. It could be he heard it from the Prophet himself. The tradition says:

"When Allah decided to take up Jesus to heaven, he came to his disciples. There were twelve of them in the house at that time. Jesus, who had just washed himself in the stream flowing down by the house where he was staying, said: One of you would disbelieve twelve times after he had believed. Then he asked which of them would like to resemble me and get killed and be rewarded with a place in the Paradise with me. The youngest of them stood up and volunteered to be killed. But Jesus told him to sit down. Again Jesus asked the same question. Again the same young man stood up. Then Jesus acquiesced and said:

1. Al-Mā'idah: 5:112-115.
2. Al-Mā'idah: 5:117.

That's you. Jesus' resemblance fell on his face while Jesus was taken away through a skylight up to heaven. When the Jews arrived there, they seized the look-like of Jesus and later crucified him. One of them disbelieved twelve times over after he had believed. Later, the people split up into three sects. One of them said: God lived with us as long as He liked and then went up to heaven. They are Jacobites. The second one said: The son of God lived with us as long as Allah willed and then Allah took him up. They are the Nestorians. The third said: The slave of Allah, a prophet, remained with us as long as Allah willed. Then Allah took him up to heaven. They were Muslims. The infidels united against this sect (the Muslims) and exterminated them. There remained no trace of Islam until Muhammadﷺ was sent."[1]

Ibn Kathīr رحمه الله quoted this narration on the authority of Ibn Abi Hātim رحمه الله and commented: The chain of narration up to Ibn 'Abbās رضي الله عنه is sound.[2]

Jesus عليه السلام was a high-minded, high-spirited, prophet, like his predecessors. His mother was a saintly woman *('siddīqah')*.[3] Jesus was truthful, in both word and act. Allah revealed to Jesus a book, the *Injīl* (Gosple), but the Gosples which are current today are not the same as the original one, neither in its language nor in its content. The extant Gosples are the works of diverse authors and, according to the Christians themselves, they have suffered from alterations, in words and meanings. Torah and the Psalms of David are not safe from alterations either. The Qur'ān refers to these alterations made in divine revelations:

﴿مِّنَ ٱلَّذِينَ هَادُوا۟ يُحَرِّفُونَ ٱلْكَلِمَ عَن مَّوَاضِعِهِۦ﴾

"Among those who are Jews, there are some who displace words from (their) right places."[4]

Christ's Sayings of Wisdom

Allah gave Jesus عليه السلام wisdom. He would preach and instruct wisely. Abu Hurairah رضي الله عنه narrated a Hadīth from the Prophet ﷺ: "Jesus عليه السلام saw a

1. Tafsīr Ibn Abi Hātim, An-Nisā: 4:157.
2. Tafsīr Ibn Kathīr, An-Nisā: 4:157.
3. Al-Mā'idah: 5:75.
4. An-Nisā': 4:46.

man stealing and told that man: 'You have stolen.' The man said: By Allah, I didn't. Thereupon, Jesus ﷺ said: I believe in Allah and do not trust my eyes."[1]

That was the way of Jesus ﷺ. He tried to make him realize the station of Allah, the High. Those who swear falsely need to be instructed in this way. He spoke softly, a style which could not fail to move the listener.

Here are some examples of his sermons and sayings:

Ibn Kathīr quoted a Hadīth collected by Ibn 'Asākir on the authority of 'Ikrimah: Jesus ﷺ said: Don't cast pearls before swine. They can make no use of them. Don't give wisdom to the one who does not seek it because wisdom is more precious than pearls. He who does not seek it is worse than swine."[2]

Jesus ﷺ is also reported to have said:

"O evil scribes, you put the world above your head and the Afterlife under your feet. Your word is a healer but your action is disease. You are like a Dafli tree (a beautiful but poisonous tree), fair to look at but fatal to eat."

Wahb bin Munabbah also narrated a saying of Jesus: 'O evil scribes, you have stationed yourselves at the doors of the paradise. Neither you enter it nor let the poor ones enter it. Surely, the vilest man in the sight of Allah is the scribe (religious scholar) who by this learning seeks worldly gains."[3]

He also narrated: Once Jesus ﷺ and another companion were standing beside a grave while a dead body was being lowered into the grave. The companion spoke of the darkness of the grave, its loneliness and narrowness. Jesus said: "You were once in the womb of your mother much narrower than the grave. Allah can widen it when He wills."[4]

Christ's Ascension

The Jews plotted his crucifixion. That, they thought, would tarnish his image and hopefully convince the people that their charges against him

1. Musnad Ahmad: 2/383.
2. Jesus' saying has now become an English proverb: To cast pearls before swine.
3. Ad-Durr-ul-Manthūr: Āl-'Imrān: 3:48.
4. Op.cit.

were true. But Allah failed their plot and smashed their hopes. Allah addressed Jesus, saying:

﴿يَٰعِيسَىٰٓ إِنِّي مُتَوَفِّيكَ وَرَافِعُكَ إِلَيَّ وَمُطَهِّرُكَ مِنَ ٱلَّذِينَ كَفَرُواْ وَجَاعِلُ ٱلَّذِينَ ٱتَّبَعُوكَ فَوْقَ
ٱلَّذِينَ كَفَرُوٓاْ إِلَىٰ يَوْمِ ٱلْقِيَٰمَةِ ثُمَّ إِلَيَّ مَرْجِعُكُمْ فَأَحْكُمُ بَيْنَكُمْ فِيمَا كُنتُمْ فِيهِ تَخْتَلِفُونَ﴾

"O 'Īsā (Jesus)! I will make you sleep and raise you to Myself and clear you [of the forged statement that 'Īsā (Jesus) is Allāh's son] of those who disbelieve, and I will make those who follow you (monotheists, who worship none but Allāh) superior to those who disbelieve [in the Oneness of Allāh, or disbelieve in some of His Messengers, e.g. Muhammad ﷺ, 'Īsā (Jesus), Mūsā (Moses), or in His Holy Books, e.g. the Taurāt (Torah), the Injīl (Gospel), the Qur'ān] till the Day of Resurrection. Then you will return to Me and I will judge between you in the matters in which you used to dispute."[1]

And Allah also said:

﴿وَمَا قَتَلُوهُ وَمَا صَلَبُوهُ وَلَٰكِن شُبِّهَ لَهُمْ وَإِنَّ ٱلَّذِينَ ٱخْتَلَفُواْ فِيهِ لَفِي شَكٍّ مِّنْهُ مَا لَهُم بِهِۦ مِنْ عِلْمٍ إِلَّا
ٱتِّبَاعَ ٱلظَّنِّ وَمَا قَتَلُوهُ يَقِينًۢا ﴿١٥٧﴾ بَل رَّفَعَهُ ٱللَّهُ إِلَيْهِ وَكَانَ ٱللَّهُ عَزِيزًا حَكِيمًا ﴿١٥٨﴾ وَإِن مِّنْ أَهْلِ ٱلْكِتَٰبِ
إِلَّا لَيُؤْمِنَنَّ بِهِۦ قَبْلَ مَوْتِهِۦ وَيَوْمَ ٱلْقِيَٰمَةِ يَكُونُ عَلَيْهِمْ شَهِيدًا﴾

"But they killed him not, nor crucified him, but it appeared so to them [the resemblance of 'Īsā (Jesus) was put over another man (and they killed that man)], and those who differ therein are full of doubts. They have no (certain) knowledge, they follow nothing but conjecture. For surely, they killed him not [i.e. 'Īsā (Jesus), son of Maryam (Mary ⁰)]: But Allāh raised him ['Īsā (Jesus)] up (with his body and soul) to Himself (and he is in the heavens). And Allāh is Ever All-Powerful, All-Wise. And there is none of the people of the Scripture (Jews and Christians) but must believe in him ['Īsā (Jesus), son of Maryam (Mary), as only a Messenger of Allāh and a human being] before his ['Īsā (Jesus) or a Jew's or a Christian's] death (at the time of the appearance of the angel of death). And on the Day of Resurrection, he ['Īsā (Jesus)] will be a witness against them.."[2]

1. Āl-'Imrān: 3:55.
2. An-Nisā': 4:157-159.

Christ's return to earth

Jesus is now in heaven but he will return to the earth, by Allah's leave, around the dawn prayer time, in the Jāmi' Damascus after the *Iqamah* has been pronounced. He will come up to the first row of the worshippers. There the *'Imām* (prayer leader) will request him to come forward and lead the prayer. But Jesus will refuse, saying: 'You are the leader, one of the other. That's the honour Allah has conferred on this *Ummah*.'[1]

The sincere among the People of the Book will believe in him. Jesus will make them a part of the *Ummah* of Muhammad (ﷺ), kill the pig, break down the cross, and abolish the *Jizyah* tax. Then he will chase the Dajjāl (Anti-Christ) and slay him at the door of Lydda, an important town, west of Jerusalem, on the Tel Aviv-Ramallah highway, where a large Israeli air base has been set up.[2] Then Jesus, following the Islamic instruction, will marry and have children. He will rule the world. His reign will be one of ideal justice. He will also invoke Allah's curse on Gogs and Magogs and they will perish.

1. Sahīh Muslim: 156.
2. Atlas Futūhāt Islamiyyah, P. 169,189 .

The Minaret of the Bride, Umayyad Mosque (Damascus)

Ancient greek Temple of Juno Hera God, Agrigento, valley of temples, Sicily, Italy

The Greek Empire

The Arabic word for Greece is *Unān* (يونان) which is the Arabicized version of Ionia. The Ionian people and their country were named after a Greek goddess called Ion. The territories of the Ioanians included Attica, the southeastern state of Greece, Aegean islands, Ionia, the western coastal area of Asia Minor, and the islands of the Ionian Sea on the western coast of Greece.[1] There is still a town called Ioannina in northwest Greece.

Greece, which lies in the southeast of Europe, is a southern extension of the Balkan Peninsula. In the east the Aegean Sea separates it from Asia Minor or Anatolia (Turkey). In the west the Ionian Sea separates it from Italy. To the south of it lies the Mediterranean Sea. To the north of Greece lie Bulgaria, Macedonia and Albania and to the northeast of

1. Oxford English Reference Dictionary, P. 741.

it lies the European part of Turkey (Thrace).

Lydia, Sparta and Solon, the Wise

In the third millennium BC the Greek tribes settled in Crete, Cyprus, the islands of the Aegean Sea, Smyrna (modern Izmir) and other places of Asia Minor. Between 800 BC and 600 BC there were already many Greek colonies in Egypt, Sicily, Italy and North Africa. In Asia Minor the Greek states of Phrygia (705 BC) and Lydia were founded. In 546 BC, Cyrus the Great *(Dhu'l-Qarnain)* defeated Croesus, the last king of Lydia, and annexed his country to his empire.

Ruins of Sardis, the capital of Lydia (Turkey)

During this time, among the Greek states, Sparta, lying in the southern part of Peloponnesus Peninsula, and Attica (Athens) gained wide reputation. In 593 BC, a wise man named Solon (639 BC – 559 BC) was the sole administrator of Athens. He wrote off the loans of mortgaged lands, manumitted slaves, and relaxed the punishments for all crimes except murder. According to his concept of democracy, he paved the way for common men (demos) to take part in the administrative affairs of the state. Modern democracy is, in fact, a modified or, say, an improved version of his concept of democracy.[1]

The historic battles of Marathon

In 498 BC the Greek states of the western coast of Asia Minor revolted against the Persian emperor. Thereupon Dara Gushtasip (Darius I) dispatched a large force to conquer Greece. In 490 BC, in the battlefield of Marathon, 22 miles off Athens, a Greek general named Meltadez routed the Persian forces. It is said that a messenger carrying the news of the victory ran nonstop for as long as 35 kilometers but when he reached Athens fell down dead. To mark this event the marathon race has been

1. Unān Ka Adabi Wirsah (the Literary Heritage of Greece) by Ahmad Aqīl Rubi, P. 15.

included in the Olympic sports.[1] Once again (480 BC) Dara's successor, Xerxes (Khushyar Shah), invaded Greece, this time with 180,000-strong army. The Iranians advanced towards Athens by way of Thrace and Macedonia but when they reached Thermopylae Pass, they found it blocked by 300 valiant soldiers under the command of Leonidas. All of them were decimated but they did give a chance to the inhabitants of Athens to make good their escape. In the meantime, the Iranian navy suffered a heavy defeat in the (naval) battle of Salamis. Xerxes succeeded in escaping back to Iran with only a remnant of his army, one-third of the original force. Next year the Iranians again took the field at Paletia but again they were routed. These battles continued right up to the time of Alexander the Great. In the meanwhile, a series of Peloponnesian battles between the Greek states of Athens and Sparta started in 460 BC and did not stop except in 405 BC when Athens was finally defeated. The Spartans pulled down the ramparts of Athens.

Historical Battlefield of Marathon

Rise of Macedonia and Alexander the Great

Philip, the ruler of Macedonia, ascended the Throne in 359 BC. He defeated the combined forces of the Greek states in 337 BC and annexed them to his kingdom, wiping off the ancient Greece from the pages of history. Afterwards, he declared war against Persia. But he was killed the next year and was succeeded by his son, Alexander III (336 BC – 323 BC) who came to be known later on as Alexander the Great. In 334 BC he set out with 32,000 infantry and 5000 mounted soldiers to conquer the world. He had also a naval fleet of 160 vessels, both large and small. He defeated the Persians in the battles of Granicus and Issus. Then he moved in the direction of Syria, Palestine and Egypt and conquered them. Then he invaded Persia again. The Persian emperor,

1. Oxford English Reference Dictionary, P. 880.

Dara III (Darius III), was defeated in the Battle of Arbela (Iraq) on 1 October, 331 BC, fled the field, but was slain by his courtiers.

Coin of Alexander the Great

Later, Alexander conquered Bakhtar or Bactria (Afghanistan) and Turkistan and there he married Roxana (رخسانة), the daughter of a chieftain. In 326 BC he invaded the Indian sub-continent, defeated Raja Porus near Jehlam (Punjab), conquered Multan and reached as far as the River Bias where his generals refused to move on further. That forced Alexander to return. On his way back, he travelled through Sind and Makran and reached Babel (Babylon) where he died. He founded 25 cities named after him in different places, Alexandria (Egypt) and Iskandron (Turkey) being the most famous of them. He is also the founder of Herat which was initially named Alexandria but later came to be known as Herat.

Alexander's successors

Among Alexander's many successors, Ptolemy and Seleucus were the most notable. Ptolemy took away Egypt and Syria and occupied them. Seleucus founded an empire with headquarter in Selucia which was later called Ctesiphon or Madā'in. In 64 BC the Roman general, Pompey, put an end to the Seleucid dynasty and annexed all its territories to the Roman empire.

Six centuries of Greek sciences

The period from the sixth to the first century BC is considered the golden age of Greek science and literature. It was the age of luminaries like Pythagoras (560 BC -480 BC), mathematician; Herodotus (b. 484 BC), historian; Pericles (495 BC – 429 BC), statesman and democrat; Socratese (469 BC – 399 BC), Unitarian philosopher; Plato (428 BC – 347 BC), philosopher; Democritus (460 BC – 370 BC), the founder of the atomic theory; Xenophon (435 BC – 354

Ancient Tablet of Pythagoras′ Geometry

BC), historian; Hippocrates (460 BC – 377 BC), the founder of medical science; Aristotle (384 BC – 322 BC), philosopher and thinker; and Archimedes (287 BC – 212 BC), mathematician and physicist. Pythagoras was the first man to say that the earth was round and the first to explain the solar and lunar eclipses. The Greeks were idolaters and hated monotheism. They hated Socratese because he preached belief in one God. In their frenzied hatred of Socratese, the preacher of monotheism, they forced him to drink a cup of poison.[1]

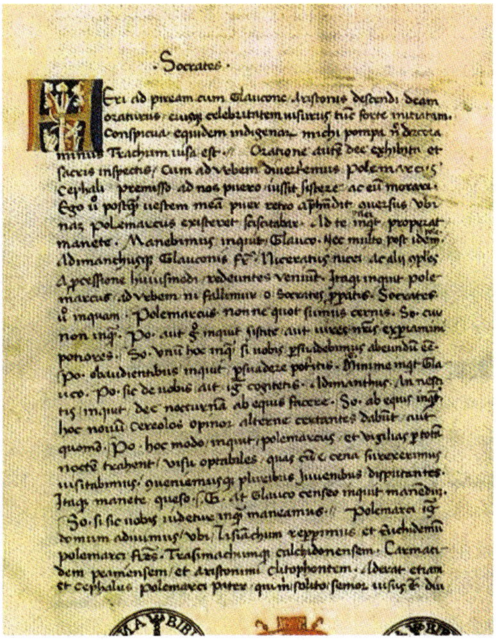
Socrates

A page from Plato's book, Republic

Plato's book, Republic, is a collection of dialogues, an excellent work in which he persevered all what he learnt from his teacher, Socratese. Plato's pupil, Aristotle, founded in 335 BC a school and library, Lyceum, outside Athens. In the nineteenth century Darwin came with his evolutionary theory which was, in fact, based on Aristotle's views. In the field of Logic, he introduced the inductive method. Alexander the Great was a pupil of Aristotle.[2]

Archimedes' contribution to knowledge was immense. His concept of density and the ratio of circumference to diameter (Pi or 22/7)[3] are some of his discoveries. During the siege of Syracuse (Sicily), he invented incendiary glass to torch the Roman ships. While he was busy drawing geometrical figures on the sand, he was killed by a Roman soldier.

1. Qadīm Mazhabi Tarīkh, P. 21; Riwāyāt-i-Tamaddun-i-Qadīm, P. 131.
2. Oxford English Reference Dictionary, P. 71.
3. Op.cit, P. 69.

Greek idolaters and Olympic sports

The Greeks were outright pagans. Socratese' preaching had no effect on them. They remained idolaters as ever. They believed that their so-called gods watch their actions and punish the guilty and that natural phenomena are the workings of their gods. Anyhow, the idea that humans are rewarded or punished after their death took hold of their minds owing to the teachings of Plato. The Greeks fancied that their gods lived either on Mt. Olympus or in their temples. Olympus was home to their renowned eleven gods. There at Olympus Zeus held his court, according to their beliefs, and that he also visited Olympia, a place in southern Greece. It was there where a sports festival was held after every four years since 776 BC. Olympic sports were banned by Christian Roman king Theodosius I in 393 CE but after fifteen centuries they were restarted from Athens in 1896.

Dionysus and Apollo

The Theatre of Dionysus on the Acropolis, Athens

Dionysus was the Greek god of wine. The festival was held in spring. Women would go out to hills, drink heavily, sing and dance wildly, and hold rallies. If they found a goat or ox, they would hold it as an incarnation of Dionysus, bite into its flesh, and chew it in the belief that by doing so the god would dissolve into their bodies. This practice took the form of the Christian rite of Eucharist in which bread symbolizes Christ's flesh and wine his blood.[1]

1. Riwāyāt-i-Tamaddun Qadīm, P. 127.

Homer in his epics speaks of goddess Athena with the face of an owl, and of goddess Hira with the face of a cow. The city of Athens is named after the former. Apollo, son of Zeus, was the Greek sun god. Music, poetic inspiration, arrow-throwing and prophesying were considered the gifts conferred by Apollo.

Diana and goddess Europa

Evora, Portugal. The iconic Roman Temple dedicated to the Emperor cult, wrongly considered as a Goddess Diana Temple, with the Loios Convent used as a Historical Hotel. UNESCO World Heritage Site.

According to Greek mythology, Apollo's sister, Artemis, was the goddess of hunting. Birth, delivery, and fertility were attributed to her. Her temple in Ephesus (Turkey) was one of the Seven Wonders of the World. Romans called her Diana. King Agamemnon even sacrificed his daughter to propitiate the goddess. The Greeks believed that Zeus assumed many forms: first, as a bull, and later, as a swan. In the latter form, he copulated with the goddess Europa, after whom the continent of Europe is named.

Phallus (male sexual organ) was worshipped everywhere in Greece. As part of the Dionysus' festive celebrations, women would go out in groups, carrying the image of phallus while chanting scurrilous songs. The Greek mythological lore mentions a worldwide deluge in which only a giant named Keleen escaped along with his wife Perha in a boat. Hellen was their son. Ancient Greeks are called Hellenes after him and their civilization Hellenistic.[1]

1. Op.cit., P. 128.

Dark side of Greek morals

Greece, the cradle of science, was morally depraved. Prostitution was an inalienable part of Greek civilization. The priestesses of the temple of Aphrodite, the Greek goddess of love, were wicked women. Praxiteles, a famous sculptor, made an effigy of his beloved, Phryne, and placed it in the temple of Apollo. Maids in nude served at banquets. Gratification of lust by unnatural means was common. Zeno, the founder of the Stoic system, was one of such men. Apelles, a sculptor, while making a statue of Alexander's beloved, Lyce, expressed his love for her. On hearing it, Alexander gave away the woman to him. The Spartan law laid down that an old man's wife, if young, shall be separated from her husband and given over to a young man to have physically strong offspring.

Aristotle said: Greeks should deal with non-Greeks as they do with beasts. Following his saying, Alexander seized twenty thousand men in Tyre (Lebanon) and ordered them to be killed. He seized another thirty thousand and had them sold as slaves in market-places.[1]

1. Qadīm Mazhabi Tarīkh, P. 53-55.

A view of Tyre (Lebanon)

The Roman Forum in Rome, Italy.

The Roman Empire

Rome and the Roman democracy

Rome, the present capital of Italy, is an ancient city. It was founded in 753 BC by Romulus. It was the seat of Roman kings but, after the abolition of monarchy, became the seat of Roman republic which was managed by Senate.

Battles between Rome and Carthage

In the third and second centuries BC Carthage (Tunisia) and Rome fought three Punic wars. In the second Punic war or Phoenician war (218 BC – 201 BC), the Carthagian general Hannibal with his 30,000 soldiers and 40 elephants crossed Spain and France and invaded Italy. He won many battles but finally had to retreat. In the Battle of Zama (Tunisia) in 202 BC he was defeated by the Romans. Hannibal fled to

Antioch and, in 183 BC, poisoned himself to death in Bithynia (Asia Minor). The Carthagians used to sacrifice their sons alive at the altar of their sun-god Ba'l Hammon. In the third Punic War (149 BC – 146 BC) the Romans set fire to their capital Carthage.[1] They also conquered Greece (147 BC – 146 BC).

Ruins of Carthage (Tunisia)

Tiberius, Caesar and Augustus

In 133 BC Tiberius carried out some agricultural reforms. So, the nobles conspired and got him killed along with 300 of his supporters during the elections. His brother also met the same fate in 121 BC. In the first century BC Rome had to fight a series of wars with Mithridates at Pontus (Asia Minor). In one of the wars (88 BC – 84 BC) he slew 30,000 Romans in a single day. Anyhow, in the third war (74 BC – 64 BC) the Romans defeated him and conquered Asia Minor, Syria and Palestine.

In 60 BC a triumvirate was set up. It was a coalition in which three generals, Pompey, Crassus and Julius Caesar, exercised supreme authority. Julius Caesar, soon after assuming power, conquered the whole of Gaul (France) and also launched an attack on Britain. Pompey

Coin of Julius Caesar

1. History of the World, P. 71.

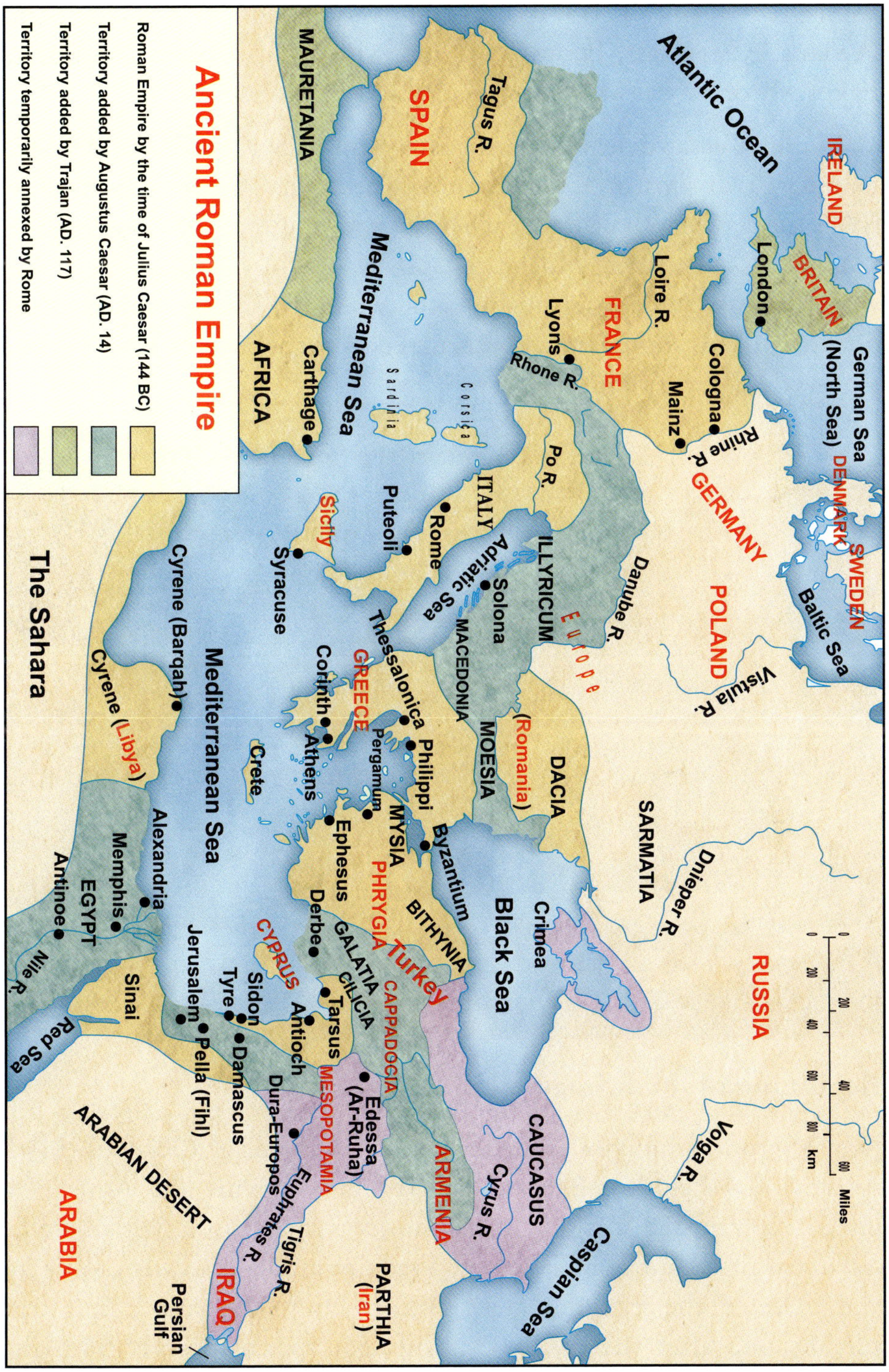
Ancient Roman Empire
Roman Empire by the time of Julius Caesar (144 BC)
Territory added by Augustus Caesar (AD. 14)
Territory added by Trajan (AD. 117)
Territory temporarily annexed by Rome
Atlantic Ocean
IRELAND
BRITAIN
London
German Sea (North Sea)
DENMARK
SWEDEN
Baltic Sea
SPAIN
Tagus R.
FRANCE
Loire R.
Lyons
Rhone R.
Cologna
Mainz
Rhine R.
GERMANY
POLAND
Vistula R.
Danube R.
Europe
MAURETANIA
AFRICA
Carthage
Mediterranean Sea
Corsica
Sardinia
Po R.
ITALY
Rome
Puteoli
Sicily
Syracuse
ILLYRICUM
Adriatic Sea
Solona
MACEDONIA
Thessalonica
GREECE
Corinth
Athens
Philippi
Pergamum
MYSIA
MOESIA
DACIA
(Romania)
SARMATIA
Dnieper R.
RUSSIA
Crimea
Black Sea
Byzantium
BITHYNIA
PHRYGIA
Ephesus
Derbe
GALATIA
Turkey
CILICIA
Tarsus
CAPPADOCIA
CYPRUS
Crete
Cyrene (Barqah)
Cyrene (Libya)
The Sahara
Mediterranean Sea
Alexandria
Memphis
EGYPT
Antinoe
Nile R.
Sinai
Red Sea
Jerusalem
Sidon
Tyre
Antioch
Pella (Fihl)
Damascus
Dura-Europos
Edessa (Ar-Ruha)
MESOPOTAMIA
Euphrates R.
Tigris R.
IRAQ
ARMENIA
CAUCASUS
Cyrus R.
Volga R.
Caspian Sea
PARTHIA (Iran)
ARABIAN DESERT
ARABIA
Persian Gulf
Miles
km

Map. 35

conquered Spain. In 53 BC Crassus was killed while fighting the Persians. Afterwards, Pompey fell out with Julius Caesar and fled to Egypt where he was killed by the minister of Ptolemy XII.

Julius Caesar defeated Mithridates' son in Syria and also defeated Pompey's two sons in Spain. By now Caesar had become an absolute ruler. On 15 March, 44 BC, when he was about to be crowned as a king, he was murdered under a conspiracy, of which Brutus, his friend, was a part. As the dagger hit him, the wounded Caesar looked in the direction of his murderer and exclaimed in surprise what later became a proverb: 'Brutus, you too'.

Temple of Mars vltor built by Augustus Caesar after the battle of Philippi

Beginning of the Roman empire

Now a second triumvirate was formed. It consisted of Octavius, Mark Antony, and Lepidus. Brutus, defeated by Octavius and Antony in Greece, committed suicide. Mark Antony went off to Egypt where he fell under the charms of Cleopatra. Thereupon, Octavius went to Egypt and defeated the Egyptian fleet. Antony and Cleopatra committed suicide, one after the other. Octavius got special powers from the

Senate in January, 31 BC. The Senate kept renewing his powers and conferred on him the title of Augustus. In January, 16 BC, he declared himself the emperor. Thus did the Roman democracy change again into monarchy. The first monarch was Augustus Caesar (Octavius).[1] During the reign of Augustus, the Roman empire was very extensive, covering Italy, France, Spain, Greece, the Balkans, Anatolia, Syria, Palestine, Egypt, Tripoli (Libya). Tunisia, Cyprus, etc. The month of August takes its name from Augustus Caesar.

It was during the reign of Augustus' successor, Tiberius (14 CE – 37 CE), that Roman governor Pilate, yielding to the insistent demands of the Jews, issued orders for Jesus to be crucified. Roman emperor Claudius (41 CE – 54 CE) conquered Britain in 43 CE. Claudius had married his niece, a widow, who bore him a son, Nero, who succeeded his father. Nero slew his mother, wife, and hundreds of men. In 64 CE a great fire broke out and burnt down a large part of Rome. It is said that this fire was set by Nero himself. A proverb says: Nero was playing the flute while Rome was burning. The same year St. Paul was killed in Rome. It was St. Paul who innovated new beliefs and made them a part of the Christian faith: the divinity of Christ and atonement through crucifixion. In 68 CE Nero, faced with riots and rebellion, committed suicide.[2] In 70 CE Roman general Titus crushed the Jewish revolt in Palestine and destroyed the Temple of Solomon.

Constantine the Great converts to Christianity

Ancient city wall of Istanbul

For three centuries the Christians suffered terrible persecutions by the Romans. The primary reason was that the Romans were pagans and hated Christianity. The first Roman king to accept Christianity was emperor Constantine the Great (306 CE – 337 CE). He declared Christianity the state

1. Oxford English Reference Dictionary, P. 89-90.
2. Encyclopedia Tarīkh-i-'Ālam: 2/114-123.

religion and convened councils of high church dignitaries who laid down beliefs and practices on which modern Christianity is based. Constantine founded, on 11 May, 330 CE, a new capital at Byzantium which was named after him, Constantinople, now called Istanbul.[1]

Ruins of Byzantine Church in Jerash, Jordan

Byzantine empire

When Roman ruler Theodosius I (388 CE – 395 CE) died, his empire was divided between his two sons.[2] The Western Roman Empire had its capital in Rome while the Eastern Roman empire retained Constantinople as its capital. Because the latter's capital was formerly called Byzantium, it is also called the Byzantine empire. The Arabs, who lived close to it, still called it the Roman empire. The word *'Ar-Rūm* which occurs in the Qur'ān refers to this very empire.

Gibbon says: During the reign of Arcadius, the first ruler of the Byzantine empire, the dead bodies of St. Andrew, St. Luke and St. Timothy were brought back to Constantinople after three hundred years and buried in the Church of the Apostles. In the same way, Prophet Ishmael's bones were allegedly brought from Palestine and carried over to Constantinople in a golden vessel draped in a silken sheet amid a lot of fanfare. To witness and take part in this festive event, visitors lined up from Palestine to Constantinople. Their belief was that the bones of

1. Op.cit., 2/125-126.
2. History of the World, P. 95.

saints and martyrs were more precious than gold and silver.[1]

Note: That is what the non-Muslims say. We know from a Hadīth that bodies of prophets of Allah remain safe and intact even after death. The Messenger of Allah ﷺ said: "Allah has forbidden the earth to eat away the bodies of (His) prophets ﷺ."[2]

Justinian and Nosherwan

Successive waves of invaders from the north sapped the strength of the Western Roman Empire till it met its final death in 476 CE while the Eastern Roman Empire (Byzantine Empire) gradually took over those areas which were once the part of the old Roman empire. Justinian (527 CE-565 CE) conquered North Africa, Italy and Spain. Then, in 540 CE, a series of Iranian-Roman battles started and continued for twelve years. Justinian built Aya Sofia cathedral in Constantinople. During the rule of his successors wars with Iran continued.

The famous Hagia Sophia mosque which was a church and now it is a museum

In 575 CE Persian emperor Nosherwan's forces laid waste the Roman territory of Cappadocia (Anatolia). When Nosherwan's grandson, Khosrau Parvez, fled from the rebels, the ruler of Constantinople, Maurice, helped him to regain his throne.[3]

Roman law of Justinian

Justinian's greatest achievement was that he completed, renewed, and codified the Roman law. His law is considered the most important milestone in the development of Roman law. Muhammad, the Messenger of Allah ﷺ, was born during the reign of his successor, Justin II.

A comparative study of the Justin law and Islamic Shariah is

1. Qadīm Mazhabi Tarīkh, P. 31-32.
2. Sunan An-Nasa'i: 1375.
3. Encyclopedia Tarīkh-i-'Ālam: 2/174.

Codex of Justinian's Roman Law

enough to impress any man with a sound mind. The Roman law, which may have contained some elements attributable to Divine inspiration, is an example of the evolution of human nature. Until that time no law of any country ever cared for equality of human beings or defined rights of men and women or gave rights to slaves and conquered people and treated them as humans. In those times women had no right to own, buy or sell property. In fact, she was herself a commodity to be owned, bought and sold. Except the Roman citizens, nobody's honour or life had any value. Trade activity was highly restricted. On the contrary, Prophet Muhammad's law, based on divine revelation, is highly advanced, judged even by the modern standard. It is just and fair. It guarantees the rights of all humans. Lawmakers of the world over have long since been following it as a model. It is impossible for a man-made law to attain to its high standard.

The Brutality of 'Emperor' Phocas

Eight years before the Prophet Muhammad ﷺ began his mission, (that is, in 602 CE), a Roman general named Phocas rebelled against Maurice, the Byzantine Roman Emperor, and seized the throne. Maurice and his family took refuge in a church but the deposed emperor, along with his five sons, were dragged out of their sanctuary. All his five sons were put to death in the sight of the emperor. When the executioner moved to cut off the throat of his infant son, a nanny, moved by loyalty to the emperor, put her own son under his sword. But this gruesome scene was overshadowed by the murder of Caesar Maurcel. Their trunks were thrown into the Bosporus, their heads suspended from the gates of Constantinople. Prince Theodosius who was carrying a message from his father to Madā'in was arrested before he could reach the Persian border and immediately put to death. Queen Constantia and her three daughters were first imprisoned in a church and later, when they were suspected of hatching a plot, were brutally murdered. First, their eyes were holed with iron bars. Then their tongues were extracted from their napes and stamped over under the feet. Then their limbs were cut off, one after the other, their nude bodies flogged, holed with lances, and thrown over into the fire of furnace.[1] And this was no abnormal event for the Romans. That was their normal practice.

Ibn 'Asākir narrated that Caliph 'Umar ﷺ sent a military contingent to the Romans. Abdullah bin Huzāfah ﷺ was one of them. The Romans arrested him and the Roman emperor told him to become a Christian or, else, he would cast him into a cauldron of copper. When he refused, the emperor ordered for a large cauldron to be brought, filled with oil, and heated. When the oil started boiling, the emperor ordered another Muslim to be brought. The emperor told him to become a Christian. When he refused, he was thrown into the boiling oil. His flesh melted down, leaving a skeleton of bones. Now the emperor turned to Abdullah ﷺ and said: Convert to Christianity or, else, I would throw you also into the cauldron. He refused, saying: I can't abandon my faith. So, the emperor ordered him to be thrown into the cauldron. When the soldiers dragged him forth, he wept. The people thought that he wept from fear. The Caesar ordered him to come back and asked him: Why do you cry? Abdullah ﷺ replied: 'Don't you ever think I cried from fear. I grieve that I have only one life to offer to my Lord. I wish I had as many lives as the hair on my body to sacrifice to my Lord.' The emperor was oddly impressed and intended to release him. So he said: Kiss my head and get free.

Coin of Caesar Phocas

1. Ghalaba-i-Rūm, P. 67-68.

Abdullah ﷺ refused. Then the emperor said: Become a Christian and I will give you my daughter in marriage to share my empire. Abdullah declined this offer also. Then the Caeser said: Kiss me on the head and I will set free eighty Muslims along with you. 'Yes', replied Abdullah, 'That's right'. Then Abdullah kissed the Caesar on his head and he set free all the Muslims. The news reached 'Umar ﷺ, the Caliph. When Abdullah bin Huzāfah ﷺ came to the Caliph, the Commander of the Faithful stood up and kissed his head.[1]

Pope's praise of a brutal Christian king

Instead of urging the callous Phocas to regret and repent his sins, Pope Gregory the Great of Rome lavished panegyrics on him, lauding his assumed piety and generosity, and said a prayer invoking blessings on him: May he be granted a long, splendid and successful reign and, at the close of his reign, a successful Afterlife! Anyhow Phocas' brutal rule came to an end only when Heraclius' army arrived in Constantinople from Egypt. Phocas was arrested and the mobs tortured him and then cut off his head and hung it at a public place where the head of Maurice and his sons had been hung once, his body flung into flaming fire.[2]

Heraclius and Khosrau Parvez

Gold coin of Heraclius

With the enthronement of Heraclius I (610 CE – 641 CE), who was of Greek extraction, a new era of Greek rule of Constantinople began. Heraclius I was a contemporary of Prophet Muhammad ﷺ and Khosrau Parvez, the emperor of Persia. The war started by Khosrau Parvez in 603 CE continued throughout the reign of Heraclius. In 613 CE the Roman army was routed by the Persians in Antioch and the latter occupied Damascus the same year. In 614 CE the Iranians occupied Jerusalem and destroyed the Holy Sepulchre, the holiest Christian

1. Tarīkh Dimashq Al-Kabīr: 29/245-246; Usad-ul-Ghābah: 2/578.
2. Ghalaba-i-Rūm, P. 73.

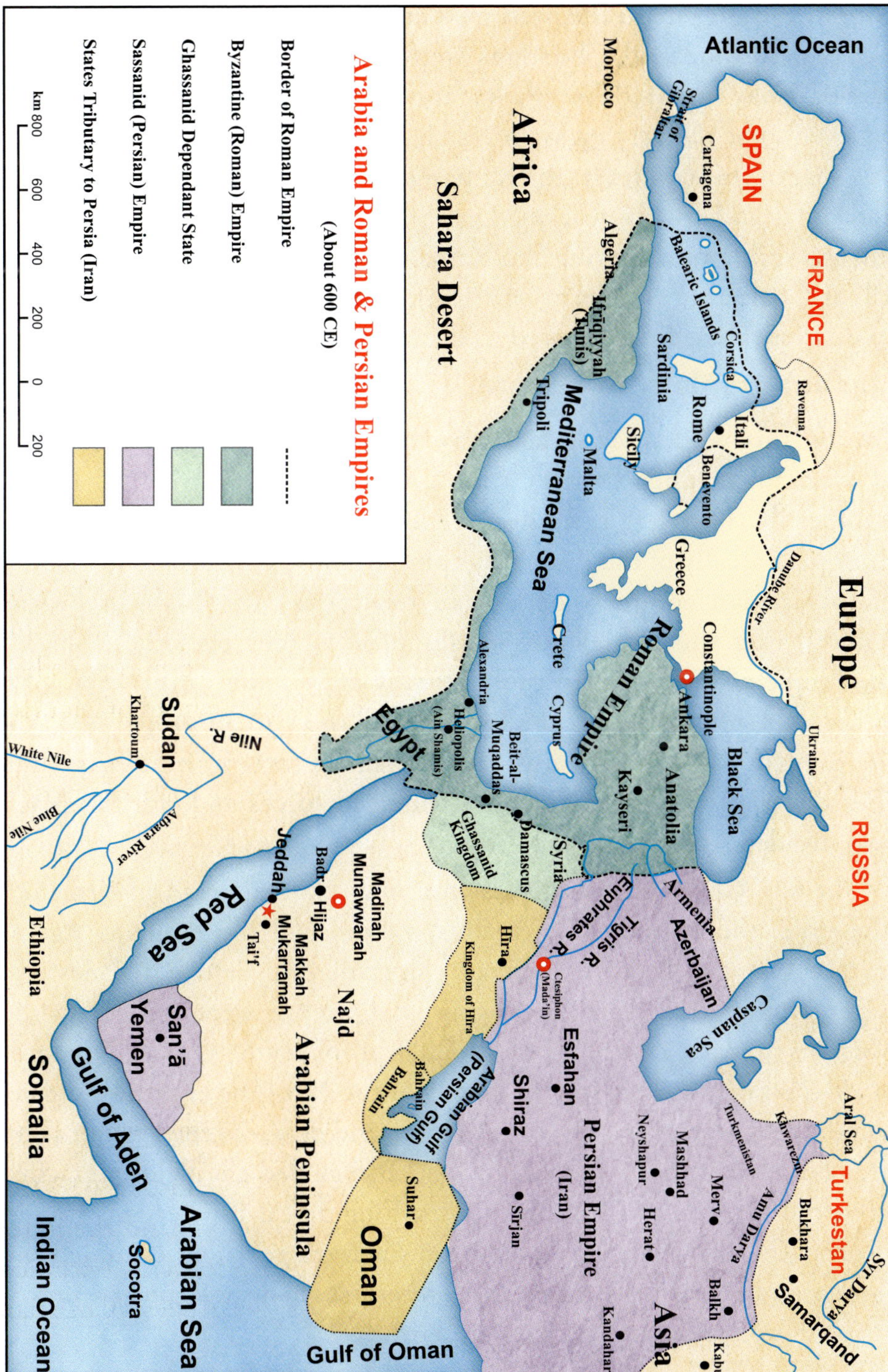
Arabia and Roman & Persian Empires
(About 600 CE)
Border of Roman Empire
Byzantine (Roman) Empire
Ghassanid Dependant State
Sassanid (Persian) Empire
States Tributary to Persia (Iran)
km 800 600 400 200 0 200
Atlantic Ocean
SPAIN
FRANCE
Europe
RUSSIA
Turkestan
Asia
Africa
Sahara Desert
Morocco
Algeria
Ifriqiyyah (Tunis)
Strait of Gibraltar
Cartagena
Balearic Islands
Corsica
Sardinia
Rome
Itali
Ravenna
Benevento
Sicily
Malta
Tripoli
Mediterranean Sea
Greece
Danube River
Crete
Cyprus
Constantinople
Roman Empire
Ankara
Anatolia
Kayseri
Black Sea
Ukraine
Alexandria
Heliopolis (Ain Shamis)
Egypt
Beit-al-Muqaddas
Damascus
Syria
Ghassanid Kingdom
Nile R.
White Nile
Blue Nile
Athara River
Khartoum
Sudan
Ethiopia
Somalia
Red Sea
Madinah Munawwarah
Badr
Hijaz
Makkah Mukarramah
Jeddah
Ta'if
Najd
Arabian Peninsula
Hira
Kingdom of Hira
Euphrates R.
Tigris R.
Ctesiphon (Mada'in)
Armenia
Azerbaijan
Caspian Sea
Esfahan
Shiraz
Sirjan
Persian Empire (Iran)
Arabian (Persian Gulf)
Bahrain
Oman
Suhar
Gulf of Oman
San'ā
Yemen
Gulf of Aden
Arabian Sea
Socotra
Indian Ocean
Aral Sea
Syr Darya
Amu Darya
Kawarezm
Turkmenistan
Bukhara
Samarqand
Merv
Mashhad
Neyshapur
Herat
Balkh
Kabul
Kandahar

Map.36

church and the site of the presumed crucifixion of Jesus.[1]

Ninety thousand Christians were slain in the city. The Persians carried away to Madā'in, their capital, the Holy Cross which was believed to be the very cross on which Jesus had been crucified. Within one year of this conquest, the Iranian forces occupied Jordan, Palestine and Sinai and finally reached Egypt. On the other side, the Iranian forces, while overpowering the Romans in Asia Minor, arrived in 617 CE at Chalcedon (modern Qazi Koi), right opposite Constantinople. In distress, Heraclius prepared to flee Constantinople.

Qur'ān's prophecy came true

During this while, Many Muslims, being persecuted by the pagans of Makkah, planned to leave their homeland. So, in 615 CE a large number of them left their hearth and home for Abyssinia (modern Ethiopia), an ally of the Roman Empire. In those days everybody talked of the Iranian conquest of Roman territories. The Makkan pagans rejoiced over the Persian fire-worshippers' victory over the Romans, the People of the Book. In those gloomy days it was unthinkable of a quick Roman victory over the Persians but the Qur'ān prophesied that the Romans would win against the Persians in three to nine years time *(Bid'a Sineen)*. At least, Heraclius collected forces and, via the Black Sea, invaded Armenia.

In 622 CE Roman and Persian armies clashed again in Armenia. Theodore, the brother of Heraclius, vanquished the Persians. Again, in 624 CE, the Persians suffered a humiliating defeat in Palestine. Right around that time the pagans of Qureysh were routed by the Muslims at Badr. Thus did the double prophecy of Qur'ān (Chapter of *Ar-Rūm* or the Romans) in favour of the Muslims and the Romans come true. Later, Heraclius invaded Iraq and defeated the Persian army near Nineveh in 627 CE. As Khosrau Parvez fled the field, Heraclius advanced and took Tabriz. At this crushing defeat the Persians turned against Khosrau Pervez. His own son Sherweh rebelled, occupied the throne and imprisoned his father, where soon he was put to death. Sherweh signed a truce on Roman terms.

1. Wikipedia Encyclopedia .

Roman Colosseum

The Dark Side of Roman and European Civilizations

Wicked and cruel Romans

The Romans were by far more wicked and more cruel than the Greeks. Lackey says: The Romans used to round up prisoners from around their conquered territories and bring them to Rome. As a result, the Roman capital turned gradually into a market-place of prostitution. The slaves from Greece and Alexandria were noted for their physical beauty. In the temple of Venus adultery was free and unrestricted. The wicked queen of the second century CE, Faustina, gave high positions to her lovers. With the approval of the Senate, she was raised to the status of a goddess. Her image was placed along with those of Juno, Venus, Ceres and other so-called gods for public worship. As in Greece, there was no bar in Rome on self-induced abortion.

In the Roman empire a father might kill his children, if he so willed. killing of offspring in public was widespread. In amphitheatres two or more swordsmen would display their skills in fencing till one slew the other. Professional swordsmen were given swords made of silver. During the reign of Tiberius (14 CE – 37 CE), the building of an amphitheatre collapsed, killing twenty thousand persons. Pairs of swordsmen fighting each other would accompany funeral processions in the fond belief that such sports would delight the departed souls!

The Romans were cruel to their slaves beyond words. Once Philamenes ordered a slave to be slain for no reason except to amuse his guest. A man named Videsiboleo used to feed his pet fish the flesh of his slaves. Brutusi had one of his debtors arrested for failing to pay a large amount of interest due on him. The defaulting borrower was starved to death in prison. The Romans had hearts harder than stone. Julius Caesar's lust for power and conquests knew no bounds. The blood of eleven hundred thousand humans could not quench his thirst for territories. The cruel Romans watched with delight the spectacle of illuminations in Nero's garden when the cloaks of Christian captives were doused with oil and set on fire. All the poor captives were burnt to death. Roman kings like Galerius and Heliogius watched with amusement prisoners being mauled by predatory beasts as they dined.[1]

Roman amphitheatres

The Roman rulers built a large, circular amphitheatre called Colosseum in the city of Rome. Its semi-circular seats rising behind and above each other round a central open space (called arena) could accommodate fifty thousand spectators. Its construction was begun by king Vespasian in 75 CE and finished by Titus. In the arena of this great building the famous gladiatorial displays, mimic battles, duels between armed warriors and

1. Qadīm Mazhabi Tarīkh, P. 56-59.

An internal view of colosseum, Rome

wild beasts used to be given.[1] Unarmed rebels and slaves were driven into the arena like herds of cattle and then hungry lions and tigers were set on them. This cruelty was fun for the Romans!

Morals of ancient Germans and Englishmen

The ancient Germans were also morally depraved. They would slay their friends and kinsmen in a state of intoxication. Ancient Scandinavians killed enemies, filled their skulls with alcohol, and drank it as mark of pride. Germans would slit the throats of their war captives on the altars of their gods. In 105 BC the Cambrians celebrating their victory at Orussio killed all their Roman prisoners to propitiate their god. In ancient Britain it was no sin marrying a step-mother. The practice continued for long in post-Christian Britain. Audbold, in spite of being a Christian, married his step mother, after the death of his father, Aethelberht, the king of England.

The immorality of ancient France

Gaul (France) was a hot point of sexual anarchy and licentiousness. In the fifth century CE, king Yourk held his court in the city of Bordeaux. The people of Heruli clan came to the court in the nude, their bodies covered only with paint. The king of Burgundy, Jundubald, ordered his three brothers to be slain and his own son Sigismund, his wife and

1. Oxford English Reference Dictionary, P. 286..

their two sons buried alive in a well in Orleans. Sigismund himself had ordered his son to be killed to please his step-mother. The famous Frank king of Gaul, Clovis, ordered all the princes of Merovangian dynasty to be slain to eliminate his rivals. Another king ordered his son, who had revolted against him, his daughter-in-law, and his granddaughter to be burnt alive.

The magistrates of Gaul, despite the evidence proving the innocence of the accused, used to expose him to fire or get him dipped into deep waters to ascertain whether he was innocent or not. Thus the accused were killed by thousands right in front of courts. In Gaul masters had the absolute right to kill their slaves. In the weddings of girls of rich families, a long row of slaves in chains accompanied them as they left the homes of their parents to join their husbands.

Pope, a supporter of cruelty

Gregory the Great, Pope of Rome, issued a papal edict ordering the purchase of slaves brought from Britain and promoted this cruel traffic in humans. On the death of the cruel king Clovis, Gregory wrote: "Clovis was a sincere believer in Trinity. The strength of his belief helped him win against the infidels". These 'infidels' also included those Christian communities whom he had defeated. When Sigismund, the killer of his own son, was slain, the pope elevated him to the rank of a saint and attributed many a miracle to him.

The dark sides of Church monasticism

Top church officials were also morally depraved. A high priest had one of his assistants buried alive to seize his property but the victim escaped from his grave anyhow. His crime was serious but he went scot-free, with only a warning. A bishop turned a man out of his house and committed adultery with his wife. A monk, rabbi Abraham, did not wash his face for as long as fifty years. A nun did not wet any part of her body except her fingers throughout her age of 60 years. A monk named St. Samuels tied a rope round his body till it cut into his flesh. The flesh rotted and stank so badly that nobody could sit near him. A monk while praying slipped and had an affair with some woman. To atone for this sin he leapt into fire and committed suicide. Edward Gibbon, a famous historian, writing about the Christian clergy of the times preceding the sixth century CE, says: "Saints, religious men, and worshippers of dead bodies destroyed the simple and pure Christian faith." Allah says:

﴿وَرَهْبَانِيَّةً ٱبْتَدَعُوهَا مَا كَتَبْنَـٰهَا عَلَيْهِمْ إِلَّا ٱبْتِغَآءَ رِضْوَٰنِ ٱللَّهِ فَمَا رَعَوْهَا حَقَّ رِعَايَتِهَا ۖ فَـَٔاتَيْنَا ٱلَّذِينَ ءَامَنُوا۟ مِنْهُمْ أَجْرَهُمْ ۖ وَكَثِيرٌ مِّنْهُمْ فَـٰسِقُونَ ﴿٢٧﴾﴾

"But the monasticism which they invented for themselves, We did not prescribe for them, but (they sought it) only to please Allāh therewith, but that they did not observe it with the right observance. So, We gave those among them who believed, their (due) reward; but many of them are Fāsiqūn (rebellious, disobedient to Allāh).." [1]

General condition of Europe

As late as the sixth and seventh centuries of the Christian era, Europe was sunk into gloom and ignorance. The states were busy with bloody wars while the people were far behind other nations in arts and sciences. Their bodies were filthy and their minds full of myths and superstitions.[2] To cleanse themselves they did not use water except rarely. Their priests and monks subjected their bodies to painful sufferings. They carried their love of seclusion to utmost limits.[3] They had not yet decided as to whether woman was a human or animal, whether she had an immortal soul or not. Women in those times had no right to own property. Robert Briefalt writes: From the fifth century CE to the tenth Century CE Europe was shrouded in pitch darkness which became still darker and more awful as years rolled on. It was like a civilization, dead and rotten. The marks of this civilization were fading. Its fate was already sealed. The countries of Europe which thrived and blossomed later, like France and Italy, were on the verge of collapse, split into petty kingdoms and princelings.[4]

1 Qur'ān: Al-Hadeed: 57:27.
2. Thilly: History of Philosophy, New York 1945.
3. Lecky. W.E.H. : History of European Morals, (New York 1855).
4. The Making of Humanity, P. 1164.

Kingdom of Ethiopia and Ethiopian Church

Modern Ethiopia, called Abyssinia in the olden times, is a landlocked country bordered by Eritrea, Sudan, Kenya, Somalia and Djibouti (formerly, French Somaliland). Prior to Eritrean independence in 1993, its territories reached up to the Red Sea. Addis Ababa is the capital of Ethiopia and Amharik its national language. Most of the inhabitants are Muslims but political power rests with the Christians since long.

The first account of how Christianity reached Ethiopia is given by the New Testament. According to it, Christianity came to Ethiopia when the apostle, Philips, administered baptism to the treasurer of Ethiopian Queen Hendeke VII while he was on a visit to Jerusalem.

New map of Ethiopa

Aksum kingdom

In the first century of the Christian Era, the immigrants from Saba (Yemen) founded the kingdom of Aksum on the Red Sea coast in Eastern Africa. This kingdom covered Eritrea and a large part of Ethiopia. The people of Aksum were pagans who worshipped their own

The stele of Aksum in Ethiopia

local deities but in about 300 CE one of their rulers, king Ezana, converted to the Christian faith at the hands of a father of peace (Abba Salamah) named Fromentes of Greek-Syrian descent. By the end of the fourth century CE most of the Ethiopians had become Christians. From there Christianity spread to other neighbouring countries and the Aksum kingdom reached up to the borders of Saba (Yemen). In those times Aksum was a great trading state. It had trade ties with Egypt, Arabia, Persia and countries as far apart as India. Their language was Ga'ez. The rulers of this kingdom, which continued to exist as late as the seventh century CE, were called Negus. Negus Ashama was a contemporary of the Prophet Muhammad ﷺ. The Prophet ﷺ wrote him a letter to accept the Islamic faith and he became a Muslim in 6 or 7 AH.

Aksum, the capital of this kingdom, mixed with Sabaean Arabs, was sited in the Ethiopian province of Tigre (14.07 degree latitude N and 38.31degree longitude E).[1] Ethiopian kings were crowned in this holy city. In the days when the Ethiopian kingdom was in full bloom, there were more than 100 four-sided tapering columns (obelisks) hewn from rocks, some reaching up to a height of 30 meters. Several of them are extant even today. Out of the giant-sized columns only one has survived. Perhaps those columns were built as monuments beside the royal tombs.[2]

Gold coin of King Ezana

1. Tarīkh Ard-ul-Qur'ān (kāmil): 2/240.
2. History of the World, P. 102; World Almanac, P. 469.

Ethiopian Orthodox Church

The Ethiopian Orthodox Church was founded during the reign of king Ezana when the patriarch of Alexandria conferred on Fromentes[1] nicknamed Abba Salamah (Father of Salamah) the title of Abuna Salamah (our father Salamah) and made him the Bishop of Ethiopia. Thus did the Ethiopian orthodox Christianity become the state religion of the Aksum kingdom. It is called the Orthodox Unitarian Christian Church of Ethiopia. It is called, in local language, *Tawhedu Beite* (Unitarian Church) because they believe that Christ had a single nature, that is, in Christ two different natures, one divine and the other human, combined and merged naturally and perfectly. On the contrary, the Roman Catholic Church and the Eastern Church (Greek Orthodox Church of Constantinople) hold that the human and divine natures of Christ are distinct, one from the other, but inseparable. The Ethiopian Orthodox Church has all along been considered a sub-branch of the Coptic Orthodox Church of Alexandria (Egypt). In the past a Coptic was always appointed the Abuna or archbishop of the Ethiopian Church. This practice continued until 1959 when Pope Sirel VIII of the Coptic Orthodox Church of Alexandria permitted the Ethiopian Church to elect their own patriarch. Ga'ez remains the official language of the Ethiopian Church[2] The Ethiopian Church has followers, besides Ethiopia, in Eritrea, Jamaica (West Indies) and Guyana (South America).[3]

Bible in Ga'ez language

1. The grave of St. Fromentes was hewn out from a cliff in Ethiopia. – (Encyclopedia of World Religions)
2. Wikipedia Encyclopedia.
3. Encyclopedia of World Religions, P. 336.

Ruins of Moenjo - Daro

India

The Indian Subcontinent, which is now divided between Bharat, Pakistan, Bangladesh, Nepal, and Bhutan, had been known for centuries as "India" up until August 1947.

The remains of ancient Indian civilizations have been found in Harappa (Punjab) and Moen-jo-Daro ('the Mount of the Dead') in Sind. Excavations have revealed that the city had been settled and re-settled several times over. The first known city dates back to 3300 BC, the second to 3000 BC, and the third to around 2900 BC. Excavations at the site have uncovered idols, instruments of copper, and drinking vessels. In Harappa, archaeologists found five thousand year old wheat grains. The greatest pyramid of Egypt (Khufo's Pyramid) was built during a period when the civilizations of Harappa and Moen-jo-Daro were at the pinnacle of their glory. The pagans of this age are known as the Dravidians.

Sind and Hind

During the period between 2000 BC to 1500 BC, the Aryan tribes from Central Asia and Persia began to cross over into the valley of Sind. The word for 'river' in their language was 'sindh,' and it is they who gave the name Sind 'Sindh' or 'Sindhu' to the River Indus. Subsequently, the surrounding region came to be known as 'Sindhu' or 'Sind.' Greek historians referred to it as 'Indus,' from which the words Ind, Hind and India have been derived.Later, the Persians and Arabs gave to the River Indus the name of Mehran; this led to Sind also being called 'the Valley of Mehran.'[1] The Arabs called the subcontinent 'Hind' which in Persian became 'Hindustan'.

Makli Graveyard. World's largest necropolis in Thatta. Sindh

The Aryans dwelt in Punjab for about five hundred years.[2] They then crossed over into the valley of the Ganges and the Jamna, which they named Aryavart, and which was known by the Purans as Bharatvarsh. The people of Siam (Thailand), Serandeep (Sri Lanka) and Burma (Myanmar) gave the name of Indria to India. The people of Sind continued to refer to their land as 'Sindh,' although foreigners began to use two different words for the subcontinent: Sind and Hind (India), keeping the former distinct from the latter.[3]The Persians had called Sind as 'Hind,' while the Greeks interchanged the initial letters h with 'humza' (I) and called it 'Ind,' which translated into English as 'India.'[4]

1. Urdu Islamic Encyclopedia: 11/329.
2. Riwāyāt-i-Tamaddun-i-Qadīm, P. 187.
3. The Aryans named Punjab and the Frontier Province 'Sapt Sindhu' (the land of seven rivers: Kabul, Sindh, Jhelum, Chenab, Ravi, Bayas and Sutlaj).
4. Tarīkh-i-Sind by Ejāz-ul-Haq Quddusi, P. 2.

Hinduism

The foreign Aryan tribes defeated the native Dravidians and settled in Sind and Punjab, during a time period known as the Age of Vedas (1500 BC – 1000 BC). During this period, four Vedas were written: Rigveda, Yajurveda, Sama Veda and Atharva Veda.

The Aryans introduced new inventions to the native civilization: imported horses, chariots, iron, and fire-worship. In turn, they borrowed deities from the natives and added them to their pantheon: Surya (the sun-god), Indra (god of rains and war), and Pirthivi (god of earth).

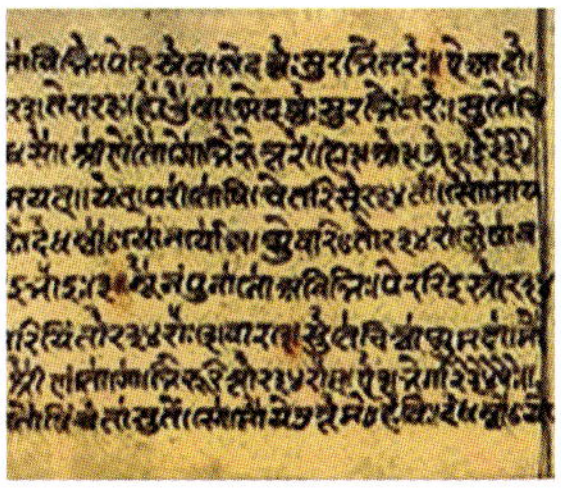

Rigveda

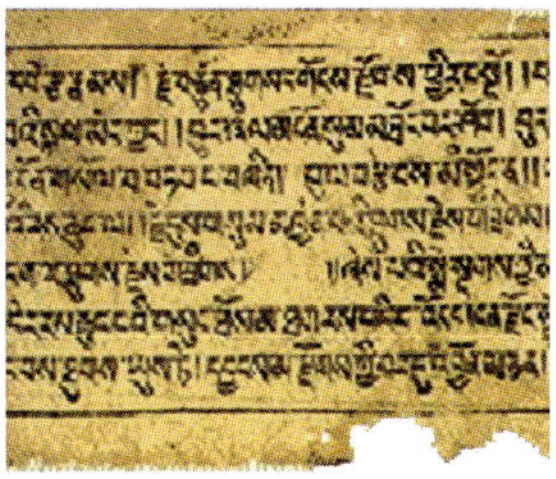

Yajurveda

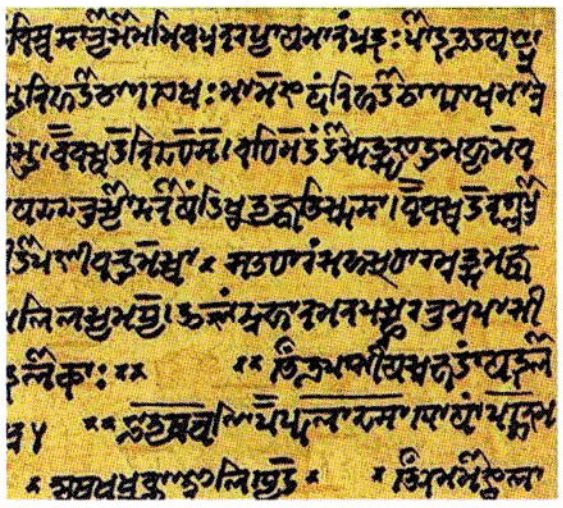

Atharva Veda

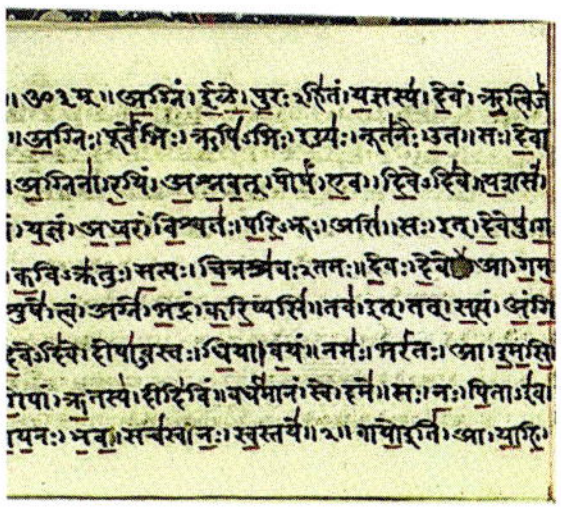

Sama Veda

During this period, the Aryan rajas carved out separate fiefdoms for themselves in the Ganges valley. During the age of the Vedas, the Indian caste system, which divided all people into four castes, was founded.[1]Ram Chandra and the Mahabharata War

Around 1000 BC, the Aryans settled in the Ganges- Jamna valley and

1. Riwāyāt-i-Tamaddun-i-Qadīm, P. 187; Qadīm Tahzīben Aur Mazāhib, P. 78-79.

A picture of 'Amlokdara' Stupa in Swat, KPK Pakistan

either enslaved the natives or drove them further south. This period is known as the Age of Valor (1000 BC – 500 BC), during which the epic of Ramayan was written. The epic narrates how Sita, the wife of Ayodhya's Raja Rama Chandra, was kidnapped by the Raja of Sri Lanka and how Rama, aided by Hanuman's forces made up of monkeys, invaded Sri Lanka and released Sita.

During this period, the famous Mahabharata Battle was fought, in which the Pandus triumphed over the Korus. It was also during this time that the Upanishads and Puranas were written. Two more gods, Vishnu and Shiva, were added to Brahma, the Creator, and a new trinity of gods, Trimurti, was evolved.

In the sixth century BC, Gautama Buddha and Mahavir revolted against the hegemony of Brahmans. They were founders of two new religions, respectively, Buddhism and Jainism. As well, the northwestern parts of the subcontinent and Punjab were occupied by the Persians, who renamed the area 'Gandhara.'[1]

1. Riwāyāt-i-Tamaddun-i-Qadīm, P. 188; Dunya Ke Bare Mazāhib, P. 32.

The Maurya Empire

When the victorious Alexander finally arrived in Gandhara, the subcontinent was a conglomeration of mini-states. After his return from the subcontinent, Chandragupt Maurya founded an extensive empire in northern India. His successor, Maharaja Ashoka the Great, extended its frontiers further up to the south of India. However, the Battle of Kalinga (265 BC) changed him greatly. He grieved over the large number of people killed during the battle, and as a result, renounced Hinduism, became a Buddhist, and devoted himself to the promotion of the new faith. Ashoka's capital was Pataliputra (modern Patna) and, save for a small area in the south, he ruled over the whole of India.

Chanakya

Chanakya (350 BC – 283 BC) was Chandra Gupta Maurya's adviser and his prime minister. According to his book "Arthashastra," his other names were Kotliya and Vishnu Gupta. He was a teacher at Takshashila (Taxila) Monastery, which was a center of meditation and philosophy. The Arthashastra is considered to be a book of statecraft and war strategy. Critics of the book point out its many negative aspects, including the advice to break pledges, practice deceit, hate neighbours, allying with the enemies of neighbours, and so on.[1]

Kushan Kingdom of Pershapura (Peshawar)

When the Maurya dynasty declined, the Bactrian Greeks extended their empire to Malwa (Central India), Gujarat and Kashmir. In the first century CE, the Kushans became a dominant power in northern India. The Maharaja Kanishka was a patron of the sciences; during his reign, Charak codified the principles of the Ayurvedic (Indian) system of medicine. Kanishka also became a Buddhist, and extended his patronage to the Buddhist faith, which encouraged many people from distant regions (notably Central and Southeastern Asia) to join the Mahayana sect of Buddhism. Kanishka's empire, with its capital at Peshawar, stretched from Central Asia to as far south as Benares and

1. Wikipedia Encyclopedia.

Takht-i-Bhai: A Buddhist monastery in Mardan

the Bindhyachal Range.

The Bindhyachal Range separates North India from the Deccan (meaning south). South of it lies the city of Bhopal, now the capital of the Indian province of Madhya Pardesh. Prior to 1947, Bhopal remained the capital of a Muslim state for as long as two hundred years.

Another coeval empire, Andhra, was located in the south of India and stretched from the Bay of Bengal to the Arabian Sea.

The Gupta Dynasty

In the fourth century CE, the Gupta dynasty gained ascendancy in the north of India. Samdar Gupta moved his capital from Pataliputra to

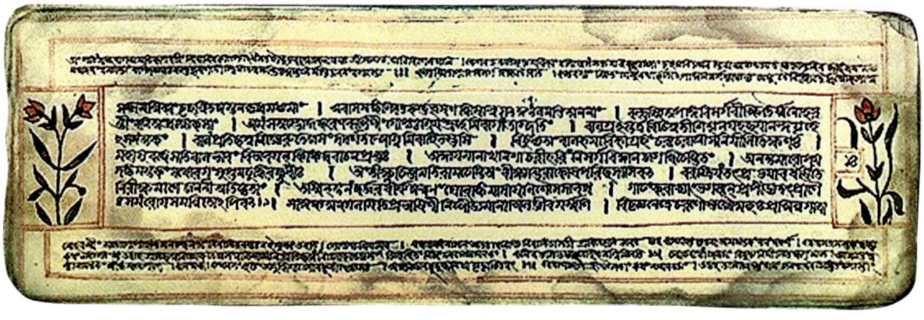

An ancient Hindu Purānas

Ayodhya. Maharaja Chandragupta II Bikramajit (376 CE – 415 CE) was considered to be the greatest monarch of the Gupta dynasty.

The Gupta reign saw the emergence of luminaries such as Kalidas, the dramatist, and Arya Bhat, mathematician and astronomer. The age of the Guptas marked the revival of Hinduism based on Puranas (religious texts). Mannu composed the Hindu religious code of law, Dharam Shastar, and the epic poems of Ramayan and Mahabharata were completed during the Gupta era. By 500 CE eighteen Puranas had been written down, containing about four hundred thousand verses. It is the standard religious textbook of the majority of the Hindus.[1]

Jawahar Lal Nehru referred to this era as 'the Hindu imperialism of the Gupta period'; this time period marked, in India, the beginning of the end of Buddhism and the rise of Hinduism, which gradually amalgamated elements of the former faith.[2]

The most important part of the Mahabharata is Bhagavad Gita, which is one of the sermons of Krishna. An account of the conditions prevailing in the times of Bikramajit was written by a Chinese traveller named Fahiyan, who had come to India in search of the remains of the academic heritage left by the Buddhists. Towards the closing years of the fifth century CE, the invasion of the Huns from the northwest put an end to the Gupta dynasty.

Hindu Deities

In the sixth century CE, idolatry was at its peak in India. It is said that the number of deities worshipped reached the millions – some say that there were up to three hundred and thirty million gods being worshipped throughout India. Every great person, each awe-inspiring natural phenomenon, and every useful tool was believed to be a deity deserving of worship. The art of carving and sculpting idols was one of the most highly developed trade of that time.[3]

O'Malley, a European scholar, says, 'The process of creating deities

1. Riwāyāt-i-Tamaddun-i-Qadīm, P. 190.
2. Tarīkh-i-'Ālam Par Ek Nazar: 1/170.
3. R.C. Dutt: Ancient India: 3/276.

did not stop here. The Hindus added an ever increasing number of deities to their pantheon, until it became difficult to keep track of the numbers of deities. Many of them were the deities of the ancient inhabitants of India, but were included in the Hindu pantheon. They numbered up to 300,000,000.'[1]

Maharaja Harsha

In the first half of the seventh century, the king (Maharajah) who ruled northern India was Harsha Vardhana (d. 648 CE). His empire stretched from the Himalayas to the Vindhyachal, with its capital in Kannauj, now a small town near Kanpur. He was a staunch follower of the Buddhist faith.

Coin of Maharaja Harsha

During his reign, a Chinese traveller named Hiuen Tsang, a Buddhist by faith, visited India (630 CE – 632 CE) and wrote an account of the conditions prevailing in India during his time.[2]

Pre-Islamic India

Before Islam reached Indian shores, the vast subcontinent had been divided into diverse principalities and small kingdoms. Previous invaders such as the Huns, Scythians, Kushans and Bakhtaris (Bactrians) had already settled in the northwestern parts of the sub-Continent. Their chieftains were called Rajputs. The Brahmans traced the lineage of those chieftains to sun and moon and acknowledged them as successors of the Khashtaris. Later, they came to be known as the Sun-Rajputs and Moon-Rajputs.

1. L.S.S. O'malley: Popular Hinduism – The Religion of the Masses (Cambridge, 1935), P. 6-7.
2. Tarīkh-i-'Ālam Par Ek Nazar: 1/196-197.

A Dark Era of Indian History

In terms of religion, morals and social conditions, the sixth century CE marked the beginning of the darkest period of Indian history.[1]

The many temples that populated the country were often the center of appalling behaviour and unlicensed lewdness. Sexuality was open and often religiously sanctified.[2] Women were accorded little to no respect, and often husbands would use their wives as gambling chips.[3]

In the event of her husband's death, a woman would either be buried or burnt alive because she was not allowed to marry again nor be treated with respect. The custom of *Sati* (burning of widows) was banned by the Muslims and finally abrogated during the British era. Nevertheless, it continued secretly and still takes place today.[4]

The Caste System

Vedic Indian society initiated the caste system, which divided society into four unequal groups:

1. Brahmans (priests)
2. Kshatriyas (warrior)
3. Vaishyas (traders)
4. Shudras (servants) or Dalits (untouchables)

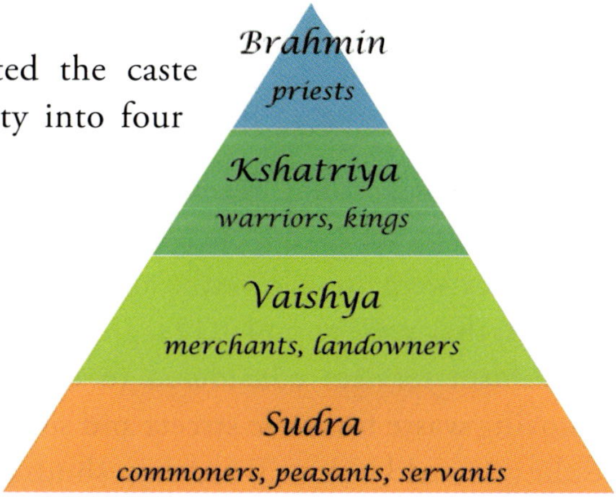

The Brahmans were the most exclusive and privileged class. They had rights that none other could claim; no one could object to their words or commands. They believed that all their sins were already forgiven, and thus they were superior to all others. They were both immune from taxes and any kind of legal punishment.

1. R.C.Dutt, Ancient India, Vol. 3.
2. Satiarath Prakash, P. 344.
3. See the opening part of Mahabharata.
4. See French traveller Berner's travelogue; History of the Rajahs of Middle Ages (Qurūn-i-Wusta Ke Rājgān Ki Tarīkh).

Qutub Minar Delhi

On the other hand, the Shudras or untouchables made up the majority of population, and suffered a great deal. It was believed that they were created from the feet of Brahma, the creator, and that it was thus their duty to serve the three classes superior to them.

The 'untouchables' received the worst treatment of all. They were considered to be filthy, such that even their shadows contaminated food. They were not allowed to attend schools, temples, or any religious services; they were completely segregated from the rest of society except to perform services considered to be impure for all others, such as removing waste from the streets and sewers. They were forbidden from reading sacred books.[1] These days shudras are called dalits.

Shudra artisans and craftsmen (called Chandals or lowly-born) lived outside the city. They were not allowed to stay overnight in cities and towns, whatever the season of the year. They would enter towns after sunrise and leave before sunset. This tyranny came to an end only during the reign of Sultan Qutbuddīn Aibak (1206 CE – 1210 CE). During his reign the boundary walls of a city remained no longer a symbol of class distinction, but were changed into ramparts. The palaces of the rich and the huts of the poor were built side by side.[2]

1. Mannu Dharam Shastar, Chapters 1,2,8-11.
2. Nabi-e-Rahmat, P. 53.

Jainism

A new religious system, Jainism, was founded in India in the sixth century BC. Its founder was Vardhaman (599 BC – 527 BC), also known as Mahawir (great hero). He was born to a Kshatriya chief near Patna (Bihar) and died in Pavapuri (Bihar).

The Mahavir opposed the caste system and various other Hindu customs. Jainism is derived from the Sanskrit word *Jai* (victory), in the sense of victory over one's base desires. It prescribes non-violence towards all living beings; *Jeo hatia,* the killing of living creatures, is forbidden. Its philosophy emphasizes the need to move one's soul towards liberation and divine consciousness by mastering one's earthly desires, in an effort to reach a state of spiritual purity.

The Jains, who have separate temples, are divided into two groups: Sivetambar (white dress) and Digambara (sky-clad or nude). These names are in reference to their followers; the former's ascetics wear

Mallikarjuna_and_Kasivisvanatha_temples_at_Pattadakal

white robes, while the Digambara forgo clothing altogether.

The two most famous Jain temples are the Chaumukha Temple of Ranakpur, Rajasthan, and Belagola temple in Karnataka. The Chaumukha Temple is famous for its architecture, with 1444 columns of intricately carved marble.

The Jains believe that their religious system was inspired by 24 Tirthankars, the first of them being Rishabha (mentioned in Vedas and Puranas), and the last of them was Mahavira, the original founder of the Jain faith. They believe that Jainism has always existed and will always exist, although some humans may forget it for periods of time.

Although Jainism rejects any idea of a supreme God, they believe in heavenly beings called Siddhas (liberated souls). They are classified into four groups: Bhavanpatis (gods dwelling in abodes), Vyantaras (intermediary gods), Jyotiskas (luminaries), and Vaimānikas (astral gods). The Jains also believe in metempsychosis (transmigration of souls).[1]

1. Merriam Webster's Encyclopedia of World Religions, P. 549-553.

Buddhism

Buddhism was founded by Siddhartha Gautama, also known as the Buddha (enlighted one). He is thought to have been born in 483 BC, according to popular belief. Tradition states that he was a prince of the Hindu state of Kapal Vastu (Nepal) but, while still young, abandoned the princely life, his wife and children, and became a hermit.

While meditating in the shade of a banyan tree in Gaya (Bihar), he is said to have received Nirvana (enlightenment). To alleviate human suffering worldwide, he founded a moral code, laid emphasis on meditation, and built Vaharas for worship and devotion. He opposed the caste-system and the superiority of Brahmans[1] but, like Hindus and Jains, believed in the transmigration of souls, a fundamental creed of the Buddhist religious system.

With the passage of time, Buddha's initial mystical teachings became entwined with idolatry, as statues of Buddha were erected and worshipped.[2]

Vedya, a Hindu scholar who wrote on the contemporary conditions during the reign of Harsha Vardhana (606 CE - 648 CE), says that Buddhism

Religious symbol of Buddhism

1. Urdu Encyclopedia of Islam: 23/174
2. Dunya Ke Bare Mazāhib, P. 107.

surpassed Hinduism in idolatry. Although Buddhism began with the rejection of God, Buddha became known as its central figure, often worshipped as a deity himself. Other figures such as Boddhisatva were included within Buddhist creed.

Among the Indian Buddhists, idolatry became so rife that in some eastern languages, the word 'Buddha' became a synonym for 'idol.'[1]

During the Kushan age, Buddhism split up into two sects: Mahayana (the larger group) and Hinayana (smaller group). The former remained forceful in northern India, and the latter in southern India.

Pundit Nehru writes in 'A glance on the World History': "Brahmanism attacked Buddhism with a big scheme. For this some terrorism was used." And, "at least Brahmanism succeeded in throwing Buddhism out of its birthplace." Now Buddhism survives outsides of India.During the Gupta period, the Hindu Brahmans worked hard to eradicate Buddhism in its original birthplace.[2]

Buddhism flourished in India for approximately eight to nine hundred years, but was suppressed and eventually minimized by Hindu extremists. Its larger sect (Mahayana) has a considerable number of adherents in Central Asia (Mongolia), China, Korea, Japan and Southeast Asia.[3] The smaller sect (Hinayana) is found only in Burma (Myanmar), Thailand, Cambodia, Vietnam and Sri Lanka.

1. History of Mediaeval Hindu India, Poona, 101/1 :1924.
2. Tarīkh-i-'Ālam Par Ek Nazar: 1/128 .
3. Urdu Encyclopedia of Islam: 23/173-174.

Marginal Notes

Encyclopedic Biography of the Prophet ﷺ, Vol 1

Eminent Personalities

Abul-Qāsim Zujāji (352-415 AH/ 963-1024 CE): Abul-Qāsim Yūsuf bin Abdullah Zujāji was a great Hadīth scholar, man of letters, and linguist; nicknamed Zujaji for his dealing in Zujāj (glass). Author of many books includīng *'Umdat al-Kitāb Wa 'Iddatu Zawi'l-Albāb, ar-Riyahīn,* and *Ishtiqāq al-Asmā'.* Died in Astrabad (Northeast Iran). *(Al-A'alām 8/239)*

Abu Mijlaz Lāhiq bin Hamīd bin Sa'īd (or Shu'bah) bin Khālid bin Kathīr Sadūsi Basri, an inhabitant of Basrah. A trustworthy narrator of *Ahādīth* who narrated several *Ahādīth*. Died before Hasan Basri, during the reign of caliph Umar bin Abdul-'Azīz. *(Wikipedia Encyclopedia)*

Abu Muhammad Yazīdi (720-817 CE): Abu Muhammad Yahya bin Mubarak Adwi Yazīdi. He was a scholar of Arabic and a great grammarian of Basrah. He was the ancestor of Yazīdi family, and was named Yazīdi for his association with Yazīd bin Mansūr. Author of *Kitāb an-Nawādir* and *al-Maqsūr wa'l Mamdūd. (Al-Munjid fi'l-A'lām, P. 619)*

Abu'l A'lā Maududi (1322-1399 AH/ 1903-1979 CE): Sayyed Abul-A'lā Maudūdi bin Sayyyed Ahmad Hasan founded Jamāt-i-Islāmi, Pakistan, in 1941. He was born in Aurangabad (Hyderabad, Deccan). He edited newspapers after his father's death, and started the magazine *'Tarjumān Al-Qur'ān'* in 1932. Author of several books on religious and political subjects. He wrote the famous commentary on the Qur'ān entitled *Tafhīm Al-Qur'ān. (Zail-ul-A'lām, P. 39-40, Wikipedia Encyclopedia)*

Abul-Fadl 'Allāmi: Abul-Fadl bin Mulla Mubārak was one of the nine ministers of the Mogul emperor Akbar (the Great).

Ashraf Qāyatbai (815-901 AH/ 1412-1496 CE): Abu Nasr Saif ad-Dīn Ashraf Qāyatbai Mahmūdi Ashrafi Zahiri, one of the Circassian (Cherkasi) sultans (kings) of Egypt, began life as a slave. He was first bought by Sultan Ashraf Barsbai in Egypt and, later, by Sultan Abu Sa'īd Zahir Chaqmāq, who manumitted him, enlisted him in his army and gave him a rank. In 872 AH the Mamālīk (Mamelukes) overthrew Sultan Tamar Bugha and appointed Ashraf Qāyatbai the new Sultan. *(Al-A'lām: 5/188)*

Ash'ath bin Qais (23 before Hijra - 40 AH/600-661 CE): Abu Muhammad Ash'ath bin Qais bin Ma'dīkarib bin Mu'āwiyah Kindi ؓ was the ruler of Kindah during pre- and post-Islamic times. In the tenth century AH, he led a 70-member delegation to the Prophet Muhammad (ﷺ) and converted to Islam. Died on the day Hasan bin Ali and Mu'āwiyah bin Abi Sufyān ؓ struck a deal and came to terms. - (Al-Isābah 1/239; Al-A'lām 1/332).

Asma'i (122-216 AH/740-831 CE): Abu Sa'īd Abdul-Mālik bin Qurayb bin 'Ali bin Asma' Bahili Asma'i رحمه الله. Born and died in Basrah. He was an Imām of Arabic language, a poet, and author of a few books including *Al-Wuhūsh wa Sifātuha, An-Nabāt wash-Shajar, Al-Khail. (Al-A'lām 4/162)*

Anas bin Mālik (10 before Hijra - 93 AH/ 612-712 CE): Abu Hamza Anas bin Mālik bin Nadar bin Damdam Ansāri Khazraji ؓ belonged to the tribe of Banu Najjār. He was the Prophet Muhammad's servant until his death. The Messenger of Allah ﷺ supplicated for Anas ؓ, that he would be blessed in his wealth, his age, and that he would enter Paradise. Allah answered this prayer, and Anas ؓ was known for being very wealthy, having many children, and lived for over a hundred years. He was the last of the Companions living in Basrah. He narrated a total of 2286 Ahādīth. *(At-Tabāqat li-Ibn Sa'd 7/17-26; Al-A'lām 2/24)*

Iyād: Iyād bin Nazār bin Ma'd bin 'Adnān was the ancestor of Banu Iyād who consists of many tribes including Banu Hudhāfah, Banu Du'mi and Banu Tammāh. They dwelt around the precincts of the House of Allah in Makkah and in regions between Tihāmah and the borders of Najrān.-(Al-A'lām 2/32).

Al-Hāfiz Ibn Kathīr (701-774 AH/1302-1373 CE): Abul-Fida' 'Imād-ad-Dīn Ismā'īl bin Umar bin Kathīr bin Dau' bin Dār' Qurashi Busrawi Dimashqi. He was a famous commentator of the Qur'ān, historian, Hadīth scholar, and jurist. He was born in Qaryah Mujaidal, a suburb of Busra (Syria) but later moved along with his brother to Damascus. He was a pupil of Ibn Taymiyyah and travelled widely to acquire knowledge. He died in Damascus. Author of many books, the most famous of them being *Tafsīr al-Qur'ān al-Adhīm, Al-Bidāya wa'n-Nihāyah,* and *Al-Bā'ith al-Hathīth. (Al-A'lām 1/320; Ad-Durar al-Kāminah 1/373-374)*

'Abdur-Rahman bin Nasir Sa'di (1307-1376 AH/1889-1956 CE): Born in 'Unaizah (Saudi Arabia). He was a great religious scholar and many benefited by his learning and scholarship. Author of several books including *Tafsīr as-Sa'di,* his most famous work. *(Wikipedia Encyclopedia)*

'Abdullah bin Salām (d. 43 AH/663 CE): Abu Yūsuf Abdullah bin Salām bin Hārith Qainuqā'ī was a Companion of the Prophet Muhammad (ﷺ) and alleged to be a descendant of Prophet Yūsuf (Joseph). He was an ally of Banu Khazraj. Before Islam, his name was Hazīn; later, the Messenger of Allah ﷺ renamed him Abdullah. He was with 'Umar bin Khattāb in the peaceful conquest of Jerusalem and at Jābiyah. He narrated 25 Ahadīth. *(A-Isābah: 4/102, Al-Istī'āb P. 460, Al-A'lām 4/90)*

'Abd Kalīl: King of Yemen. His name was 'Abd Kalīl (or Abd Kalāl) bin Muthawwib (Yanuf) Himyari. He was christian and became the king of Yemen after 'Amr bin Tubān bin As'ad. His reign spanned a period of 64 years. A contemporary of Imra al-Qais' father. *(Al-A'lām 4/57)*

Adi bin Zaid 'Ibādī (590 CE): 'Adi bin Zaid 'Ibādī Tamīmī. He was a pre-Islamic poet and an expert in Arabic and Persian languages. He pioneered Arabic writings in Khosrau's court and was Khosrau's Arabic translator. - (Al-A'lām 4/220, An-Nujūm az-Zāhirah 1/249, Al-Kāmil li-Ibn-il-Atheer 1/71)

'Atā' bin Abi Rabāh (27-114 AH/647- 732 CE): Abu Muhammad 'Atā' bin Aslam bin Safwān Qurashī was a slave of Banu Fihr or Banu Jumh. He was of Nubian extraction, was born in Yemen and grew up in Makkah. He acquired religious knowledge from the Companions living in Makkah and Madīnah and later became known as the Mufti and Muhaddith of Makkah. Mujāhid, Auzā'ī,

Ibn Jarīr, Abu Hanīfah and Laith narrated Ahadīth from him. He was counted amongst the great jurists. *(Tahdhīb at-Tahdhīb 7/179-183; Wafiyāt al-A'yān 3/261-262; Al-A'lām 4/235)*

Allamah Maqdasī (336-380 AH/947-990 CE): Abu Abdullah Shams Ad-Dīn Muhammad bin Ahmad bin Abu Bakr al-Banna' Maqdasi Bashshārī. He was a famous geographer and traveler and was named al-Maqdasī after al-Quds, his birthplace. Author of a famous work, *Ahsan at-Taqāseem Fi Ma'rafat al-Aqāleem. (Al-A'lām 5/312)*

'Alā' bin Hadramī (d/ 21 AH/642 CE): 'Alā' (Abdullah) bin Hadramī (Imād) bin Akbar bin Rabī'ah Hadrami was born in Makkah and resided in Hadhramaut. In 8 AH/ 629 CE, Prophet Muhammad (ﷺ) appointed him the governor of Bahrain, an office he continued to hold during the caliphates of Abu Bakr and 'Umar. Later on, 'Umar sent him to Basrah but he died on the way. *(Al-Isabah 4/445; Usd al-Ghāba 3/272; Al-A'lām 4/245)*

'Amārah bin 'Aqīl (182-239 AH/ 798-853 CE): 'Amārah bin 'Aqīl Yarbū'ī Tamīmī was a poet noted for his eloquence. He was the grandson of the famous poet Jarīr, from his mother's side. The grammarians of Basrah studied language under him. He became blind in his old age and his *Qasā'id* have been collected and edited by Shākir al-'Āshoor. *(Al-A'lām 5/37; Al-Munjid fi'l A'lām P.379; Tāreekh Baghdād 12/282)*

'Amr bin Luhayy: 'Amr bin 'Āmir bin Luhayy bin 'Āmir bin Rabī'ah bin 'Amir bin Qaam'ah bin Ilyās bin Mudār. His lineage is controversial; some say that he was Qahtānī while others say that he was an Adnānī, although the prevailing view is that he was an Adnānī Arab. He is responsible for corrupting the monotheistic creed of Prophet Ibrāhīm عليه السلام and introducing idol-worship in Arabia. *(Al-Jamharah li-Ibn Hazm; P. 233-235; Al-A'lām 5/84; Wikipedia Encyclopedia)*

'Amr Muzaiqiyā: 'Amr Muzaiqiyā bin 'Āmir Mā' us-Samā' bin Hārithah al-Ghatrīf is counted among those who belong to the Tubba' dynasty. He was a king of Ma'rib although the recurrent assaults of the Kahlāni nomads forced him to leave for Banu Ghassan. He later moved to 'Akk where he died. Among his descendants was Tha'labah Bahlool, the ancestor of the Ansar (the Helpers) of Madīnah. *(Taj Ul-'Uroos: see under 'Mazq'; Al-A'lām 5/80)*

'Antarah bin 'Amr bin Shaddād (d. 22 before Hijra/600 CE): 'Antarah bin 'Amr bin Shaddad bin 'Amr bin Mu'āwiyah 'Absi. He was a very generous and brave Arab, a warrior and a famous cavalier. He belonged to the first rank of Arab poets. The collection of his poetry is entitled *Mu'allaqah adh-Dhahabiyyah. (Ash-Shi'r wash-Shu'arā', P. 87; Al-A'lām 5/91; Al-Munjid fi'l A'lām, P. 381)*

Barā' bin 'Āzib ﷺ: He was a Companion of the Prophet Muhammad (ﷺ), as was his father, 'Āzib bin Hārith ﷺ. Barā' took part in many *Ghazwāt* (military expeditions) including those of *Uhud* and the *Trench*. In 24 AH he conquered Rai (Iran). *(Usd Al-Ghaba 1/199, 2/506)*

Baidāwī (d. 685 AH/1286 CE): Abu Sa'eed Nasir ad-Dīn Abdullah bin 'Umair bin Muhammad bin Ali Baidāwi Shīrāzī ﷺ was born in Baidā', near Shiraz. He was the *Qadi* (judge) of Shiraz for some time. Author of *Anwār at-Tanzeel wa Asrār at-Ta'weel,* a commentary on the Qur'ān, popularly known as *Tafsīr Al-Baidawi.* Among his other notable works are *Minhāj al-Wusul ila 'Ilm al-Usūl* and *Tawāli'-al-Anwār. - (Mu'jam Al-Mu'allifeen 6/97-98; Al-Munjid fi'l-A'lām, P. 161)*

Firdausi: Abul-Qāsim Firdausi ranks among the five great poets of Iran. The Iranians call him *Sha'ir-e-Shahnama*. Firdausi was born in 329 or 330 AH in Paz, a suburb of Tūs. He wrote his *Shahnama* in 365 AH, tracing the history of Iran, based on Iranian mythology, from the beginning of the creation to his own times. His style is moving and eloquent although many of his historical details do not have any supporting evidence. He died in 411 or 416 AH.

Hārithah bin 'Amr Muzaiqiyā: Hārithah Ghatrīf was grandfather of 'Amr Muzaiqiya bin 'Āmir Mā' us-Samā'. His grandson was Hārithah bin 'Amr Muzaiqiya, the chief ansestor of Aus and Khazraj. *(Saba'ik-udh-Dhahab, P.281)*

Hajjāj bin Yūsūf (40-95 AH/660-714): Abu Muhammad Hajjāj bin Yūsūf bin Hakam bin Abu 'Aqīl bin Mas'ūd Thaqafi, nicknamed Kulaib. Born and raised in Tā'if. He was a loyal ally of the *Ummayad* rulers. He taught children in Tā'if until he moved to Damascus, where he joined the army during the reign of Abdul-Mālik bin Marwān. In 71 AH, he laid siege to Makkah and, in the ensuing battle, Abdullah bin Zubayr ﷺ died as a martyr fighting against him. Abdul-Mālik appointed Hajjāj the governor of Iraq for his administrative skills. He remained a governor for 20 years. He died of stomach cancer in Wāsit.

(Al-Ma'ārif li-Ibn Qutaibah, P. 173, Al-'Aqd-ul-Farīd 5/13, Murooj adh-Dhahab 3/151, Tarīkh Baghdād 8/240)

Harb bin Umayyah: Abu Amr Harb bin Umayyah bin Abd Shams bin Abd Manaf bin Qusayy Qurashi was the father of Abu Sufyan. Harb was a contemporary of Abdul-Muttalib bin Hashim and a commander of the Quraish forces in the War of Fijar. He died in Syria in 586 CE, a few months after the last battle of the War of Fijar. *(Tarīkh Al-Ya'qūbi 2/12, Murooj Adh-Dhahab 2/174, Ar-Raud Al-Anf 1/319)*

Haudhah bin Ali Hanafi (d. 8 AH/630 CE): Haudhah bin Ali bin Thamamah bin 'Amr Hanafi belonged to the tribe of Bakr bin Wa'il. He was a king of Yamamah and a Christian. He was also a poet and a preacher in pre-Islamic times. Prophet Muhammad (ﷺ) wrote him a letter inviting him to the faith of Islam, but he refused. *(Al-A'lām 8/102; Wikipedia Encyclopedia)*

Ibn Is'hāq (d. 150 AH/ 768 CE): Imām Abu Abdullah Muhammad bin Ishāq bin Yasār Muttalabi Madyani رحمه الله is an authority (Imām) on *Siyar* and *Maghāzī* (Prophet's biography and his military campaigns). His grandfather, Yasār, was a freed slave of Qais bin Makhrama Muttalabi. He was of Persian origin. He resided in Medinah, travelled to Al-Jazeerah, Iraq, Kufa, Baghdad and Rai and, later, took residence in Baghdad, where he died. *(At-Tabaqāt li-Ibn Sa'd 7/321-322; Wafiyāt-ul-A'yān 4/276-277; Tarīkh Baghdād 1/215-234)*

Ibn Al-Qayyim (691-751 AH/ 1291-1350 CE): Shams-ad-Dīn Abu Abdullah Muhammad bin Abu Bakr bin Ayyub bin Sa'd bin Jarīr Dimashqi Zur'i Ibn Qayyim, surnamed Al-Jawziyyah. A pupil of Ibn Taimiyyah رحمه الله. He was a paragon of piety and devoutness, who suffered hardships and imprisonment along with Ibn Taimiyyah. Author of several valuable books like *Zād Al-Ma'ād, I'lām Al-Mūaqi'een, Badāi' al-fawā'id. (Zail Tabaqat-ul-Hanābilah 4/447; Al-Badr-ut-Tāli' 2/137; Ad-Durar-ul-Kāminah 3/400; At-Taj-ul-Mukallal, P.425)*

Ibn Jarīr Tabari (d. 310 AH/923 CE): Abu Ja'far Muhammad bin Jarīr bin Yazeed Tabari رحمه الله was born in Amul, capital of Tabaristan (Iran). He was an authority on *Tafsīr* (Quranic commentary) and history. After completing his education, he settled in Baghdād and lived there until his death. Author of great works such as *Tafsīr At-Tabari* and *Tarīkh At Tabari. (Tarīkh Baghdād 2/166;*

Mu'jam-ul-Udabā' 5/275; Wafiat-ul-A'yan 4/191)

Ibn Hajar al-'Asqalānī (773-852 AH/1372-1449 CE): Abul-Fadl Shihāb-ud-Dīn Ahmad bin Ali bin Muhammad Kinani 'Asqalānī Misri رحمه الله came to be known as Ibn Hajar. He was an *Imām* of Hadīth, History, *Ilm ar-Rijāl* (Biographical Science) and literature. He travelled to Yemen and Hijaz for studies. Author of nearly 150 books, the most famous of them being *Fath al-bāri, Al-Isābah, Tahdhīb at-Tahdhīb. (Ta'jeel-ul-Manfa'ah, P.19; Ad-Durar-ul-Kāminah 4/492; Mu'jam-ul-Mu'allifeen 2/20)*

Ibn Hauqal (d. 371AH/981 CE): Abul-Qasim Muhammad bin Hauqal, a famous historian, geographer and traveler of the tenth century CE. He was born in Nasībīn (southern Turkey) and lived in Baghdād. His famous book *Surat al-Ard* is a summary of Astakhri's book *Masālik wa'l-Mamālik. (Al-Munjid fi'l-A'lām P.7; Wikipedia Encyclopedia)*

Ibn Abdul-Barr (368-463 AH/ 978-1071 CE): Abu Umar Yūsuf bin Abdullah bin Muhammad bin Abdul-Barr Qurtubi. He was born in Cordova (Qurtubah). He was a companion of Ibn Hazm, who learnt Hadīth sciences from him. Some of his well-known works are *Al-Isti'āb, At-Tamheed* and *Al-Istidhkar. (Siyar A'lām an-Nubalā' 18/153-163; Wafiyat-ul-A'yān 7/66)*

Ibn Najjār (578-643 AH/1183-1245 CE): Abu Abdullah Mohibb ad-Dīn Muhammad bin Mahmud bin Hasan bin Hibat-Allah bin Mahāsin Baghdādi رحمه الله, surnamed Ibn Najjār. He was a great Hadīth scholar *(Muhaddith), Hafiz,* and historian. Author of several books including *Al-Qamar al-Munīr fi'l-Musnid Al-Kabīr, Kanz al-Anām fi's-Sunan wa'l-Ahkām. (Shadhrāt-udh-Dhahab 5/226-227; Al-A'lām 7/86)*

Ibn Hishām (d. 213 AH/828 CE): A famous biographer of the Prophet ﷺ. His name was Abu Muhammad Abdul-Mālik bin Hishām bin Ayyub Himyari Ma'āfirī رحمه الله popularly known as Ibn Hishām. His book *Seerat Ibn Hishām* is a rendition and summary of Ibn Ishāq's *Siyar wa Maghāzi.* He also wrote a book on the genealogy of Himyari kings. He died in Egypt. *(Ar-Raud-ul-Unf 1/22, Wafiyat-ul-A'yān 3/177)*

Ibn Ya'qūb Hamdani (280-334 AH/893-945 CE): Hasan bin Ahmad bin Ya'qūb was a Yemeni; also called Ibn Ya'qūb, Ibn Ha'ik and Ibn Dhu Damīnah.

He was an expert in many fields. Author of books on geography, history, genealogy, and other subjects, the famous among them being *Sifatu Jazeerat Al-Arab* and *Al-Ikleel.* *(Sifatu Jazeerat Al-Arab, P.7-33, Al-A'lām 2/179)*

Imām Ibn Qutaibah (213-276 AH/ 828-889 CE): Abu Muhammad Abdullah bin Muslim bin Qutaibah Dīnawarī. Born in Baghdād and lived in Kufah. He was the judge of Dīnawarī for some time. Author of *Al-Ma'ārif, Adab al-Kātib,* and *'Uyoon Al-Akhbār*. Imām Adh-Dhahabi mentions 28 of his books. He died in Baghdād. *(Siyar A'lām an-Nubalā' 13/296-302; Wafiyāt al-A'yān 3/42-44)*

Imām Mālik (93-179 AH/ 712-795 CE): Imām Dār Al-Hijra Abu Abdullah Mālik bin Anas bin Mālik Himyari Asbahi Madani was the founder of one of the four schools of Islamic jurisprudence. He was a contemporary of Imām Abu Hanīfah, Imām Shāfi'i, Mu'ammar, and Abu Dawood. He taught and gave rulings on points of law beginning in his early youth. He was known for always washing and perfuming himself before giving lessons in Ahadīth. His book, *Al-Muwatta,* ranks as the most accurate book next to *Sahīh Al-Bukhāri* and *Sahīh Muslim*. Born and died in Madīnah and was buried in *Baqee'.* *(Siyar A'lām an-Nubalā' 8/48-135, Tahdhīb at-Tahdhīb 10/5)*

Imām Muslim (204-261 AH/820-875 CE): Al-Hafiz al-Muhaddith Imām Abu Husain Muslim bin Hajjāj bin Muslim bin Ward Qushairi Neshapuri. Born in Neshapur and studied in Hijaz, Iraq, Syria, Egypt and Baghdād. He was a pupil of eminent scholars such as Imām Bukhāri and Imām Ahmad bin Hanbal. He selected, out of three hundred thousand Ahadīth, a total of 3033 Ahadīth, without repeating anyone of them, to write his Sahīh Muslim. Buried in Nasrabad, a residential district of Neshapur. *(Tarīkh Baghdād 13/100, Wafiyat al-A'yān 5/194-195)*

Imran bin 'Amr: In tribe of Imran bin 'Amr Muzaiqyiā bin 'Āmir Ma' us-Samā', Banu Atīk belongs to the offspring of Atīk bin Usd, a grandson of 'Imrān. They lived in a region now called Oman. The reigning king of Oman also belongs to this tribe. *(Sabā'ik Adh-Dhahab P.285; Mu'jam Qabā'il-ul-Arab 2/753)*

Jabir bin Abdullah (16 before Hijra-78 AH/607-698 CE): Jabir bin Abdullah bin 'Amr bin Harām Khāzraji Salami. He was born in Madīnah and became Muslim along with his father, during the Second Pledge of 'Aqabah.

He took part in 19 *Ghazwāt* along with Prophet Muhammad (ﷺ), and narrated 1540 *Ahadīth. (Usd al-Ghāba 1/294, Al-Isābah 1/546)*

Jarīr bin Abdullah Bajali: (d. 51 AH/671 CE): There is controversy over the date of his conversion to Islam. He was a very handsome man; 'Umar bin al-Khattab used to call him 'the *Yūsuf* of this *Ummah.'* The Messenger of Allahﷺ called him Mālik Al-Yemen, and appointed him governor of some parts of Yemen. He destroyed the idol named Dhu'l Khalasah and took part in the battle of Qādisiyyah. He was an emissary during the negotiations between Ali and Mu'āwiyah. Died in Qurqaisiyāh, near the Euphrates. *(Al-Isābah 1/581-583; Usd-ul-Ghābah 1/319-321; Siyar A'lām-un-Nubalā' 2/530-537)*

Kalbi (d. 204 AH/819 CE): Abu Mundhir Hishām bin Muhammad bin Sa'ib Kalbi of Kufah. His ancestral line, back in the eighth generation, leads to Imra' ul-Qais, the famous pagan poet. While in Baghdād, he used to narrate Ahadīth and was known as an expert in Hadīth and genealogy sciences. Author of about 150 books. *(Tarīkh Baghdād 14/45; Wafiyat al-A'yān 4/309-313 and 6/82-84)*

King Abdul-Azīz (1293-1373 AH/1876-1953 CE): Abdul-Azīz bin Abdur-Rahman bin Faisal bin Turki bin Abdullah bin Muhammad bin Sa'ud belonged to the tribe of Rabī'ah, a branch of Dhuhl bin Shaibān. He was the founder of the modern kingdom of Saudi Arabia. He was born in Riyadh and lived in exile along with his father in Kuwait. He later attacked Ār-Rasheed (who controlled Arabia at the time) and seized Ar-Riyadh in 1319 AH/1902 CE. Within the next 30 years he conquered most of the Arabian Peninsula and named it the Kingdom of Saudi Arabia in 1351 AH/ 1932 CE. Oil was discovered during his reign. *(Al-A'lām 4/19-20; Al-Mausoo'ah al-Arabiyyah al-Maisarah 2/1183; Al-Munjid fi'l A'lām, P.366)*

Mutanabbī (303 – 354 AH/915 - 965 CE): Abu Tayyib Ahmad bin Husain bin Hasan bin Abdus-Samad Ju'fī Kindī Mutanabbī was a distinguished Arab poet. He was called Kindi because he was born in Kindah, a residential quarter of Kufah. He grew up in Syria and studied in *Badiat ush-Sham*. He once claimed to be a prophet but later repented. He left a collection of poetry called *Diwan Al-Mutannabi*. He is lauded for his virtues as well as condemned for his drawbacks. - (Al-A'lām 1/115)

Muhammad bin Qāsim (62-98 AH/681-717 CE): Muhammad bin Qāsim bin Muhammad bin Hakam bin Abu 'Aqīl Thaqafi was a conqueror of Sind, a great leader and a distinguished personality of the reign of Bani Marwān. He was given the charge of the conquest of Sind by Hajjāj bin Yūsuf in 92 AH/711 CE. He launched attack on Sind via Makran, conquered Daibul and defeated Raja Dahir in the Battle of Rawar (93 AH/712 CE). He conquered many territories until he reached Multan. He was very young at that time. He died in captivity in Wāsit during the reign of Suleyman bin Abdul-Mālik. *(Futuh Al-Buldān li'l-Baladhari, P.224; Al-A'lām 6/333; Urdu Encyclopedia of Islam: 19/347)*

Mas'udī (d. 346 AH/957 CE): Abul-Hasan Ali bin Husain bin Ali Mas'udī Baghdādī Misrī was a descendant of Abdullah bin Mas'ud (the Prophet's Companion). He was an expert in historical research work. Born in Baghdād and died in Egypt. He was a Mu'tazilite (adherent of the school which introduced speculative dogmatism into Islam); some consider him to be a Shi'ite. His name occurs in *A'yān ash-Shi'ah*. Among his famous books are: *Murooj adh-Dhahab, Akhbār az-Zamān, At-Tanbeeh wa'l-Ishrāf. (Al-Fihrist li-Ibn an-Nadeem, P.171; Siyar A'lām an-Nubalā' 15/569; Tabaqat ash-Shāfi'iyyah 3/456)*

Mugheerah bin Shu'bah (20 before Hijra- 50 AH/ 603-670 CE): Abu Abdullah Mugheerah bin Shu'bah bin Abu 'Amir bin Mas'ud Thaqafi (a companion of the Prophetﷺ) was born in Ta'if. He was known to the Arabs as Mugheerat ar-Ra'y and converted to Islam in 5 AH/626 CE. He took part in the Expedition of Hudaybiyya and the *Ghazwāt* that followed it. He also partook in the Battles of Nahawand and Hamadan. Umar ibn Al-Khattab appointed him governor of Basrah and Kufah, successively. He did not take sides in the Ali - Muā'wiyah dispute but served as an arbiter. Muā'wiyah appointed him governor of Kufa and he died in that office. Narrator of 136 Ahadīth. *(Al-Isabah 6/156-158; Usd Al-Ghabah 4/181; Al-A'lām 7/277)*

Mahdi Abbasi (127-169 AH/744-785 CE): Abu Abdullah Mahdi-Billah Muhammad bin Abdullah Mansūr bin Muhammad bin Ali Abbāsī was born in Ahwāz. He succeeded the caliphate after the death of his father, in 158 AH – 169 AH/ 775 CE-785 CE. He was very generous and brave and built *Ar-Rasāfah,* a congregation mosque, in Baghdād. *(Murooj adh-Dhahab 4/377; Al-Kāmil li-Ibn-*

il-Atheer 5/259; Al-A'lām 6/221)

Nu'mān bin Mundhir (d. 15 before Hijra/ 608 CE): Abu Qabūs Nu'mān bin Mundhir bin Imra ul-Qais Lakhmī was a king of Hirah. He founded the town named Numāniyyah on the right bank of the Tigris. He earned the wrath of Khosrau Parvez who sent him to prison where he died. *(Al-A'lām 8/43)*

Qatādah (60-117 AH/680 – 736 CE): Abu Khattāb Qatādah bin Da'āmah bin Qatādah bin Azīz Sadūsī Basrī ﵀ was a commentator of the Qur'ān, Hadīth scholar, writer and linguist. He was inclined to the Qadri School (which asserts man's free will) and, while narrating Ahadīth, committed imposture *(Tadlees)*. He was an expert in language, genealogy, and history of Arabs. He became blind in his old age and died of plague in Wāsit. *(Siyar A'lām an-Nubāla' 5/269 – 283; Wafayāt al-A'yān 4/85; Meezān al-I'tidāl 3/385)*

Qudā'ah: Great ancestor of Banu Qudā'ah. Some historians say he was an Adnānī although most of them consider him a Qahtānī. His lineage is: Qudā'ah bin Mālik bin 'Amr bin Murrah bin Zaid bin Mālik bin Himyar. Banu Qudā'ah worshipped an idol called *Uqaisar* during Pre-Islamic Age of Ignorance. *(Nihāyat al-'Arab P.358; Mu'jam-ul-Qabā'il-il-Arab 3/957; Al-A'lām 5/199)*

Qais bin Khārijah bin Sannān Dhabyani: Some scholars include him among the Prophet's Companions. He is also the narrator of one Hadīth. *(Al-Isābah 5/353; Usd-al-Ghābah 3/494; Al-Jamharah li-Ibn Hazm, P.252)*

Qais bin Makhramah: Abu Muhammad Qais bin Makhramah bin Muttalib bin Abd-Manāf bin Qusayy Qurashi Muttalibi ﵁ (a Companion) was born in the Year of the Elephant ('Ām al-Feel). The Prophet ﷺ also gave him corn out of the spoils of Kheybar. *(Jāmi' at-Tirmidhī 3619; Usd al-Ghābah 3/510; Al-Isābah 5/379)*

Sa'eed bin Jubair (45-95 AH/665-714 CE): Abu Abdullah Sa'eed bin Jubair bin Hishām Asadi ﵀ was one of the great *Tābi'een* of Kūfah. He was a pupil of Ibn Abbās and Ibn Umar ﵄. He sided with Abdur-Rahman bin Ash'ath Kindī in the Battle of Deir Jamājam, fled to Makkah, and was arrested there. Hajjāj bin Yūsuf slew him when he was fifty years old. *(At-Tabaqāt li-Ibn Sa'd 6/256-267; Ath-Thiqat li-Ibn Hibbān 4/275; Wafayāt Al-A'yān 2/371)*

Sa'eed bin Musayyib (d. 91 AH/710 CE): Abu Muhammad Sa'eed bin Musayyyib bin Hazn Qurashi Makhzūmī, known as the chief of *Tabi'een,* was one of the seven famous jurists of Madīnah. He was born in the second year of 'Umar ibn Khattāb's caliphate. He lived a life of piety and self-denial, and was known to be a good interpreter of dreams. He died in Madīnah, at age 75. *(At-Tabaqāt li-Ibn Sa'd 5/119-143; Wafayat al-A'yān 2/375-378; Siyar A'lām an-Nubalā' 4/245)*

Salama bin Akwa' (d. 74 AH/693 CE): Salama bin Amr bin Sannan Akwa' Aslami was a Companion of the Prophet ﷺ who was known for his bravery, excellent marksmanship, and sprinting. He took part in seven battles with the Messenger of Allah (ﷺ). He lived for some time in Rabadhah and died in Madīnah. He narrated 77 *Ahadīth. (Al-Isabah 3/127; Usd Al-Ghābah 2/353, Al-A'lām 3/113)*

Samu'āl bin Adiā' (d. 65 before Hijra/ c. 560 CE): Samu'āl (Shamuel) bin Ghareed bin Adiā' Azdi belonged to Banu Dayyyān. He was a Jew of Pre-Islamic Age of Ignorance, and was known as a poet and physician. He lived until the beginning of the 6th century CE and was a resident of Kheybar who owned a palace named Ablaq. He was known for his loyalty to Imra ul-Qais. A collection of his poetical works *(Diwān)* is still extant. *(Al-A'lām 3/140; Al-Munjid fi'l A'lām, P. 309; Wikipedia Encyclopedia)*

Samhūdi (844-911 AH/1440-1506 CE): Abul-Hasan Nūr Ad-Dīn Ali Bin Abdullah bin Ahmad Hasani Shāfi'ī Samhūdī Misrī. Born in Samhūd (Upper Egypt) and grew up in Cairo. Came to Madīnah in 873 AH and became known as *Mufti* and historian of Madīnah. Died in Madīnah. Most of his works were destroyed by fire although one of his several works, *Wafā' ul-Wafā',* is widely known. *(Shadhrāt adh-Dhahab 8/50-51; Al-A'lām 4/307; Al-Munjid fi'l A'lām, P.309; Wikipedia Encyclopedia)*

Sahl bin Sa'd (d. 91 AH/710 CE): Sahl bin Sa'd bin Mālik Sā'idi Khazrajī. Both he and his father were companions of Prophet Muhammad (ﷺ). Sahl was fifteen years old when the Messenger of Allah ﷺ died. He lived for about a hundred years, and was the last of the Companions who died in Madīnah. He narrated 188 Ahadīth. *(Al-Isābah 3/167; Usd al-Ghābah 2/390; Al-A'lām 3/143)*

Sayyed Tantāwi (1347-1431 AH/1928-2010 CE): Dr. Muhammad Sayyed Atiyyah Tantāwi. He was born in Sūhāj (Egypt). He received primary education in Alexandria and belonged to the Shāfi'ite school of Islamic jurisprudence. He taught in the Islamic University of Madīnah and later became the rector of Al-Azhar University. He was the Grand Mufti of Egypt from 1996 until his death. Author of *Al-Waseet,* a commentary on the Qur'ān and received the King Faisal Award from King Abdullah bin Abdul-Azīz in 2010. He died of heart failure in Saudi Arabia on 24 Rabī' al-Awwal, 1431 AH. His funeral prayer was offered in the Prophet's mosque and he was buried in *Baqee' Al-Gharqad. (Wikipedia Encyclopedia)*

Shah Abbas (1578 CE-1629 CE): Shah Abbas Safawi, ruler of Persia (Iran), was a contemporary of the Mogul kings Akbar and Jehangir.

Shuja' bin Wahb Asadi: Abu Wahb Shuja' bin Wahb bin Rabī'ah bin Usd Usdi Ghanami was a famous Companion. He was an Ally of Banu Abd-Shams and took part in both emigrations to Abyssinia. Prophet Muhammad (ﷺ) appointed him commander of forces several times. He was with the Prophet ﷺ in all the battles and military expeditions. In 7 AH he delivered the Prophet's letter to Hārith bin Abi Shamar Ghassani. In 12 AH/633 CE he fell as a martyr in the Battle of Yamāmah. *(At-Tabaqāt li-Ibn Sa'd 3/94-95; Al-Isābah 3/256; Usd al-Ghābah 2/414; Al-A'lām 3/158)*

Shareef Makkah Al-Hussain (1270-1350 AH/1854-1931 CE): Husain bin Ali bin Muhammad bin Abdul-Mu'een bin 'Aun Hashimi Hasanī. He was the last Hashimite governor of Hijaz. He was born in Istanbul and appointed governor of Makkah in 1326 AH/1908 CE. When Ibn Saud seized Tā'if in August 1924, Hussain appointed his son, Ali, the governor and left for Jeddah. In 1344 AH/1925 CE he went to Cyprus and from there to Amman (Jordan) where he died. He was buried in Bait al-Maqdis (Jerusalem). *(Al-A'lām 2/249-250)*

Shukāmah bin Shabeeb: Shukāma bin Shabeeb bin Sakūn bin Ashras Kindī of Banu Qahtān was the ancestor of Banu Shukamah. The king of Dūmat al-Jandal, Ukaidār, who became a Muslim on receiving a letter from the Prophet Muhammad (ﷺ), belonged to Banu Shukāmah. *(Nihāyat al-Arab, P.280-281, Al-A'lām 3/171)*

Tarfah (86-60 before Hijra/ 538-564 CE): Abu 'Amr Tarfah bin Abd bin Sufyān bin Sa'd Bakri Wa'ili is counted amongst the greatest poets of the Pre-Islamic Age. He was born in *Badi'yat ul-Bahrain* and travelled widely in Nejd. King 'Amr bin Hind included him among his companions; later, the king charged him to deliver a letter to his subordinate, Muka'bar, governor of Bahrain. The latter slew him in Hajar (هجَر) because he had written a satiric poem against him. Many of his *Qasā'id* are found in books; one of them is amongst the Seven Suspended *(Al-Mu'allaqāt as-Sab'ah)*. Satire and wisdom are the two of the main features of his verses. *(Ash-Shi'r wash-Shu'arā', P. 59-60, Al-A'lām 3/225, Al-Jamharah li-Ibn Hazm, P.320)*

Umaim: He was the person who pioneered the use of wood for roofing. He was a king and known to Persians by the name of Adam. He had a son named Wabar. The tribe of Banu Umaim perished in a fierce desert storm. There is no trace of them now. *(Website: Al-Islam)*

Wā'il bin Hujr (d. 50 AH/670 CE): Abu Hunaidah Wa'il bin Hujr bin Rabī'ah bin Wā'il bin Ya'mar Hadramī Qahtānī رضي الله عنه was a companion of Prophet Muhammad (ﷺ). His father was a king of Yemen. When Wā'il رضي الله عنه came to see the Prophet ﷺ, he prayed for him and appointed him the governor of Hadramaut. When Wā'il رضي الله عنه went to see Mu'āwiyah رضي الله عنه, the latter seated him next to him. Ibn Khaldūn, the famous historian, was one of his descendants. *(Al-Isābah 6/466-467; Usd al-Ghābah 4/305-306; Al-A'lām 8/106)*

Wajj bin Abdul-Hayy: The founder of the city of Tā'if and a brother of Aja'a after whom the mountains of Aja'a and Salma (Ha'il) are named. *(Mu'jam al-Buldān: see under 'At-Ta'if; Ar-Raud al-Unf 4/317-318)*

Wahshi bin Harb (d. 25 AH/ 645 CE): Abu Dasmah Wahshi bin Harb Habshi, *Maula* (associate) Banu Naufal رضي الله عنه, is a famous Companion. He was one of the Sudanese slaves of Makkah, who killed Hamza bin Abdul-Muttalib رضي الله عنه in the Battle of Uhud. Wahshi converted to Islam and came with the delegation of the people of Tā'if to see Prophet Muhammad (ﷺ), who could not bear to see his face. He later killed Musailamah the Liar in the Battle of Yamamah. He died in Homs during the caliphate of 'Uthmān bin 'Affān رضي الله عنه. *(Sahīh al-Bukhari: 4072; Al-Isābah 6/470; Usd-al-Ghābah 4/307-309; Al-A'lām 8/111)*

Waleed bin Abdul-Malik (48-96 AH/ 668-715 CE): Abu Abbas Waleed bin Abdul-Malik bin Marwan bin Ha'kam bin Abi Al-'Aas bin Umayya رحمه الله was born in 48 AH. He succeeded his father to the caliphate (86 AH – 96 AH) and was counted amongst the *Tabi'een*. He built the Umayyad congregation mosque in Damascus (Syria) and carried out extension works in the Prophet's Mosque in Madinah and in the Holy Mosque of Makkah. He died in Der Maran and was buried in Damascus. He wore a finger ring on which the following words were engraved: 'O Waleed, you are destined to die'. *(Al-Bidāya Wa'n-Nihaya 9/168-173; Al-A'lām 8/121)*

Yaqūt Hamawi (574-626 AH/1178-1229 CE): Abu Abdullah Shihāb ud-Dīn Yaqūt bin Abdullah Rūmi Hamawi رحمه الله was a reliable historian and a geographer. He was also an expert of language and literature. Of Roman extraction, he was a slave of a Hamawi merchant of Bagdad who manumitted him in 596 AH. He was a calligrapher and used to write books in exchange for wages. He made journeys to Khorasān, Khwarzam, Mosul and Halab (Aleppo) in pursuit of knowledge. The most famous of his works is *Mu'jam Al-Buldan. (Al-A'lām 8/131; Wafayāt al-A'yān 6/127-139)*

Yazeed bin Zam'ah Asadi (d. 8 AH/630 CE): His lineage is: Yazeed bin Zam'ah bin Aswad bin Muttalib bin Usd bin Abdul-'Uzza Usdi Qurashi رضي الله عنه was a Companion of the Prophet Muhammad ﷺ. He was one of the most notable chieftain of Quraish during the Pre-Islamic Age. He was also one of the earliest converts to Islam and one of those who migrated to Abyssinia. He was martyred in the Battle of Hunain or the Battle of Tā'if. *(Al-Isabah 6/515; Usd-ul-Ghābah 4/339; Al-A'lām 8/183)*

Zakariyyā bin Muhammad Qazweeni (605-682 AH/ 1208-1283 CE): Zakariyyā bin Muhammad bin Mahmūd Ansāri Najjāri Qazweeni رحمه الله was a descendant of Anas bin Mālik رضي الله عنه (the Prophet's companion). He was a famous historian and geographer who travelled to Syria and Iraq. He was the *Qadi* (Judge) of Wāsit and Hillah during the reign of Musta'sim-Billah. *Āthar al-Bilād wa Akhbār al-'Ibād* is the most famous of his works. *(Al-A'lām 3/46)*

Zuhair (13 before Hijra/609 CE): Zuhair bin Abi Salma bin Rabī'ah bin Abi Rabāh Muzani Mudāri was a famous pre-Islamic poet. Some literary critics give him precedence over all the other poets. His father, aunt, both his sisters (Salma and Khansā') and both his sons (Ka'b and Bajeer) were poets. Zuhair lived in Hājir (Nejd). A collection of his poems (Qasā'id) is entitled *Al-Hauliyyāt. (Al-A'lām 3/52)*

Places

Abu Qubais: A mountain east of Makkah and the one nearest to the Holy Mosque of Makkah. *(Al-Munjid fi'l A'lām, P.21)*

Arhab: An agricultural region in Yemen, named after a large tribe of Hamdan. *(Mu'jam Al-Buldan: See under 'Arhab')*

Jordan (Arabic: Urdun): Once a part of ancient Syria. It is bordered in the west by River Jordan, Dead Sea, and Palestine, in the south by Saudi Arabia and Gulf of Aqabā, in the east by Iraq, and in the north by Syria. Its capital city is Amman. Several Companions of the Prophet (ﷺ) are buried there. The site of the Battle of Mūtah, near Al-Kark, lies in Jordan. Area: 90740 sq km. Its historical cities are Al-Kark, Ajlon, Azraq and Amman. *(Mausoo'ah al-'Ālam al-Islami, PP 54-58; Al-Munjid fi'l A'lām PP 36-37)*

Al-Ahsa: Eastern part of Saudi Arabia, between Kuwait and Qatar. It is included in the Eastern Region of Saudi Arabia. Among its chief cities are Al-Qateef, Al-Khobar, Jubail, Az-Zahran, etc. Site of large oil deposits. *(Al-Munjid fi'l A'lām, P. 28)*

Al-Bā'hah: This province lies in the southwest of Saudi Arabia. To the northwest of it is the province of Makkah and to the southeast of it the province of Aseer. Its area is 10362 sq km. The Shareef of Makkah called it 'the Garden of Hijaz'. *(Atlas Al-Mamlakah al-Arabiyyah as-Saudiyyah wal-'Ālam, PP 18-19)*

Al-Jauf: Mr. Abdul-Mālik Mujāhid, Managing Director, Dārussalam, writing on his travels through Dūmat-ul-Jandal in the magazine, Diyā'-e-Hadīth, says: "Al-Jauf is the name of the province. The historical town of Dūmat Al-Jandal is nearly 1200 km away from Riyadh and nearly 250 km away from the Jordanian border. The capital of Al-Jauf is Sakakah, 60 km off Dūmat Al-Jandal". *(the monthly Diyā'-e-Hadīth, Lahore, May 2011)*

As-Sulaimi: A town in the province of Ha'il, north of Wadi ar-Rumma and 170 km off the city of Hā'il. *(Wikipedia Encyclopedia)*

Ash-Shurabbah: An ancient part of Nejd, between As-Saleelah and Ar-Rabadhah, west of Al-Qaseem. A wooded region with plenty of trees. *(Mu'jam Al-Buldān: See under 'Ash-Shurabbah')*

Al-Qateef: A town 25 km northwest of the coastal city of Dammam. The Karmathians, who stole the Black Stone from the Ka'bah, came from this city. It is now the center of the petro-chemical industry. *(Mu'jam Al-Buldān: see under 'Al-Qateef')*

Al-Midh'nab: A town of the Saudi province of Al-Qaseem, 65 km south of the city of Al-Qaseem and about 300 km north of Ar-Riyadh. In Pre-Islamic times, it was called Faihān or Adh-Dhanā'ib derived from the Arabic word Dhanab meaning 'tail'. *(Mu'jam Al-Buldān: See under 'Al-Midhnab')*

Al-Mandab: An important harbor of Yemen. The Straits of Bab ul-Mandab, which is named after it, connects the Gulf of Aden and the Arabian Sea with the Red Sea, separates Asia from Africa, and Yemen from Djibouti. *(Mu'jam Al-Buldān: see under 'Al-Mandab)*

Al-Wadee'ah: This desert town, situated in the Empty Quarter, within the territorial limits of Saudi Arabia, is about 350 km southeast of the city of Najran and about 460 km north of the Yemeni port of Al-Mukallah. *(Wikipedia Encyclopedia)*

Armenia: This country lies south of Caucasus. It used to be a part of the Soviet Union until December, 1991. Its total area is 29,800 sq. km. Capital: Yerevan. Its neighbours are Azerbiajan, Georgia, Turkey, and Iran. *(Al-Munjid Fi'l A'lām, P.39)*

Basrah: A town of Iraq, 90 km south of the confluence of the Euphrates and the Tigris, on the bank of Shatt-el-Arab. Founded in 636 CE during the reign of 'Umar ibn al-Khattāb ﷺ. It became a center of language and culture during the Abbasids. Al-Fao, Al-Qarna, Umm Qasr are some of its outlying areas. *(Al-Munjid Fi'l A'lam, P. 129)*

Baqee' al-Gharqad: Baqee' is the name of a place in Madīnah, while Gharqad means: thorny bush, called 'the tree of the Jews' in a Hadīth. This tree was found in abundance in Baqee‘, hence the name of its graveyard. Baqee‘ al-Gharqad is the cemetery of Madīnah and lies east of the Prophet's Mosque. Many Companions of the Messenger (ﷺ) were buried in this cemetery. *(Sahīh Muslim 2922; Mu'jam Al-Buldān: see under 'Baqee‘'; Al-Munjid Fi'l A'lām, P. 132)*

Bi'r Ma‘ūnah: It is sited between Harrah Banu 'Āmir and Harrah Bani Sulaim, closer to the latter. While on way from Madīnah to Makkah, one comes across it in the mountains of Ubla. The event of Rajee‘ Expedition took place near it. *(Mu'jam Al-Buldān: see under 'Bi'r Ma'ūnah')*

Tan‘eem: The name of a place near Makkah, outside the precincts of the Sacred Mosque, on the Makkah - Madīnah highway. It is the place where the 'Ayeshah Mosque is sited. It is named Tan‘eem because there is a mountain named Nu‘aim on the right-hand side of it, another in the north of it named Na‘im, while the Wadi is named Na‘mān. *(Mu'jam Al-Buldan: see under 'Tan'eem; Mu'jam Lughat Al-Fuqaha', P.148)*

Khorasan: In the past, Khorasan was the name of a vast and extensive province in eastern Iran. Its border reached up to Tūran and Ma-warā' an-Nahr. Balkh (Bakhtar) was the capital of the province. Other famous cities were Sarkhas, Herat, Merv, Tūs and Neshapur. The Khorasan of today is the eastern province of Iran and is much smaller in area.

Rumiyah: The name given by the Arabs to the capital (Rome) of the ancient Roman Empire or to Istanbul (Constantinople) in relation to the Eastern Roman Empire. Ahadīth also refer to Istanbul as the 'City of Heraclius.' *(Musnad Ahmad 2/176; Sunan ad-Dārmī 503; As-Silsilah as-Sahīhah: 4; Mu'jam-ul-Buldān: 3/100)*

Siraf: This city was situated on the coast of Persian Gulf, 240 km off Bushehr and 380 km off Bunder Abbas. It took seven days to travel from Siraf to Basra. This city was destroyed by a powerful earthquake in 977 CE. *(Mu'jam al-Buldān: see under 'Siraf; Al-Munjid fi'l A'lām, P. 320)*

Sudair: Its old name is Wadi Faqi. It is 120 km north of Ar-Riyadh. *(Mu'jam ul-Buldān: See under 'As-Sudair', Wikipedia Encyclopedia)*

Sūr (Tyre): A historical city in South Lebanon, on the Mediterranean coast, 83 km south of Beirut. An ancient city of the Phoenicians, it fell to the Muslims without a battle during the reign of 'Umar ibn Al-Khattāb رضي الله عنه. The names of Tyre (Sūr) and Sidon (Saidā') occur often in the Bible. *(Mu'jam al-Buldān; see under 'Tyre'; Oxford English Reference Dictionary P. 1558, Wikipedia Encyclopedia)*

Saidā' (Sidon): This city, founded by the Phoenicians, lies on the Mediterranean coast. It is the capital of the Lebanese province of the same name. It is 50 km off Beirut and 40 km off Tyre. It is also called Sidon; its Hebrew name is Saidu. The city is named after Saidūn bin Sadqā' bin Kan'ān (Canaan). Conquered in 46 AH/667 CE. *(Mu'jam al-Buldān: see under 'Saidā', Wikipedia Encyclopedia)*

Sa'dah: An ancient city 243 km north of San'ā', the capital of Yemen. It is also a provincial capital that receives heavy rainfall. It is 1800 m above sea level. There are many Zaidi Shi'ites who reside there. *(Al-Munjid fi'l A'lām, P. 345; Al-Mausu'ah al-Arabiyyah al-Muyassarah 2/1123)*

Daba (ضَبَا): A town in the province of Tabūk on the Red Sea coast. Once upon a time, it was the harbor for the Egyptian Hajj pilgrims coming by sea. The Mameluke king Ashraf Qāyatbai, who passed through it, built a magnificent building which came to be known later on as Dār as-Sultan. Today it is a large center of commerce. *(Wikipedia Encyclopedia)*

Aden: It is the largest seaport of Yemen on the coast of the Gulf of Aden. The city of Aden is sited in the Aden Peninsula, at the foot of a 550 m-high volcanic mountain named 'Urr Aden. It is also known as Aden Abyan. It is said that Aden was founded by Shaddad bin 'Ād. Ali bin Abi Tālib رضي الله عنه visited Aden in 10 AH/ 631 CE and delivered a sermon from the pulpit of a mosque.

'Aseer: A province in the southwest of Saudi Arabia. The provincial capital is Abha. It is bordered in the south by Yemen and the province of Jazan, in the north by the province of Ar-Riyadh and the province of Makkah, in the east by the province of Najran, and in the west by the province of Al-Baha and a part of the province of Makkah. It is a beautiful and fertile mountainous region. *(Al-Mausoo'ah al-Arabiyyah al-Muyassarah 2/1212; Al-Munjid fi'l A'lām, P. 375)*

Ghalafiqah: It was a busy harbor on the Bahr-ul-Yemen (Red Sea) coast, opposite Zabīd, in the southwest of Yemen. The harbor exists no longer but its remains can still be seen today. *(Mu'jam al-Buldān: see under 'Ghalāfiqah'. Urdu Encyclopedia of Islam 2 – 14/550-551)*

Qatar: Yaqūt writes, "There is a town named Qatar, opposite to Bahrain, between 'Umān (Oman) and 'Uqair. Ostriches of Qatar (النعام قَطَرِيَّة) are so called because they are hunted in sands of Yabreen and brought to Qatar which adjoins by land." Qatar is a small peninsula, east of the Arabian Peninsula. Its southern frontier meets the territory of Saudi Arabia. On the remaining three sides it is surrounded by sea (Persian Gulf). Total Area: 11, 438 sq. km. The capital town is Doha. Qatar won its independence from Britain in 1971. *(Mu'jam al-Buldān: see under 'Qatar'; Wikipedia Encyclopedia)*

Kazimah: A historical town on the Kuwait Creek, 40 Km off the Kuwait town of Al-Jahra.' It was the dwelling-place of Banu 'Iyād and Bakr bin Wa'il. It is the site of the Battle of Dhat As-Salāsil (12 AH/ 633 CE) in which Khālid bin Waleed ﷺ was victorious. Excavations carried out recently have discovered the relics of the ancient town. *(Mu'jam Al-Buldan: see under 'Kazimah', Wikipedia Encyclopedia)*

United Arab Emirates: This country is bordered in the north by the Arabian Gulf (Persian Gulf), in the east by Gulf of Oman and the Sultanate of Oman, and in the south and the west by Saudi Arabia. Its total area is 92,100 sq km. This state consists of seven emirates: Abu Dhabi, Dubai, Ras-Al-Khaimah, Ajmān, Umm-ul-Qaiween, Ash-Shariqah (Sharjah), and Al-Fujairah. Abu Dhabi is the capital of UAE. *(Mausoo'ah al-'Ālam al-Islami, P. 62-64)*

Madārij al-'Arj: A large town of Bilād Huzail in a suburban valley of Tā'if (Wadi al-'Arj). The poet of Āl Uthmān, Abdullah bin 'Umar bin Abdullah bin 'Amr bin Uthmān bin Affān al-Arji, belonged to this town. Here begins the region of Tihāmah. There is a distance of 78 miles between al-Arj and Tā'f. *(Mu'jam Al-Buldān: See under 'Al-Arj')*

Madyan (Midian): The name of a region adjoining the Gulf of Aqabah and Red Sea coast, about 200 km west of the province of Tabūk (Saudi Arabia). Its modern name is Maghāyir Shu'aib. It was the land of Prophet Shu'ayb عليه السلام and his people. Madyan is also the name of a tribe. *(Mu'jam Al-Buldān: see under 'Madyan; Mu'jam Qabāil al-Arab 3/1062; Atlas Al-Qurān (Urdu), P. 129)*

Kan'ān: The land of Kan'ān (Canaan) refers to the land of Palestine and Phoenicia which is named after Canaanites, the offspring of Kan'ān bin Sām (or Kan'ān bin Ham) bin Nūh. The Canaanites were the ancient inhabitants of southeast Arabia who migrated to Palestine and Syria in the fourth and the third millennium BC. Some of their famous towns were Shechem (Nablus), Majdu, Areeha (Jericho), Baisān, Akkā (Acre), and Yafa. *(Mu'jam al-Buldān: see under 'Kan'ān' (Canaan); Sabāi'ik adh-Dhahab, P. 30; Holy Bible (Genesis) 10:6-20; Mu'jam Mufradāt Muqarrar, Maddah At-Tarīkh, P.226)*

Mesopotamia: The name given to the land lying between the Tigris and the Euphrates. It is also called al-Jazeerah or *Ma Bain an-Nahrain*. Mesopotamia is a Greek word consisting of Mesos (middle) and Potomos (river), that is, the land between the two rivers. *(Atlas Al-Qur'ān (Urdu), P. 22)*

Wadi Hanīfah: Its old name is Al-'Ird. It is the name of a stream of Al-'Ārid (Nejd) which passes through Al-Kharj, the territory of Banu Hanīfah. It is 120 km long. Sados, Dār'iyah, 'Uyainah, al-Ha'ir, al-'Amāriyah and Manfūhah are some of the towns of this wadi. *(Mu'jam al-Buldan: see under 'al-'Ird', Wikipedia Encyclopedia)*

Wadi 'Uranah: This wadi lies east of Makkah, close to the land of Arafat, right between Arafāt and the Namirah Mosque. It is not included within the precincts of the Holy Mosque (Haram). *(Mu'jam al-Buldān: See under "Uranah'; Buhūth fi'l Fiqh al-Ma'āsir)*

Wajrah: The name of a place northeast of Makkah, close to Dhat 'Irq, the *Mīqāt* of Irāq (92 km off Makkah). It was the land of Banu Sulaim. *(Mu'jam al-Buldān: see under 'Wajrah')*

Yalamlam: The name of a wadi and it is 92 km south of Makkah. It is the *Mīqāt* of the pilgrims coming from Yemen and other countries further south. – (Mu'jam al-Buldān: see under 'Yalamlam', Wikipedia Encyclopedia)

Yanbu': It is a large city of the province of Madīnah Munawwarah on the Red Sea coast. It is 250 km off the city of Madīnah and 350 km north of Jeddah. It takes its name from the abundance of springs (370 in numbers) in that region. The name is a variant of the original Arabic word for spring (Yanboo'). It is the outlet for petroleum exports. *(Mu'jam al-Buldān: see under 'Yanbu'', Wikipedia Encyclopedia)*

Tribes

Al-Ma'āfir: A Kahlani Yemeni tribe named after their ancestor, Ma'āfir bin Ya'fur bin Mālik bin Hārith bin Murrah. The province of Ma'āfir is named after the tribe. *(Mu'jam Al-Buldan: see under 'al-Ma'āfir'; Mu'jam Al-Qabā'il-il-Arab 3/1115)*

Ās Safwan: They are Banu Jumh who include Umayyah bin Khalaf, Ubayy bin Khalaf, and Wahb bin Khalaf. *(Al-Jamharah li-Ibn Al-Kalbi; PP 94-95)*

Āl Mundhir: This tribe is named after Mundhir bin Hārith bin Jablah Ghassāni. Mundhir bin Hārith was a chieftain of *Bādiyat ash-Sham* and paid tribute to the Romans during the Pre-Islamic times. He fought several battles with the kings of Hirah, who were under the sponsorship of the Persians. Later, he was killed by the Romans through deceit. *(Al-A'lām 7/292,293)*

Bāriq: An Azdī Qahtānī tribe, the offspring of Banu Bāriq bin Adi bin Hārithah bin Amr Muzaiqiyā. The poetess, Umm Al-Khair bint al-Hareesh Al-Bāariqiyyah, who delivered an eloquent sermon against Mu'awiyah ؓ on the eve of the Battle of Sīffīn, belonged to this tribe. – (Nihāyat al-'Arab, P. 162; Mu'jam Qabā'il-il-'Arab 1/57).

Bāhilah: It is a large tribe of Qais bin 'Ailān, who belonged to Banu Adnān. The name of Bāhilah is Munabbih bin Sa'd bin Qais 'Ailan. They lived in Yamama. *(Mu'jam Qabā'il-il-Arab 1/60)*

Bajīlah: A very large Qahtāni tribe. Their lineage is Banu Anmār bin Arāsh bin Kahlān. They are named after their mother, Bajīlah bint Sa'b bin Sa'd. In the Pre-Islamic times they lived in Hijaz and Bahrain. They worshipped an idol called Dhul-Khalasah. When Muslim conquests increased, the majority of this tribe fled their dwelling-area. The Companion Jarīr bin 'Abdullah Bajali ؓ belonged to this tribe. *(Nihāyat al-'Arab, P. 164; Al-A'lām 2/43)*

Banu Asad: A well-known tribe of Banu Adnān, their lineage is as follows: Banu Asad bin Rabī'ah bin Nizār bin Ma'dd bin Adnān. Usd had three sons: Jadīlah, 'Anzah, and 'Ameerah. Tareef bin Abān of Banu 'Ameerah joined a delegation that met the Prophet ﷺ. From among the descendants of Tareef, one named 'Amir bin Muslim fell as a martyr along with the Prophet's grandson, Hussain. – (Al-Jamharah li-Ibn Hazm: 293)

Banu Asad bin Khuzaimah: This tribe is related to Asad bin Khuzaimah bin Mudrikah bin Ilyās bin Mudār Adnāni. They lived in Karkh, a region of Nejd, in the neighbourhood of Banu Tayy. Later, they left for Iraq where they lived from 19 AH to 588 AH. A delegation of these tribesmen came to see the Prophet ﷺ in 9 AH. *(Nihāyat al-Arab, p. 47; Mu'jam Qabā'il-il-'Arab 1/21-23)*

Banu Aslam: A branch of Khuzā'ah. Their lineage is as follows: Banu Aslam bin Afsa bin Hāritha bin 'Amr bin 'Āmir, who belonged to the Qahtāni tribe. One of their settlements was named Wabrah, a cluster of date-palm groves outside Madīnah. *(Mu'jam Qabā'il-il-Arab 1/26)*

Banu Bakr: A large Adnāni tribe named after Bakr bin Wa'il bin Qāsit. They lived in an area stretching from Yamāmah further beyond in the direction of Bahrain and Iraq. One of the warlike tribes who fought several historical battles, both before and after Islam. *(Mu'jam Qabā'il-il-Arab 1/93-98)*

Banu Tujaib: It is a sub-tribe of Banu Sakūn. Their lineage is: Banu Ashras bin Shabeeb bin Sakun bin Ashras bin Kindah. Tujaib was the name of the mother of 'Adi and Sa'd, the sons of Ashras. They lived in an area called Kasr in the middle of Hadramaut. A 13-member delegation from the tribe of Tujaib came to see the Prophet Muhammad (ﷺ) and also brought *Zakaah* with them. The Prophet ﷺ was delighted and received them with honor. *(Mu'jam Qabā'il-il-Arab 1/116; Mu'jam al-Buldān: see under 'Tujaib')*

Banu Abdul-Qais: Banu Abdul-Qais bin Afsa bin Dumiyy bin Jadeelah bin Asad is a branch of the Adnāni tribe. Initially, they lived in Tihāmah but later moved to Bahrain. They are divided into several sub-tribes, all of whom accepted Islam. *(Nihāyat al-Arab, P. 307; Al-A'lām 4/49)*

Banu 'Adwān: They are the descendants of the Adnāni tribe of Qais 'Ailān. Adwān's name was Hārith bin 'Amr bin Qais and was known as Banu 'Adwān because he had killed his brother unjustly. Banu 'Adwān lived in Tā'if. Overcome by Thaqeef, they made their way to Tihamah. *(Nihāyat Al-'Arab, P.322)*

Banu Nadeer: One of the Jewish tribes of Madīnah. They broke the treaty they had made with the Prophet Muhammad (ﷺ) after the Battle of Badr (2 AH). The Prophet ﷺ thus banished them from Madīnah and their properties were later confiscated. *(Al-Munjid fi'l-A'lām, P. 574)*

Banu Umayyah: Named after Umayyah bin Abd-Shams bin Abd-Manāf bin Qusayy, the ancestor of the Umayyads of Quraish. Umayyah commanded the forces of Quraish in battles. He lived long after the birth of the Prophet Muhammad (ﷺ). *(Al-A'lām 2/23)*

Banu Tameem: This great Adnani tribe is named after Tameem bin Murr bin Udd bin Tābikhah bin Ilyās bin Mudār bin Nizar bin Ma'dd bin 'Adnān. They lived in Nejd and later spread to as far as Basrah, Bahrain and Yamamah. They were divided into several branches like Hārith, 'Anbar, Zaid Manāt, Mālik, 'Amr, Sa'd, Hanzalah, 'Auf, Yarbū', Riyūh, Imra ul-Qais, Hārith al-'A'raj, and Rabī'ah.

Banu Tameem were settled in Nejd but later spread out to surrounding areas. In the regions of Nejd and Jabal Shammar only three of their branches remain now: Hanzalah bin Mālik bin Zaid Manāt bin Tameem, Sa'd bin Zaid Manat bin Tameem, and 'Amr bin Tameem. In the Battle of Qadsiyyah (Iraq), Banu Tameem performed extraordinary feats of valor and turned the tide of the battle to the Muslims' favour. Imām Muhammad bin Abdul-Wahhab bin Suleman (1115-1206AH/ 1703-1792 CE) belonged to Banu Hanzalah, a branch of Banu Tameem. He was born in the town of 'Uyainah (Nejd), 40 km northwest of Ar-Riyadh. To pursue his studies, he travelled to Syria, Basrah and Hijaz. He succeeded his father as the *Qadi* (Judge) of Huraimalah. In 1143 AH he started his missionary work from his native town of 'Uyainah, where many reformers joined him on his mission. In 1157 AH/1744 CE he went to Dār'iyah and met Muhammad bin Sa'ud to further spread his message. The British initiated the use of the word *'Wahhabi'* as a label for his followers. Muhammad bin Abdul-Wah'hāb died in Dār'iyah. His offspring are known as Āl ash-Sheikh. He wrote many theological and reformatory books including *Kitāb at-Tawheed, Kashf ash-Shubhāt* and *Nawāqid ul-Islam*. For more details, see 'Muhammad bin Abdul-Wahhāb: a maligned and oppressed reformer' by Mas'ūd Alam Nadvi (Urdu). *(Al-A'lām 6/257; Wikipedia Encyclopedia)*

Banu Jumah: This Quraishi tribe descended from Banu Husais, who were Adnānis. Their line of descent is: Jumah bin 'Amr bin Husias bin Ka'b bin Lu'ayy bin Ghālib bin Fihr. They were known for a fierce and bloody battle they fought with Banu Muhārib bin Fihr at a place called Radm. *(Mu'jam Qabā'il-il-Arab 1/202,203)*

Banu Sa'd: An Adnāni tribe. Their lineage is as follows: Sa'd bin Zaid Manāt bin Tameem. Their settlements in central Arabia were in Yamamah, Dahnā', and Jarbah'. They clashed with Banu Shaibān and were victorious. Their king was Ma'dīkarab bin Hārith bin 'Amr. *(Mu'jam Qabā'il-il-Arab 2/515)*

Banu Sakūn: A sub-tribe of Kindah, who were Qahtānis. Their lineage is: Banu Sakūn bin Ashras bin Thaur (Kindah) bin 'Ufair bin 'Adī bin Hārith bin Murrah. Banu Sakun were the kings of Dūmat al-Jandal. The Prophet (ﷺ) sent Khalid ibn Waleed to a king of Dūmat al-Jandal named 'Ukaider. Khalid bin Waleed seized him and brought him as a prisoner to the Prophet ﷺ. Later, a settlement was reached whereby he agreed to pay *Jizyah* and was set free. *(Mu'jam Qabā'il-il-Arab 2/528,529)*

Banu Sahm: A Quraishi tribe. Their lineage is: Sahm bin 'Amr bin Husais bin Ka'b bin Lu'ayy bin Ghālib bin Fihr bin Mālik. The Banu Sahm tribesmen settled in al-Fustāt (Egypt). (Al-Fustat was an ancient Muslim city which have been merged in Cairo). A group of them settled in Upper Egypt. The Prophet's companion, 'Amr bin 'Ās Sahmi, who was the governor of Egypt, built a mosque (Jami' 'Amr bin 'Ās) in al-Fustāt. That mosque was sited in an area where Banu Sahm were settled. *(Mu'jam Qabā'il-il-Arab 2/560)*

Banu Sulaim: This tribe is named after Sulaim bin Mansur bin 'Ikramah bin Khasafah bin Qais 'Ailan. They were Adnānis; those who belong to this tribe are called Sulaimi. They dwelt in Upper Nejd, Harrah Bani Sulaim, Harrāt An-Nar, Wadi al-Qura, and Taimā'. *(Nihayat Al-Arab, P.271)*

Banu Shaibān: This Qahtāni tribe, a branch of Himyar, is named after Shaibān bin 'Auf who belonged to Bani Zuhair bin Abyan bin Humaisa' bin Himyar bin Sabā. *(Nihāyata al-Arab, P/283)*

Banu 'Adī: An Adnāni tribe. Their lineage is: Banu 'Adī bin Ka'b bin Lu'ayy bin Ghālib bin Fihr. 'Adī had two sons: Ruzāh and 'Uwaij. 'Umar bin Khattāb, the second Caliph, belonged to Banu Ruzāh while another Prophet's companion, Nu'aim bin Abdullah surnamed al-Nukām, belonged to Banu 'Uwaij. *(Nihayat Al-Arb, P.325)*

Banu Ghatfan: The ancestor of this Adnāni tribe was Ghatfān bin Sa'd bin Qais bin 'Ailan bin Mudār bin Nizār bin Ma'dd bin Adnān. His offspring multiplied and branched off into several tribes, the chief of them being Ashja', 'Abs, and Dhabyān. *(Nihāyat al-Arab, P.348; Mu'jam Qabā'il-il-Arab 3/888)*

Banu Kalb: Their lineage is: Kalb bin Wabrah bin Taghlib bin Hulwān bin 'Imran bin Ilhāfi bin Qudā'ah. There were many other tribes of this name but this one became most widely known. Their settlements were in as-Samāwah, between Kūfah and Damascus. They had set up an idol named 'Wadd' in Dūmat Al-Jandal. They were the allies of Banu Umayyah. Mu'awiya ibn Abi Sufyān, had married a woman named Maisūn from the tribe of Banu Kalb. *(Nihāyat Al-Arab, P. 365; Mu'jam Qabā'il-il-Arab 3/991, 992; Al-Jamharah li-Ibn Hazm, P. 455)*

Banu Makhzum: This Quraishi tribe descended from Banu Yaqzah bin Murrah bin Ka'b. 'Umar (or 'Amr) bin Makhzūm was the ancestor of Prophet's companion Khālid bin Waleed. The Prophet's arch enemy Abu Jahl ('Amr bin Hishaām bin Mugheerah) also belonged to this tribe. *(Nihāyat al-Arab, P. 371; Al-Jamharah li-Ibn al-Kalbi, P. 85)*

Bahrā': Bahra' is a sub-tribe of Qudā'ah. Their lineage is: Bahrā' bin 'Amr bin Ilhaf bin Qudā'ah bin Mālik bin Himyar. This tribe thrived and prospered and their men settled in Syria, Abyssinia (Ethiopia), Iraq and several other countries. They split up into many clans including the clan ('Asheerah) of Miqdad, to which belonged the famous Companion Miqdad bin Aswad, the clan of Qumzan, and the clan of Bu Muheyr. *(Wikipedia Encyclopedia)*

Tanūkh: According to Jauhari, Tanūkh is a Qahtani tribe of Yemen. Mu'ayyad, a historian, says that Tanukh belonged to Qudā'ah. Abu Obaid holds that Tanūkh is a collective name of three tribes: Nizār, Ahlāf and Fahmi. They are so named because they pledged at Tatnakh, a place in Syria, to live together. *(Nihāyat al-Arab, P. 178; Al-Jamharah li-Ibn Hazm, P. 453)*

'Āmilah: Banu 'Āmilah is a Qahtāni tribe, named after Hārith ('Āmilah) bin Murrah bin Udad bin Zaid bin Yashjub bin Zaid bin Kahlān. Hārith was a brother of Lakhm and Judham. Banu 'Āmilah lived in Jabal 'Āmilah in Syria. They worshipped an idol named Uqaisar, which they used to make pilgrimage to. *(Nihāyat al-Arab, P. 303; Mu'jam Qabā'il-il-Arab 2/714; Al-Mufassal fi Tāreekh-il-Arab Qabl-al-Islam 6/275)*

'Abīl: An extinct Arab tribe named after 'Ubail Bin Mahlail bin 'Aud bin Iram bin Sām bin Nūh. They dwelt in Madīnah (Yathrib). *(Nihāyat al-Arab, P. 317; Mu'jam Qabā'il-il-Arab 2/748; Lisan al-Arab: see under 'Abl)*

'Udhrah: The ancestor of Banu 'Udhrah, a branch of Banu Qudā'ah, was 'Udhrah bin Sa'd Hudhaim bin Zaid bin Laith. Banu 'Āmir, Kāhil, 'Iyās, 'Auf and Rafā'ah are the branches of Banu 'Udhrah. They were known for their loving nature and virtuousness. In pre-Islamic times they worshipped an idol named 'Shams'. *(Sabā'ik adh-Dhahab, P.87; Nihayāt al-Arab, P.326; Mu'jam Qabāil-il-Arab 2/768)*

'Adal (Banu Qārah): Banu 'Àdal is a branch of Banu Kinana. Their ancestor was 'Adal bin Hūn bin Khuzaimah bin Mudrikah bin Ilyas Mudāri. His and his brother's children mixed up and became very intimate with each other. They were named Banu Qārah after their grandmother, whose name was Qārah. They were known for consummate skill in archery. *(Nihāyat-al-Arab, P.329; Mu'jam Qabā'il-il-Arab 2/787; Al-A'lām 4/234,235)*

Ghāmid: The ancestor of this tribe was 'Amr bin Abdullah bin Ka'b bin Hārith Azdi. They were a branch of the Qahtāni tribe of Banu Azd. Their territory was *Jibāl as-Sarat. (Al-Jamharah li-Ibn al-Kalbī P. 277; Mu'jam Qabā'il-il-Arab 3/876)*

Ghutaif: A sub-tribe of Banu Tayy. Lineage: Ghutaif bin Hāritha bin Sa'd bin Hashraj bin Imra al-Qais bin 'Adī bin Akhzam bin Hazumah bin Rabī'ah bin Jarwal at-Tā'i. *(Taj Al-'Urus: see under 'Ghatf')*

Qais 'Ailān: Those who trace their ancestry to Qais bin 'Ailan bin Mudar bin Nizār bin Ma'dd bin Adnān are known as Qais 'Ailān. Hawāzan, Sulaim, Ghatafān, Māzan, Fahm, 'Adwān, Bāhila and Ghaniyy-- all of them are a part of Banu Qais 'Ailān. The words 'Qais of Yemen' are understood to include all the Adnani tribes. The Prophet ﷺ is reported to have said, according to some narrations: "May Allah have mercy on Qais. No doubt, they followed the faith of our father Ismā'īl عليه السلام." *(Nihāyat al-Arab, P. 362; Al-Jamharah li-Ibn Al-Kalbi, P.311; Al-A'lām 5/207; Mu'jam Qabā'il-il-Arab 3/972)*

Murād: Their lineage is: Murād bin Mālik (Mazhij) bin Udad bin Zaid bin Yashjub. They are a Kahlāni Qahtāni tribe. They lived near Zabīd, a region of Yemen. A famous battle, called the Day of Razm, took place between them and Hamdan in pre-Islamic times. *(Nihāyat al-Arab, P.373; Mu'jam Qabā'il-il-Arab*

3/1066)

Hudhail: They are the offspring of Hudhail bin Mudrikah bin Ilyas bin Mudar bin Nizār. They are Adnānis. They were settled in a wide area extending to as far as Mt. Ghazwan (Tā'if). They also lived in Nejd and Tihāmah. Their two main branches are Sa'd bin Hudhail and Lihyan bin Hudhail. *(Nihāyat al-Arab, P. 387; Mu'jam Qabā'il-il-Arab 3/1213; Al-A'lām 8/80)*

'Aba'hilah: They were the kings of Yemen whom the Prophet Muhammad (ﷺ) decreed to continue as kings. The Prophet ﷺ sent a letter to Aqyāl (kings) and 'Abahilah (lords) by the hand of Wā'il bin Hujr ؓ. *(Tāj al-'Uroos: see under 'Abhal')*

Miscellaneous

Ebla: A settlement which existed 55 km southwest of Aleppo (Halab). Today it is called Tel Mardeekh. *(Wikipedia Encyclopedia)*

'Ātām: Plural of 'Utum or 'utm meaning 'castle, fortress, edifice, high-rise building.' This word is mostly used for the forts of Madīnah. *(Al-Qāmoos al-Waheed: see under 'Utm'; Mu'jam Al-Buldan: see under 'Utum')*

Bahr Qulzum: Qulzum is the Arabicized form of the Latin word Kelezma, the old Roman name of the Red Sea which lies between the Arabian Peninsula and Africa. In the south, it links with the Arabian Sea via Bab-el-Mandab and, in the north, it branches off into the Gulf of Aqabāh and the Gulf of Suez. In ancient times there was a port named Qulzum or Kelezma at the tip of the Gulf of Suez (Suwais) The some is now called Suwais (Suez) It is 1900 km long and 200 to 325 km across. Its total area is 450,000 sq km. *(Mu'jam al-Buldān: see under 'Al-Qulzum'; Al-Munjid fi'l A'lām, P. 113)*

Sea of Lot: It is also called *Al-Bahr al-Mayyit* (the Dead Sea) in Arabic. Its water is extremely salty. It lies between Palestine and Jordan. Its maximum depth is 393 m. *(Al-Munjid Fi'l A'lām, P. 114)*

Sub'h al-A'sha: The name of a book written by Ahmad bin Ali bin Ahmad bin Abdullah Qalqashandi. The book provides information about the rules and regulations of dictation and about history and geography. His other books are *Nihāyat al-Arab fi Ma'rafati Ansāb-il-Arab* and *Hilyat al-Fadl wa Zain al-Karam.* *(Mu'jam al-Muallifeen 1/317; Al-Munjid fi'l A'lām, P.343)*